SMITH, HOGAN, AND ORMEROD'S
ESSENTIALS OF CRIMINAL LAW

SMITH, HOGAN, AND ORMEROD'S
ESSENTIALS OF
CRIMINAL LAW

Fourth Edition

John Child

Reader in Criminal Law, Birmingham Law School
Co-Director of the Birmingham Centre for Crime, Justice and Policing
Co-Director of the Criminal Law Reform Now Network

David Ormerod CBE, QC (Hon)

Professor of Criminal Justice, University College London
Deputy High Court Judge
Barrister, Bencher of Middle Temple
Door Tenant at Red Lion Chambers

OXFORD
UNIVERSITY PRESS

OXFORD
UNIVERSITY PRESS

Great Clarendon Street, Oxford, OX2 6DP,
United Kingdom

Oxford University Press is a department of the University of Oxford.
It furthers the University's objective of excellence in research, scholarship,
and education by publishing worldwide. Oxford is a registered trade mark of
Oxford University Press in the UK and in certain other countries

First edition 2015
Second edition 2017
Third edition 2019
Impression: 1

Public sector information reproduced under Open Government Licence v3.0
(http://www.nationalarchives.gov.uk/doc/open-government-licence/open-government-licence.htm)

Published in the United States of America by Oxford University Press
198 Madison Avenue, New York, NY 10016, United States of America

British Library Cataloguing in Publication Data
Data available

Library of Congress Control Number: 2020947871

ISBN 978-0-19-886996-2

Printed in Great Britain by
Bell & Bain Ltd., Glasgow

Preface

Smith, Hogan, and Ormerod's Essentials of Criminal Law is a textbook designed for undergraduate students of criminal law. Being targeted at that audience means that the book is focussed on teaching and learning. It devotes space to explanations of criminal law concepts in a step-by-step manner, and avoids assumed knowledge. The book highlights complexities and/or points of common confusion so that readers can understand the problem areas. The text is complemented throughout by numerous visual aids, including flow charts, case boxes, and offence charts, in order to help those who learn more effectively through visual representations. We also address student concerns with assessment by providing guidance in each chapter focussing on potential problem questions; as well as including sections dedicated to debate about reform, focussing on potential essay questions.

Our emphasis on teaching and learning and accessible presentation is supported by the quality of the content, with the book maintaining the ideals for which *Smith, Hogan, and Ormerod* criminal law books are renowned: exposing and analysing the complexities of the law, setting the law in the context of surrounding academic debate, and highlighting potential reform options that might steer the law towards greater coherence and fairness. Our aim is to provide readers with an understanding of the essentials of criminal law, in a way that is accessible to all students.

We would like to thank all those involved in the production of this latest edition, including reviewers and those working at Oxford University Press.

New to this Edition

Within this new (4th edition) of *Smith, Hogan, and Ormerod's Essentials of Criminal Law* we have further refined our discussion of topics across the book to improve student comprehension. We have added and updated material in line with important legal developments. We have also further developed the book's accompanying online resources, and for this element we welcome Ms Chaynee Hodgetts (Bangor University) to the team and we are grateful for her work in significantly enhancing the interactive features of the e-book, as well providing an overhaul of the resources that are available alongside the book.

The recent legal developments that we have incorporated in this new edition include a host of new academic, statutory, and case law materials. The most important cases include:

Barton on property offences and dishonesty;

A on causation and foreseeability;

Islam and *Sargeant* on loss of control;

Foy and *Hussain* on diminished responsibility;

Broughton and *Kuddus* on gross negligence manslaughter, omissions, and causation;

Melin, Veysey, and *Sidhu* on offences against the person;

Lawrance, Gabbai, and *Richards* on deception and sexual offences;

Whatcott, Bush, D, and *Smith* on fraud;

Johnson and *Alstom* on conspiracy;

N and *Towers* on complicity;

GB on defences to modern slavery;

Williams and *Cheeseman* on the 'householder' defence.

Getting the most out of Smith, Hogan, & Ormerod's Essentials of Criminal Law

Smith, Hogan, & Ormerod's Essentials of Criminal Law offers a rich learning experience, supporting and reinforcing your understanding through a range of features and online resources, taking you from first principles though to preparing you for assessment. This guided tour shows you how to utilise the textbook fully and get the most out of your study.

 www.oup.com/he/child-ormerod4e

Navigate the Criminal Law

Each chapter begins with a clear **Table of Contents**, breaking down the topics you will cover, including page numbers for easy reference.

Audio recordings introduce each chapter, highlighting key areas to focus on.

Focus on Key Principles

Evans [2009] EWCA Crim 650

D, V's half-sister, supplied her with heroin which she se[lf-]
overdose. D stayed with V but did not alert the authoriti[es]
the drugs. V died and D was charged with gross negligenc[e]
to aid V. The duty arose from her contribution to the dan[ger.]
• Crown Court: guilty of gross negligence manslaughter.

All **key cases** are highlighted across the chapters with a brief summary of the main facts and judgment.

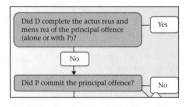

Did D complete the actus reus and mens rea of the principal offence (alone or with P)? — Yes

No

Did P commit the principal offence? — No

Tables and figures, including **animated diagrams**, are presented across the book. These will help your learning and revision, by graphically presenting some of the key concepts and principles to be considered in your study of criminal law.

? *Don't be confused ...*

When we compare the criminal law of different jurisdic[tions]
criminal law'. International criminal law (discussed at **1.**
criminalisation that applies across multiple States (eg the [crime of]
international agreement. Just as this textbook is focussing [on England]
and Wales, our discussion of comparative law here is focus[ed on]
national jurisdictions.

'Don't be confused' boxes discuss common pitfalls to avoid and other areas of confusion for those new to the law.

 Point to remember ...

The possibility of multiple causes is particularly important [in some]
cases, it will often be another party who begins the course [of events]
so there is often at least one other obvious cause. However, [another]
other cause is V herself[86]). As long as D's omission satisfies th[e rules, it]
is a factual cause if D would have prevented the result by ac[ting and it]
would not have come about 'but for' her omission).

'Point to remember' boxes highlight key things to remember as you continue your studies.

Terminology ...

When we refer to categories of offences such as 'homicide of
with a distinct actus reus and mens rea. Rather, we are si
group of offences that share certain characteristics (other
property offences; etc). It is not accurate to say D is liable fo
is liable for a homicide offence such as murder or manslau

'*Terminology*' boxes clarify legal jargon, ensuring
that you understand the key terms.

Broaden Your Knowledge

Videos (with transcripts) by David Ormerod
explain key concepts to deepen your understanding.

7.10 Reform

With much of the law in this area still govern
unsurprising that there have been several call
amendments.[194] The Law Commission, for exan
on grounds both of effectiveness and of justice'.[1]
Below we provide a brief overview of some

The penultimate section of each chapter covers **law
reform**. These sections include noted academic criticism of the law and other recent calls for reform,
preparing you for essay question assessments.

Extra detail ...

The Draft Criminal Code, as with all Law Commission draft
ence when evaluating the law or seeking alternatives to it. H
the law, and should never be presented as such: they ar
where a new statute is based on a prior Law Commission d
between the two.

'*Extra detail*' boxes offer you additional insights
into the law and suggest sources for further reading.

A selection of **annotated weblinks and further
reading** references chosen by the authors allow you
to delve deeper into topics which are of interest to
you and prepare for essay assignments.

Legal updates are provided, giving access to
recent cases and developments in the law that have
occurred since publication of the book.

Prepare for Assessment

7.11 Eye on assessment

In this section we discuss the potential applic
within a problem question. The same structu
have discussed in previous chapters.

STEP 1 Identify the potential criminal

Each chapter ends with an **eye on assessment** section dedicated to assessment advice, including how
to approach problem questions and correctly apply
your knowledge of the law.

Assessment matters ...

When discussing the potential intervention of third part
focus is the liability of D: if X's acts break the chain of
then D remains the cause and may be liable. The only r
the liability of D. You are not addressing X's liability, bu
chain of causation between D and the result. Having dis
on *separately* to discuss the potential liability of X, but t
liability of the other.

Throughout the chapters, '*Assessment matters*'
boxes offer you advice on how to approach a given
topic in essay or exam assessment.

Over 400 **self-test questions**, arranged by chapter, allow you quickly to assess your knowledge quickly of the various topics in criminal law.

 A selection of author **videos** (and transcripts) from John Child and Chaynee Hodgetts are available for each chapter, explaining how to approach key topics in your assessments.

 Each chapter is accompanied by two sample **examination questions with answer guidance** from the authors to help hone your assessment skills.

 Chapter summaries are available for every chapter, summarising the key points for your revision.

Outline Contents

Detailed Contents

Table of Cases

CASES OF OTHER JURISDICTIONS

Australia

Canada

European Court of Human Rights

Hong Kong

New Zealand

South Africa

United States

Table of Legislation

1

Introduction

1.1 Focussing on the substantive criminal law

In this textbook we will be exploring the criminal law of England and Wales. Many aspects of the criminal law feature in the news and debates in the media every day, which is useful and important because it reminds us about the vital role played by the criminal law in society. It makes the study of criminal law more interesting, and it can also high-light conflict and potential problems for the law. However, readers need to be aware that the focus of these debates and discussions is commonly very different from that involved in the study of substantive criminal law. The debates will often relate to sentencing, pro-cedure, police investigation, and criminal justice matters generally. Our focus in this textbook is on *substantive* criminal law. It is about how offences like theft and murder are defined, not about who commits them or why (criminology), how they are investigated by the police (policing and criminal procedure), how they are prosecuted and proved in court (evidence), or how they are sentenced (sentencing). Take the following example:

> The defendant (D) kicks the victim (V) hard in the shin. D commits an offence.

Our focus involves an analysis of what D did, what circumstances she did it in, and what effect it had on V. Did V suffer serious injury or minor injury? Did D mean to kick V, or was it an accident? Was V consenting to being kicked or the risk of being kicked (eg was it in a football match)? Questions like these lead us to identify the correct category of possible offences. Having identified the category, our task is then to explore the specific offences in detail, asking precisely what conduct is made criminal within each offence, and comparing the offence requirements with D's behaviour. Following this, if we find the elements of an offence are satisfied, we then explore possible defences.

Although our central study in this textbook relates to the definitions of criminal offences and defences, in this introductory chapter it is important for us to set this in context. The following sections provide short descriptions of related matters that it is helpful for readers to be aware of in order to understand the distinct role played by sub-stantive criminal rules, and to evaluate them effectively.

1.1.1 Theories of criminalisation: What should be criminalised?

When studying the substantive criminal law, it is natural to question the basis upon which certain conduct is criminalised and other conduct is not. We may ask *why* certain conduct has been made criminal (eg why is it an offence for D to kick V?);[1] we may also ask why particular conduct *should* be criminal (eg why should it be an offence for D to kick V?).[2] These questions and challenges are important areas of research for those concerned with law reform and criminal law policy. If we recommend that a new offence should be created, or a present offence be abolished or amended, we need to be able to explain a principled basis for our view. That basis is most often found in moral and political philosophy.[3]

Questions about the legitimate objectives for criminalisation are perhaps inevitably imprecise. There is no single, agreed, criterion for deciding when something 'should' be criminalised or what makes a 'good' criminal offence. That is not to suggest that exam-ining how and why things are criminalised is unimportant. It is extremely important to

---

[1] This is referred to as a 'descriptive challenge': seeking an explanation for a current state.

[2] This is referred to as a 'normative challenge': questioning the rights or wrongs of a current state.

[3] See eg Simester and Von Hirsch, *Crimes, Harms and Wrongs: On the Principles of Criminalisation* (2011); Hörnle, 'Theories of Criminalization' (2016) 10 Crim L & Phil 301.

study what is being criminalised because to criminalise behaviour is the most serious step a State can take: it prohibits conduct and backs that prohibition with a stigmatising label and a criminal penalty (eg fines, imprisonment, etc). Criminal offences bring with them intrusive powers of investigation, search, and arrest. Criminalisation should not, therefore, be justified as a response to every form of conduct we find distasteful or anti-social, it must be reserved for only the most serious transgressions that justify the State in harming D's interests.

Traditionally, where theorists have attempted to explain and justify criminalisation, they have focussed on the targeting of 'harm': conduct from D that infringes the autonomy of V (physically or otherwise), or causes serious offence.[4] Harm is a useful target because, unlike older theories based on *moral* wrongs, harm is at least relatively objective: harms can generally be observed, tested, and measured. However, although this approach is readily applicable to offences against the person such as murder, rape, or battery (eg D kicking V), it is much more difficult to present harm as the rationale for pre-emptive offences (eg liability for attempting to commit a crime[5]) or the many regulatory offences (eg failing to have a valid road traffic licence for a vehicle[6]). As a result, the advocates of a 'harms' approach are left with a difficult choice: maintain a narrow view of harm and fail to explain a large part of the criminal law that does not target such harm, or interpret harms widely enough to encompass all offences (eg endangering/harming public order) but in doing so risk the concept of harm becoming so broad that it is no longer useful.[7] Where the latter approach is preferred, it is common to see reference to 'harms' or 'wrongs'.

Harm-based approaches to criminalisation (including those expanded to wrongful conduct) also have a threshold problem: we may target harms and wrongs, but we do not want to criminalise *all* harmful conduct, regardless of the context or degree. In order to address this, Duff has outlined a useful distinction between what he terms 'private wrongs' (wrongs that are not legitimate targets for criminalisation) and 'public wrongs' (which are).[8] For example, if D finishes a relationship with V in an unkind manner, we can say that D has acted wrongfully and we may even say that she has harmed V. However, D's wrong is a private wrong: answerable to V, and perhaps to friends and family, but one where the State, and thus the criminal law, has no legitimate role. In contrast, where D kicks V, it may be that the damage done to V, and society's legitimate interest in protecting others, means that D's wrong is public and deserving of criminalisation. The problem here of course, recognised by Duff, is that the distinction between a private wrong and a public wrong is politically and morally subjective, and lacks clear criteria.[9]

---

[4] For discussion and development of the 'harm principle', see Mill, *On Liberty* (1859); Feinberg, *Harm to Others* (1984).

[5] Criminal Attempts Act 1981.

[6] Road Traffic Act 1988, s87.

[7] See Duff, *Answering for Crime* (2007) Ch6. For a modern defence of the harm principle, see Horder, 'Harmless Wrongdoing and the Anticipatory Perspective on Criminalisation' in Sullivan and Dennis (eds), *Seeking Security* (2012) 79; Horder, 'Bribery as a Form of Criminal Wrongdoing' (2011) 127 LQR 37.

[8] Duff, *Answering for Crime* (2007).

[9] For critique of approaches based on 'public wrongs', see Edwards and Simester, 'What's Public about Crime?' (2017) 37 OJLS 105. And for the response to this critique, see Duff and Marshall, 'Crimes, Public Wrongs, and Civil Order' (2019) 13 CrimL&P 27.

However, although this is a problem for those who want to establish a clear separation of legitimate and illegitimate targets of the criminal law, it may be no more than an accurate description of the political process.[10]

Theories of criminalisation provide a fascinating area for research in their own right. However, as we analyse the substantive rules of law in later chapters, such theories are rarely of direct relevance. This is not to suggest that they should be forgotten or ignored, but it is important to think about how such theories can be used when analysing the substantive criminal law. Drawing on theories of criminalisation to discuss why conduct has been legitimately criminalised can help in our central task (analysing the substantive criminal law) in a number of important ways. Three clear examples will suffice:

A) When interpreting an imprecise offence/defence: Where an offence or defence is imprecise, it is common for the courts to consider the intentions of the legislature in order to clarify and apply the rule. In the context of offences, the aim is to identify the mischief that the offence was designed to target, ensuring that it is interpreted in order to capture only that. For example, in the case of *Wilson*,[11] at his wife's (V's) request, D consensually branded his initials onto her buttocks with a hot knife. D was convicted of an offence against the person, and appealed on the basis that V's consent should have precluded liability. As we discuss later in this textbook,[12] the current law regarding consent in this area is far from clear. However, the Court of Appeal allowed D's appeal and quashed his conviction, stating firmly that the criminal law had no place interfering in the private lives of the married couple when they engaged in this activity.

B) When we are evaluating the effectiveness of an offence: It may also be useful to consider the mischief (harms and/or wrongs) that an offence was designed to target when we are considering whether it is working well. Having identified the mischief of the offence, we can ask whether the offence definition has successfully targeted that mischief, and if it has, whether it has gone beyond that target to criminalise other conduct inappropriately. Indeed, the evaluation of an offence will often focus on its over-inclusivity (criminalising more than intended) or under-inclusivity (criminalising less than intended), and this analysis only makes sense once we have identified the mischief targeted.

As we will see, the potential for overly broad criminalisation in particular is a criticism that has been made of several modern statutes. A useful example can be seen in the drafting of sexual offences.[13] In an effort to meet concerns about the ineffectiveness of some sexual offences (including concerns over seemingly low conviction rates), a succession of reforms have expanded several key offence definitions. However, despite the legitimate rationale for these reforms, questions now emerge about whether they have gone too far; whether the wide reach of these offences risks over-criminalisation.

---

[10] For a more ambitious attempt to set limits on legitimate criminalisation, see Husak, *Overcriminalisation* (2008).

[11] [1996] Crim LR 573.

[12] **Chapter 7.8.2**.

[13] Discussed in **Chapter 8**. See also our discussion of the Fraud Act 2006 in **Chapter 10**, and the Serious Crime Act 2007 in **Chapter 11**.

C) **When discussing the potential for a new offence:** In several places in this textbook we discuss proposals for new criminal offences. When we do so, it is useful to consider the mischief that those new offences would be looking to target, to consider whether they are deserving of criminalisation, and whether they are adequately covered by existing law. For example, when discussing the offences against the person,[14] we consider the offences relating to domestic violence introduced in 2015, and the potential for offences to tackle the transmission of disease.

1.1.2 Criminology: Why do people commit crime?

Exploring the reasons why people commit crimes, which types of people commit them, and whether certain groups are over-represented in criminal statistics, is a valuable pursuit.[15] For example, the reasons why a particular defendant assaulted or harassed a particular victim may help us to identify ways, whether legal or otherwise, to prevent such conduct in the future. It may also help us identify appropriate penalties. However, this is the focus for studies in criminology, and will not be central to the discussions in this textbook.

Questions about why people make bad choices are not generally relevant to the substance of the law, unless those reasons are explicitly recognised as criminal defences. D may have a good reason (a good motive if you like) for committing an offence, but unless this is recognised within the legal rules, it is irrelevant to her criminal liability.[16] It is important to remember that the courts are measuring D's liability with regard to set criminal rules, they are not judging whether D is a good or a bad person.

1.1.3 Criminal evidence: How can we prove a crime has been committed?

When we consider how the criminal law is applied in practice, issues of procedure and evidence are extremely important (eg how can we prove D kicked V, or that D intended to do so?).[17] Indeed, in order to practise in the area of criminal law, the study of criminal evidence is essential. However, again, criminal evidence is not directly relevant to the identification of legal rules governing the substantive criminal law—the definition of offences and defences.

Understanding evidential issues can, however, help our analysis and evaluation of the substantive law because it sheds light on how well criminal offences operate in practice. For example, if an offence requiring proof that D *intended* a particular result is too hard to prove (evidentially), this should lead us to consider whether the offence should be limited to proof of an intention. Similarly, where the law seeks to target criminal preparation, by creating offences which are triggered by conduct that arises before substantive criminal harms are caused, we must consider whether the conduct targeted will (evidentially) be sufficient to demonstrate that D would have gone on to cause the relevant harms.[18]

---

[14] **Chapter 7.**
[15] Case et al, *Criminology* (2017); Finch and Fafinski, *Criminology Skills* (2019).
[16] Although good reasons may provide mitigation affecting D's sentencing, this issue only arises *after* D has been found guilty for the relevant offence.
[17] Munday, *Evidence* (2019); Campbell et al, *The Criminal Process* (2019).
[18] We discuss this further in **Chapter 11.**

Assessment matters . . .

Where the facts of a problem question state what D is thinking, it is tempting to ask how this could be proved in real life. For example, where D kicks V in a game of football, you may be told in the problem that D did so 'intending to hurt V'. You may then question how the police and Crown Prosecution Service could ever know or prove this. However, this does not affect your application of the substantive criminal law. The method by which D's state of mind can be proved in court is a separate issue, and not one you need to deal with. Your task is to discuss and apply the definition of battery (the offence committed) on the facts you are given, and if you are told that D intended to kick V, then you should take this as a fact.

1.1.4 Sentencing: What are the punishments for committing crimes?

Where D is found guilty of a criminal offence (eg for battery when kicking V), D will be subject to a criminal sanction, most commonly a fine, a community penalty, or prison sentence. Some basic understanding of punishment and sentencing is useful when discussing the substantive criminal law, although this is not usually part of a criminal law course and is not part of our study in this textbook.[19]

What may be important in the course of your study of criminal law is to note the relative gravity of offences, by reference to their maximum sentence. For example, where D intentionally kicks V without V's consent, D will have committed the relatively minor offence of battery; if V suffers some harm (eg bruising) D commits the more serious offence of assault occasioning actual bodily harm;[20] and if V suffers serious harm (eg a broken leg) D may have committed the even more serious offence of causing grievous bodily harm with intent.[21] The seriousness of these offences is graded on the basis of the maximum sentence available upon conviction. Therefore, although we are not concerned with theories of punishment, or even the precise methods employed by judges when setting a sentence in individual cases, it is important to understand some basic sentencing law to understand the (logically prior) role of the substantive law in setting rules at the liability stage. This will help you to decide, for example, on the appropriate offence to discuss if D's conduct satisfies the requirements of multiple overlapping offences.

In practice, the substantive criminal law is concerned with one question: is D guilty of an offence or not. If the elements of an offence are satisfied then D has committed the crime, if not, she hasn't. There is no grey area between these two final outcomes. However, if convicted, there is much greater flexibility at the sentencing stage. D's punishment will vary depending upon the offence committed,[22] with different offences allowing for different maximum sentences, and the circumstances of D's offence will also be considered when setting the sentence below that maximum.

---

[19] Easton and Piper, *Sentencing and Punishment* (2016).
[20] Offences Against the Person Act 1861, s47.
[21] Ibid, s18.
[22] Some offences specify a mandatory sentence, but even these have exceptions.

Extra detail . . .

In 2018, the Law Commission published a report and draft Bill containing a New Sentencing Code designed to bring greater clarity and consistency to this area of the law.[23] The Sentencing Act 2020 was enacted in October 2020.[24]

1.1.5 Civil law: What is the difference between criminal and civil law?

It is important to distinguish a criminal offence from potentially similar torts (civil law).[25] For example, in harassment, the criminal law offence and the tort of harassment share common definitions. This may also be relevant where certain offences are based on torts, as with false imprisonment.

Although offences and torts may share definitions and/or a common history, the civil and criminal law systems are distinct. As with the criminal law, tort cases often centre on harms that one private party has caused to another, as where D kicks V. In tort, the injured party is seeking monetary compensation from D, and if the court is satisfied that such compensation is appropriate, it will require D to make a payment to V in proportion to the harm she has suffered. V must prove her case on the balance of probabilities (the civil standard of proof). Criminal cases, in contrast, represent an action by the State (as prosecutor) against the defendant, with a successful prosecution leading to the *punishment* of D. The criminal law's focus on the wrongful conduct of D, as opposed to the compensation of V, provides an important context to our study of the substantive rules. Here, the State must prove its case against D beyond reasonable doubt (the criminal standard of proof). The criminal and civil law operate in parallel with one another, serving different priorities of justice.

1.1.6 Comparative law: What is the criminal law in other jurisdictions?

This textbook explores the substantive criminal law in England and Wales; it is not therefore directly concerned with the substantive criminal law in other jurisdictions.[26] However, some discussion and comparison with other jurisdictions will aid our analysis of the law, and such comparison will arise regularly throughout this textbook. Where this is the case, comparison will generally be made with other common law jurisdictions such as those in the Republic of Ireland, the United States of America, Australia, New Zealand, and Canada. This is because with these jurisdictions employing similar systems of criminal law to our own, with a common tradition, comparisons are most easily drawn. Indeed, as the criminal law in these jurisdictions was previously administered by

---

[23] Law Commission, *The Sentencing Code—Volume I: Report; Volume II: Draft Legislation* (No 382, 2018).

[24] See Harris and Roberts, 'Sentencing in Transition: Recent Developments' [2020] Crim LR 369. The Act came into force on 1 December 2020.

[25] Deakin and Adams, *Markesinis & Deakin's Tort Law* (2019).

[26] Certain serious offences are extraterritorial in the sense that D can be convicted under English criminal law even where she has committed the criminal act in another jurisdiction.

Britain, there are still a number of areas where offence definitions remain identical, or certainly very similar, to our own.

Our study of the substantive criminal law is aided by international comparison in two principal ways:

A) When interpreting the law: The substantive law in another jurisdiction has no bearing on the criminal law in this country. The criminal law in England and Wales, as discussed later, is established through a combination of (i) statutes defining offences and defences, and (ii) the decisions of the courts interpreting the law and, *historically*, creating offences and defences through common law. However, the domestic courts can still find foreign legal decisions helpful when considering a problem that has arisen in that country and is now under scrutiny in the courts in England and Wales. What the foreign courts have decided does not have to be followed by the English courts, but it may be persuasive in identifying the best approach.[27]

B) When evaluating the law: In the years since other common law jurisdictions (eg those mentioned previously and others) have been independent from Britain, they have created and interpreted their own domestic criminal law. It is helpful to look to these countries to examine how their laws are developing and to consider whether or not English law compares favourably. As a result, where we consider potential reform in this textbook, we will often consider the approaches of other common law jurisdictions.

> **? Don't be confused . . .**
>
> When we compare the criminal law of different jurisdictions, we are not discussing 'international criminal law'. International criminal law (discussed at **1.2.5**) is concerned with a distinct form of criminalisation that applies across multiple States (eg the offence of genocide) and is created through international agreement. Just as this textbook is focussing on the domestic criminal law of England and Wales, our discussion of comparative law here is focussing on the domestic criminal law of other national jurisdictions.

1.1.7 Process: What is the process and procedure in trying a criminal case?

Our final topic in this section relates to the administrative structure through which the substantive criminal law is interpreted and applied.[28] For this, we are going to introduce the main actors within the criminal process and their roles (police, Crown Prosecution Service, defence representatives, judge, and jury), and we will also introduce the court and appeals structure. The actors and the administrative structures within the criminal justice system rarely have a direct effect on the substance of criminal rules, but an awareness of both is essential in order to understand those rules in context.

---

[27] The reference to foreign case law is particularly common within smaller jurisdictions (eg the Republic of Ireland and Scotland) where the volume of cases, and therefore the body of previous case law nationally, is lower.
[28] Campbell et al, *The Criminal Process* (2019).

1.1.7.1 The main actors within the criminal justice system

As we discuss the main actors in the criminal justice system, it should be remembered that a criminal case is an action between the State/Crown (as prosecutor) and a private party (as defendant). The victim of the offence, where relevant, may be simply a witness for the court.[29] This is why, unlike within civil law, the victim is not on our list of main actors.

A) **The police:** Where there is suspicion that an offence has been committed, the role of the police is to investigate the suspected offence to obtain evidence for any potential criminal trial. Where, for example, there is a complaint that D kicked V, the police will arrest and interview D; try to obtain CCTV footage of the incident; locate any witnesses; record the injuries to V; and so on.

B) **The Crown Prosecution Service (CPS):** The CPS act as prosecutors on behalf of the State/Crown.[30] The head of the CPS, the Director of Public Prosecutions (DPP), is accountable to the Attorney General (AG) who, in turn, is directly accountable to Parliament.

Before any criminal trial commences the CPS has a duty to review the evidence gathered by the police in order to assess whether a prosecution is viable: whether there is sufficient evidence that D kicked V; whether this amounted to a particular offence; and whether it is in the public interest to prosecute.[31] At trial, the CPS presents that evidence to the court. In order to obtain a conviction, the CPS must demonstrate D's guilt 'beyond reasonable doubt'—the criminal standard of proof.

 Don't be confused . . .

Civil law cases typically involve two private parties in opposition and are therefore referred to using both parties' names (eg *Jones v Smith*). In contrast, criminal law cases typically include only one party name (eg *R v Smith*). This is because in criminal cases the action is between the State as prosecutor (Regina: R) and a private defendant (party name).

C) **The defence:** The defendant (D) is the party alleged to have committed the offence. She will be represented in court by her own legal team, where possible.[32] As the prosecution have the burden of proving D's guilt 'beyond reasonable doubt', it is the aim of the defence to raise a 'reasonable doubt' within any essential element of the prosecution's case.

Where D wishes to raise a defence (eg D kicked V in self-defence) she must satisfy what is called an evidential burden: she must provide some evidence that could lead a jury to believe the defence is satisfied. This form of evidential burden should not be

---

[29] As criminal justice reform continues to move towards a victim-focussed system, the victim is included throughout the process. However, the main action remains between the State and D.

[30] There are many other agencies with prosecution powers (eg SFO, Defra, FCA, etc) but most prosecutions are conducted by the CPS. It is also possible for individuals to bring private prosecutions, on which see Elvin and De Than, 'Private Prosecution: A Useful Constitutional Safeguard or Potentially Dangerous Historical Anomaly?' [2019] Crim LR 656.

[31] Prosecution of Offences Act 1985, s10.

[32] Defence representation is paid for privately, or through State-assisted legal aid.

confused with the legal burden on the prosecution, and is placed on the defendant principally for reasons of efficiency. It avoids wasting the court's time by the court having to consider multiple defences that have no chance of success. It is for the prosecution to prove the elements of the offence beyond reasonable doubt: to prove, in our example, that D kicked V intending to make contact or having foreseen the risk of making contact, and that V suffered some minor harm as a result. If D is able to present some evidence as to a defence, satisfying the evidential burden, it is also for the prosecution to prove the absence of that defence beyond reasonable doubt.

D) **The jury:** Only Crown Court trials involve a jury. The jury is made up of 12 people.[33] The role of the jury is to decide matters of fact and not matters of law. For example, if the law makes it an offence for D to kick V, it is the jury's job to decide if D did in fact kick V. If the definition of the offence requires proof that D intended to injure V, the jury must decide whether D did so intend. The judge decides on matters of law. For example, it may be that D claims she kicked V accidentally in the course of a football match. The judge would rule as a matter of law whether consent by V in playing football was *capable* of providing D with a defence. The jury would then decide whether, on the facts, it was a football match, and whether V did consent or may have done so.

E) **The judge:** The judge must adjudicate on any legal conflict between the opposing advocates relating to rules of evidence and admissibility, as well as any other matter of law. The judge is also responsible for summing up the facts and directing the jury on the law before they retire to consider their verdict. If D is found guilty of an offence, the judge is responsible for setting the appropriate sentence.[34]

In the magistrates' courts, which operate without a jury, the magistrate must make decisions about the evidential rules, the law, *and* the facts as well. They are assisted in the first two of these by a qualified legal advisor. The magistrates are also responsible for sentencing.

Decisions of higher courts (eg the Divisional Court, the Court of Appeal, and the Supreme Court) are made by panels of judges and do not include a jury. In accordance with the doctrine of precedent, the legal interpretations and decisions of these courts then bind the future interpretations of the courts below them.

1.1.7.2 The burden of proof in criminal trials

It is for the prosecution to prove D's guilt, which is known as the 'criminal burden of proof'; and they must do so beyond reasonable doubt, which is known as the 'criminal standard of proof'. This is designed to limit the risk of innocent people being wrongly convicted.[35] It also recognises the inequality of the resources of the parties, with the State possessing vast resources for investigatory powers and personnel. The legal burden placed on the prosecution means that the defendant is presumed innocent until proven

[33] Jury members are randomly selected from the voting register up to the age of 75: Criminal Justice and Courts Act 2015, s68. Only those who are mentally incapable, or those with specified (serious or recent) criminal convictions, are excluded: Criminal Justice Act 2003, s321.

[34] The role of the judge is usefully summarised in *Wang* [2005] UKHL 9, [3] and [8].

[35] This is a position neatly encapsulated in the ratio attributed to William Blackstone writing in the 1760s which maintains that 'it is better that ten guilty persons escape than that one innocent suffer'.

guilty. This is a long-established principle of English law,[36] also found in Article 6(2) of the European Convention on Human Rights (ECHR).

Although the prosecution bearing the legal burden of proving every element of D's liability may be considered fundamental to the criminal law, it is not an absolute rule. In several instances, the legal burden is 'reversed' and D bears the burden of proving a particular element or defence. An example is where D claims to have been insane when kicking V. In that case D must prove that she was insane.[37] Reverse burdens of proof remain controversial within the law, not least for their effect on D's right to a fair trial (Art 6 ECHR). However, the use of reverse burdens in certain contexts remains commonplace.[38]

To understand the role of reverse burdens of proof, two aspects require discussion. The first concerns the standard of proof. As highlighted previously, where the burden of proof is on the prosecution, they must prove D's liability 'beyond reasonable doubt'. However, where D bears a reverse burden, she need only prove the relevant element to the civil standard of proof: 'on the balance of probabilities'.[39]

Secondly, where reverse burdens arise, this is usually in the context of defences as opposed to offences (eg insanity[40] and diminished responsibility[41]). This is important because defences only become relevant if the prosecution have already provided evidence that D has committed the elements of the offence. Asking D to prove some element of defence once the prosecution have already provided evidence of D's wrongdoing is not directly contrary to the presumption of innocence: the presumption only protects D 'until proven guilty'. In contrast, where reverse legal burdens impose an obligation on D to establish her innocence before the prosecution have provided evidence of wrongdoing, the presumption of innocence is infringed. In fact, in many cases where there appeared to be a reversed legal burden, even if this only applied to a single element within an offence, the courts have rejected it and interpreted it instead as an evidential burden to ensure compliance with Article 6 ECHR.[42] This arrangement provides some protection for D's Article 6 rights but remains problematic, particularly as the pivotal distinction between defences and offences lacks objective criteria. For example, the non-consent of V is an element of the offence in the context of sexual offences, but the consent of V is generally considered to be a defence in the context of other non-fatal offences against the person.[43]

The greatest effect of a reverse burden is as a matter of practice and procedure. However, it may also be directly relevant to the substantive definition of the offence. This is apparent in relation to certain mischiefs that, although deserving of criminalisation, are particularly difficult for prosecutors to prove. For example, as we will discuss in **Chapter 8**, this is true of sexual offences: although involving serious wrongs, it is difficult

---

[36] *Woolmington v DPP* [1935] AC 462.

[37] We discuss the insanity rules in **Chapter 13.4**.

[38] See Dennis, 'Reverse Onuses and the Presumption of Innocence' [2005] Crim LR 901; Stumer, *The Presumption of Innocence: Evidential and Human Rights Perspectives* (2010).

[39] Proving simply that it is more likely than not.

[40] See the *M'Naghten* Rules (1843) 10 Cl & Fin 200, 210.

[41] Homicide Act 1957, s2(2).

[42] The courts do so using the interpretive powers within the Human Rights Act 1998, s3. See eg *Lambert* [2001] UKHL 37 relating to the possession of drugs.

[43] See **Chapters 7** and **8** respectively. It may be that consent is wrongly classified in the context of the non-fatal offences (**7.10.3**).

to prove offences that invariably take place in private, and often come down to dispute over D's and/or V's state of mind as to consent. The temptation to employ a reverse burden as to aspects of the offence (eg consent) is obvious: where we are discussing D's state of mind, surely D is in a better position to present evidence of this than the police or CPS. Indeed, within the Sexual Offences Act 2003, we already see a movement in this direction with the use of reversed rebuttable *evidential* burdens as to consent.[44] However, despite their potential practical utility, whether such reform serves the interests of justice remains a separate question.[45]

1.1.7.3 The criminal court structure and appeals process

In this section we consider the structure of the criminal appeals system.[46] It is important to understand this structure, as reference to the different stages of appeal will arise regularly in our discussion of the law. It is also necessary to understand this structure when considering the doctrine of precedent. Just as legislation is binding on all courts, the doctrine of precedent dictates that interpretations of the law made by higher courts will bind (must be applied by) lower courts in future cases. Essentially, the doctrine of precedent is a common law system to ensure consistency between courts and to make future interpretations of the law more predictable. It is on this basis that when looking to identify substantive rules of law we will often do so by discussing the interpretations of the Court of Appeal (Criminal Division) and the Supreme Court (formerly the House of Lords[47]) in particular. When doing so, it is necessary, albeit not always straightforward, to distinguish legal interpretations that were required by the court to reach their decision (referred to as the *ratio decidendi* of the case, and capable of creating binding precedent) and interpretations that were additionally made, but not necessary to reach the decision (referred to as *obiter dicta*, creating only a persuasive and non-binding precedent).

 Extra detail . . .

Traditionally, only statements made within the *ratio* of a case will create binding precedent for lower courts. However, an emerging convention, usefully discussed in *Barton*,[48] holds that *obiter* comments within the Supreme Court are capable of binding lower courts, where those comments amount to a clear and unanimous direction from the Supreme Court Justices.[49]

In **Table 1.1**, we set out the role of each court within the criminal appeals system. We also highlight the potential for appeal between the courts.

---

[44] Sexual Offences Act 2003, s75.
[45] See Ashworth and Blake, 'The Presumption of Innocence in English Criminal Law' [1996] Crim LR 306; Ashworth, 'Four Threats to the Presumption of Innocence' (2006) 10(4) E&P 241.
[46] See Spencer, 'Does Our Present Criminal Appeal System Make Sense?' [2006] Crim LR 667.
[47] The Supreme Court replaced the Appellate Committee of the House of Lords as the highest court in the UK in October 2009.
[48] [2020] EWCA Crim 575, paras 93–109.
[49] Discussed in Horder, 'The Courts' Development of the Criminal Law and the Role of Declarations' (2020) 40(1) LS 42.

Table 1.1 Criminal courts and appeals process

Magistrates' court	The magistrates' courts are the lowest criminal courts in England and Wales. They are usually made up of volunteer magistrates who are not legally qualified, and who are intended to represent the community. They rely on a legal advisor for legal guidance. In some courts there are legally qualified magistrates who sit alone (known as 'District Judges (Magistrates' Court)'), and they tend to hear the more serious cases in the magistrates' courts. The sentencing power of the magistrates' court is limited to six months' imprisonment for each offence (12 months overall), and unlimited fines.
	All 'summary only' offences (eg assault and battery) are tried in the magistrates' court. Other offences, known as triable either way offences (offences of which the seriousness can vary considerably on their facts, eg theft and criminal damage) are tried in the magistrates' court unless D elects to be tried in the Crown Court or the magistrates think the case deserves to be tried in the Crown Court. All the most serious cases (triable on indictment only) that are tried in the Crown Court also pass through the magistrates' court. In fact, over 95% of all criminal cases will be settled in the magistrates' court without appeal.
Appeal from magistrates' court	• *D may appeal her conviction to the Crown Court.* This route is available if D pleaded 'not guilty' in the magistrates' court, but was found guilty. This appeal will result in a rehearing of the case in the Crown Court.
	• *D may appeal the level of her sentence to the Crown Court.* Again, this will result in a rehearing.
	• *D and/or the Crown can appeal by 'way of case stated' to the High Court.* Such an appeal must contend that the magistrates made a mistake in law or acted in excess of their jurisdiction, but there can be no appeal on factual matters.
	• *D and/or the Crown can apply for judicial review to the High Court.* This application must contend that the magistrates acted beyond their power (ultra vires).
Crown Court	A Crown Court case will include both a professional judge (High Court Judge, Circuit Judge, or recorder) and a jury. In exceptional cases, it can be tried by judge alone—usually where the jury is discharged by the judge. The role of the judge is to decide matters of law, and the role of the jury is to decide matters of fact. The sentencing power of the Crown Court is only limited by the individually prescribed maximum sentence for each offence. In practice the judge follows guidance from the Sentencing Council.
	We discuss very few Crown Court rulings in this textbook. This is partly because cases at this level are not always reported, and partly because of their limited precedent value when it comes to clarifying the substantive law.

(Continued)

Table 1.1 Continued

Appeal from Crown Court	• *D and/or the Crown can make an interlocutory appeal on the judge's rulings relating to the way the trial will be conducted.* The appeal is made to the Court of Appeal before the Crown Court trial commences.

- *The prosecution can make an interlocutory appeal to the Court of Appeal on a point of law, if this is made before the trial judge begins summing up.* This route is only available to trials on indictment, and requires leave from the trial judge or Court of Appeal. If leave to appeal is refused, or the Court of Appeal accepts but upholds the trial judge's ruling on the disputed point of law, then D is acquitted. If the appeal is successful, then the point of law will be corrected and the case will resume at the Crown Court on those amended terms. Thus, this route entails significant risks for the Crown and is rare.

- *D may appeal her conviction to the Court of Appeal.* The court will examine the appeal having regard to all its circumstances, 'in the round'. If the Court of Appeal finds the conviction 'unsafe' it will allow the appeal, quashing the conviction and ordering a retrial in the Crown Court as appropriate.

- *D may appeal the level of her sentence to the Court of Appeal.* The court has the power to quash and substitute any sentence or order as appropriate, although it may not increase its severity if D appealed. The Court of Appeal will only make such a substitution if the sentence is manifestly excessive or wrong in principle, not justified in law, or where matters were improperly considered or ignored.

- *D's conviction and/or sentence can be referred to the Court of Appeal by the Criminal Cases Review Commission.* If D has had an appeal rejected (or leave for appeal refused), and the CCRC believe there has been a potential miscarriage of justice (relating to conviction or sentence), it can refer it to the Court of Appeal for consideration at any time.

- *The Crown may not appeal D's acquittal.* Founded in the logic of double jeopardy (the principle that D should not face trial for the same crime twice), prosecutors cannot appeal an acquittal in the hope of convicting D. However, changes in the law relating to double jeopardy have created a narrow exception to this. If D was acquitted of one of a list of serious specified offences (eg murder or rape), and if new and compelling evidence is discovered making it more likely that D committed the offence, and if the DPP consents, the Court of Appeal may quash an acquittal and allow for new proceedings to be brought against D in the Crown Court.

- *If D is acquitted, the AG can refer a point of law to the Court of Appeal (AG's Reference cases).* Where D has been acquitted the Crown cannot appeal against this acquittal. However, if the Crown Court's decision to acquit was based on a potentially mistaken interpretation of law, the lack of an appeal risks further damage (other courts applying similar reasoning). Therefore, the AG may refer a point of law that emerged at trial to the Court of Appeal. D's acquittal is not at issue, and will remain in place irrespective of the Court of Appeal's decision. However, the mistaken point of law (if there is one) can be corrected for future cases. Because the prosecution can bring an interlocutory appeal, this scheme of bringing references after acquittal has become practically redundant.

	• *The AG can appeal the level of sentence to the Court of Appeal.* Where D has been convicted and sentenced for certain offences identified by Parliament, the AG (on behalf of the prosecution) can refer the case to the Court of Appeal if the AG believes the sentence is 'unduly lenient'. The court is empowered to quash the previous sentence or order and replace it as appropriate, including the potential for a more severe penalty.
Court of Appeal (Criminal Division)	When the Court of Appeal sits to hear an appeal it is usually comprised of three judges presided over by a Lord Justice of Appeal (senior judge). Decisions of the Court of Appeal create precedent that binds the future interpretations of lower courts and, generally, future interpretations in the Court of Appeal as well. Occasionally, however, where a case is taken before an expanded Court of Appeal panel of five judges the court is more open to departing from its own precedents.

The majority of the cases that we discuss in this textbook are Court of Appeal cases. |
| **Appeal from Court of Appeal** | • *D and/or the Crown may appeal to the Supreme Court.* Appeals to the Supreme Court will only be available where the disputed point of law is of 'general public importance'. Leave must be granted by the Court of Appeal or the Supreme Court. Where leave is granted, the Supreme Court may also, at its discretion, consider related issues of law that are not directly connected to the point appealed. |
| **Supreme Court** | The Supreme Court is the highest court in the UK (formerly that was the Judicial Committee of the House of Lords). There are 12 Justices of the Supreme Court, but the Court usually sits with five Justices in a hearing. Decisions of the Supreme Court create binding precedent for all lower courts, including the Court of Appeal. The Supreme Court also considers itself bound, although it may depart from its own precedent where appropriate. Supreme Court (House of Lords) cases will be discussed throughout this textbook. Creating the strongest judicial precedent, these decisions form a central part of our identification of the substantive law. |
| **Privy Council** | At a number of points in this textbook we will consider opinions of the Judicial Committee of the Privy Council. The Privy Council is based in the Supreme Court building, with roughly the same set of judges sitting in both courts. However, the Privy Council is not part of the criminal court structure for cases originating in England and Wales. Rather, the Privy Council is the court of final appeal for UK overseas territories and Crown dependencies, and for those Commonwealth countries that have retained the appeal to Her Majesty in Council or, in the case of republics, to the Judicial Committee.

As the Privy Council is not directly applying the law of England and Wales, opinions of the Board have no binding effect on the courts within the structure outlined above. However, when interpreting areas of law that are identical or similar to those in this jurisdiction, bearing in mind that the judges in the Privy Council are usually also Supreme Court Justices, the Board's opinions can have a strongly persuasive effect. |

1.2 Sources of the substantive criminal law

Having spent some time setting the substantive criminal law in context, and distinguishing other approaches to the study of crime, it is now possible to narrow our focus to the substantive rules themselves. The first part of this involves a discussion about the sources of the criminal law. Before we begin to interpret and apply the substantive law, we must first learn how to identify it.

Recognising the sources of the criminal law is extremely important. For example, when D kicks V causing harm, D commits a public wrong that is deserving of criminalisation. However, the fact that certain conduct *deserves* criminalisation does not tell us whether it *is* criminal, and does not tell us the precise *definition* of the offence. For this, we need to identify the source of law.

1.2.1 Statute

Most of the substantive criminal laws in England and Wales are now set out in statutory form, the principal binding source of criminal law. There are two main benefits to this. First, as the criminal law defines and controls such an important area of interaction between State and citizen, it is appropriate that these rules should be constructed through a democratically accountable process. Secondly, statutes are more accessible to all, at least by comparison with the common law discussed later. Particularly since the development and consolidation of online resources (eg www.legislation.gov.uk), it is now possible for citizens to have access to statutory rules quickly and easily. However, a degree of caution is needed:

A) **Quantity of legislation:** Although statutes are accessible, the sheer quantity of legislation makes it impossible for the legal practitioner, let alone the public, to be fully informed.[50] Problems can also be created where, as is very common, new statutes include multiple amending provisions that make patchwork changes to other legislation.

 Point to remember . . .

When using older sources to identify the law, or even newer ones such as www.legislation.gov.uk, care must be taken to ensure that you are aware of any subsequent amendments that may affect the text (even the online resources can take time to be updated).

B) **Form and detail of legislation:** Although there are formal parliamentary procedures for the creation of legislation, there are very few rules defining the form an Act must take. As a result, you will find that different statutes vary greatly from one another in their level of detail and manner of presentation. This can lead to problems of interpretation. For example, the law that criminalises D as a secondary party to an offence committed by another is set out in the Accessories and Abettors Act 1861.[51] Section 8 states, simply:

> 8. Whoever shall aid, abet, counsel or procure the commission of any indictable offence . . . shall be liable to be tried, indicted, and punished as a principal offender.

[50] Chalmers and Leverick, 'Tracking the Creation of Criminal Offences' [2013] Crim LR 543.
[51] We discuss accomplice liability in **Chapter 12**.

Although the simplicity of this provision may be superficially appealing, it quickly becomes clear that it is rather more unhelpful and misleading. With the provision leaving so many questions unanswered (eg what is it to aid, abet, counsel, or procure?), the true definition of the offence is left to the common law. On the other hand, the modern trend in favour of very detailed provisions in statutes should be approached with equal caution. As we will explore in later chapters, although these statutes have been designed to pre-empt disputes and to clarify the law, some have had the opposite effect and have tended towards unnecessary complexity and impenetrability.[52]

C) **Type of legislation:** As long as a statute containing the offence in question is enacted and in force, then so are its provisions. In this textbook, we will not dwell on the types of legislation employed. However, it is worth highlighting two concerns in this area. First, criminal offences are often created in statutes that are not primarily concerned with the criminal law (eg the Insolvency Act 1986). This makes those offences more difficult to find and set in context. Secondly, and more worryingly, a great many criminal offences are created through subordinate or secondary legislation. Such legislation does not receive full parliamentary scrutiny, and therefore lacks some democratic legitimacy.[53]

1.2.2 Common law

The law in England and Wales, both civil and criminal, owes its ancient origins to societal customs and traditions. Some of these customs and traditions were formalised within codifying legislation. However, the greater part of these rules have not been codified, and rely on recognition and enforcement through the courts directly. Through the courts, and the system of precedent, these customs-turned-laws create a body of rules known as the 'common law'.[54] Even today, these common law rules still form the basis of the criminal law in England and Wales, as well as other 'common law jurisdictions': former British colonies that were administered using the same system. The common law system can be contrasted with the 'civil law' system that dominates most of Europe, a system that is based firmly on the creation and interpretation of legal codes (legislation that attempts to codify all areas of law) rather than law created and developed in the courts.

Significantly, despite the common law system in England and Wales, it is now firmly accepted (and has been for many years) that courts are no longer at liberty to create new offences or defences[55] or to abolish such rules.[56] This is uncontroversial. Although the development of new common law offences and defences served to create an essential body of rules, it is accepted that such rules are now more appropriately dictated by a democratically accountable Parliament. A further reason for preferring statutory law is that court-made law can be criticised as retrospective: if D's conduct is declared to be

---

[52] See eg discussion of the Serious Crime Act 2007 in **Chapter 11**. Spencer, 'The Drafting of Criminal Legislation: Need It Be So Impenetrable?' (2008) 67 CLJ 585.

[53] Criticised in Law Commission, *Criminal Liability in Regulatory Contexts* (Consultation 195, 2010) para 3.114.

[54] Holmes, *The Common Law* (2012).

[55] *Jones et al* [2006] UKHL 16.

[56] See *Goldstein and Rimmington* [2005] UKHL 63, where the House of Lords denied having power to abolish the offence of public nuisance.

criminal for the first time by the court which is trying her, then D's lack of prior warning means she is treated unfairly. Such retrospectivity may allow the law to punish a certain mischief, but if that wrong was not yet recognised as a criminal wrong we cannot claim that D has *chosen* to break the law.

Although the common law no longer creates or abolishes offences or defences, it remains the source for a significant part of the current criminal law. Thus, for example, when discussing offences such as murder and manslaughter, and defences such as duress, insanity, and necessity, the relevant rules are not all defined in statute. Rather, as with many other offences and defences, we have to look to the common law and individual leading cases. This is obviously a challenge for those studying the substantive criminal law within a common law jurisdiction, but it should not be overstated. Indeed, as highlighted earlier, even when offences and defences are codified in a statute, the courts still have an important role in interpreting such legislation in practice (whether the legislation is detailed or otherwise). The difference is that legislation at least allows the democratic lawmakers to choose what discretion to leave to the courts, to control the framework of the law, and to promote consistency. With the common law, all such decisions are judge made.

 Assessment matters . . .

If in an assessment you are dealing with a statutory offence/defence then your identification of the substantive rules should *always* begin with the statute. From here, you then explore case law in order to resolve any ambiguities from the statute and to see how the rules are applied in practice: the courts 'put meat on the bone'. With a common law offence/defence you need to do exactly the same thing, but this time your only source is the case law.

1.2.3 European Convention on Human Rights

The UK ratified the ECHR in 1951, allowing individual petition to the European Court of Human Rights (ECtHR) from 1966: essentially a rights-based challenge to decisions of the UK courts. The Human Rights Act 1998 further incorporated the ECHR by allowing the Convention to be applied directly in domestic courts. The effect of the ECHR on substantive criminal law, as elsewhere, has been extensive.[57] However, unlike the statute and common law sources discussed earlier, the ECHR does *not* create any new criminal offences or defences. Rather, it sets out a number of 'rights' that the UK is obliged to protect in the creation and application of the law.

The role of the Human Rights Act 1998 (HRA) in particular, has been to highlight and prioritise rights jurisprudence and the ECHR at every stage of the legal process. Section 1 of the HRA formally incorporates ECHR rights into domestic law. This ensures the ECHR's influence from the earliest stages: every new piece of legislation, including criminal law matters, require a government minister to make a statement to Parliament of compatibility between the proposed legislation and the ECHR.[58] Beyond this, and very importantly, there is also an obligation on domestic courts to take account of ECHR rights when interpreting and applying *all* areas of law (not simply relying on potential

---

[57] Ashworth, Emmerson, and MacDonald, *Human Rights and Criminal Justice* (3rd edn, 2012).
[58] HRA 1998, s19.

appeal to the ECtHR in Strasbourg). Through section 3 HRA, domestic courts at all levels must *as far as is possible* interpret domestic legislation to give effect to ECHR rights. Under section 4, higher courts also have the power to make a 'declaration of incompatibility' where there is an inconsistency with ECHR rights and no obvious interpretive (s3-based) solution. Section 4 does not provide the courts with the power to strike down or invalidate the incompatible domestic law, and has been exercised sparingly, but provides a strong incentive to maintain consistency in interpretation.[59]

The main role of the ECHR with regard to the substantive criminal law, facilitated by the HRA, has been in terms of interpretation and evaluation. Below is a list of ECHR rights, and some examples of their effect on the law. The specific influence of the ECHR within each area of criminal law will be discussed throughout this textbook.

- Article 2: The right to life. Article 2 has affected the definition of homicide offences (murder and manslaughter),[60] abortion, euthanasia,[61] as well as leading to challenges where D kills V in self-defence.[62]

- Article 3: The prohibition of torture and inhuman and degrading treatment. Article 3 has been relevant to offences relating to parental (and school-based) application of corporal punishment,[63] as well as the treatment of criminal suspects.

- Article 4: The prohibition of slavery and forced labour. Article 4 led to the creation of a slavery offence in 2009,[64] and is particularly relevant to the discussion of human trafficking and sex workers.

- Article 5: The right to liberty and security. Article 5 has greatest effect on any defendant who has not yet been convicted (eg D's pre-trial detention, false imprisonment, and unfitness to plead), as well as D who is found not guilty by reason of insanity.[65] It might also affect the definition of offences such as false imprisonment.

- Article 6: The right to a fair trial. Article 6, including the presumption of innocence, is central to the debate concerning reverse burdens of proof.[66]

- Article 7: The prohibition on criminal laws being applied retrospectively is found in Article 7. At its strongest, it applies if an offence is created and made to apply to conduct that was not criminal at the time the conduct was performed. In such a situation it would not be permissible to convict D for her conduct before the offence was created. Article 7 provides strong support for the codification of criminal law and the limitation of judicial discretion which (inevitably) is applied after the event.

- Article 8: The right to respect for private and family life. Article 8 is relevant, in particular, to offences that criminalise consensual sexual violence.[67]

---

[59] See *AG's Reference (No 4 of 2002)* [2004] UKHL 43, [28].
[60] See **Chapters 5** and **6**.
[61] See **Chapters 11** and **12**.
[62] See **Chapter 14**.
[63] See **Chapter 7.3.1**.
[64] See **Chapter 7.9.3**.
[65] **Chapter 13**.
[66] See, in particular, **Chapters 13** and **14**.
[67] See **Chapter 7.8.2**.

- **Article 9:** Freedom of thought, conscience, and religion. Article 9 provides a framework for religiously aggravated offences,[68] as well as potential public order offences involving public worship.

- **Article 10:** Freedom of expression. Article 10 is relevant to the application of several offences and defences where D's acts are expressing protest (eg criminal damage and public order offences).

- **Article 11:** Freedom of assembly and association. Article 11 is most obviously relevant to public order offences as they apply to assemblies.

- **Article 12:** The right to family life. Article 12 has affected debates about whether married couples should be liable for an offence if they conspire (agree to commit a crime) with one another.[69]

- **Article 13:** The right to an effective remedy for breaches of Convention rights. Article 13 is most relevant to the civil law, but will also have an impact on what is known as restorative justice.[70]

- **Article 14:** The right to non-discrimination under Convention rights.

Articles 2 and 3 are absolute (do not allow for discretion) in the negative obligations they provide.[71] However, many of the other rights listed above are subject to important qualifications. This means that, even if there is an apparent breach of a Convention right, it can be justified by the State if it is: (a) prescribed by law; (b) necessary in the pursuit of a specified objective (eg public order, health or morals, or the freedom of others); and (c) proportionate to that objective. In view of the substantive criminal law, such qualifications are obviously essential. Substantive offences prohibiting D from performing certain acts will inevitably restrict her expression (Art 10), as well as depriving or restricting her liberty (Art 5) where she breaks the law. Therefore, when discussing the impact of these rights on the substantive criminal law, such qualifications should always be considered.

1.2.4 European Union

Following the UK's decision to leave the European Union (EU), the future influence of the EU on UK law is uncertain.[72] A proportion of law in the UK has been generated either directly from EU institutions[73] or indirectly through mutual recognition and cooperation. However, traditionally such provisions have not affected domestic criminal law. This is because, as the EU was originally conceived as a trade and economic union,

---

[68] See **Chapter 7.9.2**.

[69] See **Chapter 11**.

[70] Restorative justice involves a novel approach to criminal processes and sentencing that focusses on the role of the victim and the community. As it is not directly relevant to the substantive criminal law, it is not considered further in this textbook.

[71] This is not the case where a claimant alleges a breach of a positive obligation, eg the potential right to assisted death under Art 2, *Pretty v UK* (2002) 35 EHRR 1.

[72] Davidson, 'Brexit and Criminal Justice: The Future of the UK's Cooperation Relationship with the EU' [2017] Crim LR 379.

[73] Secondary law from the EU takes the form of regulations, decisions, and directives. Art 288 Treaty on the Functioning of the European Union (TFEU).

criminal law was not within its competencies. As the EU has developed, however, particularly in relation to the protection of fundamental rights, its spheres of competence have expanded well beyond their original trade-based limits.

 Don't be confused . . .

Although all Member States of the EU are signatories to the ECHR, the EU is not the author of the Convention; this is the separate European body, the Council of Europe. Therefore, our discussion of ECHR rights in the previous section must be distinguished from our discussion of the EU.

The expansion of EU competencies has begun to affect domestic criminal law in Member States.[74] Importantly, criminal law remains primarily an issue for individual States, with the EU gaining only limited competence. However, with the increased flow of people across borders, and the ease of technology connecting people together, there is much that can be gained from linking (or at least coordinating) criminal jurisdictions that have traditionally remained separate and insular. Coordination through the EU has therefore targeted offences that commonly involve a cross-border element (eg terrorism, human trafficking, corruption, and other organised crimes), preventing criminal groups from taking advantage of the patchwork of legal inconsistencies across Europe.[75] Such coordination has made particular strides in relation to criminal evidence and procedure,[76] and is likely to continue notwithstanding the UK exit.

Despite this expansion of EU competence, the vast majority of the substantive criminal law remains a preciously guarded area of national competence and sovereignty. Therefore, although we see an increased internationalisation of criminal offending in almost every area of the criminal law, the EU's competence remains relatively narrow and specific, with what we might call the more traditional offences (eg murder, offences against the person, etc) strictly excluded. As these more traditional offences are the subject of this textbook, we will largely set the influence of the EU to one side from this point forward.[77]

1.2.5 International law

International law, whether criminal or otherwise, is the product of agreements between States, and applies across those States. In this way it is fundamentally different from domestic law that is created and applied at a national level.

International law has had an effect on the substantive criminal law in England and Wales in two main ways. The first is the most direct influence, through the creation of international crimes that are applied domestically. Through Part 5 of the International Criminal Court Act 2001, a number of international offences defined in the Rome

---

[74] Criminal law emerged as a third pillar (basis for intergovernmental cooperation) within the Maastricht Treaty. Following the Lisbon Treaty, specified criminal matters come within the competence of the EU institutions. TFEU, Title V, Ch4.

[75] Art 83 TFEU.

[76] Art 82. Examples of this include measures on extradition and the European Arrest Warrant.

[77] For a wider discussion, see Mitsilegas, *EU Criminal Law After Lisbon* (2016).

Statute[78] have been incorporated into national law. The Rome Statute focusses on a relatively small core of internationally recognised war crimes such as genocide. These offences are therefore now part of the domestic criminal law as well. However, they are not discussed further in this textbook.[79]

The second area of influence arises from softer sources of international law: conventions arising from groups such as the United Nations (UN), EU, Council of Europe, and the Organisation for Economic Co-operation and Development (OECD), where the UK agrees to create criminal offences to tackle certain agreed mischiefs.[80] In this manner, although several areas of substantive criminal law have been directly influenced or mandated by the signing of such conventions, their binding source remains the national statute (discussed earlier). Reference to such *origins* of national law, and an examination of their ambitions, can be useful when evaluating the domestic offences that implement them. Such evaluation is similar to our earlier discussion of criminal wrongs: identifying the mischief which the offence is trying to tackle in order to evaluate how effectively it has been criminalised.

1.2.6 The Law Commission and the Draft Criminal Code

The work of the Law Commission and the Draft Criminal Code are not binding sources of criminal law. However, in different ways, both provide a powerful and pervasive influence affecting the reform of criminal offences and defences, as well as the interpretation of substantive rules within the courts. Both will be discussed throughout this textbook, and thus both require some introduction.

A) The Law Commission of England and Wales:[81] The Law Commission is a national law reform body, sponsored by the Ministry of Justice but independent from government. The Commission has been prolific, particularly in recent years, consulting on several areas of the substantive criminal law and producing reports, including draft legislation, that have directly led to several of the major reforms that will be discussed in later chapters. Where Law Commission projects have been successfully taken forward by government the Commission's papers can provide a useful background to this reform, explaining the rationale behind it and discussing examples of how it might be applied.[82] Even where the Commission's recommendations are not taken forward, these papers are also useful as summaries and evaluations of the current law, as well as providing alternative approaches that can be compared with the current position.[83] In either case, the

---

[78] The Rome Statute 1998 is an international agreement, creating the International Criminal Court and defining core international criminal offences.

[79] See Grady, 'International Crimes in the Courts of England and Wales' [2014] Crim LR 693; O'Keefe, *International Criminal Law* (2017).

[80] eg the Bribery Act 2010 was conceived with explicit reference to several international obligations. Law Commission, *Reforming Bribery* (Consultation 185, 2007) Appendix A.

[81] Law Commissions Act 1965. Law Commission publications can be downloaded from www.lawcom.gov.uk.

[82] See eg assisting and encouraging crime (**Chapter 11**), fraud (**Chapter 10**), and corporate manslaughter (**Chapter 6**).

[83] See eg parties to crime (**Chapter 12**), attempts and conspiracy (**Chapter 11**), intoxication (**Chapter 13**), and, more recently, insanity and automatism (**Chapter 13**), hate crime, offences against the person (**Chapter 7**), kidnapping and false imprisonment (**Chapter 7**), and unfitness to plead (**1.5.3**).

accessible and authoritative nature of Law Commission material makes it a vital source for the study of criminal law.[84]

B) **The Draft Criminal Code:** Criminal codes have become prevalent, even among common law jurisdictions. Within a code, all the major criminal offences and defences can be brought together in a single document (referred to as the 'special part' of the code), as well as general provisions such as definitions of common language (referred to as the 'general part' of the code).[85] The most recent attempt to construct a criminal code for England and Wales was published by the Law Commission in 1989,[86] following earlier proposals from an academic team in 1985.[87] The 1989 Draft Code is an exceptional piece of work, and its detailed yet succinct definitions continue to influence debate. However, very importantly, despite support from successive Lord Chief Justices, the Draft Code has never been taken forward by government and adopted into law. The approach of the Commission in recent years, since 2009, has been focussed on the reform and codification of individual areas of the law, as we see most recently in the context of sentencing (**1.1.4**). This offers many potential benefits, but the lack of a criminal code remains regrettable.[88]

Extra detail . . .

The Draft Criminal Code, as with all Law Commission draft Bills, can provide a useful point of reference when evaluating the law or seeking alternatives to it. However, such material does not represent the law, and should never be presented as such: they are simply reform recommendations. Also, where a new statute is based on a prior Law Commission draft, be careful to look out for differences between the two.

1.3 The internal structure of offences and defences

Having discussed the sources of criminal offences and defences, it is useful to provide a brief introduction to the structures or forms they take. Strictly speaking, there are very few rules that restrict how offences or defences should be framed, which is partly due to the lack of a criminal code. However, certain patterns and conventions have emerged in interpreting criminal offences, both within the common law and from statute, which can help to make sense of the law. These conceptual tools provide a framework for those drafting the law, for the courts applying the law, for the academic evaluating it, as well as for the student trying to do all three.

---

[84] Dyson et al, *Fifty Years of the Law Commission* (2016); Smith, 'Criminal Law and the Law Commission 1965–2015' [2016] Crim LR 381.

[85] The language of 'general' and 'special' parts was coined by the criminal law academic Glanville Williams.

[86] Law Commission, *A Criminal Code for England and Wales*, 2 vols (No 177, 1989).

[87] Law Commission, *Codification of the Criminal Law: A Report to the Law Commission* (No 143, 1985).

[88] Dennis, 'RIP—The Criminal Code (1968–2008)' [2009] Crim LR 1. The potential benefits of a criminal code are set out in the Law Commission's Draft Code documents. See also de Búrca and Gardner, 'Codification of the Criminal Law' (1990) 10 OJLS 559.

The most important structural devices for analysing *offences* are:

- Actus reus (guilty act): Discussed in **Chapter 2**, the actus reus of an offence describes the wrongful conduct and/or consequences required for liability in proscribed circumstances. For example, when D kicks V she may have committed the crime of battery, the actus reus of which prohibits D making unlawful physical contact with another.

- Mens rea (guilty mind): Discussed in **Chapter 3**, the mens rea of an offence describes the state of mind or fault that D must have when completing the actus reus. For battery, for example, D must either intend to make unlawful contact or at least foresee the risk that her conduct will result in contact with V, where that contact is unjustifiable.

Defences, on the other hand, do not involve guilty acts or guilty minds (quite the opposite). Thus, in this context we simply speak of the 'elements' of a defence.

- Defence elements: Discussed in **Chapter 14**, a defence will be available where its elements (its requirements) are fulfilled. For example, if D kicks V to prevent V from attacking her, she may rely on the defence of self-defence. This defence requires two core 'elements': first, that D acted with an honest belief in the need for preventative force and, secondly, that the force used (the kick) was a reasonable response based on the facts as D believed them to be.[89]

In many ways, understanding the structures of the criminal law is the most important part of our study, particularly in the context of offences. There are now well in excess of 10,000 offences known to the law of England and Wales, only a small number of which can ever be included in a textbook of this kind. Therefore, as well as studying the offences in their own right, our focus (particularly in the early chapters) is to develop methods of analysis that can be used to understand any offence within the law. It should be remembered, however, that these methods and conceptual tools are not essential parts of the law, they are simply methods developed to analyse it. As a result, areas of inconsistency and uncertainty have emerged within the techniques as they have been applied to different offences.

As we discuss each new offence, we will employ the structures of analysis traditionally employed in relation to that offence. This usually involves the simple separation of actus reus, mens rea, and defences, but this will not always be the case. It is important to reflect any different forms of analysis so that when you read court judgments and other academic material that are likely to use these approaches and terminology, you are familiar with them. However, in order to provide you with a *consistent* structure of analysis, we will also highlight how every offence could be analysed using an approach which we will call 'element analysis'. This approach will be explored fully over the following three chapters. Based on the separation of actus reus and mens rea, element analysis further subdivides an offence into conduct, circumstances, and results. It is an approach that can be set out using simple charts, as in **Table 1.2**.

---

[89] Self-defence is discussed in **Chapter 14.5**.

Table 1.2 Offence elements chart (eg battery)

	Actus reus	**Mens rea**
Conduct element	Any physical acts or omissions required for the offence. For battery, D's act of kicking	Any mens rea required as to D's acts or omissions. For battery, that D's conduct was performed voluntarily by her
Circumstance element	Any factual circumstances required for the offence. For battery, that V is a person	Any mens rea required as to those facts or circumstances. For battery, that D knew that what she was kicking was a person
Result element	Any consequences of D's action/omission required for the offence. For battery, the physical contact with V	Any mens rea required as to those consequences. For battery, that D intended contact with V or foresaw a risk of that and took the risk unjustifiably

We have chosen to employ this analytical approach as our consistent tool for two main reasons. First, it allows us to explore offences in more detail than the traditional approach of analysing just actus reus and mens rea. Secondly, when we come to discuss the general inchoate offences (eg attempts and assisting and encouraging) in **Chapter 11**, as well as certain other areas,[90] the use of element analysis is essential in order to apply the law. Thus, becoming familiar with it from an early stage will be very useful.

1.4 The principles of the substantive criminal law

Reference to the 'principles' of criminal law, common in case law and academic debate, draws upon the idea that there are certain common ideals or aims underpinning the substantive rules. Led most recently by the work of Andrew Ashworth,[91] the identification and discussion of legal principles has become very important to the study of crime. Such principles are primarily employed as evaluative tools. For example, the principle of fair warning states that criminal offences should be clearly constructed and communicated in order to guide the actions of society.

The ECHR (discussed at **1.2.3**) provides minimum thresholds to the quality of the law, particularly in relation to the presumption of innocence (Art 6) and in terms of basic clarity (Art 7). However, academic discussion of the principles of criminalisation provides clearer guidance on the *ideal* qualities of the criminal law, providing points of reference that can be used to commend or criticise individual offences or defences as appropriate. As certain principles have become more widely accepted, it is clear that

---

[90] eg reform proposals in relation to the intoxication rules (**Chapter 13**) and complicity (**Chapter 12**).
[91] Horder, *Ashworth's Principles of Criminal Law* (9th edn, 2019).

they also play a role in the interpretation of the law, with certain approaches preferred by judges over others in line with underpinning principles.

The principles of criminal law have a two-pronged effect. First, they affect the substance of the law by influencing the manner of its interpretation and, secondly, they affect the reform of the law through evaluation. In the following sections we highlight a selection of the most important principles that are closely connected to the substantive criminal law.

 Don't be confused . . .

The principles of the criminal law are useful tools for evaluating the quality of an offence or defence. However, they do not affect its validity as law. As long as an offence or defence has originated from a binding source (statute or the common law), it is valid regardless of its quality in terms of legal principles and regardless of its format within element analysis or otherwise.

1.4.1 The principle of fair warning

This principle requires clear communication of the law to the public. As stated earlier, the criminal law aims to deter people from certain wrongful activities, and to punish those who *choose* to pursue wrongful ends in disregard of the law. However, to achieve either of these aims, there is an implicit assumption that the public are aware of the law in the first place: to be guided by it, or to deserve punishment for choosing to break it.

The principle of fair warning is used to discuss and evaluate how effectively offences are communicated to the public. It is a discussion that engages with several areas of debate. For example, the principle of fair warning is central to the contention that offences existing in the common law should be codified in statute, and ideally within a criminal code. In each case, public access to the law would be improved.

Fair warning is also a principle that guides *how* offences should be codified. On the one hand, offences and statutory drafting must be sufficiently detailed to allow the public to know what exactly is being criminalised, and allow them to moderate their behaviour accordingly. For example, imagine an offence drafted in simple terms such as 'it is a crime to make unlawful contact with another'. Such an offence would inform D that kicking V *may* be criminal, but without a definition of 'unlawful' the only way D could moderate her behaviour to be sure to avoid liability would be to make no contact with others at all. Hardly an ideal message! On the other hand, offences and statutory drafting should avoid being overly complex. For example, as we will discuss in **Chapter 8**, several sexual offences (eg voyeurism) have been defined in an extremely complex manner. The complex nature of the statutory drafting does little to provide fair warning to the legal expert trying to predict the law, let alone the public.

Alongside the principle of fair warning is the duty on citizens to be aware of the criminal law, such that ignorance of the law is no excuse. This means that it is no defence, when D has committed a criminal wrong, to claim that she did not know (even reasonably) that the offence existed. This rule is controversial, especially when we consider the failures of fair warning in several areas of the law,[92] and the potential for moral ignorance (where D rejects the moral ambitions of an offence),[93] but it remains a stable tenet of the law.

---

[92] See eg Ashworth, 'Ignorance of the Criminal Law, and Duties to Avoid it' (2011) 74 MLR 1.
[93] See Husak, *Ignorance of the Law* (2016).

Extra detail . . .

For those researching this area in greater depth, some exciting work has been done by the American academic Paul Robinson. Robinson advocates the creation of multiple criminal codes, with 'rule articulation' (a code written in accessible language to tell the public what they cannot do), separated from other necessarily more complex codes that would focus on 'liability assessment' and 'grading' (codes written for those administering the law).[94]

1.4.2 The principle of fair labelling

The principle of fair labelling requires accurate correlation between the name of an offence and the conduct it criminalises.[95] The rationale for this principle can be linked with that of fair warning in the previous section. The knowledge most people have of substantive crimes will not go far beyond their awareness of offence names and the implications of those names (eg kidnapping, rape, etc). Therefore, the fairness of the label dictates the fairness of the warning. However, the principle is perhaps more important when it is applied to someone after they have been convicted. This is because, as well as D being sentenced appropriately (fines, prison, etc), it is important that the name of D's offence labels her accurately in the eyes of the public. D is not simply sent to prison for a certain duration, she is labelled as a murderer, a thief, a robber, etc.

The role of criminal labelling is not straightforward; it has both positive and negative aspects. Labels can be very useful in terms of the clear stigma and message created: allowing the State to condemn the accused in language that the public, on whose behalf the State acts, can understand. However, labelling and stigmatisation are difficult to control and quantify, relying on changeable social constructions and attitudes. Thus, in terms of the additional punishments they provide, they cannot be objectively prescribed.

What can be controlled, however, is that we can ensure the label given to D's offence is at least accurate, and in *this* sense fair. It is here that the principle engages most directly with the substantive law. First, it demonstrates the importance of separating different mischiefs into different offences with different labels. For example, if D1 steals V1's car, and D2 sets V2's car on fire, both Ds have caused the loss of a car. However, the mischiefs committed by D1 and D2 are different, and their conduct should be separately labelled: D1 has committed theft; D2 arson. This debate arises in later chapters, for example when we consider the creation of new offences that relabel conduct already criminalised elsewhere (eg the recognition of *domestic* violence/abuse as a separate offence[96]).

The aim of fair labelling also has a direct effect on the content of offences and defences whose names are well known to the public, for example rape and robbery. This is because, as well-known labels can communicate more clearly to the public, there is often a desire that they should be maintained, even when the substantive content of the offence is changed. This is partly why, for example, there has been debate about whether the

---

[94] Robinson, 'A Functional Analysis of Criminal Law' (1994) 88 Nw UL Rev 857; Robinson, *Structure and Function in Criminal Law* (1997).

[95] Chalmers and Leverick, 'Fair Labelling and Criminal Law' (2008) 71 MLR 217; Williams, 'Convictions and Fair Labelling' (1983) 42 CLJ 85.

[96] See **Chapter 7.10.1**.

offence 'rape' was rightly extended to include non-consensual anal or oral penetration.[97] The concern here is that if such labels are used inappropriately, not only is D unfairly labelled if convicted, but because D's conduct does not fit with society's general understanding of the label there is a risk that a jury might acquit a defendant who fulfils the elements of the offence, and who should, therefore, be found guilty. We see this rationale, for example, behind changes in Canadian criminal law where the label of 'rape' was removed from sexual offences entirely.[98]

1.4.3 The principle of autonomy

Where we discuss the principle of individual autonomy, we are usually referring to the autonomy of a potential offender. Again, it is a principle that can arise in various contexts. In simple terms, it can be used as a principle of minimum criminalisation. To have autonomy is to be free to act and pursue our goals unrestrained. The criminal law, by design, restricts our options by criminalising certain conduct. Indeed, in the context of criminalising failures to act, the law is limiting *all* of our options and requiring a certain course of conduct.[99] Therefore, if we see autonomy as something that should be preserved and maximised, criminal offences, particularly those involving omissions liability, should be kept to a minimum.[100]

The principle of autonomy is also the primary vehicle for the promotion of 'choice' as an essential ingredient of both moral and legal blame. The impact of this can be seen in two main areas. First, we should not criminalise conduct that D cannot avoid. The most basic implications of this would rule out the criminalisation of, for example, belonging to a certain race, breathing, or sleeping, where we have no choice at all. More interestingly, it may also affect debate on the fairness of criminalising unrealistic choices. For example, the defence of duress applies where D commits an offence to avoid threatened serious violence. However, even if we recognise that a reasonable person would have acted as D did, and therefore D's choice was in some sense a reasonably unavoidable one, duress is never allowed as a defence to murder. Thus, where D kills V whilst acting under duress and is convicted of murder, we may question the law's respect for her autonomy.[101]

Secondly, autonomy and choice are also central to debates about mens rea. At a minimum, this can be seen in the proposition that all offences should involve voluntary or intentional action: if D kicks V involuntarily, for example whilst having an epileptic seizure or when tripping over, there should be no offence.[102] Taken more widely, we could similarly contend that every element of an actus reus should require a corresponding mens rea. For example, if D kicks V and V dies, should D only be liable for an offence related to that death if D intended or at least foresaw, in

---

[97] **Chapter 8.**
[98] Criminal Code of Canada, Part VIII.
[99] Williams, 'Criminal Omissions—The Conventional View' (1991) 107 LQR 86; Ashworth, *Positive Obligations in Criminal Law* (2013).
[100] Husak, *Overcriminalisation* (2008).
[101] The Law Commission raises the principle of autonomy to support its recommendation that duress *should* be a defence to murder. This is discussed in **Chapter 14.3.**
[102] Discussed in **Chapter 3.3.**

some sense chose, that level of harm? Or perhaps this level of foresight is not necessary, and we should require only intentional conduct performed in circumstances where D *should* have recognised the risks she was running? This debate is central to much of the discussion of mens rea in **Chapter 3**, and the distinction between what is termed subjective (choice-based) and objective (results-based) approaches to the law.

1.4.4 The principle of welfare

The principle of welfare promotes the role of law in protecting society from harm. From a potential victim's perspective, the welfare principle is therefore in line with the autonomy principle discussed previously: for an individual to be autonomous and free to pursue her goals, she must be protected from others who would unfairly interfere with her, physically or otherwise. However, the protection of V requires the restriction of D. Thus, from D's perspective, the welfare principle provides a counterbalance to that of autonomy, and one that could justify a highly restrictive criminal law. For example, if D kicks V during an epileptic seizure the principle of autonomy would point towards there being no liability, D has not chosen to cause harm to V. However, D's kick has still interfered with the welfare of V. Therefore, if D is prone to such seizures, and particularly if they regularly result in injury to others, the welfare principle could be used to favour criminalisation.

The challenge for the criminal law is to find balance to promote maximum autonomy and welfare by creating the conditions, through minimum criminalisation, that allow and support people in the pursuit of legitimate social goals.[103] How effectively the law finds this balance within individual offences and defences is something for evaluative debate. Examples were highlighted in our earlier discussion of autonomy, including the criminalisation of unrealistic choices (eg affecting the defence of duress), criminalising involuntary harms (affecting the requirement of voluntary conduct) as well as unforeseen harms or circumstances (affecting mens rea more generally). In each case, balancing the welfare principle reminds us to consider the objective results of D's conduct as well as what D intended or foresaw. Where the result is serious harm to V, it may be that criminalisation is justified even where D has not chosen every aspect of the offence.

A final example that demonstrates the difficulty of finding balance is the defence of insanity.[104] This defence means that D is not criminally liable where a defect of reason arising from a disease of the mind leads her to commit an offence. However, as such defects are often more than temporary, and as D may therefore pose a continuing danger to others, a successful insanity defence will not result in simple acquittal. Rather, D is 'not guilty by reason of insanity', and a range of disposal orders, including involuntary detention in hospital, become available to the court. D is not guilty because her 'insanity' means that she did not choose to offend; but she may still have her autonomy sacrificed in the name of societal welfare.

---

[103] Lacey, 'Community in Legal Theory: Idea, Ideal or Ideology?' (1996) 15 Studies in Law, Politics and Society 105.

[104] Discussed in **Chapters 13.4** and **14.2**.

Don't be confused . . .

The principles discussed here provide useful tools for evaluating the law, but they are not exhaustive. Think of the principles as useful prompts, but try to maintain a broader focus as well: in terms of basic fairness, ask yourself whether the 'offence' you are evaluating captures *only* conduct that is fairly criminalised; and in line with basic rule of law concerns, ask yourself whether it does so in a way that does not create or perpetuate bias.[105]

1.5 The subjects of the substantive criminal law

As well as considering the content of the criminal law, it is also important to remember who it is aimed at: whose behaviour it seeks to regulate, and who is subject to punishment for breaking the law. The typical subject of the criminal law is a natural person. However, as we discuss briefly in the following sections, the criminal law will also apply to legal persons (ie corporations, partnerships, and unincorporated associations), and will not apply, or at least not in the same way, to natural persons in certain circumstances (eg minors and those unfit to plead).

1.5.1 Corporations

Where a natural person commits an offence in the course of acting on behalf of a corporation or other legal entity, she will be liable directly for that offence.[106] However, additionally, and sometimes even in the absence of individual liability, the corporation itself (as a legal person) may be liable for an offence in its own right. This is referred to as corporate criminal liability.

 Extra detail . . .

Beyond corporate criminal liability (targeting public limited companies (plc), private limited companies (Ltd), and limited liability partnerships (LLP)), the criminal law can also target unincorporated associations. However, in the absence of a legal personality, the rules governing such liability are often unclear.[107]

Most criminal offences are capable of being committed by legal as well as natural persons,[108] with the exception of murder[109] and a few others. Indeed, in many cases, the legal *and moral* case in favour of convicting the corporation may be considerably stronger

---

[105] Ormerod, 'Racism in the Criminal Justice System (Editorial)' [2020] Crim LR 659.
[106] See generally Law Commission, *Criminal Liability in Regulatory Contexts* (Consultation 195, 2010).
[107] See discussion in *L* [2008] EWCA Crim 1970.
[108] The term 'person' must be interpreted in this manner, unless the contrary is specified. Interpretation Act 1978, s5 and Sch 1.
[109] Murder cannot be committed by a corporation because it carries a mandatory life sentence, a sentence that cannot apply to a corporate entity.

than any individual involved. For example, where the negligence of a particular employee leads to harm, corporate liability may be more appropriate when that negligence is set in the context of a company that encourages risk taking and dangerous practices on a wider scale.[110]

Corporate criminal liability raises two central challenges for the law. First, in the absence of a physical entity, where do we look for the actions and mental states of the company? And secondly, where we find liability, how can we punish the company in an effective manner? In the study of substantive criminal law, we focus on the first of these concerns.[111]

1.5.1.1 Vicarious criminal liability of corporations

Vicarious liability, common in the context of tortious claims for damages, allows the liability of an employee acting in the course of their duties to be attributed to the organisation they are working for. In the context of the civil law, the doctrine serves a crucial role to enable victims to be adequately compensated for their losses, with the organisation being considerably more likely than the employee to be able to bear costs.

 Don't be confused . . .

Vicarious liability does not require the organisation to have assisted, encouraged, or contributed to the actions of the employee. In this way, vicarious corporate liability should not be confused with criminal complicity.[112]

In the context of criminal law, where the primary aim is to punish/deter D rather than to compensate V, vicarious liability makes little sense. Where D (the organisation) has acted in a criminally blameworthy fashion then it should be targeted directly, and where it has not, the use of vicarious liability is surely unfair. However, the law does allow for the vicarious criminal liability of organisations in relation to a number of offences,[113] mainly of a regulatory nature.

1.5.1.2 Direct criminal liability of corporations

There are three primary routes to the direct criminalisation of corporate conduct: (A) specific corporate offences; (B) the identification doctrine; and (C) liability for a failure to prevent.[114]

A) Specific corporate offences: Arguably the most efficient way to regulate corporations by criminal law is through the specific criminalisation of certain conduct. Thus, rather than attempting to reinterpret legislation drafted with natural persons in mind, corporate offences can be tailor-made: by removing mens rea requirements, by including

---

[110] Gobert, 'A Corporate Criminality: New Crimes for New Times' [1994] Crim LR 722.
[111] On the problem of effective punishment, see Jefferson, 'Corporate Criminal Liability: The Problem of Sanctions' (2001) 65 JCL 235.
[112] See **Chapter 12.**
[113] *Tesco Stores Ltd v Brent LBC* [1993] 2 All ER 718.
[114] See generally Cavanagh, 'Corporate Criminal Liability: An Assessment of the Models of Fault' (2011) 75 JCL 414.

due diligence defences, and so on. Such offences are often preferred, for example, when criminalising failure to meet certain health and safety standards. The disadvantages of such offences are that they can be perceived as purely regulatory, and thus not 'true' crimes, which can undermine the stigmatising effect of the law.

B) **Identification doctrine:** The identification doctrine is a mechanism created at common law to attribute criminal liability to corporations where such liability includes both actus reus and mens rea requirements. Essentially, the doctrine provides that a corporation can be liable for a crime of mens rea if that mens rea was possessed by an officer in the corporation of sufficient seniority to be considered by the court a 'controlling mind'—someone whose actions and mens rea can fairly be said to represent that of the corporation as a whole.[115] The major disadvantage of this doctrine, however, is that identifying a 'controlling officer' who had mens rea can be very difficult, particularly where the corporation is large and complex such that the 'controlling officers' are unlikely to be involved with those working at lower levels.[116]

C) **Failure to prevent:** Partly as a reaction to the perceived inadequacies of the identification doctrine, modern statutes have begun to develop a form of corporate liability based around a failure to prevent. Modelled on the tort of negligence, this doctrine does not seek to blame the corporation criminally for something it has done or thought via the identification doctrine, but rather for its failure to provide adequate procedures and mechanisms to prevent the harms caused by those employed or associated with the corporation. We can see variations of this model in place with the offences of corporate manslaughter,[117] of bribery,[118] of facilitating tax evasion,[119] etc; and depending upon its success, it is an approach that has the potential to be expanded across almost all financial crimes.[120]

A procedural development that has impacted on the criminalisation of corporations is the emergence of deferred prosecution agreements (DPAs).[121] DPAs were introduced in 2014,[122] and first used in 2015.[123] They are available to the CPS and the Serious Fraud Office (SFO), allowing these agencies to reach agreements with a corporation that defers prosecution on the proviso that the corporation agrees to a set of measures that will prevent future harms and legal violations. DPAs are controversial, and only apply to legal (as opposed to natural) persons, but can provide an efficient procedural means of regulating corporate bodies.

---

[115] Developed and discussed in *Bolton* [1956] 3 All ER 624; *Tesco v Nattrass* [1972] AC 153; *Re Supply of Ready Mixed Concrete (No 2)* [1995] 1 AC 456; *X Ltd* [2013] EWCA Crim 818; *SFO v Barclays* [2018] EWHC 3055 (QB).

[116] For a recent critique, see Lööf, 'Corporate Agency and White Collar Crime—An Experience-led Case for Causation-based Corporate Liability for Criminal Harms' [2020] Crim LR 275.

[117] See **Chapter 6.4.1**.

[118] The Bribery Act 2010, s7.

[119] See the Criminal Finances Act 2017 and Laird, 'The Criminal Finances Act 2017—An Introduction' [2017] Crim LR 915.

[120] Wells, 'Corporate Failure to Prevent Economic Crime—A Proposal' [2017] Crim LR 426.

[121] King and Lord, *Negotiated Justice and Corporate Crime* (2018); Laird, 'Deferred Prosecution Agreements and the Interests of Justice: A Consistency of Approach?' [2019] Crim LR 486; Bisgrove and Weekes, 'Deferred Prosecution Agreements: A Practical Consideration' [2014] Crim LR 416.

[122] Crime and Courts Act 2013, Sch 17.

[123] Padfield, 'Deferred Prosecution Agreements' [2016] Crim LR 449.

1.5.2 Minors

Section 50 of the Children and Young Persons Act 1933 creates a *conclusive* presumption that children under the age of 10 years cannot commit a criminal offence. Therefore, in substance, no criminal prosecution can apply to this group. This will be the case regardless of the circumstances, eg even where D (under 10) has acted intentionally and caused even serious harm or death. Those under 10 years require protection and support, and this can be gained through the civil law. They do not deserve, at this young age, the punishment and stigma of the criminal law.

Once D reaches the age of 10, the criminal law will apply regardless of her level of maturity.[124] Prior to 1998,[125] a rebuttable presumption was recognised at common law doctrine (*doli incapax*) that those between 10 and 13 years were not capable of forming a criminal mens rea: rebutted only where the prosecution could prove that D knew that her acts were 'seriously wrong' as opposed to merely 'naughty'. The abolition of this common law doctrine, combined with the comparatively low age of criminal responsibility in England and Wales compared to other jurisdictions, has led to cogent criticism of the overcriminalisation of children.[126]

1.5.3 Defendants who are unfit to plead

In the Crown Court, D is 'unfit to plead' (or unfit to be tried) if, because of a disability, she is incapable of being tried within the normal criminal court process.[127] The conditions for 'unfitness' were set out in *M*,[128] and require D to have sufficient ability to:

(a) understand the charges;

(b) understand the plea;

(c) challenge jurors;

(d) instruct legal representatives;

(e) understand the course of the trial; and

(f) give evidence (if she chooses to do so).

To establish D's unfit state (ie by showing that D lacks one or more of these abilities), the onus of proof is on the party raising the issue: if raised by the defence, then they must prove D's unfitness on the balance of probabilities; if raised by the prosecution, then the prosecution must prove it beyond a reasonable doubt.[129] The matter is decided by the judge alone. Where D is found unfit to plead, the standard criminal process ceases. This

---

[124] *T v UK* [2000] Crim LR 187: criminally punishing a 10-year-old is not contrary to Art 3 ECHR.

[125] Crime and Disorder Act 1998, s34.

[126] Brown, 'Reviewing the Age of Criminal Responsibility' [2018] Crim LR. See also Keating, 'How Should the Criminal Law Respond to the "Special Status of Children?"' in Child and Duff (eds), *Criminal Law Reform Now* (2019) 165; cf, in the same volume, critiquing the developmental model and suggesting an alternative, Yafee, 184.

[127] Where D is competent at trial, but claims to have been suffering from a defect of reason caused by a disease of the mind when committing the criminal act, the insanity rules should be applied. See **Chapters 13** and **14**.

[128] [2003] EWCA Crim 3452. See discussion in *Marcantonio, Chitolie* [2016] EWCA Crim 14.

[129] *Podola* [1959] 3 All ER 418.

is the case regardless of evidence that D committed the offence; regardless of evidence that D was of mental capacity when committing the offence; and regardless of whether D was 'fit' for some parts of the trial.[130] The fairness and legitimacy of the justice system requires a 'fit' defendant throughout.

Where D is found unfit, instead of a standard criminal trial, the case will be decided through a 'trial of the facts'. This procedure is set out in sections 4 and 4A of the Criminal Procedure (Insanity) Act 1964, as amended. A trial of the facts is a trial before a jury to determine whether D committed the acts or omissions required for the offence charged. In other words, the court will explore the actus reus of the offence, but *not* the mens rea. If it is found that D did not commit the actus reus, she will be acquitted in the normal manner. However, where D is found to have committed the actus reus, although she is not liable for the full offence, a range of disposal options become open to the court. These include a hospital order, with or without a restriction order, a supervision order, or an absolute discharge.[131]

With the greater awareness of mental health issues in the criminal justice process, so the inadequacies of the current law become more apparent.[132] Chief among these has been the fact that there is no equivalent process in the magistrates' court and youth court where some of the most vulnerable defendants are tried. In the Crown Court, where the scheme outlined above applies, there are also significant difficulties. These include, for example, finding a principled and consistent separation of acts and omissions, relevant to a trial of the facts.[133] The case of *B* provides a useful example of this where, on a charge of voyeurism, the court struggled to decide whether the relevant 'act' which would have to be proved was the simple conduct of viewing a person in a state of undress, etc, or whether it also had to be shown that the viewer was motivated to do so for sexual gratification.[134] Despite the issue of motivation seeming to go beyond an analysis of acts, the Court of Appeal held that D's sexual motivation was so essential to the 'act' of voyeurism that it remained essential even for a trial on the facts. Similar problems have also emerged in relation to potential defences.[135]

The Law Commission made recommendations for reform of the whole unfitness to plead framework in 2016;[136] including a draft Bill.[137] The Commission criticises the current law as outdated, inconsistently applied, and potentially unfair. These recommendations have been well received,[138] but whether they are taken forward by government remains to be seen.

[130] *Orr* [2016] EWCA Crim 889; Mackay, Commentary [2016] Crim LR 865.
[131] Criminal Procedure (Insanity) Act 1964, s5.
[132] Mitchell and Howe, 'A Continued Upturn in Unfitness to Plead—More Disability in Relation to the Trial under the 1991 Act' [2007] Crim LR 530.
[133] For a useful review of this area of law, including areas of legal confusion and concern, see *Wells, Masud, Hone and Kail* [2015] EWCA Crim 2; and more recently, Bevan, 'Making It Work? The Case of *Roberts* and Uneven Progress in the Reform of Unfitness to Plead Procedures' [2020] Crim LR 215.
[134] [2012] EWCA Crim 770.
[135] *Antoine* [2000] UKHL 20.
[136] Law Commission, *Unfitness to Plead. Vol 1: Report* (No 364, 2016). See also Law Commission, *Unfitness to Plead* (Consultation 197, 2010); *Issues Paper* (2014).
[137] Law Commission, *Unfitness to Plead. Vol 2: Draft Legislation* (No 364, 2016).
[138] Loughnan, 'Between Fairness and "Dangerousness": Reforming the Law on Unfitness to Plead' [2016] Crim LR 451.

1.6 Reform

In the penultimate section of every chapter we will have a separate discussion about legal reform, engaging with a wider academic and reform literature. This is not to say that we will *only* discuss reform in such sections. However, where possible, we will look to separate the discussion in this way to avoid common confusions between the current law and reform recommendations. The main aim of these sections is to help you to engage critically with the current law, moving beyond an investigation of the rules themselves, to the evaluation of those rules and the consideration of alternatives. Such material is most directly relevant to essay-type questions, which commonly require you to consider and discuss reform options. However, it will also be useful for problem questions where (as is less common) they engage with potential reform. Considering the potential reform of offences and defences is also often the best way to gain a deeper understanding of the rules themselves.

When discussing reform proposals, it is obviously important that you understand what the proposal is attempting to do. Just as your understanding of the current law requires you to be able to identify and describe the rules, the same is true for your discussion of a reform proposal. In addition, discussion of reform requires you to engage with and to evaluate the law, and this will be a major theme of these sections. Thus, you will need to consider the law on four separate levels.

- **Describe the current law:** You cannot begin to discuss the reform of an area of law before you first take time to understand it.
- **Evaluate the current law:** You need to be able to identify the problems with the current law that have motivated the creation of reform proposals, evaluating the seriousness of such problems.
- **Describe the reform proposals:** You need to know how the reform proposals seek to remedy the problems identified with the current law.
- **Evaluate the reform proposals:** To what extent would the proposals succeed in remedying the identified problems with the current law? Would the reform create any new problems?

Our discussion of reform proposals will, of course, differ within each chapter. However, the tools for evaluation (both of the current law and of reform proposals) do not change, and have been introduced in this chapter. We might ask, for example, how accurately the current law or the reform proposal targets the mischiefs that it is attempting to criminalise (**1.1.1**); how similar reforms have worked out in other common law jurisdictions (**1.1.6**); whether they conform to ECHR rights (**1.2.3**), etc. In each case, we can also apply the principles of criminalisation discussed at **1.4**, asking whether the current law or reform proposal fairly warns and labels, whether it respects autonomy, and whether it protects welfare.

The substantive criminal law should not be thought of as a static body of rules to be committed to memory. Rather, it is dynamic and changing, through judicial interpretation as well as through statutory reform. You should consider the evaluative tools discussed in this chapter as a toolbox, equipping you to grapple with the substantive law. The criminal law is clearest and most interesting and rewarding when you can not only identify and apply the rules as they stand, but do so with an understanding of how those rules have developed and how they are likely to change.

1.7 Eye on assessment

The final section of every chapter will provide an 'eye on assessment'. The idea of these sections is to discuss the *application* of the current law, particularly in the context of problem questions. Having discussed the substantive rules themselves, and having discussed potential reform, this section aims to help you to structure an answer that will demonstrate that knowledge.

Without any particular offences in mind, set out below is a generic guide to structuring a *problem question* that we will return to throughout this textbook. Although our approach may vary from this model when discussing particular offences and defences, it remains a useful structure around which these variations can be discussed and justified. It should be noted that there is no single 'right' model for answering problem questions, and so different lawyers/academics/students will prefer various approaches, but the model adopted in this textbook should provide a useful and consistent example.

INTRODUCTION

The introduction to a problem question should be brief. It can be useful to identify the offences and defences relevant to the question (ie in one or two sentences), and to say how you are going to answer the question (eg chronologically, defendant by defendant, crime by crime, etc). However, be sure to get into the body of the answer as quickly as possible.

STEP 1 Identify the potential criminal event in the facts

This is unlikely to take more than a sentence, but it is essential to tell your reader where in the facts you are focussing. For example, 'The first potential offence is committed when D kicks V'. If you go straight into an analysis of the law without highlighting the event in the facts then it is very difficult for a reader to follow your answer.

STEP 2 Identify the potential offence

Having identified the facts (eg D kicking V), you must now identify the offence you are going to apply. Usually, this means identifying the most serious offence that D might have committed. For example, 'When kicking and seriously injuring V, D may have committed a grievous bodily harm offence contrary to section 18 of the Offences Against the Person Act 1861'.

STEP 3 Applying the offence to the facts

Actus reus: What does the offence require? Did D do it?

Mens rea: What does the offence require? Did D possess it?

Remember, to be liable for the offence every element of the actus reus and mens rea must be satisfied. Thus, every element should be discussed even where it is easily satisfied and little discussion is necessary. Where there is doubt, in law or in fact, highlight and discuss areas of likely dispute between prosecution and defence. Also, if the question asks you to engage critically with the law as you apply it, take particular care to include evaluation of the law.

AR and MR are satisfied	AR and/or MR are not satisfied
Continue to STEP 4.	Return to STEP 2, and look for an alternative offence. If none, then skip to STEP 5, concluding that no offence is committed.

STEP 4 Consider defences

The word 'consider' here is important, as you should not discuss every defence for every question. Rather, think whether there are any defences that *could* potentially apply. If there are, discuss those only.

STEP 5 Conclude

This is usually a single sentence either saying that it is likely that D has committed the offence, or saying that it is not likely because an offence element is not satisfied or because a defence is likely to apply. It is not often that you will be able to say categorically whether or not D has committed the offence, so it is usually best to conclude in terms of what is more 'likely'.

STEP 6 Loop

Go back up to Step 1, identifying the next potential criminal event. Continue until you have discussed all relevant potentially criminal events.

CONCLUSION

It is good practice to complete your problem question answer with a brief conclusion. This is usually no more than a few sentences highlighting where you believe offences have been committed and where they have not.

ONLINE RESOURCES

www.oup.com/he/child-ormerod4e

This chapter is accompanied by a selection of online resources to help you with this topic, including:

- **Self-test questions and scenario questions**
- **Videos** from the authors
- **Audio introduction** to the topic
- **Chapter summary sheet**
- **Two sample examination questions with answer guidance**
- **Further reading and weblinks**

Also available on the online resources are:

- A selection of **videos** from the authors containing general advice on problem questions and essay questions
- **Legal updates**

2

Actus reus

2.1 Introduction

The term 'actus reus' is loosely translated as 'guilty act', and refers to the 'external elements' of an offence. These external elements do not simply relate to D's conduct. Rather, as we will see, the actus reus of an offence includes any offence elements other than those related to the fault ('mens rea') of the offence. This will include D's acts or omissions; any surrounding circumstances or facts necessary for liability, for example, that the appropriated property *belongs to another* for theft; and any required results, for example the causing of *death* in homicide offences. Additionally, it will include the necessary links between elements, for example that the results must be *caused* by D's conduct. So, taking the simple case of an offence of battery by kicking, the actus reus involves D's kick (conduct), of a person (circumstance), making contact with that person (result).

It should be remembered that 'actus reus' and 'mens rea' are terms of art. We separate actus reus and mens rea in our analysis because breaking down offences into their elements helps us to understand them. But we must not lose sight of the fact that no matter what methods are used to distinguish the elements of an offence, D's liability depends upon the satisfaction of *all* of them as a whole. To be liable for an offence, it must be proved beyond reasonable doubt that D satisfied *all* the requirements of *both* the actus reus and the mens rea, and D did not have any defence. This is illustrated in **Figure 2.1**.

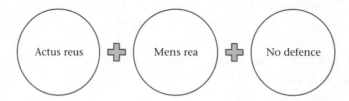

Figure 2.1 Structure of liability

The separate analysis of actus reus elements, which is the focus of this chapter, has several advantages. Most importantly, it is the physical conduct of D that typically identifies the time and location[1] of the offence. This is why the analysis of a potential offence should always begin with actus reus, as it is only after this that we can then ask if D had the requisite mens rea *at that point*. The actus reus is also the only universal feature of all criminal offences: although offences have been created in the absence of mens rea,[2] there is no liability in the absence of actus reus, there is no 'thought crime'.[3]

2.2 Separating actus reus and mens rea

Before we explore the elements that form the actus reus, we must first learn to separate them from mens rea elements. For many offences this is relatively straightforward. Whether you are analysing a statutory or common law offence, the task is to separate any offence requirement that is external from D's mental fault (actus reus elements) from anything that is concerned with such fault (mens rea elements). For example, the common law offence of murder is committed when D unlawfully causes the death of a person under the Queen's peace with the intention to kill or the intention to cause grievous (very serious) bodily harm.[4] Here, the only part of the offence that is concerned with

[1] Where the offence takes place is important in relation to jurisdictional issues. Jurisdictional discussion will arise in certain chapters, but is generally not a focus of this book.
[2] So-called strict or absolute liability offences of this kind are discussed in **Chapter 3.2.1**.
[3] See discussion in Duff, *Answering for Crime* (2009) Ch5.
[4] *Cunningham* [1982] AC 566. See **Chapter 5**.

D's state of mind or fault is her intention to kill or cause grievous bodily harm; this is therefore the mens rea. D's actions and their results—acting to cause the unlawful death of a person—are all matters other than to do with D's state of mind or fault, and therefore represent the actus reus.

However, although these simple rules of separation are capable of consistent application, this is made more difficult when dealing with terms that appear to include both fault and external requirements.[5] Examples include the terms 'appropriates',[6] 'cultivates',[7] 'abandons',[8] etc.[9] Where this is the case, we have two options: separate the fault and external aspects through the use of alternative terminology; or accept that actus reus elements occasionally include aspects that overlap with the fault or state of mind of D. It is contended that the former approach (separation) should always be preferred. However, this is not the consistent approach of the courts.

Below are two examples of terms that could be separated into actus reus and mens rea elements, but are popularly analysed as only one or the other:

- **'Sexual'**: An actus reus requirement for sexual assault,[10] as well as a number of other sexual offences,[11] is that D's conduct must be 'sexual'. Section 78 of the Sexual Offences Act 2003 states that D's conduct can be sexual (a) 'because of its nature', in the sense that a reasonable observer would describe it as sexual, or (b) if its nature may be sexual and the 'circumstances' or 'purpose' of D make it sexual. Thus, although the offence element of 'sexual' is invariably referred to as an actus reus element, where it is satisfied by the 'purpose of D', this is clearly focussing on D's state of mind.[12]

- **'Dishonesty'**: One of the main elements of theft[13] and fraud[14] (and many other offences) is the requirement that D acted 'dishonestly', an element that is almost universally referred to as a mens rea requirement.[15] However, the common law definition of dishonesty set out in *Ivey*[16] contains both internal and external elements: the jury must first ascertain the defendant's state of mind as to any relevant facts or circumstances (internal), and then, with regard to D's state of mind, determine the dishonesty of her conduct by the standards of ordinary decent people (external).

This kind of imperfect separation of actus reus and mens rea will arise within several of the offences discussed in later chapters. It is far from ideal, and has caused considerable confusion. However, without a criminal code or some other codified source setting out the definitions of actus reus and mens rea elements,[17] such inconsistency is largely

---

[5] Lynch, 'The Mental Element in the Actus Reus' (1982) 98 LQR 109.

[6] See **Chapter 9**.

[7] *Champ* [1982] Crim LR 108 and commentary.

[8] *Hunt and Duckering* [1993] Crim LR 678.

[9] See Robinson and Grall, 'Element Analysis in Defining Criminal Liability: The Model Penal Code and Beyond' (1983) 35 Stan L Rev 681.

[10] Sexual Offences Act 2003, s3.

[11] See **Chapter 8**.

[12] See recent case of AG Ref (No 1 of 2020) [2020] EWCA Crim 1665. See also Sullivan, 'Bad Thoughts and Bad Acts' [1990] Crim LR 559.

[13] Theft Act 1968, s1. See **Chapter 9**.

[14] Fraud Act 2006, s1. See **Chapter 10**.

[15] See **Chapter 3.6.1**.

[16] *Ivey v Genting Casinos (UK) Ltd* [2017] UKSC 67.

[17] See eg definitions in the US Model Penal Code 1962, §2.02.

inevitable. It is also, for the most part, an inconsistency that does not damage the application of the law: D is only liable when every element of actus reus and mens rea is proved beyond reasonable doubt, whether we call them one thing or the other. Thus, the message here is to use actus reus and mens rea terminology to help with your analysis, but recognise that the law does not maintain a precise division between the two at all times.

2.3 Actus reus elements

The broad category of 'actus reus' is usefully subdivided into elements related to conduct, circumstances, and results.[18]

- **Conduct:** D's physical acts or omissions required for liability.
- **Circumstances:** Facts surrounding D's conduct required for liability.
- **Results:** The effects of D's conduct required for liability.

As with the actus reus/mens rea distinction, the further separation of conduct, circumstances, and results within the actus reus can be useful when setting out the detail of an offence. It is also useful to employ this terminology when singling out a particular part of the actus reus for criticism or comment. As an illustration of how this subdivision works, consider the offence of criminal damage. The actus reus requires D to have completed certain acts or omissions (conduct element) to property belonging to another (circumstance element) which causes damage (result element).

2.3.1 The conduct element

The conduct element of the actus reus is concerned with the physical movement of D's body. The conduct element, therefore, focusses only on the external movement (or, as we will see, lack of movement) of D's body. This is illustrated in **Table 2.1**.

Table 2.1 Conduct element of the actus reus

	Actus reus	Mens rea
Conduct element	D's physical acts or omissions required for liability	*
Circumstance element	*	*
Result element	*	*

---

[18] Robinson and Grall, 'Element Analysis in Defining Criminal Liability: The Model Penal Code and Beyond' (1983) 35 Stan L Rev 681.

All criminal offences require a conduct element of some description as it is this element that typically locates where and when the offence happened. This is also the element that provides a nexus between D and the other elements required for liability. For example, as we consider below, whether the results were *caused by D's conduct*, and whether D has a certain mens rea *at the time of her conduct*.

 Assessment matters . . .

When assessing potential liability within a problem question you should always begin by identifying the conduct element of the actus reus: what did D do, or fail to do in breach of duty? All analysis flows from here.

The conduct required for different offences will vary considerably. For example, certain offences require quite specific acts such as penile penetration,[19] or driving.[20] However, it is also common to leave the conduct element unspecified. This is often the case when an offence is seeking to criminalise a certain harmful result no matter how it is caused by D. For example, the actus reus of murder includes *any* conduct that causes the unlawful death of a person; it does not matter if this is hitting, shooting, stabbing, pushing from a height, etc. The conduct element is still essential to D's liability, it is still the element that links D to the death, but D's method of killing is unspecified within the offence.[21]

Where a conduct element is satisfied by D's positive movements then its application is relatively straightforward. However, certain offences are defined so that liability can arise even in the absence of movement. There are three main examples:

A) Omissions liability: The major exception to any requirement of positive movement is liability based on D's omission to act. Offences satisfied by omission are extremely common in the law, and in many cases largely uncontroversial.[22] For example, there will be liability where someone, whether a human or a company, fails to comply with requirements to register or file official documents such as tax returns or licences;[23] where a motorist fails to report an accident that she was involved in;[24] or where a motorist fails to provide police with a specimen of breath when lawfully required to do so.[25] These cases are easy to deal with because the statutory offence tells us what D must do, and that if it is not done a specific crime is committed.

More controversially, beyond the *specific* omissions-based offences, many offences can be committed either by movement or omission. For example, the offence of murder is committed where D unlawfully shoots V (conduct involving movement) with the intention to kill or cause grievous bodily harm; it is also committed where D starves her child

---

[19] Sexual Offences Act 2003, s1. See **Chapter 8**.
[20] In the context of driving offences. See **Chapter 6**.
[21] Although the type of conduct may affect the sentence imposed, it will not affect D's substantive liability.
[22] This is a problem for those academics who, like Michael Moore, would prefer to represent omissions liability as a rare and mistaken option for the law: Moore, *Act and Crime* (1993) 22.
[23] See eg Companies Act 1985, s444 (Secretary of State's power to demand documents).
[24] Road Traffic Act 1988, s170(4).
[25] Ibid, s6.

(conduct involving an omission of care) with the same intention.[26] Where liability of this kind is based on an omission, three ingredients must be satisfied:

(a) *Recognised offence*: the offence charged must be recognised in law as one that is capable of being committed by omission.

(b) *Duty to act*: there must be a legally recognised duty requiring D to act in a certain manner.

(c) *Breach of duty*: D's failure to act must fall below the standard expected in the performance of the duty.

More will be said about omissions liability later in this chapter (**2.6**).[27]

B) Possession offences: Numerous offences are defined to criminalise the possession of certain dangerous material such as weapons,[28] or offensive material such as images of child sexual exploitation.[29] Possession can be reconciled with the language of acts or omissions: D may have acted to gain possession, and/or the state of possession can be presented as D's omission to dispense of the item possessed.[30] However, it is perhaps more natural to describe 'possession' as a state of affairs where the movement, or non-movement, of D's body is not the crucial factor.[31] Thus, it is acceptable to describe the conduct element of such offences as a state of possession.

C) State of affairs offences: Another category of offences that does not require positive action is referred to as 'state of affairs' or 'situational'[32] offences. Such offences should be treated with caution and can be the hallmark of tyrannical regimes that may attach criminal liability to membership of a certain political party,[33] or race, or religion. However, even within England and Wales, state of affairs offences can be identified. For example, it is an offence under section 11 of the Terrorism Act 2000 to be a member, or profess to be a member, of a terrorist organisation.[34] Other examples include offences of 'being found' in a particular situation, for example the case of *Winzar* and being found drunk in a highway contrary to section 12 of the Licensing Act 1872.

 Winzar v Chief Constable of Kent (1983) The Times, 28 March

D was taken to hospital on a stretcher, but was found to be drunk and told to leave. The police took D to their car on the highway outside the hospital. When on the highway, D was charged with being 'found drunk' in the highway.

• Magistrates' court: guilty of section 12 offence;

• Divisional Court: Conviction upheld.

---

[26] *Gibbins and Proctor* (1918) 13 Cr App R 134.

[27] See also *Smith, Hogan, and Ormerod's Criminal Law* (16th edn, 2021) Ch2.

[28] Prevention of Crime Act 1953, s1.

[29] Protection of Children Act 1978, s1.

[30] Yaffe, 'In Defence of Criminal Possession' (2016) 10 Crim L & Phil 441.

[31] Duff, *Criminal Attempts* (1996) Chs9–11; Husak, 'Does Criminal Liability Require an Act?' in Duff (ed), *Philosophy and the Criminal Law* (1998) 60.

[32] Cohen, 'The Actus Reus and Offences of Situation' (1972) 7 Is LR 186.

[33] *Scales v US*, 327 US 203 (1961) regarding communist party membership.

[34] Discussed in *AG's Reference (No 4 of 2002)* [2005] 1 AC 264.

In *Winzar*, and other similar cases,[35] we could focus on D's actions in creating the state of affairs, and/or D's omission in failing to remove herself from that state. Examining what actions by a defendant will be sufficient for an offence may also be relevant when assessing the quality and fairness of that law. For example, in *Winzar*, any actions that D performed when moving to the highway do not appear to be voluntary, and therefore liability in that case is highly questionable.[36] However, again, when applying offences of this kind it will often be more straightforward to describe the conduct element in terms of a state of affairs, and this is perfectly acceptable.

 Don't be confused . . .

In line with the Law Commission and others, we employ the term 'conduct element' to describe the part of the offence that deals with D's physical movements or omissions. However, several statutes (as we will see) prefer the term 'act', even where that term is intended to include omissions liability. Take care with this when reading and interpreting statutes.

2.3.2 The circumstance element

Whatever D's conduct, it will be surrounded by a multitude of external circumstances: surrounding facts that are not performed by D, and not caused by D's action. Circumstances might include, for example, that V is female; V is under 18 years old; a reasonable person would be offended by D's act; V is a police officer; etc. The task in interpreting and applying each offence is *not* to engage with every fact or circumstance surrounding D's conduct, but to analyse the offence charged to see which circumstances are required for that offence to be committed. This is illustrated in **Table 2.2**.

Table 2.2 Circumstance element of the actus reus

	Actus reus	**Mens rea**
Conduct element	D's physical acts or omissions required for liability	*
Circumstance element	Surrounding facts that must exist for liability	*
Result element	*	*

Every criminal offence will include some manner of circumstance element, used to focus in on the mischief targeted by the offence. For example, the actus reus of

---

[35] See *Larsonneur* (1933) 24 Cr App R 74 (D was brought into the UK against her will by police, and then charged with landing in the UK illegally contrary to the Aliens Order 1920). See Lanham, '*Larsonneur* Revisited' [1976] Crim LR 276; with response from Smith [1999] Crim LR 100, and Lanham, Letter [1999] Crim LR 683.

[36] Smart, 'Criminal Responsibility for Failing to Do the Impossible' (1987) 103 LQR 532.

murder is not satisfied simply by D's conduct causing death unlawfully; D's conduct must cause the death *of a person*. Similarly, the actus reus of criminal damage is not simply conduct causing damage, but conduct causing damage *to property belonging to another*. Indeed, every offence will contain certain core circumstance elements: that D is a natural or legal person, and that D is over the age of criminal responsibility (10 years old).

The examples of circumstances discussed so far are physical ones, but this is not always the case. It is also possible for offences to require mental circumstances to exist. Rape, for example, requires D to penetrate V with his penis (conduct) without V's consent (circumstance). In this example, V's mental state is the circumstance element.[37]

Circumstance elements will, of course, vary between offences. For example, despite the central role of the absence of consent within many sexual offences, it is irrelevant to murder. V's consent to being killed may be a circumstance of D's conduct, but it is not a circumstance element of the offence of murder and thus it has no bearing on D's liability for that offence. For each offence we explore in later chapters, an important task is to identify, from the definition of the crime in the statute and/or common law, which circumstances are elements of the offence which are legally relevant and must be proved.

 Extra detail . . .

Sexual offences such as rape provide a useful example of how important circumstances can be to the targeting of a criminal mischief. Sexual penetration in the absence of consent is a serious criminal wrong; yet when the same conduct is done with legally valid consent, it is a social good.[38]

2.3.3 The result element

Just as D's conduct will take place in the context of certain circumstances, that conduct is also likely to cause a number of results. For example, when I move my fingers on the keyboard, this results in words appearing on the computer; when I throw a stone at your window, this results in damage to your window; and so on. As with the circumstance element, however, when we refer to the result element of an offence we are not referring to *every* consequence of D's conduct. Rather, the result element of an offence is only concerned with certain consequences of D's conduct (and/or exceptionally the conduct of another[39]) that are required for liability, as illustrated in **Table 2.3**. For example, the result element of the actus reus of murder is 'death' (D's conduct must cause the death of V): if, in causing V's death, D's conduct also unlawfully harms a bystander and perhaps damages property, these other results are irrelevant to the charge of murder. Such results may give rise to additional criminal charges in their own right, but these will be separate from the issue of murder.

---

[37] See **Chapter 8**.

[38] The 'moral magic' performed by consent will be discussed in **Chapter 8**.

[39] This is the case eg in the context of vicarious liability or secondary liability. See **Chapter 12**.

Table 2.3 Result element of the actus reus

	Actus reus	Mens rea
Conduct element	D's physical acts or omissions required for liability	*
Circumstance element	Surrounding facts that must exist for liability	*
Result element	Things caused by D's conduct required for liability	*

Not all offences require a result element. For example, the offence of perjury applies where D lies in court when giving evidence.[40] When lying in this way, D's offence includes a conduct element (speaking) and a circumstance element (she is giving evidence in court; what she says is false), but nothing needs to result from D's conduct. Whether the court is caused to be misled, for example, is irrelevant: it is not a requirement of the offence. Another offence of this kind, with no result element, is the general inchoate offence of attempt.[41] D is liable for attempt as soon as she goes beyond mere preparation in trying to commit a crime; she is liable as soon as she acts in these circumstances, without reference to any results.

Some of the most prominent offences in the criminal law, however, will require a result element. For example, murder requires D's conduct to *cause death*; offences against the person are structured around D's conduct *causing various levels of bodily harm*; criminal damage requires D's conduct to *cause damage*; and so on. Where this is the case, it is important to remember that we are not simply asking whether these results came about. Rather, the result element requires proof that the relevant results have been *caused* by D's conduct.

Therefore, whenever an offence includes a result element, this includes the requirement that the result must be causally connected to D's conduct. There are two stages that must be satisfied to establish causation:

- **Causation in fact:** There must be a logical connection in fact. Thus, if the result would have come about in the same manner regardless of D's conduct, there is no factual causation.

- **Causation in law:** A variety of legal principles have developed to limit a finding of causation to conduct that had a substantial effect; was blameworthy; and was not superseded by subsequent events.

Causation between D's conduct and results will only be found where *both* stages of this test are satisfied. There is considerably more to say about how causation rules operate and this will be continued later in this chapter (**2.7**).[42]

---

[40] Perjury Act 1911, s1. Perjury also applies where D believes she is lying but is in fact telling the truth.

[41] See **Chapter 11.2**.

[42] See also *Smith, Hogan, and Ormerod's Criminal Law* (16th edn, 2021) Ch2.

Assessment matters . . .

It is common for students to think of causation as a separate issue from the actus reus. This is not correct. Causation is an essential part of the actus reus of any offence that includes a result element. It is the essential link between the conduct element and result element.

2.3.4 Separating conduct, circumstances, and results

Although the separation of conduct, circumstances, and results provides a useful structure through which to view and discuss the law, it remains controversial. The main problem is that adopting a precise and consistent separation of elements is often very difficult.[43]

In the absence of a criminal code or some other unified source setting out the definitions of offence elements,[44] such inconsistency is again largely inevitable. It may be, however, that a lack of consistency can be tolerated. As we discussed in relation to the problems with the actus reus/mens rea distinction, it is important to remember that D's liability requires proof of *every* element of an offence. Therefore, in practice, the criminal law will be unaffected by whether we label an offence requirement as conduct, circumstance, or result; it must still be proved in the same way. However, as a device for discussing the law, it is only useful if it represents a reasonably common language: the more difference between interpretations, the less useful the technique becomes.

Below we highlight two areas where the separation of elements has proved to be particularly problematic:

A) **Expanding the conduct element:** In this textbook, when we refer to the conduct element we will be focussing on the physical movement of, or omission to move, D's body.[45] This is criticised by those who prefer to view action in its social context, for example that D's conduct is 'shooting'; not simply 'moving a finger'.[46] However, if we expand the definition of the conduct element beyond a focus on D's body, it is very difficult to know where to stop. For example, if D's conduct becomes 'shooting', why not 'shooting a person'? Such expansion would undermine the separation of actus reus elements.

B) **Expanding the result element:** In this textbook, when we refer to the result element, we will be focussing only on events *caused* by D's conduct. However, there is always a temptation to include circumstances within a discussion of the result element. For example, the academic Michael Moore would include a basic 'moral criterion' that would add further detail (eg the result of sexual assault would not simply be described as 'sexual contact', but 'sexual contact with a person').[47] Glanville Williams would also add

---

[43] Buxton, 'The Working Paper on Inchoate Offences: (1) Incitement and Attempt' [1973] Crim LR 656; Buxton, 'Circumstances, Consequences and Attempted Rape' [1984] Crim LR 25; and Duff, *Criminal Attempts* (1996) 12–14.

[44] See eg definitions in the US Model Penal Code 1962, §2.02.

[45] In line with Robinson and Grall, 'Element Analysis in Defining Criminal Liability: The Model Penal Code and Beyond' (1983) 35 Stan L Rev 681.

[46] Duff, *Criminal Attempts* (1996) Ch9.

[47] Moore, *Act and Crime* (1993) 208.

to the result element based on what is 'customarily regarded' within elements.[48] Both approaches lack the necessary precision for maintaining the separation of actus reus elements.

 Assessment matters . . .

When applying the general inchoate offences it is essential to use the terminology of conduct, circumstances, and result.[49] However, when discussing other offences you should only use it if it is useful. For example, if you wish to make a particular point about one part of an offence, then the subdivision can be helpful to identify the part of the offence you mean. However, when making more general points about the law, or summarising the requirements of an offence, it will often be easier and less cumbersome to talk of actus reus and mens rea only.

2.4 Categories of offences

The actus reus of an offence is made up of a combination of elements: the conduct element; circumstance element; and result element. However, as we have already noted, although all offences will include conduct and circumstances, not all offences will include a result element. Whether an offence includes a result element or not has been used to distinguish two categories of offences.

2.4.1 Conduct crimes

Conduct crimes are so called because they do not include a result element. Examples include perjury and attempts liability. The actus reus of these offences are complete as soon as D performs certain conduct in certain proscribed circumstances. As there is no result element, there is also no need to apply the rules of causation: D's conduct does not need to cause anything to satisfy the requirements of the offence.

2.4.2 Result crimes

Result crimes, unsurprisingly, are so called because they require a result element. Examples include murder and criminal damage. The actus reus of these offences is complete when D performs conduct in certain proscribed circumstances, with that conduct causing a certain proscribed result. As the result must be caused by D's conduct, the rules of causation must be applied to these cases. It is common for result crimes to specify certain circumstances and results, but to leave the conduct element unspecified. For example, the offence of murder requires the unlawful killing (result) of a person (circumstance), but it does not specify D's conduct: it must be conduct of D that has caused the result, but it does not matter what this was (eg shooting, stabbing, omitting to feed, etc) as long as the killing was unlawful.

---

[48] Williams, 'The Problem of Reckless Attempts' [1983] Crim LR 365, 369.
[49] Explored in **Chapter 11**.

Assessment matters . . .

All result crimes require D's conduct to have caused the result element. However, your discussion of causation does not need to be equally detailed in every case. For example, in a case where D wounds V by cutting her with a knife, D's conduct and the wounding happen simultaneously. As there is no space in time or proximity between conduct and result, there is little room for doubting the causal connection between the two, and so discussion of causation can be brief. In contrast, where D attacks V and V dies some time later, the gap between D's conduct and the result (death) means that an extended discussion of causation is more likely to be required.

2.5 Summary

We have provided an overview of actus reus elements, including conduct, circumstances, and results. In later chapters, a significant part of our study will be to identify the actus reus requirements of various offences, both from statute and from the common law, and to learn how they are/should be applied in practice. Understanding the elements of the actus reus in general terms will help with both.

The next two sections of this chapter revisit two areas already introduced: omissions and causation. It is important to remember the role that these play in the context of the previous discussion. However, as each of them raises a number of important issues, and has attracted significant judicial and academic attention, they require some additional examination.

2.6 Omissions liability

When looking to identify the conduct element of an offence, you should begin with D's movement as opposed to her omission to move. Although certain offences can *only* be committed by omission,[50] most offences can be committed by act or omission, or by action alone, with a marked reluctance from both courts and the legislature to impose liability for omissions.

A common illustration of legal reluctance in relation to omissions liability, and one that provides a useful starting point for discussion, is that *without more* there will be no liability in English law if D watches a child drown in a shallow pool, even if D could easily save the child, and even if D omits to help because she intends the child to die.[51] If the child had died as a result of D's positive action in these circumstances (eg D holding the child under water), D would be liable for murder without further enquiry.

---

[50] eg a motorist failing to provide police with a specimen of breath when properly instructed to do so, contrary to the Road Traffic Act 1988, s6.

[51] Ashworth, 'The Scope of Liability for Omissions' (1989) 105 LQR 424. Liability will only arise where D has responsibility for the child (Children and Young Persons Act 1933, s1), or a legal duty to act (discussed in the following pages).

However, in the absence of a positive action, D's omission will not satisfy the conduct element of murder and therefore the crime will not be complete.

There are several justifications for this restrictive approach when it comes to omissions liability.[52] Although we might see D's failure to save the drowning child as morally blameworthy, nevertheless, with limited criminal law resources we may see the conduct of the other party who pushed the child as a more pressing target. Also, whereas a positive action makes it easy to identify the particular defendant who may be liable, D's omission to save is logically one that is shared with everyone else in the world, and so it is difficult to construct laws to isolate particular *criminal* omissions: it creates problems for fair warning, certainty, and coherence. Perhaps the most important reason for reluctance relates to respect for D's autonomy in the sense of her right to pursue personal goals without undue interference from the law.[53] Let us imagine that, at any one time, D has 100,000 options when it comes to her movements (go left; right; sit; go to the shops; to work; and so on). When a criminal offence imposes liability for a positive action, D now has 99,999 options: she can act as she wishes, as long as she does not act in the proscribed manner. In contrast, when a criminal offence imposes liability for an omission to act, D has only one option: she must act in the manner required by the offence to avoid liability.[54]

Thus, although D's omission may be morally wrongful, the question of criminalisation must weigh D's wrongful omission (favouring criminalisation) against issues of practicality and respect for D's autonomy (weighing against criminalisation). This is illustrated in **Figure 2.2**.

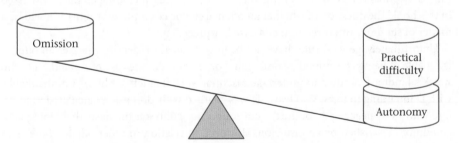

Figure 2.2 Weighing up omissions liability

In contrast to liability based on movement, D's omission alone will not generally be enough to satisfy the conduct element of an offence. However, this is not to say that there is no liability for omissions, it is simply to highlight that for omissions liability to be found further ingredients are required to tip the balance. These include:

(a) D's offence must be capable of commission by omission;

(b) D must have a legally recognised duty to act; and

(c) D must have unreasonably failed to act on that duty.

---

[52] Williams, 'Criminal Omissions—The Conventional View' (1991) 107 LQR 86.

[53] See discussion of the principle of autonomy in **Chapter 1.4.3**.

[54] There are, of course, a number of problems with this illustration. However, it serves to highlight (in general terms at least) the core of the autonomy argument.

This is illustrated in **Figure 2.3**.

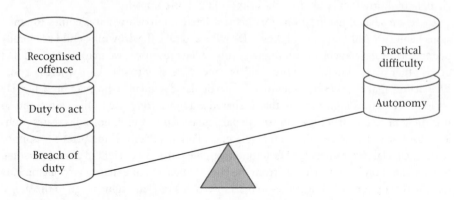

Figure 2.3 Where omissions liability is justified

For D's omission to satisfy the conduct element of an offence, each of these three requirements must be found. Following this, as long as the other offence elements are also satisfied, D will be criminally liable.

2.6.1 Offences capable of commission by omission

In certain cases it will be clear from the statutory wording that an offence can be committed by omission. However, for the majority of offences, including all those discussed
in this book, the question of whether an offence can be committed by omission will be a
matter of statutory interpretation and case law precedent.

Unfortunately, general rules have not been developed to identify whether an offence
is capable of being committed by omission. For example, in the case of *Ahmad*,[55] D, who
was V's landlord, omitted to undertake essential work that left V's home uninhabitable,
with D intending to force V to leave. D was charged with 'doing acts calculated to interfere with [V's] peace and comfort',[56] but found not guilty on the basis that 'doing acts'
could not be satisfied by an omission. However, in relation to other offences, the term
'act' within a statute has not prevented liability for omissions. For example, where D
remains motionless in response to sexual touching from a child, it has been held that he
commits a sexual offence even where the terms of that offence require D to have acted.[57]

In the absence of general rules relating to statutory terms such as 'act', it is now clear
that each offence must be assessed individually. This will be done in detail in later chapters, but a few illustrations may be useful:

- **Homicide (murder and manslaughter offences)**: It has long been recognised that
  most homicide offences can be committed by omission. For example, in *Gibbins and
  Proctor*,[58] a man and woman were convicted of murder on the basis of their omission
  to feed the man's child (V). They had a duty to feed the child, they breached that duty,

---

[55] (1986) 84 Cr App R 64.
[56] Protection from Eviction Act 1977.
[57] *Speck* [1977] 2 All ER 859. See **Chapter 8.4**.
[58] (1918) 13 Cr App R 134.

and they also satisfied the mens rea of murder because they had an intention to cause serious harm.

- **Non-fatal offences against the person:** Employing terms such as 'assault', 'wound', and 'battery', there has been a reluctance to find omissions liability in relation to non-fatal offences.[59] However, liability has been found. For example, in *Santana Bermudez*,[60] D misinformed a police officer that he did not have any needles on his person, and was therefore liable when the officer (V) was pricked during the personal search. This approach, finding omissions liability in such cases, is surely correct. With reference to *Gibbins* above, for example, it would be absurd if D was liable for causing death to her child by omission, but would avoid any liability for lesser crimes if the police had intervened at a stage when V was seriously harmed but not yet dead.

- **Property offences:** Again, despite some doubt,[61] omissions liability has been found in relation to certain property offences. For example, in *Miller*,[62] D was convicted of arson when, having inadvertently started a fire, he did not act to try and put out the fire or call for assistance.

There appears to be a trend towards accepting omissions liability for an ever greater range of offences. However, this expansion remains controversial.[63] It is also far from complete; for example, there is still no liability for offences *attempted* by omission,[64] or for unlawful act manslaughter.[65] As such, when applying omissions liability within a problem question, some consideration of whether the offence is capable of commission by omission remains essential.

2.6.2 Duties to act

Having established that the offence charged is capable of commission by omission, the next requirement is that D must have a legally recognised duty to act.[66] It is this duty that narrows the law's focus from *all* those who failed to act, which could be everyone in the world, to isolate those few whose omissions are criminal. In this regard, duties are not simply imposed on those who are in a position to help, such as those who know about the danger and are able to provide assistance: that approach may seem appealing in order to catch D who watches the child drown for example, but it would also catch anyone who watches an aid appeal on television and chooses not to donate in the knowledge that lives could be saved. Rather, the law will only impose a duty to act in very narrow categories. These include offence-specific duties; contractual duties; familial duties; duties based on an assumption of care; and duties created through endangerment.

Unfortunately, despite the importance of these categories, the boundaries of each are far from certain. As the common law develops, we can identify core cases, but application outside these core cases remains challenging.

---

[59] **Chapter 7.**
[60] [2004] Crim LR 471.
[61] The 1989 Draft Criminal Code eg would not have allowed omissions liability for property offences.
[62] [1983] 2 AC 161.
[63] See criticism from Williams in 'Letter to the Editor' [1982] Crim LR 773.
[64] See **Chapter 11.2.**
[65] See **Chapter 6.3.**
[66] See Alexander, 'Criminal Liability for Omissions: An Inventory of Issues' in Shute and Simester (eds), *Criminal Law Theory* (2002) 121.

Assessment matters . . .

A 'duty to act' sounds like, and is often confused with, a 'duty of care'. A duty of care is a tort law concept essential to the tort of negligence, and identifies all those we must take care to avoid harming by our conduct. Indeed, we will discuss duties of care when we analyse the crime of gross negligence manslaughter,[67] a crime that borrows heavily from the tort of negligence. In contrast, 'duties to act' identify a considerably narrower set of duties where D's criminal liability can be based on an omission. Where a duty to act is found, there will always be a duty of care; however, a duty of care will not always indicate a duty to act. Therefore, whenever D's liability is omission-based, a duty to act must be identified.

2.6.2.1 Duties to act based on the specifics of an offence

Where an offence is specifically drafted to allow for omissions liability, or may only be capable of commission by omission, it is straightforward to identify the duty to act that is created. Statutory examples include section 170(4) of the Road Traffic Act 1988, which makes it an offence to fail (ie omit) to report a motor accident in which D is involved. If an accident is not reported, we can say that everyone has omitted to report it. However, the statute creates a special duty on those involved in the accident: only their omission to report is singled out as a potentially criminal omission which will satisfy the conduct element of the offence. There are also examples, albeit rare ones, in the common law. For example, the case of *Dytham* and the common law offence of misconduct in public office.[68]

 Dytham [1979] 3 All ER 641

D, a police officer, was charged with misconduct in public office when, while on duty, he failed to intervene in an incident in which V was kicked to death by a nightclub bouncer 30 yards away. The offence of misconduct in public office creates a clear duty for public officials to act in a reasonable manner.

• Crown Court: guilty of misconduct in public office.
• Court of Appeal: conviction upheld on appeal.

Offence-specific duties of this kind are unproblematic, but they are also rather narrow: they apply only in the context of the individual offence that creates them. Liability of this kind is expanding, particularly with regard to corporate and/or professional offences, but this expansion is not yet systematic and has been criticised for its inconsistency.[69] The other duties to act (discussed below), in contrast, can apply to provide omissions liability across multiple offences, even those that are more typically committed by positive actions (eg murder).

---

[67] See **Chapter 6.3**.
[68] See also *AG's Reference (No 3 of 2003)* [2004] 3 WLR 451.
[69] See Ashworth, 'A New Generation of Omissions Offences?' [2018] Crim LR 354; Laird, 'The Criminal Finances Act 2017—An Introduction' [2017] Crim LR 915.

2.6.2.2 Duties to act based on a contract

Where D has a contractual duty to act, such a duty is also capable of being recognised in criminal law as a basis for omissions liability. Contracts can give rise to duties between the parties where D is contracted to protect V or her property, as well as third parties such as carers and health professionals. Most commonly, as in *Pittwood*, this will involve contracts of employment.

 Pittwood (1902) 19 TLR 37

D, a railway crossing gate-keeper, opened the gate to let a cart cross the lines and then went to lunch, forgetting to close it again. As a result, a subsequent cart collided with a train, killing the train driver. D was charged with manslaughter based on his omission (contractual duty to close the gate).

• Trial court: guilty of gross negligence manslaughter.

Certain contractual duties to act, particularly in relation to the caring professions, are now firmly established. However, outside these core examples, uncertainty remains. For example, how strictly will a court adhere to the terms of a contract? If a lifeguard is contracted until 5 pm, for example, is there a duty to act if she spots someone drowning at 5.05 pm as she leaves her shift?

2.6.2.3 Duties to act based on a familial relationship

Core examples where a duty to act has been found between family members include a parent's duty to care for their child, as was the case in *Gibbins and Proctor*[70] (**2.6.1**), and between a married couple, as was the case in *Hood*.

 Hood [2004] 1 Cr App R 431

D omitted to summon help for three weeks after his wife (V) fell and suffered broken bones. V died as a result. D was charged with manslaughter on the basis of breaching his familial duty to assist.

• Crown Court: guilty of gross negligence manslaughter.
• Court of Appeal: conviction upheld on appeal.

Beyond these core examples, however, a lack of case law has (again) led to considerable uncertainty. First, although duties have been recognised between parent and child, and between a married couple, it is difficult to predict what other relationships will give rise to similar duties. For example, if the duty is family-based, will it extend to siblings or the wider family?[71] On the other hand, if the duty is based on dependence, which is arguably a more justifiable basis,[72] will it extend to unmarried couples or even cohabiting

---

[70] (1918) 13 Cr App R 134.
[71] There is some indication of this in *Stone and Dobinson* [1977] QB 354.
[72] Fletcher, *Rethinking Criminal Law* (1978) 613.

friends?[73] A second layer of uncertainty relates to the boundaries of a duty within a recognised relationship. For example, will a parent still owe a duty to a fully emancipated child over the age of 18,[74] or a wife to her husband if they have been separated although perhaps not yet divorced? Again, it may be better to focus on dependence as opposed to formal relationships, but this simply leads to another question: how much dependence?[75]

2.6.2.4 Duties to act based on an assumption of care

Assumption of care duties will arise when D has voluntarily undertaken to care for V whatever the formal relationship between D and V, in circumstances where V becomes dependent upon that care.[76] A duty to act will arise where the promise of care is explicit, as in *Nicholls*.

Nicholls (1874) 13 Cox CC 75

D, V's grandmother, agreed to take care of V after the death of V's mother. V was neglected by D and died. D was charged with gross negligence manslaughter based on the duty arising from an explicit assumption of care.

• Trial court: guilty of gross negligence manslaughter.

A similar duty will also arise where the promise of care is implicit, as in *Instan*.

Instan [1893] 1 QB 450

D, V's niece, moved into V's house. V became extremely unwell with a gangrenous leg and was unable to look after herself. D continued to live in the house and eat V's food, etc, but she did not care for V or summon help. V died and D was charged with gross negligence manslaughter based on the duty arising from an implicit assumption of care.

• Crown Court: guilty of gross negligence manslaughter.

Although the imposition of a duty to act in these cases seems broadly just, assumption of care duties can be problematic. Most importantly, it remains unclear exactly how much, or how little, D must do before a duty will arise. Useful examples of relatively minor acts of attempted assistance leading to the creation of a duty to act include *Ruffell*,[77] in which D briefly and unsuccessfully attempted to revive a fellow drug user after an overdose, and *Stone and Dobinson*,[78] in which D, of low intelligence, tried ineffectually to assist V before her death.

Aside from issues about when this kind of duty will arise, there is also the related problem of when it will end. It may be supposed, for example, that D could extinguish

---

[73] There is some indication of this in *Sinclair, Johnson and Smith* (1998) 21 August, CA.
[74] *Sheppard* (1862) Le & Ca 147 suggests not.
[75] Discussed in Ashworth, 'Manslaughter by Omission and the Rule of Law' [2015] Crim LR 563.
[76] Mead, 'Contracting into Crime: A Theory of Criminal Omissions' (1991) 11 OJLS 147.
[77] [2003] EWCA Crim 122. Note, however, this conclusion is muddied by the fact that the court also stresses the close friendship between D and V.
[78] [1977] 2 All ER 341.

the duty by informing the authorities that she will no longer be caring for V, or perhaps if V expressly releases D from the duty.[79] However, without clarifying case law, these propositions are far from clear.

Finally, it should be highlighted that a duty to act arising from an assumption of care gives rise to an uncomfortable contrast: D who tries to help V will create a duty to continue acting that can lead to serious criminal liability if breached; D who does not try to help will not create a duty and will not therefore risk liability. The legal message, it could be said, is not to try.[80]

2.6.2.5 Duties to act based on endangerment

A duty to act will arise where D's previous conduct has created or contributed to a dangerous situation. Having created the danger, whether inadvertently or otherwise, D must act to try to prevent harm coming about.

 Miller [1983] 2 AC 161

D, a squatter in V's house, went to sleep holding a lit cigarette. He awoke to find the mattress smouldering, but did nothing except move to an adjoining room. The fire caused extensive damage, and D was charged with criminal damage based on his omission to tackle the smouldering mattress or alert the authorities. The duty to do so arose from his inadvertent creation of the dangerous situation.

- Crown Court: guilty of criminal damage.
- Court of Appeal: conviction upheld on appeal.
- House of Lords: conviction upheld on appeal.

Miller establishes a duty to act based on endangerment, arising at the point D becomes aware of the danger she has created. It is also a useful reminder that omissions liability is not restricted to cases of murder and manslaughter.[81] It should be remembered that omissions liability is not offence-specific, and may satisfy the conduct element of any offence that is capable of being committed by omission.

The *Miller* principle has been extended by the case of *Evans*.

 Evans [2009] EWCA Crim 650

D, V's half-sister, supplied her with heroin which she self-administered. V showed symptoms of an overdose. D stayed with V but did not alert the authorities for fear of personal liability for supplying the drugs. V died and D was charged with gross negligence manslaughter on the basis of her omission to aid V. The duty arose from her contribution to the dangerous situation through drug supply.

- Crown Court: guilty of gross negligence manslaughter.
- Court of Appeal: conviction upheld on appeal.

---

[79] There is some indication of this in *Smith* [1979] Crim LR 251.

[80] If this is the message, it is not indefensible. eg when D begins to aid V, it may be that others stop helping in view of D's presence and/or that V stops asking for help. Thus, if D's assistance is then stopped, V may be worse off as a result.

[81] Murder and manslaughter are over-represented in omissions case law because the serious harm involved encourages prosecutors to find creative routes to liability.

Evans clarifies (and extends) the duty recognised in *Miller* in two important ways. First, it is clarified that D need only *contribute* to the dangerous situation as opposed to being its *cause*; Evans does not cause V to take the drug, but her supply of it clearly contributes to the taking. Secondly, we are told that D need not be subjectively aware of the danger created (which had been assumed from *Miller*), but that a duty may also arise where D objectively *should have realised* that a danger was created.[82] In *Lewin v CPS*,[83] a case that preceded *Evans*, a challenge to the CPS's decision not to prosecute D failed where D had left a heavily intoxicated friend (V) in his car in extremely hot conditions abroad leading to V's death. The court held that D did not owe a duty to V after he had parked his car. However, applying *Evans*, it could now be argued that leaving V in the car *contributed* to a dangerous situation and that D *should have realised* the risk to V's life, creating a duty to act and potential liability.

Assessment matters . . .

Within several cases mentioned previously, the courts have discussed more than one possible duty to act. For example, in the case of *Evans* there is discussion of potential duties based on a relationship (D was V's half-sister), assumption of care (when D begins to look after V), as well as a duty arising from endangerment. Indeed, certain cases are unclear upon which basis the duty has been found, or whether it is found from the combination of possible duties. With this in mind, when answering a problem question, try to highlight all possible duties to act that may give rise to D's liability. Additionally, as these are common law duties, remember that the list of duties to act currently recognised by the courts is not exhaustive: if you cannot find a recognised duty but you think liability should be found, you may wish to highlight the possibility that one of the existing duties may be extended or the, admittedly rather remote, possibility that a new duty may be recognised.

2.6.3 Breach of duty to act

After it has been established that D's offence was capable of commission by omission, and that D had a recognised duty to act, the next requirement is that D breached that duty. This requirement is useful to focus our minds on an obvious (but easily confused) point about omissions liability: D does not satisfy the conduct element because at the relevant moment she was perfectly still (it is very likely that D will have been moving her body in one way or another); she omits in law because she fails to do what the duty to act requires of her. Thus, to test whether D has breached her duty to act, we must question what the particular duty to act required her to do.

In general terms, a duty to act obliges D to do what is *reasonable*. What is reasonable is a question for the jury. In the case of *Miller*, for example, a reasonable response would have meant D attempting to put out the smouldering mattress or contacting the fire brigade if this was not possible; in *Evans* to contact the emergency services; in *Dytham* to intervene in the bouncer's attack on V or at least call on other officers for backup.

Importantly, the duty to act does not require *more* than what is reasonable. For example, if Miller awoke to a roaring inferno, he would not have had a duty to charge into the

---

[82] See Williams, 'Gross Negligence Manslaughter and Duty of Care in "Drugs" Cases: *R v Evans*' [2009] Crim LR 631.
[83] [2002] EWCA 1049.

fire and attempt to put it out single-handedly. In such a case, there would be a duty to act, but this would probably be satisfied by a call for help. Thus, even where harm is caused, this will not necessarily mean that D has breached her duty to act, and the question of breach must always be discussed.

Some confusion, however, should be highlighted. This is illustrated through the case of *Stone and Dobinson*.

Stone and Dobinson [1977] 2 All ER 341

D1 (a man of low IQ) and D2 (described as 'ineffectual and inadequate') took in D1's sister (V) to live with them. V suffered from anorexia nervosa which led her to avoid food; eventually she became confined to her bed. D1 and D2 made some incompetent efforts to feed and clean V, and contact a doctor, but eventually stopped. V later died in appalling conditions. D1 and D2 were charged with gross negligence manslaughter on the basis of their omission. The duty was created by a voluntary assumption of care.

- Crown Court: guilty of gross negligence manslaughter.
- Court of Appeal: conviction upheld on appeal.

This case is important because the extremely low functioning of D1 and D2 made it difficult for them to look after themselves, let alone care for V. Therefore, even after a duty to act is found on these facts, it is surely questionable what D1 and D2 were duty bound to do given their lack of capacity. If the test is whether they acted reasonably based, *subjectively*, on their impaired ability to act, then there appears to be no clear breach. However, the little attention given to this question by the court may suggest that the test was rather: did they do what is, *objectively*, reasonable based on the standards of reasonable competent people? If the current law is represented by this latter test (the judgment was not clear), then it is easy to see why liability was found, but there is potential for considerable injustice. Just as we should not require Miller to act beyond the capabilities of the reasonable man by tackling an inferno single-handedly, surely it is equally unfair to demand things from Stone and Dobinson that are beyond their abilities.

Assessment matters . . .

If a scenario akin to *Stone and Dobinson* were to arise in a problem question where D's acts fall below the standards of a reasonable person, but potentially not below a standard reasonable for them personally, you should apply *Stone and Dobinson* (an objective, reasonable person standard) as the most closely applicable case. However, it would also be useful to highlight in your discussion that this issue was not directly addressed by the court and that the unfairness it entails may well lead a future court to adopt a different approach, at least allowing the reasonable standard to take account of D's physical and mental limitations.

2.6.4 Causation by omission

If it is established that D's offence is capable of commission by omission; that D had a recognised duty to act; and that D breached that duty; then D's omission will fulfil the requirements of the conduct element. Where D's offence is a conduct crime such as a failing to report type offence, the question then becomes whether D's omission is accompanied by the circumstances and mens rea required for the offence to be complete. However, where D's offence is a result crime, such as a homicide offence, it must also be demonstrated that a certain result came about, and that it was *caused* by the conduct element. We discuss causation in detail later (**2.7**). However, it is worth highlighting here the unusual issues that arise where D's causing conduct element is an omission.

It is arguable that an omission to act can never cause a result element. The point here is that although D's omission may allow for the result to happen, it has not materially contributed to the result any more than D's omission has contributed to every other event that takes place at that point in time.[84] This is not, however, the approach taken by the law, and it is clear that an omission can be found to have caused a result element. Although D's omission may not be the only cause, and may not even be the most significant cause, this is not determinative of the issue or of liability. Additionally, accepting the potential for omissions to cause results in certain cases does not mean that we have to conclude that D has caused (by failing to prevent) *all harms* going on in the world: the restrictive nature of duties to act will have already narrowed D's potential liability to only those events where the law requires D to act.[85]

For D to commit a result crime by omission, the causation rules must be applied. This is not an empty requirement. The prosecution must show that it is because D failed to act in line with her duty that the result came about, and that if she had acted in line with her duty it would not have done so.[86] For example, if the duty in *Evans* was for D to call an ambulance as soon as it became obvious that V was suffering a drugs overdose, it must be demonstrated by the prosecution that had she done so V would not have died of that overdose. If, *hypothetically*, V died immediately after self-injecting the drug, then it is highly unlikely that D could have been liable for causing death: even if she had acted in line with her duty (calling for help), V would still have died.

In the recent case of *Broughton*,[87] the Court of Appeal found that even where D denies V a 90% chance of survival by omitting to call for help, the 10% chance that V would have died anyway undermines any finding of causation. Fanciful possibilities aside, it much be clear that the harm *would not* have resulted *but for* D's omission.

 Assessment matters . . .

Having established a conduct element through D's omission (relevant offence; duty to act; breach of duty), it is common for students to forget to discuss a requirement of causation. Remember, even if D has omitted in breach of her duty, unless that omission has causally contributed to the result there can be no liability for a result crime. Think about what D's duty to act required her to do and ask yourself the following—if D had acted in line with her duty, would it have prevented the result? If yes, causation can be found; if no, there is no causation.

---

[84] Hogan, 'Omissions and the Duty Myth' in Smith (ed), *Criminal Law: Essays in Honour of JC Smith* (1987) 85. Moore, *Act and Crime* (1993) 267.

[85] Leavens, 'A Causation Approach to Criminal Omissions' (1988) 76 Cal LR 547.

[86] Simester describes this as D's failure to break a harmful chain of causation. Simester, 'Causation in (Criminal) Law' (2017) 133 LQR 416, Part III.

[87] [2020] EWCA Crim 1093: Discussing gross negligence manslaughter where D failed to call for help while V suffered, to whom D owed a duty, a drugs overdose and eventually died.

2.6.5 Distinguishing acts and omissions

In the majority of cases it will be obvious whether D has acted or omitted to act, and it will be a case of assessing her liability on that basis. However, this will not always be the case. For example, if D and V are playing tug-of-war and D lets go of the rope (causing V to fall and hurt herself), has D acted (letting go) or omitted (stopped pulling)? If a doctor turns off a life-support machine, has she acted (turning off) or omitted (stopped treatment)? And so on.[88]

The grey area of uncertainty between acts and omissions is capable of causing problems for the law. It is obviously crucial where the offence charged cannot be committed by omission (eg attempts). However, even where the offence (as is increasingly the case) can be committed by act or omission, it is important to remember that omissions liability is still more restrictive. For example, if D acts by movements to kill V then the conduct element of murder is satisfied immediately. However, if D kills V by omission, the conduct element requires further ingredients: a duty to act and a breach of that duty. Where there is no duty to act, D will avoid liability in the second (omissions-based) example where she would have been potentially liable in the first.

Without a rule of interpretation to guide courts in this area, it seems that the decision whether to classify D's conduct as an act or omission is one that is made on a case-by-case basis. This gives rise to inconsistency. For example, in *Fagan* [89] where D accidentally drove onto a police officer's foot and then rested the car there intentionally, D's conduct was interpreted as an action: driving on and staying on the foot, rather than an omission to move off the foot. This allowed for straightforward liability without consideration of duties to act. However, where D's behaviour has a strong social utility, courts are much more likely to interpret the conduct as an omission. For example, in termination of medical care cases such as *Bland* [90] (doctor's decision to terminate care) and *Re B (A Minor)* [91] (parents' decision to terminate care), it has been held that stopping treatment will be an omission even if it involves acts such as turning off machines, and that such omissions might not breach D's duty to act where V's best interests are not served by further treatment. The issue here is not whether these cases reached the correct outcomes, but the unprincipled basis upon which they were distinguished.[92]

 Assessment matters . . .

If you are faced with conduct in a problem question that could be interpreted as an act or an omission it will usually be necessary, at least briefly, to consider both options. First, explain that the conduct element could be satisfied if we interpret D's conduct as an act. Then consider the omissions alternative, highlighting whether it is likely that D had a duty to act and breached that duty. Finally, discuss which approach you believe the court is likely to take on the basis of similar cases.

---

[88] Kennedy, 'Switching Off Life Support Machines: The Legal Implications' [1977] Crim LR 443.
[89] [1969] 1 QB 439. Discussed further in **Chapter 4**.
[90] *National Health Service Trust v Bland* [1993] 1 All ER 821.
[91] [1981] 1 WLR 1421.
[92] Keown, 'Restoring Moral and Intellectual Shape to the Law after *Bland*' (1997) 113 LQR 481.

2.7 Causation

When assessing liability for conduct crimes such as perjury, attempts liability, etc, there is no result element and therefore no requirement that it should be *caused* by D's conduct. In contrast, when assessing liability for a result crime such as homicide offences, criminal damage, etc, a result element must be found, and so it is also essential to demonstrate a causal link between D's conduct and that result. If D's conduct element (action or omission) did not cause the result element, there will be no liability for a result crime.

It is often quite straightforward to demonstrate that D's acts caused a particular result. For example, if D throws a stone at V's window and it breaks, there seems to be little room for dispute: the damage was caused by D's act. In such cases, the judge will direct the jury simply to apply their common understanding of causation. However, in real life (*and particularly in problem questions*), examples may not be this straightforward. For example, what if the window was only broken because the glass was unusually thin? What if D was not aiming for the window, but the stone was caught by a strong gust of wind? What if another stone, thrown by X, would have smashed the glass a split second later, or even made contact at the same time? In such cases, the issue of causation (whether D's conduct caused the result) is likely to be disputed between prosecution and defence. This time, although the judge will again direct the jury to apply their common understanding of causation, the judge will also guide the jury's deliberation with a number of legal principles.[93]

Assessment matters . . .

Your approach to problem questions should mirror the approach of the court. If causation is readily satisfied in your discussion of a result crime, then there is no need to discuss the full detail of the causation rules. You should highlight the presence of causation, but need not elaborate. A full discussion of the causation rules, the legal principles developed to assist with difficult cases, is only required where there are, or may be, problems identifying causation.

Legal principles have developed in the courts to assist juries where a common-sense understanding of causation does not provide a clear answer. These principles are applied via a two-stage test:

- **Causation in fact:** Did the result come about because of D's conduct?
- **Causation in law:** Was D's conduct a substantial; blameworthy; and operating cause?

Importantly, the answer to *both* these questions must be 'yes' in order to find causation. We will discuss each in turn.

2.7.1 Causation in fact

Factual causation is always the starting point for a discussion of the causation rules, asking generally whether the result came about because of D's contributory act or her failure (omission) to prevent the result. Another way to express this is through the commonly

---

[93] *Pagett* (1983) 76 Cr App R 279. See also Judicial College, *Crown Court Compendium* (2020) 7.33–7.37.

used 'but for' test:[94] *but for* D's conduct, would the result have come about? If 'no', the result would not have happened without D's intervention, then D is the cause in fact. The 'but for' test should not be applied too rigidly, however, as D will still be a factual cause where she contributes to a result alongside other causes that may have independently brought about the result.

If D's conduct is not a factual cause, as in *White*, there can be no causation.

 White [1910] 2 KB 124

D put poison in his mother's (V's) drink intending to kill her. It was unclear on the facts whether V drank any of the poison, but she died shortly afterwards. Regardless of her potential consumption of the poison, however, medical evidence demonstrated that V died due to an unrelated heart condition.

• Crown Court: D was not guilty of murder (result crime requiring causation), but was guilty of attempted murder (conduct crime not requiring causation).
• Court of Criminal Appeal: conviction upheld on appeal.

In *White*, D had completed acts intending to cause death (conduct element of murder), and death came about (result element of murder), but liability for murder failed because of the lack of causation linking D's conduct with the result. D's conduct did not causally contribute to the death of V in any way: he was not the factual cause. Drawing on our previous stone-throwing example, this would also rule out liability where a stone from X hits and smashes the window a split second before the stone thrown by D. Since the window is already broken and D's conduct has caused no further damage, her conduct has not in fact caused criminal damage.

The test of factual causation, therefore, will rule out liability for a result crime in cases such as *White*. However, the test remains extremely wide. This is particularly clear in two regards.

• Accelerating the result: As long as D's conduct caused the result to come about when it did, she is the factual cause; it is irrelevant if it would have come about later without D's involvement. For example, if V had died as a result of the poison in *White* or D's stone had hit before X's in our criminal damage example, factual causation would be established: the results may have occurred just seconds later without D's involvement, but D is still the factual cause of the result that did come about.[95] This rule holds certain logic, particularly in homicide cases: as we will all die at some point, D can never do more than speed up this process.
• More than one cause: Again, as long as D's conduct contributed as a factual cause of the result, it is not necessary to show that D was the only or even the main cause. This is illustrated in the case of *Benge*.

---

[94] Also referred to as a '*sine qua non*' cause.
[95] *Dyson* [1908] 2 KB 454.

Benge (1865) 4 F & F 504

D, a railways foreman, misread a train timetable when taking up sections of track. A train arrived when the track was up and V was killed. D contended that death could have been avoided if his 'flagmen' (stationed along the track to warn unexpected trains) had placed themselves at the proper distance from the worksite, and also if the train driver had kept a proper lookout.

• Court: D was guilty of gross negligence manslaughter.

In *Benge* it may be that other actors were also 'but for' causes of V's death, and may have been independently liable for it. However, the presence of multiple causes does not undermine the fact that D was a factual cause as well. Unlike the civil law, criminal liability does not seek to apportion blame or look for dominant causes, it simply asks whether each defendant individually facing the prospect of liability was a factual cause. In relation to our criminal damage example, this would be the case where D, a 12-year-old, is allowed to throw the stone by her father (D2): both D (by her act) and D2 (by his omission to stop D) are factual causes of the damage.

Point to remember . . .

The possibility of multiple causes is particularly important in relation to omissions liability. In such cases, it will often be another party who begins the course of events that will lead to the result, and so there is often at least one other obvious cause. However, this is irrelevant to D's liability (even if the other cause is V herself[96]). As long as D's omission satisfies the requirements of the conduct element, it is a factual cause if D would have prevented the result by acting in line with her duty to act (the result would not have come about 'but for' her omission).

2.7.2 Causation in law

The basic test for factual causation is supplemented with a test for legal causation to avoid an overly broad catchment. For example, where D throws a stone and breaks V's window, she is the factual (but for) cause of the damage. However, we could also say that V is a factual cause if, but for V's action in annoying D, D would not have sought revenge and thrown the stone. Similarly, we could say the glass manufacturer is a 'but for' cause as, but for their creation of the glass, it would not be there to be damaged; and even D's parents might be a factual cause as, but for their decision to have children, there would be no D; and so on. The test for legal causation seeks to narrow the catchment of causation rules in terms of *fairness*: when is it fair to blame D for causing a certain result?

The role and ambition of legal causation is unproblematic. However, unlike the relative objectivism of 'but for' factual causation, any test that is formulated with reference to abstract notions such as 'fairness' is always likely to be controversial, and so it has proved.[97] Through common law case-by-case development, several principles of legal causation have been established. However, such is the inconsistency of their

---

[96] *Swindall and Osborne* (1846) 2 Car & Kir 230.
[97] Hart and Honoré, *Causation in the Law* (1985).

interpretation and application that several commentators have concluded that talk of established principles is misguided, with the so-called principles being used by courts to reach a *desired* conclusion in the absence of rules.[98] We discuss the principles of legal causation, insofar as the courts have declared principles of any certainty, in the following sections.

2.7.2.1 Legal cause must be 'substantial'

Probably the least controversial principle of legal causation is that D's conduct must have made a substantial contribution to the result. The term 'substantial' should not, however, imply that D must be the main cause. In fact, as long as D's role is not *de minimis* it will satisfy this requirement: D's role must be more than 'slight or trifling',[99] 'negligible',[100] 'insubstantial or insignificant'.[101]

Having been established as a factual cause of the result, it will be rare that D's conduct will not also be at least more than a *de minimis* cause. However, the fact that D's conduct is a factual cause will not automatically satisfy this requirement. For example, if D pricked V with a pin seconds before she was stabbed to death by X, it is possible to describe D's conduct as a 'but for' cause of death: where V dies of blood loss, D's conduct has caused a slight loss of blood that will have marginally speeded up the time of death. Without D's conduct V would have died only a split second later, but (as discussed previously) this does not prevent D's conduct being described as a factual cause of the death *at the time it did happen*.[102] It would be similar if D telephoned V, only for V to be startled by the ring tone and drop a vase:[103] D may not play a major role in the damage, but she remains a factual cause. In each case, we may assume that legal causation will not be found because the role played by D was negligible (*de minimis*).

2.7.2.2 Legal cause must be 'blameworthy'

When a result crime is created, this is typically in an attempt to target wrongful or blameworthy conduct that leads to a harmful result. For example, criminal damage criminalises D's conduct performed whilst intending or foreseeing the risk of harming another's property (blameworthy conduct) which causes damage to that property (result). Gross negligence manslaughter criminalises D's conduct performed in a grossly negligent manner (blameworthy conduct) which causes death (result). In each case, as with almost all result crimes, the mischief of the offence is established by a link not simply between conduct and result, but between blameworthy conduct and result.

The question for the courts, and our focus here, is whether this pattern represents a rule of legal causation, or simply a common feature of offences designed to criminalise blameworthy conduct. The answer remains controversial,[104] but recent judgments of the Supreme Court suggest that blameworthiness *should* be applied as a rule of causation

---

[98] Williams eg describes legal causation as a 'moral reaction': Williams, *Textbook of Criminal Law* (2nd edn, 1983) 381.

[99] *Kimsey* [1996] Crim LR 35.

[100] *L* [2010] EWCA Crim 1249.

[101] *Cato* [1976] 1 All ER 260.

[102] Perkins and Boyce, *Criminal Law* (1982) 779.

[103] Based on an example from Hall, *General Principles of Criminal Law* (1960).

[104] See Simester, 'Causation in (Criminal) Law' (2017) 133 LQR 416.

within all result crimes. This means that, to prove legal causation, the prosecution must establish that D (a) performed blameworthy conduct, (b) caused the result, and (c) the blameworthiness of D's conduct was central to causation. One of the first cases to recognise this principle was *Dalloway*, a challenging case in which D satisfied (a) and (b), but not (c).

 Dalloway (1847) 2 Cox CC 273

D was driving a horse and cart on a highway, whilst negligently allowing the reins to lie on the horse's back rather than keeping control of them. A small child (V) ran into the road a few yards ahead of the cart and was killed. Even if D had control of the reins, he could not have stopped in time to save V.

• Court: D was not guilty of gross negligence manslaughter.

In *Dalloway*, D was negligent in his driving and, in that sense, his conduct was blameworthy. He was also the factual cause of V's death. However, his *blameworthy conduct* was not the cause of the death: V would have died even if D was not driving negligently. The crime (gross negligence manslaughter) is seeking to criminalise deaths that are brought about because of grossly negligent behaviour; it is not intended to target deaths (as in *Dalloway*) where D's negligence has no causal effect. Thus, D was not guilty of gross negligence manslaughter.[105]

In most cases it will be readily apparent that D's blameworthy conduct caused the result, and so the blameworthy cause rule is rarely litigated. However, around 10 years ago there was a flurry of cases relating to driving offences in which the rule was doubted in the Court of Appeal,[106] before being reaffirmed by the Supreme Court in *Hughes*.

 Hughes [2013] UKSC 56

D (driving without insurance or a full licence) was involved in a fatal collision with V. V was entirely responsible for the accident, having veered onto the wrong side of the road whilst under the influence of drugs. D was charged with causing death when uninsured and without a full driving licence contrary to section 3ZB of the Road Traffic Act 1988.

• Crown Court ruling: D did not cause death.

• Court of Appeal: prosecution appeal allowed, finding liability under section 3ZB. The offence is one of strict liability, requiring no mens rea or blameworthiness as to the causing of death.

• Supreme Court: appeal allowed, restoring the Crown Court decision. Offence requires some more than minimal fault/blameworthiness causing the result.

The approach in *Hughes* has been reaffirmed by a seven-member Supreme Court in *Taylor*,[107] a case that also involved causing death with a motor vehicle. In a unanimous

---

[105] Imagine a hypothetical where V jumps from a bridge to commit suicide and happens to land on D's car who is driving dangerously. If V landed on the car before the road, it is possible to say that D caused V's death (ie it happened fractionally sooner than it would otherwise), but it would surely be wrong to convict D of causing death by dangerous driving.

[106] *Williams* [2010] EWCA Crim 2552; *H* [2011] EWCA Crim 1508. Prompting academic criticism: Ormerod [2011] Crim LR 468; Sullivan and Simester, 'Causation Without Limits: Causing Death While Driving Without a Licence, While Disqualified, or Without Insurance' [2012] Crim LR 753.

[107] [2016] UKSC 5.

judgment, the court held that D's liability required 'at least some act or omission in the control of the car which involved some element of fault, whether amounting to careless/inconsiderate driving or not, and which contributed in some more than minimal way to the death'.[108] The Supreme Court, however, left open the possibility that regulatory offences (as opposed to 'true crimes') might be constructed to dispense with the blameworthy cause requirement. This qualification is problematic, both in terms of its uncertain principled basis, and the practical issue of separating regulatory and other offences that is not standardised within English law.[109]

 Assessment matters . . .

It should be remembered that for the vast majority of cases, where D causes a criminal harm, it will be very obvious that the cause was a blameworthy cause. In such cases, you need only highlight that this requirement is satisfied. Only discuss the blameworthiness requirement where the result (although factually caused by D) was in some sense unavoidable, and could/would have happened if D was acting innocently.

2.7.2.3 Legal cause must be 'operative'

As well as being substantial (more than *de minimis*) and blameworthy, D's conduct must also be the operative cause of the result. The term 'operative' means that D's conduct must still be a significant cause of the result at the time it comes about; the chain of causation between conduct and result elements must not be broken. For example, where D supplies V with a dangerous drug and V voluntarily self-injects causing death, D is not the legal cause of the death.[110] D is the factual cause (but for the supply of the drug V would not have died); plays a substantial role (obtaining the drug is a major step on the way to death); and her conduct is clearly a blameworthy cause (she is likely to know that the drug is dangerous); but the conduct of V breaks the chain of causation between D's conduct and the result. It is V's free and voluntary choice to self-inject the drug, and by making that choice V becomes the sole author of the results. This is illustrated in **Figure 2.4**.

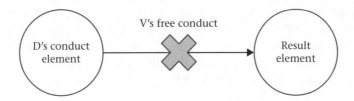

Figure 2.4 Breaking the chain of causation

We are looking for actions or events capable of breaking the chain of causation between D's conduct and the criminal result. These are known as a *novus actus interveniens*. Whilst not categorically ruled out by the courts, it is unlikely that omissions can break

---

[108] At [32].
[109] Discussed in Laird, 'The Decline of Causation Without Limits' [2016] Crim LR 566.
[110] *Kennedy (No 2)* [2007] UKHL 38.

a chain of causation.[111] Breaks can arise from certain subsequent actions of D; natural events; actions of V; or actions of a third party. Each will be discussed.

Lord Hoffmann stated in *Empress Car*[112] that 'it is of course the causal significance of acts of third parties . . . or natural forces that gives rise to almost all the problems about the notion of "causing" and drives judges to take refuge in metaphor [eg causal chains] or Latin [*novus actus*]'. This quotation highlights two important issues. The first is that cases of this kind arise often in the courts, and certainly more than cases questioning the 'substantial' or 'blameworthiness' of causes. The second is that judges have found these cases difficult, with legal principles often applied inconsistently or developed in open contradiction with one another, particularly in the context of homicide and other serious cases where major policy concerns arise.

Intervention from defendant

It will be very rare for D's own subsequent conduct to break the chain of causation between her initial conduct and the result. For example, where D stabs V and then shoots V within the same attack, the second act will certainly not break the chain: all of D's acts will be grouped as a single transaction causing death. The exceptional situation where a break may be found is where D's subsequent acts are part of a separate transaction. For example, D, having wounded V, visits her in hospital and accidentally infects her with smallpox from which she dies.[113] Here, D's original conduct (wounding) is effectively superseded by the operative cause of death, the infection. D remains liable for a wounding offence, but as the wounding did not cause death, it cannot give rise to liability for a homicide offence. To explore D's potential liability for a homicide offence we would have to focus on her second action (ie when infecting V), but as D infected V accidentally (ie lacking mens rea) it is unlikely that liability will be found. Where rare cases of this kind arise, it is therefore important to identify the limits of a transaction (a grouping of acts within a single event). We explore such interactions between actus reus and mens rea elements later.[114]

Intervention from naturally occurring events

Naturally occurring events (or 'acts of God') will only break the chain of causation if they are unforeseen by D and unforeseeable to the reasonable person. For example, if D assaults V and then leaves her on the beach at low tide, it is foreseeable that the tide will come in and V may drown. The natural event (tide) will not break the chain of causation: D's original conduct (assault) is the legal cause of V's death.[115] Equally, if D attacks V (conduct) and leaves her in a coma, making V more vulnerable to potential infection, any subsequent infection (natural event) that kills V will not break the chain. D's original conduct (attack) is the legal cause of death.[116]

---

[111] See Simester, 'Causation in (Criminal) Law' (2017) 133 LQR 416, Part III.

[112] [1999] AC 22.

[113] See *Le Brun* (1991) 94 Cr App R 101, on quite different facts, citing *Smith and Hogan's Criminal Law*.

[114] See **Chapter 4.3**.

[115] Example from *Perkins* (1946) 36 J Cr L & Cr 393; followed in the New Zealand case *Hart* [1986] 2 NZLR 408.

[116] *Gowans* [2003] EWCA Crim 3935.

However, where D attacks V and then leaves her in an apparently safe environment, only for V to be killed when struck by lightning, or a falling tree, or caught in a freak earthquake, the unforeseen and unforeseeable event *will* break the causal chain.[117] Here, D remains liable for what she has caused (namely the harm from the initial attack), but is not liable for the death. D's original conduct (attack) is not the legal cause of V's death.

Intervention from victim

As with our drugs supply example at the beginning of this section, it is clear that the acts of V can break the chain of causation between D's conduct and the result. Three main principles have emerged from judgments dealing with these cases, and they focus on: (A) the foreseeability of V's acts; (B) the voluntariness of V's acts; and (C) the unique vulnerabilities of V. We will discuss each, as well as (D) the apparent inconsistency between them:

A) **Foreseeability:** As with natural events, the foreseeability of the intervention (this time the actions of V) is key to whether that intervention will break the causal chain. For example, if D jumps out and scares V who is perched on a window ledge, and V falls from the window and dies, D is the legal cause of death: V's response in fright, leading to a loss of balance, is foreseeable. However, if D jumps out and scares V who is sitting on the sofa in her living room, and V then jumps, runs up some stairs to find a window, and then jumps out, it is likely that D's conduct will not be the legal cause of death: V's response was unforeseeable and, to use the language of various cases, 'daft'. The key then, when applying this rule, is to identify the tipping point between reactions of V that are foreseeable and do not break the causal chain, and those that are daft that will break the chain. As *Roberts* illustrates, courts will rarely interpret V's conduct as daft.

Roberts (1972) 56 Cr App R 95

D, driving V home after a party, began making unwanted sexual advances towards her, threatening her, and touching her coat. V jumped out of the moving car and suffered bodily harm. D was charged with assault occasioning actual bodily harm, contrary to section 47 of the Offences Against the Person Act 1861.

• Crown Court: guilty of section 47 offence.

• Court of Appeal: conviction upheld on appeal.

D's conviction in *Roberts* demonstrates the broad interpretation that courts apply to the test of foreseeability. It is also clear that the test will vary in line with V's age, mental capacity, and other circumstances. For example, where V is intoxicated, the court will ask if V's response was within the range of foreseeable responses for an intoxicated person.[118]

B) **Voluntariness:** Following D's conduct, if the result comes about because of V's free, voluntary, and informed act, the chain of causation *will* be broken. For example, if D supplies V with a hammer, and V uses the hammer to commit criminal damage, D is not the legal cause of the damage: D is a factual 'but for' cause of the damage, but the chain of causation is broken by V's free, voluntary, and informed choice to use the

---

[117] Examples from *Perkins* and Hart and Honoré, *Causation in the Law* (1985).

[118] *Corbett* [1996] Crim LR 594.

hammer in this way. In contrast, where V's acts are not free, voluntary, and informed, they will not break the chain. For example, where D gives V a poisoned apple and V eats it being unaware of the poison, D will remain the legal cause of death: the chain of causation is not broken because, although V acted freely and in some sense voluntarily when eating the apple, her actions were not informed.

Problems emerge where V's acts fall between these extremes, where V's acts are *partially* free, voluntary, and informed, as in *Kennedy (No 2)*.

Point to remember . . .

Problems emerge for the courts when cases fall between extremes, but these are exactly the cases that help us the most: they indicate the borderline between acts that break the chain of causation and those that do not.

Kennedy (No 2) [2007] UKHL 38

D supplied V with a prepared syringe of heroin. V self-injected the drug and died as a result. D was charged with manslaughter on the basis that his unlawful conduct (drug supply) caused V's death.

- Crown Court: guilty of constructive manslaughter.
- Court of Appeal: conviction upheld on appeal.
- House of Lords: quashing D's conviction on appeal—D was not guilty because he was not the legal cause of V's death.

Assessment matters . . .

Take care when discussing *Kennedy (No 2)* in assignments. The precedent that an informed and voluntary act by a responsible adult will break the chain of causation is *Kennedy (No 2)*—NOT *Kennedy*.[119]

In *Kennedy (No 2)* D's conduct was held not to be the legal cause of death because V's free, voluntary, and informed choice to self-inject the drug broke the chain of causation.[120] In reaching that conclusion, the court overruled a number of previous cases that had found liability in these circumstances.[121] *Kennedy (No 2)* demonstrates a relatively broad interpretation of what is free, voluntary, and informed: V's acts were seen as free and voluntary despite his addiction to the drug supplied. For liability to be found in these circumstances post-*Kennedy (No 2)*, it would have to be shown that D participated in the administration of the drug (so V was not acting independently),[122] or to focus on D's behaviour *after* the self-administering to locate an alternative conduct element (**2.6**).[123]

[119] In *Kennedy* [1999] Crim LR 65, the Court of Appeal held that D *had caused* V to take the noxious substance despite free and informed consent. *Kennedy (No 2)* arose following intervention from the Criminal Cases Review Commission.

[120] Ormerod and Fortson, 'Drug Suppliers as Manslaughterers (Again)' [2005] Crim LR 819. For an alternative view (supporting liability), see Jones, 'Causation, Homicide and the Supply of Drugs' (2006) 26 LS 139.

[121] Including *Rogers* [2003] Cr App R 10; *Finlay* [2003] EWCA Crim 3868.

[122] *Burgess* [2008] EWCA Crim 516.

[123] eg an omission to assist where D has a duty to do so.

C) **Vulnerabilities:** It is a long-established principle in criminal law, as in civil law, that D must 'take his victim as he finds him'. Where D punches V in a way that would ordinarily cause no more than minor bruising, but V's 'egg-shell skull' means that she suffers much greater harm and even death, D will be the legal cause of that greater harm: V's unique vulnerability will not break the chain of causation, even if unknown to D. The same principle will apply where D's stone only smashes a window because the glass is unusually thin: D remains the legal cause of the damage. Where, as with these examples, V's vulnerabilities are physical, there is little problem. However, as in *Blaue*, the principle is capable of wider application.

Blaue [1975] 3 All ER 446

D stabbed V. V required a blood transfusion to save her life, but refused on religious grounds (being a Jehovah's Witness). V died and D was charged with her manslaughter.

- Crown Court: guilty of manslaughter.
- Court of Appeal: conviction upheld on appeal—V's refusal did not break the chain of causation.

In *Blaue*, following *Holland*,[124] V's refusal of medical care was interpreted as part of her character rather than a separate, potentially intervening, event. The court held that D must take V as she is found, which meant her whole person, not just her physical person, and therefore V's refusal to accept a potentially life-saving blood transfusion could not break the causal chain: D remained the legal cause of death. The question becomes, if V's religious convictions are part of V, what other characteristics can be treated in the same way? For example, what if V simply did not like doctors, was afraid of needles, scared of catching blood-borne diseases, or even maliciously refused treatment in order to increase D's liability? The *Blaue* precedent opens the *possibility* that V's refusal in such circumstances will not break the causal chain.

D) **Inconsistency between principles:** Having set out the three principles relating to foreseeability, voluntariness, and vulnerabilities, it should be highlighted that there is a certain tension between them. For example, in *Roberts* we can accept that V jumping from a car is foreseeable. But it also seems to be voluntary (breaking the causal chain as per *Kennedy (No 2)*). It may be that V's act was not *fully* voluntary in the sense that she was under threat from D, but is this any less voluntary than the consumption of drugs by an addict? Equally, in *Blaue* we could say that V's refusal of a blood transfusion was both unforeseeable (breaking the causal chain as per *Roberts*) and voluntary (breaking the causal chain as per *Kennedy (No 2)*). Perhaps the difference is that V's refusal in *Blaue* was an omission, but this is not clear. The issue here is whether the courts are using the principles to make a decision in line with the rule of law, or choosing between principles in order to justify a prior moral decision about D's culpability.[125]

A useful illustration of this concern is the courts' response to cases where V commits suicide following an attack from D. We have a set of cases where D injures V and then V

---

[124] (1841) 2 Mood & R 351. In *Holland*, the state of medical safety at that date made the refusal of treatment potentially reasonable. In *Blaue*, the court clarified that reasonableness is irrelevant.

[125] See generally Hart and Honoré, *Causation in the Law* (1985).

acts to exacerbate that injury and cause death. For example, in *Dear*,[126] D's conviction for murder was upheld where V intentionally aggravated his wounds that had been inflicted by D. In such cases, V's acts appear voluntary, and they are certainly unforeseeable, but liability may *perhaps* be justified as an extension of *Blaue*: V is acting (rather than omitting), but D's acts would have caused death anyway if untreated. However, what about cases where V would have survived her injury? This has been debated, for example, where V commits suicide to escape long-term domestic abuse.[127] It was also the focus of the recent case *Wallace*.

 Wallace [2018] EWCA Crim 690

D attacked V with a corrosive substance, leaving him with catastrophic injuries and in a state of considerable suffering. V survived the attack, but moved to Belgium and decided to end his life at a euthanasia clinic (legal in Belgium). On a charge of murder, the question was whether D caused V's death?

• Crown Court: May J made a terminating ruling that causation could not be found on these facts. The prosecution appealed against that ruling.

• Court of Appeal: allowing the appeal, finding that causation was possible. Retrial ordered.

The Court of Appeal's decision in *Wallace* seems correct in the sense that we might *want* to find causation in certain cases of this kind, but the underlying reasoning remains problematic.[128] The Court of Appeal focussed its analysis on foreseeability and voluntariness. Foreseeability represents a significant hurdle in cases of this kind, demonstrating that D should have foreseen that V might commit suicide/seek euthanasia as a result of the attack, but in certain cases (eg particularly those involving domestic abuse) it may well be satisfied. It is noted that, at Wallace's retrial, the question of foreseeability was put to the jury; the jury found Wallace not guilty of murder, but guilty of a serious non-fatal offence (ie an offence that did not require causation of death).[129] However, it is questionable whether foreseeability should have been the main focus of this case. V made what appeared to be a free and voluntary decision to die, and the doctors (X) made a free and voluntary decision to act on that decision, both potential breaks in the causal chain as per *Kennedy (No 2)*. The Court of Appeal, however, held that the circumstances of ongoing suffering from D's attack made V's and X's decision in some sense *involuntary*, and the issue was not presented to the jury at retrial. The fine line between this and the apparently voluntary choice of an addicted V to take drugs in *Kennedy (No 2)* appears vanishingly small.

Intervention from third parties

We have already discussed the possibility of multiple causes. For example, where D, aged 12, smashes V's window and X (D's parent) allows this to happen in breach of the parental duty to control D, it may be that both D and X have caused the damage. Where this

---

[126] [1996] Crim LR 595.

[127] See *Dhaliwal* [2006] EWCA Crim 1139; Horder and McGowan, 'Manslaughter by Causing Another's Suicide' [2006] Crim LR 1035; Munro and Aitken, 'Adding Insult to Injury? The Criminal Law's Response to Domestic Abuse-Related Suicide in England and Wales' [2018] Crim LR 732.

[128] See Simester and Sullivan, 'Causing Euthanasia' (2019) LQR 21.

[129] See **Chapter 7**.

is the case, both D and X can be independently liable for criminal damage. However, there will also be cases where, following D's conduct, the result element only comes about because of the conduct of X. In such cases, the acts of X take on responsibility for the results and break the chain of causation between D and the result element.[130] For example, where D supplies X with poison, and X then poisons and kills V, D is not the legal cause of V's death: the causal chain is broken by the acts of X. As in the previous section, the principles of (A) foreseeability and (B) voluntariness play an obvious role in the case law. However, more controversially, (C) the status of X and (D) the type of offence charged, also seem to be important considerations.

Assessment matters . . .

When discussing the potential intervention of third parties it is important to remember that our focus is the liability of D: if X's acts break the chain of causation, D is not liable; if they do not, then D remains the cause and may be liable. The only reason you are discussing X is to ascertain the liability of D. You are not addressing X's liability, but simply whether X's conduct breaks the chain of causation between D and the result. Having discussed the liability of D, we may then go on *separately* to discuss the potential liability of X, but the liability of one has no bearing on the liability of the other.

A) Foreseeability: As with the intervention of V, to break the chain of causation the acts of X must be unforeseen by D and unforeseeable to the reasonable person.[131]

B) Voluntariness: To break the chain of causation, the acts of X must also be free, voluntary, and informed. For example, if D asks X to deliver a cake to V and the cake contains a secret bomb, and X does so, D is the legal cause of V's death: X has not acted in a free, voluntary, and *informed* manner. This was illustrated in the case of *Michael*.[132] D, the mother of V, sought to kill V by providing X who was V's nurse with a large dose of poison and telling her that it was medicine for V. The 'medicine' was eventually administered to V by Y, a small child living at the house. Despite the acts of both X and Y following from D, there was no break in the chain of causation: the third party acts were not free, voluntary, and informed as they did not know the substance was poison.

C) Status of X: When applying these principles, it has become clear that the courts apply different standards depending upon the status of X, the potentially intervening party. This is most obvious where X is a doctor, treating V as a result of D's previous attack. In such circumstances, negligent treatment from X that leads to greater harm will only break the chain of causation if the court considers it 'palpably wrong', and that the injuries inflicted by D are largely healed, as in *Jordan*.

---

[130] *Latif* [1996] 2 Cr App R 92.

[131] For a recent discussion on the detail of what must be foreseeable, see *A* [2020] EWCA Crim 407: whether the circumstances of a collision on the hard shoulder of a motorway were foreseeable.

[132] (1840) 9 C & P 356.

Jordan (1956) 40 Cr App R 152

D stabbed V. In hospital, at a stage when V's wound was largely healed, X (a doctor) administered a large quantity of a drug to which V had shown he was intolerant. The treatment was described as 'palpably wrong'. D was charged with murder.

- Crown Court: guilty of murder.
- Court of Criminal Appeal: allowing the appeal and quashing D's conviction—X's acts broke the chain of causation such that D was not the legal cause of death.

Jordan demonstrates that the conduct of doctors *can* break the chain of causation, but its potential was narrowed considerably in two later cases of *Smith* and *Cheshire*.

 Smith [1959] 2 QB 35

D stabbed V in a fight between soldiers from different regiments. When carrying V to the medical reception, X dropped him twice. Y (a doctor) failed to note that the wound had pierced a lung and provided treatment later described as 'thoroughly bad'. D was charged with manslaughter.

- Crown Court: guilty of constructive manslaughter.
- Court of Criminal Appeal: upholding D's conviction—D remained a legal cause of V's death.

In *Smith*, despite poor treatment from two third parties, D remained a legal cause. The distinction here is that, unlike *Jordan*, the wounds inflicted by D were not largely healed and remained a significant and operative cause of death. As long as the injury inflicted by D is still ongoing and not 'merely part of the history' leading to injurious acts from X or Y, D will remain a legal cause.

 Cheshire [1991] 3 All ER 670

D shot V. In hospital, V was treated and the wounds ceased to be life threatening. However, following a negligently performed tracheotomy by a doctor (X), V's windpipe narrowed and he died. D was charged with murder.

- Crown Court: guilty of murder.
- Court of Appeal: upholding D's conviction—D was still a legal cause of V's death.

In *Cheshire*, unlike *Smith* (but in common with *Jordan*) V's wounds had largely healed at the point of X's negligent intervention. However, despite this, X's acts did not break the chain of causation. The court clarified that the test was not about X's mens rea, but rather whether X's act was 'so independent of [D's] acts, and in itself so potent in causing death, that [the jury] regard the contribution made by [D's] acts as insignificant'. Exactly how 'so independent' and 'so potent' should be interpreted is unclear. However, although the possibility of doctors breaking the chain of causation remains open, as demonstrated in *Jordan*, it seems that *Cheshire* has further narrowed the already rather narrow circumstances in which it may be found.

To claim that such cases involve foreseeable and involuntary acts on the part of doctors is only possible if those principles are stretched to insignificance. Rather, the courts appear to be acting on the *understandable* basis of policy: D's acts led to V requiring care and so D should take the full consequences if things go wrong.[133] As we see in *Pagett*, it is a policy that may not be isolated to doctors.

  Pagett (1983) 76 Cr App R 279

D, to resist lawful arrest, held V in front of him as a human shield and shot at police (X). X returned fire and killed V. D was charged with the manslaughter of V.

- Crown Court: guilty of constructive manslaughter.
- Court of Appeal: upholding D's conviction—D was still a legal cause of V's death.

In *Pagett*, as with previous cases, we can understand the policy grounds on which the courts would not want to say that X's act broke the chain of causation, as this would prevent D being liable for a homicide offence. However, in order to achieve this end, the legal principles of causation are compromised. The court held that X's instinctive reaction to return fire was in some sense 'involuntary', as well as holding more generally that acts done in line with a duty to prevent crime would never break the chain of causation.

D) Type of offence: It has become apparent that, as well as special categories of X distorting the principles of causation, there may be a similar issue with certain types of offence.[134] We see this in *Empress Car* in relation to pollution offences.

  Empress Car Co Ltd [1999] 2 AC 22

D, a company, allowed oil to be stored on its site and failed to take precautions to prevent the foreseeable danger that someone would release it into the river. X (an unidentified stranger) released the oil. D was charged with offences related to the pollution of the river.

- Crown Court: guilty of pollution offences.
- Court of Appeal: conviction upheld on appeal.
- House of Lords: upholding conviction—D remained a legal cause.

In *Empress Car*, despite the presumably free and voluntary act of a third party, the chain of causation was not broken. The House of Lords in *Kennedy (No 2)* has since clarified that the *Empress Car* precedent is isolated to pollution cases alone.[135] However, in allowing the exception, there is further erosion of the principles of causation.

---

[133] Although understandable, it may be argued that attempt liability may be more appropriate: punishing D for what she was trying to do rather than maintaining the fiction that her acts achieved that end.

[134] Padfield, 'Clean Water and Muddy Causation: Is Causation a Question of Law or Fact, or Just a Way of Allocating Blame?' [1995] Crim LR 683.

[135] The application of *Empress Car* is also discussed in *Day* [2014] EWCA Crim 2683, [23], suggesting that it could be applied more widely.

Summary

It is important to remember the basic structure of the legal question: is there a break in causation between D's conduct and the results? See **Figure 2.5**.

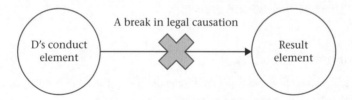

Figure 2.5 A break in legal causation

In order to answer this question, we must consider the circumstances of the potential break, illustrated in **Table 2.4**. Varieties of intervening acts

Table 2.4   Varieties of intervening acts

Type of intervention	Principles
Intervention from D	(1) Will only break the chain if it is part of a new transaction
Intervention from naturally occurring events	(1) Will only break the chain if it is unforeseen by D and unforeseeable by a reasonable person
Intervention from victim	(1) Will break the chain if it is unforeseen by D and unforeseeable by a reasonable person; and (2) will break the chain if it is free, voluntary, and informed; but (3) D must take the victim as he finds him
Intervention from third party	(1) Will break the chain if it is unforeseen by D and unforeseeable by a reasonable person; and (2) will break the chain if it is free, voluntary, and informed; but (3) special categories of third parties and offences will apply different rules

These principles should be applied to every case. However, it is equally important to discuss potential conflicts between principles. In some cases, with reference to academic discussion, it may be useful to identify the outcome you think the court would prefer on policy grounds, and then discuss whether the principles of causation will allow for that outcome.

2.8 Reform

With essay-type questions in mind, it is useful to pick up on three major debates that have arisen during the chapter. These include (a) the availability of omissions liability; (b) the role of results within offences; and (c) the extent of the courts' discretion when applying legal causation. We provide a brief overview of each, highlighting potential options for reform.

2.8.1 Omissions

The central debate regarding omissions is to what extent the law should recognise a duty to act. It will be remembered that, unlike positive acts that will always satisfy the conduct element of an offence,[136] omissions will only do so if: (a) the offence is capable of commission by omission; (b) D has a recognised duty to act; and (c) D breached that duty. Thus, notoriously, if D stands and watches a small child drown in a shallow pool she will not be liable for any offence in relation to the death—even if she could easily save the child, and even if she chose not to act because she wanted the child to die. D will only be liable if she comes within a narrow legal category creating a duty to act as, for example, where she is V's parent.

Examples of this kind have led several academics to contend that liability for omissions should be expanded. There are two main examples of how this could be achieved. First, we could create a new omissions-based offence for failure to perform an 'easy rescue', of the type seen in several other jurisdictions.[137] This so-called 'bad Samaritan' offence criminalises those who fail to avert serious harm where such harm could be easily and safely prevented.[138] Secondly, building upon duties to act recognised within the current law, we could introduce a new duty to act based on 'citizenship'. Alongside duties based on familial relationships, etc, a citizenship duty to act would mandate reasonable action (preventing harm) whenever D was in a position to do so for the benefit of other citizens. With D's omissions much more likely to satisfy the conduct element of an offence, the focus would then be on other offence elements to see what, if any, offence is committed. For example, if D fails to save the drowning child with the intention that V should die, her breach of a citizen's duty to act would make her liable for murder.

The case for expanding omissions liability is put most convincingly by Ashworth.[139] He terms this approach the 'social responsibility view'. For Ashworth, the current approach to omissions, which he terms the 'conventional view', falls into two main errors.

First, it assumes a moral difference between acts and omissions that is not present. In certain cases an omission may be more culpable than an act. For example, consider V1 who is caught in a house fire when D1 fails to press a button to set off a sprinkler system that would save V1; and contrast that with D2 who, seeing that V2 will die in

---

[136] The only exception being where the offence can only be committed by omission.

[137] Including France and a number of US states: Ashworth and Steiner, 'Criminal Omissions and Public Duties: The French Experience' (1990) 10 LS 152.

[138] The specified level of potential harm to V and the ease of D's potential acts both vary between jurisdictions.

[139] Ashworth, *Positive Obligations in Criminal Law* (2013); Ashworth, 'The Scope of Criminal Liability for Omissions' (1989) 105 LQR 424.

considerable pain, and with no way to rescue her, shoots V2. Who is more culpable? Additionally, in many cases it will be difficult to determine if D has acted or omitted. For example, as discussed earlier (**2.6.5**), where D releases his grip of the tug-of-war rope, is D acting to let go or omitting to hold on?

Secondly, Ashworth contends that the autonomy argument against omissions liability is misconceived. Although omissions liability restricts D's options more than act-based liability (**2.6**), bearing in mind that a duty will only arise in exceptional circumstances where V is in considerable danger, and bearing in mind the low expectation of D, over-all autonomy is respected. Indeed, a lack of rescue will severely restrict V's autonomy (through injury) and D will also benefit from the potential for similar assistance in the future.

The social responsibility view of omissions advocated by Ashworth has several benefits, including the potential for improved 'fair warning'.[140] Under the current law there are a number of duties to act, but in each case the law is very unclear as to the boundaries where these duties arise. As a result, D has to wait until after the event to find out if the court will identify a duty or not. It could be argued that a new easy-rescue offence, or a more general citizenship duty, would be fairer, clearer, and simpler.[141] The clear warning would be that omissions liability is possible whenever D unreasonably fails to act.

The arguments against such an expansion, effectively supporting the status quo, are numerous. They are also usefully summarised by Glanville Williams who, in response to Ashworth, defends the conventional view.[142] Central again is the autonomy argument: whereas act-based liability stops D pursuing one course of action, omissions liability stops her pursuing *all* courses of action that are not the action required to avoid liability. But there are also other concerns. First, despite the occasional counter-example, it is contended that omissions are less culpable than actions: D is not making the world worse; she is *merely* failing to make it better. Secondly, and following from this, if the criminal law has limited resources (both in detection and punishment) it should focus on acts as the most blameworthy conduct. Thirdly, Williams contends that a citizenship duty, or specific offence of failure to rescue, would be too uncertain with no common standard of social responsibility to provide fair warning of when people may become liable for their omissions.

2.8.2 Results

One of the most interesting tensions within the criminal law is found between subjectivism (focussing on D's individual culpability) and objectivism (focussing on the harms caused by D's conduct).[143] When discussing the result elements of offences, this tension is readily apparent. On one side, results are central to liability because they usually represent the harm caused by D (objectivism); but on the other side, they are almost redundant because they are not fully controlled by D and are therefore an imperfect reflection of her culpability (subjectivism). The current law represents an *often uncomfortable* compromise between the two.

---

[140] See **Chapter 1.4.1**.
[141] Cobb, 'Compulsory Care Giving: Some Thoughts on Relational Feminism, the Ethics of Care and Omissions Liability' (2008) 39 Cam LR 11.
[142] Williams, 'Criminal Omissions—The Conventional View' (1991) 107 LQR 86.
[143] See discussion in **Chapter 1.4**.

Starting with the subjectivist approach, the logic of this position is simple. Let us imagine that D1 shoots at V1 with the intention to kill. Meanwhile, D2 shoots at V2 with the intention to kill. If D1 kills V1, but D2 does not manage to kill V2 (because, for example, V2 is saved by doctors), the difference between D1 and D2 is simply a matter of luck. And, as luck is not a reflection of D's culpability, both D1 and D2 are equally culpable and should be punished in the same way.[144] Indeed, on this basis, *all* result crimes could be remodelled into 'acting with intent' conduct crimes: focussing liability on what D controls (ie her acts and her mens rea) and not being distorted by luck.[145] The subjectivist position can be seen in several areas of the law. For example, where D attempts to commit an offence with intention, but is not successful in that attempt, the same maximum sentence will generally apply to the attempt as to the principal offence attempted.[146]

An objectivist approach, in contrast, contends that *results matter*.[147] Although D1 and D2 in our example have performed the same acts, our reaction to them will be very different: we condemn D1 for her acts *and* for causing the death of V; we condemn D2 for her acts, but we are relieved that death did not result.[148] Results are therefore perceived as an additional harm for which D is responsible. It is also contended that holding D1 responsible for the result is not punishing her on the basis of luck. As Duff makes clear, 'if I [behave in a particular way] with the intention of bringing X about ... I have control over X's occurrence in that it depends to a significant degree on me and on what I do; X will not ensue if I do not [behave in that particular way]'.[149] The objectivist position can also be seen in several areas of the law. For example, when we discuss the non-fatal offences against the person in **Chapter 7**, it will be seen that a ladder of offences is used to label and punish D principally with reference to the seriousness of the harm inflicted upon V. An objectivist approach can also be seen in the absence, in this jurisdiction, of any general offence of reckless endangerment.[150] If D acts with the intent to cause harm she may be liable for attempt; but if she acts merely foreseeing the risk of harm, even where this is sufficient mens rea for the principal 'result-based' offence, she will not be liable for a general endangerment offence where the result does not come about.[151]

More recently, Edwards and Simester have explored something of a mid-way position, in which we recognise D1 and D2 as equally culpable (ie they both demonstrate the same evil intents), but still blame D1 more (and consider greater punishment to be justified)

---

[144] Ashworth, 'Belief, Intent and Criminal Liability' in Eekelaar and Bell (eds), *Oxford Essays in Jurisprudence* (1989); Ashworth, 'Taking the Consequences' in Shute, Gardner, and Horder (eds), *Action and Value in Criminal Law* (1993); Ashworth, 'Defining Offences Without Harm' in Smith (ed), *Criminal Law: Essays in Honour of JC Smith* (1987). See also Alexander and Kessler Ferzan, *Crime and Culpability: A Theory of Criminal Law* (2009).

[145] Although this is the logical conclusion of a subjectivist approach, few academics would support this extreme.

[146] Criminal Attempts Act 1981, s4. The only exception is attempted murder, where there is a discretionary, as opposed to mandatory, life sentence.

[147] Moore, *Placing Blame: A General Theory of the Criminal Law* (1997); Moore, *Causation and Responsibility* (2009).

[148] Duff, *Criminal Attempts* (1996) Ch4.

[149] Duff, *Answering for Crime* (2007) 63.

[150] Duff, 'Criminalising Endangerment' in Duff and Green (eds), *Defining Crimes* (2005).

[151] The English law contains several specific endangerment offences (eg speeding offences), but no general offence (akin to attempt) to catch reckless endangerment beyond these.

because of the greater harm caused.[152] Choosing between competing approaches can quickly draw us back to foundational debates about the purpose of criminal law and punishment,[153] but such choices remain essential to our critique of the law and its potential reform: to critique the law effectively, we need to have a sense of a normative ideal.

2.8.3 Causation

The causation rules dictate the required connection between the conduct and result elements of a result crime: D's conduct must cause the result in fact ('but for' test) *and* in law (significant, blameworthy, and operative). As we have seen earlier, the development and application of causation rules within the common law has been and remains highly problematic. In response, several alternative approaches have been advanced.

Hart and Honoré, for example, suggest an alternative based on a distinction between what they term 'normal' causal conditions such as environmental factors (not legal causes) and 'abnormal' causal conditions such as voluntary intervention (which will constitute legal causes), and may also break the chain of causation if performed by another.[154] There is much to commend this approach, but it may be that the central distinction remains too vague and subjective to perform the objectifying role intended. More recently, Simester has outlined an approach to causation that would distinguish what he terms 'direct causes' (where D initiates a causal chain that provides the mechanical route to a result) from 'indirect causes' (where D initiates a causal chain that leads to a result through its intersection with a separate causal chain).[155] Adopting this approach would involve fundamental changes in the way the courts understand and apply causation rules.[156]

A more modest and practical option for reform can be found within the Law Commission Criminal Law Team's 2002 Working Paper on causation, set out in its draft Bill.

(1) Subject to subsections (2) to (5), a defendant causes a result which is an element of an offence when—

   (a) he does an act which makes a substantial and operative contribution to its occurrence; or

   (b) he omits to do an act, which he is under a duty to do according to the law relating to the offence, and the failure to do the act makes a substantial and operative contribution to its occurrence.

(2) (a) The finders of fact may conclude that a defendant's act or omission did not make a substantial and operative contribution to the occurrence of a result if compared with the voluntary intervention of another person, unless:

   (i) the defendant is subject to a legal duty to guard against the very harm that the intervention or event causes; and

   (ii) the intervention was not so extraordinary as to be unforeseeable to a reasonable person in the defendant's position; and

   (iii) it would have been practicable for the defendant to have taken steps to prevent the intervention.

---

[152] Edwards and Simester, 'Crime, Blameworthiness and Outcomes' (2019) OJLS 50.
[153] See **Chapter 1.1**.
[154] Hart and Honoré, *Causation in the Law* (1985).
[155] Simester, 'Causation in (Criminal) Law' (2017) 133 LQR 416.
[156] Simester's approach is also problematic, as it is questionable whether complex human events will ever occur in the absence of an interaction of causal chains, and therefore ever exist within the 'direct cause' category.

(b) The intervention of another person is not voluntary unless it is:

    (i) free, deliberate and informed; and

    (ii) performed or undertaken without any physical participation from the defendant.

(3) (a) The finders of fact may conclude that a defendant's act or omission did not make a substantial and operative contribution to the occurrence of a result if compared with an unforeseeable natural event;

    (b) A natural event is not unforeseeable unless:

        (i) the defendant did not foresee it; and

        (ii) it could not have been foreseen by any reasonable person in the defendant's position.

The substance of the team's proposals is largely a reflection of the current law, and so it would do little to resolve many of the uncertainties discussed earlier. But codification of the basic structure of causation would have advantages: creating a settled basis for the law and, equally importantly, a settled terminology. However, as the Commission has not taken these proposals forward, reform of this kind is unlikely in the near future.

Extra detail . . .

This is the first time, of many, that we have quoted Law Commission material. Remember that these do not represent the current law and you should not apply them as if they do. Rather, they are reform suggestions and should be discussed only in that context.

2.9 Eye on assessment

This section sketches a structure for analysing the actus reus of an offence when applying the law in a problem-type question. Drawing on the structure outlined at the end of **Chapter 1**, we are focussing on the first part of Step 3.

STEP 1 Identify the potential criminal event in the facts

This should be simply stated (eg 'The first potential criminal event arises where D kicks V'). The role of this stage is to highlight which part of the question you are answering before you begin to apply the law.

STEP 2 Identify the potential offence

State this simply (eg 'When breaking the vase, D may be liable for criminal damage'). The role of this stage is to highlight which offence you are going to apply.

> ### STEP 3 Applying the offence to the facts
>
> Having highlighted a possible offence, Step 3 requires you to both identify the actus reus and mens rea of that offence, *and* apply them to the facts.

Step 3 will probably require most analysis within a problem question (although Steps 1 and 2 should not be forgotten). It includes the identification and application of both actus reus and mens rea elements. This should always begin with the actus reus: the actus reus of an offence locates it in time and space and provides a base from which to ask if D had the required mens rea *at that point*. Our analysis of actus reus requires us to answer two (deceptively) simple questions.

(1) What is the actus reus of the potential offence?

(2) Did D complete the actus reus (did she do it)?

The answer to these questions will vary between offences (question 1) and between factual scenarios (question 2). The answer to the first question will be discussed in relation to each offence covered in this textbook: gleaned from a combination of statutory and common law sources. However, the structure of application (question 2) is common between offences and can be usefully introduced at this point through **Table 2.5**.

Table 2.5 Applying the actus reus to problem facts

Actus reus	
A) Conduct element: what did D physically do?	Although there is some flexibility in stages B and C, application of the actus reus should always begin with the conduct element. This is because you need a conduct element before you can ask if the required circumstances were present when D acted or omitted, and whether D's conduct caused the result. Your analysis of the conduct element will vary between conduct and result crimes.
	Conduct crimes: conduct crimes (offences not including a result element) will usually specify a particular act or omission that D must have done. The question is therefore simple: did D do it?
	Result crimes: result crimes are a little trickier because you are usually looking for any (non-specific) conduct that caused the result. Where D performs several acts and omissions, you may have a choice of potential conduct elements. When choosing between them, look for an action (as opposed to an omission) if possible.
	Only focus on D's omission if: D has not acted (eg *Gibbins and Proctor*), D acted but there is an obvious problem with mens rea at that point (eg *Miller*), or D acted but there is an obvious problem with causation from that conduct (eg *Evans*). If you are forced to move on to consider omissions liability in this manner, always tell your reader the reason you are forced to do so. If there is no problem with finding liability based on D's acts, there is no need to consider her omissions as well (eg if D shoots V intentionally, then fails to get medical help and V dies—there is no need to consider D's omission to get help).

B) Circumstance element: were the required circumstances present?	All offences (conduct and result crimes) include circumstance elements (eg that D does not own the property damaged for criminal damage). Typically, the question is whether the circumstance is present at the time of the conduct element.
C) Result element: did D's conduct element cause the required result?	This will only be required, of course, for result crimes. This part of your analysis has two parts. First, you have to ask if the result (whatever is specified in the offence) actually happened. Secondly, you must ask if it was caused by D. Having identified the conduct element (act or omission) that is most likely to have caused the result, you must now apply the causation rules (factual and legal causation) in relation to that conduct element. Thus, if D has acted but you have chosen to focus on her omission (eg because the act was involuntary), your question is whether her omission caused the result.

To illustrate this structure, take the facts of *Miller* (**2.6.2.5**): D fell asleep with a lit cigarette, awoke to find it smouldering on the mattress, but simply left the fire to spread rather than attempting to put it out or summon help. The potential criminal event here relates to the damage to the property (Step 1) and the most likely offence is arson (Step 2). Arson is discussed in **Chapter 9**, but the actus reus essentially requires D to damage another person's property by fire.[157]

When applying this, our first task is to identify the conduct element. As D has set fire to the mattress we should begin here, with the act of dropping the cigarette. However, it is apparent that this act is not a suitable conduct element: although it causes the damage, it is done when D is asleep and is not accompanied by mens rea. Therefore, we must look for an alternative conduct element. In this case, the alternative arises when (having realised the danger) D wakes up and fails to try and prevent further damage. At this point D is most likely to have the mens rea for the offence. Focussing on this point, D's conduct element is an omission. As an omission, liability will require D's conduct to satisfy additional requirements: arson must be capable of commission by omission (*Miller* shows that it is), D must have a duty to act (D has created a dangerous situation and therefore has a duty to try to mitigate that danger), and D must have breached that duty (a reasonable person would be expected to try and put out the fire or summon help; by doing neither, D breaches his duty). D therefore satisfies the conduct element of criminal damage.

The next question is whether D's omission caused damage (result) to the property of another by fire (circumstance). It is clear from the facts that the fire does damage the property of another, so our focus turns to the causal relationship between this damage and the omission of D. Applying the causation rules, it is evident that D's omission is a factual cause of the damage: but for D's omission to take reasonable steps, the fire would not have spread and caused such extensive damage. D's omission was a blameworthy cause (he chose not to act despite foreseeing the danger), it was a substantial cause

---

[157] Criminal Damage Act 1971, s1.

(certainly more than *de minimis*), and it was an operative cause (there were no actions or events that could have broken the chain of causation). Therefore, the actus reus of arson is satisfied.

Assessment matters . . .

In this example, the bulk of our discussion related to the conduct element of the actus reus. This is because the facts of *Miller* present a challenge when locating a suitable conduct element, but are quite straightforward when it comes to circumstances, results, and causation. In another example, the conduct element may be straightforward and there may be more discussion of other elements. It is important that your answer covers the full actus reus, but you need only discuss issues in detail where there is some uncertainty.

 ONLINE RESOURCES

www.oup.com/he/child-ormerod4e

This chapter is accompanied by a selection of online resources to help you with this topic, including:

- **Self-test questions** and **scenario questions**
- **Videos** from the authors
- **Audio introduction** to the topic
- **Chapter summary sheet**
- Two **sample examination questions** with answer guidance
- **Further reading and weblinks**

Also available on the online resources are:

- A selection of **videos** from the authors containing general advice on problem questions and essay questions
- **Legal updates**

3

Mens rea

3.1 Introduction

The Latin term 'mens rea' is loosely translated as 'guilty mind'. Where actus reus focusses on the external elements of an offence, mens rea focusses on state of mind or fault: did D *intend* to do it, *believe* it would happen, *foresee a risk* it might happen; and so on.

As with our discussion of actus reus, it should be remembered from the outset that these terms (actus reus and mens rea) are terms of art. The ambition of the criminal law is to define *offences* which are combinations of actus reus and mens rea elements that criminalise wrongful events.[1] However, the separation of actus reus and mens rea elements is helpful when discussing and applying the criminal law, and is almost universally adopted by the courts as well as within academic writing. Mens rea is a core component of criminal law, illustrated in **Figure 3.1**.

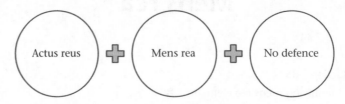

Figure 3.1 Elements of criminal liability

3.1.1 Identifying mens rea elements

If the actus reus/mens rea distinction were strictly applied, then the identification of mens rea within a statutory or common law offence would be straightforward: any requirement external to D's state of mind or fault would be an actus reus requirement, and anything internal to D's state of mind or fault would be a mens rea requirement. This remains a useful rule of thumb. For example, the common law offence of murder criminalises D who unlawfully causes the death of a person under the Queen's peace (external actus reus requirement), with the *intention* to kill or cause serious bodily harm to a person (internal mens rea requirement). However, as we have already discussed in the context of the actus reus, the precise labelling of external requirements as actus reus and internal requirements as mens rea is not always as consistent as we might hope. There are certain offence requirements that are *internal* to the mind of D and yet are traditionally referred to as part of the actus reus; as well as requirements that are *external* to the mind of D and yet are traditionally referred to as part of the mens rea.[2]

Within the broad class of mens rea terms, recognising something of the diversity just discussed, it is useful to make a further division between two categories:

- **Subjective mens rea:** The term 'subjective' is used to indicate a mens rea requirement that is looking (internally) to the mind of D. For example, criminal damage requires a mens rea of at least recklessness as to the causing of damage.[3] To satisfy this mens rea, the prosecution must prove that D personally foresaw a risk of causing damage. It is not enough to show that she should have done, or that a reasonable person would have done.

- **Objective mens rea:** The term 'objective' is used to indicate a requirement that need *not* identify a certain state of mind held by D; judging D instead by an external standard of reasonableness. For example, certain offences require proof that D was 'negligent'. Negligence is a mens rea term, but rather than focussing on D's internal thoughts, the focus is on what a reasonable person in D's position would have known.

[1] Discussed in **Chapter 1.1.1**.
[2] Discussed in **Chapter 2.2**.
[3] Criminal Damage Act 1971, s1.

Don't be confused . . .

When a jury are asked to apply subjective mens rea requirements it is, of course, impossible for them to look inside D's mind. Therefore, just as a jury will look to objective factors when applying objective mens rea terms (eg what would a reasonable person have foreseen in these circumstances?), the application of subjective mens rea terms will often involve a similar process. However, important differences remain. For example, let us consider a mens rea requirement of 'foresight of damage' where the jury believe a risk of damage would have been obvious to a reasonable person.

- **Objective test:** the fact that it was obvious to a reasonable person is determinative. D satisfies the offence requirement without needing to consider whether she actually foresaw it or not.
- **Subjective test:** the fact that the jury think it would have been obvious to a reasonable person is evidence that may encourage them to think that D also foresaw it. However, if they believe D's claim that (for whatever reason) she did not foresee it at the time, or they think that she may not have foreseen it, the offence requirement will not be satisfied.

Identifying the mens rea of an offence is not, therefore, a case of surgically separating internal from external requirements. Rather, it is a case of identifying those offence requirements that are focussing, in general terms, on D's state of mind or fault, whether these are subjective or objective requirements.[4] In more practical terms it is also about learning the vocabulary of mens rea terms that has developed in the common law (eg 'intention'; 'recklessness'; 'malice'; 'knowing'; 'belief'; etc), and looking to pick them out from the definition of an offence.

A final point to remember, when identifying and applying mens rea elements, is that your task is not a moral one. The term mens rea may imply some kind of moral evaluation (ie, *guilty* mind) and the law *is* seeking to criminalise wrongful or guilty behaviour. However, the absence of moral fault should not affect how you identify and apply the law in practice: if D's behaviour satisfies the elements of an offence, then she commits that offence. Discussion of the morality of D's behaviour is relevant, if anywhere, only to a critique of the law. For example, where D kills V at V's request, in order to relieve V from some manner of incurable illness or painful condition, her action is popularly referred to as a 'mercy killing'. For many people, the actions of D in these circumstances would not be considered wrongful or guilty. However, in law, D is still likely to have committed the offence of murder: D unlawfully causes V's death (actus reus), with the intention to kill (mens rea), and with no legal defence. We may criticise the law and say that the offence should not apply in these circumstances (this is a reform discussion), but this will not affect the application of the *current* law.[5]

---

[4] An alternative terminology has been to label subjective mens rea as 'mens rea', and objective mens rea as 'fault'. However, this approach is not consistently applied by courts or academics. Eg the Law Commission consistently employs the term 'fault element' as a simple substitute for 'mens rea', whether subjective or objective.

[5] See *Kingston* [1994] 3 WLR 519: liability was found despite D only committing the offence due to the wrongful actions of others.

Extra detail . . .

The same logic underpins the classical maxim that 'ignorance of the law is no excuse'. If D satisfies the actus reus and mens rea and has no defence, she has committed the offence: it is irrelevant to her liability if she or anyone else considers what she did to be morally justifiable (as with mercy killers), and it is irrelevant whether she knew that what she was doing was a crime.

3.1.2 The role of mens rea elements

Offences are created in an attempt to criminalise wrongful behaviour. In this regard, if offences focussed only on the conduct of the accused they would be rather blunt weapons. Actus reus elements can define harmful conduct and/or consequences, such as causing death, causing damage, taking another's property, etc, but such harms alone will not necessarily justify punishing D and labelling her as a criminal. Rather, before we can properly blame D for what she has done, it is often necessary to know whether she meant to do it; knew the risk it would happen; should have known the risk; and so on. This is the role of mens rea.

Compare the following examples in which D shoots and kills V:

(a) D1 shoots and kills V1, intending by her acts to cause death;

(b) D2 shoots at a shooting range target. V2 is (unknown to D) hiding behind the target, and is killed.

In both examples, D1 and D2 have completed the actus reus of a homicide offence: their action has unlawfully caused the death of a person. However, the difference between their states of mind (D1 intending to kill; D2 knowing nothing of V2) means that our reaction to the two events is likely to be very different. D1 has killed intentionally and we therefore blame her for the death, we want her to be punished and to prevent her from acting in this manner again. D2, on the other hand, has simply shot at a target, with the death of V2 following as a terrible accident. Here, rather than blame D2 we are more likely to feel sorry for her, as someone having to live with the consequences of the accident, and we are much less likely to want to stop her doing the same thing again (ie shooting at a target). D2's conduct was not blameworthy.

The way the law distinguishes these events is through mens rea requirements. D1 has committed the offence of murder, she has unlawfully killed a person *with the intention to kill or cause serious harm*.[6] D2, in contrast, is unlikely to have committed any offence: a terrible result may have occurred (the death of V2), which is the same result caused by D1, but D2 lacks the mens rea for a homicide offence.

Extra detail . . .

If we think back to the principles of criminalisation,[7] these would (predominantly) support the current law in criminalising D1 and not D2.

- Fair warning: a warning not to kill by accident could only be heeded by stopping doing anything potentially dangerous. As such activities are common and often beneficial (eg driving), this would not be a useful message. A warning not to kill intentionally avoids such problems.

---

[6] *Cunningham* [1982] AC 566. See Chapter 5.
[7] Discussed in **Chapter 1.4.**

- Fair labelling: our different moral reactions to the conduct of D1 and D2 means that they should not be labelled in the same way.

- Autonomy: criminalising D2 where she does not choose to kill, or even to risk the death of V2, would not respect her autonomy.

- Welfare: a focus on welfare may encourage us to look at the objective results (death in both cases) ahead of mens rea. Thus, such an approach may favour the criminalisation of D1 and D2.

When thinking about the role of mens rea, and the construction of offences, we should not fall into the trap of being overly simplistic. The difference between D1 who intended to kill and D2 who had no knowledge of V2 is quite straightforward; and we can appreciate the role of mens rea to catch D1 within an offence and to exclude D2. However, these examples are at the very clear ends of what is otherwise a rather murky spectrum. For example, what if, when D2 shot V2:

- D did not want to kill V, but recognised that she was virtually certain to do so, for example because she saw V standing behind the target;

- D did not want to kill V, but recognised that there was a risk she might do so, for example because of her bad aim?

- D did not know V was behind the target, but only because she failed to check the target as the gun range staff had informed her to do?

In these examples, D does not intend to kill or cause serious bodily harm to V in the conventional sense because she was not shooting in order to bring that result about (discussed at **3.4.1**). However, we may still want to find liability for murder, or some other homicide offence. Thus, the mens rea of an offence must define which states of mind within the spectrum will be enough to satisfy the particular offence and which will not. To do so, the common law has developed a rich language of mens rea terms including 'intention', 'knowledge', 'belief', 'recklessness', 'negligence', 'dishonesty', and many more. Much of this chapter will be spent discussing what each of these terms means in law, allowing you to understand them when they are used within an offence and apply them to problem facts.

3.2 Mens rea in context

Although most of this chapter will be spent discussing the legal meaning of the central mens rea terms (eg 'intention'; 'recklessness'; etc), it is first important to introduce how these terms work in the context of a whole offence. The actus reus of an offence can be viewed independently, without reference to mens rea: we can ask whether D unlawfully caused death; damaged another's property; had non-consensual intercourse; and so on. However, this is not the case with mens rea terms, which on their own are unhelpful. For example, if you heard that a friend, D, had hurt one of your other friends, V, it would be natural to ask D what she was thinking. If D answered simply 'intention' or 'recklessness', this would be entirely unhelpful: even understanding the terms, they need context to provide any assistance. It makes no sense for D to intend, for example, in the abstract. However, if D were to explain that she 'intended to hurt V' or 'meant to' or realised her actions 'might hurt V', then this tells us a lot.

The same is true with the mens rea of an offence. Mens rea terms carry the same meaning across different offences: 'intention' in relation to murder means the same as 'intention' in relation to theft.[8] However, what must be intended in each case will be very different: in murder D must intend to kill or cause GBH; in theft D must intend to deprive V permanently of the property. The mens rea relates to the actus reus elements for the offence in question.[9] Take the offence of criminal damage set out in **Table 3.1**.[10]

Table 3.1 Criminal damage

	Actus reus	**Mens rea**
Conduct element	Any act (or omission) that causes the result	Voluntary
Circumstance element	The property damaged belongs to another	Intention or recklessness
Result element	Damage or destruction	Intention or recklessness

If we were to state the mens rea of criminal damage it would not be accurate to say that D must 'intend or be reckless': these words alone tell us nothing. Rather, we should say that D must 'intend or be reckless as to causing damage to another's property'.

As with criminal damage, most offences require some mens rea to correspond with each element of the actus reus. In such cases, as long as you know what the mens rea terms mean (discussed later), and as long as you know which element of the actus reus they correspond with, then you will understand the mens rea of the offence. However, there are two exceptions to this rule: two categories of offences where mens rea will not correspond with every element of the actus reus. Each requires some introduction.

3.2.1 Strict liability: actus reus with no corresponding mens rea

Certain offences are constructed to require actus reus elements with no corresponding mens rea. This can arise in two different ways, each of which will be discussed further in **Chapter 4**.

A) **Strict or absolute** *offences*: There are some offences in which the only mens rea required is that D's conduct must be voluntary, with no mens rea required as to any other element of the offence. Offences of this kind are usually dealing with regulatory matters

---

[8] There are, however, unhelpful exceptions to this within certain offences: Stark, 'It's Only Words: On Meaning and Mens Rea' (2013) 72 CLJ 155.

[9] See also discussion of the correspondence principle in **Chapter 4.2**.

[10] Criminal Damage Act 1971, s1.

and attract limited punishments to reflect the lack of mens rea. Examples include D selling defective products, or failing to observe regulatory formalities in her business.[11] Since these offences punish D for things that happen (actus reus) without regard to D's choices in bringing those things about (D's state of mind), they are criticised as lacking respect for the principle of autonomy.[12]

B) **Strict liability** *elements*: Much more common are offences which require mens rea as to certain actus reus elements, but not to all. Where mens rea is not required as to an element of the actus reus, it is said that liability for that element is 'strict'. Offences of this kind are generally less controversial than absolute offences where no mens rea is required as to circumstances *and* results. Nevertheless, strict liability remains problematic with regards to the principle of autonomy: liability is still possible in the absence of choice as to an essential part of what D is being blamed for.

3.2.1.1 The presumption in favour of mens rea

Although strict liability is common within many criminal offences, its controversial nature means that it will only be applied by a court if it is obvious in the drafting of the offence that it is what was intended by Parliament. Where an offence sets out a certain actus reus and is simply silent as to mens rea, there is a *presumption* that mens rea is required as to that element. As stated in the House of Lords:

> the test is not whether it is a reasonable implication that the statute rules out mens rea as a constituent part of the crime—the test is whether it is a *necessary* implication.[13]

In the case of K,[14] D was convicted of the (now repealed) offence of indecent assault,[15] an offence that criminalised sexual touching with victims under 16 years old. One element of the actus reus was that V must be under 16. The offence did not state that D had to 'know' or 'intend' or be 'reckless' about V's age, the statute was silent. The lower courts interpreted the element as strict: if V was under 16 it did not matter what D's state of mind about V's age was. However, the House of Lords held that the presumption of mens rea should be applied. It was for the prosecution to prove that D lacked mens rea as to V's age, even where the terms of the offence in the statute were silent as to its requirement.

If statutory offences were carefully drafted explicitly to set out every actus reus and mens rea requirement then the presumption of mens rea would be unnecessary. Unfortunately, this has never been the case with criminal legislation where political compromise, or simple oversight, will often result in ambiguous and incomplete definitions. Therefore, a presumption of mens rea is useful to ensure such oversight does not result in overly broad legislation that criminalises without due respect for the principle of autonomy. However, the presumption can be problematic. For example, despite the sweeping language of the House of Lords in B and K, the courts have not always been consistent in

---

[11] Baldwin, 'The New Punitive Regulation' (2004) 67 MLR 351. See also Law Commission, *Criminal Liability in Regulatory Contexts* (Consultation 195, 2010).

[12] See **Chapter 1.4.3**.

[13] *B (A Minor) v DPP* [2000] 2 AC 428 (emphasis added).

[14] [2002] 1 AC 462.

[15] Sexual Offences Act 1956, s14 (repealed).

their application of the presumption.[16] Further, although it is generally accepted that the presumption will require a mens rea of at least recklessness,[17] this *rather important detail* is rarely made explicit in the case law.[18]

3.2.2 Ulterior mens rea: mens rea with no corresponding actus reus

Ulterior mens rea, which is more commonly termed 'ulterior intention', describes a mens rea requirement that does not correspond to a conduct, circumstance, or result element of the actus reus. For example, to be liable for the offence of theft, D must appropriate the property of another (actus reus) dishonestly and with the intention to permanently deprive V of that property (mens rea).[19] Here, the requirement that D must 'intend to permanently deprive V' is an ulterior mens rea requirement: D must intend something (permanent deprivation) that does not have to actually happen for the offence to be committed, something that is not part of the actus reus of the offence.

Where we see ulterior mens rea within offences, the mens rea standard that is invariably required is intention (hence the common use of the term 'ulterior intention'). However, this is not always the case.[20] For example, section 1(2) of the Criminal Damage Act 1971 criminalises D who destroys or damages property (actus reus) intending or being reckless as to whether any property would be destroyed or damaged, *and* intending or being reckless as to whether the life of another would be thereby endangered (mens rea). The second part of this mens rea, that D must be at least reckless as to the endangerment of the life of another, constitutes ulterior mens rea: it is irrelevant whether another's life is endangered in fact as endangerment is not part of the actus reus of the offence.

3.2.3 Conclusions on mens rea in context

In **Chapter 2** we concluded that when identifying the actus reus of an offence, it can be useful to identify the separate elements of which it is made up: the conduct element, the circumstance element, and for result crimes the result element. In general terms, the same approach should be taken when identifying the mens rea of an offence. Thus, in most cases the mens rea can be discussed broadly (eg the mens rea for murder is the intention to kill or cause grievous bodily harm). However, where necessary, the mens rea of an offence can also be discussed more precisely as it relates or corresponds to each element of the actus reus, as set out in **Table 3.2**.

[16] Horder, 'How Culpability Can, and Cannot, Be Denied in Under-Age Sex Crimes' [2001] Crim LR 15. See also *Brown* [2013] UKSC 43 (NI).

[17] *G* [2008] UKHL 37. This is also the level of mens rea preferred within the Law Commission's 1989 Draft Criminal Code, cl20.

[18] See eg *Tolson* (1889) 23 QBD 168, which talks ambiguously of states of mind that can make wicked acts into innocent ones.

[19] Theft Act 1968, s1.

[20] Child, 'The Structure, Coherence and Limits of Inchoate Liability: The New *Ulterior* Element' (2014) 34 LS 537.

Table 3.2 Elements of an offence

	Actus reus	**Mens rea**
Conduct element	Any physical acts or omissions required for the offence	Any mens rea required as to D's acts or omissions
Circumstance element	Any factual circumstances required to exist for the offence	Any mens rea required as to those facts or circumstances
Result element	Any consequences of D's action/omission required for the offence	Any mens rea required as to those consequences
Ulterior mens rea element	*	Any mens rea required as to something that is not part of the actus reus

3.3 Voluntary act requirement

When identifying the mens rea of an offence, we are generally looking to find which mens rea term (eg 'intention', 'recklessness', 'negligence', and so on) is required to be proved against D in relation to each element of the actus reus she performed. For example, the offence of battery is committed by D who makes unlawful contact with V (actus reus), with a corresponding intention or recklessness as to that contact (mens rea). The same pattern is repeated when discussing potential mens rea as to circumstances, results, and ulterior mens rea.

However, mens rea as to the conduct element is different. Whether we are discussing D's movement or omission to move her body, it is not intuitive to think of D desiring to move; believing she is moving; foreseeing a risk of moving; and so on. The standard mens rea terms, defined and discussed later, are inappropriate. Rather, for the conduct element of the actus reus, it is more common to inquire as to the 'voluntariness' of D's movement or omission to move.[21] Just as *all* offences include a conduct element within their actus reus,[22] so must this conduct be voluntary.[23]

---

[21] Some courts and academic writers refer to an 'intention' to move. However, in this context, 'intention' is being used to mean 'voluntariness'.

[22] Discussed in **Chapter 2.3.1**.

[23] See Child, 'Defence of a Basic Voluntary Act Requirement in Criminal Law from Philosophies of Action' (2020) 23(4) New Crim LR 437.

Don't be confused . . .

Voluntariness is often presented as part of the actus reus of the conduct element rather than a separate corresponding mens rea requirement.[24] This is because many academics believe that the definition of action inevitably includes voluntariness, effectively merging the concepts. However, this is not the approach preferred within this textbook. Just as we attempt to separate internal and external offence requirements in relation to circumstances and results, the same approach can also be useful with the conduct element (for reasons of consistency if nothing else). The only difference with regard to the conduct element, as opposed to circumstances and results, is that we only ever have to apply a single mens rea term: voluntariness.

3.3.1 The test for voluntariness

This is the mens rea requirement for the conduct element of every offence. There is a great deal of philosophical and neurological debate as to the meaning of 'voluntary action'.[25] However, although this debate will influence and inform a legal definition, where possible the courts prefer to use terms in their 'natural' or 'everyday' meaning, and this is certainly easier when directing a jury. The test of voluntariness, then, is simply whether D had control over her conduct (act or omission) at the relevant time.

In a majority of cases it will be obvious that D's movement or omission to move was voluntary. This will be the case where D has considered her options before acting, as well as cases where D acts instinctively in a fight, for example. In fact, it is so unlikely that D lacked control of her body that within the criminal law there is an established presumption of voluntariness. Rather than the prosecution having to prove that D's conduct was voluntary in every case, it will be *presumed* that D's conduct was voluntary unless D can produce evidence to suggest that it was not. It is only when D has discharged this evidential burden that the prosecution will then have to prove beyond reasonable doubt (the criminal standard of proof) that D's acts were in fact voluntary.[26]

A claim, by the defence, that D's conduct was involuntary can take several forms. Most obviously, this will be the case where D was unconscious or semi-conscious as, for example, where D broke an object whilst sleepwalking. However, it is not limited to such cases. For example, if D moves her arm and stabs V because X is pushing her arm, then D's conduct will not be voluntary and she will not be liable for an offence. The same is true where D omits to move, for example, because she is physically restrained from doing so by X. Involuntariness can also result from reflex or spasm. For example, if while driving D acts on reflex because she is attacked by a 'swarm of bees' or a 'malevolent passenger',[27] her driving will not be voluntary. Similarly, if D strikes V while suffering from a 'spasm' or 'convulsion',[28] again, liability will fail because D has not acted voluntarily.

---

[24] See, for support of the actus reus approach, Patient, 'Some Remarks About the Element of Voluntariness in Offences of Absolute Liability' [1968] Crim LR 23.

[25] Moore, *Act and Crime* (1993); Lacey, 'Responsibility without Consciousness' (2016) 36 OJLS 219; and references therein.

[26] See **Chapter 1.1.7.1**.

[27] Examples from *Bell* [1984] 3 All ER 842.

[28] Examples from *Bratty v AG for NI* [1961] 3 All ER 523.

The only exception to these examples of involuntariness is that D cannot claim to have acted involuntarily if the reason for her lack of control was self-induced. For example, where D voluntarily became intoxicated or where she was driving when tired and fell asleep.

Don't be confused . . .

Where D claims to have acted involuntarily, she is attempting to avoid liability by denying an element of the offence (mens rea as to the conduct element). However, because the presumption of voluntary movement places an evidential burden on D to provide some evidence of involuntariness, claims of this kind are more commonly referred to as defences: defences of automatism, intoxication, and insanity. We discuss how D can avoid liability on this basis (including issues of prior fault) in **Chapter 13**.

3.3.2 The role of voluntariness

When discussing the actus reus we explained that the conduct element represents a basic ingredient of every crime:[29] we can only blame D for harmful results because they were caused by her act, and for circumstances because they were associated with her action, and so on. Thus, with all responsibility and liability flowing from D's conduct, the requirement that this conduct should be at least voluntary is fundamental to the law's respect for D's autonomy. Even where the offence charged is a strict or absolute liability offence where no mens rea as to circumstances and results is required, we can at least say that the basic ingredient of action was one that D must have controlled. As stated by Hart, 'unless a man has the capacity and fair opportunity to adjust his behaviour to the law, its penalties ought not to be applied to him'.[30]

Despite the vital role of voluntariness, however, there are a few absolute offences that do not seem to require any mens rea, even voluntary conduct. For example, it was an offence under the Aliens Order 1920 for D to be found in the UK when leave to land in the UK had been refused. This was the charge in *Larsonneur*.

Larsonneur (1933) 24 Cr App R 74

D was ordered to depart from the UK and travelled to the Irish Free State. However, she was then arrested and brought back to the UK against her will. Having been brought back to the UK, she was charged with the offence of being found in the UK contrary to the Aliens Order.

• Court: guilty of the offence. The offence does not require D's presence to be voluntary.

Larsonneur is already slightly exceptional because it involves one of the few offences where the conduct element is not straightforwardly based on movement or an omission, but rather on a status (being found).[31] However, the real problem with liability

---

[29] See **Chapter 2.3**.
[30] Hart, *Punishment and Responsibility* (1968) 181.
[31] See **Chapter 2.3.1**.

in this case is not the actus reus, but rather the lack of a voluntariness requirement attached to it: D is liable for being found in the UK even though her presence is not voluntary. Despite extensive criticism of the case and the offence however,[32] *Larsonneur* was followed by the more recent case of *Winzar v Chief Constable of Kent*,[33] and there is nothing in principle to prevent Parliament creating other offences of this kind in the future.

It is probably better to see exceptional offences of this kind, which do not include a voluntariness requirement, as unwelcome anomalies within the law. They should not be allowed to distort or distract our more general analysis. The requirement that D's conduct element must be performed voluntarily is all but universal within the criminal law, and certainly common between *all* the offences discussed in the later chapters of this textbook.[34] This is illustrated in **Table 3.3**.

Table 3.3 Mens rea of the conduct element

	Actus reus	**Mens rea**
Conduct element	Any physical acts or omissions required for the offence	Voluntariness

 Assessment matters . . .

As D's acts are presumed in law to be voluntary, unless D provides some evidence to rebut this presumption, the issue of voluntariness will often not be discussed by the court. Likewise, when you are applying the law to problems facts, you do not need to consider the issue of voluntariness unless there is some indication that D's acts or omissions may be involuntary. If you are told, for example, that D hates V and runs over to V and stabs her, it would be unnecessary, and rather odd, to begin a discussion about whether D's motion to stab might have been a reflex or spasm. In contrast, if you are told, for example, that the stabbing happened whilst D was suffering from some kind of seizure, then a discussion of this kind would be important.

3.4 Mens rea terms

Although there is only a single mens rea term that applies to the conduct element (voluntariness), the standard of mens rea required for other elements will vary greatly between offences. These include, but are not limited to, 'intention', 'knowledge', 'belief', 'recklessness', 'negligence', and 'dishonesty'. The relationship between elements is set out in **Table 3.4**.

---

[32] See eg Horder, *Excusing Crime* (2004) 251.
[33] (1983) The Times, 28 March.
[34] See eg *Robinson-Pierre* [2013] EWCA Crim 2396: D's appeal allowed on the basis that liability requires voluntary conduct, even where the offence is absolute.

Table 3.4 Mens rea of the other offence elements

	Actus reus	Mens rea
Circumstance element	Any factual circumstances required to exist for the offence	Any mens rea required as to those facts or circumstances
Result element	Any consequences of D's action/omission required for the offence	Any mens rea required as to those consequences
Ulterior mens rea element	*	Any mens rea required as to something that is not part of the actus reus

To understand the mens rea of an offence, it is therefore necessary to identify which mens rea terms (eg intention) are used within the definition of the offence; which part of the actus reus they are referring to (eg D must intend a result); and what that mens rea term means. The first two of these tasks have already been discussed in general terms, and will be discussed in relation to various offences in later chapters. We turn to the third task now.

The criminal law has developed a rich and varied vocabulary of mens rea terms. In the sections that follow, we will set out the most important of these terms and discuss their meaning.[35] Our aim is to clarify these terms so that when they arise in later chapters you will be able to understand them, and then to apply them in context. However, before we begin this discussion, there are three important points that should be borne in mind.

A) Mens rea terms are usually interpreted consistently between offences: Despite the occasional *and regrettable* exception,[36] the general rule is that each mens rea term can be defined independently of the offence in which it arises. Courts will often limit their engagement with mens rea terms to the specific case and offence before them, but because the same terms are used across numerous offences it is problematic to employ different interpretations, and so common definitions have developed. The idea is to identify legal definitions of mens rea terms that do not change depending upon the offence in issue.

B) The criminal law is concerned with the legal definition of mens rea terms: Although this sounds obvious, it is very easy to allow our common non-legal understanding of terms such as 'intention' and 'recklessness' to cloud our reading and understanding of their legal definitions. There is a consistent effort to align legal and non-legal definitions, particularly with the needs of jurors' understanding in mind. However, whereas it is acceptable for vague definitions to be used in everyday discourse, in the legal context the definitions need to be precise in order to be consistently applied. In an effort to provide this rigidity, legal definitions depart from non-legal understandings in several areas. To understand and apply the law you must learn and apply only these legal definitions.

[35] See also Ormerod and Laird, *Smith, Hogan, and Ormerod: Criminal Law* (16th edn, 2021) Ch3.
[36] Stark, 'It's Only Words: On Meaning and Mens Rea' (2013) 72 CLJ 155.

C) Mens rea terms are (for better and for worse) defined by the common law: Where mens rea terms are codified within a criminal code or other statute, there is an opportunity to set out a limited number of terms within a clear and defined hierarchy. We see this in the US Model Penal Code 1962,[37] for example, as well as within the 1989 Draft Criminal Code for England and Wales.[38] However, the current law in England and Wales in this area remains uncodified, with mens rea terms defined almost exclusively within the common law. There are two main consequences of this. First, the definition of mens rea terms is not fixed, but rather a matter of precedent between courts. In relation to each term, we will see that definitions have changed over time, and are not necessarily settled in their present state. Secondly, we do not have a fixed list of mens rea terms. We will discuss the most commonly used mens rea terms in this chapter, but in later chapters we will encounter other mens rea terms that have been developed by the courts.

3.4.1 Intention

Intention is the most serious standard of mens rea, demonstrating the greatest culpability and the greatest blameworthiness.[39] It can be satisfied in either of two rather different ways:

- **Direct intention:** D intends an actus reus requirement 'directly' if she acts with a *purpose* or *aim* towards it. Thus, D intends a circumstance (eg that property belongs to another for theft) where she hopes that it should be present; and a result (eg causing death for murder) where it is her purpose or aim is to bring that result about by her conduct. D's belief in the likely success of her aim is irrelevant. The leading case defining direct intention is *Moloney*.[40]

- **Oblique intention:** D intends an actus reus requirement (whether circumstance or result) 'obliquely' where it is: (a) virtually certain to arise; (b) she recognises that it is virtually certain; and (c) the jury find that this recognition amounts to an intention. The leading case defining oblique intention is *Woollin*.[41]

Despite their differences, it is important to remember that both direct intention and oblique intention are simply alternative definitions of the same mens rea term: intention. Where an offence has a mens rea of intention, this requirement can be satisfied by *either* direct or oblique intention.

 Don't be confused . . .

The mens rea for most serious offences can be satisfied by intention or recklessness. One of the few exceptions to this is murder where D must act with the intention to kill or cause serious harm (recklessness is not sufficient). As a result, you will notice that most of the cases defining intention tend to be murder cases: as only intention will suffice for this offence, it is particularly important to know where its definition starts and ends. Remember, however, that intention is also required for a variety of other offences.

---

[37] US Model Penal Code 1962, §2.02.
[38] Law Commission, *A Criminal Code for England and Wales: Report and Draft Criminal Code Bill* (No 177, 1989) cl18.
[39] See generally Lacey, 'A Clear Concept of Intention: Elusive or Illusory?' (1993) 56 MLR 621.
[40] [1985] AC 905.
[41] [1999] AC 82.

3.4.1.1 Direct intention

Direct intention is relatively uncontroversial. In line with common understanding, the law's approach to this concept holds that D intends something if it forms part of her purpose when acting (a purely internal, subjective requirement). Such intention does not require premeditation or planning, but it must be present at the time of action. For example, D smashes V's vase in retaliation for V scratching her car. Here, D commits criminal damage with intention as to both circumstance and result elements:

- D directly intends the result element of the offence (damage) because she acts in order to cause damage;
- D directly intends the circumstance element of the offence (that the property belongs to another) because she hopes that the property belongs to V.

An alternative way of expressing direct intention, promoted by Duff,[42] is to think about success and failure. Employing this approach, we can say that D directly intends the damage because her enterprise would be a failure if the vase was not damaged. Equally, she directly intends that the vase should belong to V because, if it did not, her enterprise would be a failure.

In most cases, as with the vase example, direct intention is also synonymous with 'desire'; that is, D intends to damage the vase if she desires to damage the vase. However, this is not always true. In certain cases D may directly intend an offence element as a *means to an end* even though she does not specifically desire it. For example, if D kills her mother in order to obtain inheritance we can say that she acts with the direct intention to cause death. D may not desire the death of her mother, she may be very sad afterwards, but the death is an essential means to her desired end: the inheritance. Using Duff's language, D directly intends to kill her mother because she will only succeed (her actions will only lead to the gaining of inheritance) if she causes death: if she does not cause death, her enterprise has failed. The same would be true, for example, where D burns down V's house in order to see her reaction. D directly intends to cause damage by fire, thereby satisfying the mens rea for arson, because even if she does not desire the fire in its own right, she intends it as a necessary means to a desired end: seeing V's reaction to the burning house. This interpretation of intention is confirmed in *Hyam v DPP*,[43] where Lord Hailsham states that intention clearly includes 'the means as well as the end'.

Very importantly, *unlike oblique intention discussed in the following section*, direct intention is not affected by a foreseen likelihood of success or failure. For example, D, a hopeless darts player, can throw a dart directly intending to hit a treble 20 even though D knows that she is very likely to fail. The same logic also applies to our earlier examples. Thus, if D throws V's vase in order to damage it, it is her direct intention to cause damage even if she knows that the vase is very solid and is unlikely to be broken. Where D is unsure whether the vase belongs to V, she still directly intends that it belongs to another if she hopes that it belongs to V. Equally, if D tries to gain inheritance by shooting her mother, but knows that she is a bad shot or that V may be out of range, or that the gun may not fire, etc, she still directly intends to kill when she pulls the trigger as a means to an end.[44]

---

[42] Duff, *Intention, Agency and Criminal Responsibility* (1990).

[43] [1975] AC 55.

[44] For discussion about potential differences between 'intending' and 'trying', see Horder, 'Varieties of Intention, Criminal Attempts and Endangerment' (1994) 14 LS 335.

3.4.1.2 Oblique intention

When the courts are dealing with offences that require a mens rea of intention (eg murder), the 'golden rule' for directing a jury is to avoid any elaboration on the meaning of 'intention' unless it is truly necessary.[45] Thus, the jury are left to apply their common understanding, which is likely to be broadly in line with the definition of direct intention just discussed. However, where a finding of direct intention is unlikely, it will (exceptionally[46]) be necessary to direct the jury so that they can apply a legal definition of intention that includes oblique (or indirect) intention.

 Assessment matters . . .

The courts' approach is the same one that you should take when discussing a requirement of intention in a problem question. Always start with direct intention. If D directly intends the offence element then there is no need to consider oblique intention. Only consider oblique intention if there is some doubt as to D's direct intent.

Oblique intention can arise even where an offence element (the proscribed result, for example) is not D's purpose or aim, and even where it is not a means to a separate purpose or aim. There are three parts to the definition of oblique intention, which are similar whether intent relates to results or circumstances:

- D has obliquely intended a *result* element (eg death or GBH for murder) if that result: (a) was a virtually certain consequence of her conduct; (b) she realised that it was a virtually certain consequence of her conduct; and (c) the jury find that her realisation amounted to an intention;

- D has obliquely intended a *circumstance* element (eg V's ownership of property for theft) if: (a) the circumstance was virtually certain to be present; (b) she realised that it was virtually certain to be present; and (c) the jury find that her realisation amounted to an intention.

The potential for oblique intention is very useful in practice. For example, let us imagine that D placed a bomb on a passenger plane, her intention being to blow up the plane and thereby to destroy certain insured items in the plane's hold. If the bomb explodes and kills the pilot and passengers, has D acted with the intention to kill? D does not have a *direct* intention to kill, as causing death is not her purpose or aim. Equally, she does not directly intend death as a means to an end: if, miraculously, the insured items were destroyed but the people on board were saved or parachuted to safety, her enterprise would not have failed, she would still succeed in destroying the packages on board for the insurance. The destruction of the insured items could be described as an intended means to an end (the end being the insurance claim), but that is not true of the deaths. However, the fact that deaths were a virtually certain consequence of her conduct, and the fact that she realised this and continued anyway, makes her state of mind look very much like an intention to kill. It is the three-part test for oblique intention that allows us to say that D intended to kill.[47]

The leading case, confirming the three-part test for oblique intention, is *Woollin*.

---

[45] *Moloney* [1985] AC 905, 926.
[46] *Allen* [2005] EWCA Crim 1344, [63].
[47] Pedain, 'Intention and the Terrorist Example' [2003] Crim LR 579.

Woollin [1998] 4 All ER 103

D killed his child by throwing him against a hard surface. D did not desire to kill the child. D was charged with murder, requiring a mens rea of intention to kill or cause serious bodily harm.

- Crown Court: guilty of murder—the judge directed the jury that they could find intention if they were satisfied that D realised that his actions posed a 'substantial risk' of causing death or serious injury.
- Court of Appeal: conviction upheld on appeal—direction as to intention was acceptable.
- House of Lords: allowing D's appeal. A direction in relation to 'substantial risk' is not appropriate. Oblique intention requires the result: (a) to be virtually certain; (b) to be foreseen by D as virtually certain; and (c) for the jury to find intention.

Before we provide a little more detail on the three steps of the *Woollin* test, it is important first to understand the term 'virtual certainty'.

'Virtual certainty'

The first two parts of the three-part test use the concept of a 'virtual certainty': to be intended, the actus reus element (a) must be virtually certain to arise and (b) must be foreseen by D as a virtual certainty. The level of foresight set by this term is vitally important. It is not designed to cover cases where D foresees a future event as simply likely, very likely, or even probable: these are (as we will discuss later) states of belief or recklessness, but not intention. Rather, the standard of virtual certainty is designed to catch *only* those cases where D sees the circumstance or result as practically inevitable. The word virtually is used largely because it is impossible to be completely certain about something that happens in the future. For example, when D puts her bomb on the plane, set to detonate in flight, she is likely to be virtually certain that deaths will result from an explosion whilst legitimately contending that, without the ability to look into the future, she was not and could not be completely certain.

The high threshold set by 'virtual certainty' is essential to provide a clear definition of intention (separate from belief and recklessness). This is because as soon as we start equating intention with high levels of foresight short of a virtual certainty, it is very difficult to know where to draw the line and what language to use to do it. However, despite this importance, the common law has struggled to maintain a consistent definition. This can be illustrated in the series of murder appeal cases in **Table 3.5**, the issue in each being whether D *intended* to kill or cause serious harm to V.

Table 3.5 The evolution of oblique intention as a term of mens rea

Case reference	Case facts	Level of foresight
Hyam v DPP [1975] AC 55	D put blazing newspaper through the letterbox of her rival (X) causing a house fire. D's intention was to scare X, but in fact she caused the deaths of X's children (V).	House of Lords upheld a conviction where oblique intention was defined in terms of foresight of a 'high probability'.

(Continued)

Table 3.5 Continued

Moloney [1985] AC 905	D shot his stepfather V (whom he loved) in a drunken contest that involved the quick-drawing of loaded shotguns. D's gun was directed point blank at V's head when D fired.	House of Lords quashed D's conviction because it was based on an incorrect direction that D foreseeing a mere 'probability' could amount to an intention. Despite this, however, in summing up Lord Bridge talked loosely of foresight of a 'natural consequence' being sufficient.
Hancock & Shankland [1986] AC 455	D1 and D2 (who were striking miners) pushed a concrete block from a motorway bridge intending to scare working miners travelling in taxis on the motorway below. The block hit a car and killed V.	The trial court convicted the defendants of murder, following Lord Bridge's 'natural consequence' formulation. However, the conviction was quashed on appeal. The concern of both the Court of Appeal and the House of Lords was that foresight of a 'natural consequence' may go beyond foresight of something that is certain (or at least virtually certain). However, again, some of the language used by the Lords implied that some lower threshold may be acceptable (eg Lord Scarman's statement that 'the greater the probability of a consequence the more likely it is that the consequence was foreseen and that if that consequence was foreseen the greater the probability is that the consequence was also intended...').
Nedrick [1986] 1 WLR 1025	D poured paraffin through the letterbox of X's house and set it alight. A child (V) died in the house fire.	The trial court convicted D of murder, following a direction from the judge that intention could be found where D foresaw death or injury as 'highly probable'. The Court of Appeal quashed D's conviction and clarified (Lord Lane CJ) that the jury 'are not entitled to infer the necessary intention, unless they feel sure that death or serious bodily harm was a virtual certainty (barring some unforeseen intervention) as a result of the defendant's actions and that the defendant appreciated that such was the case'.
Woollin [1998] 4 All ER 103	D killed his child by throwing him against a hard surface. It was not D's purpose to kill the child.	The court convicted D of murder, following a direction that intention could be found where D foresaw a 'substantial risk' of death or injury. The House of Lords allowed D's appeal, substituting a manslaughter conviction, and endorsed the standard of 'virtual certainty' set out by the Court of Appeal in *Nedrick*, adding it is for the jury to 'find' whether D intended in this oblique sense.

Despite this historical inconsistency, the current law (following *Woollin*) is clear that if D's foresight of a result is less than a virtual certainty, it will not be sufficient: such foresight may amount to a belief and/or recklessness, but not to an intention.[48]

Objective part: (a) the offence element must be a virtual certainty

The first part of the test for oblique intention, it will be remembered, is that the offence element must be virtually certain in fact. This is an example of an objective mens rea requirement: it is not looking to the mind of D, but rather to the objective external world.

This requirement is consistently referenced in the case law and is relatively straight-forward to apply. However, it has the potential to cause problems, and we may question if it is useful within the definition. Using the plane bomber example again, let us imagine that unknown to D the hold of the plane was lined with special bomb-proof material such that the destruction of the plane was not inevitable. Where death results despite this protective material, can we still say that D obliquely intended to kill? She may have foreseen death as a virtual certainty (part (b)), but since the protective material *may* have protected those on board, we cannot say that death was virtually certain in fact (part (a)). In effect, objective facts that are not known to D (in this case the materials of the plane) are partly defining the law's view of D's state of mind.

Whilst odd, it should be noted that the first part of the *Woollin* test will rarely cause problems in practice. This is because, where part (b) is satisfied (ie D foresees a virtual certainty), this will usually be because the element is a virtual certainty in fact. However, the example in the previous paragraph at least demonstrates the potential for a problem to arise.

 Extra detail . . .

Although the full three-stage test has been endorsed by later cases,[49] it will be interesting to see if it is followed by a case such as the variation of the plane bomber example just discussed (where D is virtually certain of an element, but it is not virtually certain in fact). It may be that the first part of the *Woollin* test will be removed as a requirement of oblique intention, and recognised instead as evidence relevant to the second question (evidence to help the jury decide whether D foresaw the element as a virtual certainty). If an example of this kind were to arise in a problem question, it would be useful to acknowledge this possibility.

Subjective part: (b) D must foresee the offence element as virtually certain

The requirement that D must foresee the offence element as a virtual certainty is clear and relatively uncontroversial. It should be remembered that this is a subjective question that looks to the mind of D. Thus, if the jury believe that D *honestly* did not foresee or might not have foreseen the offence element as a virtual certainty, even if it was virtually certain in fact (part (a)) and even if it would have been obvious to a reasonable person, this part of the *Woollin* test will not be satisfied and the jury are not entitled to find oblique intention.[50]

---

[48] The principle is usefully discussed in *Matthews and Alleyne* [2003] EWCA Crim 192.

[49] eg *Matthews and Alleyne* [2003] EWCA Crim 192.

[50] In *DPP v Smith* [1961] AC 290 the House of Lords had opened the possibility for an objective definition of intention. However, since the Criminal Justice Act 1967, s8 and *Woollin*, it is clear that this objective route has been foreclosed.

Jury part: (c) the jury may find intention

The final part of the *Woollin* test is that (*only* when the first two parts are satisfied) the jury are entitled to find that D intended the offence element. It is also the most controversial. It is controversial because the fact that the jury are 'entitled' to find, or 'may' find, means that even where the first two parts of the test are satisfied, the jury are not *obliged* to find intention. Further, although this third part creates a separate and independent question from the other two, the case law does not provide criteria to guide the jury in their decision. Having found that the offence element was virtually certain and that it was foreseen as a virtual certainty by D, the jury are then left with the question 'is that intention?': they may equate this with intention if they wish, or they may not.

 Extra detail . . .

There has been considerable academic debate about whether satisfaction of the first two parts should oblige the jury to find intention, and thus to remove discretion from this third part.[51] This arose most recently where the court in *Woollin* described the jury as 'finding' intention rather than 'inferring' it as they had in *Nedrick*, the implication being that to 'find' intention seems to contain less discretion than to 'infer' it. However, the dominant interpretation remains that this third part is not simply a rubber stamping of the first two: satisfaction of parts (a) and (b) does not equate to intention, they merely provide the basis from which the jury may, or may not, find intention.[52]

The discretion afforded to the jury within this third part (whether or not to find intention) has both positive and negative aspects. On the positive side, allowing the jury to find that D did not intend an offence element despite it being a foreseen virtual certainty, can provide useful 'moral elbow room' within difficult cases.[53]

In the civil law case *Gillick v West Norfolk*,[54] for example, the House of Lords ruled that it was not unlawful for a doctor (D) to prescribe the contraceptive pill to a girl under the age of 16 (X). Prescribing the contraception fulfilled the actus reus of an offence of assisting or encouraging underage sex, but the court, in granting the declaration that the prescription was lawful, suggested that for the purposes of the criminal law there was an absence of intention to encourage. Applying the first two parts of the *Woollin* test, we may conclude that there was an intention to encourage: it was virtually certain that X's boyfriend would be encouraged to have sex with X if he knew she was not going to become pregnant, and it is likely that the doctor will have foreseen this encouragement as virtually certain to follow his prescribing X the pill. In the case itself, the House of Lords avoided this conclusion by saying that an intention to act in a patient's medical interests cannot amount to a criminal intention.[55] However, this line of reasoning is clearly unacceptable: if D (a doctor) honestly believed that it was in the best interests of a patient to die, for example, we would not say that this negated the intention to kill. Rather, a better approach may be to rely upon the third part of the *Woollin* test, accepting that the result (encouragement of X and her boyfriend) is virtually certain; accepting that D foresees it as virtually

---

[51] Norrie, 'After *Woollin*' [1999] Crim LR 532; Williams, 'Oblique Intention' (1987) 46 CLJ 417.

[52] *Matthews and Alleyne* [2003] EWCA Crim 192.

[53] Horder, 'Intention in the Criminal Law—A Rejoinder' (1995) 58 MLR 678, 688.

[54] [1985] 3 All ER 402.

[55] Lord Scarman (at 19) states that the 'bona fide exercise by a doctor of his clinical judgement must be a complete negation of the guilty mind'.

certain; but in light of D's intention to protect his patient, allow the jury to 'find' that D did not intend to encourage such unlawful conduct. Indeed, in an analogous case, *Re A*,[56] a similar approach could have been adopted. This case involved the medical separation of conjoined twins where it was virtually certain that the operation would kill one of the twins, and the doctors (D) recognised it as such. Again, when asking if D intended to kill, it is possible that the third part of the *Woollin* test could be used to avoid this conclusion.

The main advantage of this approach, therefore, is the discretion that it allows the jury. The first two parts of the *Woollin* test cannot separate the plane bomber in the earlier example from D in *Gillick* or *Re A*: in each case the result is a virtually certain consequence of D's conduct (part (a)), and D will be aware that it is a virtually certain consequence (part (b)). It is the discretion in part (c) that allows the jury the opportunity to 'find' that the plane bomber intended to kill, but that D in *Gillick* and *Re A* did not intend the relevant results.

Unfortunately, for two reasons, this same discretion (or moral elbow room) is also highly problematic. First, it is unpredictable: without criteria to guide a jury, different juries may come to different conclusions when assessing the same or similar facts. This is objectionable from a rule of law perspective since we cannot tell in advance whether conduct will be criminal, and it is also unreliable as a method of distinguishing cases such as those described previously. We may predict (or at least *hope*) that a jury will find intention in relation to the plane bomber, and no intention in relation to *Gillick* and *Re A*, but there are no guarantees of this. It is little wonder, for example, that the court and medical profession would rather rely on a defence of necessity in cases such as *Re A* than they would rely on the unfettered discretion of a jury on whether to find intention.[57]

Secondly, the third part of the *Woollin* test has also been criticised for allowing the jury to, in effect, decide the law. The role of the jury is meant to be isolated to issues of fact.[58] The law tells us the elements of a crime, the law defines those elements, and it is then for the jury to decide whether or not D completed those elements in fact. However, with no legal rule defining and guiding the third part of the *Woollin* test, the jury are not only being asked to apply a legal rule, they are being asked to define it. This problem is limited, of course, because the discretion will only arise where the first two parts of the *Woollin* test are satisfied, so the jury do not have complete freedom to define any state of mind they wish as an intention, but it is still apparent.[59]

 Assessment matters . . .

When applying the *Woollin* test to problem facts, the third part presents particular difficulty. You may conclude from the facts that an offence element (eg death in murder) was a virtual certainty and that D foresaw it as such, but (like the jury) you have no criteria to apply in order to answer the third part. The best approach is to highlight this problem (as a criticism of the current law) and then to say what you think the jury are most likely to decide based on an assessment of the facts as a whole. For example, it is likely that a jury will have little sympathy for the plane bomber and are therefore more likely to find an intention to kill.

---

[56] [2001] 2 WLR 480.
[57] Necessity is discussed in **Chapter 14.6**.
[58] Discussed in **Chapter 1.1.7.1**.
[59] Cf Norrie, 'Legal and Social Murder: What's the Difference?' [2018] Crim LR 531, 539–540: Arguing that *Woollin* could be interpreted to allow for a finding of intention even when one or both of the first two limbs are not satisfied.

3.4.1.3 Conditional intention

D conditionally intends an offence element (eg causing death) where she decides to bring it about if a certain condition arises (eg if she can buy a gun).[60] In this manner, D is committing herself to a future act with a particular mens rea, if a certain condition arises. When discussing and applying conditional intentions, two important details should be borne in mind.

First, conditional intention will only apply to mens rea as to future events within D's ulterior mens rea (discussed at **3.2.2**). D can conditionally intend something in the future (eg to kill V if the weather is clear), but D cannot conditionally intend to complete conduct that she has already done. We can ask whether it was D's purpose to kill (direct intent) or whether it was a foreseen virtual certainty (oblique intent), but talk of conditions doesn't make sense.

Secondly, we must take care to ensure that the conditions of D's intention do not undermine the offence. For example, if D intends to smash a vase, but only if she discovers that it belongs to her, then she does not (under any condition) intend to damage the property of another. Equally, we must ensure that D has a fully formed intention. For example, if D decides that she will kill V 'if she wants to tomorrow', then we might interpret this as the delaying of a decision rather than a decided conditional intention. Equally, if D says she will kill V 'if she wins the lottery twice in a row', then the extreme unlikelihood of this coming about may cause us to doubt that D really does intend to go through with her plan (even if the conditions do arise).

 Point to remember . . .

The basic rule is that a conditional ulterior intention is still an intention. This rule is relevant to all offences that contain a requirement of mens rea as to future events, from single requirements (as with theft), to more substantial requirements (as with general inchoate offences) where D's ulterior mens rea relates to a full future offence.

3.4.2 Knowledge

The mens rea of 'knowledge' is generally seen as equivalent to 'intention' in terms of culpability. D has knowledge of an offence element if (a) she believes that it is the case and (b) she is correct in that belief.[61] This interpretation was confirmed in two cases in the House of Lords. In *Montila*:[62]

A person cannot know something is A when in fact it is B. The proposition that a person knows that something is A is based on the premise that it is true that it is A. The fact that the property is A provides the starting point. Then there is the question whether the person knows that the property is A.

---

[60] Child, 'Understanding Ulterior Mens Rea: Future Conduct Intention is Conditional Intention' (2017) 76 CLJ 311; Williams, 'Intents in the Alternative' (1991) 50 CLJ 120; Campbell, 'Conditional Intention' (1982) 2 LS 77.

[61] Shute, 'Knowledge and Belief in the Criminal Law' and Sullivan, 'Knowledge, Belief and Culpability' in Shute and Simester (eds), *Criminal Law Theory* (2007) Chs8 and 9.

[62] [2004] 1 WLR 3141, [27].

And in *Saik*:[63]

> [T]he word 'know' should be interpreted strictly and not watered down. In this context, knowledge means true belief. . . . If D1 and D2 agree they will . . . exchange money that comes into their bureau de change, they cannot be said to be agreeing to launder money which they *know* to be from a criminal source if they merely see a risk that it might be from a criminal source.

In this manner, a mens rea of 'knowledge' includes both subjective and objective parts.

The subjective part (a) focusses on D's state of mind: she must believe that the offence element is the case. For example, D must believe that the property was stolen for handling stolen goods; or that V is a person for murder; etc. As stated in the quotation from *Saik*, belief that something 'is the case' is not satisfied by a belief that it '*may be* the case'. However, it also seems that something short of virtual certainty may be acceptable. For example, in *Hall*[64] it was accepted that D could *know* goods were stolen if she was informed by someone with first-hand experience, and in *Griffiths*,[65] it was held to be enough if D has no serious doubts. In each case, we are focussing on what D actually believed (subjective mens rea), not on what she should have believed or what a reasonable person in her position would have believed (objective mens rea).

The objective part (b) focusses on the objective reality: what D believes must be true in fact before we can say that she has knowledge of it. For example, if D sells property that she believes to be stolen but in fact is not, she does not *know* that the property is stolen. This part of the legal definition is very important, and explains why the mens rea of knowledge is, *generally*,[66] only used in the context of circumstance elements. Circumstance elements typically relate to facts that must be present at the time of D's conduct (eg that, for murder, V is a person), and therefore it is possible for both parts of the 'knowledge' definition to be satisfied. For result elements, in contrast, a knowledge requirement is more problematic: D may have acted with the belief that her conduct would cause a particular result (eg death for murder), but the objective reality of that belief could not be known until *after* her action. It should be remembered that D's mens rea must be identified at the time she acts.[67]

 Don't be confused . . .

It is common for offences specifically to require a mens rea of knowledge as to a circumstance element. However, as knowledge is considered to be equivalent to intention, even where an offence specifies a mens rea of intention as to a circumstance element, knowledge will suffice.[68]

---

[63] [2006] UKHL 18, [26], drawing on Ormerod, 'Making Sense of Mens Rea in Statutory Conspiracies' (2006) CLP 185.

[64] (1985) 81 Cr App R 260.

[65] (1974) 60 Cr App R 14.

[66] A notable exception emerges in the context of accomplice liability, **Chapter 12.3.2**.

[67] Discussed further in **Chapter 4**.

[68] Discussed further in the context of the general inchoate offences, **Chapter 11**.

3.4.2.1 Wilful blindness

A state of knowledge can alternatively be found where D: (a) foresees the possibility of a certain circumstance; (b) it would be easy for D to discover the truth; (c) D deliberately avoids finding out; and (d) the circumstance is in fact present. Where this is the case, D's decision to 'shut her eyes' to the facts, or 'bury her head in the sand', is described as wilful blindness (or wilful ignorance). The status of wilful blindness as sufficient to amount to knowledge was confirmed in the House of Lords in *Westminster CC v Croyalgrange Ltd.*[69]

Although there has been relatively little case law discussing the meaning of wilful blindness,[70] it remains a useful concept.[71] For example, let us imagine that D receives a state-of-the-art stolen television from her friend P for only a few pounds. For D to commit the offence of handling stolen goods, she must *know* or believe that the property (the television) is stolen.[72] However, even where D knows that P is a burglar, and even where she suspects that the property is stolen, she may still remain unsure as to its origins: she may lack belief. In such cases, because the route to finding out (simply asking P) is straightforward and available to her, the law translates her wilful blindness into a form of knowledge that will satisfy the offence mens rea.

There are problems with the law here, some of which are obvious from the previous example. First, in the absence of case law, there is a lack of clarity as to how the stages of the definition should be applied. For example, it is unclear how much foresight D must have to satisfy (a); how easy it must be for her to discover the truth within (b); as well as how consciously (as opposed to absent-mindedly) D must have avoided finding out within (c). Secondly, there may be cases where wilful blindness does not appear blameworthy. For example, what if D in the previous example avoided asking her friend about the television because she had promised to trust her in the future. Imagine also a parent who does not inquire about the activities of their child because they want to encourage independence and respect privacy.

 Assessment matters . . .

When applying lesser developed terms such as wilful blindness to problem questions, it is important to highlight areas of doubt. You should still apply the criteria that are available from case law. However, where there is a lack of clarity, it is best to highlight this lack of clarity and then to predict in general terms whether, and why, you think the court will find the requirement satisfied.

3.4.3 Belief

'Belief' is a mens rea term that is not as culpable as 'intention' or 'knowledge'. D has belief that a circumstance exists, or that a result will be caused, where she foresees it as highly likely. This is identical to the first subjective limb of the definition of knowledge. The difference for 'belief' is that there is no objective second limb requiring D's belief to be correct

---

[69] (1986) 83 Cr App R 155.

[70] See, most usefully, *Roper v Taylor Garages* [1951] 2 TLR 284.

[71] Sarch, *Criminally Ignorant: Why the Law Pretends We Know What We Don't* (2019); Wasik and Thompson, 'Turning a Blind Eye as Constituting Mens Rea' (1981) 32 NILQ 324; Yaffe, 'The Point of Mens Rea: The Case of Willful Ignorance' (2018) 12 Crim L & Phil 19.

[72] Theft Act 1968, s22.

in fact. Thus, where D believes a fact and she is correct, we can say that she had knowledge or belief. However, where D believes a fact and she is not correct, we can only say that she had belief.[73] Unlike knowledge, it is straightforward to hold a belief that a future event will come about, and so belief may be required as to results and ulterior mens rea. However, as with knowledge, belief arises most commonly in relation to circumstance elements.

3.4.4 Recklessness

Below 'intention' and 'knowledge', and also below 'belief', 'recklessness' represents the next most culpable mens rea term. It is also one of the most important, arising in the majority of the offences discussed in this textbook. To satisfy a mens rea of recklessness, it must be demonstrated that D (a) foresaw a risk of the relevant element of the actus reus and (b) unreasonably continued to run that risk. This interpretation was confirmed by the House of Lords in G.[74]

Again, this general definition should be expressed and applied slightly differently depending upon the element of the actus reus at issue. For example:

- D is reckless as to a *circumstance* element, such as the property belonging to another for criminal damage, when she (a) foresees a risk that the circumstance is present and (b) unreasonably continues to run that risk;
- D is reckless as to a *result* element, such as property damage for criminal damage, when she (a) foresees a risk that the result will be caused by her conduct and (b) unreasonably continues to run that risk.

In this manner, the test includes a subjective part (a) and a minor *but necessary* objective part (b). We will discuss each in turn.

 Point to remember . . .

We highlighted earlier the importance of understanding and applying the legal definition of mens rea terms and not being distracted by their (often different) common non-legal meanings. The term 'recklessness' is one that students often confuse in this way. In common use, the term recklessness is often employed to describe a person's dangerous behaviour (eg she flailed her arms recklessly). However, where 'recklessness' is used as a mens rea term it is not concerned with D's physical behaviour. The test is simply: (a) did D foresee a risk of the offence element? And (b) did D continue unreasonably to run that risk? If the answer to both questions is 'yes', then a mens rea of recklessness is satisfied.

Subjective part: (a) D must have foreseen a risk of the offence element being satisfied

The first part of the 'recklessness' test focusses on D's state of mind: at the time of acting, D must have subjectively foreseen a risk of the relevant circumstance or result. Whether D foresaw the relevant risk or not is a simple question of fact for the jury. However, courts have provided some further guidance on exactly what the law means by the foresight of a risk. Four points of clarification should be noted.

---

[73] Shute, 'Knowledge and Belief in the Criminal Law' and Sullivan, 'Knowledge, Belief and Culpability' in Shute and Simester (eds), *Criminal Law Theory* (2007) Chs8 and 9.

[74] [2003] UKHL 50. The definition provided by the court is taken from the Law Commission's 1989 Draft Criminal Code, cl18.

D must foresee the risk: It must be remembered that this part of the 'recklessness' test is purely subjective: our focus is on D's state of mind alone. Thus, for example, if the jury believe that D did *not* foresee or might not have foreseen a risk then the test will not be satisfied even where the risk would have been obvious to a reasonable person in D's position. This is illustrated in *Stephenson*.

 Stephenson [1979] QB 695

D, who suffered from schizophrenia, sheltered in a haystack and made a fire for warmth. Inevitably, the fire spread and caused damage. D was charged with criminal damage, the mens rea of which requires D to be reckless as to causing damage. Medical evidence indicated that D may not have been aware of the risk of damage as a result of his condition.

• Crown Court: guilty of the offence. The trial judge directed the jury in terms of risks that would have been obvious to them.
• Court of Appeal: appeal allowed against conviction. The test is purely subjective: it was a misdirection to question the obviousness of the risk; the only question is whether D foresaw a risk.

The degree of the risk foreseen by D is irrelevant: For oblique intention, D must foresee the actus reus element as virtually certain; for belief, it must be foreseen as highly likely. For recklessness, there is no such restriction. Whether D foresees the risk as virtually certain, highly likely, likely, unlikely, etc, as long as *a* risk is foreseen, it will be sufficient. This is illustrated in *Brady*.

 Brady [2006] EWCA Crim 2413

D was drunk in a nightclub. He climbed onto a railing and then fell to the dance floor beneath, causing serious injury to V. D was charged with an offence against the person that included a mens rea of recklessness as to causing harm.[75]

• Crown Court: guilty of the offence against the person.
• Court of Appeal: appeal allowed because the definition of recklessness provided by the lower court was not sufficiently clear. D stated in appeal that the test of recklessness required foresight of 'an obvious and significant' risk. This more specific point was rejected: foresight of any risk is sufficient.

How carefully D considers the presence of the risk is irrelevant: D may have carefully considered the implications of her conduct before acting, or she may have considered them only fleetingly while acting. However, in each case D's state of mind will be sufficient for this part of the recklessness test: some foresight of the risk is all that is required, however fleeting or superficial that is. This is a sensible rule, and it avoids the court becoming bogged down in trying to distinguish between D's degrees of thought or focus. However, the basic line between foreseeing and not foreseeing can still be problematic. In certain cases, at the very edges of subjective foresight, the courts have been

---

[75] See **Chapter 7**. For discussion of the implications of D's intoxication, see **Chapter 13.2**.

willing to accept that a risk was foreseen when it was 'suppressed', or 'driven out', or where D 'closed his mind' to it. In cases such as *Parker*, the test is satisfied on the somewhat artificial basis that the risk was foreseen by D in the back of her mind.

Parker [1977] 1 WLR 600

After a very bad day, D lost his temper when he found a public telephone out of order and proceeded to 'smash down' the receiver into the dialling box. This caused minor damage. D was charged with criminal damage, the mens rea of which requires D to be reckless as to causing damage. D claimed that, in the heat of the moment, he was not aware of this risk.

• Crown Court: guilty of criminal damage.

• Court of Appeal: conviction upheld on appeal—although D's awareness of the risk of damage was suppressed by his anger, the risk still must have entered his mind.

D's attitude to the risk occurring is irrelevant: Having foreseen the risk, D may worry and hope that it will not arise; she may endorse the risk; or she may not care either way. In each case, D's state of mind will be sufficient for this part of the recklessness test: some foresight of the risk is all that is required, however indifferently D may view it. This question used to arise in the context of rape and other sexual offences, before the definition of those offences changed, where D performed sexual acts and 'could not care less' whether V consented or not.[76] In such cases, it has been consistently held that D's state of mind will satisfy the test for recklessness: D may not attach any weight to the risk, but it is still foreseen.[77]

A more difficult case is where D claims that she had so little regard for her potential victims that she did not even consider the possible risks of her actions, a so-called cognitive void.[78] This is problematic because, unlike earlier examples, despite D's obvious culpability, she is claiming that she did not foresee the risk before choosing to ignore it. There is some support for the proposition that D's state of mind would still be sufficient to satisfy a mens rea of recklessness: Lord Goff in *Reid*, for example, suggested that D could be recklessly indifferent to a risk without being aware of it.[79] However, the better view, in light of *G* and other subsequent case law, is that D would not be reckless in these circumstances. The basic subjective ingredient of this mens rea term is that D must have foreseen a risk.

Objective part: (b) D must have unreasonably continued to run the risk

Having established (a) that D foresaw a risk of the circumstance or result element, it must also be demonstrated (b) that D *unreasonably* chose to run that risk. This second part of the test is objective: it does not matter whether D thought it was reasonable to

---

[76] The issue no longer arises in such cases because the mens rea of these offences no longer requires recklessness. See discussion in **Chapter 8.2.2**.

[77] *Satnam and Kewal Singh* (1984) 78 Cr App R 149.

[78] Ben-David, 'Cognitive Void in Relation to Attendant Circumstances as Subjective Mens Rea' [2015] New Crim LR 418.

[79] (1992) 95 Cr App R 391. Leigh, 'Recklessness after *Reid*' (1993) 56 MLR 208.

run the risk, the question is whether the court thinks it was reasonable based on the standards of reasonable people acting in D's circumstances. For example, D may believe that it is reasonable to throw stones at her friend's window, because she wants to get her friend's attention, even though she foresees a risk of damage. The question for the court, however, is whether such conduct would be considered reasonable by others in her position. In this case, unless she has the permission of V, or she is trying to rouse V whose house is on fire, the answer is likely to be 'no': meaning that recklessness as to causing damage would be found.[80]

In many cases it will be obviously unreasonable to run the risk of causing damage or injury, and this part of the test will be easily satisfied. However, this will not always be the case. For example, a car driver may foresee a risk of someone jumping out in front of their car and being injured; when a doctor performs an operation, they may foresee a chance that the patient will die; etc. The law does not want to discourage socially useful activities such as driving and performing operations. In such cases, D will not have a mens rea of recklessness as to causing harm: she foresees the risk she is running (a), but it is not unreasonable to run that risk (b).

3.4.4.1 Historical background: the rise and fall of objective recklessness

To understand the current definition of recklessness just described, it is useful to bear in mind the common law journey that has been taken to get there.[81] This is set out in **Table 3.6**.

Table 3.6 The evolution of recklessness as a term of mens rea

Case reference	Case facts	Definition of 'recklessness'
Cunningham **[1957] 2 QB 396**	D tore a gas meter from the wall in order to steal money from it. Gas escaped into his neighbour's house and was inhaled by V. D was convicted of an offence against the person, including a mens rea of malice (which is the same as recklessness) as to the endangerment of life. This was quashed on appeal.	*Subjective beginnings* The Court of Criminal Appeal quashed D's conviction because the trial judge had defined the offence term 'malicious' (meaning the same as 'reckless', see **3.4.4.1**) as synonymous with 'wicked'. The Court of Criminal Appeal set out a test for recklessness that is similar to the current law, including that D must foresee the risk. This is why the current subjective test for recklessness is often referred to as *Cunningham* recklessness.

---

[80] Consent would also raise the possibility of a statutory defence. See discussion in **Chapter 9.7.3**.
[81] Davies, 'Lawmakers, Law Lords and Legal Fault' (2004) 68 JCL 130; Crosby, 'Recklessness—The Continuing Search for a Definition' (2008) 72 JCL 313.

Caldwell [1982] AC 341	D, who had been drinking heavily, started a fire in a hotel as part of an ongoing dispute. D was convicted of aggravated criminal damage, including a mens rea of recklessness as to the endangerment of life. The House of Lords upheld this conviction.	*Objective recklessness* With Lords Wilberforce and Edmund-Davies dissenting, the House of Lords expanded the *Cunningham* definition of recklessness to include what is referred to as 'objective recklessness'. Under this new test, set out by Lord Diplock, D would be reckless where: (a) she foresees a risk (in line with *Cunningham*); or (b) she failed to foresee a risk that would have been obvious to the reasonable person. The second possibility here is objective because it does not look to the mind of D: it asks if the reasonable person would have foreseen the risk and allows the court to find recklessness on this basis. This is often referred to as *Caldwell* recklessness.
Lawrence [1982] AC 510	This case involved reckless driving, including a mens rea of recklessness as to associated dangers.	*Expanding objective recklessness* Lord Diplock reiterated his objective definition of recklessness, adding that the obvious risk must also be serious. The use of objective recklessness in this case demonstrated its general application outside criminal damage cases.
Elliott [1983] 1 WLR 939	D (a 14-year-old girl with learning difficulties) started a fire in a garden shed. The fire spread and caused damage. D was charged with criminal damage, including a mens rea of recklessness as to the damage. D claimed that she did not foresee the damage.	*Unfairness of objective recklessness* D was liable for criminal damage in this case because although she did not foresee damage (she was not subjectively reckless), the damage would have been obvious to a reasonable person. Thus, recklessness was found using the *Caldwell* test. D was liable despite not foreseeing the risk of damage, and despite her age and learning difficulties making it impossible for her to appreciate the foresight that the objective reasonable person would have.

(Continued)

Table 3.6 Continued

G [2003] UKHL 50	D (children aged 11 and 12) set fire to some newspapers under a wheelie bin. They left the fire and it spread to surrounding buildings. They were convicted of criminal damage of the buildings, on the basis of their mens rea of recklessness as to the damage. They had not foreseen the chance of the fire spreading and damage being caused, although that would have been obvious to a reasonable person.	*Full circle: overruling* Caldwell *and back to* Cunningham The House of Lords allowed the appeal and quashed the convictions. Following extensive criticism of *Caldwell*, the House of Lords took the opportunity to overrule it and to restate the subjective recklessness test set out in *Cunningham*.
AG's Reference (No 3 of 2003) [2004] EWCA Crim 868	The case involved the offences of manslaughter and misconduct in public office. The latter including an element of recklessness.	*Expanding* Cunningham; G; *subjective recklessness* This case is useful because it confirms 'general principles' laid down in *G*: that 'recklessness' should be interpreted in a subjective manner for all offences where the term is used.

In this manner, the common law definition of recklessness has completed a full circle: from subjective to objective to subjective. Importantly, you should be clear that objective (*Caldwell*) recklessness has been overruled in *G*, and so the term 'recklessness' should now always be interpreted in its subjective form (see further discussion at **3.5**).

3.4.4.2 Maliciously and wilfully

The mens rea term 'maliciously' arises in several offences against the person.[82] The mens rea term 'wilful' also arises in a host of offences, including wilfully obstructing a police officer[83] and misconduct in public office.[84] Where such terms are applied to circumstance or result elements, it is now settled that their meaning is the same as 'recklessness'.[85] The fact that different mens rea terms are used to mean the same thing is obviously not ideal,

[82] Discussed in **Chapter 7**.
[83] Police Act 1996, s89.
[84] *AG's Reference (No 3 of 2003)* [2004] EWCA Crim 868.
[85] For 'maliciously' see *Cunningham* [1957] 2 QB 396. For 'wilfully' see *D* [2008] EWCA Crim 2360. In the absence of explicit authority, there remains some doubt as to whether 'malice' should be interpreted to apply the objective limb of recklessness as well as the subjective limb. However, it is contended that both should be applied.

and has the potential to cause confusion. However, aligning their meanings with reck-lessness in this manner at least reduces the complex variety of mens rea definitions that are present in the common law.

3.4.5 Summary of mens rea terms

Despite their general focus on the mind of D, mens rea terms will often include objective as well as subjective parts within their definition. For example, 'oblique intention' requires that the offence element was not only subjectively foreseen as a virtual certainty, but that (objectively) it was a virtual certainty; 'knowledge' requires subjective belief in a circumstance, and also that (objectively) the belief is true; 'recklessness' requires subjective foresight of a risk, and also (objectively) a consideration of reasonableness; and so on. However, despite these objective considerations, the core of each term still focusses on the subjective mind of D. In each case, the prosecution must prove that D brought the relevant circumstance or result to mind in some manner before mens rea can be established.

When we discuss and apply the subjective parts of these mens rea terms, it is important to remember that they are not all about the foresight of a risk. Two forms of subjective mens rea should be distinguished.

- Where D acts in order to bring about a certain result, or a certain circumstance: This form of subjective mens rea only applies in the context of direct intention. Crucially, this form of subjective mens rea does not focus on degrees of foresight; the only question is whether the result or circumstance is D's purpose or aim.

- Where D acts foreseeing a result being caused, or the presence of a circumstance: This form of subjective mens rea requires us to assess the degree to which D foresaw the circumstance or result. Depending upon the degree of foresight, we might conclude that D is obliquely intending, has knowledge, belief, and/or recklessness.

Where D possesses the first form of subjective mens rea it is clear that she is directly intending. However, where D foresees a circumstance/result within the second form, but does not have it as her aim or purpose, we need to be able to identify the relevant mens rea across several options. The most effective way of doing this is to think about D's foresight as a spectrum between foresight of a virtual certainty at the top and lack of foresight at the bottom. At the top of the spectrum D's foresight will satisfy the test for several mens rea terms, and this will reduce as we move down the spectrum. This is set out in **Tables 3.7** (results) and **3.8** (circumstances); it can be useful to keep this in mind when applying mens rea terms, as well as discussing the differences between them.

Table 3.7 Mens rea as to the result element

D's foresight that her conduct will cause a certain result	Mens rea term
Virtually certain	Intention; belief; recklessness
Very likely	Belief; recklessness

(Continued)

Table 3.7 Continued

Likely	Recklessness
Possible	Recklessness
Unlikely (but still a risk)	Recklessness
Not foreseen	No subjective mens rea

Table 3.8 Mens rea as to the circumstance element

D's foresight that a certain circumstance will be present	Mens rea term
Virtually certain	Intention; knowledge (if true); belief; recklessness
Very likely	Knowledge (if true); belief; recklessness
Likely	Recklessness
Possible	Recklessness
Unlikely (but still a risk)	Recklessness
Not foreseen	No subjective mens rea

? Don't be confused . . .

Despite the overlap of mens rea terms, many offences list more than one mens rea term that will satisfy the offence. For example, offences will often specify a mens rea of 'intention or recklessness'. Here, as D cannot intend without being reckless as well, it is advised that you focus on the minimum requirement (recklessness) only. It is a bit like a sign on the beach saying 'no swimming' and also 'no swimming breaststroke': they are both accurate, but the second is unnecessary because the prohibition is covered by the first.

3.5 Objectifying 'subjective' mens rea terms

It is important to understand and analyse mens rea terms in their context (ie any qualifications written into the offence). Since 2003 and the decision in G bringing about the demise of objective recklessness, each of the core mens rea terms ('intention', 'knowledge', 'belief', and 'recklessness') are now defined to require some degree of subjective mens rea. In each case, the mens rea term will only be satisfied if D herself possessed a certain purpose or certain foresight. However, although this positively serves the principle of autonomy,[86] it also makes the finding of mens rea more difficult: proving that D possessed a certain state of mind at the relevant time, not simply that a reasonable person in her position would have done so, can be challenging.

The greater difficulty of proving a subjective mens rea may be acceptable in view of the serious consequences of criminal prosecution, and the need for certainty that D is deserving of those consequences. However, for certain offences, where proving subjective mens rea has been particularly difficult,[87] or where Parliament simply deems it necessary, the construction and context of mens rea terms can be adapted to reduce (or even to eliminate) their subjective parts. These offence constructions are not claiming to redefine the mens rea term more generally, and will not affect its definition when used in other offences, but they do affect the way it should be applied within that particular offence.

As the process of objectifying mens rea terms does not affect their general definitions, we will not discuss them in detail here. Rather, this will be done as they arise in relation to particular offences in later chapters. However, by way of introduction, such constructions will usually take one of two forms:

- **Objectifying the subjective part:** For certain offences you will find the subjective part of a mens rea term can alternatively be satisfied by a finding that a reasonable person in D's position would have had that mens rea. For example, harassment offences require D to know that her behaviour will cause harassment, or that she *ought to have* known.[88] The first part of this applies the standard (subjective) use of the mens rea term 'knowledge', but the second alternative allows for a purely objective mens rea. The qualifying statement 'ought to have' means that, in this context, an objective test is to be applied.

- **A lack of positive belief:** An even stricter mens rea construction is to require D to have a positive and reasonable belief. For example, to commit rape D must have penetrated the vagina, anus, or mouth of V with his penis and without V's consent.[89] Mens rea as to V's non-consent is satisfied where D 'does not reasonably believe that [V] consents'. There are two aspects to this. First, there is a positive obligation on D to have held a belief in consent: if D did not believe that V consented because he did not care, for example, D will satisfy the mens rea.[90] Secondly, even where D did believe that V was consenting, that belief must be reasonably (objectively) held: unless a reasonable person in D's position would have so believed, D will satisfy the mens rea.

 Point to remember . . .

The use of objective constructions is common in the law. Therefore, when identifying the mens rea of an offence, as well as looking to spot mens rea terms, it is equally important to consider their context: are they being used in the standard manner or are they adapted or objectified in some way?

---

[86] See **Chapter 1.4.3**.
[87] eg sexual offences or terrorism offences.
[88] Protection from Harassment Act 1997. See **Chapter 7.9.1**.
[89] Sexual Offences Act 2003, s1. See **Chapter 8.2**.
[90] This will be the case even if a reasonable person would have believed that V was consenting.

3.6 Other mens rea terms

In this section we discuss the terms 'dishonesty' and 'negligence'. Although both are described as mens rea terms, they are importantly different from the more common mens rea terms discussed previously. This is because, unlike intention and recklessness, for example, they do not correspond to separate requirements within the actus reus of an offence. Rather, they include both external and internal requirements, and so they stand alone within an offence definition.

Don't be confused . . .

For the mens rea terms discussed previously (eg intention and recklessness), it has been important to identify a corresponding actus reus element. This is because it is essential to know what D must intend or foresee in order to apply the requirement to problem facts. Crucially, this is not a necessary requirement for dishonesty and negligence: an offence may require dishonesty and/or as stand alone elements, where they need not correspond with specific actus reus elements.

3.6.1 Dishonesty

A mens rea requirement of dishonesty appears regularly in the context of property offences,[91] and much of its detail can be left for consideration at this later stage. However, it is useful to provide a brief introduction.

The definition of dishonesty was recently modified by the Supreme Court in *Ivey*,[92] overruling *Ghosh*.[93] Although *Ivey* concerned a civil law dispute, Lord Hughes (delivering the unanimous judgment) stated clearly that the definition should be applied consistently in criminal courts as well; [94] and this has been confirmed by a specially constituted five-member Court of Appeal (Criminal Division).[95] To apply the test in *Ivey*, the jury must consider two questions:

(A) What was the actual state of D's knowledge or belief as to the facts?

(B) In the context of (A), was D's conduct dishonest by the standards of ordinary decent people?

Although it is not often necessary to set out the full test when directing a jury,[96] both parts are essential for dishonesty to be found. The two parts combine both subjective and objective considerations:

A) Subjective part: The first part is subjective, and focusses on the mind of D. The issue here is not simply whether D believes her conduct is honest or dishonest; the court in

---

[91] See **Chapters 9** and **10**.

[92] *Ivey v Genting Casinos Ltd* [2017] UKSC 67. See Laird, 'Case Comment' [2018] Crim LR 395; Laird and Ormerod, '*Ivey v Genting Casinos*—Much Ado About Nothing?' (2018) Supreme Court Yearbook; Ormerod and Laird, 'The Future of Dishonesty–Some Practical Considerations' (2020) 6 Archbold Review 8.

[93] [1982] QB 1053.

[94] At [74].

[95] *Barton* [2020] EWCA Crim 575.

[96] *Roberts* (1985) 84 Cr App R 177. This is likely to continue to be the case post-*Ivey*.

Ivey makes clear that assessments of this kind are not determinative of dishonesty. However, D may hold (or lack) certain knowledge or belief that is relevant to an assessment of her conduct. The court gives the example of a tourist who comes from a country where public transport is free, and reasonably believes that it is free in the UK as well. This reasonably held belief can and should influence a jury's evaluation of D's conduct (eg when boarding public transport without paying) under the second objective part.[97]

B) Objective part: The second part is objective, and now the focus of the dishonesty test. The question for the jury is deceptively simple: was D's conduct dishonest by the standards of honest and reasonable people? In this regard, it is not open to D to argue that a practice is honest within a specific sub-group or industry of which she may be a member, the test is whether it is honest across society.[98] The test is *deceptively* simple because, as academics and others have highlighted with regard to previous tests, an assumed common standard of honesty across society is surely at best vague and at worst a fiction.[99]

3.6.2 Negligence

Negligence is used to describe a certain type of behaviour from D that drops below the standards that we expect from reasonable people. A requirement of negligence most commonly arises in relation to regulatory and driving offences.[100] In these cases, D is performing a lawful act (eg driving) that entails obvious risks to others. Rather than focussing on D's state of mind (eg did she foresee the risk?), a negligence requirement asks simply whether her behaviour in relation to those risks was reasonable. The assumption behind negligence as a mens rea element is that *even if* D did not foresee the relevant risk, the failure of foresight is itself culpable in certain circumstances.[101]

To identify these 'certain circumstances', the test for negligence in the criminal law is similarly constructed to the tort of negligence. Thus, a negligence requirement entails the following questions:

(A) What was D's duty of care?

(B) Did D breach that duty of care?

Both of these questions are objective, focussing on external standards and conduct.

A) What was D's duty of care? This question encourages us to consider who D owes a duty to, and also, what standard of care is required. Certain statutory negligence offences will specify this within the offence, but this will not always be the case. The question of 'who' D has a duty towards, if unspecified within the offence, will be interpreted very widely in line with civil law (ie D must consider the safety of all those potentially affected

---

[97] At [60].

[98] See *Hayes* [2015] EWCA Crim 1944, where D attempted (unsuccessfully) to argue that he should be judged by the standards of other investment bankers, where the practice of manipulating lending rates was common and perceived by many as legitimate.

[99] For a discussion of the problems identifying such a universal standard, see Griew, 'Dishonesty— The Objections to *Feely and Ghosh*' [1985] Crim LR 341.

[100] eg the offence of driving without due care and attention: Road Traffic Act 1988, s3.

[101] For discussion of negligence as a culpable failure of belief (foresight), see Stark, *Culpable Carelessness: Recklessness and Negligence in the Criminal Law* (2016).

by her conduct). It should be remembered that this is *not* the same as the 'duty to act' required for omissions liability; a duty to act is interpreted very narrowly.

The more difficult question is to assess the standard of care required. Here, the general rule is that D must act *reasonably* or in the manner that would be expected of the reasonable person. Where D is performing a skilled activity or holds specialised knowledge, she will be judged against the standard of a reasonable person with that knowledge. For example, negligent driving is measured against the standard of a 'competent and careful driver', and so D can be held to have driven negligently even if a reasonable non-driver could not have performed better.[102] Likewise, a surgeon must perform an operation to the standard of a reasonable surgeon, not to the standard of a reasonable layperson handed the scalpel!

Although the standard of reasonableness increases to take account of D's specialised knowledge, the same will not be true in the other direction. Therefore, when assessing the standard of the reasonable person, the jury may not take account of characteristics that may lead to D's inability to meet that standard through no fault of D. For example, it would be no defence to a charge of careless driving for D to say she was a learner driver and therefore unable at that moment to achieve the standard of the 'competent and careful driver'. Equally, if D walks into something and causes damage or injury, it will be no excuse to a negligence-based offence for D to point out that she is blind. The strict application of the reasonable person standard in such cases has attracted criticism,[103] and there is some indication that it may be softening to allow for the age of D to be considered,[104] but the basic position remains largely unchanged.

B) Did D breach that duty of care? Negligence also requires D to have breached the duty of care. A breach requires the prosecution to prove that D's conduct was performed below the reasonable standard required of her. When applying this question to problem facts, some harm or injury resulting from D's conduct is an indication that D has breached their duty of care, but it is not definitive. For example, if a car (driven by V) brakes suddenly in front of D and she crashes into it, this is an indication that D may have been driving negligently by driving too fast or being too close to V's vehicle. However, it is also possible that D was driving competently, and that the crash could not have been avoided or, at least, a reasonable driver may have had the same accident.[105]

 Assessment matters . . .

When applying a negligence-based offence to problem facts, it can be easy to equate resulting harm with a breach of duty. Take care: this is not always the case. Always discuss whether D's conduct fell below, or is likely to have fallen below, the standard of the reasonable person.

---

[102] *McCrone v Riding* [1938] 1 All ER 721.
[103] Simester et al, *Simester and Sullivan's Criminal Law* (6th edn, 2016) 162.
[104] *R (RSPCA) v C* [2006] EWHC 1069 (Admin). See also *obiter* statements in *Hudson* [1966] 1 QB 448.
[105] Discussed in *Simpson v Peat* [1952] 2 QB 24, 28.

3.6.2.1 Gross negligence

Gross negligence has no equivalent in the civil law and arises in the criminal law in relation to one offence only: gross negligence manslaughter.[106] To be found to have been 'grossly negligent', D must fulfil the conditions of negligence discussed earlier, and D's negligence must be sufficiently extreme to be considered by the jury as 'gross'. This definition was set out in the House of Lords in the leading case *Adomako*.[107]

> Simple lack of care such as will constitute [standard civil negligence] is not enough. For the purposes of the criminal law there are degrees of negligence, and a very high degree of negligence is required to be proved before [gross negligence] is established.

It is therefore for the jury to consider whether D's negligence is sufficiently serious to be considered 'gross'.

Extra detail . . .

This is another area where the law is criticised for asking the jury to decide issues of law as well as issues of fact. In this respect it is like the final part of the *Woollin* test for intention. This is because, when deciding if D's negligence is 'gross', the jury are given only a limited definition of grossness to apply. If the jury believe that D's behaviour is really bad (if they want her to be criminalised) then they will call it gross; and if they think that it does not deserve criminalisation then they will say that it is not gross. In this manner, the jury are deciding (not applying) the boundaries of the offence.

3.7 Establishing mens rea based on previous blameworthy conduct

Where an offence requires a certain mens rea and that mens rea is absent, the standard result will be no liability for the offence charged. This seems straightforward and correct. However, in certain cases the application of this rule without exception could lead to unfairness. This may be the case, for example, where D only lacks mens rea (eg foresight of a risk) because she was voluntarily intoxicated. In *Lipman*,[108] for example, having taken LSD (a hallucinogenic drug) as well as other drugs, D killed his sexual partner under the delusional belief that he was fighting snakes. In this case, D lacked voluntariness in his movements, as well as any other relevant mens rea.

Responding to cases such as *Lipman*, common law rules have developed to allow the court (in certain circumstances) to ask whether D's lack of mens rea was a result of her own 'prior-fault', and potentially reconstruct missing mens rea where this is the case. Thus, in *Lipman*, D was liable for manslaughter: although D did not act with mens rea when killing V, his prior blameworthy choice to take a dangerous drug (leading to

---

[106] **Chapter 6.3.2.**
[107] [1995] 1 AC 171. In *Sellu* [2016] EWCA Crim 1716, the high threshold for this test was emphasised, with the court describing only 'truly exceptionally bad' negligence as sufficient.
[108] [1970] 1 QB 152.

his involuntary state) was substituted for that missing mens rea so that liability could be found. The circumstances where prior-fault analysis has been allowed have so far focussed on voluntary intoxication (as in *Lipman*) and other external causes of involuntariness. These are discussed fully in Chapter 11.

3.8 Reform

With essay-type questions in mind, it is useful to pick up on two issues in particular that have been discussed within this chapter. The first is the potential benefit of codifying mens rea terms and thereby removing their core definitions from the common law. The second is to look in slightly more detail at the relative merits of subjective mens rea requirements on the one hand, and objective mens rea requirements on the other.

3.8.1 Codifying mens rea terms

Although most criminal law academics favour general codification of the criminal law, there is always a balancing of benefits (eg consistency and clarity) against the loss of flexibility within the common law. However, when it comes to the codification of mens rea terms, there are few if any who would oppose having statutory definitions and the chance to have avoided the continuously changing definitions that have dogged the criminal law over the past 50 years. As highlighted at various points in this chapter, these changes have come in a range of forms. Some have been subtle changes, and others full redefinitions. Some have been the product of careful consideration, and some simply from an imprecise choice of words. However, in each case the general application of mens rea terms, which potentially apply to many hundreds of offences, magnifies and exacerbates problems in the law.[109]

The codification of mens rea, in a manner seen in other jurisdictions,[110] remains no more than an aspiration in England and Wales. Despite notable attempts by the Law Commission within the 1989 Draft Criminal Code,[111] and later when suggesting reforms to the offences against the person,[112] the Commission's recommendations have not been taken forward into law.[113] Probably the three main reasons in favour of codification are: (A) creating a set mens rea vocabulary; (B) creating settled core definitions; and (C) creating the clarity of definition necessary to improve the law:

A) **A settled vocabulary:** One of the main advantages of the US Model Penal Code, for example, is that it reduced the amount of mens rea terminology to four key terms:

---

[109] For a discussion of the problems caused by a lack of codification in this area, see Law Commission, *Report on the Mental Element in Crime* (No 89, 1978).

[110] See eg Australian Model Criminal Code (1992) Div 5; US Model Penal Code 1962, §2.02; Gainer, 'The Culpability Provisions of the Model Penal Code' (1987) 19 Rut LJ 575.

[111] Law Commission's 1989 Draft Criminal Code, cl18.

[112] Law Commission, *Offences Against the Person and General Principles* (No 218, 1993) cl1.

[113] The most recent move was a 1998 Home Office Consultation Paper. See Smith, 'Offences Against the Person: The Home Office Consultation Paper' [1998] Crim LR 317. The Law Commission decided not to include definitions of mens rea terms in its most recent report on offences against the person (No 361, 2015).

intention, knowledge, recklessness, and negligence.[114] By this simple act, the host of terms that were rarely used within the law, and not well understood, were removed. The terms that remained were defined to recognise a spectrum of mens rea, but also to provide a useful core set of well understood definitions.

B) A settled definition: Codification of mens rea terms does not eliminate all discretion for the court, and there remains room for disagreement through interpretation.[115] However, a statutory definition can at least provide a core definition that will be protected from change within the common law. Thus, although we might still disagree on the exact level of foresight required for belief, for example, we would not have the dramatic redefinition of core terms between subjective, to objective, to subjective, as we have had with recklessness over the last 40 years.[116]

Settled core definitions are important to protect against retrospective lawmaking (ie where D's state of mind fulfils the mens rea only due to its redefinition).[117] Additionally, statutory definitions protect the democratic will of Parliament, ensuring that if Parliament creates offences with a certain mens rea in mind, that the mens rea term it uses in drafting will continue to have the same meaning when the offence is applied. Indeed, this was one of the central criticisms of the *Caldwell*[118] objective redefinition of recklessness, as Parliament had created the Criminal Damage Act 1971 on the basis of the then subjective definition of recklessness.[119]

C) A clear definition: One of the main problems with common law definitions is that it is easy for precise meanings to be lost within a court's judgment, and even easier if a definition is gleaned from a combination of several judgments across multiple cases. This has been problematic, for example, in the context of oblique intention and the meaning of 'virtual certainty' (discussed at **3.4.1.2**). Codification, in contrast, has the potential to make a definition considerably clearer, which also makes it easier to spot problems within the law and to correct them.

A useful example of improved clarity and evaluative potential can be seen in the context of oblique intention, where D obliquely intends a result element (eg unlawful killing for murder). It will be remembered that the *Woollin* definition of oblique intention requires: (a) that the result be a virtual certain consequence of D's act; (b) that D realises it is a virtually certain consequence of her act; and (c) that the jury choose to 'find' intention. Developing this, the Law Commission defined intention within the 1989 Draft Criminal Code as:

> act[ing] in order to bring [the result] about or being aware that it would occur in the ordinary course of events.

---

[114] Gainer, 'The Culpability Provisions of the Model Penal Code' (1987) 19 Rut LJ 575.

[115] See, on the US Model Penal Code, Simons, 'Should the Model Penal Code's Mens Rea Provisions be Amended?' (2003) 1 Ohio JCL 179.

[116] Davies, 'Lawmakers, Law Lords and Legal Fault' (2004) 68 JCL 130.

[117] Contrary to the principle of fair warning, see **Chapter 1.4.1**.

[118] [1982] AC 341.

[119] McEwan and Robilliard, 'Recklessness: The House of Lords and the Criminal Law' (1981) 1 LS 267.

In response to this clear statement of the (recommended) law, an interesting debate emerged that was previously hidden within the inconsistency of the common law. Even accepting that the result must be virtually certain, and that D must foresee the result as virtually certain, a question emerges as to what the *cause* of this virtual certainty must be. The most obvious answer, and that implied in the *Nedrick* and *Woollin* directions, is that the result must be a virtually certain consequence of D's conduct. However, this can be problematic. To go back to our plane bomber examples, what if D sets a bomb in order to destroy insured property on a plane, but thinks there is a 50 per cent chance that the bomb will malfunction and fail to explode? If the question is whether it is virtually certain that death will arise from D's *conduct* (planting the bomb), and whether it is foreseen as a virtual certainty of that *conduct*, then the answer is 'no': there is only a 50 per cent chance that the bomb will explode. However, D's purpose in acting (direct intent) is for the bomb to explode and the property to be destroyed, and if this happens then it is virtually certain (and foreseen as virtually certain) that death will result. Therefore, the Law Commission's definition of intention was adapted in their later report,[120] applying where:

(a) It is [D's] purpose to cause [the result]; or

(b) although it is not [D's] purpose to cause it, he knows that it would occur in the ordinary course of events if he were to succeed in his purpose of causing some other result.

Under the new definition, D in the previous example would satisfy an intention to kill. It is not D's purpose to kill, but she knows that death will occur in the ordinary course of events, in other words would be virtually certain, if she succeeds in her purpose (blowing up the items).

 Assessment matters . . .

If an example of this kind were to arise in problem facts, it is not clear whether the courts would interpret the *Woollin* definition in line with the Law Commission's adapted approach. However, highlighting this possibility would impress examiners.

3.8.2 Subjective vs objective mens rea

As we have seen, a subjective approach to mens rea requires the prosecution to prove that D had a particular purpose or foresight at the time of acting. In contrast, an objective approach to mens rea focusses on reasonableness, asking whether a reasonable person in D's shoes would have foreseen a particular risk, and finding D culpable on that basis. As mens rea terms have developed within the common law, there has often been an apparent conflict between these two approaches. When discussing mens rea in this manner, it is important to remember that both approaches have their own advantages and disadvantages. Equally, the ideal test may well be one that incorporates elements of both.[121]

[120] Law Commission, *Offences Against the Person and General Principles* (No 218, 1993) cl1.
[121] Tur, 'Subjectivism and Objectivism: Towards Synthesis' in Shute, Gardner, and Horder (eds), *Action and Value in Criminal Law* (1993) 213.

A convenient way to set out and compare the relative merits of subjective and objective approaches is to look back to our discussion of 'recklessness' (**3.4.4**). It will be remembered that, following its subjective beginnings, the case of *Caldwell*[122] (and Lord Diplock in particular) redefined recklessness in an objective manner: applying where D foresaw a risk (subjective), but also where she unreasonably failed to do so (objective).

Caldwell attracted considerable criticism because of the apparent judicial lawmaking involved, but also simply on the basis that it employed an objective approach. Sir John Smith, for example, wrote that 'the decision sets back the law concerning the mental element in criminal damage in theory to before 1861'.[123] The concern was, *and remains*, that before we are ready to convict D of a serious offence, we should be sure she has chosen to commit, or at least chosen to risk committing, that offence.[124] D will be reckless under the *Caldwell* test even where she has not made such a choice, because she has not foreseen the risk of the offence element (in this case, the risk of causing damage), it will be enough that she *should have done so*. The objection is made considerably stronger when we realise that D will be reckless under this definition even in cases where it would be impossible for her to have lived up to that reasonable standard. For example, if a blind D were to walk into and damage another's property, she will be (objectively) reckless as to that damage as long as a reasonable (sighted) person would have foreseen the risk of causing damage.[125] D is liable for a criminal offence despite not choosing to commit it; not choosing to risk it; on the basis of a reasonableness standard that was impossible for her to meet.

Criticism of *Caldwell* and the objective test led directly to it being overruled by the House of Lords in *G*,[126] with the law reverting to the old subjective test: D will only be reckless when she has foreseen the risk (in this case, of causing damage). However, the obvious problems with the purely objective test should not imply that a purely subjective one is necessarily the perfect answer. For example, what about D who damages the property of another and does not foresee the risk of damage because she could not care less about the risk to others, or because she was angry? In such cases, D may not have consciously chosen to risk the offence, but the reason for this lack of choice is in great measure D's own fault.[127] These criticisms are further strengthened by recognition that in *some* circumstances, the current law will find recklessness despite D not foreseeing the risk in the conventional sense, as for example when D is intoxicated, or when the court says D must have foreseen the risk 'in the back of her mind' (as we discuss at **3.4.4** and **3.7**). If these exceptions are allowed, why not also allow recklessness where D failed to foresee a risk because of her selfishness and lack of concern for others?

Much of the current academic work in this area is not promoting complete subjectivism or complete objectivism, but rather looking for compromise approaches between them. For example, allowing recklessness to be found in cases where D has not foreseen

---

[122] [1982] AC 341.

[123] Smith, 'Comment on *Caldwell*' [1981] Crim LR 393.

[124] For discussion of the principle of autonomy, see **Chapter 1.4.3**.

[125] See *Elliott* [1983] 1 WLR 939, at **3.4.4.1**.

[126] [2003] UKHL 50.

[127] Even on the facts of *G*, the majority of the general public would support liability being found. Keating, 'Reckless Children' [2006] Crim LR 546.

a risk, but only if this lack of foresight was something D could be blamed for. In this manner, the blind D who causes damage will not be measured against the standard of the reasonable sighted person. However, on the other hand, D who does not care about others will not be able to rely on her callous attitude to avoid liability either.[128]

3.9 Eye on assessment

This section sketches a structure for analysing the mens rea of an offence when applying the law in a problem-type question. Drawing on the structure outlined at the end of **Chapter 1**, we are focussing on the second part of Step 3.

STEP 1 Identify the potential criminal event in the facts

This should be simply stated (eg 'The first potential criminal event arises where D kicks V'). The role of this stage is to highlight which part of the question you are answering before you begin to apply the law.

STEP 2 Identify the potential offence

Again, state this simply (eg 'When breaking the vase, D may be liable for criminal damage'). The role of this stage is to highlight which offence you are going to apply.

STEP 3 Applying the offence to the facts

Having highlighted a possible offence, Step 3 requires you to both identify the actus reus and mens rea of that offence, *and* apply them to the facts.

Step 3 includes the identification and application of both actus reus elements and mens rea elements. As we discussed in **Chapter 2**, this should always begin with the actus reus elements, ensuring that your analysis answers two core questions.

(1) What is the actus reus of the potential offence?
(2) Did D complete the actus reus (did she do it)?

---

[128] See Ben-David, 'Cognitive Void in Relation to Attendant Circumstances as Subjective Mens Rea' [2015] New Crim LR 418; Lacey, 'Responsibility Without Consciousness' (2016) 36 OJLS 219; Duff, *Intention, Agency and the Criminal Law* (1990); Tadros, 'Recklessness and the Duty to Take Care' in Shute and Simester (eds), *Criminal Law Theory* (2002) 248.

If you conclude that D has *not* completed the actus reus of the offence, there is no need to continue to discuss mens rea elements: if there is no actus reus then there is no crime. However, if you conclude that D has completed the actus reus, or (*as is more likely in a problem question*) if you conclude that D is likely to satisfy the actus reus elements, then it is correct to move on to discuss mens rea. Again, your analysis should focus on two core questions.

(1) What is the mens rea of the potential offence?

(2) Did D have that mens rea at the point in time of her relevant conduct?

The answer to these questions will vary between offences (question 1) and between factual scenarios (question 2). The answer to the first question will be discussed in relation to each offence covered in this textbook: gleaned from a combination of statutory and common law sources. However, the structure of application (question 2) is common between offences and can be usefully introduced at this point. It involves the stages of analysis set out in **Table 3.9**.

Table 3.9 Applying mens rea to problem facts

Mens rea	
A) Mens rea as to the conduct element?	As we discussed earlier (**3.3**), (*almost*) all offences require D's acts to be voluntary. Thus, you must always consider whether, at the point of acting, D was in control of her movements or lack of movements.
	Although this must be considered, you do not always have to discuss it in your answer. There is a common law presumption that D's acts are voluntary. Thus, although voluntariness is a requirement for liability, and although you should always consider this (keep it in mind) when applying the law, you do not need to discuss it in your answer unless there is some indication in the facts that D's acts were not voluntary.
B) Mens rea as to the circumstance element?	All offences (conduct and result crimes) include circumstance elements (eg that the property belongs to another for criminal damage). Examine the offence to see if these requirements must be intended; be known; believed; foreseen; or if any mens rea is required.
	If the mens rea is obviously satisfied on the case facts then do not spend time on it, simply say that it is likely to be present and move on. For example, if D stabs and kills V, it is unlikely that you need a lengthy discussion about whether D *knew* V was a person. However, if the issue is not straightforward, discuss it.

(Continued)

Table 3.9 Continued

C) Mens rea as to the result element?	Only result crimes will include a result element (eg that D's acts must cause death for murder). Where such an element of the actus reus is present, examine the offence to see if it must be intended; be known; believed; foreseen; or if any mens rea is required.
	As with mens rea as to circumstances, make sure you discuss the facts of the problem to see if the required mens rea is satisfied. If it is obviously satisfied, then highlight this briefly; if it is not obviously satisfied, then discuss what is likely.
D) Ulterior mens rea?	Only certain offences will include an ulterior mens rea requirement (eg the intention to permanently deprive for theft). As above, make sure you clearly identify what mens rea term is required (intention, etc), and then apply it to the facts.

Although we have set out the table using element analysis (separating acts, circumstances, and results), this is not necessary within your answer. For example, when discussing murder, it is more common to talk generally of a mens rea of 'intention to kill or cause serious harm to a person' than it is to separate mens rea as to the unlawful killing (result) from mens rea as to the fact V is a person (circumstance). Discussing mens rea in such general terms is perfectly acceptable (*and often more straightforward*), but you must still remember to cover every mens rea requirement within the offence: D only commits the offence if every element is satisfied. With this in mind, it can be useful to employ the language of element analysis to pinpoint certain elements for particular comment (eg if D intended to kill but did not think she was unlawfully killing a person), and it can also be useful to have it in the back of your mind as a checklist to make sure you have not left anything out.

Three final points should be noted:

- **Liability requires D to complete every element of the offence:** As with actus reus elements, if *any* element of the mens rea is or may be missing then D has not committed the offence (assuming those elements cannot be reconstructed through D's prior-fault, as discussed at **3.7**). You may then consider if D has committed an alternative (lesser) offence.

- **Don't be afraid of the unknown:** Problem question facts are often incomplete. Particularly when applying the mens rea terms, you will often find that you are unsure if D satisfies the term or not. A common mistake students make is to pretend they are sure—stating that intention, for example, is clearly satisfied or clearly absent. In such a case, where it is not clear, this is wrong. It is much better to talk of likelihoods, particularly when predicting if a jury will find mens rea or not. Thus, unless you are very sure (eg the facts say that D intends or does not intend) then discuss whether mens rea will be proved in terms of what you think is more likely and why.

- **Intention (again):** This is a repetition from the discussion of intention, but it relates to a common mistake and so it is worth repeating. If the mens rea of an offence requires D to intend, always begin your discussion with direct intention (ie was it D's purpose or aim). Only if this is not found should you then consider oblique intention (ie was it foreseen as a virtual certainty) as a backup alternative definition.

ONLINE RESOURCES

www.oup.com/he/child-ormerod4e

This chapter is accompanied by a selection of online resources to help you with this topic, including:

- **Self-test questions** and **scenario questions**
- **Videos** from the authors
- **Audio introduction** to the topic
- **Chapter summary sheet**
- Two **sample examination questions** with answer guidance
- **Further reading and weblinks**

Also available on the online resources are:

- A selection of **videos** from the authors containing general advice on problem questions and essay questions
- **Legal updates**

4

Interaction of actus reus and mens rea

4.1 Introduction

In **Chapters 2 and 3** we discussed actus reus (external requirements) and mens rea (internal/fault requirements) as largely separate concerns. However, it is important to remember that criminal liability can only be found when these two requirements are proved together in relation to the same offence. This is illustrated in **Figure 4.1**.

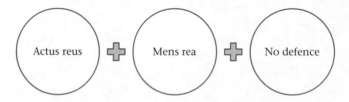

Figure 4.1 Elements of criminal liability

In this chapter, our aim is to provide some more detail about this structure, bringing together the interaction of actus reus and mens rea.

We consider the interaction of actus reus and mens rea elements in two separate contexts. First, it is important to understand how actus reus and mens rea elements relate to one another within the structure of an offence. We introduced this issue at the start of **Chapter 3**, but some more detail will be useful. Secondly, interaction issues also emerge when applying offence requirements to a set of problem facts. In this second context, we focus in particular on cases where actus reus and mens rea elements appear to be satisfied, but they do not take place at the same time and/or are not focussed on the same target. We discuss each in turn.[1]

4.2 Interaction within the structure of an offence

When identifying actus reus and mens rea elements within an offence, it is useful to remember how these elements interact with one another. We are looking for mens rea elements that *correspond* with elements within the actus reus.

The correspondence principle is the name given to the basic idea that each element within the actus reus of an offence should have a mens rea element that corresponds/couples with it. For example, the offence of criminal damage requires D to cause damage (actus reus) and intend or be reckless as to causing damage (mens rea).[2] Such correspondence allows us to understand D's actus reus (her causing damage) as a culpable expression of her agency: she has not only caused damage, which may have been accidental, but has (at least) chosen to risk unjustifiably doing so (been reckless about it), and may therefore be legitimately blamed for it. Such correspondence is also essential to our understanding of mens rea. As highlighted in **Chapter 3.2**, it is nonsense to inquire if D intends or is reckless in the abstract; we need to know the corresponding element of the actus reus. Our question for criminal damage is not 'is D intending or reckless', but 'is D intending or reckless as to causing damage to property belonging to another'.

When discussing an offence, it is therefore useful to think about the required correspondence of actus reus and mens rea within each offence element. The example of criminal damage is set out in **Table 4.1**.

Table 4.1 Criminal damage

	Actus reus	Mens rea
Conduct element	Any act (or omission) that causes the result	Voluntary
Circumstance element	The property damaged belongs to another	Intention or recklessness
Result element	Damage	Intention or recklessness

Every element of this offence (conduct, circumstance, and result) includes an actus reus requirement and a corresponding mens rea requirement.

---

[1] See also *Smith, Hogan, and Ormerod's Criminal Law* (16th edn, 2021) Ch3.3.
[2] Criminal Damage Act 1971, s1.

4.2.1 Exceptions to the correspondence principle

The correspondence principle does not represent a universal rule of offence construction. Exceptions arise in two forms. First, an offence may contain actus reus elements without corresponding mens rea elements. These are called strict liability elements, arising most commonly within strict or absolute liability offences and constructive liability offences. Secondly, an offence may contain mens rea elements without corresponding actus reus elements. These elements are called ulterior mens rea elements. Both are common within the current law, but remain controversial.

4.2.1.1 Actus reus without corresponding mens rea: strict liability

We discussed strict liability in **Chapter 3.2.1** to mean, simply, an absence of corresponding mens rea. Where an offence contains elements of strict liability—that is, where there are actus reus elements without corresponding mens rea—that offence can be seen as contrary to the correspondence principle.[3]

Strict liability is a label that is used in three main contexts. First, where an offence requires no mens rea beyond voluntary movement, it is referred to as a 'strict or absolute liability offence'. Secondly, where an offence requires mens rea for each element apart from one, this element (where no mens rea is required) is referred to as a 'strict liability element'. Thirdly, in the context of 'constructive offences'. Constructive offences include a basic offence with full actus reus and corresponding mens rea, but also include an additional actus reus element alone which is *constructed* on the basic offence to make a more serious crime.

Strict or absolute liability offences

Strict or absolute liability offences require no mens rea beyond voluntariness as to the conduct element. An example is the offence of driving when over the prescribed alcohol limit, set out in **Table 4.2**.[4]

Table 4.2 Driving when over the prescribed alcohol limit

	Actus reus	**Mens rea**
Conduct element	Bodily movement required to drive, attempt to drive, or be in charge of vehicle	Voluntary
Circumstance element	Being in a 'motor vehicle'; being on a road or in a public place; being over the prescribed alcohol limit	None

Strict or absolute liability offences are controversial because they criminalise D for acting in circumstances (and sometimes causing results) without proof of choice or control. D

---

[3] See generally Simester (ed), *Appraising Strict Liability* (2005).
[4] Road Traffic Act 1988, s5.

need not intend them, foresee them, or even negligently fail to guard against them. For example, D would commit the driving offence in **Table 4.2** even if she did not realise that she was over the alcohol limit when driving, and even if she was not negligent as, for example, where her drink was spiked. As long as her actions satisfy the actus reus, and as long as she is voluntary in her movements, she has committed the offence.

Strict liability elements

It is common to find offences that require mens rea as to certain actus reus elements, but not to others. Where no mens rea is required to a certain element, this is commonly referred to as a strict liability element. An example is the offence of causing a child (V) to watch a sexual act, set out in **Table 4.3**.[5]

Table 4.3 Causing a child to watch a sexual act

	Actus reus	**Mens rea**
Conduct element	Any act (or omission) that causes the result	Voluntary
Circumstance element	D is over 18 And	None
	(V is under 16	Lack of reasonable belief V is over 16
	or	
	V is under 13)	None
Result element	Causing V to watch a third person engaging in a sexual activity or an image of sexual activity	Intention
Ulterior mens rea	*	Intention to gain sexual gratification

This offence provides a useful example because it includes several mens rea requirements: D's acts must be *voluntary*; she must *intend* the result element—to cause V to view sexual activity; and she must intend an ulterior mens rea requirement—to gain sexual gratification. Moreover, if V is between 13 and 16, D must also have mens rea as to this circumstance element. However, if V is under 13, the statute is clear that mens rea as to this element is strict: it is irrelevant if D intended V to be under 13; foresaw that as a risk; should have foreseen it; or had no way of knowing.

---

[5] Sexual Offences Act 2003, s12.

Offences of this kind, where liability is strict as to isolated elements, are generally less controversial than strict liability offences where no mens rea is required as to circumstances *and* results. However, they remain problematic. After all, D is still being blamed and criminalised without choosing to cause or even risk an essential part of the actus reus.

Constructive liability offences

Constructive liability offences have an interesting and unique offence structure. At their base is a full offence that includes both actus reus and corresponding mens rea elements. At this stage there is no exception to the correspondence principle. However, in addition to this base offence, constructive crimes also include additional actus reus elements, usually in the form of result elements, that construct upon the base offence to make a more serious crime. These additional constructing elements have no corresponding mens rea, they are strict liability elements. Thus, if D satisfies the elements of the base offence, and the additional actus reus element, she becomes liable for the constructive and more serious offence.

Probably the most well-known constructive crime is murder.[6] Murder is committed as a constructive offence where D intentionally causes serious harm to V (base offence), and V dies as a result (additional actus reus). This is set out in **Table 4.4**.

Table 4.4 Murder and constructive liability

	Actus reus	**Mens rea**
Conduct element	Any act (or omission) that causes the result	Voluntary
Circumstance element	V is a person under the Queen's peace	Knowledge
Result element	**Death of V**	Intention to cause death *or* **intention to cause grievous bodily harm**

The *minimum* mens rea required of D is that she voluntarily and intentionally caused grievous bodily harm to a person. If D acted in line with this intention (intentionally causing grievous bodily harm) she would commit a serious offence against the person.[7] Constructing upon this base offence of intentionally causing grievous bodily harm, the offence of murder also requires an additional actus reus element: that D caused death. However, this additional actus reus element does not require any additional corresponding mens rea. In effect, the grievous bodily harm offence (actus reus and mens rea) + death (additional actus reus) = murder.

---

[6] See **Chapter 5**.
[7] Offences Against the Person Act, s18.

Extra detail . . .

Although many offences include elements of strict liability, make sure that you check the case law for a particular offence to ensure that it has been interpreted in this manner. As discussed at **3.2.1.1**, the presumption of mens rea means that several offences that appear to lack mens rea requirements have been interpreted by the courts as requiring mens rea.

4.2.1.2 Mens rea without corresponding actus reus: ulterior mens rea

In contrast to strict or constructive liability where an offence contains actus reus elements without corresponding mens rea, ulterior mens rea describes mens rea elements that lack corresponding actus reus.[8] For mens rea to make sense, it must still relate to something (eg we cannot understand an intention requirement without knowing *what* D must intend). However, the object of D's ulterior mens rea, what she must intend, does not form part of the actus reus and thus does not need to come about for the crime to be completed.

For example, to be liable for the offence of theft, D must appropriate the property of another (actus reus) dishonestly and with the intention to permanently deprive V of that property (mens rea).[9] Here, the requirement that D must 'intend to permanently deprive V' is an ulterior mens rea requirement. This is illustrated in **Table 4.5**.

Table 4.5 Theft

	Actus reus	**Mens rea**
Conduct element	Any act (or omission) causing the result	Voluntary
Circumstance element	What is appropriated is property	Knowledge
	What is appropriated belongs to another (ie not exclusively to D)	Knowledge
	D's appropriation is objectively dishonest	In context of D's knowledge and belief
Result element	Appropriation of V's property	Intention
Ulterior mens rea element	*	**Intention permanently to deprive V of the property**

---

[8] See Horder, 'Crimes of Ulterior Intent' in Simester and Smith (eds), *Harm and Culpability* (1996) 153.

[9] Theft Act 1968, s1.

The offence requirement that D must 'intend permanently to deprive V' is an ulterior mens rea element because it lacks a corresponding actus reus element: D must *intend* permanently to deprive, but whether D permanently deprives V of her property in fact is irrelevant.

Ulterior mens rea requirements are relatively common in the criminal law. Some of the advantages of ulterior mens rea include:

A) Where corresponding actus reus would be impractical: With offences such as theft, it is obviously impractical to include an actus reus requirement that D must 'permanently deprive' V of her property: the offence could never be complete unless the property was destroyed, because D would always have the option of returning it and thereby negating the actus reus. However, without the mens rea requirement of an intention to permanently deprive, the offence would be too wide, criminalising non-consensual borrowing.

B) Where we wish to intervene to prevent harm: Many offences, such as the general inchoate offences of attempt, conspiracy, and assisting and encouraging, seek to criminalise D for taking steps towards committing a future offence (trying to commit it; agreeing to commit it; assisting or encouraging another to commit it) with the intention, or in some cases recklessness, that the future offence will be completed. In these cases, we do not want to wait for the future offence to be completed before we can act to criminalise D, so the offences punish D for taking steps towards the future offence (actus reus) with ulterior mens rea as to it coming about.[10]

C) Where D has already committed a certain offence, but she does so with the intention to commit another: Where this is the case, certain offences have been drafted to criminalise D for a more serious offence that takes account of her ulterior intention. For example, section 62 of the Sexual Offences Act 2003 criminalises D who commits an offence with the (ulterior) intention to commit a sexual offence. Again, this future sexual offence does not need to come about in fact, so it is not part of the actus reus, it must simply be intended.

 Point to remember . . .

It is important for you to understand the terminology of strict and constructive liability, and of ulterior mens rea. However, this is simply to highlight them as exceptions to the correspondence principle. Although common within the law, you will see that offences that have been constructed in these forms are often some of the most controversial.

4.3 Interaction within the application of an offence

Having explored the different ways actus reus and mens rea elements can interact within the structure of an offence, this second part of the chapter explores their interaction when applied to case facts. In practice, and in a problem question, we are looking to identify a criminal event, an event in which D completes all the actus reus and mens rea elements of an offence.

---

[10] **Chapter 11.**

Assessment matters . . .

In most cases, as long as the offence requirements are understood, and as long as the facts are clear, the application stage can be quite straightforward. Your task is to work through the offence elements: if they are all satisfied then D has committed the offence; if one or more of them is missing then she has not committed the offence.

In a minority of instances, however, problems relating to the interaction of actus reus and mens rea will emerge. In these cases, although D completes all the actus reus and mens rea elements, the two parts do not 'mesh' with one another. There are two main examples of this. First is the case where D's actus reus is directed at one object (eg D hits V), but her mens rea is directed at another (eg she intended to hit X). Here, the question is whether we can we use D's mens rea directed at X as sufficient mens rea for an offence against V. Can we bring the elements together to create a single *whole* offence? The second set of cases is where D completes the actus reus and mens rea elements of an offence, but they do not appear to coincide with one another because they come about at different times. As highlighted in **Chapters 2 and 3**, D's mens rea must correspond with the conduct element of the actus reus. However, in a case where D has possessed that mens rea, either before or after her act, is there any way we can find liability?

4.3.1 Actus reus and mens rea at different objects: transferred malice

When D completes the actus reus of an offence (eg causing damage or injury) for which mens rea is required, that mens rea must correspond with the actus reus elements (eg D must intend to cause that damage or injury). In some cases, D's mens rea will be indiscriminate. For example, D may detonate a bomb intending to kill *anyone nearby*, or set a fire intending to *cause general damage*. Where D's mens rea is indiscriminate in this way, it is straightforward to find that D's mens rea corresponds with the actus reus and satisfies the offence. If D's bomb kills V, for example, we can say that D intended to kill V because V was within the group ('anyone nearby') that D intended to kill. Equally, if V survived and V2 was killed, we can say that D intended to kill V2 as well (V2 is within the same group).

Problems can emerge, however, where D acts with a specific target in mind. For example, D may detonate a bomb intending to kill V in particular, or start a fire intending to damage specific property. Where D succeeds in her plan, then liability is straightforward. However, where D explodes the bomb intending to kill V in particular but also kills V2, or misses V and only kills V2, then we have a problem; and if D's fire spreads in an unexpected way and damages property other than that intended, we have the same problem. In these cases, we have actus reus (death and damage), and we have mens rea (intention to cause death and damage), but the targets of the two are different: D intends to kill or damage one target, but actually kills or damages another. Is D liable for an offence?

Where D's actus reus and mens rea target different objects in this manner, liability is found through the doctrine of 'transferred malice' or, more accurately, 'transferred mens rea'. Essentially, D's targeted mens rea (eg D's intention to kill a particular person or intention to damage particular property) is *transferred* to the object that was the victim of D's actus reus (eg the actual person killed or property damaged). This was discussed in *Latimer*.

Latimer (1886) 17 QBD 359

D swung a belt at V attempting to hit him, but only caught him slightly. Missing V, the main force of the belt hit a woman (V2), who was severely injured. D had clearly committed an offence against V. However, D was charged with a more serious offence against the person in relation to V2's injuries.[11]

- Court: guilty of offence against V2. D's malice (mens rea) directed at V could be transferred to V2, satisfying the mens rea of the offence in relation to V2.

In the absence of transferred malice, D would not escape liability altogether. D would still be liable, for example, for his attempt to injure V seriously. However, attempt liability alone in these circumstances would seem odd. After all, D not only tried to cause serious injury, but he did so, albeit to an unforeseen V2. It is this intuition that D deserves liability for the full offence that has given rise to the doctrine of transferred malice, a legal manipulation (a 'legal fiction'[12]) that allows D's mens rea to be moved from one target to another. With both actus reus and mens rea now focussed on the same target, using transferred malice, liability can be found. This is illustrated in **Figure 4.2**.

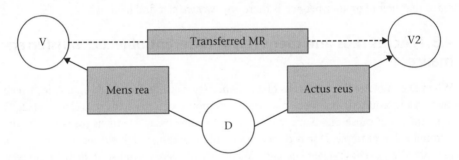

Figure 4.2 Transferred mens rea

The criminal law's rules which allow for the transfer of mens rea ensure liability by linking actus reus and mens rea elements that would otherwise lack for coincidence on a single object. This will apply for assault cases such as *Latimer*, homicide cases where D kills an unintended target,[13] as well as a host of other offences such as criminal damage where D may cause damage to an unintended target. In each case, as made clear in *Latimer*, it is not necessary for D to have foreseen harm to V2, or even for D to have been negligent in failing to foresee it. Rather, it is D's mens rea towards V that is simply transferred to bring together the elements of liability.

---

[11] Offences Against the Person Act 1861, s20. See **Chapter 7.5**.

[12] 'Legal fiction' is a term used to describe an untrue rule or assertion that is accepted as true for legal purposes. In the context of transferred malice, this arises from the redirection of mens rea. We see another example of a legal fiction when discussing the intoxication rules at **Chapter 13.2**. Such rules can be extremely useful in achieving certain policy ends, but are, as we discuss, also controversial.

[13] *Mitchell* [1983] QB 741.

4.3.1.1 Limitations to the doctrine of transferred malice

There are two important limitations to the doctrine of transferred malice. First, D's mens rea can only be transferred where it relates to the same crime as her actus reus. For example, D throws a stone at V, a person, but misses and causes property damage. In this case, although D's intention to cause harm to V is hardly to her credit, an intention to hurt a person is categorically different from intention or recklessness as to property damage, and transfer of mens rea is therefore unavailable.[14] The same is true where D shoots at a dog (property) in an attempt to kill it, but misses and kills its owner, V2. D does not murder V2 because an intention to kill a dog is categorically different from an intention to kill or seriously injure a person. This is illustrated in **Figure 4.3**.

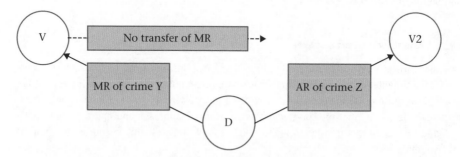

Figure 4.3 No transferred mens rea between different crimes

The second limitation to the doctrine is where liability would require a double transfer of malice. In *AG's Reference (No 3 of 1994)*,[15] D stabbed his pregnant girlfriend, V, several times with the intention required for murder. As a result of this, V gave birth prematurely to V2. V2 later died, largely as a result of the premature birth. The House of Lords rejected D's liability for the murder of V2 because such liability would require a double transfer of mens rea: from the mother, V, to her foetus, X, and then from the foetus to its changed status as a person at birth, V2.[16] This is illustrated in **Figure 4.4**.

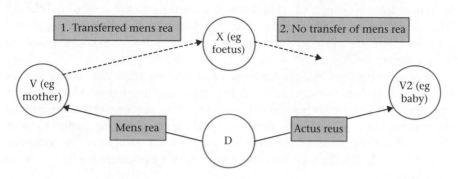

Figure 4.4 No double transfer of mens rea

---

[14] *Pembliton* (1847) LR 2 CCR 119.

[15] [1996] 1 Cr App R 351.

[16] D was not liable for murder. However, D was liable for manslaughter, as the offence is wide enough to be satisfied on these facts without reliance on a transfer of malice. See **Chapter 6.3.1.3**.

Despite these two limitations, the doctrine of transferred malice remains controversial. For some, the doctrine remains too open and should be limited further. Horder has criticised the doctrine for allowing a transfer of mens rea, potentially, even where the victim of the harm (V2) was unintended *and* the manner of the harm was unanticipated. For example, D shoots a gun at V; V2, who is hiding in the bushes nearby, is startled by the noise and dies of a heart attack. Horder recommends the introduction of a 'remoteness' limitation.[17] Beyond this, others have questioned whether, given that the doctrine is a legal fiction, it is necessary at all. In most cases involving transferred mens rea, it would be possible without the need for transfer to find attempt liability in relation to D's intended target V, and possibly a reckless or negligence-based offence in relation to the actual harm caused to V2.[18]

 Assessment matters . . .

Horder's article is particularly interesting here. If a case of this kind arose in problem facts (where V2 is both unintended as a victim and suffers harm in an unforeseen manner), the current law would suggest that D's mens rea towards V could be transferred to V2 to complete an offence. However, it may be that the court would accept Horder's approach and find a further limitation to the doctrine of transferred malice. Highlighting this possibility in your essay would be very useful.

4.3.2 Actus reus and mens rea at different times: coincidence principle

When discussing transferred malice, we highlighted the need for mens rea and actus reus to coincide, or come together, in relation to the same object (V). Beyond this, it is also essential that they should coincide at the same point in *time*—this is traditionally described as respecting the coincidence principle. For example, D forms the intention to kill her husband (V) by poisoning his food. When D is driving home from work someone runs in front of her car and is killed; it is V. D has not committed murder. Although D has caused V's death, which is the actus reus of murder, and she intends in general terms to kill him, she lacks the mens rea in the form of an intention to kill *by this act* and *at this point in time*.

The need for temporal coincidence is the reason why our application of criminal law to problem facts should always begin with the actus reus. Once it is established that the actus reus of an offence has been completed, we can then inquire whether D possessed the mens rea for the offence *at the point in time* that she completed the conduct element. Whether or not she possessed the mens rea at some other point in time is irrelevant; liability demands that she must have possessed it at that particular time for liability to be established.

---

[17] Horder, 'Transferred Malice and the Remoteness of Unexpected Outcomes from Intentions' [2006] Crim LR 383. See also Eldar, 'The Limits of Transferred Malice' (2012) 32 OJLS 633.

[18] Ashworth, 'Transferred Malice and Punishment for Unforeseen Consequences' in Glazebrook (ed), *Reshaping the Criminal Law* (1978) 77.

It is worth stressing here that we are talking about coincidence between mens rea and the *conduct element* of the actus reus (D's act or omission) rather than with the actus reus more generally. For example, if D laces V's food with poison with the intention to kill, and causes V's death, she has committed murder even if she changes her mind before the poison takes effect and V dies. Indeed, she may even change her mind the split second after lacing V's food, well in advance of V ingesting the poison. As long as D's conduct is the cause of V's death, and as long as D had the required mens rea when completing that conduct, there will be coincidence and the offence will be committed.

In **Figure 4.5** the point of coincidence is represented by the vertical dotted line.

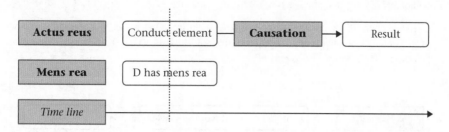

Figure 4.5 Coincidence of actus reus and mens rea

Coincidence is an absolute rule of law to which there are *no exceptions*: a lack of coincidence will mean a lack of liability. However, in rare cases where an apparent lack of coincidence is at issue, it can be very difficult to accept this conclusion. D has the mens rea for the crime at some point in time, and has completed the actus reus at some point in time, and so it can be very appealing to try to find ways around the rule. Indeed, this is what we have seen in several cases; *not* exceptions to the coincidence principle, but the courts finding often ingenious ways to identify coincidence where it looks like there is none. Such cases can be split into two categories: where actus reus seems to precede mens rea, and where mens rea seems to precede actus reus.

4.3.2.1 Actus reus preceding mens rea

The first example of a potential lack of coincidence arises where D's conduct causing the result (actus reus) precedes the point in time at which D holds the required mens rea. This is illustrated in **Figure 4.6**.

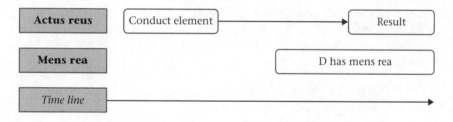

Figure 4.6 Lack of coincidence—actus reus then mens rea

Where this problem has emerged, the courts have developed two possible methods of finding coincidence.

The first, the *continuing act* approach, is exemplified in *Fagan* (see **Figure 4.7**).

 Fagan v MPC [1969] 1 QB 439

D accidentally drove his car onto a policeman's (V's) foot and, when he became aware of this, intentionally took his time moving the car in order to cause further pain. When discussing Fagan's potential liability for an offence against the person, the problem became apparent: when performing acts within the actus reus (driving onto the foot) D lacked mens rea; but when he gained mens rea (intentionally causing pain) these acts were already complete.

- Divisional Court: (by a majority) guilty of offence against the person. D's 'act' did not stop when driving onto the foot, but continued when on the foot. Thus, D's act did coincide with a time when he possessed the required mens rea.

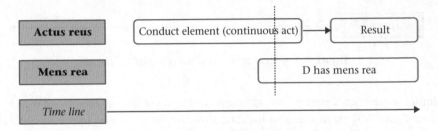

Figure 4.7 Understanding the approach in *Fagan*

By extending the conduct element, coincidence between actus reus and mens rea can be found. The courts are not creating an exception to the coincidence principle, but they are manipulating the definition of the conduct element in order to find it.

Although the continuing act approach reaches the desired conclusion, its operation can be criticised as rather artificial. With this in mind, perhaps a better approach to the problem, as outlined in more recent case law, is to abandon a focus on D's initial acts, and to focus instead on her later omission.

The second approach, the *omissions approach*, is exemplified in *Miller* (see **Figure 4.8**).

 Miller [1983] 2 AC 161

D, a squatter in V's house, went to sleep holding a lit cigarette. He awoke to find he had dropped the cigarette and the mattress was smouldering, but did nothing other than move to an adjoining room. The fire caused extensive damage, and D was charged with criminal damage based on his omission to tackle the smouldering mattress or alert the authorities (a duty arising from his inadvertent creation of a dangerous situation).

- Court: guilty of criminal damage.
- Court of Appeal: conviction upheld on appeal.
- House of Lords: conviction upheld on appeal.

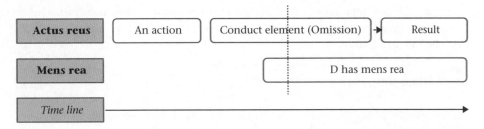

Figure 4.8 Understanding the approach in *Miller*

The fire was caused by D's positive act of dropping the cigarette. However, if the court were to focus on this act then a coincidence problem emerges: when D acted to cause the fire he lacked mens rea as he was asleep, and when he had the mens rea (foreseeing the possibility of damage) his action was complete. Rather than trying to reinterpret and lengthen D's acts as in *Fagan*, the House of Lords instead focussed on D's omission to act having become aware of the danger. As discussed previously,[19] omissions liability is only applicable where D has a duty to act. However, in this case, having created a dangerous situation and become aware of that danger, D has a clear duty to take reasonable steps to prevent the harm. In failing to do so, and thereby breaching that duty, Miller's omission satisfied the actus reus of the offence, and did so at a time that he possessed the requisite mens rea. Again, we have coincidence, and so we have liability.

 Point to remember . . .

As the continuing act approach (*Fagan*) and the omissions approach (*Miller*) both provide answers to the same problem, it is tempting to think of them interchangeably. However, you should be careful not to do so. As set out previously, they are alternatives. It is often good to acknowledge both options, but remember that they are not the same.

4.3.2.2 Mens rea preceding actus reus

The second example of a potential lack of coincidence arises where D acts with the requisite mens rea for the offence, but it is her later action without mens rea that forms the actus reus of the offence. This is illustrated in **Figure 4.9**.

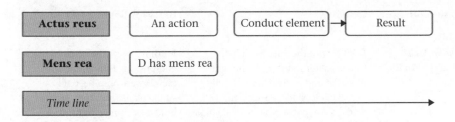

Figure 4.9 Lack of coincidence—mens rea then actus reus

---

[19] See **Chapter 2.6**.

Where this problem has emerged, the courts have sought to find coincidence using the *single transaction* approach. An early example of this is the Privy Council case *Thabo Meli* (see **Figure 4.10**).

Thabo Meli [1954] 1 All ER 373

D and others hit V over the head and then, as they had planned, attempted to disguise their crime by pushing his corpse over a cliff. However, it was later discovered that V had not died from the initial blows, but rather from exposure at the bottom of the cliff. Thus, D had the mens rea for murder when striking the initial blows that did not cause death, but when completing the later act that did cause death he lacked mens rea. There was no further intention to kill because D thought V was already dead.

- Court: guilty of murder.

- Privy Council: conviction upheld on appeal. Rather than looking at each individual action separately, D's actions were better analysed as part of a general plan to cause death and to hide the body: a series of acts that could be linked within one logical transaction. Analysed in this way, since D possessed the mens rea for murder at one point during this single transaction, coincidence was found.

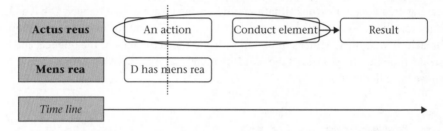

Figure 4.10 Understanding the approach in *Thabo Meli*

Within this small class of cases, where D acts with intent to kill by initial conduct but actually causes death by subsequent conduct, the single transaction approach has become firmly established.

There is an appealing logic about this approach, and there is little doubt that D deserves to be found liable. However, there is also some uncertainty. Chiefly, this uncertainty relates to the basis upon which courts link D's acts within the transaction. A series of cases in **Table 4.6** set out how the courts have approached this task.

Table 4.6 Developing cases on single actus reus transactions

Case reference	Case facts	Basis for linking acts
Thabo Meli [1954] 1 All ER 373	D hit V with the intention to kill (mens rea for murder). D thought V was dead and pushed him off a cliff to make it look like an accident. D died from exposure following the fall. A single transaction links D's initial attack (with mens rea) to pushing V off the cliff (actus reus causing death).	Hitting D over the head (act 1) and pushing him off the cliff (act 2) were both part of D's single plan. Thus, they can be linked as a single transaction.

(Continued)

Table 4.6 Continued

Church [1966] 1 QB 59	D fought and began to strangle V until she passed out (with mens rea for manslaughter). D thought V was dead and threw her body into a river to hide it (no mens rea as he thought she was dead). V drowned; D was convicted of manslaughter on the basis of linking his first act (with mens rea) to his second act (causing death) to find coincidence.	There was no 'plan' linking D's first act (attacking V) and second act (throwing her in the river). However, the Court of Criminal Appeal still found that they could be linked within a single transaction. It did not explain why.
Le Brun [1992] QB 61	D hit his wife (V) causing unconsciousness (with the mens rea for manslaughter). D realised that V was not dead. D dragged V home to try and cover up his offence, but dropped her accidentally and caused further head injuries from which she died. D was convicted of manslaughter on the basis of linking his first act (with mens rea) to his second act (causing death) to find coincidence.	There was no 'plan' linking D's first act (hitting V) and second act (dropping V). Also, unlike the previous cases, D did not believe V was dead. However, the Court of Appeal still found that D's acts could be linked as a single transaction on the basis that D's acts were of the same type. Thus, if D had dropped V trying to take her to a doctor, this act may not be linked with the former. However, as he was trying to conceal his crime, it could.

In the light of these cases, it seems clear that the courts have adopted a flexible approach in deciding whether D's acts can be linked within a single transaction or not. If they decide that D's acts remain of the same type, which they seem to regard in general terms as meaning they remain 'bad', then they are likely to link D's acts in order to allow for coincidence. It is only if D accidentally causes harm when later trying to help, for example, by dropping V when taking her to a hospital, that the courts are unlikely to link D's acts.

 Extra detail . . .

An alternative approach to this second problem of coincidence is to focus solely on D's initial action and to establish a chain of causation from there. For example, in *Le Brun*, 'but for' D's initial attack, D would not have dragged V and she would not have died when dropped (ie D's initial action was causally connected to V's injuries). The attraction of this approach is that D's second action when dropping V (that does not coincide with mens rea) becomes irrelevant. Through the causation rules, we can say that D's first act also caused the death, and find coincidence with mens rea at this point.

This approach was discussed in *Le Brun*, but the court preferred the single transaction approach. However, were a similar case to arise on problem facts, it would be useful to highlight this as an alternative approach.[20]

---

[20] Arenson, '*Thabo Meli* Revisited: The Pernicious Effects of Result-Driven Decisions' (2013) 77 JCL 41.

4.4 Reform

In many ways, the correspondence principle remains an ideal of criminalisation: offences should consist of harmful behaviour (actus reus) that D has chosen to bring about, or chosen to risk bringing about (mens rea).[21] To the extent that this is true, the topics discussed earlier represent at least partial failures to meet that ideal:

- Through offence definitions:

  ▷ strict and constructive liability—offences containing actus reus elements without corresponding mens rea;

  ▷ ulterior mens rea—offences containing mens rea elements without corresponding actus reus.

- Through the application of offences:

  ▷ transferred malice—finding liability even though D's actus reus and mens rea were targeted at different objects;

  ▷ coincidence—finding liability even though D's actus reus and mens rea, as ordinarily understood, occurred at different times.

With this in mind, it is unsurprising that each of these areas has given rise to considerable debate. Such debates have already been highlighted within our previous discussion of the law, and we do not propose to repeat them. However, when thinking about potential reform in this area, it is useful to structure your thinking, by separating two importantly distinct questions:

- **Do we want liability in these circumstances at all?**

  This is what we might call a threshold question. If we agree that offences *should only* be committed where D demonstrates blameworthiness in both act and mind, and that these should focus on the same object and occur at the same time, are we willing to tolerate any exceptions? For example, in the context of constructive liability, if D's acts cause an additional harm, for example death, should we define offences to punish D for this even if she only foresaw causing a lesser harm?[22] In the context of transferred malice, where D hits V2 when intending to hit V, should we allow a rule that artificially transfers the mens rea from V to V2, or should we reject it? In this latter example, such rejection seems even more appealing when we could still charge D with an attempt offence in relation to V, and possibly a reckless or negligence-based offence in relation to V2.[23]

---

[21] Horder, 'A Critique of the Correspondence Principle' [1995] Crim LR 759; Mitchell, 'In Defence of a Principle of Correspondence' [1999] Crim LR 195.

[22] Several jurisdictions repealed offences of constructive liability. Eg the Republic of Ireland reform of the offences against the person: Non-Fatal Offences Against the Person Act 1997. The Law Commission of England and Wales has made similar recommendations for the reform of offences against the person (see **Chapter 7.10**).

[23] Ashworth, 'Transferred Malice and Punishment for Unforeseen Consequences' in Glazebrook (ed), *Reshaping the Criminal Law* (1978) 77.

- If we do want liability in these circumstances, what is the least objectionable way to secure it?

This question is based on an acceptance that (in certain cases) constructive and strict liability, ulterior mens rea, transferred malice, or the stretching of coincidence can be acceptable. In the context of strict liability, constructive crimes, and ulterior mens rea, the debate then becomes how *widely* the practice should be available. Are such offences acceptable generally, or are they only acceptable in certain exceptional circumstances, for example to combat particularly serious harms,[24] or only where finding mens rea is particularly difficult.[25] In the context of transferred malice and coincidence, the same question arises: if these techniques can be used, where should we place the limits (eg the additional restrictions to transferred malice suggested by Horder, discussed at **4.3.1.1**)? However, in addition to this, transferred malice and coincidence also raise issues of *method*: how are we to make sense of mens rea transfers, and how can we find coincidence when it appears to be absent? This second issue is also discussed earlier, and particularly in the context of coincidence where the common law seems to have developed multiple and alternative methods for addressing the same problem. Again, here your task is to discuss these methods and comment on which, if any, you believe is the most appropriate.

4.5 Eye on assessment

This section focusses on problem-type questions, and how the topics discussed previously should be structured into your answers. To do so we need to distinguish between those topics relating to the elements of an offence (strict, constructive liability, and ulterior mens rea), and those relating to the application of an offence (transferred malice and coincidence).

4.5.1 Offence content

The content of an offence provides you with the offence elements of actus reus and mens rea that you must apply in a problem question. It may therefore be useful to highlight whether the offence is one that contains elements of strict liability or ulterior mens rea in order to explain why it is not necessary to identify certain corresponding mens rea in the context of strict liability, or actus reus in the context of ulterior mens rea. However, unless the question specifically asks you to evaluate or discuss the law as you apply it, there is no need to enter a debate about the rights and wrongs of the offence. In most cases, you are asked to 'discuss potential liability', not to 'discuss the merits of the law'.

---

[24] This is often a justification for punishing ulterior harmful intentions before any corresponding action is completed. See **Chapter 11**.

[25] This is often the justification for regulatory offences (especially those targeting companies) being strict. See **Chapter 3.2.1**.

4.5.2 Offence application

The rules relating to coincidence of actus reus and mens rea, that is coincidence on the same object and at the same time, are essential to the application of the law. They are therefore essential considerations within all problem questions. However, although essential, it is relatively rare that a problem question, *and very rare that a real case*, will involve problems in this area. The ideal approach to a problem question will therefore be to ensure coincidence, but not to waste unnecessary time discussing it unless such discussion is required.

As with **Chapters 2 and 3**, we are focussing on the third step of the problem question structure introduced in **Chapter 1**.

STEP 1 Identify the potential criminal event in the facts

This should be simply stated (eg 'The first potential criminal event arises where D kicks V'). The role of this stage is to highlight which part of the question you are answering before you begin to apply the law.

STEP 2 Identify the potential offence

Again, state this simply (eg 'When breaking the vase, D may be liable for criminal damage'). The role of this stage is to highlight which offence you are going to apply.

STEP 3 Applying the offence to the facts

Having highlighted a possible offence, STEP 3 requires you to both identify the actus reus and mens rea of that offence, *and* apply them to the facts.

As discussed in **Chapter 2.9**, your analysis within Step 3 should always begin with the actus reus of the offence. Identify the act/omission that D has completed, the relevant circumstances, and where necessary the unlawful results of those acts. Remember, where the actus reus does specify results, you must also show that D's acts *caused* those results.

Having examined the actus reus of the offence, you now know the point in time that D completed the relevant acts/omissions. Thus, when moving to mens rea (discussed in **Chapter 3**) you can ask more precisely whether D satisfies the mens rea at the *time* she completes the conduct element and whether it was *directed* at the relevant object.

The issues discussed in this chapter should be considered when applying mens rea elements. There are two possibilities:

- **If D satisfies the mens rea at that time and directed at that object:** There is no problem with coincidence. You do not need to say more on the topic: by explicitly identifying the mens rea at that relevant time and directed at that relevant object you have already demonstrated that coincidence is present.

- If D does not satisfy the mens rea at that time and/or directed at that object: There is a problem with coincidence. You can now highlight the problem; moving on to a full discussion of transferred malice and/or the reinterpretation of acts in order to see if coincidence can be found.

ONLINE RESOURCES

www.oup.com/he/child-ormerod4e

This chapter is accompanied by a selection of online resources to help you with this topic, including:

- **Self-test questions** and **scenario questions**
- **Videos** from the authors
- **Audio introduction** to the topic
- **Chapter summary sheet**
- Two **sample examination questions** with answer guidance
- **Further reading and weblinks**

Also available on the online resources are:

- A selection of **videos** from the authors containing general advice on problem questions and essay questions
- **Legal updates**

5

Murder

5.1 Introduction

From this point in the book our focus narrows from the general principles and structures of criminal law, to explore particular offences and defences. We begin with a category of crimes known as homicide offences (offences which involve the killing of a person), and with the offence of murder in particular.

 Terminology . . .

When we refer to categories of offences such as 'homicide offences', we are not referring to an offence with a distinct actus reus and mens rea. Rather, we are simply referring to a label that describes a group of offences that share certain characteristics (other categories include, eg, sexual offences; property offences; etc). It is not accurate to say D is liable for homicide. Rather, if liability is found, D is liable for a homicide offence such as murder or manslaughter.

D commits murder where she, a person,[1] unlawfully causes the death of V, also a person, under the Queen's peace, with the intention to kill or cause grievous (serious) bodily harm (GBH). Murder is generally considered the most serious crime. The harm involved does not simply affect the interests of V, but undermines V's potential to experience any future 'worldly' interests of any kind. Even within the law's class of 'homicide' offences, murder is distinguished as the most serious by the requirement of proof of intent: D has not simply killed V, she has done so *intending* to kill or cause GBH. It is because of its gravity as an offence that murder was until relatively recently punished with the death penalty,[2] and now results in a mandatory life sentence.

 Don't be confused . . .

A mandatory life sentence will rarely equate to a lifetime in prison. Rather, a life sentence is made up of a tariff period (ie a minimum period in prison reflecting the circumstances of the killing), followed by a licence period during which time D is released from prison but is monitored and may be restricted in various ways.[3] The sentence is a 'life sentence' because the licence period restrictions continue for the life of D. The typical tariff period for a single murder in unexceptional circumstances is 15 years' imprisonment.

Despite the perceived position of murder at the apex of criminal law, it remains a problematic and controversial offence. Indeed, the Law Commission has described it as a 'rickety structure set upon shaky foundations'.[4] This is both a criticism of the offence itself, discussed in this chapter, as well as a criticism of its position and definition in the context of the other homicide offences.[5]

5.2 Defining murder

The Homicide Act 1957, the Coroners and Justice Act 2009, and the Corporate Manslaughter and Corporate Homicide Act 2007 have put on a statutory footing several offences and defences within the wider group of homicide offences. Crucially, however, the offence of murder remains a common law offence (ie formed through case precedent).

---

[1] Murder cannot be committed by a corporation or other organisation. See **Chapter 6.4.1** for the possibility of corporate manslaughter.

[2] Murder (Abolition of Death Penalty) Act 1965 marked the end of a mandatory death sentence for all convicted murderers.

[3] Sentencing Code 2020, Sch 21. See Padfield, 'Tariffs in Murder' [2002] Crim LR 192. For recent crticisms of the Sch 21 tariffs, see Roberts and Saunders, 'Sentencing for Murder: The Adverse and Unintended Effects of Schedule 21 to the Criminal Justice Act' [2020] Crim LR 900.

[4] Law Commission, *A New Homicide Act for England and Wales* (Consultation 177, 2005) para 1.4.

[5] Discussed in **Chapter 6**. See also *Smith, Hogan, and Ormerod's Criminal Law* (16th edn, 2021) Chs 12–15.

The definition of murder still quoted widely by the courts derives from a seventeenth-century book by Coke:[6]

> Murder is when a man of sound memory, and of the age of discretion, unlawfully killeth within any country of the realm any reasonable creature *in rerum natura* under the King's peace, with malice aforethought, either expressed by the party or implied by law, so as the party wounded, or hurt, etc die of that wound or hurt, etc within a year and a day after the same.

Despite its continued citation, the archaic and increasingly inaccurate definition contained in this quotation should not be applied straightforwardly in a modern context. Rather, although it establishes authority for the offence of murder, a contemporary translation and clarification of the offence elements is essential.

In modern language, the offence of murder requires D unlawfully to kill another person under the Queen's peace, and to do so intending to kill or cause GBH (serious bodily harm). The elements of murder are set out in **Table 5.1**.

Table 5.1 Murder

	Actus reus	**Mens rea**
Conduct element	Any conduct that causes the result	Voluntary
Circumstance element	V must be a person;	Knowledge
	under the Queen's peace;	Knowledge
	killing must be unlawful	Lack of belief in lawfulness
Result element	Death of V	Intention to kill or cause GBH

This represents the current definition of murder: modernising the language from Coke's definition and recognising important changes within the law. For example, contrary to what was stated by Coke, the modern definition of murder does not include a requirement for V's death to follow 'within a year and a day' of D's conduct. This requirement made some sense historically where a long delay before death would make it almost impossible to demonstrate a causal link from V's death back to D's original conduct. However, with advances in medical science, not only has demonstrating such a causal link become easier, but the likelihood of delay before death has also increased through the use of life-support machines, etc. The rule was abolished by the Law Reform (Year and a Day Rule) Act 1996.[7] The present position is that as long as causation can be established, D may now be liable for murder regardless of the delay between her original conduct and the death of V. The only remaining restriction is that where there is considerable

---

[6] 3 Inst 47.
[7] Yale, 'A Year and a Day in Homicide' (1989) 48 CLJ 202.

delay between D's conduct and V's death (over three years), or where D has already been prosecuted for a non-fatal offence relating to the same incident, the Attorney General must consent to the prosecution for murder.[8]

Despite the seriousness of murder as a crime, it is important to recognise that cases caught within the definition will not always be morally straightforward. As with other offences, where D satisfies the actus reus and mens rea elements she is liable irrespective of her motive.[9] Thus, murder is committed where D kills due to hatred or spite, but it is also committed in more morally ambiguous cases such as so-called 'mercy killings' where D intentionally kills, often with V's consent, in order to relieve V's pain or suffering. The moral diversity of these cases is useful to keep in mind when discussing the precise requirements of the offence. It is also something that we will return to when we consider potential reforms in this area, not least the continued application of a mandatory life sentence to all murder cases (**5.6.1**).

5.3 Actus reus of murder

The actus reus of murder is satisfied where D unlawfully kills another person under the Queen's peace. We discuss each element in turn.

5.3.1 D's conduct

As with other result crimes[10] murder does not specify particular conduct that D must perform (eg shooting, stabbing, etc). Rather, the actus reus is satisfied by *any* conduct that causes the death of a person. Thus, it is necessary to identify some conduct by D, but, as long as it causes V's death, the type of conduct is irrelevant. D may also commit murder by omission, as in *Gibbins and Proctor*, as long as the requirements of omissions liability are satisfied.[11]

Gibbins and Proctor (1918) 13 Cr App R 134

D1 (Gibbins) and his new partner D2 (Proctor) failed to feed D1's 7-year-old child (V), resulting in V's death. D1 and D2 acted with an intention to (at least) cause serious bodily harm to V.

- Crown Court: D1 and D2 convicted for murder.
- Court of Criminal Appeal: conviction upheld on appeal. D1 liable for his omission to feed based on a familial duty owed to V; D2 based on her assumption of a duty (she was in charge of buying food).

5.3.2 Necessary circumstances

The actus reus of murder also requires proof of several circumstances that must be present for D to be liable. In most cases these will be clear, and very little discussion will be required. However, problem cases can arise.

[8] Law Reform (Year and a Day Rule) Act 1996, s2.
[9] The only exception is where D's reasons/motives satisfy the elements of a criminal defence.
[10] For discussion of 'result crimes', see **Chapter 2.4.2**.
[11] See **Chapter 2.6**.

5.3.2.1 Under the Queen's peace

Where soldiers kill alien enemies 'in the heat of war, and in actual exercise thereof',[12] the killing is not under the Queen's peace and is not, therefore, murder. This exception is important, particularly as section 9 of the Offences Against the Person Act 1861 makes any murder or manslaughter committed by a British citizen, *committed on any land outside the UK*, an offence that can be tried and punished in England. It is, however, a narrow exception. Where a soldier kills another, even an alien enemy in a war zone, and it is *not* done in the heat of battle, this will be considered as having been committed under the Queen's peace and D will satisfy the actus reus of murder.[13]

5.3.2.2 Unlawful killing

To say that the killing must be 'unlawful' is simply to stress that it must satisfy all actus reus and mens rea elements, and be done without lawful defence. Thus, for example, where D kills in self-defence, she is not liable for murder. We discuss defences to murder at **5.5**.

 Point to remember . . .

As we will see in **Chapter 14**, some defences do not apply to murder (eg duress and duress of circumstance).

5.3.2.3 V must be a person

For murder, as with other homicide offences; offences against the person; etc, the victim must be a human being. This sounds straightforward, and in the vast majority of cases it will be. However, the status of the victim as a person will occasionally require discussion. This discussion focusses on two questions: when does life as a human being begin? And when does this status end?

A) When does V begin to be a person: An unborn child (foetus) is not a person within the criminal law. Thus, where D kills an unborn child she may commit offences of child destruction or procuring a miscarriage,[14] but she cannot commit murder. In law, V only becomes a person when she is 'fully expelled from the womb' and alive.[15] Whether the umbilical cord and/or afterbirth have been expelled is irrelevant, as long as the whole of the baby's body is removed.[16] This position may be criticised in purely biological terms, the difference between a late-term foetus and a neonate is only (as Simester and Sullivan put it) a matter of location.[17] However, it is a distinction that has rarely troubled the courts.[18] The exclusion of murder from prenatal deaths is also useful to allow for specific offences that can be tailored to the unique issues that arise in this area

---

[12] Hale, *The History of the Pleas of the Crown* (1736) vol I, 443.

[13] Hirst, 'Murder Under the Queen's Peace' [2008] Crim LR 541; Rowe, 'The Criminal Liability of a British Soldier Merely for Participating in the Iraq War' [2010] Crim LR 752.

[14] Infant Life (Preservation) Act 1929, s1 or Offences Against the Person Act 1861, s58.

[15] *Poulton* (1832) 5 C & P 329.

[16] *Reeves* (1839) 9 C & P 25.

[17] Simester et al, *Simester and Sullivan's Criminal Law: Theory and Doctrine* (7th edn, 2019) 389.

[18] The Criminal Law Revision Committee identified the last case where this was directly relevant to have been in 1874: *Handley* (1874) 13 Cox CC 79.

and avoid conflict with legal termination procedures. Despite Article 2 of the European Convention on Human Rights (ECHR) protecting the right to life, the European Court of Human Rights (ECtHR) has left the issue of when life begins to Member States' margin of appreciation.[19]

The focus on birth gives rise to a notable issue: prenatal harms that cause postnatal death. Where D harms a foetus that is subsequently born alive, but then dies as a result of those injuries, D has caused the death of what is a person at the time of death. Courts have long accepted that such cases satisfy the actus reus of murder,[20] although, interestingly, this has not been applied to cases where a mother injures her own foetus through neglect.[21]

Don't be confused . . .

Where prenatal harm causes postnatal death, the actus reus of murder is satisfied. However, mens rea will often be problematic. Where D acts with the intent to injure seriously or kill the foetus, this is not the mens rea for murder (it is not an intent to injure seriously or kill a *person*). Additionally, where D intends to injure seriously or kill the mother, a transfer of malice to the baby is ruled out by the double transaction (from the mother to the foetus to the baby).[22] Murder, as opposed to manslaughter, will only be available in cases of this kind where D intends the foetus to be killed or seriously injured after being born alive. This will be extremely rare.

B) When does life end for the purposes of the offence: Identifying the definitive point where life comes to an end, where V is no longer a person, has become increasingly difficult. There is no authoritative definition of death within the criminal law, but courts will often refer to medical definitions to assist them. In this regard, however, it is clear that death should not always be assumed where V stops breathing, or even where V's heart stops, as such occurrences can, if treated in good time, often be reversed.

The borderline problem becomes acute where V's body can be kept 'alive' by medical techniques despite little or even no chance of recovery. In such cases, V will be considered medically dead at the point of 'brain death' (complete and irreversible non-functioning of the brain stem), and this status has been accepted by the House of Lords in *Bland*.[23] Where V's condition falls short of brain death, for example a persistent vegetative state; a profound and permanent coma; etc, V will not be considered dead and therefore remains a 'person' capable of being murdered.

---

[19] *Vo v France* [2004] 2 FCR 577; O'Donovan, 'Taking a Neutral Stance on the Protection of the Foetus' (2006) 14 Med L Rev 115.

[20] *Senior* (1832) 1 Mood CC 346.

[21] *Knights* (1860) 2 F & F 46. More recently, the Court of Appeal has applied this rule to dismiss an action relating to foetal alcohol syndrome: *CP (A Child) v First-Tier Tribunal* [2014] EWCA Civ 1554.

[22] See discussion of transferred malice and *AG's Reference (No 3 of 1994)* [1997] 3 All ER 936 in **Chapter 4.3.1.1**.

[23] [1993] 1 AC 789.

5.3.3 Causing death

To complete the actus reus of murder, D's act or omission must *cause* V's death. This requires application of the general rules of factual and legal causation already discussed.[24] There is no need to repeat that discussion here.

One issue that should be highlighted, however, is that 'causing death' will include any 'acceleration of death'. For example, the killing of a terminally ill patient or someone who, for whatever reason, has only a short time to live, will still satisfy the actus reus of murder. As death will come to us all at some point, the act of 'causing death' must be logically synonymous with 'accelerating death'. Thus, where a doctor, family member, or anyone else intentionally ends the life of V in order to relieve pain or suffering, believing that V would not have lived long anyway, D still commits murder. This may be perceived as a problem if we believe that so-called 'mercy killing' should be permissible, but the current law offers no exception of this kind.[25]

5.4 Mens rea of murder

Coke's definition describes the mens rea of murder as 'malice aforethought', and this term is still often used. However, malice aforethought is now simply a term of art, with its modern interpretation bearing little resemblance to the original words. For example, it is now clear that D's mens rea need not be 'malicious': that is, need not demonstrate an evil character.[26] Similarly, it need not involve 'aforethought': as long as D has the mens rea when acting, there is no requirement of pre-planning.[27] Rather, at the time of conduct causing death, the current law requires D to have an intention to kill or cause GBH (serious bodily harm).[28]

We have already discussed meaning of the term 'intention',[29] and this definition applies to murder as it does to other offences requiring intention. We will not repeat the detail of that discussion here. D intends to kill or cause GBH where her conduct is carried out in order to bring about that result (direct intent); and/or where her conduct is virtually certain to cause that result, she foresees it as a virtual certainty, and the jury choose to find intention (oblique intent). At one time, the House of Lords expanded the definition of oblique intention in murder to include cases where D did not foresee a virtual certainty, but a reasonable person in D's position would have done so.[30] This created a form of objective intention. However, this no longer represents the law in England and Wales, having been reversed by section 8 of the Criminal Justice Act 1967. The current law defining intention will require *subjective* purpose or *subjective* foresight of a virtual certainty in every case.[31]

---

[24] **Chapter 2.7.**
[25] *Inglis* [2010] EWCA Crim 2637.
[26] eg so-called 'mercy killing' will still constitute murder.
[27] Mitchell, 'Thinking about Murder' (1992) 56 JCL 78.
[28] *Cunningham* [1982] AC 566; *Moloney* [1985] AC 905.
[29] **Chapter 3.4.1.**
[30] *DPP v Smith* [1961] AC 290.
[31] *Woollin* [1999] AC 82.

Don't be confused . . .

As we will see in later chapters, most serious offences require a mens rea of intention or recklessness as to a certain result. For such offences, the divide between intention and recklessness is unproblematic: either will suffice for liability. As murder is only satisfied by an *intention* to kill or cause GBH (recklessness is insufficient), the divide between these mens rea terms becomes very important. This is why most of the cases discussed in **Chapter 3.4.1**, attempting to define intention, were murder cases.

The fact that the mens rea for murder can be satisfied by an intention to cause GBH, as an alternative to an intention to kill, is very important. D acts or omits to act with the intention to cause GBH if she intends, directly or obliquely, to cause serious bodily harm: 'grievous' being given its ordinary meaning of 'serious' or 'really serious'.[32] For example, an intention to break a major bone or severely wound V would amount to an intention to cause GBH.[33] The jury must assess what D was thinking: how much harm was D intending to cause V? Having assessed the degree of harm subjectively intended by D, the jury must then decide whether this is equivalent to the legal definition of (at least) GBH.

Allowing liability for murder where D acts with the intention to cause GBH means that murder is a constructive liability offence. Where D acts with intention to kill, as in **Table 5.2**, there is uncontroversial correspondence between actus reus (causing death) and mens rea (intending to do so).

Table 5.2 Murder and intention to kill

	Actus reus	**Mens rea**
Result element	Death of V	Intention to kill

However, where D acts with intention to cause 'merely' GBH, this does not correspond straightforwardly with the actus reus of causing death. Rather, D's mens rea corresponds with an actus reus of causing GBH, with the additional actus reus element 'causing death' constructing upon this. D is liable for murder on the basis of constructive liability,[34] illustrated in **Table 5.3**.

Table 5.3 Murder and intention to cause GBH

	Actus reus	**Mens rea**
Result element	Death of V	Intention to cause GBH

---

[32] *Bollom* [2003] EWCA Crim 2846.
[33] We discuss this further in **Chapter 7.6** in relation to offences of causing GBH with intent.
[34] Constructive liability is discussed in **Chapter 4.2.1.1**.

The possibility for constructive liability in murder, where D intends to cause GBH, has attracted severe criticism from academics[35] and appeal court judges[36] alike. Such criticism arises because, in these cases, D does not *choose* to kill or perhaps even to risk killing, and therefore arguably lacks the culpability to deserve liability for murder. For example, consider the case of D, a paramilitary, who shoots V in the knee as a punishment for V's disloyalty. D intends to cause GBH, but definitely does not want V to die: D wants V to be a walking deterrent to disloyal members. D is liable for a serious offence against the person.[37] However, where V dies as a result of the shot, for whatever reason, whether it be lack of treatment, infection, etc, D's liability increases to murder and the mandatory life sentence is applied.[38] Under the current law, D satisfies the mens rea for murder even if she has no anticipation that her conduct risks killing V, as long as D intends a certain level of harm that the jury interpret as GBH. This will be discussed further in the context of possible reforms (**5.6.2**), along with the counter-argument that is common to constructive liability: that as soon as D intends any harm her normative position changes and she is legitimately blamed for *all* the consequences that follow.

5.4.1 Other mens rea requirements

As will be noted from **Table 5.1** setting out the offence, the mens rea of murder includes elements beyond an intention to kill or cause GBH. Most importantly, as with all other criminal offences, D can only commit murder if her act or omission causing death was performed voluntarily. Additionally, she must intend or know that what she is killing is a person under the Queen's peace.

 Assessment matters . . .

In most cases, and most problem questions, it will be straightforwardly apparent that D acts voluntarily and she is aware that V is a person, and in these cases discussion of mens rea need not go beyond the required intention to kill or cause GBH. However, where there is uncertainty (eg where a spasm in D's finger causes her to pull the trigger of a gun; or where D shoots at a figure unsure if it is a person; etc) then these elements will require specific discussion.

5.5 Defences to murder

If the actus reus and mens rea elements of murder are satisfied, the next step is to explore the possibility of a defence.

---

[35] Mitchell, 'In Defence of the Correspondence Principle' [1999] Crim LR 195; cf Horder, 'A Critique of the Correspondence Principle in Criminal Law' [1995] Crim LR 795.
[36] *Hyam* [1975] AC 55, see the reasoning of Lord Diplock.
[37] See **Chapter 7.6**.
[38] In theory, if D simply intends to prick V with a pin and V is a haemophiliac, this could lead to liability for murder (whatever D's impression, a reasonable jury are likely to see the intended pin-prick as an intention to cause serious harm to someone with this condition).

5.5.1 General defences

Most of the *general* defences (so called because of their application across multiple offences) will potentially apply to murder, with the notable exception of duress and duress of circumstances. These are fully discussed later in two separate chapters. In **Chapter 13** we discuss denials of offending: D contends that he lacks responsibility for the offence due to some form of mental abnormality, whether internally or externally caused. In **Chapter 14** we discuss the general defences: D contends that her actions were justified or should be excused because she lacked a *viable* choice not to offend. Satisfying the elements of one of these defences will lead to a complete acquittal.[39]

5.5.2 Doctors and the treatment of terminally ill patients

Over a number of years, with the increased use of powerful pain-relieving medication in hospitals, a category of cases has emerged that has put a strain on the law of murder. These cases involve the prescription of pain-relieving drugs to terminally ill patients, where doctors are aware that the patient's life expectancy will be reduced as a side effect. Such practices are very common and relatively uncontroversial in their medical context. However, to the extent that they satisfy the definition of murder, it seems that the avoidance of liability is now best explained as a form of specific defence for medical professionals.

It is important first to understand how the elements of murder can be satisfied in these cases. The doctor satisfies the actus reus of murder because her conduct in prescribing drugs accelerates the patient's death, and as discussed at **5.5.3**, causing death includes doing an act that accelerates death. In terms of mens rea, although the doctor does not *directly* intend to kill or cause GBH because she does not act in order to bring about that result, the shortening of life is a virtually certain consequence of her conduct and her knowledge of this is likely to amount to an *oblique* intention to kill.[40] Thus, the elements of murder are satisfied.

This problem arose in *Adams*, although the solution offered by the court did not rely on criminal defences.

Adams [1957] Crim LR 365

D, a doctor, was charged with murder having 'eased the passing' of several patients including V with strong pain-relieving drugs.

• Crown Court: not guilty. Devlin J directed the jury that there was no special defence for doctors, but that 'he is entitled to do all that is proper and necessary to relieve pain and suffering even if measures he takes may incidentally shorten life'.

---

[39] The only exception being the insanity defence, which leads to the special verdict of 'not guilty by reason of insanity'. This is discussed in **Chapter 13**.

[40] *Woollin* [1998] 4 All ER 103. We may hope that despite D's foresight the jury will choose not to 'find' intention, but this is not certain: see **Chapter 3.4.1.2**. Cf *Moor* (1999, unreported) discussed in [2000] Crim LR 31 and 568.

The principle applied in this case is sometimes referred to as the doctrine of double effect, which holds that intentionally causing a harmful result (eg death) can be morally defensible where it is a side effect of promoting a good end (eg pain relief) as the dominant aim. Crucial to this is Devlin J's focus on the *incidental* shortening of life. The same act completed by another party, for example to hasten the collection of inheritance, or by a doctor where the shortening of life was the main purpose, would lead to conviction.[41] However, the direction and the principle are problematic: it is unclear whether it is actus reus (causation) or mens rea (intention) that is being displaced. It is also unclear how it is displaced: what exactly does it mean to 'incidentally shorten life'?

In line with the result of *Adams*, but moving away from the reasoning of Devlin J, we should now see this exception as a special common law defence. In *Bland*,[42] Lord Goff referred, *obiter*, to:

> the established rule that a doctor may, when caring for a patient who is, for example, dying of cancer, lawfully administer painkilling drugs, despite the fact he knows that an incidental effect of that application will be to abbreviate the patient's life.

Constructed as a defence, the rule may still lack some clarity, but it is able to provide specific protection for doctors within this category of cases. It is also able to do so without distorting the general rules of causation, or relying upon the vagaries of oblique intention.

5.5.3 Partial defences

As well as the complete defences that, if satisfied, will lead to D's acquittal, the law of murder also includes three partial defences. If one of these partial defences is satisfied then D's liability for murder will be reduced to voluntary manslaughter, an offence which still carries a maximum life sentence, but at the discretion of the court rather than as a mandatory sentence. These partial defences are *not* general defences, and apply *only* to the offence of murder.

The three partial defences to murder are:

- **Loss of self-control:** D kills while out of control owing to fear of serious violence or by extremely grave circumstances giving her a justifiable sense of being seriously wronged.[43]

- **Diminished responsibility:** D's recognised medical condition led to an abnormality of mind and substantially impaired her capacity, causing her to kill.[44]

- **Suicide pact:** D kills V in pursuance of an agreement that they will both die together.[45]

Each of the partial defences will be discussed in detail in **Chapter 6**, as their satisfaction will lead to liability for manslaughter.

---

[41] See eg *Cox* (1992) 12 BLMR 38, where the 'defence' did not apply to a doctor who prescribed non-therapeutic drugs with the principal intention of causing death. The charge was one of attempted murder.

[42] [1993] 1 AC 789.

[43] Coroners and Justice Act 2009, s54.

[44] Homicide Act 1957, s2 (as amended by the Coroners and Justice Act 2009, s52).

[45] Homicide Act 1957, s4.

Assessment matters . . .

When considering defences to murder, students often skip straight to discussion of the partial defences. However, remember that these defences will still lead to liability for manslaughter. Therefore, you should always consider the complete defences first. Only if D lacks a complete defence would she want to consider the partial defences.

5.6 Reform

Despite sustained criticism of several aspects of the offence of murder, and despite numerous reform recommendations, the law has remained largely unchanged over the past 50 years.[46] In this section, we provide some additional discussion of the two main areas of criticism identified earlier, and sketch some of the recommendations for reform that have been offered. These relate to the maintenance of the mandatory life sentence and, secondly, the scope of the mens rea for murder. Although the law of homicide seems to have slipped from the current agenda in England and Wales,[47] it is noted that the Scottish Law Commission are currently engaged in a five-year project reviewing the Scottish offences.[48] Though quite different in substance from their English equivalents, it is possible that this will regalvanise reform debates south of the border as well.

5.6.1 Reforming the mandatory life sentence

In order to achieve the partial removal and subsequent abolition of the death penalty,[49] the substitution of a mandatory life sentence of imprisonment was a necessary political compromise.[50] The death penalty could be removed, but there was, and remains, maintenance of the idea that murder as the ultimate crime should be punished with some comparable level of 'ultimate' punishment.

In the majority of cases, the mandatory life sentence does not lead to imprisonment for the rest of the offender's life. However, its terms remain uniquely draconian. Depending upon the circumstances of the murder, the minimum period of imprisonment will be set by the court at between 15 years and a whole-life term: this is known as the tariff period.[51] Importantly, and unlike standard sentences, the tariff period must be served in full before D's release is considered by a parole board. At the end of the tariff, a parole board will then decide whether D should stay in prison because she represents

---

[46] See generally Horder, *Homicide and the Politics of Law Reform* (2012).
[47] The Justice Committee held a one-off evidence session on the law of homicide on 14 September 2016, but things have not moved forward from this point.
[48] Announced as part of the Scottish Law Commission, *Tenth Programme of Law Reform* (2018).
[49] Homicide Act 1957, s5 singled out certain types of murder that continued to attract the death penalty, before abolition through the Murder (Abolition of the Death Penalty) Act 1965.
[50] Wasik, 'Sentencing in Homicide' in Ashworth and Mitchell (eds), *Rethinking English Homicide Law* (2000) 167.
[51] Sentencing Code 2020, Sch 21.

a continued risk to particular persons or to the public, or be released into the community.[52] Even where D is released, this is only a release on a life-long licence: allowing administrative (not judicial) action to call D back into prison where necessary.

Despite the original utility of the mandatory life sentence as a compromise in the abolition of the death penalty, arguments against preservation of the mandatory sentence are overwhelming. Central to this is that the law of murder does not target a single specific 'ultimate' mischief, but is, rather, broad enough to catch conduct across a wide moral spectrum: from cold-blooded serial killers or sexually motivated killers, to the morally ambiguous mercy killing. This is common to most criminal offences, for example there is similar disparity between D who recklessly breaks another's pen and D who intentionally smashes another's computer, and yet both are liable for the same offence of criminal damage.[53] The difference, of course, is that a judge can reflect the moral disparity in criminal damage cases within the court's sentencing discretion from discharge to ten years' imprisonment, supplemented with aggravated forms of the offence.[54] For murder, in contrast, such discretion is removed. Over time, reflecting such criticisms, attitudes towards the mandatory life sentence have hardened academically,[55] judicially,[56] within Parliament,[57] and even among the general public.[58]

However, despite hardening attitudes against the mandatory life sentence, the current political reality is that the sentence is unlikely to be reformed.[59] We have seen this, for example, in the Law Commission's terms of reference relating to its review of murder in 2005 and 2006 where the mandatory sentence was not open for the Commission to consider.[60] In light of this reality, focus has turned to the reform of murder itself and the rules relating to it, the aim being to remove behaviour from the offence that does not warrant the mandatory sentence. Three areas are of particular interest:

- **Narrowing the definition of murder:** This possibility is discussed in the next section.

- **Reforming the partial defences:** Satisfying a partial defence allows D's liability to be mitigated from murder to manslaughter and thereby avoids the mandatory life sentence. We discuss the partial defences in the next chapter.[61]

- **Extenuating circumstances mitigation:** The idea of 'extenuating circumstances' has been introduced in other jurisdictions to allow the mandatory life sentence not to

---

[52] For a useful critique of this process, see Padfield, 'Justifying Indefinite Detention—On What Grounds?' [2016] Crim LR 797.

[53] Criminal Damage Act 1971, s1. Discussed in **Chapter 9.7.**

[54] Criminal Damage Act 1971, s4.

[55] Mitchell, *Murder and Penal Policy* (1990); Mitchell, 'Identifying and Punishing the More Serious Murders' [2016] Crim LR 467.

[56] See eg *Howe* [1987] 1 All ER 771, 781.

[57] House of Lords, Select Committee on Murder and Life Imprisonment (1989) HL Paper 78, paras 108–118: recommending the removal of the mandatory sentence.

[58] Law Commission, *A New Homicide Act for England and Wales?* (Consultation 177, 2005) Appendix A (Mitchell); Mitchell and Roberts, *Public Opinion and Sentencing for Murder* (2010): empirical work finding majority public support for removing the mandatory sentence.

[59] Horder, *Homicide and the Politics of Law Reform* (2012).

[60] Law Commission, *Murder, Manslaughter and Infanticide* (No 304, 2006) para 1.1.

[61] **Chapter 6.2.**

apply for certain exceptional murder cases.[62] However, despite a similar proposal (outlined by John Spencer) being advocated in this country, and even put forward as an amendment to a Bill in the House of Lords in 2009, it has not been adopted.[63] Indeed, this option seems unlikely to gain political traction, as it is perceived as an erosion of the mandatory sentence.

5.6.2 Reforming the mens rea of murder

Debates about the appropriate boundaries of murder have generally focussed on mens rea elements: adapting the mens rea in order to target more effectively those seen as deserving of the label of murderer and, of course, in view of the mandatory life sentence. Three examples provide useful illustration:

A) **Lord Goff:** In a wide-ranging article published in 1988, Lord Goff recommends reforming the mens rea of murder in a manner that would at the same time: (a) *narrow* the current law by removing liability where D intends GBH, as opposed to death, and by narrowing an intention to kill to direct intention only, and also (b) *widen* it by allowing liability where D is 'wickedly reckless' as to death.[64] Goff would narrow the law, excluding those who intend to cause GBH, because he believes such defendants are inappropriately labelled as murderers: 'it seems very strange that a man should be called a murderer even though not only did he not intend to kill the victim, but he may even [in certain cases] have intended that he should not die'.[65] Conversely, Goff would find liability where D is wickedly reckless as to death, a concept borrowed from Scottish criminal law. This would apply where D did not necessarily act with the purpose of killing V, but her actions demonstrated a callous or careless disregard for V's life. To understand these proposals, it is useful to also see the meticulous rebuttal of Goff's approach in the reply article of Glanville Williams.[66]

B) **The Law Commission:** The most recent comprehensive review of murder has come from the Law Commission.[67] The Commission sets out recommendations for a new ladder of homicide offences including first degree murder (punished with a mandatory life sentence); a new offence of second degree murder (punished with a discretionary life sentence); and manslaughter (punished with a discretionary life sentence).[68] The separation of first and second degree murder allows the Commission to narrow the offence of first degree murder and, thereby, the mandatory sentence.

- **First degree murder:** Where D kills (a) with the intention to kill, *or* (b) with the intention to cause serious injury where D was aware that her conduct involved a serious risk of causing death;

---

[62] eg in Israel and the French Penal Code, art 345.

[63] Hansard, HL, 26 October 2009, cols 1008–9.

[64] Goff, 'The Mental Element in the Crime of Murder' (1988) 104 LQR 30.

[65] Ibid, 48. See also Wilson, 'Murder and the Structure of Homicide' in Mitchell and Ashworth (eds), *Rethinking English Homicide Law* (2000).

[66] Williams, 'The Mens Rea of Murder: Leave It Alone' (1989) 105 LQR 387.

[67] Law Commission, *A New Homicide Act for England and Wales?* (Consultation 177, 2005); Law Commission, *Murder, Manslaughter and Infanticide* (No 304, 2006).

[68] See Ashworth, 'Principles, Pragmatism and the Law Commission's Recommendations on Homicide Law Reform' [2007] Crim LR 333.

- **Second degree murder:** Where D kills (a) with the intention to cause serious injury; *or* (b) with the intention to cause injury or fear or risk of injury where D was aware that her conduct involved a serious risk of causing death; *or* (c) cases described in the current law as voluntary manslaughter;[69]
- **Manslaughter:** Cases described under the current law as involuntary manslaughter.[70]

Despite the merits of these recommendations, they have yet to be acted upon by the government and (at the time of writing) appear unlikely to be acted upon.

 Assessment matters . . .

When and if you discuss Law Commission (or any other) recommendations in an essay, remember that they are just that: recommendations. It is very easy to refer to such policies inaccurately as if they represent the current law. Do not fall into this trap.

C) **Alan Norrie:** In a more recent article, Norrie discusses the divergence between legal and social definitions of murder.[71] In view of the Grenfell Tower disaster, Norrie examines the claims of those calling for murder (as opposed to manslaughter) liability. The article focusses on the current law, asking whether and how the law of murder might be interpreted more expansively to meet 'social' demands. In doing so, it provides an important counterbalance to the prevailing reform debate: although we might seek to narrow murder liability to limit the potential unfair application of the mandatory life sentence, such narrowing risks removing a powerful label that remains important within society.

5.7 Eye on assessment

The offence of murder is one of the most commonly used offences within problem scenarios. This is because, not only is the offence important and interesting in its own right, but it is also a useful vehicle through which to focus discussion on several matters. Murder is one of the few offences that is only satisfied by a mens rea of intention as opposed to recklessness; it gives rise to the most difficult issues of causation with most reported causation cases involving murder. Additionally, murder scenarios can involve a wide variety of defences, with the potential application of *both* partial and general defences.

Despite the range of potential issues, however, as with all problem questions it is important to work through the problem/offence methodically in order to discuss liability:

---

[69] Voluntary manslaughter is found where D commits murder, but satisfies the terms of a partial defence. Discussed in **Chapter 6.2**.

[70] Involuntary manslaughter is found where D does not commit murder, but does satisfy the elements of a manslaughter offence. Discussed in **Chapter 6.3**.

[71] Norrie, 'Legal and Social Murder: What's the Difference?' [2018] Crim LR 531.

> **STEP 1 Identify the potential criminal event in the facts**
>
> This is unlikely to take more than a sentence, but it is essential to tell your reader where in the facts you are focussing.

In the context of murder, or other potential homicide offences, Step 1 simply requires you to point out a death in the facts that may be connected with D. For example, 'We will first examine the potential liability of Lucy for the death of Tom'.

> **STEP 2 Identify the potential offence**
>
> Having identified the facts (eg D potentially killing V), you must now identify the offence you are going to apply. Usually, this means identifying the most serious offence that D might have committed.

Whenever there is a death in a problem question that may have been caused by D you should *always* begin with a consideration of murder, even if it is reasonably clear that an element within the offence will not be satisfied.[72] If murder is satisfied, you can then move to a discussion of defences, both full and partial. If not, depending upon which elements of murder are missing, this will lead you to the consideration of an alternative offence.

> **STEP 3 Applying the offence to the facts**
>
> Actus reus: What does the offence require? Did D do it?
>
> Mens rea: What does the offence require? Did D possess it?
>
> Remember, to be liable for the offence, every element of the actus reus and mens rea must be satisfied. Where there is doubt, in law or in fact, highlight and discuss areas of likely dispute between prosecution and defence. Also, if the question asks you to engage critically with the law as you apply it, take particular care to include evaluation of the law.

A) Actus reus: When discussing the actus reus of murder you are looking for an act or omission that has caused V's death. This will involve the standard rules of causation and, where necessary, omissions liability. If D satisfies the actus reus of murder, continue to discuss mens rea.

If D does not satisfy every element of the actus reus she will not be liable for murder or any other homicide offence. If the question only asks you to consider liability for murder or homicide offences, then this is the end of the story: no liability. However, if the question asks you to consider D's liability more generally, having concluded that she did not cause death, your next question will be whether she has criminally contributed to the death. For example, has she assisted, encouraged, or caused another person to kill V

---

[72] The only exception being where the problem question tells you to *only* discuss some other offence.

(leading to potential liability as a secondary party[73]); or has she assisted or encouraged V to kill herself (leading to potential liability for assisting or encouraging suicide[74])?

B) **Mens rea:** The mens rea of murder is only satisfied where D acts or omits to act with the intention (direct or oblique) that her conduct will cause death or GBH (serious bodily harm). It is useful to think of this as a tick-box exercise, with any one of four states of mind sufficient, illustrated in **Table 5.4**.

Table 5.4 Mens rea for murder

Intention . . .	to cause death . . .	or to cause GBH
Direct	1	2
Oblique	3	4

When applying the mens rea for murder to problem facts, it is useful to follow this ordering. If you find that D has acted with the direct intention to cause death (1), then there is no need to discuss the GBH rule in any detail and certainly no need to discuss the complex rules of oblique intention.[75] If it is necessary to discuss oblique intention as, for example, where D does not want to harm V at all, but recognises that her actions are extremely likely to do so, it is good practice to lead your reader to that point: tell the reader (drawing on the facts of the problem) why you think a court would be unlikely to find a direct intention. If D satisfies the mens rea for murder by one of these four means then the offence is complete; continue to discuss defences.

If D lacks mens rea then she will not be liable for murder. If the question asks you to consider liability for murder only then this is the end of the story: no liability. However, where the question is more general and asks you to consider liability for homicide offences, or all potential offences, then, assuming the actus reus was satisfied, you will now move to consider potential liability of an offence of involuntary manslaughter. These offences require the same actus reus as murder, but are much less restrictive in terms of mens rea.[76]

STEP 4 Consider defences

The word 'consider' here is important, as you should not discuss every defence for every question. Rather, think whether there are any defences that *could* potentially apply. If there are, discuss those only.

---

[73] See **Chapter 12**.
[74] See **Chapter 11**.
[75] This approach, only discussing oblique intention where necessary, is described by Lord Bridge as a 'golden rule' in *Moloney* [1985] AC 905, 926.
[76] See **Chapter 6.3**.

When discussing defences, always begin with the complete defences as these usually lead to a complete acquittal.[77] Remember that the defences of duress and duress of circumstances do not apply to murder. If none of the complete defences applies, or there is some doubt over their application, also continue to discuss the partial defences.[78]

STEP 5 Conclude

This is usually a single sentence either saying that it is likely that D has committed the offence, or saying that it is not likely because an offence element is not satisfied or because a defence is likely to apply. It is not often that you will be able to say categorically whether or not D has committed the offence, so it is usually best to conclude in terms of what is more 'likely'.

STEP 6 Loop

Go back up to STEP 1, identifying the next potential criminal event. Continue until you have discussed all the relevant potentially criminal events.

 ONLINE RESOURCES

www.oup.com/he/child-ormerod4e

This chapter is accompanied by a selection of online resources to help you with this topic, including:

- **Self-test questions** and **scenario questions**
- **Videos** from the authors
- **Audio introduction** to the topic
- **Chapter summary sheet**
- Two **sample examination questions** with answer guidance
- **Further reading and weblinks**

Also available on the online resources are:

- A selection of **videos** from the authors containing general advice on problem questions and essay questions
- **Legal updates**

---

[77] See **Chapters 13–14**.
[78] See **Chapter 6.2**.

6
Manslaughter

6.1 Introduction

As with murder, manslaughter is a common law homicide offence: an offence with an actus reus of unlawful conduct causing the death of a person. The scope of the offence is much wider than for murder, however, covering almost all unlawful killings that fall short of murder. The sentencing options for manslaughter are also considerably wider than those for murder: with murder, the judge must pass a *mandatory* life sentence; with manslaughter, the judge has discretion up to a *maximum* of life imprisonment.[1] As the types of conduct and fault caught within the offence of manslaughter can differ greatly

---

[1] Consistency in such sentencing discretion is managed through sentencing guidelines issued by the Sentencing Council.

in terms of blameworthiness, sentencing discretion allows the court to reflect those differences more effectively at the sentencing stage.

Although manslaughter is a single offence label at common law, one of its complexities lies in the fact that it can be committed in a variety of ways. The different forms of manslaughter are separated into two distinct categories. In the first category (known as 'voluntary manslaughter'), D satisfies both the actus reus and the mens rea of murder, but also fulfils the elements of a partial defence that reduces her liability to manslaughter. In the second category (known as 'involuntary manslaughter'), D does not satisfy the mens rea for murder, but becomes liable for manslaughter because her conduct and mental state satisfy the elements of a lesser involuntary manslaughter offence. Thus, voluntary manslaughter involves a *partial defence* to murder, whereas involuntary manslaughter involves a separate *offence*.

 Assessment matters...

When applying the law to a problem question, begin by considering liability for murder. Whether the elements of murder are satisfied or not will then lead to a discussion of the appropriate category of manslaughter. We discuss this further when considering assessments (**6.6**).

The structure of homicide offences is illustrated in **Figure 6.1**.

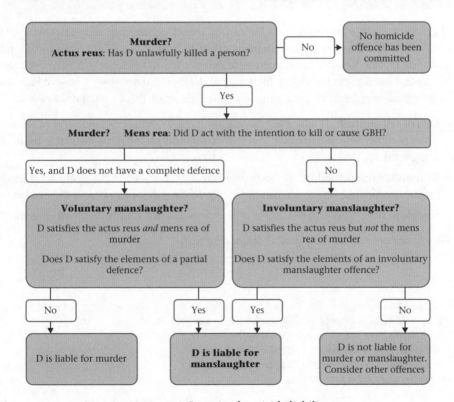

Figure 6.1 Locating homicide liability

Don't be confused . . .

The categories of voluntary and involuntary manslaughter mark an important distinction between the two routes to liability for manslaughter. However, do not be misled, the labels 'voluntary' and 'involuntary' are simply terms of art. The distinction between the two categories has nothing to do with the voluntariness or otherwise of D's conduct. Indeed, we have already discussed the fact that all offences require voluntary conduct,[2] and so-called involuntary manslaughter is no different.

Although murder and manslaughter are the only homicide offences at common law, separate statutory homicide offences have been created, particularly in recent years, to address perceived weaknesses with the common law. Some of these have employed the term manslaughter (eg corporate manslaughter[3]), whereas others have avoided it (eg causing death by dangerous driving[4]). There are also offences that apply to the killing of a foetus as opposed to a legal 'person' (eg child destruction[5]). Each of these offences exists outside the common law definitions of murder and manslaughter. We will discuss these bespoke offences at **6.4**. However, we begin with a discussion of the core common law offence of manslaughter, and the categories of voluntary and involuntary manslaughter.

6.2 Voluntary manslaughter

The first category of manslaughter (voluntary manslaughter) can only arise where D satisfies *both* the actus reus and the mens rea of murder. After this is established, and assuming that D does not have a complete defence (eg self-defence[6]), it then becomes relevant to discuss the possibility for a partial defence: a defence that may reduce D's liability from murder to voluntary manslaughter. There are three partial defences:

- **Loss of self-control:** D kills while having lost her self-control owing to fear of serious violence or because of extremely grave circumstances giving her a justifiable sense of being seriously wronged.[7]

- **Diminished responsibility:** D's recognised medical condition led to an abnormality of mental functioning which substantially impaired her capacity and caused her to kill.[8]

- Suicide pact: D kills V in pursuance of an agreement that they will both die together.[9]

We will discuss each of these partial defences in turn.

---

[2] **Chapter 3.3**.
[3] Corporate Manslaughter and Corporate Homicide Act 2007, s1.
[4] Road Traffic Act 1988, s1 (as substituted by the Road Traffic Act 1991, s1).
[5] Infant Life (Preservation) Act 1929, s1.
[6] These defences are discussed in **Chapters 13** and **14**.
[7] Coroners and Justice Act 2009, s54.
[8] Homicide Act 1957, s2.
[9] Ibid, s4.

Assessment matters . . .

The partial defences are *only* defences to murder and should not therefore be discussed or applied in the context of any other crime. In practical terms, it can be useful to think of them as mechanisms for avoiding the mandatory sentence for murder, because if the defence is satisfied it will mitigate D's offence to manslaughter and thereby allow the court discretion in sentencing.

6.2.1 Loss of self-control

The partial defence to murder of 'loss of self-control' (LOC) is defined in sections 54 and 55 of the Coroners and Justice Act 2009 (C&JA 2009).[10] The basic rationale of the partial defence is that where D kills with the intention required for murder, D's level of culpability is lower when she does so in circumstances of justified anger or acute fear, and is (in some sense) overwhelmed by a violent passion likely to have similarly affected others in her position. Paradigm examples, where the defence is intended to apply, include cases where D kills V upon discovering V abusing D's child; or where D reacts to personal bullying or abuse by killing, in circumstances where the complete defence of self-defence does not apply.

The statutory defence represents a codification and substantial reform of the previous common law partial defence of provocation (abolished by the C&JA 2009, s56).[11] Despite relative clarity within core examples, the development of the defence of provocation at common law was characterised by uncertainty and perceived unfairness. This uncertainty was often compounded by inconsistent interpretations within the appellate courts.[12] Therefore, following a number of Law Commission papers and recommendations,[13] the new partial defence of LOC was created.

 Assessment matters . . .

When discussing and evaluating the LOC defence, it can be useful to refer to pre-C&JA 2009 cases and Law Commission material. Indeed, we will do so in this chapter. However, although useful for comparison and evaluation purposes within essay-style assessments, take care *not* to present pre-C&JA 2009 cases as current legal authorities, and avoid them altogether when applying the current law in problem questions.[14]

---

[10] Norrie, 'The Coroners and Justice Act 2009—Partial Defences to Murder (1) Loss of Control' [2010] Crim LR 275; *Smith, Hogan, and Ormerod's Criminal Law* (16th edn, 2021) 13.1. A useful summary of the current law is also provided in the recent case *Goodwin* [2018] EWCA Crim 2287.

[11] For a detailed discussion of the old common law defence of provocation, see Ormerod, *Smith and Hogan's Criminal Law* (12th edn, 2008) Ch15. See also Horder, *Provocation and Responsibility* (1992).

[12] For a useful summary of these problems, see Law Commission, *Partial Defences to Murder* (Consultation 173, 2003) Part 4.

[13] Law Commission, *Partial Defences to Murder* (Consultation 173, 2003); *Partial Defences to Murder* (No 290, 2004); *A New Homicide Act for England and Wales* (Consultation 177, 2005); *Murder, Manslaughter and Infanticide* (No 304, 2006).

[14] *Gurpinar* [2015] EWCA Crim 178, [4] and [17].

The current LOC partial defence is defined, principally, within section 54 of the C&JA 2009.

> 54(1) Where a person ('D') kills or is a party to the killing of another ('V'), D is not to be convicted of murder if—
>
> > (a) D's acts and omissions in doing or being a party to the killing resulted from D's loss of self-control,
> >
> > (b) the loss of self-control had a qualifying trigger, and
> >
> > (c) a person of D's sex and age, with a normal degree of tolerance and self-restraint and in the circumstances of D, might have reacted in the same or in a similar way to D . . .
>
> (7) A person who, but for this section, would be liable to be convicted of murder is liable instead to be convicted of manslaughter.

In line with section 54(1), the LOC partial defence is made up of three elements, set out in **Table 6.1**. All three must be satisfied for the defence to apply.

Table 6.1 Partial defence of LOC

A) D's role in the killing must have resulted from a loss of self-control

B) D's loss of self-control must have been caused by a qualifying trigger:
   i) a fear of serious violence from V against D or another, *or*
   ii) a thing or things done or said (or both) which constituted circumstances of an extremely grave character, *and* caused D to have a justifiable sense of being seriously wronged

C) A hypothetical person, of D's age and sex, might have reacted in the same way

Where an issue of LOC arises,[15] the legal burden is on the prosecution to prove beyond reasonable doubt that one or more of these elements is absent. If the prosecution are unable to disprove the defence, then D will be liable for manslaughter and not for murder.

 Don't be confused . . .

Although we are again speaking of 'elements', the terms actus reus and mens rea are not applicable to defences. This is because, when discussing the elements of a defence, as opposed to the elements of an offence, we are focussing on factors that make D's conduct less blameworthy.

We will explore each element of the partial defence in turn. However, first we consider an important qualifier to the defence: D's conduct must not be motivated by a considered desire for revenge.

[15] The defence will only be left to the jury (become an issue for their determination) where the judge is satisfied that there is sufficient evidence that a reasonable jury may find every one of the defence elements satisfied. Coroners and Justice Act 2009, s54(6); *Martin* [2017] EWCA Crim 1359; *Gurpinar* [2015] EWCA Crim 178. If there is no sufficient evidence the defence must not be left to the jury: *Islam* [2019] EWCA Crim 2419.

6.2.1.1 Exclusion: D must not act in a considered desire for revenge

Section 54(4) excludes the defence where D acts in a considered desire for revenge. In many cases, such a 'considered' desire will be evidence that D did not lose her self-control and so D will also lack a vital element of the defence. However, crucially, even if D satisfies the elements of the defence, the defence will not be available and D will be liable for murder if she acted in a considered desire for revenge. For example, D kills V following a verbal attack by V, giving D a justifiable sense of being seriously wronged. Even where D is out of control at the moment of causing death, if the attack was 'thought about and considered' in advance, D will still be excluded from the defence.[16] This exclusion has been seen as vital to prevent the defence being used inappropriately by revenge killers.

The exclusion, however, can also cause problems. A significant criticism of the pre-C&JA 2009 defence of provocation was that it failed to provide a partial defence to victims of abuse who killed their abusers. Particularly in the context of abused women, such defendants will not generally react on impulse, but may be driven to kill over a period of time, and choose to kill at a time when they do not endanger themselves or their children (eg when V is asleep).[17] The exclusion within the current law provides a significant hurdle for defendants of this kind trying to rely on the LOC partial defence.[18]

Point to remember . . .

It is useful to begin a discussion of the LOC defence with this exclusion because, when it applies, there is no need to move on to a discussion of the defence elements.

6.2.1.2 Element 1: D must have lost self-control

The first element of the partial defence, and perhaps its central feature, is the requirement that D's conduct (which caused V's death) must have resulted from a lack of self-control. This is a *subjective* requirement: we ask whether D herself lost self-control; it is irrelevant (for this element) whether a reasonable person in D's position would have done so or not.

There is a problem, however, in knowing exactly what the law means by 'a loss of self-control', and the term is not defined in the 2009 Act. Loss of self-control should not be interpreted too strictly by isolating it to cases where D fully lacks control over her physical bodily movement: such cases are already catered for within the *complete* defence of insanity, or a claim of automatism.[19] However, we must also avoid adopting an interpretation that applies too widely, and it is clear that a loss of self-control is not synonymous with simple panic or fear.[20] As the Court of Appeal accepted in *Jewell*, the term should be interpreted to require extreme emotion and/or a loss of rationality.[21] The court, adopting the wording of the 13th edition of *Smith and Hogan's Criminal Law*, defined loss

---

[16] See *Evans* [2012] EWCA Crim 2.

[17] Dressler, 'Battered Women Who Kill Their Sleeping Tormentors' and Horder, 'Killing the Passive Abuser: A Theoretical Defence' in Shute and Simester (eds), *Criminal Law Theory* (2002).

[18] Withey, 'Loss of Control, Loss of Opportunity?' [2011] Crim LR 263.

[19] See **Chapters 13** and **14**. Sorial, 'Anger, Provocation and Loss of Self-Control: What Does "Losing It" Really Mean?' (2019) 13 CrimL&P 247.

[20] *Martin* [2017] EWCA Crim 1359, [47].

[21] [2014] EWCA Crim 414.

of self-control as the 'loss of the ability to act in accordance with considered judgement or a loss of normal powers of reasoning'.[22] In this manner, a loss of self-control is not a claim that D lacked the mens rea for murder, but rather, it is an explanation why she had it.

Under the pre-C&JA 2009 defence of provocation, there was a further requirement that D's loss of self-control be 'sudden and temporary'. *This is no longer the case.* The old requirement of a sudden and temporary loss of self-control was heavily criticised for its perceived gender bias: whilst men are more likely to react immediately to provocation, women, although similarly affected, may react later after a slow-burn period. This was particularly evident in cases where female victims of domestic abuse were denied the partial defence having killed their abuser, not because they were acting for revenge or in circumstances of rational control, but because they killed at a time they were not facing an immediate threat (ie when it was safe for them to do so).[23] Because the 'sudden and temporary' requirement has been removed from the defence, there is greater potential for slow-burn defendants to be able to satisfy the test. However, it remains uncertain whether in practice they will succeed. Although there is no 'sudden and temporary' condition within the current law, it is difficult to make sense of what the loss of self-control requirement means if it is not understood in its ordinary sense (ie a 'rush of blood' or 'emotional surge') and without taking account of the time delay between provocation and reaction: a long delay implies that the trigger has not caused a loss of self-control.[24] Indeed, we see this to a certain extent in the case of *Jewell*.

 Jewell [2014] EWCA Crim 414

D killed V, a workmate, after an extended period of perceived intimidation by V. D gave evidence that he was unable to sleep in the preceding days, and was gradually 'shutting down' before he acted to kill, describing his final acts as having been done in a dream-like state. D was charged with murder.

- Crown Court: guilty of murder. LOC was not left to the jury, with the judge finding no basis for the defence.
- Court of Appeal: conviction upheld on appeal. The planning that preceded the killing undermined a claim of loss of self-control.

The approach taken in *Jewell* confirms that the requirement of loss of self-control will remain a significant hurdle for those wishing to make use of the defence, particularly in the most difficult cases such as those involving abused women. For example, if D kills her partner following domestic abuse, she may not have done so in a manic/rush

---

[22] Per Rafferty LJ at [23]. It should be noted that the Lord Chief Justice declined to endorse this approach in *Gurpinar* [2015] EWCA Crim 178, leaving the point for future consideration (at [19]).

[23] Exemplified in *Ahluwalia* [1992] 4 All ER 889 (pre-C&JA 2009): D killed her husband after years of domestic abuse, but was denied the partial defence because the killing did not result from a sudden event (V was asleep at the time). For a discussion of the law after *Ahluwalia*, but pre-C&JA 2009, see Wells, 'Battered Women Syndrome and Defences to Homicide: Where Now?' (1994) 14 LS 266.

[24] This is recognised in the 2009 Act's Explanatory Notes, para 337 and in parliamentary debates prior to reform.

of blood-type manner, but she may have felt, as a result of the abuse, that she lacked control in the sense of seeing no alternative options to protect herself. Interpreting the definition of loss of self-control in this expansive manner has an obvious appeal in the context of people who kill their abusers, and even perhaps for so-called mercy killers who are driven to kill their loved ones believing it is the only way they can assist them.[25] However, as we see in *Jewell*, it is unlikely that such an expansion will find favour within the current law.[26]

6.2.1.3 Element 2: there must be a qualifying trigger

D's loss of self-control must have been caused by a 'qualifying trigger'. Where D loses self-control and kills in the absence of such a trigger, the LOC defence will not apply. Section 55 of the 2009 Act sets out two qualifying triggers for the defence: a fear of serious violence, and/or a sense of being seriously wronged by things said or done. Although each trigger provides a separate, alternative route into the defence, many cases will involve a combination of the two.[27]

A) Fear of serious violence from V (s55(3)): The first qualifying trigger arises where D loses self-control in fear of serious violence against herself or another identified person (eg her child). This is a *subjective* requirement: D must react to a genuine fear, and it must be a fear of *serious* violence, but this fear need not be based on a correct assessment of the facts (ie there does not need to be an actual threat) and D's fear need not be reasonable (ie a reasonable person in D's position may have realised there was no need to fear). This trigger, which did not feature in the common law provocation defence, is partly designed to remove gender bias from the defence. It extends qualifying triggers from classically masculine responses to verbal or physical affronts, to include reactions to fear of serious violence. This trigger is intended to be employed, for example, in the context of abused women who kill their abusers in fear of future violence.

It is useful to consider how this trigger (and the LOC *partial* defence more generally) will operate alongside the *complete* defence of self-defence.[28] Of course, in cases where D might raise self-defence then this will be her priority: successfully pleading self-defence will result in acquittal. However, where D kills in fear of serious violence and self-defence is not available (eg because the threat to D from V was not imminent; or because the force used was unreasonably excessive; etc) then the partial defence of LOC may provide a useful safety net, reducing D's liability to manslaughter.[29]

---

[25] *Cocker* [1989] Crim LR 740 (pre-C&JA 2009): a tragic case in which D's hesitation when killing his terminally ill wife demonstrated that he was not out of control, and thus outside the provocation defence.

[26] The current uncertainty as to the definition of 'loss of self-control' was discussed in *Gurpinar* [2015] EWCA Crim 178, but the court declined to provide further guidance.

[27] Coroners and Justice Act, s55(5); *Dawes* [2013] EWCA Crim 322, [56].

[28] Self-defence is discussed in **Chapter 14.5**.

[29] LOC is not, however, an *automatic* back-up to self-defence, and will not be put to the jury unless there is evidence of each of its elements: *Martin* [2017] EWCA Crim 1359.

Extra detail . . .

Whether D fears violence is a subjective question that does not rely on reasonableness. However, where that belief is unreasonable and only arises as a result of voluntary intoxication, it is unclear whether this would qualify as a trigger under the current law. Subjective requirements in self-defence, for example, apply an exception in relation to beliefs formed from voluntary intoxication, not allowing such beliefs to satisfy the defence.[30] However, in line with the old common law of provocation,[31] it is contended that even intoxicated beliefs should be sufficient (should not be excluded) in the context of the LOC defence as a *partial* defence to murder.

The 'fear of serious violence' trigger has an important qualification set out in section 55(6) (a): it will not apply where D has consciously caused the conditions of her own defence. D causes the conditions of her own defence, in this context, where she has incited V to act (causing D to fear) in order to have an excuse to use violence against V. This would be the case, for example, where D provokes V to punch her, intending to incite V into an attack in order to kill V and rely on the partial defence. Blocking the defence in these cases is an important restriction, but will only apply where D has *purposively* manipulated the circumstances. Where D acts in a manner that is likely to provoke violence, but is not doing so consciously in order to gain an excuse to react violently, then the defence may still operate. This interpretation was confirmed in *Dawes and Others*.

 Dawes and Others [2013] EWCA Crim 322

D discovered his estranged wife asleep with another man (V), and stabbed V with a kitchen knife, causing death. D was charged with murder and raised the defence of self-defence.

- Crown Court: guilty of murder. The jury did not accept the defence of self-defence, and the judge refused to allow the partial LOC defence to go to the jury because: (a) if D did kill in reaction to an attack from V then this only happened because D had provoked the attack; and (b) there was no evidence of a loss of self-control; D was acting in an angry but controlled manner.
- Court of Appeal: as part of a combined appeal with two other cases, Dawes's conviction was upheld. Importantly, the court clarified that the Crown Court had been wrong on point (a): although D may have provoked the attack from V, this will only undermine a LOC defence where it is done consciously in order to provide a defence for retaliatory violence. That was not the case here. However, the Crown Court was still correct not to leave LOC to the jury on the basis of point (b).

B) A sense of being seriously wronged by things said or done (s55(4)): The second qualifying trigger arises where D loses self-control as a result of a 'justifiable sense of being seriously wronged' by 'things said or done' (not necessarily by V[32]) that were of an 'extremely grave character'. This trigger requires D to identify specific actions or comments which caused the loss of self-control, with mere circumstances (eg losing money on the stock market, or a farmer losing her crops to flood) being insufficient.[33]

---

[30] See discussion of self-defence in **Chapter 14.5**.
[31] *Letenock* (1917) 12 Cr App R 221.
[32] eg *Davies* [1975] QB 691 (pre-C&JA 2009): D killed his wife after being provoked by her lover.
[33] *Acott* [1997] 2 Cr App R 94 (pre-C&JA 2009).

This trigger is partly *subjective* (D must personally feel seriously wronged) and partly *objective* (the feeling of wrong must be objectively justifiable, and the circumstances must be objectively grave).

The inclusion of objective requirements within this trigger, new to the C&JA 2009, was designed to prevent the partial defence being used (or even raised[34]) in circumstances where D is provoked by trivial events (eg a crying baby[35] or a poorly cooked steak[36]), or by events that are only grave for D because of something objectionable about her character (eg a white supremacist provoked by a lack of deference from V, a black man[37]). In such cases, it is clear that a trivial event is not one of an 'extremely grave character', and a racist perception can never result in a '*justifiable* sense of being seriously wronged'. There is a useful discussion of this in *Dawes and Others*, concerning the linked appeal of Barry Bowyer.

 Dawes and Others [2013] EWCA Crim 322

Bowyer (D) and V were both romantically involved with the same woman (X). D broke into V's house to steal items to sell. V returned home, found D, and attacked and insulted him. D retaliated, killing V. D was charged with murder.

- Crown Court: guilty of murder. The trial judge allowed the LOC defence to go to the jury, but they did not accept it.
- Court of Appeal: as part of a combined appeal with two other cases, Bowyer's conviction was upheld. The court confirmed the accuracy of the trial judge's direction on LOC, but also stated that the judge should not have left the defence to the jury at all. On the issue of the qualifying trigger, the court stated that 'it is absurd to suggest that the entirely understandable response of the deceased to finding a burglar in his home [ie attacking and insulting D] provided the appellant with the remotest beginnings of a basis for suggesting that he had a justifiable sense of being wronged, let alone seriously wronged' [66].

The objective standards within this trigger are useful to exclude cases of this kind. And the appellate courts have been clear that trial judges should take this role seriously, evaluating the evidence rigorously before it is left to the jury.[38] However, the terms used ('extremely grave'; 'justifiable sense'; 'seriously wronged') are regrettably vague for such an important defence element. This results in considerable leeway for judges and juries when applying the law, and through this, the potential for inconsistency.[39]

---

[34] A judge will not allow the defence to go to the jury unless there is sufficient evidence upon which it might be accepted. Section 54(6); and **6.2.1**.

[35] *Doughty* (1986) 83 Cr App R 319 (pre-C&JA 2009).

[36] Example from Law Commission, *Murder, Manslaughter and Infanticide* (No 304, 2006) para 1.47.

[37] The Commission, and government, were similarly keen to exclude so-called honour killings: eg where D kills his daughter because she has had a sexual relationship before marriage. *Mohammed* [2005] EWCA Crim 1880 (pre-C&JA 2009).

[38] *Gurpinar* [2015] EWCA Crim 178, [12]–[14]. Where the LOC defence is withdrawn by a trial judge following an appropriate examination, the Court of Appeal will be reluctant to overturn that decision: *McDonald* [2016] EWCA Crim 1529.

[39] Withey, 'Loss of Control, Loss of Opportunity?' [2011] Crim LR 263, 271–274; Storey, 'Loss of Control: "Sufficient Evidence" (Again)' (2015) 79 JCL 154.

Two exclusions apply to this trigger. First, as with the fear of serious violence trigger, D cannot rely on things said or done where she has incited them in order to use violence in response.[40] For example, if D encourages V to shout abuse at her so that she (D) has an excuse to react violently, the defence will not be available.

Additionally, section 55(6)(c) specifically excludes things said or done constituting 'sexual infidelity'. This exclusion was added by the government to send a clear message that killing in response to sexual infidelity should never be sufficient to ground a defence to murder, as it had in a number of pre-C&JA 2009 Act provocation cases.[41] However, the exclusion has been highly controversial.[42] Criticism of the exclusion has focussed on the principle itself: why should sexual infidelity be singled out for exclusion among the many reasons for a violent loss of control, particularly as LOC is only a partial defence? More damagingly, criticism has also focussed on the coherence of the exclusion: the lack of a definition of 'sexual infidelity' (eg does fidelity assume a certain status of relationship between D and V?); the potential for mixed issues (eg where D discovers her husband sexually abusing their daughter); the ambiguous drafting of things said or done that 'constituted' sexual infidelity (eg would this include V telling D that she planned to be unfaithful in the future?); and so on. These problems were discussed by the Court of Appeal in *Clinton*.

 Clinton [2012] EWCA Crim 2

D killed his wife following an argument in which she informed him that she was having an affair; that she had had sexual intercourse with a number of other men during their marriage; and she taunted him about his previous failed attempts to commit suicide. D accepted that he had completed the elements of murder, but claimed a LOC defence.

- Crown Court: guilty of murder. LOC was withdrawn from the jury because of the sexual infidelity exclusion.

- Court of Appeal: appeal allowed, and retrial ordered. Where sexual infidelity is not the sole trigger said or done (as here), it should be allowed to go to the jury alongside all other factors.

In a well-reasoned judgment, the court in *Clinton* exposed the poor drafting of the exclusion, and revealed that for coherence it could not apply in the manner that many had expected.[43] Where the sole trigger relied on by D is something said or done which amounts to sexual infidelity, then this will not apply as a qualifying trigger. However, whenever there are additional potential triggers, as will invariably be the case in complex real-world relationships, then sexual infidelity will *not* be excluded from those other factors when they are considered by the jury, with a cumulative approach employed. Therefore, in most cases involving sexual infidelity, the courts are likely to focus more on the general objective standards for exclusion rather than the specific terms of section 55(6)(c).

[40] Coroners and Justice Act, s55(6)(b); *Dawes* [2013] EWCA Crim 322, [56].
[41] Hansard, HC, 9 November 2009, col 82.
[42] Reed and Wake, 'Sexual Infidelity Killings' in Reed and Bohlander (eds), *Loss of Control and Diminished Responsibility: Domestic, Comparative and International Perspectives* (2011) 117.
[43] Morgan, 'Loss of Self-Control: Back to the Good Old Days' (2013) 77 JCL 119.

Extra detail . . .

Although D must have been provoked, there is no requirement that this was by V. For example, D may be taunted by X about the behaviour of V, causing D to lose control and kill V. Equally, if D loses control and attempts to kill X, but misses and kills V, D's defence may transfer to the killing of V in a manner similar to transferred malice.[44]

6.2.1.4 Element 3: a person of normal tolerance and self-restraint might have reacted similarly

The third and final element within the LOC partial defence is that D's reaction to the qualifying trigger must have been *objectively* understandable in the sense that 'a person of D's age and sex, with a normal degree of tolerance and self-restraint, and in the circumstances of D, might have reacted in the same or in a similar way to D'.[45] This element is core to the rationale of the LOC defence: it is not simply that D has a good reason for losing self-control and killing, it is also that anybody might have reacted as she did in the same circumstances. This element is necessary to show that D's offence was, at least partially, not a reflection of an evil character. We are not saying that D acted correctly, but we can understand and partially excuse D's conduct on the basis that, as the old adage goes, 'there but for the grace of God go I'.

Despite the importance of the objective test, there remains some uncertainty about the precise standard against which D's conduct should be measured (ie which of D's characteristics can be considered within the normal person test?). We could measure D's conduct against the standard of a normal adult, but this would be unfair to younger defendants who do not have the same capacity for tolerance and self-restraint.[46] This is why section 54(1)(c) explicitly allows for D's age and sex to be taken into account: the question is not whether the generic normal person might have reacted as D did, but whether someone of D's age and sex might have done so.

 Extra detail . . .

Taking account of 'age' seems sensible: it is logical that we might expect a higher degree of tolerance and self-restraint from an older person, and to hold a child to an adult standard would seem unfair. However, the inclusion of 'sex' seems to be an odd legacy from the pre-C&JA 2009 common law, as there is no evidence that men and women have different levels of 'normal' tolerance or self-restraint.[47]

---

44 *Gross* (1913) 23 Cox CC 445 (pre-C&JA 2009): D was provoked by her husband X, shot at him, but missed and hit V. D could use the partial defence in relation to the killing of V. Transferred malice was discussed in **Chapter 4.3.1**.

45 Coroners and Justice Act, s54(1)(c).

46 *Camplin* [1978] AC 705 (pre-C&JA 2009): recognising this in a case where D (a 15-year-old boy) killed V after being raped and then mocked by his rapist.

47 Its maintenance within the C&JA 2009 may even be harmful. See Cobb and Gausden, 'Feminism, "Typical" Women and Losing Control' in Reed and Bohlander (eds), *Loss of Control and Diminished Responsibility* (2011).

Having accepted qualifications to the 'normal person' standard in age and sex, the next question is how and when should a line be drawn: which *other* characteristics of D can (or cannot) be taken into account? This question caused significant difficulties for the pre-C&JA 2009 common law, with case law diverging to various extremes before the law was clarified to take account of age and sex only.[48] The C&JA 2009 goes beyond the old common law position because section 54(1)(c) makes reference, in addition to age and sex, to 'the circumstances of D'. But in order to know which circumstances, we must look to further detail in section 54(3) which defines 'the circumstances of D' as:

> all of D's circumstances other than those whose only relevance to D's conduct is that they bear on D's general capacity for tolerance and self-restraint.

The qualification here is quite subtle, but vitally important. It requires us to examine any potential circumstance individually to see if the jury should take it into account. Having identified a circumstance of D that impacted on her ability to control herself, the court must consider whether that circumstance was *only* relevant to D's self-control, in which case it should not be taken into account, or whether it was also relevant to some other aspect of D's defence, in which case it should be taken into account. Unfortunately, and crucially, the statute does not clarify *what* other aspects of D's defence must be impacted on in order for her circumstances to become relevant, nor *how* such circumstances should be taken into account.

The leading case interpreting this part of the C&JA 2009 is *Rejmanski*, a combined appeal questioning the relevance of mental disorders within the objective third element of LOC.[49]

 Rejmanski & Gassman [2017] EWCA Crim 2061

Rejmanski (a Polish army veteran) killed V after the latter made a series of insulting comments about his military service. D was suffering with Post Traumatic Stress Disorder (PTSD) at the time, and argued LOC on the basis that a reasonable person suffering with the same condition might have reacted similarly. In the conjoined appeal, but entirely separate case, Gassman killed when suffering Emotionally Unstable Personality Disorder (EUPD), a condition that caused intense anger. Again, D wanted her EUPD to be considered within the objective limb of the LOC partial defence.

• Crown Court: both guilty of murder.

• Court of Appeal: convictions upheld on appeal. In both cases it was found that D's mental condition was not relevant to the objective limb of the LOC defence.

Rejmanski provides several useful points of clarification. Perhaps most importantly, the court highlights that even when D's circumstances are relevant to an understanding of her qualifying trigger (ie the second element of LOC), this will not mean that such

---

[48] The law was clarified in *AG for Jersey v Holley* [2005] UKPC 23 (pre-C&JA 2009). For discussion of the legal divergence preceding this case, and evaluation of the case itself, see Macklem and Gardner, 'Compassion Without Respect: Nine Fallacies in *R v Smith*' [2001] Crim LR 623; Mitchell, Mackay, and Brookbanks, 'Pleading for Provoked Killers: In Defence of *Morgan Smith*' (2008) 124 LQR 675.

[49] Laird, Commentary [2018] Crim LR 665. Applied recently in *Sargeant* [2019] EWCA Crim 1088.

circumstances become relevant to the third limb as adjustments to the objective standard of the normal person.[50] Thus, it was correct for the jury in *Rejmanski* to consider D's PTSD when assessing the gravity of V's insults about his military service, but D's response should still be measured (within the objective third element) against the standard of a normal person not suffering from PTSD. For the Court of Appeal, whether a circumstance goes beyond D's general capacity for tolerance and self-restraint should be assessed separately on the facts of each case, and courts should act 'with some care' to avoid the objective test being undermined by the inclusion of too many of D's characteristics.[51]

A similar point is made in *Asmelash*, where it is confirmed that D's voluntary intoxication will not typically represent a relevant circumstance within the objective third element.

 Asmelash [2013] EWCA Crim 157

D and V spent the day drinking and arguing, culminating in D stabbing V twice and killing him. D was charged with murder.

- Crown Court: guilty of murder. Directing the jury as to LOC, the judge explained that they should ask whether a reasonable person sharing D's characteristics, *but not intoxicated*, might have acted in the same way.
- Court of Appeal: conviction upheld on appeal. Voluntary intoxication was only relevant to D's general capacity of self-control and was therefore rightly excluded.

Rejmanski and *Asmelash* therefore provide some useful clarity on what is excluded from the objective test, but, regrettably, they are much less helpful on which circumstances are included and how they should be considered. Rather than additional circumstances being included as qualifications to the reasonable person standard (ie asking whether a normal person with 'relevant circumstance' might have acted similarly), it seems that the best D can hope for is that the objective standard (accounting for age and sex only) will be applied in view of a qualifying circumstance (ie asking whether the trigger, in view of the 'relevant circumstance', might have caused a normal person to act similarly). Within this limited role, the courts highlight circumstances affecting the gravity of the trigger as the most likely to qualify.[52] But little more is said on this; and the potential for circumstances to qualify via alternative routes was avoided as irrelevant to the present issue.[53] Such omissions are regrettable, not least when reflecting on the chaos similar uncertainty engendered within the pre-C&JA 2009—chaos that was a major catalyst for the reform that followed.

[50] At [26]. This is important partly because relevance within the second element of LOC had been interpreted as a gateway into the objective element at certain points within the pre-C&JA 2009 law. See *Camplin* [1978] UKHL 2.
[51] See also *McGrory* [2013] EWCA Crim 2336: D's depression reduced his ability to deal with taunting from V, but as this characteristic related to a general capacity for self-restraint, it was not relevant to the objective test.
[52] At [27].
[53] At [28]. Examples might include, it is submitted, exceptionally low IQ that leads D to misinterpret the gravity of provocation and hinders her ability to consider alternatives to the use of violence, or traumatic historical experiences (eg abuse) that lead D to misinterpret the severity of a present attack.

We are left with a test that measures D's reaction in killing against the objective standard of what a normal person of her age and sex might have done. It is possible for other circumstances of D to be relevant to this assessment, but each one must be individually assessed in light of the restrictive interpretations from the Court of Appeal. Where D has a mental condition that leads to reduced capacity for self-restraint and a loss of self-control, the appropriate partial defence will usually be diminished responsibility.

 Point to remember . . .

The last part of the third element of LOC 'might have reacted in the same or in a similar way' should not be forgotten. Two points are important. First, it is not necessary that a normal person 'would' have reacted in a similar way, only that one 'might' have (a lower standard). Secondly, even if a 'normal' person might have lost control and killed as D did, you must still look at the 'way' it was done. For example, if D lost control and killed V in a particularly brutal or prolonged attack, in a manner in which a normal person would never do, then she may fall outside the defence.[54]

6.2.2 Diminished responsibility

As with LOC, diminished responsibility (DR) is a partial defence to murder (and only to murder[55]) that reduces D's liability from murder to 'voluntary' manslaughter, thereby avoiding the mandatory life sentence.[56] For the LOC defence, as we have seen, D claims that she should be partially excused for the killing on the basis that a 'normal' person might have reacted as she did. For DR, in contrast, D is claiming a partial excuse on the basis that she should not be held to the standard of a 'normal' person because of her medical condition.[57]

Where D's medical condition creates a defect of reason that *completely* undermines her ability to understand the nature or quality of her acts, or to know if they are wrong, then she will have a complete defence of insanity.[58] No liability is appropriate in such cases. DR is different. Where D's medical condition causes her an abnormality of mind that *substantially* impairs her abilities, she will commit an offence. However, instead of being treated as a murderer, D is held liable for manslaughter.

The elements of the DR partial defence, contained in section 2 of the Homicide Act 1957, were effectively substituted by section 52 of the C&JA 2009. The pre-C&JA 2009 DR defence was defined broadly and imprecisely to apply where D's 'abnormality of mind' substantially impaired her 'mental responsibility'. This was welcomed in certain cases, allowing for flexibility and legal equity, essentially allowing courts and juries to interpret and apply the law as they wished to find a 'fair' result—as between murder and manslaughter. However, as discussed by the Law Commission, this flexibility also

---

54 *Van Dongen* [2005] Crim LR 971 (pre-C&JA 2009): D's acts demonstrated abnormal savagery and fell outside the defence.

55 *Campbell* [1997] Crim LR 495 (pre-C&JA 2009): will not apply to attempted murder.

56 The maximum sentence for manslaughter is life imprisonment, but (unlike for murder) this sentence is not mandatory. Sentencing options for diminished responsibility manslaughter are likely to include detention in a secure hospital.

57 Horder, *Excusing Crime* (2004) Ch1.

58 *M'Naghten* (1843) 10 Cl & Fin 200, 8 Eng Rep 718. See **Chapter 14**. Although the verdict will be the 'special' one of 'Not Guilty by Reason of Insanity'.

resulted in 'chaotic' use of the partial defence, with it being 'grossly abused' and resulting in a 'lottery' between cases.[59] In view of these problems, the Commission made recommendations for reform,[60] many of which were adopted within the 2009 Act.

The current DR defence is set out (as substituted) in section 2 of the Homicide Act 1957:[61]

> 2(1) A person ('D') who kills or is a party to the killing of another is not to be convicted of murder if D was suffering from an abnormality of mental functioning which—
>
> (a) arose from a recognised medical condition,
>
> (b) substantially impaired D's ability to do one or more of the things mentioned in subsection (1A), and
>
> (c) provides an explanation for D's acts and omissions in doing or being a party to the killing.
>
> (1A) Those things are—
>
> (a) to understand the nature of D's conduct;
>
> (b) to form a rational judgment;
>
> (c) to exercise self-control.

 Don't be confused . . .

Both LOC and DR defences have been reformed by the 2009 Act. For LOC, as the old provocation defence (replaced by LOC) existed at common law, the new defence is located in the 2009 Act itself. In contrast, as the old DR defence was already fully codified within the Homicide Act 1957, the 2009 Act simply amended that statute. Therefore, when referring to the current DR defence, you should still refer to section 2 of the 1957 Act.

DR can be separated into four elements, set out in **Table 6.2**. All four must be satisfied for the defence to apply.

Table 6.2 Partial defence of diminished responsibility

A) D must demonstrate an abnormality of mental functioning
B) The abnormality must have arisen from a recognised medical condition

C) The abnormality must have substantially impaired D's ability to:
   i) understand the nature of her conduct; *or*
   ii) form a rational judgement; *or*
   iii) exercise self-control

D) The abnormality must provide an explanation (or cause) of the killing

[59] Law Commission, *Partial Defences to Murder* (No 290, 2004) Part 5.

[60] Law Commission, *Murder, Manslaughter and Infanticide* (No 304, 2006).

[61] See Mackay, 'The New Diminished Responsibility Plea' [2010] Crim LR 290; Mackay and Mitchell, 'The New Diminished Responsibility Plea in Operation: Some Initial Findings' [2017] Crim LR 18.

In common with the insanity defence, but in contrast to LOC, the burden of proving these elements is on the defendant and not the prosecution.[62] As we have discussed, where the burden of proof is reversed in this manner, the defence only have to prove their case to the civil standard: on the balance of probabilities.[63] D must prove every element of the DR defence, and only then will liability be reduced from murder to 'voluntary' manslaughter. We will explore each element in turn.

6.2.2.1 Element 1: D must have had an abnormality of mental functioning

The term 'abnormality of mental functioning' is not defined in the statute and remains somewhat vague. In line with the old law, the element is designed to require a link between D's medical condition and some impact on her mind.

The language of 'mental functioning' (as opposed to 'abnormality of mind' under the pre-C&JA 2009 law[64]) demonstrates a move towards medical/psychiatric definitions that are likely to standardise the potential application of the element. The defence has always required medical evidence to succeed, but since the C&JA 2009, with the move to more medicalised elements, that has become more dominant.[65]

6.2.2.2 Element 2: the abnormality must have arisen from a recognised medical condition

The required link between D's abnormal mental functioning and a recognised medical condition is one of the most important and clearly medicalising elements of the partial defence. Whether a condition is 'recognised' remains ultimately a question for the court; but courts will be guided by medical recognition within glossaries such as the World Health Organization's *International Statistical Classification of Diseases and Related Health Problems* (ICD 10) and the American Medical Association's *Diagnostic and Statistical Manual* (DSM), and potentially outside of these where supported by a reliable body of expert opinion. Both psychiatric and purely physical conditions are *capable* of satisfying this element, although of course purely physical conditions are less likely to satisfy the other defence elements.

 Extra detail . . .

Although D must have a recognised medical condition, there is no threshold of seriousness. Thus, as long as the other defence elements are satisfied, even mild depression would be sufficient.

The rationale for linking this element of DR to medical definitions is to ensure that the legal test is not left behind by developments in medical science. However, as medical definitions are not specifically designed to assist the criminal law, courts retain the ultimate power to exclude or include conditions as *legally* appropriate.

---

[62] Homicide Act 1957, s2(2).

[63] See **Chapter 1.1.7.2**. The reverse burden for DR has been found to be compatible with the Art 6 ECHR right to a fair trial: *Lambert* [2001] 1 Cr App R 205; *Foye* [2013] EWCA Crim 475; *Wilcocks* [2016] EWCA Crim 2043.

[64] In *Byrne* [1960] 2 QB 396 (pre-C&JA 2009), Lord Parker CJ described the then test as 'a state of mind so different from that of ordinary human beings that the reasonable man would term it abnormal' (403).

[65] See *Bunch* [2013] EWCA Crim 2498; *Golds* [2016] UKSC 61, [38].

A) **Included:** The most common conditions used to found a DR defence include schizophrenia, depression, and personality disorders.[66] However, as discussed by Hughes LJ in *Dowds*,[67] medical dictionaries may also include 'conditions' that would be inappropriate for a DR defence (eg 'unhappiness', 'anger', and 'paedophilia'). In view of this, the court provides a further filter as to what conditions may be recognised within the DR defence.

 Dowds [2012] EWCA Crim 281

D killed his partner whilst heavily intoxicated, inflicting 60 stab wounds. D attempted to use the DR defence, relying on his 'acute intoxication' (extreme drunkenness) which is a medical condition recognised by the World Health Organization.

- Crown Court: guilty of murder. The judge refused to allow DR.
- Court of Appeal: conviction upheld on appeal. Although acute intoxication was a medically recognised condition, it will not qualify as such within the DR defence.

B) **Excluded:** Pre-C&JA 2009, the vague terms of the DR defence meant that it could be used flexibly in the context, for example, of abused women who kill and so-called mercy killers. The current law, however, will not allow for the inclusion of such cases unless D is suffering from a recognised medical condition.[68] This is a real restriction on the scope of the defence, but should not be exaggerated. First, many defendants in such cases *will* be suffering from a recognised anxiety- or depression-related condition. Further, where there is no such condition, there are strong grounds to maintain that D's case should not come within the defence: the rationale of the defence is to provide a partial excuse for those acting as a result of their medical affliction; not as a method for courts to engage with a debate on euthanasia or other defences they might want to create (in the guise of DR) in the absence of statutory recognition of such defences by government.[69]

More troubling is the potential exclusion of developmental immaturity, particularly with young defendants: this will sometimes coincide with a recognised condition (eg autism), but will not always do so. The Law Commission recommended that developmental immaturity should be explicitly included as an alternative to a recognised medical condition.[70] This was rejected by the government as unnecessary. The government stressed the general overlap with recognised conditions. Despite this, the omission is unfortunate, and may lead to unfairness.

6.2.2.3 Element 3: the abnormality must have substantially impaired D's mental ability to . . .

Although the defence is still called 'diminished responsibility', the pre-C&JA 2009 requirement of a 'substantially impaired mental responsibility' has been replaced with an

[66] Mackay and Mitchell, 'The New Diminished Responsibility Plea in Operation: Some Initial Findings' [2017] Crim LR 18.

[67] [2012] EWCA Crim 281.

[68] Kennefick, 'Introducing a New Diminished Responsibility Defence for England and Wales' (2011) 74 MLR 750; evidence of 'Dignity in Dying' to the Joint Committee on Human Rights, 8th Report, 2008–9, para 1.150.

[69] A point made in Horder, *Ashworth's Principles of Criminal Law* (8th edn, 2016) 277–278.

[70] Law Commission, *Murder, Manslaughter and Infanticide* (No 304, 2006) paras 5.125–5.137.

element that makes no reference to 'responsibility' at all. Rather, D's 'substantial' impairment must be shown to relate to one of three rather more precise abilities (each capable of medical assessment). Whether D's abnormality has substantially impaired her in a relevant way remains a question for the jury, but this will inevitably be guided by the weight of expert medical evidence.[71]

The term 'substantial' is not defined in the 2009 Act, and has led to some uncertainty. Adopting a similar definition to 'substantial' in the context of causation,[72] it had been assumed that substantial simply required a 'more than merely trivial' effect.[73] However, following the Supreme Court ruling in *Golds*,[74] this is no longer the case. Rather, when asking if D was significantly impaired, the jury (and expert witnesses) must assess whether such impairment was 'weighty', 'important', and 'significant'. The court's interpretation effectively raises the bar for defendants, and has the potential to further depress the already decreasing numbers of those successfully relying on the defence.[75] Curiously, the Court of Appeal in *Squelch* has subsequently endorsed a jury direction that described substantial as 'less than total and more than trivial'.[76] However, it is likely that courts will now take care to avoid reference to 'more than trivial', highlighting the higher standard required from *Golds* where a definition is needed.[77]

 Extra detail . . .

Following the decision in *Golds*, the term 'substantial' now has a different meaning in causation (more than trivial) and DR (significant). Care must be taken to apply the correct definition in the correct context. The inconsistency here is regrettable, not least because courts in both contexts have stressed that (as a standard English word) a definition will rarely be required when directing a jury. How exactly a jury are expected to intuitively reach these quite different interpretations without direction is not explained.

. . . understand the nature of D's conduct

This first possibility carries an obvious echo of the insanity defence: which also refers to an inability to understand the nature of one's own conduct.[78] However, unlike insanity, where there must be a complete inability, DR is satisfied by a substantial impairment. An

---

[71] Such is the vital role of expert evidence, there remains a question about whether a trial judge should remove murder from the jury where the prosecution does not raise evidence to challenge expert defence evidence of a relevant impairment. *Golds* [2016] UKSC 61, cf *Brennan* [2014] EWCA Crim 2387; commentary by Fortson [2015] Crim LR 291. However, more recently in *Hussain* [2019] EWCA Crim 666, the Court of Appeal held that the Supreme Court in *Golds* did not suggest that a trial judge should withdraw a murder charge from the jury simply on the basis that the medical evidence pointed one way and that reliance should not be placed on any judgment predating *Golds* on that issue.

[72] See **Chapter 2.7.2.1**.

[73] See *Ramchurn* [2010] EWCA Crim 194.

[74] *Golds* [2016] UKSC 61. Laird, Commentary [2017] Crim LR 316.

[75] Gibson, 'Diminished Responsibility in *Golds* and Beyond: Insights and Implications' [2017] Crim LR 543.

[76] [2017] EWCA Crim 204, [38].

[77] *Golds* emphasises that 'substantial' is a word of common use and understanding, and so it will rarely be necessary for a definition to be given when directing a jury.

[78] See **Chapter 13.4.2**.

example, adapted from the Law Commission, is a child with a mental illness who obsessively plays violent video games and then kills in the belief that the victim will regenerate as they do in her games.[79] Here, D may understand the physical dynamics of her action, but she does not understand its impact on V.

Mackay and Mitchell found this factor to be the least likely to be relied on by defendants as the sole factor.[80] To address this perceived underuse, Mackay contends that the interpretation of this factor could be expanded to include a lack of *moral* understanding as to the wrongfulness of D's conduct,[81] though this has not yet been adopted by the courts.

. . . form a rational judgement

The second possibility is where D's abnormality substantially impairs her ability to form a rational judgement. As the Law Commission highlights,[82] this is the most likely route within DR for an abused person who kills their abuser, or for a so-called mercy killer; in each case the pressure of the circumstances may substantially impair D's ability to make rational choices.[83]

Mackay and Mitchell found this factor to be the most likely to be relied on by defendants. However, some concern was noted that 'rational judgement' was being confounded with 'decision'. We are looking for effects upon D's reasoning power, not simply her resulting choice.[84]

. . . exercise control

The final possibility within this element, where D's ability to exercise control is substantially impaired, has the potential to be interpreted very widely. The availability of this option makes it possible to restrict the LOC defence to cases where a person of 'normal' self-restraint might have reacted similarly. Where D is incapable of living up to the standard of 'normal' self-restraint, her defence (if she satisfies all the elements) should be DR.

Extra detail . . .

Although impairment of any one of these factors will satisfy this element of the defence, it is important to note that in practice they will often be pleaded together.

6.2.2.4 Element 4: the abnormality must provide an explanation (or cause) of the killing

The final element of the DR partial defence requires a causal link between D's abnormality and the killing. Although section 2(1)(c) only states that the abnormality must provide an 'explanation' for the killing, section 2(1B) clarifies that an 'explanation' will be found 'if

---

[79] Law Commission, *Murder, Manslaughter and Infanticide* (No 304, 2006) para 5.21.
[80] Mackay and Mitchell, 'The New Diminished Responsibility Plea in Operation: Some Initial Findings' [2017] Crim LR 18.
[81] Mackay, 'The Impairment Factors in the New Diminished Responsibility Plea' [2018] Crim LR 462, 466.
[82] No 304, para 5.121.
[83] The issue is really about whether D was able rationally to make a choice rather than whether the choice made was a rational one. Cf *Conroy* [2017] EWCA Crim 81.
[84] *Conroy* [2017] EWCA Crim 81. See Mackay, 'The Impairment Factors in the New Diminished Responsibility Plea' [2018] Crim LR 462, 468–469.

it causes, or is a significant contributory factor in causing, D to carry out the conduct'. In this manner, the DR defence does not partially excuse D simply because of her abnormality of mental functioning and/or her recognised medical condition. It is rather because these elements combine to have affected her conduct and caused her to kill.[85]

Demonstrating a causal link of this kind is far from straightforward. Causation in criminal law, as we discussed earlier,[86] usually focusses on the external causal effect of D's conduct on a particular result, and this can be very difficult to prove. Causation in the context of DR requires something even more challenging: assessment of the causal effect of an abnormality *within* the mind of D upon her choice of conduct. Even with the help of medical experts, this is far from an exact science,[87] and empirical evidence demonstrates that experts have shied away from engaging with this issue in their psychiatric reports.[88] It is for the defendant to prove.

Another difficulty when applying this element is the chance, which is not uncommon, of multiple causes/motivations (eg D kills as a result of her abnormality and her anger at losing her job). When applying the law to such facts, it is clear that D's abnormality can be a substantial cause without being the sole cause, satisfying this element of the defence. However, it will be necessary for D to demonstrate, on the balance of probabilities, that her condition was not merely incidental. There is a useful discussion of this in the combined appeals of *Joyce and Kay*.[89]

    Joyce and Kay [2017] EWCA Crim 647

Both cases involved Ds who suffered from schizophrenia and killed whilst under the influence of alcohol and other drugs. Both were charged with murder and raised the partial defence of DR.

- Crown Court: Kay was found guilty of murder; Joyce was found guilty of manslaughter on grounds of diminished responsibility.

- Court of Appeal: both appeals focussed primarily on sentencing, but the court took some time to repeat and confirm matters of general principle. Kay was correctly liable for murder because his schizophrenia did not have a significant impact on the killing, and his intoxication (which did have a significant impact) was not related to a medical condition (ie he was not an addict); Joyce was able to rely upon the DR defence because, regardless of his intoxicated state, his schizophrenia continued to play a substantial causative role.

Where, as in *Joyce and Kay*, one of the causes of D's killing is intoxication, three situations should be carefully separated when applying the defence:

(a) First, as confirmed in *Dowds* (discussed earlier), acute intoxication is not a *legally* recognised condition for the purposes of DR, and so intoxication alone cannot provide a basis for the DR defence.

---

[85] Confirmed in *Golds* [32]. Cf Laird [2017] Crim LR 316.

[86] **Chapter 2.7.**

[87] Miles, 'A Dog's Breakfast of Homicide Reform' [2009] 6 Arch News 6.

[88] Mackay and Mitchell, 'The New Diminished Responsibility Plea in Operation: Some Initial Findings' [2017] Crim LR 18, 34.

[89] Confirming the pre-C&JA 2009 case *Dietschmann* [2003] 1 AC 1209. Storey, 'Drug-Free Zone: Court of Appeal Confirms that Voluntary Intoxication is not Relevant in Cases of Diminished Responsibility' (2017) 81 JCL 258.

(b) Secondly, where D is intoxicated and has a separate recognised condition (as in *Joyce and Kay*), the jury should ask whether D's recognised condition caused the killing and, as far as possible, exclude the intoxication from their consideration.

(c) Thirdly, where D has a recognised condition that caused the intoxication (eg drug or alcohol dependency), the jury may take account of *both* the condition and the intoxication related to that condition when considering causation.[90]

6.2.3 Suicide pact partial defence

The third partial defence to murder arises where D kills V pursuant to an agreement that they will die together (a suicide pact). Section 4 of the Homicide Act 1957 states:

(1) It shall be manslaughter, and shall not be murder, for a person acting in pursuance of a suicide pact between him and another to kill the other or be a party to the other . . . being killed by a third person . . .

(2) For the purposes of this section 'suicide pact' means a common agreement between two or more persons having for its object the death of all of them, whether or not each is to take his own life, but nothing done by a person who enters into a suicide pact shall be treated as done by him in pursuance of the pact unless it is done while he has the settled intention of dying in pursuance of the pact.

There are two main elements to this partial defence, set out in **Table 6.3**. Both must be satisfied for D's liability to be reduced from murder to voluntary manslaughter.

Table 6.3 Partial defence of suicide pact

A) D must have agreed with V that they will die together
B) D must intend, at the point of killing V, to die herself in line with the agreement

As with the DR defence, the burden of proof is on D to establish the elements of the defence on the balance of probabilities.[91]

 Assessment matters . . .

When applying the law to apparent suicides, take care to identify the correct offences. Where D kills V, then you are right to apply homicide offences and, where relevant, the partial defence of suicide pacts. However, where D assists or encourages V to kill herself, D will not have committed a homicide offence (she has not caused death). Rather, you should apply the offence of assisting or encouraging suicide.[92] The act of suicide or attempted suicide is not an offence.

---

[90] *Stewart* [2009] EWCA Crim 593 (pre-C&JA 2009), confirmed in *Joyce and Kay*, and *Foy* [2020] EWCA Crim 270.

[91] Homicide Act 1957, s4(2). This is compatible with D's right to a fair trial under Art 6 ECHR: *AG's Reference (No 1 of 2004)* [2004] 1 WLR 2111.

[92] Discussed in **Chapter 11.6.1**.

6.3 Involuntary manslaughter

Involuntary manslaughter has nothing to do with 'involuntariness'. Rather, the label 'involuntary' is used to differentiate this second form of manslaughter liability from the first (voluntary manslaughter) discussed previously. Crucially, whereas voluntary manslaughter arises where D commits murder and then relies on a partial *defence*, involuntary manslaughter arises where D does not satisfy the mens rea of murder, so does not commit murder, but does commit a lesser manslaughter *offence*.[93]

Three main involuntary manslaughter offences will be discussed in this section. All exist at common law.

- **Unlawful act manslaughter:** D commits a criminal act in dangerous circumstances, and this causes the death of V.
- **Gross negligence manslaughter:** D causes V's death through criminal negligence.
- **Reckless manslaughter:** D causes V's death, being reckless as to causing death or GBH.

 Don't be confused . . .

A fourth involuntary manslaughter offence is that of corporate manslaughter. However, as this offence requires a different actus reus from other manslaughter offences, it will be discussed separately at **6.4.1**.

The main point of contention within involuntary manslaughter offences has been breadth of the forms of mens rea capable of giving rise to liability. Although courts have a wide sentencing discretion, from absolute discharge to life imprisonment, it remains questionable whether all the conduct currently captured within these offences deserves the label manslaughter. Indeed, the Law Commission has cautioned against this category becoming a 'residual, amorphous, "catch-all" homicide offence'.[94]

6.3.1 Unlawful act manslaughter

Unlawful act manslaughter (UAM) is also referred to as 'unlawful and dangerous act manslaughter' or 'constructive manslaughter'. D commits UAM when she acts to commit a criminal offence (the base offence), the base offence carries an objective risk of some physical harm to V, and V dies as a result. The current state of the law is presented in **Table 6.4**.

Table 6.4 Unlawful act manslaughter

	Actus reus	**Mens rea**
Conduct element	Any acts causing the results	Voluntary

---

[93] See flowchart in **Figure 6.1**.
[94] Law Commission, *Murder, Manslaughter and Infanticide* (No 304, 2006) para 2.9.

Circumstance element	Any circumstances required for the base offence	As required for the base offence
	A sober and reasonable person in D's position would recognise a risk of some harm to V	None
Result element	Any results required for the base offence	As required for the base offence
	Death of V	None

The elements of UAM can be alternatively, and more simply, presented as the combination of three core requirements (illustrated in **Figure 6.2**). The presentation and analysis of UAM in this three-part structure (as opposed to a more traditional discussion of actus reus and mens rea) is the most common approach taken by courts and academics.

Figure 6.2 Unlawful act manslaughter

From the outset, the potential breadth of UAM should be highlighted. At one end of the spectrum, where D's conduct is most blameworthy, UAM will apply to cases just short of liability for murder. For example, where D's conduct causes V's death with D foreseeing that her act is likely to kill or cause GBH, but not foreseeing it as a virtual certainty,[95] UAM is most likely to be applied.[96] In contrast, at the other end of the spectrum, UAM can also be satisfied by conduct which is significantly less blameworthy. For example, where D commits a relatively minor offence without foreseeing significant risks to V, but V is killed as a matter of 'bad luck'. The most common example of the latter (less blameworthy) scenario involves the so-called 'one punch killer' who commits UAM when she hits V (commits a battery), V falls, hits her head, and dies.[97]

As both **Table 6.4** and **Figure 6.2** make clear, liability for UAM does not require D to have any mens rea as to the dangerousness of her action, or as to the resulting death. UAM is a constructive liability offence; with dangerousness and the death of V

---

[95] Where D foresees causing death or GBH as a virtual certainty, it is possible that she satisfies the mens rea for murder. See **Chapter 5.4**.

[96] D is alternatively liable for reckless manslaughter (**6.3.3**).

[97] *Mallett* [1972] Crim LR 260. Mitchell, 'More Thoughts About Unlawful and Dangerous Act Manslaughter and the One Punch Killer' [2009] Crim LR 502.

constructing upon the base offence to create liability for UAM.[98] We will discuss each of these three elements in turn.

6.3.1.1 The unlawful act (base offence)

We must first identify the charge that D would have faced if no one died. We call this the base offence. Historically, this base offence was interpreted very widely to include all criminal offences, and even civil wrongs.[99] However, under the current law, only *criminal* offences will be sufficient.[100]

The most common base offences within UAM are offences against the person (eg D physically attacks and kills V without the mens rea for murder, but with the mens rea for an offence against the person).[101] However, other criminal offences will also qualify. For example, UAM convictions have been based upon criminal damage (eg *Farnon & Ellis*:[102] where a homeless man was killed following a basement fire); and burglary (eg *Watson*:[103] where an elderly homeowner had a heart attack during a burglary). There are two important restrictions on the types of base offence that will satisfy this element.

A) **The base offence must be one requiring subjective mens rea:** In the case of *Andrews v DPP*,[104] at trial, a charge of UAM was constructed upon a negligence-based dangerous driving offence (D having killed a pedestrian whilst overtaking another car). However, on appeal to the House of Lords, it was stated that the base offence for UAM requires an intrinsically criminal offence, not satisfied by 'a lawful act with a degree of negligence that the legislature makes criminal'. The original meaning of this dictum is ambiguous and troublesome. However, it has been interpreted to mean that offences satisfied by a mens rea of negligence (eg dangerous driving),[105] or strict liability offences,[106] will not qualify as potential base offences for UAM.[107] Thus, where D acts negligently to cause death, the appropriate course will be to consider liability for gross negligence manslaughter (**6.3.2**).

B) **The base offence must have been completed by an act rather than an omission:** Until this issue is revisited in the courts (when we anticipate it will be reversed) it is currently the case that the base offence within UAM must have been completed by an action as opposed to an omission.[108] In *Lowe*,[109] the Court of Appeal held that D was not guilty of UAM where his base offence was one of *omitting* to care for his child (an offence

---

[98] Constructive crimes are introduced in **Chapter 4.2.1.1**.

[99] eg *Fenton* (1830) 1 Lew CC 179: involving civil trespass; Buxton, 'By Any Unlawful Act' (1966) 82 LQR 174.

[100] *Kennedy (No 2)* [2007] UKHL 38.

[101] See **Chapter 7**.

[102] [2015] EWCA Crim 351.

[103] [1989] Crim LR 730.

[104] [1937] AC 576.

[105] *Lamb* [1967] 2 QB 981.

[106] There is no direct authority on this point, but it is generally accepted and must surely follow from the exclusion of negligence-based offences.

[107] See useful discussion in Freer, 'We Need to Talk About Charlie: Putting the Brakes on Unlawful Act Manslaughter' [2018] Crim LR 612.

[108] Dennis, 'Manslaughter by Omission' (1980) 33 CLP 255; Taylor 'The Contours of Involuntary Manslaughter—A Place for Unlawful Act by Omission' [2019] Crim LR 205.

[109] [1973] QB 702.

under section 1(1) of the Children and Young Persons Act 1933). Liability in this case could have been rejected because D's base offence was satisfied by negligence (see point A). However, the court instead focussed on the lack of a physical act by D.

With respect, the use of the act/omission distinction in this context lacks any coherent basis: if the criminal law outside UAM places harm caused by omission in breach of duty alongside harm caused by action, why should it be different in this context?[110] Indeed, as we have discussed,[111] the distinction between acts and omissions is often difficult to define, and so the use of the distinction here simply adds unnecessary complexity to the law.

Assessment matters . . .

Most omissions cases can be dealt with under the alternative involuntary manslaughter offence of gross negligence manslaughter, where liability can be found for omissions. However, criticism of the act/omission rule has been included above because, if applying UAM to omissions within a problem question, it would be sensible to highlight the criticism of the rule and the potential that it may not survive future appellate decisions.

Having identified a potential qualifying base offence (ie a criminal offence; requiring subjective mens rea; committed by D's acts), it remains essential that D satisfied every element of that base offence, and lacks a valid defence. Although this sounds self-evident for an *unlawful* act, it is easily neglected, even by the highest courts.[112] The requirement is illustrated in *Lamb*.[113]

Lamb [1967] 2 QB 981

D pointed a loaded revolver at V as a joke. Neither D nor V understood how a revolver worked, and so when D pulled the trigger neither realised that the barrel of the gun would revolve and the bullet would be fired. It did, and V was killed.

- Crown Court: guilty of unlawful act manslaughter.
- Court of Criminal Appeal: appeal allowed. The base offence (assault or battery) was not complete because D lacked mens rea, he did not intend or foresee a risk of harm to V or a risk of causing V to apprehend harm.

When identifying the relevant base offence upon which to construct UAM liability, it should be remembered that the general doctrines of criminal law will still apply to this offence. This includes rules that can be used to create liability, such as the intoxication rules discussed in **Chapter 13**, as well as the rules relating to defences discussed (principally) in **Chapter 14**:

Creating liability: where D commits the actus reus of a base offence (eg hits V), but lacks mens rea due to voluntary intoxication, D remains liable for basic intent offences

---

[110] Ashworth, 'Editorial' [1976] Crim LR 529.

[111] See **Chapter 2.6.5**.

[112] *DPP v Newbury* [1977] AC 500: where the House of Lords fail to specify the offence at the base of the UAM conviction.

[113] See also *Arobieke* [1988] Crim LR 314: D caused V's death, but not through a completed base offence; there was no liability for UAM.

because the intoxication rules serve to replace the absent mens rea. With all elements of the base offence now satisfied, D may be liable for UAM.[114]

Defences: where D commits a base offence but satisfies the elements of a complete defence, there is no crime upon which to construct UAM liability.[115] As many UAM cases involve base offences against the person, the most common defences to consider are self-defence and consent.[116] In *Slingsby*, for example, there was no battery, and therefore no UAM, where V *consented* to acts of sexual touching, even though those acts resulted in the unexpected injury and infection from which V died.[117] However, care should always be taken to question whether a potential defence is satisfied. For example, in the case of *A*,[118] D threw V into a river as part of a post-exam celebration, and V drowned. D claimed that V was consenting, but the Crown established that V was not consenting on the facts and D was liable for UAM.

 Extra detail . . .

There has been considerable debate in recent years about a so-called 'rough sex defence'. This has arisen from cases where D kills V, but claims that death was an accidental result of consensual violence during sex (ie claims a 'consent' defence to the base crime of violence). Rejecting this line of defence, legislation has recently been introduced to clarify that V cannot consent to serious violence for reasons of sexual gratification;[119] and so V's consent is legally invalid, and D's potential defence is undermined.

6.3.1.2 The base offence must be dangerous to V

The second element of 'dangerousness' is important, but easily misunderstood. It is not simply a requirement that D's actions are dangerous in fact: as they have caused death, such a requirement would be self-evident and unnecessary. Rather, it is the requirement that a sober and reasonable person in D's position would have foreseen that her acts carried a risk of harm to V at the time D acted. It should be noted that this is an objective requirement. Thus, although the base offence will require some manner of subjective mens rea, the dangerousness element does not.

The full test of the dangerousness of D's conduct is usefully set out by Edmund Davies J in *Church*:[120]

[T]he unlawful act must be such that all sober and reasonable people would inevitably recognise that it must subject the other person to, at least, the risk of some harm resulting therefrom, albeit not serious harm.

It is important to understand and apply this test of recognition carefully. In particular, four core questions should be borne in mind.

---

[114] *Lipman* [1970] 1 QB 152.

[115] *Scarlett* (1994) 98 Cr App R 290.

[116] See **Chapter 14.5** on self-defence, and **Chapter 7.3.2–7.3.3** and **7.8.2–7.8.3** on consent to an offence against the person.

[117] *Slingsby* [1995] Crim LR 570.

[118] (2005) CACD, reported as a case note at 69 JCL 394.

[119] Domestic Abuse Bill 2020, cl65. At the time of writing, the Bill is in its final stages of parliamentary approval. See, for background to the rough sex provision, https://assets.publishing.service.gov.uk/government/uploads/system/uploads/attachment_data/file/909931/Consent_to_serious_harm_for_sexual_gratification_not_a_defence-_AUG_2020.pdf.

[120] [1996] 1 QB 59, 70.

A) Recognising danger to whom? The *Church* definition states that D's conduct must be dangerous to the 'other person' and, importantly, this other person should be interpreted as V. Despite some inconsistent authorities,[121] it is now clear that the first element of UAM (the base offence) does not need to be directed or targeted at V. For example, in *Watson*,[122] D's base offence of burglary was not directed at the elderly homeowner (V), but nevertheless D was liable for UAM when V died from a stress-induced heart attack. In contrast, the second element (dangerousness) will only be satisfied if danger *to V* is foreseeable. For example, let's imagine that the frail householder in *Watson* died from a heart attack having watched television news footage of a violent crime perpetrated by D. In such a case, D should not be liable for UAM in relation to V unless, at the time of D's acts, there was a foreseeable risk of harm to V, and not just a risk to the more immediate victim of her violent attack. There is support for this approach in *Carey*.[123]

B) What type of recognition? The requirement is that a sober and reasonable person would have recognised/foreseen danger to V, *not* whether D herself foresaw it. The test is objective, it is a strict liability element,[124] and not a question of D's personal perception or mens rea. Taking *Watson* as our example again, the test for dangerousness was satisfied in this case because a reasonable person would have foreseen the risk of causing a heart attack when restraining an elderly person and stealing from them. It is irrelevant whether D personally foresaw the risk of danger, and even whether D was capable of foreseeing the risk (eg due to low IQ).[125]

The only exception, where we take account of D's subjective mind, is where D has 'special knowledge' of risks to V that may not be obviously apparent to a reasonable person. For example, if the victim in *Watson* had been apparently young and healthy then the risk of harm from a non-violent burglary may not have been foreseeable to the sober and reasonable individual. However, if D had known (special knowledge) that the apparently healthy victim had a fragile heart condition, then this could be taken into account within the test, and would be likely to make danger foreseeable in the *Church* sense.

Although a risk of harm will often be foreseeable (it usually is where death has resulted!), this will not always be the case. This is illustrated in *Dawson*.[126]

Dawson (1985) 81 Cr App R 150

D and others attempted to rob a petrol station using an imitation gun. V was not elderly, was in apparent good health, and protected behind bullet-proof glass. V suffered a heart attack and died, owing in part to an underlying heart condition. D was charged with UAM.

- Crown Court: guilty of UAM. Jury directed to consider the risk of danger from the perspective of a reasonable person knowing what they (the jury) knew, which included knowledge of the heart condition.
- Court of Appeal: appeal allowed. Direction was wrong to include facts that were known to the jury, but would not have been apparent to a reasonable person in D's shoes at the time of the attempted robbery.

---

[121] *Dalby* [1982] 1 All ER 916.

[122] [1989] Crim LR 730.

[123] [2006] EWCA Crim 17: an affray (involving danger/harm to others) was not foreseeably dangerous to V.

[124] See **Chapter 4.2.1.1**.

[125] *Farnon & Ellis* [2015] EWCA Crim 351; commentary at (2015) 79 JCL 234.

[126] See also *Carey* [2006] EWCA Crim 17: death of an apparently healthy young woman when fleeing from an affray. No foreseeable risk of danger to V; therefore no UAM.

In cases of this kind, D has clearly completed a relevant base offence (attempted robbery); and caused death. However, as harm to V was not objectively foreseeable, the dangerousness element was not satisfied and there could be no liability for UAM.

C) **What degree of recognition?** The *Church* test speaks of '*all* sober and reasonable people . . . *inevitably*' recognising a risk to V.[127] From this, it is clear that the potential for risk/danger should not be interpreted too widely to include a mere possibility of harm (where harm is possible, but unlikely). The risk must be one that a reasonable person *would* have foreseen rather than *may* have foreseen.

D) **Recognition of what?** We have so far spoken loosely of foresight of a risk of harm or danger. However, precisely what must be foreseen is crucial. Starting again with the quotation from *Church*, we are told that D must foresee 'the risk of some harm . . . albeit not serious harm'. *Church* is therefore important authority that the foreseeable risk of harm need not be a risk of serious harm, and certainly need not be a risk of life-threatening harm. For example, if D hits V, where a reasonable person would foresee the risk of some minor bruising only, this element would be satisfied.

 Extra detail . . .

Although danger of some harm to V must be objectively foreseeable, this danger does not need to be the sole or principal cause of her death. For example, in *JM and SM* ,[128] V (a doorman) died after a fight with D. The fight carried an objectively foreseeable risk of harm: standard risks from fighting. However, V did not die as a result of this danger, he died due to a heart attack resulting from a rush of blood during the fight combined with an undiagnosed heart condition. D was liable for UAM.

Although there is no requirement for a foreseeable risk of *serious* harm from D's base crime, a foreseeable risk of a legally recognised harm is essential. In this regard, a foreseeable risk of unlawful physical contact with V (potentially causing various levels of bodily injury) will obviously qualify. Equally, it is clear from the case law that a base crime can be foreseeably dangerous even if no physical contact with V is anticipated, where, for example, bodily harm is still likely (eg from heart attack).[129] Although there is no UAM case to settle this point, it is likely that a foreseeable risk of psychiatric harms would also be sufficient: psychiatric harms (recognised psychiatric conditions) have been accepted as bodily harms in the context of the offences against the person, so there is no reason why they would be excluded here.[130] However, a foreseeable risk of psychological or emotional harms short of psychiatric injury (eg fear or distress) will not be sufficient.[131]

---

[127] Emphasis added.
[128] [2012] EWCA Crim 2293. See, more recently, *Tarasov (Valodia)* [2016] EWCA Crim 2278.
[129] *Watson* [1989] Crim LR 730.
[130] *Ireland and Burstow* [1998] AC 147. See **Chapter 7.4.1**.
[131] *Dhaliwal* [2006] EWCA Crim 1139, [32]: no UAM liability in case involving psychological abuse causing distress (short of a recognised psychiatric disorder) and ultimately suicide.

Assessment matters . . .

Proving that sober and reasonable people would inevitably foresee a risk of D's acts causing a psychiatric disorder will always be extremely difficult. In practice, when courts are looking for potential dangerousness, we will almost always be talking about objective foresight of a risk of unlawful contact, or shock/distress causing physical injury (eg heart attack). Further, even in extreme cases where a risk of psychiatric injury is objectively foreseeable (eg potentially following prolonged domestic abuse), other elements of UAM (eg *causing* death) remain major hurdles.[132]

6.3.1.3 The base offence must cause the death of V

The third and final element of UAM is the requirement that D's base offence, as well as foreseeably endangering V, should *cause* V's death. As with the requirement of dangerousness, this is a strict liability element: D's base offence must cause death, but there is no requirement for D to have intended; known; foreseen; or had any mens rea at all as to this result. This was discussed in *AG's Reference (No 3 of 1994)*.

AG's Reference (No 3 of 1994) [1998] AC 245

D stabbed his girlfriend (M), with the intention required for murder and knowing that she was pregnant. Although M survived, the attack later caused her to enter premature labour. M's baby (V) was born, but only survived for four months in intensive care before it died. D was charged with the murder of V.

- Crown Court: no liability for murder or UAM. As D was acquitted, the AG appealed the point of law.
- Court of Appeal: D should have been liable for murder using transferred malice—transferring D's intent to kill M to V.
- House of Lords: D should not have been liable for murder as there can be no double transfer of malice.[133] However, D should have been liable for UAM.

Don't be confused . . .

Liability for murder was not possible in *AG's Reference (No 3 of 1994)* because of the difficulty of demonstrating mens rea as to the death of V. However, UAM should have been found because no such mens rea is required: D need only complete a base offence (the assault of M); for that base offence to be objectively dangerous to V (clearly satisfied); and for that base offence to cause the death of V (satisfied on the facts).

The causation element of UAM requires us to apply the standard causation rules discussed previously.[134] D's act must be the cause of death in fact (the 'but for' cause); and

---

[132] Munro and Aitken, 'Adding Insult to Injury? The Criminal Law's Response to Domestic Abuse-Related Suicide in England and Wales' [2018] Crim LR 732.

[133] See **Chapter 4.3.1.1.**

[134] **Chapter 2.7.**

the cause of death in law (proximate; substantial; and operating). In cases such as *AG's Reference (No 3 of 1994)*, where there is a significant gap in time between D's acts and the death of V, then a causal link can be more difficult to prove. However, as long as it is proven, as it was in this case, liability will be found.[135]

Within the general rules of causation, there are three areas of particular interest for UAM:

A) **Fright and flight:** V flees from the scene of a crime (base offence) committed by D, and dies when in flight. This can result, for example, from a heart attack brought on from the exertion; tripping and falling injuries; running in front of a car; etc. D's probable lack of mens rea as to death or serious injury in these cases will undermine liability for offences such as murder, and should direct you towards the strict elements of UAM. When applying UAM, however, there are two main barriers to liability. First, where D appears healthy and there are no obvious physical hazards, it may be difficult to demonstrate an objectively foreseeable risk of harm in flight, as in *Carey*.[136] Secondly, it must be shown that V's conduct in taking flight has not broken the chain of causation between D's base offence and V's death: V's response must not be 'wholly disproportionate' or 'daft'.[137] This is discussed in *Lewis*.[138]

B) **Drug supply:** V voluntarily takes controlled drugs supplied by D (supply being the base offence), and dies from their effects. Following several years of confusion, the case of *Kennedy (No 2)* has now clarified that there can be no liability for UAM in these cases.

  Kennedy (No 2) [2007] UKHL 38

D supplied V with a prepared syringe of heroin. V self-injected the drug and died as a result. D was charged with UAM on the basis that his unlawful conduct (drug supply) caused V's death.

- Crown Court: guilty of UAM.
- Court of Appeal: conviction upheld on appeal.
- House of Lords: quashing D's conviction on appeal—D was not guilty because he was not the legal cause of V's death.

In such cases, V's free and voluntary act in self-administering the drug will break the chain of causation between D's base offence (supply) and V's death. It is also debatable whether the act of drug supply alone can give rise to an objectively foreseeable risk of

---

[135] *AG's Reference (No 3 of 1994)* [1998] AC 245: Lord Hope stated that UAM would be committed even if the death was 'many hours, days or even months' after the base offence.

[136] [2006] EWCA Crim 17: no UAM where V (an apparently healthy young woman) died from a heart attack when fleeing from an affray.

[137] See **Chapter 2.7.2.3**.

[138] [2010] EWCA Crim 151: V was killed running into a road to escape an ongoing assault from D. That caused death. The manner of escape was foreseeable and therefore did not break the causal chain. See also *Tarasov (Valodia)* [2016] EWCA Crim 2278: V's choice to jump out of a window (causing death) did not break the causal chain despite a gap of over one hour from D's original attack.

bodily harm.[139] Therefore, to find liability for UAM in these cases it will be necessary to show that D administered the drug directly to V:[140] this base offence is foreseeably dangerous, and does not require the voluntary acts of V to cause death.

C) **Suicide:** V is distressed by D's base offence (eg D's physical abuse of V) to such an extent that she commits suicide. Two categories of cases should be distinguished. The first is where D's base offence causes physical injury to V, and V either fails to treat or exacerbates that injury in some manner to cause death. In these cases, causation (and thus liability for UAM) has been found on the basis that D's original offence remains a substantial and operating cause of death; V has no duty to limit the harm caused by D; and D must take her victim as she found her, as in *Blaue*.[141] The second category is where D's base offence causes psychiatric harm or where V's injuries are healed at the point of suicide. In these cases, it will be much more difficult to demonstrate that V's suicide was not a free and voluntary act that breaks the chain of causation, as discussed in *Dhaliwal*.[142]

6.3.2 Gross negligence manslaughter

Generally, liability for serious offences will be imposed only where D makes the *choice* to harm or to risk harm: punishing D for the harms caused, but also for her blameworthy *choice* in bringing them about. This approach respects the principle of autonomy.[143] As a result, there are not many serious offences in English law based on negligence, other than those in a regulatory context.[144] However, gross negligence manslaughter (GNM) stands as an extreme exception, punishable with a maximum of life imprisonment.

GNM arises where D's conduct is seriously negligent (unreasonably careless or inattentive), and where that negligence causes death. For example, if D tests her new gun in a busy park and causes death, failing to foresee any potential harm to others because she does not care about and therefore does not consider the safety of others, she is likely to be liable for GNM. Liability of this kind has been recognised for many years,[145] but has developed inconsistently at common law, particularly during the 1970s and 1980s where the then objective definition of recklessness caused confusion between GNM and reckless manslaughter (discussed later, **6.3.3**).[146] The law was clarified in the leading House of Lords authority *Adomako*.

---

139 Wilson, 'Dealing with Drug Induced Homicide' in Clarkson and Cunningham (eds), *Criminal Liability for Non-Aggressive Deaths* (2008).
140 Offences Against the Person Act 1861, s23.
141 (1975) 61 Cr App R 271: refusal of medical treatment on religious grounds. See also *Dear* [1996] Crim LR 595: reopening of wounds caused by D.
142 [2006] EWCA Crim 1139: V committed suicide following sustained domestic abuse from D. See also *Wallace* [2018] EWCA Crim 690; Horder and McGowan, 'Manslaughter by Causing Another's Suicide' [2006] Crim LR 1035; Munro and Aitken, 'Adding Insult to Injury? The Criminal Law's Response to Domestic Abuse-Related Suicide in England and Wales' [2018] Crim LR 732.
143 See **Chapter 1.4.3**.
144 See **Chapter 3.6.2**.
145 *Finney* (1874) 12 Cox CC 625; *Bateman* (1925) 94 LJKB 791.
146 See **3.4.4**. *Stone and Dobinson* [1977] QB 354; *Seymour* [1983] 1 AC 624; *Kong Cheuk Kwan* (1986) 82 Cr App R 18.

Adomako [1994] 3 All ER 79

D (an anaesthetist) failed to notice that a tube supplying oxygen to his patient (V) had become detached. As a result, V died. D was charged with GNM on the basis that his conduct fell dramatically below the standards expected of a reasonable anaesthetist.

- Crown Court: convicted of GNM—negligence test applied without reference to objective recklessness.
- Court of Appeal: conviction upheld on appeal.
- House of Lords: appeal dismissed—correct test requires a duty of care between D and V; a breach of that duty; that D's conduct caused death; and that D's conduct was 'gross' in its negligence.

Since *Adomako*, cases have further clarified that GNM cannot be found unless D's conduct created a serious and obvious risk of death to V,[147] and that it was reasonably foreseeable that D's breach of duty gave rise to such a risk.[148] The elements of GNM can be set out to separate actus reus and mens rea, as in **Table 6.5**.

Table 6.5 Gross negligence manslaughter

	Actus reus	**Mens rea**
Conduct element	Any conduct causing the results	Voluntary
Circumstance element	There must be a duty of care between D and V	Knowledge of facts establishing a duty
	D's breach of duty must pose a serious and obvious risk of death which is reasonably foreseeable	None
	D's breach of duty must be 'grossly negligent'	None
Result element	D must breach her duty of care	None
	Death of V	None

Setting out GNM in this manner highlights the lack of subjective mens rea required. However, partly because of this lack of mens rea, and partly because of its links with the civil law concept of negligence, GNM is more commonly presented and applied (as in *Adomako*) as the six core elements in **Figure 6.3**.

---

147 *Kuddus* [2019] EWCA Crim 837. Laird, commentary [2019] Crim LR 1055. Laird, 'The Evolution of Gross Negligence Manslaughter' [2018] 1 Arch Rev 6.
148 *Misra* [2004] EWCA Crim 2375; *Rose* [2017] EWCA Crim 1168.

Figure 6.3 Gross negligence manslaughter

We will discuss each of these elements in turn.

6.3.2.1 Duty of care

The first element of GNM requires the prosecution to prove that, at the time of D engaging in the conduct that causes death, D owed V a duty of care. Core examples of duties of care include doctors to patients;[149] transport carriers to passengers;[150] employers to employees;[151] etc. However, duties will be recognised far beyond these examples. With the definition of a 'duty of care' taken largely from the civil law, it has been interpreted broadly to apply wherever D's conduct carries a foreseeable risk of death to those around her.[152]

The criminal law is not, however, bound to follow the civil definition of 'duty of care'. As illustrated in *Wacker*, the criminal law has taken a more expansive approach to recognising duties.

 Wacker [2003] QB 1203

D was engaged in smuggling 60 illegal immigrants into the UK. D shut the air vent to the container carrying the immigrants, and 58 of them suffocated as a result. D was charged with GNM.

• Crown Court: convicted of GNM.

• Court of Appeal: conviction upheld on appeal. Although the joint criminal venture between D and the victims would undermine any duty of care in civil law, this was not the case in criminal law.

The ability of the criminal law to recognise duties of care outside those recognised in civil law is important because it allows criminal courts (as in *Wacker*) to avoid complex civil rules/exclusions that do not serve the interests of the criminal law. The aims of the two bodies of law are different. Civil law is structured around private compensation between individuals and the consent of both parties to a risky activity or crime may, therefore, undermine a civil claim; whereas the criminal law is structured more generally around the prevention and punishment of wrongs, with blame coming from the State, rather than in the form of compensation to another non-innocent party.[153]

---

[149] *Adomako* [1994] 3 All ER 79.
[150] *Barker* [2003] 2 Cr App R 110.
[151] *Dean* [2002] EWCA Crim 2410.
[152] *Evans* [2009] EWCA Crim 650; Herring and Palser, 'The Duty of Care in Gross Negligence Manslaughter' [2007] Crim LR 24.
[153] See also *Willoughby* [2005] Crim LR 389: death of V when helping D to commit arson, leading to UAM liability.

Extra detail . . .

Whether a relationship is capable of giving rise to a duty of care is a legal question for the judge. The jury will be directed that a duty exists if they find certain facts to be present and (where there is dispute on facts) to not find a duty if they find other facts to be present.[154]

Unlike UAM, GNM can be committed by act or *omission*. Where D's positive acts cause death (eg negligent mistreatment by a doctor), then it is sufficient to demonstrate a duty of care as discussed. However, where D's omissions cause death (eg negligent lack of treatment by a doctor), then the standard rules of omissions liability will also apply.[155] This means that as well as a duty of *care*, the court must also identify a duty from the much narrower categories of duties to *act*. We have already discussed the limited duties to act recognised in law: statutory; contractual; relationship-based; where D assumes a duty by caring for V; where D has created or contributed to a dangerous situation.[156] Although *both* a duty to act and a duty of care will be required for omission-based GNM, the duties to act within the narrower category will always also satisfy a duty of care. Thus, in practice, it is only necessary to identify a duty to act, which will then double as a duty of care as well.[157]

A leading case in relation to omission-based GNM is *Evans*.[158]

Evans [2009] EWCA Crim 650

D, V's half-sister, supplied her with heroin which she self-administered. Seeing symptoms of an overdose, D stayed with V but did not alert the authorities for fear of personal liability for supplying the drugs. V died and D was charged with GNM on the basis of her omission to aid V (duty arising from her creation of a dangerous situation when supplying the drugs).

- Crown Court: guilty of GNM.
- Court of Appeal: conviction upheld on appeal.

Evans provides a useful illustration of GNM liability by way of an omission. In doing so, it also demonstrates the novel way in which GNM has been used to find liability in a drug supply and overdose case. As we discussed earlier, UAM cannot operate in these cases as V's voluntary self-injection will break the chain of causation. In cases like *Evans*, by focussing on D's negligent omission *after* the self-injection, there is the potential for a causal link between this 'conduct' and V's death. This is illustrated by **Figure 6.4**, with the cross representing V's self-injection (the break in the causal chain).

154 *Evans* [2009] EWCA Crim 650, [45].
155 See **Chapter 2.6**.
156 See **Chapter 2.6.2**.
157 For critical discussion, see Ashworth, 'Manslaughter by Omission and the Rule of Law' [2015] Crim LR 563.
158 Williams, 'Gross Negligence Manslaughter and Duty of Care in "Drugs" Cases: *R v Evans*' [2009] Crim LR 631.

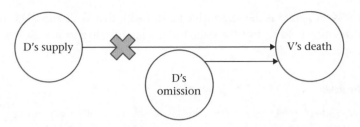

Figure 6.4 Breaking the chain of causation

The approach in *Evans* makes it much easier to find liability where D supplies V with a drug, V self-administers, and V dies. However, finding a duty to act (necessary for omissions liability) will not always be straightforward, and should be assessed with care. For example, if D in *Evans* had simply supplied the drug to V and left (ie not becoming aware of the overdose), it would have been much harder to establish a duty.[159] It would also be very difficult to establish the other elements of GNM on such facts. In *Broughton*,[160] D supplied his girlfriend, V, with a cocktail of controlled drugs at a festival. She experienced a violent reaction, but D did not call for medical assistance, despite pleas from others to do so. Instead, he video-recorded V's 'trip' as her condition deteriorated. D was convicted inter alia of manslaughter by gross negligence. The Court of Appeal quashed his conviction. There was no clear evidence that V died because of D's neglect. There was only evidence that this had 'drastically reduced her chances of survival', but that alone cannot suffice. A medical expert gave evidence that, had V received medical attention by a particular time in the evening, she would have stood a 90 per cent chance of survival. In a case concerning negligent lack of medical attention, in order to establish that a breach of duty was a substantial and operative cause of death, the prosecution had to prove that the victim *would* have lived. The Court of Appeal articulated the applicable test in the following terms:

> The prosecution must prove to the criminal standard that the gross negligence was at least a substantial contributory cause of death. That means that the prosecution must prove that the deceased would have lived in the sense that life would have been significantly prolonged.

On the evidence there was a 10 per cent chance she would have died. A jury could not be sure to the criminal standard that D's conduct was the cause of death.

6.3.2.2 Breach of duty of care

The second element of GNM is the requirement that D breaches her duty of care, and duty to act in the context of omission-based GNM. Again, this requirement mirrors negligence in the civil law, and similar principles apply. The question is whether D's conduct fell below that expected of a reasonable person in her position. For action-based GNM, we ask whether a reasonable person would have refrained from the acts carried out by D, and/or whether a reasonable person would have acted differently. For omission-based GNM, we ask how a reasonable person in D's position would have behaved. As with the civil law, where D purports to exercise a certain skill, the standard against which

---

[159] See **Chapter 2.6.2**.
[160] [2020] EWCA Crim 1093.

D's conduct is measured is the reasonable person with that skill. Thus, D's conduct in *Adomako* was measured against the standard of a reasonable anaesthetist, not simply a reasonable person.

Extra detail . . .

The consent of V to D's conduct is not relevant to the issue of breach; although it may be relevant to the final element of 'grossness' discussed later. For example, the victims in *Wacker* discussed in the previous section consented to the obviously dangerous venture of attempting to be smuggled in a lorry container. Their consent did not undermine the fact that D's conduct, including the shutting of the vent which led to their deaths, was a breach of his duty to them.

6.3.2.3 Serious and obvious risk of death

When breaching her duty of care, it is now clear that D's conduct must pose a risk of death to V which is both serious and obvious, as well as being reasonably foreseeable. The first aspect of this element is usefully discussed in *Kuddus*.[161]

Kuddus [2019] EWCA Crim 837

D, the chef and owner of a curry house, prepared a curry for takeaway delivery. It included peanuts. Unknown to him, V, the 15-year-old who had ordered the food on the internet had stated that she had a peanut allergy. V ate the meal, suffered an allergic reaction and died. The person responsible for taking the orders in the curry house (X) failed to pass that information to D (X was also convicted of manslaughter and did not appeal). V had previously only ever experienced mild allergic reactions to nuts. D argued that since V was only mildly allergic there was no serious and obvious risk of death to her.

- Crown Court: guilty of GNM. On the reasonable foreseeability of a serious and obvious risk, the trial judge directed the jury to consider what was foreseeable to a reasonable restaurateur given the knowledge of the restaurant as a whole (ie following the notification from V).
- Court of Appeal: conviction quashed. The question was whether a reasonable chef with the knowledge that D had about the customer would have foreseen the serious and obvious risk of death, so the knowledge of the restaurant (which was informed of the risk) should not have been conflated with that of D (who was not).

Kuddus provides useful guidance on the element of reasonable foreseeability, discussed separately at **6.3.2.4**. However, for present purposes, it also provides useful guidance on the requirement of a 'serious and obvious risk of death'. The reasonable foreseeability of a risk of death has been the focus of several recent cases, but as the court makes clear in *Kuddus*, care should be taken not to neglect the *separate* requirement that that risk must also be factually present—'put simply, you cannot foresee something that does not exist' (at [54]). Whether the risk of death was serious and obvious is a question of fact for the jury.

One issue on appeal in *Kuddus* was whether the serious and obvious risk of death must be to the specific V. As V had only experienced mild allergic reactions in the past, Kuddus' defence argued that this element of the offence was not satisfied—there was no

---

[161] Laird, Commentary [2019] Crim LR 1055.

serious and obvious risk of death *to V*. This argument was rejected by the appeal court (at [69]–[73]). When applying the serious and obvious risk of death requirement, the question is whether there was such a risk to *the class of persons* to whom D owed a duty. As nut products pose a serious and obvious risk of death to those with nut allergies, and V had a nut allergy, this element was satisfied. D's appeal was successful because the risk, though present, may not have been reasonably foreseeable to someone in his position (ie due to the conflation of the restaurant's knowledge with his own).

6.3.2.4 Reasonably foreseeable risk of death

Not only must the risk of death exist in fact, but it must also have been one that the reasonable person would have foreseen. This is an objective requirement: it is not necessary to demonstrate that D foresaw the risk herself. This requirement was confirmed in *Gurphal Singh*[162] and *Misra*,[163] and is usefully illustrated in *Rose*.[164]

 Rose [2017] EWCA Crim 1168

D (an optometrist) performed an eye test on V (a seven-year-old), recording no problems. Five months later, V became ill and died suddenly, death caused by a long-standing condition involving a build-up of fluid in the brain (hydrocephalus). Evidence was given that a competent eye test would have revealed V's condition when it was still treatable, but D did not view the correct scans of V's eye structure during the test and so the condition was missed. D was charged with GNM.

- Crown Court: guilty of GNM.

- Court of Appeal: appeal allowed. At the point D breached her duty to V, it was not reasonably foreseeable that the breach posed a serious and obvious risk of death.

In allowing D's appeal, *Rose* reveals important details about how this element of GNM should be applied. Crucially, the court confirmed that the foresight test must be applied at the moment D breaches her duty to V, and may only include facts that would have been obvious to a reasonable person at that time. Thus, although a reasonable optometrist would have known that a negligently performed eye test *might* risk *something serious* being missed, and although further tests *would have* revealed an obvious risk, neither is sufficient for this element of the test. In each case, it will be for the jury to decide if a reasonable person in D's position, at the time of the breach, knowing only those facts available to D, would have foreseen a serious and obvious risk of death. There is further useful discussion of this point in the recent case of *Winterton*,[165] where liability for V's death was found when several people had pointed out to D the dangerous nature of the trench for which he was responsible and which ultimately collapsed and killed V.

---

[162] [1999] Crim LR 582.

[163] [2004] EWCA Crim 2375.

[164] Laird, Commentary [2018] Crim LR 76; and lamenting the lack of appeal to the Supreme Court [2018] Crim LR 241. Cf Stark, 'In Praise of *Rose*' [2019] 8 Arch Rev 7.

[165] [2018] EWCA Crim 2435: D (construction site manager) should have foreseen the obvious risk that an excavation tunnel would collapse, risking the death of anyone trapped within.

Extra detail . . .

Rose makes it more difficult to convict individuals of GNM where they negligently fail to take steps that might identify a serious risk of death: without taking steps to identify the risk (eg doing the eye test properly) the risk is not revealed, and this element of GNM will not be satisfied.[166] The same issue may be pertinent to potential GNM charges surrounding the Grenfell Tower disaster: if D does not appropriately examine faulty building cladding, for example, the risks of death posed by the material remain *possible* rather than *obvious*. In cases of this kind, D's course of conduct becomes important: was she alerted to the problem previously;[167] can we group her course of conduct within a single transaction, within which *cumulatively* the risk becomes obvious?[168]

6.3.2.5 Causing death

After it is established that D owed V a duty of care (including a duty to act in omission cases), that D breached that duty, that the breach entailed an obvious and serious risk of death, and that that risk was reasonably foreseeable, it must be proved that D's breach caused V's death. For example, where a doctor, D, breaches a duty of care to her patient with negligent treatment, and V dies, it must still be shown that V would not have died in the same way if she had been treated reasonably.[169] This requires the standard causation rules discussed previously: D's conduct must be a cause of death in fact (a 'but for' cause); and a cause of death in law (proximate; substantial; and operating).[170]

Even where D's conduct is omission-based, causation must still be found. For omission-based GNM, the question of causation requires us to ask what a reasonable person in D's position would have done, and whether that action would have prevented V dying in the manner she did. For example, D was liable for GNM in *Evans* because she failed to act reasonably to try to save V's life, watching V die of an overdose over the course of hours without calling medical help. However, if we vary the facts of *Evans*, such that V died almost instantly, and so even if D had called for help this could not have prevented V's death, then there would have been no causation and no liability.

6.3.2.6 Grossly negligent

The final element of GNM requires D's negligence to be sufficiently 'gross' (ie sufficiently bad) to be deserving of criminal as opposed to simply civil liability. This is a question for the jury. Lord Mackay sets out the question in *Adomako* as follows:

> [H]aving regard to the risk of death involved, [was] the conduct of the defendant . . . so bad in all the circumstances as to amount to a criminal act or omission?

---

[166] Cf Stark, 'In Praise of *Rose*' [2019] 8 Arch Rev 7.

[167] See *Zaman* [2017] EWCA Crim 1783: liability for GNM where D (a restaurant owner) failed to guard against customers suffering allergic reactions, despite previous incidents, where V died from such a reaction.

[168] Something like this is attempted by Norrie in the context of oblique intention and murder: 'Legal and Social Murder: What's the Difference?' [2018] Crim LR 531. The difficulty in both contexts would be to establish the transaction across a necessarily large time-span, see **Chapter 4.3.2.2.**

[169] See *Broughton* [2020] EWCA Crim 1093.

[170] See **Chapter 2.7.**

Lord Mackay's question, as stated, needs qualification. After all, D's negligent conduct may satisfy a negligence-based criminal offence such as careless or dangerous driving, and yet still not be sufficiently gross for such a serious offence as GNM. Therefore, the grossness element is not simply about distinguishing non-criminal conduct; instead, it asks the jury if D's behaviour warrants liability for manslaughter.

The term 'gross' is rather ambiguous as an offence element, and so it is useful to consider what factors a jury should take into account when applying it to the facts of a case. The Court of Appeal discussed this point in *Sellu*,[171] encouraging trial judges to set out the details of this element more clearly when directing a jury, to avoid relying on the term 'gross' alone, and to recognise the important role played by expert evidence (eg helping the jury quantify the seriousness of a breach). Although the court did not attempt a definition of grossness, the description of requiring a 'truly exceptionally bad' breach provides useful emphasis that the bar for liability is (and should be) set high.

When assessing D's breach within this element, the jury are required to look at all the surrounding circumstances in order to make their assessment; for example, what were D's motives; was she acting maliciously; how did she explain her conduct; and so on. The discretion given to the jury here can be useful to ensure only those deserving, all things considered, of GNM liability are brought within the offence. However, the absence of clear criteria makes it difficult to predict the outcome of cases, and has given rise to powerful criticism about the potential for inconsistency[172] with different juries applying the test differently, and about the role of the jury more generally.

The latter criticism, about the role of the jury, focusses on whether the grossness element is asking the jury to establish facts, which is the correct role of the jury, or whether it is asking them to establish matters of law, which is the correct role of the judge.[173] When applying elements of a crime, the jury should be given the legal definition of that element by the judge and then be asked to decide whether, on the facts as they believe them to be, that element is satisfied. With regard to the grossness element, it can appear as if this division of expertise has broken down: the jury are told to find the grossness element as having been satisfied if they find the facts to be criminal in nature, and to find the facts criminal if they find them gross. This test is circular and, in effect, it is asking the jury to define the offence (the law) as they apply it. However, despite the apparent circularity, the test has survived challenges on human rights grounds and remains valid.[174]

6.3.3 Reckless manslaughter

Reckless manslaughter is the last of the three common law involuntary manslaughter offences. D will be liable under this offence where she causes V's death by act or omission and is at least reckless as to causing death or GBH. The elements are set out in **Table 6.6**.

---

[171] [2016] EWCA Crim 1716.
[172] Such inconsistency can also be reflected in decisions to prosecute. Quick, 'Prosecuting "Gross" Medical Negligence: Manslaughter, Discretion and the Crown Prosecution Service' (2006) 33 JLS 421.
[173] See **Chapter 1.1.7.1**.
[174] See Lord Justice Judge's attempt to explain the test in a non-circular way in *Misra* [2004] EWCA Crim 2375, [62]–[63].

Table 6.6 Reckless manslaughter

	Actus reus	Mens rea
Conduct element	Any act or omission causing the result	Voluntary
Circumstance element	V is a person	Knowledge
Result element	Death of V	Recklessness as to death or GBH

The offence of reckless manslaughter is rarely prosecuted, and so there are few appeal cases discussing its interpretation.[175] It is rarely prosecuted because cases coming within this offence will almost always alternatively satisfy the elements of either UAM or GNM and, as these two offences do not require subjective mens rea as to death or serious harm, they will usually be easier to prosecute. The only cases where D commits reckless manslaughter *and not* UAM or GNM, arise where D kills by omission (thus no UAM), and where D's omission does not pose an objectively foreseeable risk of death (thus no GNM).

Mitchell and Mackay found that reckless manslaughter is occasionally charged where the facts of a case involve culpability just short of murder, where it is clear that D foresaw a high risk of causing death or GBH, but it would be difficult to demonstrate that it was foreseen as a virtual certainty (ie difficult to prove the intention required for murder).[176] This makes sense, both in relation to the law in practice and as an approach to problem questions. If it is clear that D foresaw death or GBH as highly likely, then a jury may find foresight equivalent to virtual certainty and thus find liability for murder, but will at the very least find a foresight that will satisfy the requirements of reckless manslaughter. In a more recent article, contrary to Mitchell and Mackay, Stark denies the existence of the offence within the current law. However, he moves on to contend that its use could provide benefits in terms of fair labelling and at sentencing.[177]

6.4 Statutory offences of unlawful killing

This chapter has focussed on the traditional manslaughter conviction: voluntary manslaughter resulting from a partial defence to murder, and involuntary manslaughter resulting from a common law manslaughter offence. However, the criminal law also recognises a number of other offences of unlawful killing, some of which employ the label manslaughter. These offences are discussed briefly in this section, and their differences from the traditional forms will be highlighted.

---

[175] One of the few exceptions is *Lidar* [2000] 4 Arch News 3.

[176] Mitchell and Mackay, 'Investigating Manslaughter: An Empirical Study of 127 Cases' (2011) 31 OJLS 165.

[177] Stark, 'Reckless Manslaughter' [2017] Crim LR 763. See also Taylor, 'The Contours of Involuntary Manslaughter—A Place for Unlawful Act by Omission' [2019] Crim LR 205.

6.4.1 Corporate manslaughter

The Corporate Manslaughter and Corporate Homicide Act 2007 (CMA 2007) creates a separate homicide offence applicable to corporate defendants,[178] and abolishes GNM for companies.[179] The offence is commonly presented as a form of involuntary manslaughter alongside the traditional common law offences, but has been separated in our discussion here because, unlike those offences, corporate manslaughter does not require the standard actus reus of murder to have been committed (the killing of a person, by a person). Rather, corporate manslaughter can be satisfied where a variety of acts or omissions within the corporation, potentially from many different individuals, combine to cause death.

The CMA 2007 is based indirectly on preceding Law Commission recommendations.[180] The Commission and others were critical of the way the common law had failed to find GNM in relation to companies. This was because, particularly with respect to large and complex companies, it would often be impossible to identify a 'controlling mind' (ie very senior figure) within the company who was individually[181] responsible in GNM for V's death. In the absence of such a figure, even if a general culture of negligence was found within large parts of the corporation, and these were found to have caused V's death, the common law identification doctrine could not link liability to the corporation.[182] The CMA 2007 sought to address these problems within the new offence. However, it is noteworthy that the few successful prosecutions under the offence have also (so far) focussed on smaller corporations.[183]

 Extra detail . . .

Directors and other individuals within a corporation cannot be charged with the corporate manslaughter offence, and cannot be a secondary party to a corporate manslaughter offence. However, they can still be individually liable under one of the standard common law involuntary manslaughter offences, or for health and safety offences.[184]

The corporate manslaughter offence is set out in section 1(1) of the CMA 2007. Where D (a corporation) is found liable under this section, it will face an unlimited fine,[185] potentially combined with a remedial order and/or a publicity order.[186]

---

[178] See **Chapter 1.5.1**. Ormerod and Taylor, 'The Corporate Manslaughter and Corporate Homicide Act 2007' [2008] Crim LR 589.

[179] CMA 2007, s20.

[180] Law Commission, *Involuntary Manslaughter* (No 237, 1996).

[181] The old law would not allow the acts of employees to be aggregated together and viewed as the acts of the corporation: *AG's Reference (No 2 of 1999)* [2000] QB 796.

[182] Wells, 'Corporate Manslaughter: Why Does Reform Matter?' (2006) 123 SALJ 646.

[183] *Cotswold Geological Holdings Ltd* [2011] EWCA Crim 1337; Dobson, 'Shifting Sands: Multiple Counts in Prosecutions for Corporate Manslaughter' [2012] Crim LR 200.

[184] Antrobus, 'The Criminal Liability of Directors for Health and Safety Breaches and Manslaughter' [2013] Crim LR 309.

[185] CMA 2007, s1(6).

[186] Ibid, ss9–10.

(1) An organisation to which this section applies is guilty of an offence if the way in which its activities are managed or organised—

(a) causes a person's death, and

(b) amounts to a gross breach of a relevant duty of care owed by the organisation to the deceased.

The structure of this offence is similar to GNM, and its analysis and application should be approached in a similar manner. The elements are set out in **Figure 6.5**.

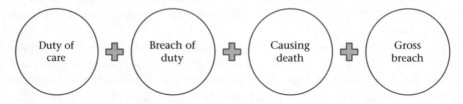

Figure 6.5 Corporate manslaughter

Before discussing these elements, it is necessary first to identify which organisations are capable of committing the offence. This is set out in section 1(2) to include most corporations, police forces, partnerships, trade unions, or employers' associations, as well as various government departments.

6.4.1.1 Duty of care

D (the relevant organisation) must owe a duty of care to V (the person killed). As with GNM, the duty requirement will be interpreted in line with established civil law duties. As set out in section 2 of the CMA 2007, the most relevant duties will be to employees; visitors on premises; customers; etc. As with GNM, it is for the judge to decide as a matter of law what is capable of giving rise to a duty of care.[187]

The scope of this element and, therefore, the offence, is severely limited by a number of exceptions where a duty of care will not be found. For example, section 3 excludes public policy decisions. This will exclude a number of cases, including where government departments make potentially negligent decisions to remove funding from projects and people die as a result (eg the funding of certain medical drugs). Section 4 excludes military activities; section 5 excludes certain police activities; section 6 excludes certain activities of the emergency services; and section 7 has a similar role for child protection and probation services. In each case, these provisions are unnecessarily complex in their construction.

6.4.1.2 Breach of duty of care

This element requires D (the relevant organisation) to have breached its duty to V by failing to perform in a reasonable manner, to the standard of a relevant reasonable organisation. Importantly, and in contrast to the old identification doctrine approach described earlier, this breach does not need to be identified in the conduct of a single representative of the organisation, but can be found through an aggregation of the organisation's activities as a whole.

---

[187] Ibid, s2(5).

The crucial restricting qualification to this is that a 'substantial element' of the breach must be traceable to 'the way in which [D's] activities are managed or organised by its senior management'.[188] This is not as restrictive as the identification doctrine: 'senior management' is interpreted more broadly than those who would have qualified as controlling minds;[189] 'senior management' allows aggregation across those in that class; and their impact only needs to be 'substantial' as opposed to sole or even dominant. However, any restrictions of this kind relating to senior figures will inevitably make the prosecution of larger and more complex organisations difficult.

6.4.1.3 Causing death

As with GNM, the standard rules of causation will apply.[190]

6.4.1.4 Gross breach of duty

Finally, it must be established that D's (the relevant organisation's) breach of duty was 'gross'. As with GNM, this is a question for the jury. However, unlike with GNM, the CMA 2007 provides significant guidance for the jury in their assessment. Section 1(4)(b) states that:

> a breach of a duty of care by an organisation is a 'gross' breach if the conduct alleged to amount to a breach of that duty falls far below what can reasonably be expected of the organisation in the circumstances.

Section 8 then goes on to provide factors for the jury to consider, including the seriousness of D's failure and how foreseeable it was that a risk of death would be created. Additional factors listed in section 8 also include an assessment of the culture towards risk within the organisation, as well as any breaches of health and safety law.[191]

6.4.2 Driving causing death

There are many statutory offences involving causing death by driving. Where D kills V with her car, there is nothing to stop her being charged with murder or manslaughter at common law, provided the relevant elements of the offence can be proved (ie including mens rea). However, for reasons of fair labelling, and in order to tailor offences to secure convictions for road-based homicides, a series of bespoke offences has been created.[192] It should be noted that these offences do not extend to cyclists who cause death, a potential lacuna in the law that has attracted debate.[193]

---

[188] Ibid, s1(3).
[189] Ibid, s14(c) defines 'senior management' as those having significant roles in managing significant activities or parts of the organisation.
[190] See **Chapter 2.7**.
[191] Wright, 'Criminal Liability of Directors and Senior Managers for Deaths at Work' [2007] Crim LR 949.
[192] Cunningham, 'The Reality of Vehicular Homicides: Convictions for Murder, Manslaughter and Causing Death by Dangerous Driving' [2001] Crim LR 679.
[193] Freer, 'We Need to Talk About Charlie: Putting the Brakes on Unlawful Act Manslaughter' [2018] Crim LR 612.

6.4.2.1 Causing death by dangerous driving

Section 1 of the Road Traffic Act 1988 (RTA 1988)[194] makes it an offence to cause death by driving a 'mechanically propelled vehicle dangerously on a road or other public place'.[195] The elements are set out in **Table 6.7**.

Table 6.7 RTA 1988, s1

	Actus reus	**Mens rea**
Conduct element	Causing the result by driving	Voluntary
Circumstance element	D's driving of a vehicle in public is dangerous	None
Result element	Death of V	None

As the table demonstrates, causing death by dangerous driving is a negligence-based offence. All that is required is that D's driving caused V's death, employing the standard rules of causation,[196] and that D's driving, at the relevant time, was objectively dangerous.

D's driving will qualify as 'dangerous' where 'the way he drives falls far below what would be expected of a competent and careful driver, *and* it would be obvious to a competent driver that driving in that way would be dangerous' (ie would risk injury or serious property damage).[197] This also includes cases where the mechanical state of the car makes driving dangerous, and this would have been obvious to a reasonable driver.[198] As with other negligence-based offences, D's ignorance of the factors making her driving dangerous is irrelevant to her liability if such facts would have been obvious to a reasonable person.[199] The only exception is one working against D: where she has special knowledge of potential danger beyond that of a reasonable driver, as for example where she is a mechanic and recognises signs of danger, her driving may be found to be dangerous on that basis.

6.4.2.2 Causing death by careless driving

Section 2B of the RTA 1988 makes it an offence to cause death by driving a 'mechanically propelled vehicle on a road or other public place without due care and attention, or without reasonable consideration for other persons using the road or place'.[200] The elements are set out in **Table 6.8**.

---

[194] As amended by the Road Traffic Act 1991.

[195] The Legal Aid, Sentencing and Punishment of Offenders Act 2012, s143 inserted a new offence in the RTA 1988, s1A of causing GBH by dangerous driving. Applying similar terms to s1, this offence applies where D causes serious harm which falls short of death.

[196] See **Chapter 2.7**.

[197] RTA 1988, s2A (emphasis added).

[198] Ibid, s2A(2) and (3); *Strong* [1995] Crim LR 428.

[199] *Roberts and George* [1997] Crim LR 209.

[200] Road Safety Act 2006, s30.

Table 6.8 RTA 1988, s2B

	Actus reus	Mens rea
Conduct element	Causing the result by driving	Voluntary
Circumstance element	D's driving of a vehicle in public is without due care and attention, Or without reasonable consideration for others	None None
Result element	Death of V	None

Filling the perceived gap below the section 1 offence, here D's driving does not need to carry an obvious objective risk of causing harm to the person or property. Rather, it is enough that D was driving in a careless manner,[201] and that she caused death.

6.4.2.3 Causing death by careless driving when under the influence of drink or drugs

Section 3A of the RTA 1988 makes it an offence to cause death by driving a 'mechanically propelled vehicle on a road or other public place without due care and attention, or without reasonable consideration for other persons using the road or place, and he is, at the time when he is driving, unfit to drive through drink or drugs, *or* he has consumed so much alcohol that the proportion of it in his breath, blood or urine at that time exceeds the prescribed limit, *or* he is . . . required to provide a specimen . . . but without reasonable excuse fails to provide it, *or* he is required by a constable to give his permission for a laboratory test of a specimen of blood taken from him . . . but without reasonable excuse fails to do so'. The elements are set out in **Table 6.9**.

Table 6.9 RTA 1988, s3A

	Actus reus	Mens rea
Conduct element	Causing the result by driving	Voluntary
Circumstance element	D's driving of a vehicle in public is without due care and attention, or without reasonable consideration for others	None

(Continued)

---

[201] Defined at RTA 1988, s3ZA.

Table 6.9 Continued

Circumstance element	And	
	D is unfit to drive through drink or drugs; or she exceeds the alcohol limit; or she fails to provide a specimen; or she does not give permission for a specimen to be tested	None
Result element	Death of V	None

This offence constructs upon the section 2B offence, leading to more serious liability where one of the aggravating factors is present.

6.4.2.4 Causing death while driving unlawfully

Section 3ZB of the RTA 1988[202] makes it an offence to cause death whilst driving without a valid driving licence, or whilst uninsured. The elements are set out in **Table 6.10**.

Table 6.10 RTA 1988, s3ZB

	Actus reus	Mens rea
Conduct element	Causing the result by driving	Voluntary
Circumstance element	D is driving a vehicle in public; and	None
	D has no licence; or D is uninsured	None
Result element	Death of V	None

Alongside this offence, and with the same construction, section 3ZC of the RTA 1988 includes an offence of causing death whilst disqualified from driving.[203]

These offences have been controversial because, read literally, they appear to criminalise D for causing death even where she is not a blameworthy cause (ie where her driving is faultless). Indeed, this is how section 3ZB was originally applied.[204] However, following academic criticism,[205] the Supreme Court has now confirmed that D's driving must

[202] Road Safety Act 2006, s21.
[203] As amended by the Criminal Justice and Courts Act 2015, s29.
[204] *Williams* [2010] EWCA Crim 2552.
[205] See Ormerod [2011] Crim LR 473, and Sullivan and Simester, 'Causation Without Limits: Causing Death Whilst Driving Without a Licence, While Disqualified, or Without Insurance' [2012] Crim LR 754.

have caused death through some fault on her part.[206] This confirms the general principle of causation that all causes must be blameworthy.[207]

6.4.3 Infanticide

The infanticide rules apply to cases in which D (a mother) kills V (her child) within the first year of its life where, at the time of killing, D's mind was disturbed due to the birth or due to her lactation as a result of the birth.[208] Infanticide rules are specifically designed to distinguish killings of this type from traditional homicide offences. To this end, infanticide can operate *either* as an offence in its own right, *or* as a partial defence to murder or manslaughter. The law is set out in section 1 of the Infanticide Act 1938.[209]

6.4.3.1 The offence of infanticide

Section 1(1) of the 1938 Act makes it an offence:

> Where a woman by any wilful act or omission causes the death of her child being a child under the age of twelve months, but at the time of the act or omission the balance of her mind was disturbed by reason of her not having fully recovered from the effect of giving birth to the child or by reason of the effect of lactation consequent upon the birth of the child, then . . . she shall be guilty of . . . infanticide, and may for such offence be dealt with and punished as if she had been guilty of the offence of manslaughter of the child.

The elements of infanticide are set out in **Table 6.11**.

Table 6.11 Infanticide

	Actus reus	**Mens rea**
Conduct element	Act or omission causing the result	Voluntary
Circumstance element	D is the mother of V; and	None
	V is under 12 months old; and	None
	D's mind was disturbed by the effects of giving birth, or her lactation from giving birth	None
Result element	Death of V	None

---

[206] *Hughes* [2013] UKSC 56; *Taylor* [2016] UKSC 5.

[207] See **Chapter 2.7.2.2**.

[208] Mackay, 'The Consequences of Killing Very Young Children' [1993] Crim LR 21; Wilczynski and Morris, 'Parents Who Kill Their Children' [1993] Crim LR 31; Brennan, 'Beyond the Medical Model: A Rationale for Infanticide Legislation' (2007) 58 NILQ 505.

[209] As amended by the Coroners and Justice Act 2009, s57.

Where D satisfies these elements, she will be liable for infanticide regardless of whether she satisfies the elements of any other homicide offence (the *offence* of infanticide is free-standing and independent of other offences).[210] The offence will often be charged where D kills V when suffering from postnatal depression, and sentences are usually relatively low.[211] It should be noted that the rather artificial link to the physical birth of the child or D's lactation has been criticised, but it seems that the courts will interpret these requirements broadly to allow appropriate cases to come within the offence.[212] *Tunstill*[213] clarified that infanticide can apply even where a relevant mental disturbance (ie birth-related) is accompanied or exacerbated by other pre-existing mental conditions.

6.4.3.2 The partial defence of infanticide

Section 1(2) of the 1938 Act states that:

> Where upon the trial of a woman for the murder of her child, being a child under the age of twelve months, the jury are of opinion that she by any wilful act or omission caused its death, but that at the time of the act or omission the balance of her mind was disturbed by reason of her not having fully recovered from the effect of giving birth to the child or by reason of the effect of lactation consequent upon the birth of the child, then the jury may, notwithstanding that the circumstances were such that but for the provisions of this Act they might have returned a verdict of murder, return in lieu thereof a verdict of infanticide.

The effect of this section is that even where D is charged with, and satisfies, the elements of murder or manslaughter, if the court finds the elements of infanticide to be satisfied as well, they should find liability for infanticide only. D has an evidential burden to raise the defence, and it is then for the prosecution (if they so choose) to disprove the elements beyond a reasonable doubt.

Extra detail . . .

The infanticide rules only apply to biological mothers within the first year of birth. Outside this (eg fathers who kill), D will be potentially liable for the traditional homicide offences, and will have to rely on defences such as diminished responsibility.

6.4.4 The killing of a foetus

The unlawful killing of a foetus does not represent a homicide offence because a foetus is not a person in law until it is fully independent of its mother, by being fully expelled from the womb.[214] The abortion of a foetus under 24 weeks in certain conditions, or after this point in more exceptional conditions, has been a legal practice for some time.[215] However, outside this regulated procedure, the killing of a foetus is likely to constitute an offence under one of two headings.

---

[210] *Gore* [2008] Crim LR 388: clarifying that infanticide does not require mens rea as to death.
[211] The maximum sentence is life imprisonment, but most cases result in community orders.
[212] *Kai-Whitewind* [2006] Crim LR 348.
[213] [2018] EWCA Crim 1696. Laird, Commentary [2019] Crim LR 163.
[214] See **Chapter 5.3.2.3**.
[215] Abortion Act 1967, s1.

A) **Section 1 of the Infant Life (Preservation) Act 1929:** This section creates the offence of 'child destruction': the intentional killing of a foetus capable of being born alive. A foetus is capable of being born alive where it would be capable of independent breathing, usually from around 26 weeks.[216] The offence is punishable with a maximum of life imprisonment.

B) **Section 58 of the Offences Against the Person Act 1861:** This section creates the offence of attempting to procure a miscarriage: where D (whether the mother of V or any other person) intentionally attempts to cause a miscarriage at any stage by means of ingestion of a noxious thing (eg poisons) or other means.[217] The offence may be committed even where the 'mother' is not in fact pregnant, where D (any person other than the 'mother') acts with the intent to cause a miscarriage.

 Extra detail . . .

As discussed earlier, although the killing of a foetus will not amount to a homicide offence, liability for a homicide offence may be possible where the foetus is injured by D when in the womb and dies later after birth (**6.3.1.3**). As long as the foetus is born alive before it dies, it becomes a 'person' within the meaning of the law.

6.5 Reform

In this section we will highlight a number of ongoing debates in relation to manslaughter and the potential for further reform. We begin with debates about voluntary and involuntary manslaughter, we then consider the overall structure of manslaughter.

6.5.1 Reforming voluntary manslaughter

Despite the extensive reform of loss of control and diminished responsibility within the C&JA 2009, considerable debate remains about the role and construction of these partial defences. This is perhaps inevitable, with the partial defences playing such a vital role in removing deserving cases from the label (and mandatory life sentence) of murder. It is also for this reason that the potential for new partial defences is commonly debated.[218]

Beginning with the partial defence of loss of control, it is useful to look back (see **Table 6.12**) on three controversial points identified in relation to the pre-C&JA 2009 law and see whether they remain a concern for the current law.

---

[216] *Rance v Mid-Downs Health Authority* [1991] 1 QB 587; Foster, 'Forty Years On' (2007) 157 NLJ 1517.

[217] *Ahmed* [2010] EWCA Crim 1949.

[218] See eg Wake, 'Human Trafficking and Modern Day Slavery: When Victims Kill' [2017] Crim LR 658; Keating and Bridgman, 'Compassionate Killings: The Case for a Partial Defence' (2012) 75 MLR 697.

Table 6.12 Evaluating the current partial defence of LOC

What types of conduct can qualify as provocation (or, under the current law, as 'triggers')?	The 2009 Act defines 'qualifying triggers' in a way that both narrows and expands the previous law. It narrows the trigger based on provocative acts or omissions to only those creating a 'justifiable sense' of D being 'seriously wronged'. It expands the law by introducing a new fear of serious violence trigger. These general categories, although rather vague, have been generally welcomed (**6.2.1.3**). However, the specific exclusion of sexual infidelity has not been successful.[219]
What characteristics of D can be taken into account when deciding if her reaction should qualify for the defence?	This question was problematic under the old law, and has not been resolved within the 2009 Act. It is clear that D's 'age' and 'sex' may be considered within the normal person test, but the ambiguous reference in the statute to 'in the circumstances of D' continues to cause uncertainty (**6.2.1.4**).[220]
Is the defence gender-biased in its operation?	Significant efforts were made to make the defence more gender-neutral within the 2009 Act, including the new fear of serious violence trigger and the removal of the 'sudden and temporary' requirement for D's loss of control. However, the government's choice to retain the requirement that D should have lost control in fact (contrary to the Law Commission's recommendations) continues to present a significant hurdle for female defendants who are much less likely to react through a loss of control (particularly in the context of abused women) (**6.2.1.2**).

The current LOC defence is a significant improvement on the previous common law, and has been further strengthened by a series of useful Court of Appeal judgments. However, uncertainties remain.[221]

For diminished responsibility, it is useful to start with the general scope and aim of the defence. This is because the medicalisation of the elements of DR will almost inevitably restrict its use as a flexible (undefined) tool of legal equity: a tool for avoiding murder and the mandatory life sentence in 'deserving' cases. In this regard, we may think the law should have remained broadly defined, thereby allowing flexibility to deal more sensitively with women who kill their abusers; and potentially others,

---

[219] For a useful discussion of specific and general exclusions, see Crofts and Loughnan, 'Provocation, NSW Style: Reform of the Defence of Provocation in NSW' [2014] Crim LR 109.

[220] Mitchell, Mackay, and Brookbanks, 'Pleading for Provoked Killers: In Defence of *Morgan Smith*' (2008) 124 LQR 675.

[221] See eg Sorial, 'Anger, Provocation and Loss of Self-Control: What does "Losing It" Really Mean?' (2019) 13(2) CrimL&P 247; Parsons, 'The Loss of Control Defence—Fit for Purpose? (2015) 79 JCL 94.

such as so-called mercy killers. On the other hand, we may think the law should be strictly defined, that Parliament should be responsible for creating partial defences for these classes of defendants where necessary. As the number of defendants success-fully raising the defence continues to decline,[222] one's view of the new defence, and the appropriateness of future reform, will chiefly depend upon which side of this debate is preferred.

Accepting that the current law has adopted a relatively precise definition of DR, there is also room to question that detail. Two areas stand out. First, there remains a concern that developmentally immature defendants without an associated learn-ing disability will fall outside the defence. The Law Commission's recommendations extended the defence to the developmentally immature (**6.2.2.2**). Secondly, having established the first three limbs of the defence (abnormality of mental functioning; caused by a recognised condition; substantially impairing D's ability to control or understand her actions), it is arguable that the further requirement of a causal link between D's abnormality and the killing is both medically incapable of being proved and morally unnecessary.[223]

6.5.2 Reforming involuntary manslaughter

The common law offences of UAM and GNM are some of the most controversial in the criminal law. In both cases, the offences label and punish D for manslaughter without requiring her to have foreseen the possibility that her acts will cause death: they both include elements of strict liability.[224]

For UAM, this led the Law Commission at one time to recommend abolition of the offence without replacement.[225] However, more recently, the Commission has made recommendations that reduce the constructive nature of the offence by requiring *some* mens rea as to death or injury, but leaving its basic structure largely intact.[226] For those opposed to constructive liability, this remains inadequate.[227]

Similar criticisms can be made of GNM. Indeed, as GNM does not require D to have committed a base offence with necessary mens rea, it is capable of criminalis-ing D for manslaughter where she has not chosen to commit, or risk committing, any offence at all. Rather, it will be enough that her behaviour is classified by a jury as falling grossly below the level expected. The Law Commission has consistently recommended the maintenance of GNM, although it would like it to be codified in legislation, and to make D's ability (capacity) to appreciate the risk of death as an express element.[228]

---

[222] Mackay and Mitchell, 'The New Diminished Responsibility Plea in Operation: Some Initial Findings' [2017] Crim LR 18.

[223] Mackay, 'The New Diminished Responsibility Plea' [2010] Crim LR 299.

[224] See generally Clarkson and Cunningham (eds), *Criminal Liability for Non-Aggressive Death* (2008).

[225] Law Commission, *Involuntary Manslaughter* (Consultation 135, 1994).

[226] Law Commission, *Murder, Manslaughter and Infanticide* (No 304, 2006) para 2.163.

[227] Keating, 'The Restoration of a Serious Crime' [1996] Crim LR 535.

[228] Law Commission, *Murder, Manslaughter and Infanticide* (No 304, 2006) para 3.60.

6.5.3 Reforming the structure of manslaughter offences

The Law Commission has recommended a restructuring of murder and manslaughter into three tiers (a ladder) of offences.[229] This was introduced in the context of murder in the previous chapter, where we acknowledged the unlikelihood of this structure being adopted into legislation.[230] However, the recommendations provide a useful insight into how that law might be rationalised. The structure recommended by the Commission is as follows:

> . . . first degree murder should encompass:
>
> (1) intentional killings, and
> (2) killings with the intent to cause serious injury where the killer was aware that his or her conduct involved a serious risk of causing death.[231]

 Extra detail . . .

First degree murder is expanded beyond intentional killing to include a killing with the intention to cause serious harm (as with the current law). However, the requirement that D must foresee a serious risk of death would, if enacted, reduce the scope of the offence as where D stabs V in the leg causing GBH, but V dies following an unforeseen medical complication. The mandatory life sentence would apply to first degree murder.

> . . . second degree murder should encompass:
>
> (1) killings intended to cause serious injury; or
> (2) killings intended to cause injury or fear or risk of injury where the killer was aware that his or her conduct involved a serious risk of causing death; or
> (3) killings intended to kill or to cause serious injury where the killer was aware that his or her conduct involved a serious risk of causing death but successfully pleads provocation, diminished responsibility or that he or she killed pursuant to a suicide pact.[232]

Extra detail . . .

The proposed offence of second degree murder would carry a maximum (non-mandatory) life sentence. This offence would encompass certain cases currently dealt with as murder (1), but also the more serious cases currently dealt with as manslaughter (2 and 3).

---

[229] Law Commission, *Murder, Manslaughter and Infanticide* (No 304, 2006); Ashworth, 'Principles, Pragmatism and the Law Commission's Recommendations on Homicide Law Reform' [2007] Crim LR 333.
[230] See **Chapter 5.6.2**.
[231] Law Commission, *Murder, Manslaughter and Infanticide* (No 304, 2006) para 9.5.
[232] Ibid, para 9.6.

. . . manslaughter should encompass:

(1) killing another person through gross negligence ('gross negligence manslaughter'); or

(2) killing another person:

   (a) through the commission of a criminal act intended by the defendant to cause injury, or

   (b) through the commission of a criminal act that the defendant was aware involved a serious risk of causing some injury ('criminal act manslaughter').[233]

 Extra detail . . .

The least culpable form of homicide would retain the label of manslaughter, with a maximum (non-mandatory) life sentence. This would cover reformed versions of the current involuntary manslaughter offences.

Debates about the best structure for homicide offences continue, both within England and Wales,[234] and beyond. The Scottish Law Commission, for example, is midway through an examination of Scottish homicide offences.

6.6 Eye on assessment

In this section we discuss the potential application of manslaughter within a problem question. The same structure of analysis should be employed as we have discussed in previous chapters.

STEP 1 Identify the potential criminal event in the facts

This is unlikely to take more than a sentence, but it is essential to tell your reader where in the facts you are focussing. For homicide offences, point out where a person has died (eg 'The first potential criminal event arises where Mary shoots at Vicky and Vicky dies').

STEP 2 Identify the potential offence

Having identified the facts (eg D potentially killing V), identify the offence you are going to apply. Usually, this means identifying the most serious offence that D might have committed.

---

[233] Ibid, para 9.9.
[234] eg Kyd, 'Done to Death? Reform of Homicide Law' in Child and Duff (eds), *Criminal Law Reform Now* (2019) 101, and comment from McKay 124.

When applying Step 2, keep in mind the flowchart with which we began the chapter, repeated in **Figure 6.6**.

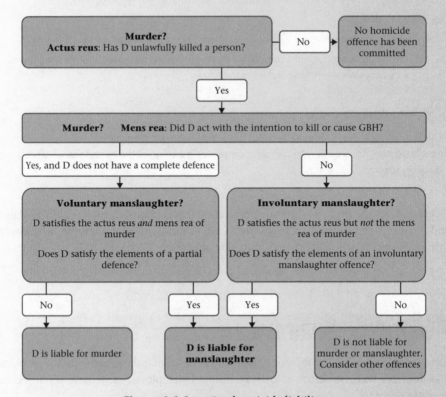

Figure 6.6 Locating homicide liability

In line with the flowchart, unless the question isolates a specific offence for discussion (eg 'Discuss Mary's potential liability for UAM'),[235] begin with the most serious potential offence: murder.

STEP 3 Applying the offence to the facts

Actus reus: What does the offence require? Did D do it?

Mens rea: What does the offence require? Did D possess it?

6.6.1 Where the elements of murder are satisfied

Where the elements of murder are satisfied, move to discuss potential defences.

---

[235] Where a specific offence is isolated by the question, the elements of this offence (and potential defences to it) are all that should be discussed.

STEP 4 Consider defences

The word 'consider' here is important, as you should not discuss every defence for every question. Rather, think whether there are any defences that *could* potentially apply. If there are, discuss those only.

When discussing defences, always begin with the complete defences (**Chapters 13** and **14**) as these usually lead to an outright acquittal. Remember that the defence of duress does not apply to murder. If none of the complete defences apply, or there is some doubt over their application, continue to discuss the partial defences to murder.

When discussing the partial defences, it is appropriate to discuss loss of control first and then go on to consider diminished responsibility (reflecting current court practices). As both defences are statute-based, your discussion should be structured around the elements of the defences as stated in the statute. Cases that post-date the statute should be used to identify how the courts apply the defence elements in practice. Remember that cases predating the C&JA 2009 are not binding precedent and should not be presented as such.

When applying the partial defences, take care to acknowledge areas of uncertainty. Particularly in relation to diminished responsibility, many of the questions for the jury are likely to be led by expert medical evidence. If you are not told medical details about D within the problem facts (eg that she is suffering from clinical depression, etc), then you should highlight this omission of essential information. You can still apply the law on the facts that you are given, and you can still predict *likely* outcomes based on those facts, but your answer should be expressly qualified (eg 'on the facts available it seems likely that . . .').

STEP 5 Conclude

This is usually a single sentence either saying that it is likely that D has committed the offence or saying that it is not likely, either because an offence element is not satisfied or because a defence is likely to apply. It is not often that you will be able to say categorically whether or not D has committed the offence, so it is usually best to conclude in terms of what is more 'likely'.

STEP 6 Loop

Go back up to STEP 1, identifying the next potential criminal event. Continue until you have discussed all the relevant potentially criminal events.

6.6.2 Where the elements of murder are not satisfied

Where the actus reus of murder is not satisfied, then you need to look for other potential offences beyond homicide. Where the actus reus of murder is satisfied, but the mens rea is lacking, you should apply the involuntary manslaughter offences. Remember that the three common law involuntary manslaughter offences are separate and should not be confused. Apply them to the facts one at a time.

When selecting which offence to apply first, the following distinction is useful:

A) D lacks mens rea for murder, but she clearly foresaw the risk of death or GBH: Where D's mens rea is just short of that required for murder, it is logical to step down to the offence of reckless manslaughter. This is because reckless manslaughter shares a similar structure to murder, with the only difference being that D need not intend to cause death or GBH (recklessness being sufficient). Thus, there is no need to demonstrate a base offence (required for UAM), or duty of care and grossly negligent conduct (required for GNM). Rather, you can simply refer back to your discussion of several elements of murder (particularly the actus reus), and then apply the reckless-ness-based test for mens rea to demonstrate liability.

B) D lacks mens rea for murder, and it is unclear if she foresaw a risk of death or GBH: In many cases, the simple step down to reckless manslaughter will not be possi-ble. In these cases, reflecting the approach generally taken in the courts, it is good prac-tice to apply UAM first, and then to apply GNM where UAM is not satisfied. In certain cases you can skip over UAM very briefly (eg where D's conduct is an omission, or there is clearly no base offence).

Where you do not find liability for any offence, then move to Step 5. Where you find a likelihood of liability, move to Step 4.

STEP 4 Consider defences

The word 'consider' here is important, as you should not discuss every defence for every question. Rather, think whether there are any defences that *could* potentially apply. If there are, discuss those only. Remember that the partial defences cannot apply here—they can only potentially apply where D commits murder.

STEP 5 Conclude

This is usually a single sentence either saying that it is likely that D has committed the offence, or saying that it is not likely, either because an offence element is not satisfied, or because a defence is likely to apply. It is not often that you will be able to say cate-gorically whether or not D has committed the offence, so it is usually best to conclude in terms of what is more 'likely'.

STEP 6 Loop

Go back up to STEP 1, identifying the next potential criminal event. Continue until you have discussed all the relevant potentially criminal events.

ONLINE RESOURCES

www.oup.com/he/child-ormerod4e

This chapter is accompanied by a selection of online resources to help you with this topic, including:

- **Self-test questions** and **scenario questions**
- **Videos** from the authors
- **Audio introduction** to the topic
- **Chapter summary sheet**
- Two **sample examination questions** with answer guidance
- **Further reading and weblinks**

Also available on the online resources are:

- A selection of **videos** from the authors containing general advice on problem questions and essay questions
- **Legal updates**

7

Non-fatal offences against the person

7.1 Introduction

One of the central values upon which the criminal law is constructed is bodily autonomy: the right not to be physically interfered with against your will.[1] We have already discussed the role of this value in the context of murder (**Chapter 5**) and manslaughter (**Chapter 6**), where D's conduct results in the ultimate loss of V's bodily autonomy through death. However, the criminal law's protection of bodily autonomy extends to conduct well short of that causing death. Grouped within the 'non-fatal offences against the person', a variety of offences have been designed to criminalise behaviour that ranges from the infliction of serious (non-fatal) injuries, through to the potential targeting of any non-consensual contact. For the purposes of our discussion, these offences can be usefully separated into two categories, result-focussed and conduct-focussed.

The offences in the result-focussed category are defined largely by reference to the *degree* of harm suffered by V. These offences can be presented as an imperfect 'ladder', with the most serious at the top and the least serious at the bottom.

(a) Wounding with intent to cause grievous bodily harm (GBH), or causing GBH with intent.

(b) Maliciously wounding or inflicting GBH.

(c) Assault occasioning actual bodily harm (ABH).

(d) Assault and battery.

The second category of non-fatal offences is 'conduct-focussed'. Although offences in this category are still concerned with D causing harm to V, they are equally concerned with the *manner* in which that harm is inflicted. This can be illustrated, for example, with harassment and poisoning offences. In each case, the behaviour in question could have been criminalised by use of offences within the first category, or new ones in the same form, focussing on the degree of harm suffered by V. However, to do so would be to ignore the special circumstances of D's offending. By employing the more specific offences of harassment and poisoning, offences which can be defined and labelled to highlight the particularly harmful methods D has employed, the law can send a clear message to both the individual offender as well as society more generally.

---

[1] Respect for bodily autonomy is enshrined in Art 8 ECHR (respect for private life). For more serious infringements the protection lies in Art 3 (freedom from torture, inhuman and degrading treatment), Art 4 (freedom from slavery), Art 5 (freedom from unlawful deprivation of liberty), and Art 2 (right to life). See **Chapter 1.1.1** and **1.4** for a more general discussion of the values protected by the criminal law. See also Wilson, *Central Issues in Criminal Theory* (2002) Ch1.

As will become clear, unlike the result-focussed category of non-fatal offences, the conduct-focussed category does not attempt to target a particular spectrum of resulting harms. Rather, offences in this conduct category have been developed in an ad hoc manner, arising to fill gaps within the result category as well as reflecting social and political priorities. It is within this conduct-focussed category that we might also locate the sexual offences, a series of offences that are defined independently to reflect the uniquely serious manner of their commission. However, owing to the importance and complexity of these offences, they will be discussed separately in **Chapter 8**.

 Extra detail . . .

Only a natural 'person' can be a victim of an offence against the person. The meaning of 'person' has already been discussed in relation to homicide,[2] and these rules apply equally to the non-fatal offences (eg an unborn foetus or someone who is legally dead cannot be the victim of an offence against the person).

Although we use the language of 'victim' for the person offended against, the implications of this label can appear inappropriate for certain non-fatal offences. For example, as we will discuss, it is possible for D to commit a non-fatal offence even when the 'victim' has consented to, and even gained pleasure from, D's actions. Think about this when evaluating the offences: if the label 'victim' seems inappropriate, does this mean you think the law is in need of reform; if not, who is the law protecting?

The Law Commission published a report in 2015 discussing the current law on the offences against the person, and making recommendations for fundamental reform. We make reference to the report throughout this chapter; but it repays reading in full.[3]

7.2 Assault and battery

Within the result category of non-fatal offences, at the bottom of our imaginary ladder of harms, are the offences of assault and battery. Many of the offences in this category are defined in the Offences Against the Person Act 1861(OAPA). However, the offences of assault and battery are not defined in statute. The power to charge assault and battery derives from section 39 of the Criminal Justice Act 1988,[4] but they are *defined* at common law. This has given rise to a technical dispute as to whether these offences should be *referred to* as statutory or common law offences, but for our purposes, little turns on this question.[5]

---

[2] See **Chapter 5.3.2.3**.
[3] Law Commission, *Reform of Offences against the Person* (No 361, 2015). See also *Smith, Hogan, and Ormerod's Criminal Law* (16th edn, 2021) Ch16.
[4] 'Common assault and battery shall be summary offences and a person guilty of either of them shall be liable to a fine . . . , to imprisonment for a term not exceeding six months, or to both.'
[5] Assault and battery are also torts. As a result, the definition of these offences has been partly derived from civil law cases, and some of these cases are discussed later.

7.2.1 Assault

An assault involves any conduct by D that, intentionally or recklessly, causes V to *apprehend* imminent unlawful personal violence. In contrast, a battery (discussed at **7.2.2**) is any conduct by which D, intentionally or recklessly, *inflicts* unlawful personal violence upon V. The elements of assault are set out in **Table 7.1**.

Table 7.1 Assault

	Actus reus	**Mens rea**
Conduct element	Any conduct causing the result	Voluntary
Circumstance element	V is a person	Knowledge
Result element	V apprehends an imminent threat of unlawful force	Intention or recklessness

7.2.1.1 Actus reus of assault

In contrast to the everyday/non-legal meaning of 'assault', the legal definition does *not* require D to make any physical contact with V. Such contact is only required for the distinct offence of 'battery'. The actus reus of assault is satisfied as soon as D causes V to apprehend or believe that V is about to suffer some personal violence. The actus reus of assault is therefore less concerned with the conduct of D, and rather more concerned with the effect of that conduct on V. The test is not whether D's conduct was likely to cause another to apprehend unlawful violence, but whether it had this effect in fact. For example, if D motions to strike V (ie performs conduct that would usually cause V the relevant apprehension), but V does not so apprehend, perhaps because she is asleep or she knows D is bluffing, the actus reus will not be satisfied.

To clarify this central point, several questions must be considered:

A) **What do we mean by 'unlawful personal violence'?** Unlawful personal violence includes any non-consensual contact with V. The actus reus of assault will therefore be satisfied where V is caused to apprehend even low-level violence; V need not believe that the 'violence' would be serious or cause injury.[6] This is commonly expressed as causing V to 'fear' injury, but care should be taken with the use of this term: V can be caused to fear without apprehending imminent violence (eg D shows V a scary film); and V may be caused to apprehend imminent violence without fear (eg V is much stronger than D). In each case, for the purposes of this offence, the only relevant question is whether D caused V to apprehend imminent personal violence.

B) **How imminent must V believe the violence will be?** V must be caused to apprehend immediate or imminent unlawful personal violence. Threats of violence at some non-imminent point in the future (eg 'I will beat you up next month'), however serious,

---

[6] *Ireland* [1998] AC 147.

will not constitute an assault. The distinction between imminent violence, which does satisfy the actus reus, and non-imminent violence, which does not, is therefore crucial. The courts have applied a part subjective and part objective approach:

- Subjective: we ask what facts V is caused to believe; what V believes the nature of the threat is.

If D points an unloaded or imitation gun at V, causing V to believe that she is about to be shot, then D has completed the actus reus of assault. In reality, under any definition of 'imminence', there is no imminent threat of V being shot by a gun that cannot be fired. However, based on the facts that V is caused to believe, a finding of imminence is possible.[7]

- Objective: based on the facts that V is caused to believe, whether this belief amounts to an apprehension of *imminent* violence is an objective one for the court.

If V is caused to believe she will be shot in one hour, whether this is imminent will be a question for the court. The tendency of the court has been to interpret the requirement of imminence very broadly, allowing for liability even where V knows that the threat will involve some delay.[8] This approach has been adopted consistently by the courts,[9] as illustrated by the case of *Constanza*.

Constanza [1997] 2 Cr App R 492

D harassed V over a period of 20 months, sending threatening letters, writing on her front door, and taking items from her laundry. V suffered clinical depression as a result. D was charged with assault causing actual bodily harm, which as we will see is an offence that requires an assault to have been committed (discussed at **7.4**). D claimed that the letters could not have caused V to anticipate an *immediate* threat.

- Crown Court: guilty of assault, and thus assault occasioning actual bodily harm.
- Court of Appeal: conviction upheld on appeal. The court found assault on the basis that V was caused to apprehend violence 'at some point not excluding the immediate future'.

Assessment matters . . .

When applying cases such as *Constanza* to the facts of a problem question, a very wide definition of 'imminence' should be employed. However, take care not to fall into the trap, which the courts argu- ably have, of confusing an imminent anticipation of violence at some point in the future (not enough to satisfy the actus reus) with an anticipation of imminent violence (which will satisfy the actus reus). It is not disputed that the cases discussed earlier displayed the former, but it is debatable whether they should have been held to include the latter.

---

[7] *Logdon v DPP* [1976] Crim LR 121.

[8] See Virgo, 'Offences Against the Person—Do-It-Yourself Law Reform' (1997) 56 CLJ 251.

[9] *Logdon v DPP* [1976] Crim LR 121: D showed V a pistol in a drawer, saying he would keep her hostage; *Smith v Chief Superintendent of Woking Police Station* (1983) 76 Cr App R 234: D seen looking through a window at V; *Ireland* [1998] AC 147: D made phone calls to V.

C) **Can the result be caused indirectly?** Most assaults will involve a threatened battery, as where D threatens to punch V in the face. However, although D must cause V to apprehend imminent unlawful violence it is not necessary that such apprehension should involve violence *from D*. Thus, where D threatens V with a dog,[10] or even attack from another person, D's conduct will satisfy the actus reus.

D) **Can the conduct element be satisfied by words alone, or by omission?** Words alone are capable of causing V to apprehend unlawful imminent violence, and so it is clear they are capable of fulfilling the conduct element of assault, whether communicated orally or in written form.[11] It is also *likely* that assault can be committed by omission, although this has not yet been clarified at common law.

Assault by omission could arise where D inadvertently causes V to apprehend imminent violence, and then omits to correct the situation. For example, D is checking the sights on her gun when V walks into the room, and then D intentionally omits to withdraw the threat by lowering the gun. D does not commit assault by her act (when aiming the gun) as she does not possess mens rea at this point; she commits assault when omitting to lower the gun, in breach of a duty to act,[12] with the required mens rea. This example could be analysed as assault by omission *or* assault by continuing act.[13]

E) **Can the threat be implied or conditional?** Implied or conditional threats are most likely in the context of a verbal assault as, for example, where D says to V 'if the coin-toss lands on heads then I will hit you'. As before, provided D's threat causes V to apprehend imminent violence, the actus reus of assault will be satisfied.[14] The only exception to this is where the communicated condition undermines *any chance* of the threat being carried out. For example, D shouts at V 'I would hit you if you weren't already ugly'. D's conduct may be threatening, but her statement makes clear that there will be no imminent attack, and therefore there is no assault.[15]

7.2.1.2 Mens rea of assault

The mens rea for assault requires D to intend *or* be reckless as to causing the result: D must intend or foresee the possibility that her act will cause V to apprehend imminent unlawful violence. This was established in *Venna*.[16] D must also possess mens rea as to the other offence elements: D's conduct must be voluntary,[17] and she must have been aware that her victim, V, was a person.

---

[10] *Dume* (1986) The Times, 16 October.
[11] As in *Constanza*.
[12] D has a duty to act to remedy her inadvertent creation of a dangerous situation: *Miller* [1983] AC 161. See **Chapter 2.6**.
[13] For discussion of these alternative approaches, see **Chapter 4.3.2.1**.
[14] See Williams, 'Assault and Words' [1957] Crim LR 219.
[15] See *Tuberville v Savage* (1669) 1 Mood Rep 3: D's potential assault (putting hand on sword) was undermined by the accompanying statement: 'if it were not assize time I would not take such language'.
[16] [1976] QB 421. This case involved a battery that caused actual bodily harm, but it remains good authority for the mens rea of both assault and battery.
[17] See **Chapter 3.3**.

Assessment matters . . .

Although D's mens rea as to the result of causing V to apprehend imminent violence should always be discussed in a problem answer, this is not true of the other mens rea requirements. It will usually be self-evident that D acted voluntarily and is aware that V is a person, and so these requirements need only be explicitly discussed if there is some room for doubt. This applies equally to all offences discussed in this chapter.

7.2.2 Battery

A battery is any conduct by which D, intentionally or recklessly, inflicts unlawful personal violence upon V.[18] The elements of battery are set out in **Table 7.2.**

Table 7.2 Battery

	Actus reus	**Mens rea**
Conduct element	Any conduct causing the result	Voluntary
Circumstance element	V is a person	Knowledge
Result element	Unlawful physical contact with V	Intention or recklessness

7.2.2.1 Actus reus of battery

The actus reus of battery consists of the infliction of unlawful personal violence. The term 'violence' in this context will encompass *any* unlawful contact with another. As Blackstone explained:

> The law cannot draw the line between different degrees of violence, and therefore prohibits the first and lowest stage of it; every man's person being sacred, and no other having a right to meddle with it, in even the slightest manner.[19]

It is useful to focus on a few questions that have arisen for clarification in the courts:

A) **Does battery require physical contact?** Unlike assault, where D can cause V to apprehend violence through any means, including words, battery will *always* require physical contact with V. This is a fundamental difference between the two offences. However, although some force must be applied, it will be satisfied even if V is unaware of the touching, as where V is asleep, and will include touching V's clothes, as illustrated in *Thomas*.

---

[18] *Rolfe* (1952) 36 Cr App R 4.
[19] *Commentaries*, iii, 120, cited in *Collins v Wilcock* [1984] 3 All ER 374, 378.

Thomas (1985) 81 Cr App R 331

D (a school caretaker) touched the hem of a 12-year-old pupil's skirt. He was charged with the (now repealed) sexual offence of indecent assault which, like battery, required a touching.

- Court: guilty of indecent assault.
- Court of Appeal: appeal allowed on the basis that the touching was not indecent. However, it was confirmed that there was a touching: 'There could be no dispute that if you touch a person's clothes while he is wearing them that is equivalent to touching him.'[20]

Despite this wide interpretation, the requirement of contact can be problematic. For example, where D causes bodily harm in the form of psychiatric injury, this may be inflicted without any physical impact on V's body. In such a case, because there is no physical force, there will be no battery.[21]

B) **Can the result be caused indirectly?** Many cases will involve *direct* contact between D and V, as where D hits V with her fist or with a weapon. However, battery will also be found where contact is caused *indirectly*, as where D hits V by throwing things at V or spitting on V, or where D's contact with a third party impacts on V (eg D punches X, causing her to drop V, her baby[22]); commenting at the height of the Covid-19 pandemic, the DPP has also asserted that coughing on V will suffice. Several cases confirm the potential for battery by indirect means. In *DPP v K*,[23] for example, D committed battery when he poured acid into a toilet hand-dryer, causing the next user to be sprayed; in *Martin*[24] it was agreed that battery could be found where D digs a pit for V to fall into, or causes injury through the placing of an obstruction. Other cases involve battery where D sets his dog[25] or other animal[26] on V.

C) **Can the conduct element be satisfied by an omission?** Battery will invariably involve an act, and it has been assumed that acts are required for liability.[27] However, as with assault (**7.2.1.1**), it is likely that the courts will find battery can be committed by omission. Support for this can be found in *Santana-Bermudez*.

Santana-Bermudez v DPP [2004] Crim LR 471

D assured V, who was a policewoman, that he was not carrying any 'sharps' (hypodermic needles) before she searched him. He was, and V was injured. D was charged with battery occasioning actual bodily harm (discussed at **7.4**), an offence where battery must be demonstrated.

- Magistrates' court: guilty of battery occasioning actual bodily harm.

---

[20] At 334.
[21] Ormerod and Gunn, 'In Defence of *Ireland*' [1996] 3 Web JCLI.
[22] *Haystead v Chief Constable of Derbyshire* (2000) 164 JP 396. Liability could *alternatively* be found through transferred malice.
[23] [1990] 1 All ER 331, overruled on *other* grounds by *Spratt* [1991] 2 All ER 210.
[24] (1881) 8 QBD 54.
[25] *Murgatroyd v Chief Constable of West Yorkshire* [2000] All ER 1742.
[26] eg where D causes a horse to bolt: *Gibbon v Pepper* (1695) 2 Salk 637 (*obiter*).
[27] *Innes v Wylie* (1844) 1 Car & Kir 257.

- Crown Court: not guilty—no actus reus.
- Divisional Court: no retrial was ordered, but the court confirmed that D's omission was capable of giving rise to a battery.

Omissions liability, it should be remembered, requires D to have omitted in breach of a duty to act.[28] In *Santana-Bermudez*, this is established by D's creation of a dangerous situation: having sharp objects in his pocket and assuring V that he did not.[29]

7.2.2.2 Mens rea of battery

The mens rea of battery requires intention or recklessness as to causing the result: the application of unlawful force to the body of V. This was established in *Venna*.[30] D must also perform her conduct voluntarily, knowing that V is a 'person'.

7.2.3 Hostility as an element of assault or battery?

It is generally accepted that hostility is *not* an element of assault or battery. Lord Lane CJ has described battery as:

an intentional touching of another person without the consent of that person and without lawful excuse. It need not necessarily be hostile, or rude, or aggressive, as some of the cases seem to indicate.[31]

Some doubt was raised by the House of Lords in *Brown*,[32] where the majority indicated that hostility *is* required. However, the definition of 'hostility' applied in *Brown* means that it is likely to have little impact. The facts of *Brown* involved sadomasochistic acts that were consented to for the mutual satisfaction of those involved, and such acts could not, in plain English, be described as hostile. To find hostility in this case, the House of Lords effectively emptied the word of its meaning: saying the acts were hostile because they were unlawful.[33] Under this approach, hostility does not seem like an offence element at all, but rather a description of events that have been found to be criminal on other grounds.

7.2.4 The relationship between assault and battery

Assault and battery are two separate offences. However, this was not always the case, and they are still often referred to interchangeably, inconsistently, and/or cumulatively in cases, academic discussion and statute. The main reason for this continued problem is that, without an acceptable verb to correspond with the noun of 'battery', the term 'assaulted' is used to describe D who commits both assault and/or battery. Take care not to be confused by this when reading cases and commentary: 'D assaulted V' can mean D committed assault, battery, or both.

---

[28] See **Chapter 2.6**.
[29] *Miller* [1983] AC 161.
[30] [1976] QB 421.
[31] *Faulkner v Talbot* [1981] 3 All ER 468, 471.
[32] [1994] AC 212.
[33] Per Lord Jauncey.

7.3 Defences to assault and battery

Where D has satisfied the offence elements of assault or battery, she will nevertheless avoid liability if she has a specific defence of 'lawful chastisement', 'consent', or 'belief in consent'.

> **Assessment matters . . .**
>
> When considering defences, it is usually good practice to begin with specific defences. However, if these do not apply, remember that D can also avoid liability if she satisfies one of the general defences that apply across a greater part of the criminal law. See **Chapter 13**, where we discuss denials of offending, and **Chapter 14**, where we discuss the general defences.

7.3.1 Lawful chastisement of children

A lawful chastisement or 'corporal punishment' defence has traditionally applied at common law to allow parents and teachers to use physical force to discipline children.[34] However, the definition of this defence at common law was uncertain, and the subject of challenges in the ECtHR.[35]

The defence is now codified within section 58 of the Children Act 2004, and considerably restricted in scope. The defence will: (a) only apply for parents; (b) only apply to assault and battery (ie none of the more serious offences against the person); and (c) only apply where the force used was reasonable and proportionate in the circumstances, involving no cruelty.

Following section 549(4) of the Education Act 1996, a member of school staff has no defence to any offence against the person committed on a pupil by way of punishment. This includes assault or battery. However, the Act does make clear that reasonable force can be used to restrain violent pupils (s550A), those who are endangering themselves and/or property (s548(5)), or where the teacher needs to search for a weapon (s550AA).

7.3.2 Consent to assault and battery

The defence of consent is vitally important in relation to non-fatal offences against the person.[36] Where D makes *consensual* contact with V (eg shaking V's hand), or causes V to apprehend *consensual* contact (eg motioning towards shaking V's hand), we would not want to find liability for assault or battery. Indeed, such examples are so obviously outside the behaviour that we want to criminalise that there are strong grounds for

---

[34] Keating, 'Protecting or Punishing Children: Physical Punishment, Human Rights and English Law Reform' (2006) 26 LS 394; Barton, 'Hitting Your Children: Common Assault or Common Sense?' (2008) 38 Fam L 65.

[35] *A v UK* [1998] TLR 578; Phillips, 'The Case for Corporal Punishment in the UK—Beaten into Submission in Europe' (1994) 43 ICLQ 153.

[36] There is a vast literature on this subject. See Law Commission, *Consent and Offences against the Person* (Consultation 134, 1994), on which see Ormerod, 'Consent and Offences Against the Person: LCCP No 134' (1994) 57 MLR 928; and Law Commission, *Consent in Criminal Law* (Consultation 139, 1995), on which see Ormerod and Gunn, 'Consent—A Second Bash' [1996] Crim LR 694. See also Reed et al (eds), *Consent: Domestic and Comparative Perspectives* (2017).

contending that 'non-consent' should be classified as an offence element, meaning that such conduct would not require a consent defence at all. And there is some uncertainty here at common law, with examples of contradictory classifications found in the courts and surrounding commentaries. We discuss this in the 'reform' section later (**7.10.3**). In what follows, for the sake of consistency, and in line with a slight predominance in the case law,[37] we analyse consent as a defence.

The structure of the defence of consent, as it applies to assault or battery, is set out in **Table 7.3**.

Table 7.3 Defence of consent

A) V's consent must be expressed or implied to D in a legally recognised manner
B) V's consent must be effective: V must have the capacity, freedom, and information required to make a choice

As we go on to discuss the more serious offences against the person from **7.4**, a third element to the consent defence emerges (**7.8.2.1**): the context of V's consensual harm must come within a legally accepted category (eg surgery). In the context of assault and battery, however, due to the low levels of harm involved, no such additional limitations apply. Even where we perceive D's conduct as socially unacceptable, such as where D and V engage in a consensual fight, V's effective consent will preclude charges of simple assault or battery.

7.3.2.1 Element 1: expressed and/or implied consent

The most straightforward cases involving consent entail V expressly consenting to contact with D (eg when V motions to shake D's hand). However, particularly in the context of assault or battery, implied consent is very common.

Implied consent most commonly applies to touching which, although not explicitly consented to, is part of everyday life.[38] For example, where one is jostled in a busy street or when entering a crowded train; or even where one is embraced, within reason, as the clock strikes for New Year. The logic behind implied consent is that, by voluntarily participating with others in physical activity in society, we agree to be exposed to the foreseeable contact that social life entails. However, as demonstrated in *Wood v DPP*, contact must be genuinely within the realms of everyday activity.

 Wood v DPP [2008] EWHC 1056 (Admin)

D was restrained by V, a police officer, as he left a public house. V was not in the process of arresting D, but merely restraining him in order to establish his identity. D resisted, and was charged with assaulting the police officer.

• Magistrates' court: D is guilty of assault.

---

[37] This was the approach preferred by the bare majority in *Brown* [1994] AC 212.
[38] *Collins v Wilcock* [1984] 3 All ER 374.

- Crown Court: conviction upheld.
- Divisional Court: appeal allowed, and D acquitted. V is not entitled to restrain D in this manner unless carrying out a lawful arrest (no implied consent). Thus, as V was assaulting D, D's resistance was lawful.

Implied consent should also not be equated with foreseeability, clarified in *H v CPS*.[39] In this case V, a teacher at a special-needs school, was aware of the high risk of assault within the school. However, the court rejected the submission that her awareness amounted to an implied consent for D's attack.

7.3.2.2 Element 2: effective consent

For consent to be valid in law, it must be effective. For example, if V is unaware of exactly what D is planning to do, or is unable to understand, then it is highly questionable whether V's apparent acquiescence should absolve D of liability. The principal questions are the following:

- What *mental capacity* is required for V to be capable of effective consent?
- What degree of *knowledge* is required for V to be capable of effective consent?
- Can *fraud* by D undermine the effectiveness of apparent consent?
- Can *duress* or pressure from D or another undermine the effectiveness of apparent consent?

We consider each in turn.

Extra detail . . .

In the context of implied consent to touching expected in everyday social movement (eg light contact between people on a busy train), uniquely, 'effective consent' is assumed and becomes irrelevant. This assumption is clearly artificial, particularly where V is unable to understand, for example because of age or mental deficiency, the implied consent she is providing. However, despite the artificiality, bearing in mind the type of conduct involved, it is unlikely to lead to substantial problems.

Capacity

V may lack the capacity[40] to consent for a variety of reasons, including mental disorders, learning difficulties, infancy, or more temporary conditions such as intoxication. In each case, the issue of capacity should be considered.

In the interests of simplicity, it is tempting for the courts to equate a certain status with a general lack of capacity. This has been the dominant approach historically, exemplified in *Burrell v Harmer*.

---

[39] [2010] All ER 56.
[40] See Law Commission, *Consent in Criminal Law* (Consultation 139, 1995) Part 5; Law Commission, *Mental Capacity* (No 231, 1995).

Burrell v Harmer [1967] Crim LR 169

D was charged with assault occasioning actual bodily harm, an offence which required proof of a battery, after tattooing the arms of boys aged 12 and 13. D's defence was that the boys had consented, having actively instigated the tattooing.

- Crown Court: guilty of the offence. The boys, as minors, were not capable of understanding the nature of the act of tattooing (ie they lacked capacity) and therefore there was no effective consent.

With the court taking little time to explain and discuss exactly what knowledge the boys lacked, this case demonstrates the artificiality of a simple status approach.

A more nuanced approach to capacity has been set out in the Mental Capacity Act 2005, and whilst the criminal courts are not bound by it in the context of offences against the person, it has had a considerable impact on judicial reasoning.[41] The Act states that 'a person lacks capacity in relation to a matter if at the material time he is unable to make a decision for himself in relation to the matter because of a temporary or permanent impairment of, or a disturbance in the functioning of, the mind or brain'. The Act further cautions that a lack of capacity should not be inferred from '(a) a person's age or appearance, or (b) a condition of his, or an aspect of his behaviour, which might lead others to make unjustified assumptions about his capacity'.

The question of capacity must be individual and decision-specific. Capacity can change for each individual over time, and different decisions require different levels of capacity to be engaged with (ie V may lack capacity for complex decisions, but not for more simple ones). The resulting test is more difficult for the courts to apply, but respects the autonomy of the individuals involved.

Assessment matters . . .

Where the facts of a problem question state that V suffers from a certain mental condition, is a minor, or is intoxicated, it is tempting to assume that she lacks capacity to consent. This should certainly be discussed, but the best answers will also consider the possibility that she might have sufficient capacity despite her status. A conclusion should then be provided with an opinion of what is most likely based on the facts provided.

Informed consent

Beyond the *capacity* to consent to particular conduct, V must also be aware of what that conduct entails before she can exercise her capacity and make a decision. Although this requirement is logical, the amount of information V requires for effective consent it less obvious. Adopting a commonsense approach, the courts generally equate the level of knowledge required with the degree of harm to which V is consenting: the greater the harm, the more knowledge required for effective consent. It should therefore be of little surprise that most of the cases discussed here involve more serious offences than simple assault or battery. However, as the same general rules apply to assault and battery (just with a lighter touch), it is useful to have the discussion at this stage.

Informed consent to non-fatal offences was considered in the important case of *Konzani*.

---

[41] See *Re S and another (Protected Persons)* [2010] 1 WLR 1082, [53].

Konzani [2005] EWCA Crim 706

D engaged in consensual unprotected sexual intercourse with three victims. As a result of this, each contracted HIV, a condition that D was aware he had but of which fact he had not informed the complainants. D was charged with maliciously inflicting GBH (discussed at **7.5**).

- Crown Court: guilty of maliciously inflicting GBH.
- Court of Appeal: conviction upheld on appeal. The victims had consented to sexual intercourse, but, because of the lack of information made known to them, they had not consented to the risk of contracting HIV.

The court explained the role of informed consent in the following terms:

> If an individual who knows that he is suffering from the HIV virus conceals this stark fact from his sexual partner, the principle of her personal autonomy is not enhanced if he is exculpated when he recklessly transmits the HIV virus to her through consensual sexual intercourse. On any view, the concealment of this fact from her almost inevitably means that she is deceived. Her consent is not properly informed, and she cannot give an informed consent to something of which she is ignorant . . .[42]

The court in *Konzani* made a clear distinction between (a) the 'nature of the sexual intercourse' about which V was informed and as to which there *was* effective consent, and (b) the 'risk of HIV infection' about which V was not informed and as to which there was *no* effective consent. This distinction is critical because, if it is not made, then there is either consent to both and thus no liability at all, or there is no consent to either and thus D has also committed rape.[43] In this manner, *Konzani* encourages us to consider D's central activity (in this case, sexual intercourse) as *potentially* distinct from associated risks of harm (in this case, infection); and encourages us to consider V's consent separately as to each. Where D has consented to the central activity, and the analysis moves to the separate associated risks, three categories of case should be distinguished:

A) No knowledge or deception: Where D has no special knowledge of the associated risks (eg D does not know she is infected), then V's effective consent to the central activity includes consent as to the associated risks. D is not deceiving V, and V is fully informed of what D knows. Even where those risks manifest in harm, no liability will result.[44]

B) Knowledge but no deception: Where D has special knowledge of the associated risks (eg D knows she is infected), and she informs V of that fact, then V's effective consent to the central activity includes consent as to the associated risks. Even where those risks manifest in harm, no liability will result.

C) Knowledge and deception (as in *Konzani*): Where D has special knowledge of the associated risks (eg D knows she is infected) but does not inform V of that knowledge, then V's effective consent to the central activity will not include effective consent to the associated risks. Where those risks manifest in harm, liability may be found.

---

[42] At [23] per Judge LJ.

[43] For critical commentary, see Weait, 'Knowledge, Autonomy and Consent: *R v Konzani*' [2006] Crim LR 763; Munro, 'On Responsible Relationships and Irresponsible Sex' (2007) 19 CFLQ 112.

[44] D may alternatively rely on a belief in consent defence, discussed at **7.3.3**.

Extra detail . . .

Konzani involved risks associated with sexual intercourse, but the rule will apply in other contexts as well. For example, a doctor (D) injects V with a therapeutic drug, knowing, but not informing V, that the needles being used have often been found to be contaminated. V's consent to the injection includes consent to various associated risks. However, D's special knowledge means that V's effective consent to the injection may not include effective consent to the risks of contamination that were not disclosed, should they arise.

Consent procured by fraud

Fraud has the potential to undermine V's apparent consent in two main areas: fraud as to the identity of D; and fraud as to the nature of the act consented to.[45] Unfortunately, the current law has become complex and confused.

A) Fraud as to the identity of D: The basic rule is easy to apply. If D gains V's consent to being touched by impersonating X, V's consent to that touching (battery) is not legally effective. V's consent is given to X in relation to X's acts, not the impersonating D.

Problems emerge where D is not impersonating another person but, rather, D is lying about certain characteristics or qualifications. It is much less clear here if D is being fraudulent about her *identity*, and until recently, the courts maintained a narrow definition. In *Richardson*,[46] for example, despite being suspended from practising dentistry, D continued to treat patients, fraudulently presenting herself as a presently certified professional. Although initially convicted of assault occasioning actual bodily harm (discussed at **7.4**) for harms caused to her patients (ie fraud held to undermine any apparent consent), this was overturned on appeal, with the Court of Appeal asserting that fraud as to an attribute (such as a qualification) did not amount to fraud as to D's identity. The outcome from *Richardson* is troubling, as D's lack of qualifications was surely more important to V's consent than whether D claimed to be someone else. However, the law has been clarified by the recent case of *Melin*.[47]

 Melin [2019] EWCA Crim 557

D fraudulently presented himself as a medically trained doctor when giving Botox injections to two victims. Both victims consented to the treatments, but maintained that they would not have done so had they known that D was not medically trained. D was charged with maliciously inflicting grievous bodily harm (discussed at **7.5**).

- Court: guilty of maliciously inflicting grievous bodily harm. Fraud as to identity (presenting as a doctor) undermined the victim's apparent consent.
- Court of Appeal: Conviction upheld in relation to one victim, where D's comments about his medical training were made well in advance of her consent to treatment. However, D's appeal was allowed as to the second victim, where D's comments came after consent at the time of the treatment.

---

[45] See Law Commission, *Consent in Criminal Law* (Consultation 139, 1995) Part 6.
[46] [1998] 2 Cr App R 200.
[47] Laird, Commentary [2019] CrimLR 1050.

The decision of the Court of Appeal in *Melin* does not reject the previous approach from *Richardson*, but does provide important clarifications to the law on fraud as to identity. In line with *Richardson*, where D's fraud is passive (ie a failure to inform) and/ or where the subject of D's fraud does not play a causal role in V's consent (as with the second victim in *Melin*), V's consent remains intact. However, where D's fraud is active (ie the supply of misinformation) and does bring about consent (as with the first victim in *Melin*), V's consent may be undermined.

B) **Fraud as to the nature of D's conduct:** Fraud as to the nature of D's conduct is capable of undermining otherwise effective consent as, for example, where D tells V that it is customary to greet someone by punching them in the face. However, where V is not deceived as to the core nature of the act, but simply as to a collateral issue, this will not generally undermine consent. The courts have consistently interpreted the 'nature' of conduct very narrowly. For example, in *Mobilio*,[48] where V consented to D inserting an instrument into her vagina for diagnostic purposes, but D was secretly acting only for his sexual gratification, the court held that V's consent was nevertheless effective: D's fraud was not as to the *nature* of the act.

This issue has also arisen in relation to consensual sexual intercourse where D does not inform her sexual partner of a known sexually transmitted infection. This was considered in *Dica*,[49] where D infected two sexual partners with HIV. As with the more recent case of *Konzani* (discussed earlier in relation to informed consent), the Court of Appeal in *Dica* made the crucial distinction between: (a) consent as to sexual intercourse, which was both informed and non-fraudulent, and (b) consent as to the risk of infection, which was uninformed and gained through fraud.[50] Although V was not misled as to the *nature* of the sexual act, and thus D had not committed rape, V was misled as to the *nature* of the associated risk of infection (the risk of bodily harm). D was guilty of inflicting GBH.

Consent procured through duress

V's apparent consent will not be effective if it is gained by threats (duress). For example, if V submits to a light beating only amounting to a battery in order to avoid a greater one, the threat of the greater beating is likely to undermine her consent. Similar results have emerged even where D's threats were non-criminal (eg submit to this beating or be dismissed from employment;[51] or I will bring a prosecution;[52] etc). Indeed, duress may even be implied from a relationship, such as that between a teacher and pupil.[53]

Despite these examples, however, the exact test for duress in this context remains unclear. It must be demonstrated that V's apparent consent was *caused* by D's threat as opposed to other factors, and so it is important to balance the gravity of the threat against the act consented to. However, it remains unclear whether this balancing is

---

[48] [1991] 1 VR 339. Ormerod, 'A Victim's Mistaken Consent in Rape' (1992) 56 JCL 407.
[49] [2004] EWCA Crim 1103.
[50] The court in *Dica* disapplied the earlier case of *Clarence* (1888) 22 QBD 23, where the court had held that V's consent to sexual intercourse amounted to an implied consent to the risk of infection.
[51] *McCoy* 1953 (2) SA 4.
[52] *State v Volschenk* 1968 (2) PH H283; here the threat did *not* undermine consent.
[53] *Nichol* (1807) Russ & Ry 130.

a purely objective procedure (asking if a person of reasonable steadfastness would have submitted to the violence), or whether it includes a subjective dimension (eg where D knew V was particularly vulnerable through mental abnormality or alcoholism, etc).

Assessment matters . . .

To assess whether consent is effective, it is necessary to consider each of the topics discussed in this section: capacity, level of knowledge, fraud, and duress. However, applying these to the facts of a problem question is not a tick-box exercise. Therefore, again, you should fully explore and discuss where it is relevant on the facts (eg D is a minor or is tricked in some way), but you can be brief where no such indicators/issues arise.

7.3.3 Belief in consent to assault and battery

D may also avoid liability if she *believed* that V provided valid consent. Thus, even if V was not consenting, and so the consent defence does not apply, D will avoid liability if she genuinely believed that consent was present. As seen in *Jones*, this will be the case even where D's belief is unreasonable.

Jones and Others (1986) 83 Cr App R 375

The defendant schoolboys threw V into the air with the intention of catching him as part of a joke. However, they failed to catch V and he suffered severe injuries. They sought to rely on the consent of V.

- Crown Court: guilty of an offence causing GBH. The judge did not allow the defence of consent to be put to the jury.
- Court of Appeal: appeal allowed. Consent should have been left to the jury. Consent could have been a valid defence if V had consented *or* D genuinely (even if unreasonably) believed that V consented.

This defence is rarely pursued in court. D must raise enough evidence that she genuinely believed that V provided valid consent (ie express or implied, and effective).

7.4 OAPA 1861, s47: assault occasioning actual bodily harm

Section 47 is satisfied where D commits an assault or battery that causes V to suffer actual bodily harm (ABH).

47. Whosoever shall be convicted on indictment of any assault occasioning actual bodily harm shall be liable to imprisonment for not more than five years.

The elements of the section 47 offence are set out in **Table 7.4**.

Table 7.4 OAPA 1861, s47

	Actus reus	**Mens rea**
Conduct element	Any conduct causing the results	Voluntary
Circumstance element	V is a person	Knowledge
Result elements	V apprehends a threat of imminent physical contact, or, physical contact is applied And V suffers ABH	Intention or recklessness None

An alternative illustration of section 47 is provided in **Figure 7.1**.

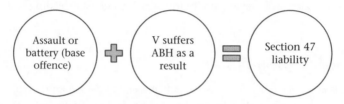

Figure 7.1 OAPA 1861, s47

7.4.1 Actus reus of s47

The actus reus of the section 47 offence requires D to commit the actus reus of assault or battery, with the additional result that V suffers ABH.

7.4.1.1 Assault or battery

The term 'assault' in section 47 should be read as 'assault or battery'. The actus reus elements of these base offences have been discussed earlier (**7.2.1–7.2.2**). Most cases will involve a battery that occasions ABH. However, a base offence of assault is also possible as, for example, where D causes V to apprehend imminent violence (assault) and V hurts herself when attempting to escape (ABH).[54]

7.4.1.2 Occasioning

Having demonstrated an assault or battery, the prosecution must prove that this assault or battery *occasioned* ABH. 'Occasioning' has been interpreted to mean nothing more than 'causing'.[55] Thus, D's conduct must have caused (a) the result element of the assault or battery, and (b) ABH.

---

[54] *Roberts* (1972) 56 Cr App R 95.
[55] Ibid. Challenged in Gardner, 'Rationality and the Rule of Law in Offences Against the Person' (1994) 53 CLJ 502, 509.

7.4.1.3 Actual bodily harm

'Actual bodily harm' is not defined in the OAPA, and so the courts have attempted to interpret it in line with the term's common meaning, influenced also by the maximum five-year sentence.[56] Distinct from mere battery, it is clear that ABH will not be found where V's injury is merely 'transient and trifling'.[57] However, ABH has been described in expansive terms to include 'any hurt or injury that is calculated to interfere with the health or comfort' of V.[58] Examples of ABH include:

- scratches, grazes, and abrasions;
- bruising and swelling;
- temporary loss of consciousness;[59]
- cutting a substantial amount of hair;[60]
- psychiatric injury; etc.[61]

The potential for ABH in the form of psychiatric injury should be applied with care. Psychiatric injury will amount to ABH where it manifests as an identified or recognised psychiatric condition (eg clinical depression). However, simple psychological harms, such as fear or anxiety, will never amount to ABH. *Ireland* is the leading case.

 Ireland and Burstow [1998] AC 147

These appeals were conjoined in the House of Lords. Ireland was charged with a section 47 offence having made a series of silent telephone calls which caused V1 to suffer psychiatric harm. Burstow was charged with an offence of causing GBH, having harassed V2, including making silent calls, and causing her to suffer severe depression.

- Crown Court: both found guilty of the offences charged.
- Court of Appeal: both convictions upheld on appeal.
- House of Lords: appeals dismissed. Psychiatric injury is capable of amounting to actual and/or grievous bodily harm.

7.4.2 Mens rea of s47

The only mens rea requirements for section 47 are those relating to the base offence of assault (intention or recklessness as to causing V to apprehend imminent violence) or battery (intention or recklessness as to making contact with V). There is no additional mens rea required for the result of ABH, as established in *Roberts*.

---

[56] *DPP v Smith* [1961] AC 290 at 334 describes the term as requiring 'no explanation'.
[57] *T v DPP* [2003] Crim LR 622.
[58] *Miller* [1954] 2 QB 282.
[59] *T v DPP* [2003] Crim LR 622.
[60] *DPP v Smith* [2006] EWHC 94 (Admin).
[61] CPS Charging Standards: www.cps.gov.uk/legal-guidance/offences-against-person-incorporating-charging-standard.

Roberts (1972) 56 Cr App R 95

D made unwanted sexual advances towards V when driving her in his car. D tried to take off V's coat (a battery), and this led to V jumping out of the moving car and sustaining grazes and concussion (ABH). D was charged with a section 47 offence. D claimed that he did not foresee the risk that V would jump out of the car, and that he should therefore avoid liability.

- Crown Court: guilty of section 47 offence.
- Court of Appeal: conviction upheld on appeal. Liability does not require D to foresee the risk that his acts will cause ABH.

The rule in *Roberts* was later thrown into doubt following a remarkable series of cases.[62] However, it has since been confirmed by the House of Lords in *Savage* and *Parmenter*.[63]

 Savage and Parmenter [1992] 1 AC 699

These appeals were conjoined in the House of Lords. Savage intended to throw the contents of her beer glass over V1, but slipped and threw the glass as well causing a wound. Parmenter handled a baby (V2) in such a way that caused serious injury. In both cases, the defendants claimed that they did not intend or foresee a risk of causing harm.

- Crown Court: both found guilty of offences involving GBH.
- Court of Appeal: appeals allowed—there was a lack of mens rea for the GBH offences. In *Savage*, liability for GBH was replaced with liability for a section 47 offence. In *Parmenter*, section 47 was not applied, the court found that mens rea was required as to causing ABH.
- House of Lords: *Parmenter* appeal allowed. *Savage* appeal dismissed. Both liable for a section 47 offence: this offence requires no mens rea as to the causing of ABH.

Section 47 is, therefore, an example of a constructive liability offence.[64]

7.5 OAPA 1861, s20: wounding, or inflicting grievous bodily harm

Section 20 criminalises malicious wounding *and/or* inflicting GBH, with at least foresight of some bodily harm.

20. Whosoever shall unlawfully and maliciously wound or inflict any grievous bodily harm upon any other person, either with or without any weapon or instrument shall be guilty of [an offence triable either way] and being convicted thereof shall be liable to imprisonment for five years.

[62] *Spratt* [1991] 2 All ER 210 (without reference to *Roberts*) held that recklessness was required as to the ABH. However, on the same day, *Savage* [1991] 2 All ER 210 (without reference to *Roberts*) held that no mens rea was required. Later, confronted with this conflict (but, again, without reference to *Roberts*), *Parmenter* (in the Court of Appeal) preferred *Spratt*.

[63] Reversing *Parmenter* and overruling *Spratt* on this point.

[64] On constructive liability, see **Chapter 4.2.1.1**. For reform discussion on this point, see **Chapter 7.10.2**.

The elements of the section 20 offence are set out in **Table 7.5**.

Table 7.5 OAPA 1861, s20

	Actus reus	**Mens rea**
Conduct element	Any conduct causing the results	Voluntary
Circumstance element	V is a person	Knowledge
Result element	V is wounded Or V suffers GBH	Recklessness as to some bodily injury

7.5.1 Actus reus of s20

The two ways of completing the actus reus of section 20 are through wounding and/or inflicting GBH.

7.5.1.1 Wounding

To constitute a wound, V's skin must be broken by, for example, stabbing.[65] The stand-ard case will involve V's outer skin, but wounding will also be found where D breaks internal membranes that are similar to the outer skin as, for example, where D punches V and splits the inside of her cheek or lip.[66] There are limits, however. First, the whole skin (every layer) must be broken. For example, a scratch that breaks the 'surface of the skin' but not every layer will not amount to a wound.[67] Secondly, wounding cannot be *purely* internal. In *Wood*,[68] for example, despite causing V's broken collarbone, as the skin remained intact, there was no wound.

Doubt remains as to whether wounding can be caused by omission, and a case of this kind would be rare. However, it is likely that omissions liability is possible. For example, D omits to put sharp knives in a safe place having foreseen the possibility that V—a young child—might injure herself with them, breaching a duty to remove the danger created. D is likely to be liable for the section 20 offence by omission if injury results.

7.5.1.2 Inflicting grievous bodily harm

In the absence of a statutory definition, GBH has been interpreted by the House of Lords to mean 'serious bodily harm'.[69] Thus, V's injuries must be more serious than ABH, which requires only 'bodily harm'. However, it is clear that GBH does not require injury

---

[65] *Moriarty v Brooks* (1834) 6 C & P 684.
[66] *Waltham* (1849) 3 Cox CC 442.
[67] *Morris* [2005] EWCA Crim 609.
[68] (1830) 1 Mood CC 278.
[69] *Smith* [1961] AC 290. See recently *Sidhu* [2019] EWCA Crim 1034.

to be permanent or life-threatening,[70] with even brief unconsciousness being potentially sufficient.[71] Classic examples include broken bones and disfigurement. It is also clear that *serious* psychiatric injuries may amount to GBH, as discussed previously in *Ireland* (**7.4.1.3**). However, as with ABH, such injury must amount to a recognised psychiatric condition; simple fear or distress is insufficient.

Extra detail . . .

As with section 47, when deciding on the degree of harm caused, the court will consider the totality of V's injuries. Thus, it is not necessary to demonstrate that V suffered ABH or GBH as a result of a single act (eg punch), provided that the harm was sustained from one attack or relevant period.[72]

Unlike the section 18 offence (discussed at **7.6**) which requires D to 'cause' GBH, section 20 uses the term 'inflict'. This has given rise to some disagreement about whether the two words require different tests, for example whether 'inflict' implies that D must cause injury through an assault or battery, as with section 47. However, it is now settled law that 'inflict' should be interpreted in exactly the same way as 'cause': D's conduct must be shown to have caused the harm to V applying the standard rules of causation, and there is *no* extra requirement of assault or battery.[73]

Assessment matters . . .

There are two distinct ways to bring about the actus reus of section 20: by wounding or by inflicting GBH. It should be remembered that although these will often overlap (eg D stabs V in the stomach), this will not always be the case. Where D breaks one of V's bones, for example, but does not break the skin, this is GBH and not a wound.[74] Conversely, a minor wound (eg injection from a needle) will amount to a wound but not GBH. Thus, when applying section 20 to the facts of a problem question, it is good practice to identify which (if not both) are caused by D.

7.5.2 Mens rea of s20

Whether the allegation is of wounding, causing GBH, or both, section 20 specifies a mens rea that D must be acting 'maliciously'. This has been interpreted to mean 'intentionally or recklessly'.[75] However, although intent or foresight of a risk is required, section 20 does *not* require D to intend or foresee the full extent of the harms caused (ie wounding or GBH). Rather, liability merely requires D to intend or foresee that *some*

---

[70] *Bollom* [2004] 2 Cr App R 50.
[71] *Hicks* [2007] EWCA Crim 1500.
[72] *Brown* [2005] EWCA Crim 359: case involving abuse over several days.
[73] *Wilson* [1984] AC 242, clarifying that assault and battery are *not* required for s20 liability.
[74] *Wood* (1830) 1 Mood CC 278 (broken collarbone).
[75] *Savage* and *Parmenter* [1991] 4 All ER 698, 721. Although the term 'recklessness' is used, it remains unclear whether D must satisfy *both* limbs of the test, or whether foresight of a risk (ie the first limb) is all that is required.

bodily harm might be caused, not necessarily amounting to a wounding or GBH. As Diplock LJ explained in *Mowatt*:[76]

> … the word 'maliciously' does import upon the part of the person who unlawfully inflicts the wound or other grievous bodily harm an awareness that his act may have the consequence of causing some physical harm to some other person. … [But] it is quite unnecessary that the accused should have foreseen that his unlawful act might cause physical harm of the gravity described in [s20], ie, a wound or serious physical injury. It is enough that he should have foreseen that some physical harm to some person, albeit of a minor character, might result.

It should be remembered, however, that intent or foresight of some harm is still necessary for liability. For example, D will not commit a section 20 offence if her intention is simply to frighten V, where D does not foresee the possibility of V suffering injury as a result.

7.5.3 Coexistence of s20 and s47

As the section 47 and section 20 offences are punishable with the same maximum of five years' imprisonment, it is arguable that their coexistence is unnecessary.[77] However, as section 20 will *usually* involve greater harms,[78] and also includes a higher requirement of mens rea, section 20 is regarded in practice as the more serious offence. In this manner, conviction for section 20 will usually result in a higher sentence than conviction for section 47.

As we highlighted earlier, one of the aims of this first category of non-fatal offences is the creation of a ladder that provides appropriate offences and sentences in relation to different levels of harm. The lack of clarity in the existing distinction between section 47 and section 20, and its reliance on prosecutors and the courts to create that distinction in practice, reflects poorly on the current law. This has been highlighted by the Law Commission,[79] and we discuss it later in the context of potential reforms (**7.10.1.1**).

7.6 OAPA 1861, s18: wounding, or causing grievous bodily harm with intent

Section 18 criminalises D who, with intention to cause GBH or resist apprehension etc, maliciously wounds *and/or* causes GBH.

> 18. Whosoever shall unlawfully and maliciously by any means whatsoever wound or cause any grievous bodily harm to any person with intent to do some grievous bodily harm to any person or with intent to resist or prevent the lawful apprehension or detainer of any person, shall be guilty of [an offence triable only on indictment], and being convicted thereof shall be liable to imprisonment for life.

---

[76] [1968] 1 QB 421, 426. Reiterated in *C* [2007] EWCA Crim 1068.
[77] Gardner, 'Rationality and the Rule of Law in Offences Against the Person' (1994) 53 CLJ 520.
[78] This will not always be the case. See reform discussion at **7.10.1.1**.
[79] Law Commission, *Reform of Offences against the Person* (No 361, 2015).

The elements of the section 18 offence are set out in **Table 7.6**.

Table 7.6 OAPA 1861, s18

	Actus reus	**Mens rea**
Conduct element	Any conduct causing the results	Voluntary
Circumstance element	V is a person	Knowledge
Result element	V is wounded Or V suffers GBH	Intention to cause GBH *or* intention to resist apprehension, etc and malice as to bodily harm

7.6.1 Actus reus of s18

The actus reus of the section 18 offence is identical to that of section 20: D's conduct must have caused V to suffer either a wound and/or GBH. There is no need to demonstrate that the elements of assault or battery were also present.

7.6.2 Mens rea of s18

The mens rea of section 18 is the same regardless of whether D has wounded V or caused GBH. The standard case of section 18 will involve D causing GBH to V with malice and an intention to cause GBH. However, section 18 is also committed where *any* of the following arises:

- wounding with malice and intent to cause GBH;
- wounding with malice and intent to resist lawful apprehension;
- wounding with malice and intent to prevent lawful apprehension;
- wounding with malice and intent to resist lawful detainer;
- wounding with malice and intent to prevent lawful detainer;
- GBH with malice and intent to resist lawful apprehension;
- GBH with malice and intent to prevent lawful apprehension;
- GBH with malice and intent to resist lawful detainer; and
- GBH with malice and intent to prevent lawful detainer.

Amongst these variations, two important details should not be missed:

A) **Role of intention:** Unlike other offences against the person, the mens rea of section 18 is only satisfied by an *intention* (recklessness is not sufficient). Therefore, the meaning of 'intention' as distinct from recklessness becomes crucial. D intends when she either (a) acts in order to bring about the result, or (b) acts with foresight that the result is a virtually certain consequence of her action, the result is in fact a virtually certain result, and the jury choose to find that she intended it.[80]

B) Mens rea and wounding: As discussed in *Taylor*, an intention to wound is *not* sufficient mens rea for section 18.

 Taylor [2009] EWCA Crim 544

D stabbed V in the back during an altercation. There was no evidence that D intended to cause GBH.

- Crown Court: guilty of a section 18 offence. The court defined the mens rea of section 18 as an intent to wound or to cause GBH.
- Court of Appeal: appeal allowed, and liability for section 20 substituted. Section 18 requires intention to cause GBH (not simply to wound), and there was insufficient evidence of such intention in this case.

7.6.2.1 Malice

'Malice' has already been discussed in relation to section 20 (**7.5.2**): it requires, broadly, D to intend or foresee the possibility of causing V bodily harm. For the section 18 offence, the role played by the malice requirement is therefore very different between (A) cases where D intends GBH, and (B) cases where D does not intend to cause GBH but does, for example, intend to resist lawful apprehension.

A) Where D intends to cause GBH: In this most common construction of the section 18 offence, the word 'maliciously' adds nothing at all. D's intention to cause GBH incorporates the less serious malice requirement, and so it need not be discussed separately.[81]

B) Where D does not intend GBH, but does intend to resist lawful apprehension, etc: Here, the 'maliciously' requirement becomes central to liability. This is because D's mens rea does not otherwise refer to harms at all. The 'maliciously' requirement means that D must foresee at least some bodily harm, and although there is no direct authority, probably also requires the foresight of GBH.[82] Thus, where D intends to prevent apprehension, etc, 'maliciously' should be interpreted to require her to *also* foresee the possibility of GBH before section 18 liability is established.

7.7 Sections 47, 20, and 18: alternative verdicts

Consistent with the 'laddering' of these offences, it has been held that a charge relating to a more serious offence against the person will include the less serious offences as alternatives. Thus, if D is charged under section 18, GBH with intent, a jury may

---

[80] See **Chapter 3.4.1**.
[81] *Brown* [2005] EWCA Crim 359, [17].
[82] This is assumed in *Morrison* (1989) 89 Cr App R 17.

alternatively find liability under section 20 or section 47 if they believe that the essential elements of liability for section 18 are unproven.[83] Thus, analysis of liability will generally focus on the most serious potential offence before working down the ladder if necessary.

Despite the utility of this approach, research (albeit now rather dated) suggests it can lead to unfortunate consequences. Principally, because of the availability of the lesser alternatives, it seems that many juries have shied away from reaching guilty verdicts for the most serious section 18 offence, even where the elements of this offence appear to be satisfied.[84] Such research demonstrates a flaw in the laddering of offences.

7.8 Defences to sections 47, 20, and 18

Where D satisfies the elements of section 47, 20, or 18, she will nevertheless avoid liability if she has a specific defence of 'consent' or 'belief in consent'. D may also avoid liability by relying on one of the general defences discussed in **Chapter 13** (denials of offending) and **Chapter 14** (general defences). Our focus in this section will be the specific defences.

It should be noted that although the defences of 'consent' and 'belief in consent' are available in relation to sections 47, 20, and 18, these defences are *not* constructed in the same way as they were in relation to assault and battery (**7.3.2–7.3.3**). To apply to the more serious offences, V's consent, or D's belief in consent, will require additional elements before being legally effective. Before discussing the consent defences, however, we discuss a separate method of defending section 47 liability.

7.8.1 Defences to the base offence for s47

The defences to assault and battery discussed earlier (including lawful chastisement, consent, and belief in consent) will not ordinarily prevent liability for a section 47, 20, or 18 offence. However, the unique construction of section 47, requiring a base offence of assault or battery that causes ABH, opens the possibility that one of these defences might apply, removing liability for the base offence. With the base offence removed, the construction of section 47 liability (assault or battery + ABH = s47) becomes impossible. Thus, in effect, a defence to simple assault or battery can act as a defence to section 47 liability.

However, where D has caused ABH, the courts have been reluctant to allow a defence to simple assault or battery (the base offence) to undermine liability. A line of authority has developed in these cases that can prevent D relying on what appears to be an effective defence to the base offence, if she has foreseen the risk of causing ABH. Where D seeks to rely on a defence to the base offence, she will be restricted to only those defences that are available for the more serious offences (discussed at **7.8.2–7.8.3**).

---

[83] *Mandair* (1994) 99 Cr App R 250.
[84] Genders, 'Reform of the Offences Against the Person Act: Lessons from the Law in Action' [1999] Crim LR 689.

Although the courts have struggled for consistency, their general approach can be summarised as follows:

A) D causes ABH, she intended or foresaw the possibility of causing ABH:

 Example...

D and V play a game trying to push each other over. V falls and accidentally hits her head on a rock, causing ABH. D had foreseen that such injuries might result, as she noticed there was a rock directly behind V.

V may have given effective consent to assault or battery, but D's foresight that she might cause ABH means that such consent will *not* prevent section 47 liability. Rather, D will only avoid liability if she satisfies the elements of the more restrictive consent defences (discussed at **7.8.2–7.8.3**). This is confirmed in *Donovan*.[85]

B) D causes ABH, she did not intend or foresee the ABH:

 Example...

D and V play a game trying to push each other over. V falls and accidentally hits her head on a rock, causing ABH. D had not foreseen that V might hurt herself in this way; she did not notice the rock as it was hidden beneath the grass.

As D does not foresee the chance of causing ABH or greater, V's effective consent to assault or battery *will* prevent section 47 liability. V has consented to the assault or battery, and there is no reason (no further fault from D) that justifies treating that consent as invalid. This is confirmed in *Meachen*.[86]

C) D causes ABH. She did not intend or foresee the ABH, although she should have foreseen it:

 Example...

D and V play a game trying to push each other over. V falls and accidentally hits her head on a rock, causing ABH. D had not foreseen that V might hurt herself in this way, but she should have done as the rock was clearly visible.

This final example is the most problematic, with conflicting authorities. *Boyea* suggests that V's effective consent to assault or battery will *not* prevent D's potential section 47 liability.[87] As with D's recklessness in (A), D's negligence as to causing ABH will undermine her defence. D will only avoid liability if the elements of the more restrictive consent defences (discussed at **7.8.2–7.8.3**) are satisfied. However, in *Meachen*,[88] the Court of Appeal cast doubt on this interpretation, suggesting that only subjective

---

[85] [1934] 2 KB 498.
[86] [2006] EWCA Crim 2414.
[87] (1992) 156 JP 505.
[88] [2006] EWCA Crim 2414, [41].

foresight of ABH (A) will prevent V's consent to simple assault or battery undermining the base offence. Case (C) should therefore be treated in the same way as (B). It is likely that the interpretation in *Meachen* will be followed.

Extra detail . . .

Section 47 cases where V consented to assault or battery, but did not consent to ABH, are rare. However, the approach of the courts, focussing on D's foresight of ABH, is interesting. It should be remembered that D need not foresee the chance of causing ABH to be liable for a section 47 offence, as it is a constructive liability offence. However, such foresight becomes a primary concern here, when deciding if defences to simple assault or battery can be used to prevent liability.

7.8.2 Consent to the more serious offences against the person

Consent can be a valid defence to offences under section 47, 20, or 18. However, in addition to the defence elements required for consent as to assault or battery (capacity, information, lack of duress, etc), consent to the more serious offences will only be available where D's conduct comes within an 'excepted category' recognised at common law. For example, D cannot avoid liability for GBH even if V asked to be shot. However, a doctor can avoid such liability if V consented to a surgical operation that was duly performed. The elements of the defence are set out in **Table 7.7**.

Table 7.7 Defence of consent to serious offences against the person

A) V's consent must be expressed or implied to D in a legally recognised manner
B) V's consent must be effective: V must have the capacity, freedom, and information to make a choice
C) The conduct and harms consented to must come within a legally recognised category

We have discussed the first two elements of the defence in the context of assault and battery (at **7.2.3**), and the same rules apply here. Therefore, our focus will be on the additional element, identifying the categories of conduct that can be validly consented to.

The third element of the defence was established in what remains the leading case, *Brown*.

Brown [1994] AC 212

D and others were involved in sadomasochistic homosexual groupings. Within the group, the men filmed various acts causing both ABH and wounding for their mutual sexual pleasure. They were charged with offences under sections 47 and 20.

• Crown Court: guilty of section 47 and 20 offences.

- Court of Appeal: convictions upheld on appeal.
- House of Lords: appeal dismissed (3:2). The court set out the additional requirement for consent in relation to sections 47, 20, and 18. They then concluded that sadomasochism did not qualify within one of the special categories.

The recognised categories, or accepted activities, where V's consent will be legally effective, have not been designed in accordance with particular legal principles or with regard to any legal or medical notions of acceptable harm.[89] Rather, as Lord Woolf rather candidly admitted in *Barnes*,[90] they have evolved as a matter of 'public policy'. This policy-based approach allows the courts flexibility to reach what they consider to be socially desirable results. However, in their attempts to do so, the list of accepted activities has developed inconsistently and, as many would now accept, incoherently. The categories that have so far been acknowledged by the courts, in certain circumstances at least, include:

- surgery;
- body modification;
- religious flagellation;
- sports;
- horseplay; and
- sexual pleasure.

We discuss each in turn.

7.8.2.1 Surgery
Surgery is a straightforward example where V can provide valid consent to what might otherwise constitute a serious offence against the person.[91] This includes both essential and non-essential (cosmetic) treatment.[92]

7.8.2.2 Body modification
Short of surgery, several cosmetic procedures also cause bodily harms—including piercing, tattooing, hair cutting, etc. These procedures can, of course, be validly consented to.[93] However, this is a category with significant grey areas, as we see in *Wilson* and *BM*.

---

[89] See Tolmie, 'Consent to Harmful Assaults: The Case for Moving Away from Category Based Decision Making' [2012] Crim LR 656; Kell, 'Social Disutility and Consent' (1994) 14 OJLS 121; Giles, 'Consensual Harm and the Public Interest' (1994) 57 MLR 101.
[90] [2005] Crim LR 381. The same acknowledgment was made in *BM* [2018] EWCA Crim 560 (discussed at **7.8.2.2**).
[91] Law Commission, *Consent in Criminal Law* (Consultation 139, 1995) Part 8; Skegg, 'Medical Procedures and the Crime of Battery' [1974] Crim LR 693 and (1973) 36 MLR 370.
[92] *Corbett v Corbett* [1971] P 83: gender reassignment surgery.
[93] Law Commission, *Consent in Criminal Law* (Consultation 139, 1995) Part 9; Elliott, 'Body Dysmorphic Disorder, Radical Surgery and the Limits of Consent' (2009) 17 Med L Rev 149.

Wilson [1996] Crim LR 573

At his wife's (V's) request, D consensually branded his initials onto her bottom with a hot knife. D was charged with a section 47 offence.

- Crown Court: guilty of section 47 offence.
- Court of Appeal: appeal allowed. D's conduct was akin to tattooing, and V's consent was therefore valid.

The Court of Appeal, in allowing the appeal in *Wilson*, was robust in making clear that this kind of activity, performed in private, was not deserving of criminal liability. This would suggest that *Wilson* was a clear case on its facts where V's consent was valid. However, the position is not so clear when compared to the case of *Brown*: some of the acts in *Brown* could equally have been treated as analogous to this category of behaviour (eg genital piercing), but the court in *Brown* found consent to be invalid.

BM [2018] EWCA Crim 560

D (a professional piercer and tattooist) began performing more extreme forms of body modification, including the removal of an ear, the removal of a nipple, and tongue splitting. It was not disputed that each V (customer) consented in fact to the procedures. D was charged with a section 18 GBH offence on the basis that such consent was not legally valid.

- Crown Court: preparatory hearing found that consent was not legally valid, giving rise to an inter-locutory appeal.
- Court of Appeal: dismissing the appeal. Body modification of this kind is akin to unlicensed surgery, and therefore not part of piercing, etc category ([42]).

BM provides some useful clarification as to the limits of this consent category. However, several problems remain. The court is clear that the practices in *BM* are unlawful, and that piercing, etc are lawful, but provide little guidance as to the myriad of procedures between (eg scarification, skin peels, branding, beading, etc).[94] At various points in the judgment the court highlights factors such as whether the harm caused is ABH or GBH, whether the activity is specifically regulated, whether it gives rise to further risks (eg infection), but we are not told how (and to what extent) such factors are determinative. It is reasonable for the court to say that the recognition of new consent categories is a matter for Parliament ([45]), but, it is submitted, guidance on the boundaries of existing categories is still a matter for the court.[95]

---

[94] These procedures may not be to everybody's taste, but they are available within tattoo studios across the country. The court's treatment of tongue-splitting (also *relatively* common) alongside the other procedures in *BM* suggests a strong possibility that consent will not be valid in these cases either.

[95] See discussion in Pegg, 'Not So Clear Cut: The Lawfulness of Body Modifications' [2019] Crim LR 579; Clement, 'Consent to Body Modification in Criminal Law' [2018] 77(3) CLJ 451; Williams, 'Body Modification and the Limits of Consent to Injury' (2019) 135 LQR 19.

Body modification is also common in a religious context (eg circumcision of Jewish and Muslim males).[96] Religious body modification gains some protection from Article 9 ECHR which respects religious freedom. However, certain cultural practices have not been accepted within this exception, for example cheek incision.[97] Such distinctions appear incoherent.

7.8.2.3 Religious flagellation

Although rarely practised, religious flagellation (beating or whipping as part of a religious ritual) is also likely to constitute an exception where V may validly consent to bodily harm.[98] This was recognised by Lord Mustill in *Brown*.

7.8.2.4 Sports

Various sports provide a clear social utility despite the high risk of bodily injury involved, for example rugby, roller derby, etc. However, although the law seeks to allow valid consent in these cases, it must take care not to exempt acts of violence carried out under the guise of sport.[99] Several principles have developed.[100]

First, we must question whether the 'sport' is recognised by the law (ie sports that can be played legally). What is included here remains, to some extent, an accident of history, and is not based on degrees or risks of harm. For example, sports like boxing allow participants intentionally to inflict GBH, and the courts recognise this as lawful.[101] However, certain activities that might once have been considered sports, such as duelling, are no longer recognised as lawful. Where injury results from an unrecognised sport, then V's 'consent' will not be legally valid, and D may be liable.

Secondly, where the sport *is* legally recognised, we examine the rules of the sport. The law will generally accept that no offence arises for conduct within the rules of a sport, played consensually. For example, if D tackles V in a game of rugby, injuring V, but not committing a foul, D will not be liable for an offence. These risks are implicitly consented to when V joins the game. One qualification here, however, is that the criminal law is not *obliged* to accede to any rule changes instituted by sporting bodies. For example, if the Football Association decided that footballers could hit each other with bats, this would not automatically mean that consent to such hitting would be legally recognised.

Thirdly, we must consider injuries that result *outside* the rules of a game. In this regard, human imperfection dictates that for sport to be played at all, consent must be valid in relation to certain forms of inadvertent or reckless behaviour, such as a late tackle in

---

[96] Gilbert, 'Time to Reconsider the Lawfulness of Ritual Male Circumcision' [2007] EHRLR 279. Female circumcision and associated conduct is criminal (Female Genital Mutilation Act 2003, as amended by the Serious Crime Act 2015).

[97] *Adesanya* (1974) The Times, 16 July; Poulter, 'Foreign Customs and the English Criminal Law' (1975) 24 ICLQ 136.

[98] Law Commission, *Consent in Criminal Law* (Consultation 139, 1995) paras 10.2–10.7.

[99] Ibid, Part 12; Cutcheon, 'Sports, Violence and the Criminal Law' (1994) 45 NILQ 267; Anderson, 'No Licence for Thuggery: Violence, Sport and the Criminal Law' [2008] Crim LR 751.

[100] For a discussion of CPS charging policy, see Livings, 'Sports Violence, "Concurrent Jurisdiction" and the Decision to Bring a Criminal Prosecution' [2018] Crim LR 430.

[101] Gunn and Ormerod, 'The Legality of Boxing' (1995) 15 LS 181; Anderson, *The Legality of Boxing: A Punch Drunk Love?* (2007).

football or a bouncer in cricket.[102] The task, then, is to distinguish what we might call *legitimate* foul play (conduct that breaches the rules, but is still impliedly and validly consented to), from *illegitimate* foul play (conduct that breaches the rules to such an extent that it is not validly consented to). This was discussed in *Barnes*.

 Barnes [2005] 1 WLR 910

D was playing in an amateur football match. D mistimed a sliding tackle against V, and caused serious injury. D was charged with a section 20 offence.

- Crown Court: guilty of section 20 offence.
- Court of Appeal: appeal allowed. D's conduct can be outside the rules of the game (within a margin of appreciation) and still be validly consented to.

When asking if the risk is impliedly consented to by those involved, even though it is outside the rules of the game, the Court of Appeal set out a number of factors that should be considered: the type of sport, the level at which it is being played, the nature of the act, the degree of force, the extent of the risk of injury, and D's state of mind.[103] With sporting sanctions and/or civil remedies often readily available, criminal prosecutions are rare and usually reserved for only the gravest conduct.

The test in *Barnes* may be usefully imagined as a target board, as set out in **Figure 7.2**.

According to *Barnes*:

- Inner circle (rules of the game): V provides valid implied consent to any non-intentional injury occurring within the rules of the game.

- Middle ring (just outside the rules of the game): V provides valid implied consent to any non-intentional injury occurring just outside the rules of the game, but within a margin of appreciation.

- Outer ring (outside the margin of appreciation): V's implied consent to the risk of harm does not include conduct that breaks the rules of the game and is outside the margin of appreciation.

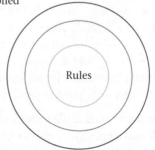

Figure 7.2 Consent and sport

Picking up on the last of the factors highlighted in *Barnes*, D's state of mind requires some special attention. This is because, with the exception of boxing and certain martial arts, playing sport should not involve D *intentionally* causing V bodily harm. Thus, although in sports such as hockey or cricket V's implicit consent will extend to the *risk*

---

[102] *Moore* (1898) 14 TLR 229.

[103] Supported by the Law Commission, *Consent and Offences against the Person* (Consultation 134, 1994). See Gardiner, 'Should More Matches End in Court?' (2005) 155 NLJ 998.

of D causing bodily harm, V has not consented to D *intentionally* causing such injury. Where D causes injury with intent, there is, therefore, no consent.[104]

7.8.2.5 Horseplay

Focussing predominantly on children, the horseplay exception goes beyond sport to recognise consent in relation to general undisciplined play. Such conduct often carries a risk of injury, and consent has been held to be legal valid even where GBH results—as long as the court is satisfied that V's consent was *genuine*.[105] Not recognising this exception would criminalise thousands of acts in playgrounds across the country and also, perhaps, deny a valuable part of growing up.[106]

The horseplay exception has been interpreted widely. For example, in *Aitken*[107] 'robust games' involved RAF officers, who were celebrating in a bar, setting fire to one another's fire-resistant clothing, eventually leading to V suffering severe burns. It was held that if V consented, such consent could be recognised within the exception.

7.8.2.6 Sexual pleasure?

Where V's consent arises in the context of conduct engaged in for sexual pleasure, as opposed to the pleasure of sport or other non-sexual play, the courts have struggled to maintain a clear or coherent approach. New legislation is in process to provide some clarification—that V cannot consent to serious harm for reasons of sexual gratification alone[108]—but as we discuss below, interpretive challenges are likely to remain.

Risk of sexually transmitted infection

It is now clear from *Dica*[109] that V may validly consent to the *risk* of even potentially lethal infection in the context of a sexual encounter, including unprotected sex with a person with HIV, as long as V was fully informed of the risk.[110] This will not, of course, include consent where either party is *intending* that the infection should be spread. This rule is confirmed in clause 65(4) of the Domestic Abuse Bill 2020.

Unlike many recognised exceptions (discussed earlier), consent to the risk of infection is not socially desirable. However, it was found in *Dica* that not recognising this exception would involve an 'impracticality of enforcement', as well as invading a part of life that remains 'pre-eminently private'.

Harm and sexual pleasure: sadomasochism

Sadomasochism (giving and receiving targeted pain for sexual pleasure) is always likely to be problematic for the law in this area.[111] An analogy could be drawn with the risk of sexual infection, allowing consent in recognition of the impracticality of enforcement

---

[104] *Bradshaw* (1878) Cox CC 83.

[105] *A* [2005] All ER 38: V was clearly not consenting.

[106] *Jones* (1986) 83 Cr App R 375.

[107] [1992] 1 WLR 1006.

[108] The Domestic Abuse Bill 2020, cl65. At the time of writing, the 2020 Bill is in its final stages of parliamentary scrutiny.

[109] [2004] EWCA Crim 1103.

[110] *Konzani* [2005] EWCA Crim 706.

[111] Law Commission, *Consent in Criminal Law* (Consultation 139, 1995) Part 10; Bamforth, 'Sadomasochism and Consent' [1994] Crim LR 661; Leigh, 'Sado-Masochism, Consent and the Reform of the Criminal Law' (1976) 39 MLR 130.

and the privacy of sexual relationships. However, unlike the risk of sexual infection and most sport, and horseplay, D is not simply *risking* bodily harm. Rather, the intentional infliction of bodily harm is essential to what both D and V are consenting to. As a matter of logic and in theory, this should not automatically disqualify V's consent as invalid. Within the recognised categories, D intends to inflict bodily harm in the context of body modification, religious flagellations, and sports such as boxing and martial arts. However, in the context of sadomasochism, the courts have felt the need to look more deeply into the perceived social utility of the practice. In doing so, the law has become confused, inconsistent, and indefensible.

The following cases provide an overview of the current legal position:

- *Brown:*[112] the leading case in this area, involving sadomasochistic homosexual encounters between a group of men resulting in prosecutions under sections 47 and 20. A majority in the House of Lords (3:2) upheld the convictions, reasoning that despite the consent of those involved, the actions were not 'sexual' but 'violent'; reflecting a cult of violence that endangered and corrupted those involved.

- *Donovan:*[113] this early case reflects many of the same public policy concerns that led to the decision in *Brown*. In this case, D beat a consenting 17-year-old girl with a cane for purposes of sexual gratification. D was convicted of both indecent assault and common assault. As D was charged with assault and not GBH it is even more astounding that a conviction resulted: as discussed earlier, valid consent for these cases should not require D's conduct to come within the recognised categories. Although such a result is unlikely to be repeated, the policy aims discussed in this case (referred to in *Brown*) remain relevant to the current law.

- *Wilson:*[114] here, D's conviction under section 47, following the consensual branding of his wife's bottom, was overturned on appeal. The Court of Appeal considered the activity to be akin to tattooing, and made clear that they did not believe that this is an area in which the criminal law should interfere: 'consensual activity between husband and wife, in the privacy of the matrimonial home, is not, in our judgment, normally a proper matter for criminal investigation, let alone criminal prosecution'.

Recognising the apparent conflict between *Brown* and *Wilson* in particular, subsequent cases have attempted to find a sensible distinction. Unfortunately, however, courts have tended to do so by focussing on the degree or nature of the harms involved.[115] This is unfortunate because, as both cases involved ABH, it is hard to identify the measurement by which the harms in *Brown* can be characterised as worse. This is particularly evident when we consider that it was only in *Wilson*, and not in *Brown*, that hospital treatment was required.

The latest twist in this debate looks to be coming in the form of legislation, with section 65 of the Domestic Abuse Bill 2020 providing that 'It is not a defence that

---

[112] [1994] AC 212.

[113] [1934] 2 KB 498.

[114] [1996] Crim LR 573.

[115] *Laskey v UK* (1997) 24 EHRR 39: claiming the injuries were not 'comparable in seriousness'; *Emmett* (1999) The Times, 15 October: V's consent to ABH was invalid because D's conduct went 'beyond that which was established in *Wilson*'.

V consented to the infliction of the serious harm for the purposes of obtaining sexual gratification'.[116] This legislation, essentially codifying the ratio in *Brown*, has been prompted by an apparent rise in sadomasochistic practices, and a concern that vulnerable people are pressured into 'consenting' in the context of abusive relationships and/or encounters.[117] Arguably, this concern provides a valid point of distinction from other consensual activities such as sports and legitimate forms of body modification. However, it remains questionable whether codifying the existing law in *Brown* will lead to changes in practice. Whilst legislation can provide emphasis, highlighting the rule to prosecutors and courts, the characterisation of an activity as 'sexual violence' (as in *Brown*) as opposed to conduct akin to tattooing or other legitimate activities (as in *Wilson*) is likely to remain contentious.

> **? Don't be confused . . .**
>
> When discussing the new legislation on consent and sexual gratification, and the surrounding case law, remember that the debate is not only semantic (ie a challenge in phrasing the rule), but also normative (ie whether the rule is desirable). The rule in *Brown*, now codified, has chosen to remove V's legal right to consent to all serious harms for reasons of sexual gratification alone. This is done to protect vulnerable people from abuse, but in doing so it also limits the freedom of others who wish to experience pain for sexual pleasure in non-abusive relationships. The ongoing question for courts and law reformers is whether it is acceptable for the freedom of those in the latter group to be restricted to protect those in the former, and whether (as was arguably the case in *Wilson*) courts will continue to try and carve out points of distinction when apparently non-abusive cases come before them.

7.8.3 Belief in consent to the more serious offences against the person

D has a defence if she believed that V provided valid consent. D's belief in V's consent must have been consistent with the legal requirements of being informed, effective, and within a recognised category. Thus, even if V was not consenting in fact, D will avoid liability if she genuinely believed that consent was present.[118] This defence is rarely pursued in practice.

7.9 Conduct-focussed offences against the person

The first category of non-fatal offences which we have examined above was primarily concerned with the *degree* of harm caused by D: creating a ladder of offences in order to label and punish the degree of harm caused most appropriately. However, in this section we discuss a new category of offences. These offences, although still concerned with

---

[116] At the time of writing, the 2020 Bill is in its final stages of parliamentary scrutiny.
[117] See HC Deb, 28 April 2020; and in particular the HC Report, 6 July 2020.
[118] *Jones* [1987] Crim LR 123.

degrees of harm, are no longer attempting to form part of the ladder explored in the result category. Rather, this group of offences is conduct-focussed: created independently in order to recognise certain specifically harmful circumstances or motives, in order to fill perceived gaps in the law, and/or to reflect political and social priorities.

There are many offences that fall within this category. In the following sections we explore a sample of these, including harassment and stalking, racially or religiously aggravating elements, torture and slavery, administering poison, and domestic abuse.

7.9.1 Harassment and stalking

The criminalisation of harassment and stalking has for many years been, and remains, a challenge for the criminal law.[119] This is because, unlike standard offences against the person, harassing conduct can take almost any form, including apparent acts of kindness such as the repeated sending of flowers. Also, whereas other offences typically focus on a single attack from D, the harms associated with harassment are usually cumulative: perhaps each one being minor viewed in isolation, but severely debilitating in combination. With this in mind, despite the broadening of the OAPA offences to include purely verbal assaults and psychiatric injuries,[120] specific offences have been required to combat the full range of potentially harassing behaviour.[121] These are provided within the Protection from Harassment Act 1997 (PHA).

7.9.1.1 PHA 1997, s2: offence of harassment

Section 2 makes it an offence to cause harassment: to pursue a course of conduct in breach of section 1(1) or 1(1A)[122] (see **Table 7.8**).

1(1)   A person must not pursue a course of conduct—

(a) which amounts to harassment of another, and

(b) which he knows or ought to know amounts to harassment of the other.

(1A)   A person must not pursue a course of conduct—

(a) which involves harassment of two or more persons, and

(b) which he knows or ought to know involves harassment of those persons, and

(c) by which he intends to persuade any person (whether or not one of those mentioned above)—

(i) not to do something that he is entitled or required to do, or

(ii) to do something that he is not under any obligation to do.

---

[119] Babcock, 'The Psychology of Stalking' in Infield and Platford (eds), *The Law of Harassment and Stalking* (2000); Addison and Lawson-Cruttenden, *Harassment Law and Practice* (1998); Finch, 'Stalking the Perfect Stalking Law: An Evaluation of the Efficacy of the Protection from Harassment Act 1997' [2002] Crim LR 702.

[120] *Ireland* [1998] AC 147.

[121] See Home Office, *Stalking the Solutions* (1996). There are also tortious remedies for harassment and a civil order (Stalking Protection Order) has been introduced under the Stalking Protection Act 2019.

[122] Section 1A was added by the Serious Organised Crime and Police Act 2005, s125.

Table 7.8 PHA 1997, s2

	Actus reus	Mens rea
Conduct element	Any course of conduct that causes the result	Voluntary
Circumstance element	V is a person	Knowledge
Result element	(s1(1)) Harassment of V Or (s1A) Harassment of V and others	Know or ought to have known Know or ought to have known
Ulterior mens rea element	*	(s1A) Intention to persuade V not to do something she is entitled to do, or to do something she is not obliged to do

Actus reus of s2

The actus reus of section 2 proscribes a course of conduct that results in V, or V and others, being harassed. The terms 'harassment' and 'course of conduct' are crucial.

A) **Harassment** is not fully defined in the PHA and leaves considerable discretion to the court to interpret the term as it is commonly understood.[123] We are told in section 7(2) that harassment includes 'the causing of alarm or distress'. However, as we are only told that harassment *includes* causing alarm or distress, it is possible that harassment can also be found without proof of either.[124] Equally, alarm and distress can be caused without harassment. This point was clarified in *O'Neill*: 'many actions that cause alarm or distress will not amount to harassment; hence, the requirement, well established in authority . . . that the conduct must also be oppressive'.[125]

We must take care to understand D's conduct in the context of the facts of each individual case. In *Curtis*,[126] for example, D undoubtedly caused alarm and distress to V through several minor assaults and other dangerous behaviour. However, although D's actions were 'oppressive, unreasonable and unacceptable', the Court of Appeal quashed his conviction for harassment, finding that the relevant six incidents spread out over a nine-month relationship between D and V, involving violence on both sides, did not amount to harassment.

---

[123] *Thomas v News Group Newspapers Ltd* [2001] EWCA Civ 1233.
[124] *DPP v Ramsdale* (2001) The Independent, 19 March.
[125] [2016] EWCA Crim 92.
[126] [2010] EWCA Crim 123.

Assessment matters . . .

The lack of a clear definition should encourage you to discuss the law when applying it to problem facts. Look for the causing of alarm or distress, and oppression, but remember that this is not conclusive.

B) A course of conduct must be shown to have *caused* the harassment. D's behaviour must be persistent, with a course of conduct requiring at least two separate incidents. The law focusses on D's conduct, and as established in *James v CPS*, even an active intervention by V will not necessarily prevent liability for D.

 James v CPS [2009] EWHC 2925 (Admin)

V, the manager of a social services team, had a duty to return the calls of D (a receiver of care) despite D's persistent abuse on such calls.

- Magistrates' court: guilty of section 2 offence.
- Crown Court: conviction upheld on appeal.
- Divisional Court: conviction upheld on appeal. V's self-exposure to the harassment was irrelevant.

When identifying the incidents within D's course of conduct, it is important to distinguish between cases involving a single victim, and cases involving multiple victims. The rules are set out in section 7:

7(3)   A 'course of conduct' must involve—

    (a) in the case of conduct in relation to a single person (see section 1(1)), conduct on at least two occasions in relation to that person, or

    (b) in the case of conduct in relation to two or more persons (see section 1(1A)), conduct on at least one occasion in relation to each of those persons.

In standard cases involving a single V under section 7(3)(a), a course of conduct will require D to repeat certain conduct on at least two occasions to that V. Although relatively simple to state, the test can cause problems, particularly where it is difficult to identify or divide incidents. For example, in *Kelly v DPP*,[127] D made three calls to V's mobile between 2.57 am and 3.02 am, leaving abusive voicemail messages on each occasion. Listening to these messages later, and without pause between messages, V was caused severe distress. *Is this more than one incident?*[128] Similarly, in an effort to find multiple incidents, the courts have also been willing, whether rightly or wrongly, to accept indirect acts of harassment. For example, in *DPP v Williams*[129] D put his hand

---

[127] [2003] Crim LR 43, DC.

[128] See also *DPP v Hardy* [2008] All ER (D) 315: 95 phone calls within a 90-minute period held to constitute a course of conduct rather than a single incident.

[129] *DPP v Williams* (DC, 27 July 1998, Rose LJ and Bell J).

through a bathroom window startling X who was in the room showering, and causing V (X's flatmate who was later *told* of the incident) to also be fearful. Later, D looked into a bedroom window, this time frightening V directly. The court held that, as V was caused distress by both incidents, the offence was made out even though the first was indirect.[130]

In cases involving multiple victims, a course of conduct will require only a single harassing act for each victim. A single act would suffice provided it impacts on at least two victims. In this manner, D's multiple acts of harassment are not excused from liability simply because they are not aimed at the same V. This provision is particularly useful in the context of protesters who harass those connected with animal breeding and testing.[131] Where D's course of conduct is based on section 7(3)(b), however, it must be remembered that the additional element of ulterior mens rea will be required.[132]

Alongside evidence of multiple acts, to establish a 'course of conduct' in either guise, it must also be demonstrated that those acts were in some way connected. In many cases, such as repeated telephone calls within a short period of time, this will be relatively easy to establish. However, what if the acts are separated by a considerable period of time, say, two birthday cards, or are of a very different nature? This was discussed in *Lau v DPP*.

 Lau v DPP [2000] Crim LR 580

The first incident involved D slapping V (his then girlfriend) on the face. The second, four months later, involved D threatening V's new partner with a brick. D was charged with a section 2 offence.

- Magistrates' court: guilty of section 2 offence.
- Divisional Court: appeal allowed. Although a course of conduct can *potentially* be found despite a lengthy gap, even up to a year, the incidents must have a logical connection. An example given was of racial harassment outside a synagogue on the Day of Atonement. In this case there was insufficient evidence of that connection or nexus.

It is clear from *Lau* that each case will turn on its facts. The question for the court is a general one: are the incidents logically connected as a single course of conduct? To fulfil the actus reus of section 2, the answer must be 'yes'.

Mens rea of s2

Applying the mens rea for section 2 again requires a distinction to be made between cases where D harasses a single V on multiple occasions (s1(1)), and cases where D harasses multiple Vs (s1(1A)). This is because it is only in the latter that there is an additional ulterior mens rea requirement.

A) Mens rea required for both s1 and s1A: At the time of acting, D must have known, or ought to have known, that her course of conduct would result in harassment. In this manner, the mens rea of section 2 can be satisfied both subjectively by D's actual

---

[130] Section 7(3A) provides the additional possibility that where D aids and abets an act of harassment that is carried out by another, the law will also treat the act as having been completed by D.

[131] Home Office, *Animal Welfare: Human Rights—Protecting People from Animal Rights Extremists* (2004).

[132] Section 7(3A) provides the additional possibility that, where D aids and abets an act of harassment that is carried out by another, the law will also treat that act as having been completed by D.

knowledge or objectively by the fact that a reasonable person would have known. The objective approach is illustrated in *Colohan*.[133]

 Colohan [2001] EWCA Crim 1251

D, who suffered from schizophrenia, sent a number of letters to his local MP (V). The letters were threatening in places and caused V substantial distress. D was charged with a section 2 offence.

- Crown Court: guilty of section 2 offence.
- Court of Appeal: conviction upheld on appeal. Although D may not have known that his letters would cause alarm or distress, a reasonable person not suffering such an illness would have done. Therefore, mens rea is satisfied.

Within this objective standard, D's lack of appreciation or inability to appreciate the effects of her conduct will not be taken into account. However, any additional information that D possesses will. This is important where D is aware of particular circumstances that make her otherwise innocuous conduct more likely to be harassing (eg D knows that V has consistently rejected her advances, and yet continues to send gifts).

B) **Mens rea required only where D harasses multiple Vs (s1(1A)):** D must intend her course of conduct to persuade the victims to refrain from something they are entitled to do, or to do something they are not (eg for an animal breeder to stop trading with a biological research lab). In the more common section 2 case, where D harasses a single victim (s1(1)), this additional intention is not required.

Defences for s2

With such a broadly defined offence it is important to consider any defences that D might raise to avoid liability.[134] A specific defence is provided by section 1(3), highlighting three cases where no course of conduct will be found:

1(3)   Subsection (1) or (1A) does not apply to a course of conduct if the person who pursued it shows—

(a) that it was pursued for the purpose of preventing or detecting crime,

(b) that it was pursued under any enactment or rule of law or to comply with any condition or requirement imposed by any person under any enactment, or

(c) that in the particular circumstances the pursuit of the course of conduct was reasonable.

A) **Defence 1(3)(a):** This defence seems tolerably clear. Although the defence is predominantly intended to protect the police and other law enforcement agencies, it can also be used by others, such as investigative journalists, and even members of the public. However, particularly where the defence is raised by people who are not acting as officials, the court will closely scrutinise whether such conduct was required.[135]

---

[133] [2001] EWCA Crim 1251.

[134] Discussed in *Hayes v Willoughby* [2013] UKSC 17.

[135] *Howlett v Holding* (2006) The Times, 8 February: D conducted a campaign against V, a local councillor, by flying banners from his aircraft referring to her in abusive terms.

B) **Defence 1(3)(b):** This defence is also relatively uncontroversial, protecting free speech and expression, for example, through public demonstrations.[136]

C) **Defence 1(3)(c):** This defence is more problematic, and more difficult to define.[137] The defence requires D to prove (on the balance of probabilities) that her harassing course of conduct was *reasonable* for her to pursue in the circumstances. For the court, particularly in protest-related cases, this will mean difficult policy decisions regarding the reasonableness of protest that causes others alarm or distress.[138]

Alongside these specific defences, the general defences must also be considered. We discuss these in **Chapters 13** and **14**.

7.9.1.2 PHA 1997, s4: causing fear of violence

Section 4 criminalises D's course of conduct that not only causes harassment to V, but *also* leads to a fear that violence will be used against V (see **Table 7.9**):

4(1) A person whose course of conduct causes another to fear, on at least two occasions, that violence will be used against him is guilty of an offence if he knows or ought to know that his course of conduct will cause the other so to fear on each of those occasions.

(2) For the purposes of this section, the person whose course of conduct is in question ought to know that it will cause another to fear that violence will be used against him on any occasion if a reasonable person in possession of the same information would think the course of conduct would cause the other so to fear on that occasion.

Table 7.9 PHA 1997, s4

	Actus reus	**Mens rea**
Conduct element	Any course of conduct that causes the result	Voluntary
Circumstance element	V is a person	Knowledge
Result element	Harassment of V	Know or ought to have known
	V fears on at least two occasions violence will be used against her	Know or ought to have known

Actus reus of s4

Section 4 shares many of the same actus reus elements as section 2, with the addition that D must cause V to fear that violence will be used against her. Section 4 is the more serious offence and carries the higher maximum sentence: 10 years' imprisonment on indictment, as opposed to six months for a summary conviction under section 2.

---

[136] *Huntingdon Life Sciences v Curtin* (1997) The Times, 11 December.
[137] *Baron v DPP* (13 June 2000).
[138] *Debnath* [2006] 2 Cr App R 25.

The requirement that D causes V to fear that violence will be used against her is therefore central to the more serious section 4 offence. In many ways, this is a similar requirement to the actus reus of assault (see **7.2.1.1**), although, importantly, section 4 does not require V to anticipate *imminent* violence.[139] Although 'violence' is not defined in the PHA, it is clear that V must anticipate that she personally will come to harm, and it is not sufficient if V anticipates violence to another.[140] The only qualification to this is where D's threats to another cause V, indirectly, to fear for her own safety.[141]

The requirement of 'harassment' (defined earlier) is not explicit in the text of section 4. However, a series of decisions have made clear that harassment *is* an essential element within the offence.[142] This means that harassment must be considered.[143] However, as causing a fear of violence will also *generally* cause alarm or distress (harassment), the requirement of harassment will be easily satisfied in most cases.

Finally, and also in common with section 2, it must be demonstrated that both of these results were caused by D's 'course of conduct' (defined earlier). An isolated event, no matter how serious, will not be sufficient. Rather, a course of conduct requires the causing of harassment and fear of violence on at least two occasions. It should be noted that, unlike the section 2 offence, a course of conduct under section 4 will only be satisfied where it is focussed on a single V. Thus, multiple acts directed at different Vs (caught within s2 through s1(1A)), will not be sufficient for section 4.

Mens rea of s4
As with the section 2 offence, D is not required to intend or even foresee a possibility that her course of conduct will cause harassment and a fear of violence. Rather, it is sufficient mens rea if a reasonable person, possessed of any special knowledge D has, would have known that the course of conduct would cause those results.

Defences for s4
As with section 2, there are a set of specific defences set out within the PHA that apply to section 4:

4(3)   It is a defence for a person charged with an offence under this section to show that—

(a) his course of conduct was pursued for the purpose of preventing or detecting crime,

(b) his course of conduct was pursued under any enactment or rule of law or to comply with any condition or requirement imposed by any person under any enactment, or

(c) the pursuit of his course of conduct was reasonable for the protection of himself or another or for the protection of his or another's property.

[139] *Qosja* [2016] EWCA Crim 1543: explaining that even the unspecified threat 'I'll come back and get you' may be sufficient, [31].
[140] *Henley* [2000] Crim LR 582: D harassed V and his family, including threats to kill. The trial judge wrongly failed to direct the jury that V must fear violence to himself and that foreseeing violence to others *only* is insufficient for s4.
[141] Ibid. See also *Caurti v DPP* [2002] Crim LR 131 and commentaries.
[142] eg *Curtis* [2010] EWCA Crim 123.
[143] *Widdows* [2011] EWCA Crim 1500: D's conviction for s4 quashed because the trial judge failed to make clear in summing up that harassment was required. However, see *Haque* [2011] EWCA Crim 1871: D's conviction was safe despite a similar failure.

The defences in section 4(3)(a) and (b) largely mirror those already discussed in relation to section 2: where D is attempting to prevent/detect crime, and where D is acting in accordance with a rule of law. However, the third specific defence in section 4(3)(c) contains an important difference. Although the corresponding defence to section 2 allows *any* reasonable excuse to act as a defence, in relation to section 4, D's reasonable conduct will only be a defence where it is directed at protecting herself or another, or for the protection of property. This represents a significant narrowing of the defence in light of the more harmful conduct that D has completed to come within section 4.

Alongside these specific defences, the general defences must also be considered. We discuss these in **Chapters 13** and **14**.

7.9.1.3 Stalking offences

Harassment offences in sections 2 and 4 of the PHA have been employed to tackle stalking. However, following an Independent Parliamentary Inquiry into Stalking Law Reform,[144] specific stalking offences were created.[145] The report concluded that since sections 2 and 4 had been interpreted so widely by the courts to include, for example, neighbourhood disputes, they were no longer fit for purpose in relation to stalking. The stalking-specific offences were therefore designed to build upon sections 2 and 4, to expose the full extent of the harm associated with stalking as opposed to simple harassment. The maximum sentences, however, remain the same as the more basic section 2 and 4 offences.

The stalking offences are set out in sections 2A and 4A of the PHA. These offences do not replace sections 2 and 4. Rather, where D commits an offence under section 2 or 4, and D's course of conduct includes conduct 'associated with stalking', D may now be alternatively liable under sections 2A and 4A. Conduct associated with stalking is left undefined in the PHA, but section 2A(3) does provide a number of illustrative examples intended to aid interpretation:

> 2A(3) The following are examples of acts or omissions which, in particular circumstances, are ones associated with stalking—
>
> (a) following a person,
>
> (b) contacting, or attempting to contact, a person by any means,
>
> (c) publishing any statement or other material—
>
>> (i) relating or purporting to relate to a person, or
>>
>> (ii) purporting to originate from a person,
>
> (d) monitoring the use by a person of the internet, email or any other form of electronic communication,
>
> (e) loitering in any place (whether public or private),
>
> (f) interfering with any property in the possession of a person,
>
> (g) watching or spying on a person.

---

[144] Justice Unions' Parliamentary Group, 'Independent Parliamentary Inquiry into Stalking Law Reform: Main Findings and Recommendations', February 2012.

[145] Gowland, 'Protection from Harassment Act 1997: The "New" Stalking Offences' (2013) 77 JCL 387.

Interestingly, the PHA does not specify any corresponding mens rea element in relation to this requirement. Thus, as long as D's course of conduct includes acts or omissions that are associated with stalking, there is no requirement for D to have realised that this was the case.

The structure of the new section 2A offence is set out in **Figure 7.3**.

Figure 7.3 PHA 1997, s2A

The structure of the new s4A offence is set out in **Figure 7.4**.

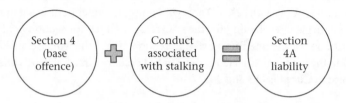

Figure 7.4 PHA 1997, s4A

Owing to a late parliamentary amendment, the section 4A offence (but *not* the s2A offence) can *also* be committed through an alternative construction. Within this alternative, the requirement that V must fear violence has been broadened considerably. This is set out in section 4A(1)(b):

4A(1)(b) either—

   (i) causes another ('B') to fear, on at least two occasions, that violence will be used against B, or

   (ii) causes B serious alarm or distress which has a substantial adverse effect on B's usual day-to-day activities.

This extension was felt necessary because using section 4 as the base offence was believed to be overly restrictive: it would not have allowed for a stalking conviction under section 4A where V did not anticipate physical attack but was nevertheless caused substantial distress.

The statute does not provide a definition of what constitutes 'serious alarm or distress' or a 'substantial adverse effect on B's usual day-to-day activities'. This has been left to the courts, with the potential to be interpreted very widely indeed. As for mens rea, as with a charge based on V fearing violence, it is clear that D's mens rea as to section 4A(1)(b)(ii) is also satisfied by knowledge that such results will be caused, or by the fact that a reasonable person, possessed of any special knowledge D may have, would have known.[146]

---

[146] PHA, s4A(3).

This alternative structure for section 4A is set out in **Figure 7.5**.

Figure 7.5 Alternative route to PHA 1997, s4A

Defences for s2A and s4A

As we have already observed, the section 2A and 4A offences are very similar to the section 2 and 4 offences discussed previously, the major difference being that the stalking offences also require D's course of conduct to include conduct associated with stalking. Consistent with this, the specific defences discussed earlier in relation to the section 2 and 4 offences are also capable of negating liability for the section 2A and 4A offences. Thus, for section 2A (as with s2), if D acts with one of the intentions listed in section 1(3) then this will negate her liability for the course of conduct; for section 4A (as with s4), if D acts with one of the intentions listed in section 4(3)[147] she will also avoid liability.

Alongside these specific defences, the general defences must also be considered. We discuss these in **Chapters 13** and **14**.

7.9.2 Racially or religiously aggravating elements

Where D's violence has been motivated by hostility towards a particular racial or religious group, it has always been open to the court to reflect this aggravating factor at the sentencing stage,[148] and this remains the case.[149] However, first the Crime and Disorder Act 1998 (in relation to race) and then the Anti-Terrorism, Crime and Security Act 2001 (amending the Crime and Disorder Act in relation to religion) adapted these aggravating factors and made them elements of a new species of offences. Although somewhat controversial,[150] in 2014 the Law Commission recommended expanding the categories of hate crime to include aggravation based on disability, sexual orientation, and transgender.[151] There has been a mounting pressure for reform,[152] particularly in relation

---

[147] This time the defences that are also explicitly repeated in s4A(4).

[148] Walters, 'Conceptualizing "Hostility" for Hate Crime Law: Minding "the Minutiae" When Interpreting Section 28(1)(a) of the Crime and Disorder Act 1998' (2014) 34 OJLS 47; Burney, 'Using the Law of Racially Aggravated Offences' [2003] Crim LR 28.

[149] Owusu-Bempah and Walters, 'Racially Aggravated Offences: When Does Section 145 of the Criminal Justice Act 2003 Apply?' [2016] Crim LR 116; 'Racially and Religiously Aggravated Offences: "God's Gift to Defence"?' [2019] Crim LR 463.

[150] For a useful discussion of religiously aggravated offences, and potential dangers to freedom of expression, see Iganski, Sweiry, and Culpeper, 'A Question of Faith? Prosecuting Religiously Aggravated Offences in England and Wales' [2016] Crim LR 334.

[151] Law Commission, *Hate Crime: Should the Current Offences be Extended?* (No 348, 2014); Bakalis, 'Legislating Against Hatred: The Law Commission's Report on Hate Crime' [2015] Crim LR 192.

[152] See eg Scott, 'Violence Against Paedophiles: A Problem for Hate Crime Law?' [2018] Crim LR 543. See generally, Walters, Owusu-Bempah, and Wiedlitzka, 'Hate Crime and the "Justice Gap": The Case for Law Reform' [2018] Crim LR 961.

to offences committed against women.[153] The Law Commission has recently consulted on extending the categories further, to include characteristics of gender or sex, of age, and potentially beyond this to certain philosophical beliefs, occupations such as sex workers, homelessness, and alternative subcultures.[154]

D commits one of these 'aggravated offences' when she perpetrates one of the offences discussed earlier (assault and battery; s47 OAPA; s20 OAPA; or harassment or stalking[155]), *and* she satisfies one of the additional racially or religiously aggravating elements. Thus, for example, a conviction for assault or harassment becomes a conviction for racially aggravated assault or religiously aggravated harassment. In each case involving offences against the person, the aggravated version of the relevant base offence has a maximum sentence that is increased.

The offences are stated in sections 29[156] and 32[157] of the Crime and Disorder Act 1998. However, it is section 28 that sets out the requirements for racial or religious aggravation:

28(1)   An offence is racially or religiously aggravated for the purposes of sections 29 to 32 below if—

(a) at the time of committing the offence, or immediately before or after doing so, the offender demonstrates towards the victim of the offence hostility based on the victim's membership (or presumed membership) of a racial or religious group; or

(b) the offence is motivated (wholly or partly) by hostility towards members of a racial or religious group based on their membership of that group.

Section 28 thereby creates two separate forms of aggravating element: actus reus-based (s28(1)(a)), and mens rea-based (s28(1)(b)). D's base offence need only satisfy *one* of these to become an aggravated offence.

7.9.2.1 Aggravated through actus reus

The model of aggravation is where, *regardless of D's mens rea*, her actions at the time of committing the base offence (eg assault) objectively demonstrate hostility towards a racial or religious group. In this manner, even where D's base offence is not motivated by racial or religious hostility as, for example, where D is angry after V took her parking space, if D acts so as to display such hostility in the course of her offence then she is caught by the aggravated form of liability. The question in each case will be whether D's demonstration of hostility is linked to her base offence. This was discussed in *Babbs*.

---

[153] Schweppe, 'You Can't Have One Without the Other One: "Gender" in Hate Crime Legislation' [2020] Crim LR 148.

[154] Law Commission, Hate Crime Laws (Consultation 250, 2020). As well as discussing each of these potential extensions of the current law on their particular merits, the Commission also provides useful analysis of why and how certain characteristics should be selected ahead of others, looking to avoid ad hoc unprincipled expansion of the law.

[155] There is no need for aggravation for s18 which carries the maximum life sentence.

[156] In relation to assault and battery, s47 and s20 OAPA.

[157] In relation to harassment and stalking.

Babbs [2007] EWCA Crim 2737

D racially abused V in a takeaway restaurant, and a scuffle broke out. Some minutes later, after D had received his food, he then headbutted V. D was charged with racially aggravated assault relating to the headbutt.

- Crown Court: guilty of aggravated assault.
- Court of Appeal: conviction upheld on appeal. Despite the delay between the racial abuse and the assault, there was sufficient proximity for the prosecution to stand.[158]

This form of aggravating element is very broad in its reach, attaching increased liability where a base offence is simply accompanied by, rather than inspired by, hostile comment or action. This was intended by its drafters, who feared that proving racial or religious hatred as a sole motive would be too difficult for prosecutors. However, it has also drawn criticism, particularly when other forms of hate will have no such effect, for example where D assaults V whilst calling him a 'fat bastard'.[159] As the statute matures it will be interesting to see if it has the effect of deterring people from using racist and other forms of discriminatory language or whether (as has been feared) it may harden the racist attitudes of those convicted.[160]

The structure of the offence is set out in **Figure 7.6**.

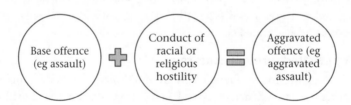

Figure 7.6 Aggravated liability (AR)

7.9.2.2 Aggravated through mens rea

The second model of aggravation is based on D's mens rea. Set out in section 28(1)(b), D is liable for the more serious offence if her commission of the base offence (eg assault) was *motivated* by racial or religious hostility. This second aggravating element is much narrower and less controversial than that in section 28(1)(a).

Although D must be motivated by racial or religious hostility to come within this aggravation, as in *Kendall v DPP*, such hostility need not be her sole motivation.

---

[158] Note, however, *Parry v DPP* [2004] EWHC 3112 (Admin), where a 20-minute delay was held to be too long.

[159] Noted by Maurice Kay J.

[160] Burney and Rose, 'Racially Aggravated Offences: How is the Law Working?' (2002) HORS 244.

Kendall v DPP [2008] EWHC 1848 (Admin)

D attached posters in public places with photos of illegal immigrants who had recently been found guilty of murder, with the heading 'Illegal Immigrant Murder Scum'. The posters also advertised the British National Party. D was charged with a public order offence, including racial aggravation under section 28(1)(b).

- Magistrates' court: guilty of aggravated offence.

- Divisional Court: conviction upheld on appeal. As long as D was partially motivated by racial hostility, it does not matter that he may have had other motives as well.

Racial or religious hostility must, however, form *part* of D's motivation. In *DPP v Howard*[161] D was charged using section 28(1)(b) after chanting 'I'd rather be a Paki than a cop' at his neighbours who were white police officers. Despite D's abusive language, it was held that he could not be liable using section 28(1)(b) because there was no evidence to demonstrate that D's words were *motivated* by hostility towards people from Pakistan, and rather more to suggest that his sole motivation was a personal dislike of his neighbours.[162]

The structure of the offence is set out in **Figure 7.7**.

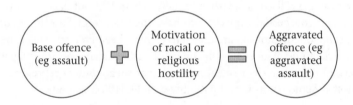

Figure 7.7 Aggravated liability (MR)

7.9.2.3 Defining terms

The terms 'race' and 'religion' are core to both models of aggravation. However, neither is defined with any detail within the Crime and Disorder Act.[163]

A) 'Race' and racial group have been interpreted by the courts in an extremely broad and non-technical manner. The interpretations will include nationality (including citizenship), ethnic origin, and colour.[164] Race will also include non-inclusive expressions, so D will have demonstrated racial hostility if she refers to V as 'foreign' or 'non-white'.[165]

---

[161] [2008] EWHC 608 (Admin).

[162] Moses LJ cautioned: 'Prosecutors should be careful not to deploy [s28(1)(b)] where offensive words have been used, but in themselves have not in any way been the motivation for the particular offence with which a defendant is charged. It diminishes the gravity of this offence to use it in circumstances where it is unnecessary to do so and where plainly it cannot be proved', [12].

[163] Partial definitions are provided: Crime and Disorder Act 1998, s28(4) and (5).

[164] This can create problems for the court, eg *White* [2001] Crim LR 576.

[165] *Rogers* [2007] UKHL 8.

B) **'Religious group'** is defined in the Act simply as a group of persons linked by reference to religious belief or lack thereof. As with the interpretation of 'race', and that employed for Article 9 ECHR, it is likely that 'religion' will be interpreted widely. Non-inclusive terms such as 'unbeliever' will also qualify as religious hostility.[166]

Three further points should be noted when applying these terms. First, the accuracy of D's assumptions about V's racial or religious status is irrelevant (eg where D calls V a 'Paki' when V is from India, D has still demonstrated racial hatred towards V);[167] secondly, racial and religious hostility can be evident even where D and V are of the same racial or religious group; and, finally, it has been held that such hostility does not require V to be aware of D's actions, or even be present at the time.[168]

7.9.2.4 Defences to the aggravated offences

There are no *specific* defences that apply solely to these aggravated offences. However, as each of these offences will include a base offence (eg assault), any specific defences that apply to those base offences (discussed earlier) will also undermine liability for the aggravated offence. The general defences should also be considered, discussed in **Chapters 13** and **14**.

7.9.3 Torture and slavery

Conduct constituting torture and/or slavery is criminalised through various offences. Where D causes bodily harm, for example, we could employ one of the non-fatal offences from the first category discussed earlier. Equally, where V is not harmed beyond being subjected to non-consensual captivity, we have the offence of false imprisonment.[169] However, specific offences of torture and slavery have been created. This is because, as with other overlapping offences, specific offences enable defendants to be labelled more appropriately, to provide a clear social message that such conduct represents a serious wrong, as well as demonstrating compatibility with ECHR obligations.

7.9.3.1 Torture

A specific torture offence was created by section 134 of the Criminal Justice Act 1988, carrying a maximum sentence of life imprisonment (see **Table 7.10**). The offence is designed in accordance with Article 3 ECHR.

134. A public official or person acting in an official capacity, whatever his nationality, commits the offence of torture if in the United Kingdom or elsewhere he intentionally inflicts severe pain or suffering on another in the performance or purported performance of his official duties.

Table 7.10 Criminal Justice Act 1988, s134

	Actus reus	Mens rea
Conduct element	Any conduct causing the result	Voluntary

[166] *DPP v M* [2004] EWHC 1453 (Admin).
[167] *Rogers* [2007] UKHL 8.
[168] *Dykes v DPP* [2008] EWHC 2775 (Admin).
[169] *Pearson-Gaballonie* [2007] EWCA Crim 3504.

Circumstance element	V is a person	Knowledge
	D is acting, or purporting to act, in an official capacity	Intention
Result element	V suffers severe pain or suffering	Intention

The Supreme Court recently considered the offence in the context of a prosecution arising from events during the Liberian Civil War. The Supreme Court held, by a majority, that an individual was capable of being 'a public official of person acting in an official capacity' even if not acting on behalf of the state.[170]

7.9.3.2 Slavery

Replacing a previous offence,[171] slavery is criminalised by section 1 of the Modern Slavery Act 2015 (MSA 2015), carrying a maximum sentence of life imprisonment (see **Table 7.11**). The offence is designed in accordance with Article 4 ECHR.

1(1)   A person commits an offence if—

(a) the person holds another person in slavery or servitude and the circumstances are such that the person knows or ought to know that the other person is held in slavery or servitude, or

(b) the person requires another person to perform forced or compulsory labour and the circumstances are such that the person knows or ought to know that the other person is being required to perform forced or compulsory labour.

Table 7.11 Modern Slavery Act 2015, s1

	Actus reus	Mens rea
Conduct element	Any conduct causing the result	Voluntary
Circumstance element	V is a person	Knowledge
Result element	V is held in slavery or servitude Or V performs forced or compulsory labour (in line with Art 4 ECHR)	Knew or ought to have known

Section 2 of the MSA 2015 sets out a complementary offence relating to human trafficking.

[170] *TRA* [2019] UKSC 52. See Cryer, Commentary [2020] Crim LR 560.
[171] Coroners and Justice Act 2009, s71.

Extra detail . . .

What about victims of slavery and/or trafficking who are compelled to commit crimes themselves? Section 45 of the MSA 2015 creates specific defences for such victim-defendants. Loosely based on the common law defence of duress,[172] defences are designed to encourage victims of slavery and/or trafficking to come forward to the police in order to undermine larger criminal organisations.[173]

7.9.3.3 Defences to torture and slavery

There are no *specific* defences for those who commit either of these offences. The general defences should be considered, particularly if D lacks capacity, but they are unlikely to apply. We discuss the general defences in **Chapters 13** and **14**.

7.9.4 Administering poison

Sections 23 and 24 of the OAPA 1861 create two specific poisoning offences. In addition to more specific labelling, these offences are designed to close a potential gap in the law: as poisoning is often non-violent, D's conduct may, for example, lack the assault or battery essential to section 47 of the OAPA.[174]

7.9.4.1 OAPA 1861, s23: administering poison so as to endanger life or cause GBH

Section 23 represents the more serious poisoning offence, punishable with a maximum of ten years' imprisonment (see **Table 7.12**):

23. Whosoever shall unlawfully and maliciously administer to or cause to be administered to or taken by any other person any poison or other destructive or noxious thing, so as thereby to endanger the life of such person, or so as thereby to inflict upon such person any grievous bodily harm, shall be guilty of [an offence] and being convicted thereof shall be liable . . . to [imprisonment] for any term not exceeding ten years . . .

Table 7.12 OAPA 1861, s23

	Actus reus	Mens rea
Conduct element	Any conduct causing the result	Voluntary
Circumstance element	V is a person	Knowledge
Result element	V takes or is administered a noxious thing And V's life is endangered or V suffers GBH	Reckless None, beyond recklessness as to some minor harm

---

172 See **Chapter 14.3**.
173 Laird, 'Evaluating the Relationship Between Section 45 of the Modern Slavery Act 2015 and the Defence of Duress: An Opportunity Missed?' [2016] Crim LR 395.
174 *Hanson* (1849) 2 Car & Kir 912.

Actus reus of s23

Two areas within the actus reus of section 23 require clarification: the alternative methods of poisoning; and the definition of a noxious thing.

   A) **Method of poisoning:** Section 23 criminalises D where she acts in one of three possible ways.[175] It should be remembered, however, that nothing substantively turns on which method is employed; they all result in liability for section 23.

(a) *D administers the noxious thing to V directly*: this is the most straightforward method, including cases where D injects V with a noxious thing, sprays it into her face, etc.[176]

(b) *D causes an innocent third party to administer the noxious thing to V*: this will cover cases where, for example, D asks X to inject V with the noxious thing (X believing that the syringe contains non-harmful medicine).

(c) *D causes V to take the noxious thing herself*: this final method has caused problems for the courts in terms of causation. The question is under what circumstances D can be said to have *caused* V to take the noxious thing. The answer requires us to examine whether V's conduct was both voluntary and informed:

   (i) if V is *not* aware that the substance she is taking is noxious (eg V believes she is drinking tea) then D has *caused* the taking: V's conduct is voluntary, but not informed;[177]

   (ii) if V *is* aware that the substance is noxious, and makes a free and informed decision to take it, this will break the chain of causation from D and point (c) will not be satisfied. This point was finally settled by the House of Lords in *Kennedy (No 2)*.[178] In this case, D was charged with unlawful act manslaughter (based on s23 poisoning), having handed a syringe containing heroin to V who self-injected causing death. D was not liable under section 23, and therefore not liable for manslaughter, because he had not *caused* V to take the heroin.

   B) **Noxious thing:** When defining a noxious thing, some distinction should be drawn between substances that are noxious per se, such as arsenic and other materials that will commonly lead to death, and those that are potentially noxious when administered in certain circumstances, or in large quantities.

(a) Where a substance is noxious per se, this requirement will be satisfied irrespective of whether D has administered a sufficient quantity to risk harm to V (eg not enough arsenic in the tea), and irrespective of whether V may have some resistance that makes the substance less harmful (eg having built up a resistance from regular use).[179]

(b) *Potentially* noxious substances have been interpreted widely. The court in *Marcus*,[180] for example, stated that '"noxious" mean[s] something different in quality from and of less importance than poison or other destructive things', going on to quote the *Shorter Oxford Dictionary* definition that includes the terms 'injurious, hurtful,

---

[175] For a useful overview, see *Kennedy (No 2)* [2007] UKHL 38.
[176] *Gillard* (1988) 87 Cr App R 189: spraying into V's face.
[177] *Harley* (1830) 4 C & P 369; *Dale* (1852) 6 Cox CC 14.
[178] [2007] UKHL 38. See **Chapter 2.7.2.3**.
[179] *Kennedy (No 2)* [2007] UKHL 38: heroin was considered noxious despite the tolerance built up through addiction.
[180] [1981] 1 WLR 774.

harmful, unwholesome'. The court also made it clear that, although a substance may be harmless in small quantities, it will be held as noxious if it is administered in sufficient quantities to endanger life or cause GBH, or to injure, aggrieve, or annoy in the context of section 24.

In the more recent case of *Veysey*,[181] the court accepted that urine and faeces (thrown at prison officers) were within the definition as being 'unwholesome'. The court held that where an issue arises as to whether a substance is a noxious thing it will be for the judge decide if it is *capable* of being 'injurious, hurtful, harmful or unwholesome'. It will be a matter for the jury whether they are satisfied that it was a noxious thing within that definition.

With this expansive definition in mind, where the substance administered has caused V's life to be endangered or GBH (or injury, grievance, or annoyance in the context of section 24), it will be the exceptional case where the substance is not deemed noxious.

Mens rea of s23

Mens rea for the result element consists of two requirements, both arising from the term 'maliciously'. First, D must intend or be reckless as to the method used: D must foresee a risk that her actions will cause the administration/taking of the noxious thing. Secondly, as before, maliciously has been interpreted to require D to foresee some risk of bodily harm.[182] However, no fault is required as to V's life being endangered or suffering GBH.[183]

The mens rea here contrasts with the section 24 offence, where D must act with 'intent to' bring about the harms suffered by V. This is extraordinary: a less culpable state of mind being required for the more serious offence (s23) than the less serious (s24).

7.9.4.2 OAPA 1861, s24: administering poison intending to injure, aggrieve, or annoy

Section 24 represents the less serious poisoning offence, punishable with a maximum of five years' imprisonment (see **Table 7.13**).

24. Whosoever shall unlawfully and maliciously administer to or cause to be administered to or taken by any other person any poison or other destructive or noxious thing, with intent to injure, aggrieve, or annoy such person, shall be guilty of a misdemeanor, and being . . . convicted thereof shall be liable to be kept in penal servitude . . .

Table 7.13 OAPA 1861, s24

	Actus reus	**Mens rea**
Conduct element	Any conduct causing the result	Voluntary
Circumstance element	V is a person	Knowledge

---

[181] [2019] EWCA Crim 1332.

[182] *Cunningham* [1957] 2 QB 396: D damaged a gas meter, causing gas to seep into the neighbouring houses and endangering life.

[183] *Cato* [1976] 1 WLR 110.

Result element	V takes or is administered a noxious thing	Reckless
Ulterior mens rea element	*	Intention to injure, aggrieve, or annoy

Actus reus of s24

D must expose V to a noxious thing. This has already been discussed in relation to section 23. However, unlike section 23, there is no requirement that this exposure should lead to life endangerment or GBH, or indeed to any harm at all.[184]

Mens rea of s24

Alongside mens rea elements already discussed in relation to section 23, section 24 also requires ulterior intention to 'injure, aggrieve, or annoy'. It will be remembered that *ulterior* intention is mens rea that does not correspond to an element in the actus reus—thus D must intend it, but whether it is caused in fact is irrelevant to her liability. In this manner, D's *motives* become central. For example, if D1 (a paedophile) administers drugs to a child in order to facilitate sexual offences, then she has intent to injure and satisfies the ulterior mens rea; however, if D2 (a parent) administers a drug to their child in order to keep them awake to see fireworks or to stay up for the other parent to return from work then, although we may question D's conduct, the ulterior mens rea will not be satisfied.[185]

7.9.4.3 Defences to s23 and s24

As with several offences against the person, there will be a specific defence where V provided valid consent, or D believed that V provided valid consent. As the issue of consent here relates to substances that have the potential to cause bodily harm, the precedent from *Brown* must be applied. Thus, to be legally valid, V's consent must be *both* effective (**7.3.2.2**) and come within one of the recognised exception categories (**7.8.2**). It is difficult to envisage how many of the recognised categories could apply in the context of poisoning.[186] However, it is certainly possible in relation to medicine, so there will be no poisoning offence where a doctor consensually administers an anaesthetic for surgery, even where V reacts to the anaesthetic and suffers serious harm. The general defences should also be considered, discussed in **Chapters 13** and **14**.

---

[184] Ashworth, 'Defining Criminal Offences without Harm' in Smith (ed), *Criminal Law Essays in Honour of JC Smith* (1987) 13.

[185] Examples from *Hill* (1986) 83 Cr App R 386. For a borderline case see *Weatherall* [1968] Crim LR 115: D put a sleeping tablet in V's drink to enable him to search her handbag for proof of adultery. Held: there was insufficient evidence of intent to injure, aggrieve, or annoy.

[186] It has even been suggested that poisoning can *never* come within one of these exceptions (*Cato* [1976] 1 WLR 110).

7.9.5 Domestic abuse

Domestic abuse can take many forms, including most of the offences discussed in this chapter and beyond.[187] However, as we have begun to understand some of the more subtle (but no less harmful) methods of abuse within intimate partner relationships, including non-violent attacks on V's ability to make her own choices and determine her own life goals, the inadequacy of traditional offences (focussing on violent events, and measuring degrees of injury) has been exposed.[188] The potential for a new all-encompassing 'domestic abuse' offence has some attraction in terms of labelling and drawing public attention, but an offence of this kind is difficult to define in precise terms.[189] In lieu of this, two important recent steps have been taken: the first is the creation of a new 'controlling or coercive behaviour' offence within section 76 of the Serious Crime Act 2015 (see **Table 7.14**);[190] and the second is the creation of various new procedural protections, as well as a new civil domestic abuse protection order, within the Domestic Abuse Bill 2020.[191]

76(1)   A person (D) commits an offence if—

(a) D repeatedly or continuously engages in behaviour towards another person (V) that is controlling or coercive,

(b) at the time of the behaviour, D and V are personally connected,

(c) the behaviour has a serious effect on V, and

(d) D knows or ought to know that the behaviour will have a serious effect on V.

Table 7.14 SCA 2015, s76

	Actus reus	**Mens rea**
Conduct element	Any repeated or continuous conduct causing the result	Voluntary
Circumstance element	D and V are personally connected	None
Result element	A serious effect on V	Knows or ought to know

---

[187] See eg Appendix C of the CPS *Domestic Abuse Guidelines for Prosecutors*. The Domestic Violence, Crime and Victims Act 2004 sets out an array of provisions to tackle domestic violence, including a new offence relating to serious harm caused within a family (s5).

[188] Tadros, 'The Distinctiveness of Domestic Abuse: A Freedom Based Account' in Duff and Green (eds), *Defining Crimes* (2005) 119.

[189] The Law Commission decided against recommending such an offence in *Reform of Offences against the Person* (No 361, 2015) paras 5.111–5.118.

[190] The offence owes much to the work of Evan Stark. See *Coercive Control: How Men Entrap Women in Personal Life* (2009). See also McGorrery, 'Criminalising "the Worst" Part: Operationalising the Offence of Coercive Control in England and Wales' [2019] Crim LR 957.

[191] At the time of writing, the 2020 Bill is in its final stages of parliamentary scrutiny. The new protection order will only be applicable to those aged 18 or over, but where it is applicable, will empower the police to exclude D from certain properties, from contacting V, and so on.

The actus reus elements are defined further within section 76(2)–(7), detailing the range of intimate partner relationships encompassed within 'personally connected', and defining 'serious effect' to include repeated fear of violence and/or serious alarm or distress which has a substantially adverse effect on V's day-to-day activities. A specific defence is also introduced by section 76(8) where D believed she was acting in V's best interests and her behaviour was reasonable.

The section 76 offence has great potential to protect victims of prolonged abuse in a way that has not been possible previously, targeting D who knows (or *objectively* should know) their conduct is having a serious impact on V's ability to live her life.[192] However, although still relatively new, a lack of section 76 convictions is already causing concern for its viability as a bespoke offence,[193] and perhaps lending renewed impetus to calls for an all-encompassing domestic abuse offence.

7.10 Reform

With much of the law in this area still governed by the OAPA of *1861*, it should be unsurprising that there have been several calls for reform going beyond piecemeal amendments.[194] The Law Commission, for example, has described the law as 'defective on grounds both of effectiveness and of justice'.[195]

Below we provide a brief overview of some of the most pressing areas of potential reform. These include:

- the case for modernisation and re-codification;
- the controversial status of constructive liability; and
- the meaning and role of consent.

 Assessment matters . . .

Try to think about these topics as they could relate to essay-type questions. Think about which positions/ideas you agree with and, more importantly, why you think they are the more convincing. It is this second part in particular that your examiners want you to discuss.

---

[192] See Bettinson, 'Criminalising Coercive Control in Domestic Violence Cases' [2016] Crim LR 165; Edwards, 'Coercion and Compulsion—Re-Imagining Crimes and Defences' [2016] Crim LR 876.

[193] Bishop and Bettinson, 'Evidencing Domestic Violence, including Behaviour that Falls Under the New Offence of "Controlling or Coercive Behaviour"' (2017) 22(1) IJE&P 3; Munro and Aitken, 'Adding Insult to Injury? The Criminal Law's Response to Domestic Abuse-Related Suicide in England and Wales' [2018] Crim LR 732.

[194] Genders, 'Reform of the Offences Against the Person Act: Lessons from the Law in Action' [1999] Crim LR 689.

[195] Law Commission, *Legislating the Criminal Code: Offences against the Person and General Principles* (Consultation 122, 1992).

7.10.1 Modernisation and re-codification

It is useful here to separate our discussion of the first category of non-fatal offences (result-focussed) and the second category (conduct-focussed).

7.10.1.1 Result-focussed offences (ladder of harms)

Several attempts at re-codification and rationalisation have been made, including within both the 1985 and 1989 Draft Criminal Codes.[196] The most recent attempt has come from the Law Commission, in its 2015 report *Reform of Offences against the Person*.[197]

Building from the structured hierarchy (ladder) of offences outlined by the Home Office in 1998,[198] the Commission's recommendations can be summarised as follows:

(1) **Intentionally causing serious injury:** A person is guilty of an offence if she intentionally causes serious injury to another, punishable with up to life imprisonment.

(2) **Recklessly causing serious injury:** A person is guilty of an offence if she recklessly causes serious injury to another, punishable with up to seven years' imprisonment.

(3) **Intentionally or recklessly causing injury:** A person is guilty of an offence if she intentionally or recklessly causes injury to another, punishable with up to five years' imprisonment.

(4) **Aggravated assault:** A person is guilty of an offence if—

(a) she intentionally or recklessly applies force to or causes an impact on the body of another, or

(b) she intentionally or recklessly causes the other to believe that any such force or impact is imminent, and injury is caused. Punishable with up to 12 months' imprisonment, triable only in the magistrates' court.

(5) **Physical assault:** A person is guilty of an offence if she intentionally or recklessly applies force to or causes an impact on the body of another, punishable with up to six months' imprisonment, triable only in the magistrates' court.

(6) **Threatened assault:** A person is guilty of an offence if she intentionally or recklessly causes the other to believe that any such force or impact is imminent, punishable with up to six months' imprisonment, triable only in the magistrates' court.

Although the Law Commission recommendations are based upon the Home Office scheme from 1998, two important differences should be highlighted. First, 'aggravated assault', triable in the magistrates' court only, is a newly conceived offence: looking to bridge the gap between the reckless causing of injury (3) and the equivalents of assault

[196] Law Commission, *Codification of the Criminal Law: A Report to the Law Commission* (No 143, 1985); Law Commission, *A Criminal Code for England and Wales* (2 vols) (No 177, 1989). See also Law Commission, *Legislating the Criminal Code: Offences against the Person and General Principles* (Consultation 122, 1992); Law Commission, *Offences against the Person and General Principles* (No 218, 1993).

[197] No 361, 2015. See Gibson, 'Getting Their "Act" Together? Implementing Statutory Reform of Offences Against the Person' [2016] Crim LR 597; Demetriou, 'Not Giving Up the Fight: A Review of the Law Commission's Scoping Report on Non-Fatal Offences Against the Person' (2016) 80 JCL 188.

[198] *Consultation Paper on Violence* (1998).

and battery (5 and 6), and aiming more accurately to label D's conduct and to move many cases involving low-level violence out of the Crown Courts.[199] Secondly, whereas the 1998 draft Bill would have merged assault and battery into a single offence, the Commission prefers the clarity of two separate offences (5 and 6).[200]

Several benefits within the proposed scheme can help to remind us of problems in the current law, as well as the relatively easy way many could be resolved.

A) **Clear/modern language:** Unlike the current law where the courts are required to interpret and translate terms such as 'maliciously', 'inflict', and 'grievous', the language proposed in this scheme is simple and comprehensible. This provides clarity for the court, as well as for the public whose behaviour is intended to be guided by the law.[201] The Commission's recommendations also explicitly cater for the inclusion of mental as well as physical injury.[202]

B) **Clear hierarchy/ladder in punishments:** It is a common criticism of the OAPA that offences under sections 47 and 20 have the same maximum sentence despite section 20 involving a more serious actus reus (GBH as opposed to ABH) and a more serious mens rea (recklessness as to some harm as opposed to simple assault or battery). The recommended scheme, from the most serious offence (1) to the least serious offences (5 and 6), creates a clear sentence divide between each step on the ladder. The new aggravated assault offence (4), discussed earlier, is also intended to fill a gap within this hierarchy.

C) **Clear hierarchy/ladder in harms:** The current law attempts to create a ladder of harms, with different offences applicable depending on the level of harm caused. However, as we highlighted, this breaks down to some extent in relation to wounding: even the prick of a small needle may count as a wound and therefore classify D's conduct alongside GBH. This was more understandable in 1861, where any wound may have risked infection and death, but it is clearly out of step with the medical realities of the modern world. The proposed scheme deals with this by talking only of 'serious injury', 'injury', and application or anticipation of 'force'.

D) **Use of constructive liability:** The proposed scheme, unlike the current law, employs very few constructive liability offences (we critique constructive liability at **7.10.2**). One of the few constructive liability offences within the scheme is the new offence of aggravated assault.

E) **Problems with section 47:** As we have discussed, there is a problem with the current law, that to commit an offence under section 47, D must be shown to have committed an assault or battery. This seems strange: if D *has caused* bodily harm, why condition liability on demonstrating physical contact or a fear of such contact? The equivalent offence within the Commission's scheme (3) does not contain such a requirement.

---

[199] Law Commission, *Reform of Offences against the Person* (No 361, 2015) paras 5.30–5.68.
[200] Ibid, paras 5.3–5.29.
[201] It has been argued that reform should go even further in this regard, specifying types of harm, such as disables, disfigures, or dismembers to provide a clearer message and label. Horder, 'Rethinking Non-Fatal Offences Against the Person' (1994) 14 OJLS 335.
[202] Law Commission, *Reform of Offences against the Person* (No 361, 2015) paras 4.117–4.126.

7.10.1.2 Conduct-focussed offences

Here, debate has centred on areas where new specific offences against the person could/ should be created. There are several examples of this, and we have already mentioned debate around new domestic abuse offences (at **7.9.5**), and potential new categories of hate crime (at **7.9.2**).

A further useful illustration is the proposal for a new offence targeting the reckless sexual transmission of HIV.[203] Debate here has partly been driven by perceived problems within the current law, and partly by a seeming reluctance on the part of prosecutors to charge standard non-fatal offences in such cases.[204] However, the potential for reform here is problematic. For example, if the new offence focussed on HIV alone, as opposed to all transmission of infections, then we must question the basis upon which the focus is justified, as well as the potential stigmatising effects that an offence of this kind may produce. The Commission discusses the potential for a new offence in this area at length in its 2015 report, concluding that the case for a specific offence has not yet been made.[205] It will be interesting, following the global Covid-19 pandemic, whether new offences of this kind (broadened to include non-sexual transmission of disease) become politically attractive.

 Assessment matters . . .

When writing about the potential for a new offence, it is a useful exercise to try and draft the actus reus and mens rea to consider what it might look like. In doing so, think about what form of behaviour you are trying to criminalise and why.

7.10.2 Constructive liability

Constructive liability describes an offence where D must cause a particular result, but there is no requirement for corresponding mens rea. For example, section 47 requires D's acts to cause an assault or battery, and to cause V bodily harm (all actus reus). However, in terms of mens rea, D need only have fault in relation to the assault or battery. The fact that D caused ABH is *constructed* upon her liability for assault or battery and makes her liable for the more serious section 47 offence even where such harm was unforeseen and potentially even unforseeable. We see a similar construction in several offences against the person (discussed earlier), in unlawful act manslaughter,[206] as well as in murder.[207]

Constructive liability is controversial for a number of reasons, principally relating to D's potential lack of choice/awareness. As we discussed in **Chapter 1**, justifications for

---

[203] Ormerod, 'Criminalizing HIV Transmission—Still No Effective Solutions' (2001) 30 CLWR 135; Weait, *Intimacy and Responsibility: The Criminalisation of HIV Transmission* (2007); Matthiesson, 'Should the Law Deal with Reckless HIV Infection as a Criminal Offence or as a Matter of Public Health?' (2010) 21 KLJ 123 (responding to Weait); Cherkassky, 'Being Informed: The Complexities of Knowledge, Deception and Consent when Transmitting HIV' (2010) 74 JCL 242.

[204] *Dica* [2004] EWCA Crim 1103; Weait, 'Criminal Law and the Transmission of HIV: *R v Dica*' (2005) 68 MLR 121; Spencer, 'Retrial for Reckless Infection' (2004) 154 NLJ 762.

[205] Law Commission, *Reform of Offences against the Person* (No 361, 2015) Part 6.

[206] See **Chapter 6.3.1**.

[207] See **Chapter 5.4** and **5.6.2**.

criminal law are often tied to the notion of autonomy: people should be free to act as they wish as long as they do not choose to break the law. The problem with constructive liability is that D's choice is treated as irrelevant. Thus, for example, if D assaults V and causes bodily harm, she will be liable under section 47 whether or not she chose to cause or risk that bodily harm. Not only does this conflict with the criminal law's general disposition towards subjectivism (requiring choice), but it also increases the role of luck. For example, D1 and D2 both intentionally push V1 and V2, each foreseeing no more harm than involved in simple contact. In the case of V1 this is all that results: D1 is liable for a minor battery offence. However, V2 falls and sustains an injury: D2 is now liable for a section 47 offence; or worse, V2 dies: D2 is now liable for unlawful act manslaughter. The liability of D1 and D2 is very different, and yet their intentions and *choices* (ie their culpability) were the same. *Is this just?*[208]

For some, of course, the answer is 'yes'. Although D2 may not have chosen to cause bodily injury or to kill, as in the example above, that is what her actions have caused. Although we may wish not to criminalise accidents, there is a persuasive argument that by choosing to commit the battery of V (the push), D has chosen to break the criminal law and D has therefore changed her normative position: she has chosen to break the law and so must accept *all* of the consequences of her actions, even unforeseen/unforeseeable ones.[209]

Whether or not we accept arguments for/against constructive liability will play a central role in future re-codification of the offences against the person. Currently the dominant view is that constructive liability should be avoided/minimised: this is illustrated in the reform recommendations from the Law Commission, and other jurisdictions such as the Republic of Ireland.[210] However, the debate remains open.

7.10.3 Consent

V's consent, or D's belief in consent, will undermine liability for most of the non-fatal offences. However, it is an area that has caused the court significant problems. By way of summary, the central problems identified include the following:

A) **Consent as a defence, or non-consent as an offence element:** We have treated V's consent as a *defence* in this chapter. However, the OAPA leaves open the possibility that non-consent could be analysed as an offence element, and this alternative has been preferred by several courts and commentators.[211] Indeed, in the leading case of *Brown*, only a bare majority of the Lords preferred to analyse consent as a defence.[212]

---

[208] Ashworth, 'The Problem of Luck' in Shute, Gardner, and Horder (eds), *Action and Value in Criminal Law* (1993) 107.

[209] Simons, 'Strict Liability in the Grading of Offences: Forfeiture, Change of Normative Position, or Moral Luck?' (2012) 32 OJLS 445; Ashworth, 'A Change of Normative Position: Determining the Contours of Culpability in Criminal Law' [2008] New Crim LR 232.

[210] The Irish Non-Fatal Offences Against the Person Act 1997 removed constructive liability from this area of law. See Charleton, McDermott, and Bolger, *Criminal Law* (1999) paras 9.77–9.185.

[211] eg Lord Woolf stated in relation to assault that 'it is a requirement of the offence that the conduct itself should be unlawful': *Barnes* [2005] EWCA Crim 3246, [16].

[212] Although Lord Jauncey, Lord Lowry, and Lord Templeman analysed consent as a defence, Lord Mustill and Lord Slynn considered non-consent as part of the offence. See Shute, 'Something Old, Something New, Something Borrowed: Three Aspects of the Project' [1996] Crim LR 684.

It would be highly desirable for this point to be clarified. It is contended that analysis of non-consent as an *offence* element represents the better view, particularly in relation to the minor offences of assault and battery.[213] The cumulative role of offence elements is to set out a specific harmful and/or wrongful event that the criminal law wishes to prevent and punish. D may be able to rely on a defence, but the event is still regrettable. In relation to V's non-consent, we believe that this requirement is an essential part to the *wrong* within the offences against the person. If V provides valid consent (eg in the context of contact sports), D is not committing a wrong that relies on a defence to justify or excuse it; when we come into consensual contact with others in our daily life, we are not committing wrongs that require justification. Rather, we believe that such conduct is only wrongful in the absence of consent and, thus, V's non-consent must form part of the offence elements rather than a defence.[214]

 Don't be confused . . .

The two options for interpretation are:
- *Offence*: requires (a) non-consent in fact and (b) a lack of belief in consent.
- *Defence*: satisfied by (a) consent in fact or (b) belief in consent.
  On either interpretation, D's liability will always require that V does not consent and that D does not believe that consent is present.

B) Effective consent: Considerable work has been done to understand and define consent in relation to sexual offences.[215] However, in the context of the offences in this chapter, the meaning of consent remains elusive, ill-defined, and too often susceptible to overly broad rules. The Law Commission does not deal with the meaning of consent within its 2015 report, but there is scope for the Commission to examine this again in the future.

C) Degree of harm that can be legally consented to: This problem arises where V is of full capacity, is informed, and has not been misled as to the anticipated harm: at what stage (if at all) should the law nevertheless say that V's consent is invalid?[216] This discussion raises difficult moral questions, and taken to its natural conclusion, requires consideration of euthanasia. Whatever moral view is preferred, the approach of the current law is clearly unacceptable—particularly when we begin to explore the recognised exception categories where valid consent is recognised, such as horseplay, body modification, and sexual gratification. In each case, people need to know the law to guide and model their behaviour. The fact that the current law (in cases like *Brown* and *BM*) fails to provide that guidance demonstrates a clear need for reform.

---

[213] This approach is reflected in the latest Law Commission Recommendations. Law Commission, *Reform of Offences against the Person* (No 361, 2015) paras 5.3–5.29.
[214] Williams, 'Consent and Public Policy' [1962] Crim LR 74.
[215] **Chapter 8.**
[216] Feinberg, *The Moral Limits of the Criminal Law, Vol 1: Harm to Others* (1984).

7.11 Eye on assessment

In this section we discuss the potential application of the offences against the person within a problem question. The same structure of analysis should be employed as we have discussed in previous chapters.

STEP 1 Identify the potential criminal event in the facts

This is unlikely to take more than a sentence, but it is essential to tell your reader which facts of the case you are focussing on. For offences against the person, this involves pointing out where a person has been hurt (eg 'The first potential criminal event arises where Mary kicks Vicky').

STEP 2 Identify the potential offence

Having identified the facts (eg D potentially injuring V), you must now identify the offence you are going to apply.

When applying Step 2, it should be remembered that the main non-fatal offences can be viewed as a ladder, with the least serious offences (assault and battery) at the bottom, and the most serious (s18 GBH) at the top. When *applying* these offences to a problem scenario, however, it is not sensible to discuss every possible offence in this way (bottom up):

 Example . . .

Take the example of D who breaks V's arm by hitting her with a bat. Here, it is likely that D will have committed assault if V saw her coming, as V is likely to have apprehended non-consensual imminent violence; D will also have committed battery, as she intentionally comes into non-consensual contact with V; D will also have committed a section 47 offence, as D's assault and battery have caused harm; D will also have committed a section 20 offence, as D has caused GBH and intends to cause harm; and D will also have committed a section 18 offence, as GBH is intentionally caused.

In this manner, D satisfies the elements of each of the offences. However, as she does so through a single act (hitting V with a bat), we would only charge with one offence. Therefore, much like Russian dolls, more serious offences subsume less serious ones committed by the same action: leaving D in our example liable for a section 18 offence only. The problem with starting our discussion at the bottom of the offence ladder, therefore, is that having discussed the elements of several offences, the only one that is relevant is the last. (*A particularly serious problem if you run out of time and miss it off!*)

When applying the offences against the person to a problem scenario, it is therefore advised that you begin by exploring the most serious *potential* offence first. The word potential here is important. Just as it is bad practice to discuss less serious offences when a more serious one has been committed, it is also important not to spend a long time discussing more serious offences if V has only suffered minor harm. Our recommended approach is set out in the flowchart at **Figure 7.8**.

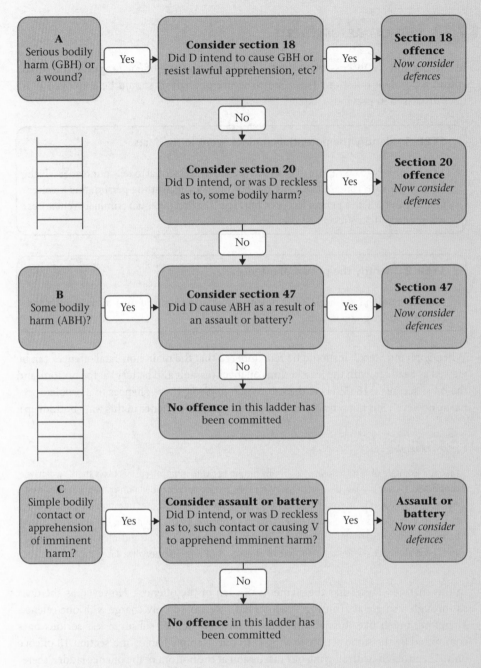

Figure 7.8 Problem question flowchart for offences against the person

 Assessment matters . . .

Although it is useful to keep in mind the types of harm that are commonly charged, such as ABH or GBH, their broad definitions make some overlap inevitable. Further, it should be remembered that V's characteristics will also play a role—what is GBH to a child, for example, might not be for an adult. Therefore, if in doubt, for example, tell your reader what the result would be 'if the court finds the level of harm to be GBH' or 'if the court finds the level of harm to be ABH'.

Having highlighted the potential criminal event (Step 1), you should assess the level of harm caused to V in order to identify the relevant entry point to the flowchart in **Figure 7.8** (A, B, or C). The relevant entry point leads you to the most serious potential offence that D may have committed (Step 2) (eg section 18 in relation to GBH, section 47 for bodily harm, etc). In line with the flowchart, the next step is to assess D's liability for that offence.

STEP 3 Applying the offence to the facts

Actus reus: What does the offence require? Did D do it?

Mens rea: What does the offence require? Did D possess it?

If D does not satisfy the elements of the most serious potential offence (eg lacks mens rea for s18), then you should go on to consider the next possible offence down the ladder. Continue this until you find an offence that D satisfies, or you conclude that D has not committed one of these offences.

AR and MR are satisfied	AR and/or MR are not satisfied
Continue to STEP 4.	Return to STEP 2, and look for an alternative offence. If none, then skip to STEP 5, concluding that no offence is committed.

STEP 4 Consider defences

The word 'consider' here is important, as you should not discuss every defence for every question. Rather, think whether there are any specific or general defences (eg consent) that *could* potentially be relevant to the facts. If there are any, discuss those only.

STEP 5 Conclude

This is usually a single sentence either saying that it is likely that D has committed the offence, or saying that it is not likely either because an offence element is not satisfied or because a defence is likely to apply. It is not often that you will be able to say categorically whether or not D has committed the offence, so it is usually best to conclude in terms of what is more 'likely'.

STEP 6 Loop

Go back up to Step 1, identifying the next potential criminal event. Continue until you have discussed all the relevant potentially criminal events.

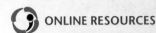

ONLINE RESOURCES

www.oup.com/he/child-ormerod4e

This chapter is accompanied by a selection of online resources to help you with this topic, including:

- **Self-test questions** and **scenario questions**
- **Videos** from the authors
- **Audio introduction** to the topic
- **Chapter summary sheet**
- Two **sample examination questions** with answer guidance
- **Further reading and weblinks**

Also available on the online resources are:

- A selection of **videos** from the authors containing general advice on problem questions and essay questions
- **Legal updates**

8

Rape and other sexual offences

8.1 Introduction

In common with the non-fatal offences against the person,[1] the core sexual offences focus predominantly on non-consensual contact. However, the additional sexual dimension within these offences makes the underlying mischiefs targeted by the criminal law rather different. Whereas offences against the person generally focus and define liability by reference to the degree of physical or psychiatric harm caused by D, even the most serious sexual offence of rape does not require injury beyond simple unlawful contact (in the case of rape, penile penetration). Rather than physical or psychiatric injury, sexual offences focus on D's invasion of V's sexual, as opposed to simply physical, autonomy. It is the intimate manner of this invasion, qualified by its nature and degree, which constitutes the central mischief of sexual offending.[2]

Sexual offences are now almost entirely codified within a single modern statute:[3] the Sexual Offences Act 2003 (SOA 2003).[4] With previous legislation variously described as 'cumbersome and inadequate',[5] and 'archaic, incoherent and discriminatory',[6] the SOA 2003 consolidated the law, modernised it in line with changing social attitudes,[7] as well as created a host of new offences. Two aspects of the SOA 2003 are particularly interesting, and usefully introduced at this point.

The first relates to the detail of the legislation. Offences within the SOA 2003 are highly, some would say excessively, detailed. As a result, the focus of this chapter will largely be on the statute itself, looking to unpack the meaning of each offence. Case law is less important to fill in gaps within the legislation, but remains essential to interpret the language of the statute and to understand how it should be applied.

Secondly, there is a trend within the substance of the sexual offences that is somewhat out of step with other offences against the person. Offences within the SOA 2003 are notable for their use of wide actus reus elements, as well as the use of objective, as opposed to subjective, mens rea requirements, and even strict liability. For example, the mens rea for rape does not require D to intend or know that V lacks consent to sexual penetration, foresee a risk of this non-consent, or even negligently fail to foresee a risk of it. Rather, mens rea is satisfied unless D holds a reasonable belief in consent (**8.2.2**).[8] This contrasts markedly with other offences against the person, and other serious offences,

---

[1] See **Chapter 7**.

[2] There is a considerable literature exploring the unique nature of sexual offending, which we return to when discussing potential reform (**8.9**). Two prominent examples include Gardner and Shute, 'The Wrongness of Rape' in Horder (ed), *Oxford Essays in Jurisprudence* (2000) and Conaghan, 'The Essence of Rape' (2019) OJLS 151.

[3] Certain sexual offences remain outside the SOA 2003 (eg those relating to prostitution and indecent images).

[4] For background, see Home Office Papers, *Setting the Boundaries: Reforming the Law on Sexual Offences* (2000) and *Protecting the Public: Strengthening Protection Against Sex Offenders and Reforming the Law on Sexual Offences* (2002).

[5] Temkin, 'Getting it Right: Sexual Offences Law Reform' (2000) 150 NLJ 1169.

[6] Lord Falconer in HL, 13 February 2003, vol 644, col 771.

[7] Both in terms of the boundaries of criminalisation, as well as the language used to construct them.

[8] The objective requirement is softened slightly to take account of D's characteristics, but remains very wide.

which typically require a minimum mens rea of subjective intention or recklessness.[9] There are several possible explanations:

- It could be that increased use of objective mens rea is a trend within legislation, and this argument can be supported by several modern statutes.[10] However, it is interesting that this trend seems at odds with the current views of the courts and Law Commission: it will be remembered that 2003 was also the year in which the House of Lords (in the case of *G*[11]) were championing the integral role of *subjective* mens rea within serious offences; and the importance of subjectivism was reiterated in the Law Commission's 2015 report on offences against the person.[12]

- It may be a reaction to the high offending rates and allegedly low conviction rates for sexual offences.[13] As sexual offences invariably take place in private, it is particularly difficult to prove to the criminal standard that D held a certain subjective mens rea at the time of offending, and so an objective standard may be justifiable to reduce the gap between offending and conviction. However, it is arguable that procedural and evidential changes may be a more appropriate way of tackling the low conviction rate.[14]

- Another possible explanation may be the unique nature of *sexual* offending in the context of wider gender inequality. By structuring offences using objective mens rea, the law is attempting to correct, or at least acknowledge, inequality by punishing D for a failure to consider the harmful consequences of his actions. Again, the extent to which this represents a contrast to other offences against the person remains debatable.

As we go on to discuss the offences in this chapter, it is useful to keep these differences in mind. If you are convinced that sexual offending is fundamentally different from other offences against the person for one of the reasons above, or for some other reason, then you should consider if these differences are accurately reflected in the law. If you are not convinced of this difference, then you should consider how the current inconsistency should be resolved: should offences against the person be structured in a more objective manner, or should sexual offences be more subjective?

With over 143 statutory sections, and seven schedules, the SOA 2003 contains in excess of 50 offences focussing on several different areas. Our main focus will be on the first four offences within the statute: rape; assault by penetration; sexual assault; and causing a person to engage in sexual activity without consent. The central feature within these offences is that V does not consent to the sexual activity. Following this, we will also briefly discuss three other categories of offences: offences against children under 13 (where consent is irrelevant); offences against young people under 16 (where consent is again irrelevant, but some awareness of age is required); and status-based and

---

[9] Bohlander, 'Mistaken Consent to Sex, Political Correctness and Correct Policy' (2007) 71 JCL 412.

[10] eg Criminal Justice and Courts Act 2015; Serious Crime Act 2015; Proceeds of Crime Act 2002; etc.

[11] [2003] UKHL 50.

[12] See **Chapter 7.10**.

[13] Home Office, *Setting the Boundaries* (2000) paras 2.3 and 2.8.5. For up-to-date statistics, see: www .ons.gov.uk/peoplepopulationandcommunity/crimeandjustice/bulletins/crimeinenglandandwales /yearendingmarch2019.

[14] Lacey, 'Beset by Boundaries' [2001] Crim LR 3.

relationship-based offences (where D is abusing a position of trust). Apart from exceptional offences involving penile penetration, these offences are gender-neutral: both men and women can be perpetrators and victims.

8.2 SOA 2003, s1: rape

The offence of rape, set out in section 1 of the SOA 2003, carries one of the most recognised and stigmatising labels within the criminal law.[15] The maximum sentence is life imprisonment.[16]

> 1(1) A person (D) commits an offence if—
>
>   (a) he intentionally penetrates the vagina, anus or mouth of another person (V) with his penis,
>
>   (b) V does not consent to the penetration, and
>
>   (c) D does not reasonably believe that V consents.

The elements of rape are set out in **Table 8.1**.

Table 8.1 SOA 2003, s1

	Actus reus	**Mens rea**
Conduct element	Penile penetration of V's vagina, anus, or mouth	Intention
Circumstance element	V does not consent	D lacks a reasonable belief in consent
Result element	None	None

 Extra detail . . .

The offence of rape is commonly described as a conduct crime. However, if we isolate the conduct element of all crimes to bodily movement alone, it is alternatively possible to describe rape as a result crime: D's bodily movement (conduct) causing penetration (result). In this chapter, we adopt the standard description of rape as a conduct crime.

8.2.1 Actus reus of s1

The actus reus of rape requires the prosecution to prove that D penetrated the vagina, anus, or mouth of V with his penis, and without V's consent.

---

[15] Discussed later (**8.9**).
[16] SOA 2003, s1(4).

8.2.1.1 'Penile' penetration

Rape is only committed where D penetrates V with his penis. If D uses anything other than his penis to penetrate V without consent he does not commit rape, although he is likely to commit an offence under section 2. The government review that led to the SOA—Sexual Offences Review—considered removing the requirement that the penetration must be penile, to achieve gender-neutrality, but decided that the limitation should remain.[17] This conclusion was based on the additional risks associated with penile penetration including pregnancy; disease transmission; etc, as well as the interests of fair labelling,[18] because rape is commonly understood to require penile penetration.

As a result of this requirement, rape can only be committed as a principal offender by a man. Under section 79(3), a 'penis' will include a surgically constructed penis: allowing conviction where D is a post-operative transsexual. Women can be accessories to rape where they assist or encourage a man to commit rape, leading to their liability for rape, but they cannot commit the offence as a principal offender.[19]

8.2.1.2 Penetration of the vagina, anus, or mouth

The historical mischief of rape was an attack on virginity, and so the actus reus focussed on penetration of the vagina only. However, as the law has developed to protect sexual autonomy more generally, this element of the offence has expanded to include anal penetration,[20] and later oral penetration.[21] Additionally, section 79(3) clarifies that 'vagina' includes a surgically constructed vagina following gender reassignment surgery. As a result of these expansions, it is now possible for a man to be the victim of rape—anally or orally.

The requirement of 'penetration' has been interpreted broadly. It is clear, for example, that penetration need not be substantial or repetitive. In the context of vaginal penetration, this requirement will be satisfied even where D's penis has only penetrated the vulva (outer part of the vagina).[22] It has also been confirmed that D's act of penetration 'is a continuing act from entry to withdrawal'.[23] This is potentially important where D penetrates V's vagina, anus, or mouth with consent, but fails to withdraw his penis after that consent is removed.[24] A narrow interpretation of penetration (entry only) would cause a problem of coincidence of timing of the conduct (penetration) and the relevant circumstance (lack of consent). At the point of penetration there is consent (no coincidence); at the time that consent is removed the penetration is complete (no coincidence). Interpreting penetration as a continuing act resolves this problem, extending the conduct element to allow for the coincidence of offence elements at any time between entry and withdrawal.[25]

---

[17] Home Office, *Setting the Boundaries* (2000) para 2.8.4.

[18] See **Chapter 1.4.2**.

[19] *Ram* (1893) 17 Cox CC 609. See **Chapter 12**. See also McKeever, 'Can a Woman Rape a Man and Why Does It Matter?' (2019) 13(4) CrimL&P 599.

[20] Criminal Justice and Public Order Act 1994, s142.

[21] SOA 2003, s1. *K* [2008] EWCA Crim 1923: charge does not have to specify which.

[22] SOA 2003, s79(9).

[23] Ibid, s79(2).

[24] *Leaver* [2006] EWCA Crim 2988. This may include where D intentionally fails to withdraw (despite having agreed to) prior to ejaculation, *F* [2013] EWHC 945 (Admin).

[25] On continuing acts, see **Chapter 4.3.2**.

8.2.1.3 Age and/or status restrictions?

Pre-SOA 2003, the age and/or status of D and V used to affect whether rape could be committed. This is no longer the case. As long as D is over the age of 10 (the age of criminal responsibility) he is capable of committing the offence on V of any age. Additionally, the relationship between D and V is also irrelevant; it does not matter that they are strangers, married, on a date, etc. To the shame of the criminal law, marital rape was only confirmed as rape as recently as 1991, and only through the courts.[26] Thus, under the SOA 2003, D's age and status are largely irrelevant.

8.2.1.4 Without V's consent

Central to the offence of rape, as well as offences under sections 2, 3, and 4, is the requirement that V lacked consent. For rape, this is the requirement that V has not consented to penile penetration of the vagina, anus, or mouth. The role consent plays within these offences is a fascinating area of law, and certainly important, but it can also be rather challenging. It is particularly important because of its vital role within the mischief of the offence: non-consensual penetration of this kind is one of the most serious offences within the criminal law, and yet sexual penetration *with* consent is generally considered a social good, and a positive aspect of social life.[27] In this manner, V's consent or non-consent exercises a legal and moral magic, marking the difference between extreme responses to behaviour.[28] It is partly because of its central role that the concept of consent is also challenging. When applying the requirement of non-consent within sexual offences, the law requires a robust concept that can provide clear guidance for the jury: clear guidance to make a binary decision between finding a lack of consent or not. However, as we discussed in the context of the offences against the person,[29] finding whether V consented or not is rarely straightforward, and will involve the weighing of a variety of factors.[30]

 Don't be confused . . .

In this section we are discussing the actus reus requirement of V's non-consent (ie did V freely agree to penetration?). We are not discussing D's mens rea as to non-consent (ie did D reasonably believe that V consented?). These are separate offence elements and you should take care not to confuse them. We will analyse actus reus elements first, and then mens rea elements.

To analyse whether V lacked consent, our focus is on the subjective mind of V. At the time of penetration, whatever the external indications, was V a willing participant to the sexual contact? The case of *McFall*, although decided pre-SOA 2003, illustrates this point well.[31]

---

[26] *R* [1991] 4 All ER 481. Confirmed by the ECtHR in *CR v UK* [1996] 1 FLR 434. Giles, 'Judicial Law-Making in the Criminal Courts: The Case of Marital Rape' [1992] Crim LR 407.

[27] Gardner, 'The Opposite of Rape' (2018) 38 OJLS 48. For an alternative and extreme view, contending that all sexual penetration *is prima facie* wrongful, see Dempsey and Herring, 'Why Sexual Penetration Requires Justification' (2007) 27 OJLS 467; Wall, 'Sexual Offences and General Reasons Not to Have Sex' (2015) 35 OJLS 777.

[28] Hurd, 'The Moral Magic of Consent' (1996) 2 LT 168.

[29] See **Chapter 7**.

[30] See Reed et al (eds), *Consent: Domestic and Comparative Perspectives* (2017), discussing consent across both OAPA and sexual offences.

[31] See also *Doyle* [2010] EWCA Crim 119.

McFall [1994] Crim LR 226 (pre-SOA 2003)

D kidnapped V, a woman with whom he had been cohabiting. D indicated that he wanted to have sexual intercourse with V and she accepted, fearing for her safety if she refused. V pretended to consent during the act and faked enjoyment. D was charged with rape.

- Crown Court: guilty of rape—despite the outwards signs, V was not subjectively consenting.
- Court of Appeal: conviction upheld on appeal.

Our focus then, is the mind of V.

Having identified this focus, however, we still need to unpack the legal definition of consent to know what test to apply. Pre-SOA 2003, there was no codified definition of consent and the approach of the courts, in line with the approach to 'consent' in the context of the offences against the person, was largely to leave the definition to the common understanding of the jury,[32] providing additional guidance only where issues of capacity or deception were involved. This approach attracted considerable criticism, with Glanville Williams highlighting the 'deplorable tendency of the criminal courts to leave important questions of legal policy to the jury':[33] the jury are not being asked to apply the facts to a legal rule with a definition of consent, they are being asked to define it as well. The reformers working towards the SOA 2003 therefore made a clear and robust definition of consent one of their primary ambitions.[34]

The definition of consent within the SOA 2003 is spread across three sections:

- **Section 76:** A set of 'conclusive presumptions' of non-consent: sets of facts which, if proved, will be enough to establish non-consent.
- **Section 75:** A set of 'evidential presumptions' of non-consent: sets of facts which, if proved, require D to provide some counter evidence to prevent a finding of non-consent.
- **Section 74:** A general definition of consent.

Alongside the general definition of consent in section 74, sections 76 and 75 are intended to provide a clear message that consent will not be present in certain circumstances and to remove or reduce the juries' discretion, speeding up trials and ensuring appropriate convictions.

 Assessment matters . . .

When applying the requirement of non-consent to problem facts, always begin with the presumptions of non-consent. If your facts come within the conclusive presumptions, then non-consent can be found without further discussion; if they come within the evidential presumptions, then you can say a finding of non-consent is likely unless D provides some evidence in rebuttal. Go on to discuss the general definition of consent if the presumptions do not apply or where an evidential presumption might to be rebutted.

---

[32] *Olugboja* [1981] 3 All ER 443 (pre-SOA 2003).
[33] Williams, *Textbook of Criminal Law* (1978) 551.
[34] Home Office, *Setting the Boundaries* (2000) Part 2.

Conclusive presumptions of non-consent: s76

If the facts of a case come within the conclusive presumptions then the actus reus require-ment of non-consent will be established without any need to consider the general defi-nition of consent (s74). The conclusive presumptions only apply in two circumstances:

> 76(2) The circumstances are that—
>
> (a) the defendant intentionally deceived the complainant as to the nature or purpose of the relevant act;
>
> (b) the defendant intentionally induced the complainant to consent to the relevant act by impersonating a person known personally to the complainant.

Extra detail . . .

Note for both (a) and (b) that D's deception must be intentional. Thus, for example, if V was inadvert-ently misled as to the nature or purpose of the act or as to D's identity, then the conclusive presump-tions are not be engaged, and the general definition of consent should be applied.

The circumstances outlined in section 76 emerged from pre-SOA 2003 case law. To illus-trate how the section is likely to be applied, therefore, some of the older case law remains a useful supplement to the growing number of cases decided under the statute.

A) Deception as to the nature or purpose of the act: V is deceived as to the 'nature' of the act where she is misled as to the physical mechanics of that act; she is deceived as to the 'purpose' of the act where she is misled as to why it should happen. In certain cases, as in *Williams*, such deception is obvious.

Williams [1923] 1 KB 340 (pre-SOA 2003)

D, a singing teacher, deceived his 16-year-old student (V) into having sexual intercourse, telling her that it was a procedure to improve her singing voice. D was charged with rape.

• Crown Court: guilty of rape. D's deception as to the nature and quality of the act undermined V's apparent consent.

• Court of Criminal Appeal: conviction upheld on appeal.

D misled V as to the dynamics of sexual intercourse, and so the court found deception as to the *nature* of the act.[35] V was also deceived as to the *purpose* of the act: it was done for D's sexual gratification and not to improve V's singing voice.[36] Thus, in either case, if decided today, the conclusive presumptions in section 76 would oblige a jury to find there was no consent.

Beyond straightforward cases of this kind, however, the presumption can be difficult to apply. This is because the terms used within the section (ie 'nature' and 'purpose') are rather ambiguous in their application, and because the conclusive outcomes that result

---

[35] See also *Flattery* (1877) 2 QBD 410 (pre-SOA 2003): D deceived V into thinking that the sexual penetration was a medical operation.

[36] See also *Green* [2002] EWCA Crim 1505 (pre-SOA 2003): D induced men to masturbate while connected to monitors as part of a bogus medical experiment. They understood the nature of the act, but were deceived as to purpose.

make courts understandably reluctant to interpret them too widely.[37] Additionally, even where section 76 does not apply, a lack of consent may still be found applying the general definition of consent within section 74.

Regarding the term 'nature', for example, it is now clear that if V understands the basic dynamics of the sexual act, deception as to associated risks will not be sufficient to engage the conclusive presumptions. This has arisen chiefly in relation to the risk of sexual infection, as in *Dica*.

Dica [2004] EWCA Crim 1103

D, knowing he was HIV-positive, had unprotected sexual intercourse with two victims, infecting both with the disease. It was clear that neither of the victims would have consented to intercourse if they had known about D's infected status.

- Crown Court: guilty of an offence against the person (not guilty of rape). V's potential consent to the risk of infection was uninformed, and so invalid: the judge removed the issue of consent from the jury.
- Court of Appeal: appeal allowed against the non-fatal offence, and a retrial ordered. The trial judge was wrong to remove the issue of consent from the jury; although V's lack of knowledge about D's HIV made consent to the risk of infection unlikely, it was still a question of fact for the jury. However, the position at trial that V was not deceived as to the 'nature' of the sexual act was confirmed; there was no rape.

It was open to the court in *Dica* to find that D's act of intercourse while he was knowingly infected was of a different 'nature' to that consented to by V, namely intercourse with someone not knowingly infected, engaging the conclusive presumption of non-consent and resulting in liability for rape. However, significantly, the court did *not* take this step. D's infection and his choice not to inform V may be relevant when considering consent under the general definition of consent (s74), but it did not affect the nature of the act: V was not deceived as to the basic physical dynamics of sexual intercourse, and so the conclusive presumptions were not engaged.

The limits of the term 'purpose' have also been addressed by the courts. For example, it is clear from *Linekar* that deception as to the purpose of the sexual act does *not* include deception as to V's purpose.[38]

Linekar [1995] 2 Cr App R 49 (pre-SOA 2003)

D had sexual intercourse with V, a sex worker, having promised to pay her £25. D never intended to pay. D was charged with rape on the basis that V would not have consented if she had known D had no intention to pay.

- Crown Court: guilty of rape—V's apparent consent was not effective due to D's deception.
- Court of Appeal: appeal allowed, consent was not undermined by D's deception.

---

[37] The case law has generated considerable academic comment. See recently Gibson, 'Deceptive Sexual Relations: A Theory of Criminal Liability' (2020) OJLS 82.

[38] Reed, 'Analysis of Fraud Vitiating Consent in Rape Cases' [1995] Crim LR 310.

The Court of Appeal recognised that V would not have consented without the promise of payment, but held that her consent remained effective: she was not deceived as to the nature of the act (she knew he was going to penetrate her vagina with his penis) or the purpose of D doing so (for him to derive sexual gratification). Thus, when interpreting the conclusive presumptions under section 76, it is likely that deception as to the purpose of the act will only include deception as to D's and not V's purpose.

Even accepting this clarification, however, the interpretation of deception as to 'D's purpose' remains ambiguous. Individual cases have brought pockets of clarity. We know, for example, that V will be deceived as to the purpose of an act if she is led to believe that it is being done for non-sexual reasons.[39] However, other cases have added to the confusion. For example, the case of *Devonald* seems to suggest that V *is* deceived as to purpose if (despite understanding the sexual context) V is deceived as to D's motives.

 Devonald [2008] EWCA Crim 527

V (a 16-year-old boy) was involved in a relationship with D's daughter. The relationship ended and D, believing V had treated his daughter badly, sought revenge. D posed as a young woman on the internet, formed a link with V, and persuaded V to masturbate in front of a webcam. D was planning to use the video to humiliate V. D was charged with an offence under section 4 of the SOA 2003 (causing a person to engage in sexual activity).

- Crown Court: guilty of sexual offence. Section 76 presumption applied: V was deceived as to D's purpose in relation to the sexual act.
- Court of Appeal: conviction upheld on appeal.

V's apparent consent was based on the understanding that he was masturbating for the sexual gratification of a young woman. D's deception therefore undermined the effectiveness of that consent. However, it is arguable that this result should have been achieved through the general definition of consent (s74) rather than applying the conclusive presumptions (s76). V was not deceived as to D's intention to induce sexual behaviour, he was only deceived as to D's intended sexual enjoyment of it. If this is now caught within section 76, as the case suggests, what about D who has sex with V pretending that it is an expression of love when he simply sees it as a one-night stand, or as a route to promotion?

 Extra detail . . .

Devonald could be seen as a case where D has mixed purposes: to induce sexual behaviour and to gain material to humiliate V. D is honest about the first, but deceives V in relation to the latter.

    Cases of this kind can cause significant problems for the application of the section 76 presumptions. For example, in *Green*, D committed an offence when he induced men to masturbate while connected to monitors as part of a bogus medical experiment.[40] But what if Green was genuinely performing a medical experiment (as he told the men involved), but he was also acting for personal sexual gratification (as he did not tell them)? Would the court apply the section 76 presumption (as they did in *Devonald*)? Would they ask what D's dominant purpose was? These questions remain unanswered.

---

[39] *Green* [2002] EWCA Crim 1505 (pre-SOA 2003): D made V believe it was medical research.
[40] [2002] EWCA Crim 1505.

B) Deception as to the identity of D: The second scenario in which the conclusive presumptions of non-consent will apply is where D intentionally deceives V as to his identity. The presumption will *not* apply where D pretends to have certain attributes such as a well-paid job, or even where he pretends to be someone who is not known personally to the victim (eg a celebrity). Such cases will be decided under the general definition of consent in section 74. Rather, the conclusive presumption will only apply where D intentionally and actively pretends (it is not enough that V simply got the wrong idea[41]) to be someone who V knows personally such as her husband; boyfriend; friend; etc. The presumption has been defined narrowly to catch only the clearest cases of wrongful impersonation.

Despite the narrow construction, two problem areas remain. First, as the statute does not expressly deal with deception as to personal attributes, we may assume that it will be interpreted in line with current case law on offences against the person. Generally, deceptions as to attributes will not constitute deception as to identity, but there may be exceptions to this. Where D lies about his employment or prospects in order to induce intercourse the jury will approach the question of consent using the general definition in section 74.[42] This also prevents any use of the conclusive presumption where D deceives V as to the risk of a sexual infection: such infection would be an attribute of D and not part of his identity.[43] More difficult will be cases of sexual touching where D fraudulently claims to be medically qualified, for example, and acting in line with that employment. In such a case, following *Melin*, it may be that a conclusive presumption of non-consent would be appropriate.[44]

Secondly, the requirement that D's impersonation must be of someone 'known personally' to V is also problematic. It is clearly intended to avoid the conclusive presumptions applying where D impersonates a celebrity, for example. However, exactly who is known personally to V may be difficult to discern. Does it include everyone who V has ever met, however briefly? Does it include relationships formed on the internet where V may not have met the person at all?[45] Such questions have not yet arisen in the courts, but have the potential to cause real problems. It may also be questioned why the SOA 2003 limited the presumption in this manner: is it less serious for V to be deceived as to the identity of D if he pretends to be her favourite musician rather than her boyfriend? And if so, why?

 Assessment matters . . .

Our discussion of section 76 has given rise to several areas of uncertainty. As we have discussed before, when learning and discussing the law, care must be taken to engage with uncertainties. If the application of the current law to a set of facts is uncertain, then this should always be acknowledged. Your task is to analyse the statute, analyse the case law, and to see if you can find general rules or trends that will help you to predict how the courts are likely to deal with the issue.

---

[41] *Elbekkay* [1995] Crim LR 163 (pre-SOA 2003).

[42] See *R(Monica) v DPP* [2018] EWHC 3508 (Admin).

[43] *B* [2006] EWCA Crim 2945.

[44] *Melin* [2019] EWCA Crim 557: deception as to medical qualification vitiated consent to Botox injections; the court distinguished *Richardson* [1998] 2 Cr App R 200 (pre-SOA 2003) where a dentist deceived patients as to his being registered to practise.

[45] *McNally* [2013] EWCA Crim 1051: D presented online as male and maintained that identity when later making sexual contact with V.

Rebuttable presumptions of non-consent: s75

If the facts of a case do not come within the conclusive presumptions (s76), the next stage of analysis is whether they come within the rebuttable presumptions (s75). Unlike section 76, the rebuttable presumptions do not establish a lack of consent. Rather, as their name suggests, if the facts of a case come within the rebuttable presumptions, then the jury will find a lack of consent *unless D provides evidence to rebut (challenge) the presumption.*[46]

For the presumption to apply it must be established that certain facts arose (discussed later), and that D had knowledge of those facts. For example, the first rebuttable presumption will arise where violence has been used against V at the time or immediately before the relevant act (taking the offence of rape as an example, 'the act' would be penile penetration). Thus, if V were to suffer violence from another, without D's knowledge, the presumption will not arise. V may still lack consent under the general definition (s74), but section 75 will be irrelevant.

  Point to remember . . .

The presumptions will arise if the facts exist and D is aware of those facts. Significantly, the prosecution do not need to demonstrate that those facts *caused* V's lack of consent. For example, if violence was knowingly used at the time of penile penetration, a rebuttable presumption of non-consent will arise without discussion of whether V would have consented if the violence was not used.

Once a presumption of this kind has arisen because the facts mirror one of the scenarios in section 75 and D had knowledge of this, the burden is then on D to provide some evidence to rebut that presumption. This rebuttal does not necessarily require D to deny the facts themselves (eg to deny that violence was used), it is enough for D to deny the implication that such facts demonstrate a lack of consent. For example, in the context of violence, D could contend that he was engaged in a sadomasochistic sexual encounter with V, and that V was consenting to both the violence and the penile penetration. Such evidence, however convincing or otherwise, will rebut the presumption. The burden of proof is then on the prosecution to demonstrate that there was a lack of consent despite D's explanation, applying the section 74 general definition.[47]

  Point to remember . . .

Evidential presumptions are not the most potent weapon for prosecutors. They were designed as a method of encouraging D to engage with the prosecution, with D having to provide an explanation for his conduct to avoid the presumption. However, they are certainly less powerful than the conclusive presumptions under section 76, and current practice has shown that section 75 is rarely used.

Section 75(2) provides six scenarios in which a rebuttable presumption of non-consent will arise. We explore each in turn.

---

[46] On rebuttable presumptions in general, see **Chapter 1.1.7.2.**
[47] *White* [2010] EWCA Crim 1929.

A) Violence:

> . . . any person was, at the time of the relevant act or immediately before it began, using violence against the complainant or causing the complainant to fear that immediate violence would be used against him.

As stated earlier, the potential for consenting sadomasochistic relationships makes it sensible that violence creates a rebuttable (as opposed to conclusive) presumption of non-consent. The width of the presumption is also to be welcomed, going beyond violence to include threats of violence,[48] as well as violence and threats from others provided D is aware of them. The requirement that D's threat be of 'immediate violence' is more troubling: why not include cases where D threatens future violence unless V submits to sexual acts? One may also question the limitation of the presumption to threats of *violence*. Prior to the SOA 2003, there was an offence based on procuring sexual intercourse by threats which covered threats of all kinds, including damage to property; threats of dismissal from employment; threats of arrest; or any other threat that induced V to submit to intercourse. Under the current law, a lack of consent may still be found in these cases applying the general definition of non-consent under section 74, but they will not give rise to a presumption under section 75.

B) Fear of violence:

> . . . any person was, at the time of the relevant act or immediately before it began, causing the complainant to fear that violence was being used, or that immediate violence would be used, against another person.

The presumption is usefully expanded to include cases where D or another inflicts violence or threatens to inflict violence on a third party. For example, D threatens to harm V's child unless she submits to intercourse. The presumption is limited in the same manner as (A) with regard to 'immediacy' and 'violence'. It may also be overly broad at times: read literally, if V watches a news report about a violent crime and then consents to intercourse, it will be presumed that she does not consent! In this example, it will be straightforward for the presumption to be rebutted, but the fact that it applies at all suggests defective drafting.

C) Unlawful detention:

> . . . the complainant was, and the defendant was not, unlawfully detained at the time of the relevant act.

This presumption is relatively uncontroversial, and rather difficult for D to rebut. It applies where V submits to sexual acts whilst the hostage of D or others.[49]

D) Unconsciousness:

> . . . the complainant was asleep or otherwise unconscious at the time of the relevant act.

---

[48] See *Dagnall* [2003] EWCA Crim 2441 (pre-SOA 2003): D dragged V from the road threatening to rape her. V responded that he could 'do what he liked as long as he did not harm her'. V was clearly not consenting.

[49] *David T* [2005] EWCA Crim 2668.

There will be relationships in which sexual contact while the other party is asleep, for example, is done with that party's consent. However, this will not often be the case, and a rebuttable presumption of non-consent is appropriate. Indeed, under the old common law, unconsciousness would have been enough to find non-consent irrespective of D's explanations.[50] It should be noted that this presumption will only apply where V is fully unconscious, and D is aware of this: where V is intoxicated, for example, but short of unconsciousness, the presumption will not apply. An interesting issue which has yet to be addressed by the courts is whether prior consent, given in a free informed manner by V of full capacity, remains valid if V is unconscious or asleep at the time of the sexual acts. V might say to her partner, D, that she anticipates being so drunk later that evening that she may be incoherent, but that she wants D to have sex with her at that time in any event.[51]

E) Disability preventing communication:

> . . . because of the complainant's physical disability, the complainant would not have been able at the time of the relevant act to communicate to the defendant whether the complainant consented.

Although V may be able to communicate with others or on other occasions (eg through sign-language), if a physical disability prevents her communicating her consent on this occasion and with this D, there will be a presumption of non-consent. This presumption reinforces the idea from the general definition of consent (discussed later) that consent should be an active expression of willingness from V rather than a lack of active opposition. However, the fact that the presumption is limited to physical disability will prevent it being used, for example, where V is too intoxicated to communicate.

F) Involuntary doping:

> . . . any person had administered to or caused to be taken by the complainant, without the complainant's consent, a substance which, having regard to when it was administered or taken, was capable of causing or enabling the complainant to be stupefied or overpowered at the time of the relevant act.

The final scenario within section 75 covers cases of so-called drug date-rape, where D or another causes V to consume unwanted stupefying substances by, for example, spiking her drink with alcohol or other drugs such as Rohypnol.[52] Importantly, the presumption will only apply where the substance is added without V's consent. Thus, if V becomes voluntarily intoxicated, even if she is encouraged to do so by D, the presumption will not arise.

General definition of non-consent: s74

> 74. For the purposes of this Part, a person [V] consents if he agrees by choice, and has the freedom and capacity to make that choice.

Many of the clearest cases of non-consent will be dealt with under the section 76 and 75 presumptions. It is therefore easy to fall into the trap of thinking that if the presumptions do not apply then any apparent consent from V must be effective. This is not the case. Rather, where the presumptions do not apply, or where a presumption under section 75

---

[50] *Larter and Castleton* [1995] Crim LR 75 (pre-SOA 2003).
[51] See Jarvis, 'The Timing of Consent' [2019] Crim LR 394.
[52] See Finch and Munro, 'Intoxicated Consent and the Boundaries of Drug Assisted Rape' [2003] Crim LR 773, and revisited [2004] Crim LR 789.

is rebutted by D, it is still vital to apply the general definition of consent under section 74. Indeed, certain cases will fall outside the presumptions and yet it will be very clear for the jury that V's apparent consent was not effective, as in *Jheeta*.

 Jheeta [2007] EWCA Crim 1699

D sent V anonymous text messages over several years, purporting to be from the police, telling her to continue having a sexual relationship with him in order to avoid fines for causing distress. D was charged with rape.

• Crown Court: guilty of rape—D's deception undermined V's apparent consent.

• Court of Appeal: conviction upheld on appeal.

In a case like *Jheeta*, D's deception is clearly sufficient to undermine V's apparent consent. However, D has not deceived V as to the nature (physical dynamics of sexual intercourse) or the purpose (his sexual gratification) of the sexual act, and so the conclusive presumptions of non-consent do not apply. Equally, the facts do not fall within the rebuttable presumptions either. V's lack of consent is clear on the basis of section 74 alone.[53]

Section 74 is designed to afford the jury some discretion in cases falling outside the presumptions, and so the definition is not overly prescriptive. However, it does provide two important clarifications.

First, the use of the language 'agrees by choice' is a clear indication that consent should be viewed as a *positive* sign of willingness, as opposed to the absence of an objection. The distinction here may be subtle, as discussed in *Watson*,[54] but it is vital as a move away from a historical view of rape as a necessarily violent encounter. As a matter of substantive law, the question of consent does not rely on V's objections or whether she physically resisted penetration, although this will be useful evidence of non-consent,[55] the absence of consent is the absence of a freely made choice to participate.

Secondly, the definition also highlights two major factors (although it does not define them) that should be applied when deciding if any apparent consent from V was legally effective. Mirroring similar considerations of effective consent in the context of the offences against the person,[56] these factors are 'capacity' and 'freedom'.

A) Capacity: To make a valid choice to consent, V must be able to understand that choice: she must have sufficient mental capacity. An assessment of capacity is specific to the individual V on the specific occasion. The test is not status-based: the simple fact that V is very young[57] or old, or that V has a mental disorder,[58] for example, will not automatically undermine her ability to consent.[59] This interpretation was confirmed in

---

[53] See similarly *B* [2013] EWCA Crim 823.

[54] [2015] EWCA Crim 559: highlighting that whilst submission is not consent, reluctant consent can be. Cf *Doyle* [2010] EWCA Crim 119.

[55] *Malone* [1998] All ER 176 (pre-SOA 2003).

[56] See **Chapter 7.3.2.2**.

[57] Very young children are, however, protected by specific offences for which consent is irrelevant (**8.6–8.7**).

[58] As with children, mentally ill victims are also protected by specific offences for which consent is irrelevant (**8.8.3**).

[59] Elliott and De Than, 'The Case for a Rational Reconstruction of Consent in Criminal Law' (2007) 70 MLR 225.

the leading case of *C*. *C* focussed on section 30 of the SOA 2003 (sexual activity with a person with a mental disorder impeding choice (**8.8.3**)), but the discussion of capacity is equally applicable to capacity in the context of effective consent.

 C [2009] 1 WLR 1786

V had a history of mental disorders manifesting themselves in manic episodes and delusions involving irrational fears for her safety. D befriended V, gave her crack cocaine, and made her perform acts of oral sex on him and another. V claimed that she only consented out of fear for her safety.

- Crown Court: guilty of the section 30 offence. Capacity undermined by fears originating from mental illness.
- Court of Appeal: allowing D's appeal. Capacity not undermined by a condition of this kind.
- House of Lords: conviction reinstated. Capacity can be undermined where V understands the nature of the act, but a mental condition prevents her making a real choice.

In her judgment in the House of Lords, Baroness Hale made several telling contributions to the jurisprudence in this area. For example, discussing a non-status-based approach to consent, she commented:

... it is difficult to think of an activity which is more person and situation specific than sexual relations. One does not consent to sex in general. One consents to this act of sex with this person at this time and in this place.[60]

Individualising the assessment of capacity, and rejecting the status-based approach, the House of Lords set out the following test for valid decision making:

a) a person must be able to understand the information relevant to making it, and

b) must be able to weigh that information in the balance to arrive at a choice.[61]

In *C*, although V was able to understand the sexual acts (satisfying the first limb of the test), her inability to weigh that information to make a choice (due to her mental disorder) meant that she could not pass the second. Thus, she lacked capacity to consent and, therefore, there was no consent.

 Point to remember ...

Although *C* involved mental disorder, this is not the only reason why V might lack capacity to consent. For example, if V is heavily intoxicated she may also fail the test for capacity set out in *C*.[62]

B) Freedom: As well as capacity to choose, V must have sufficient freedom. 'Freedom' is not defined in the SOA 2003 and the concept has little precedent within the common law.

---

[60] At [27].
[61] At [24].
[62] *Bree* [2007] EWCA Crim 804.

It therefore provides a great deal of flexibility and discretion for the court and the jury to interpret the term as they deem appropriate; the negative consequence of this breadth being the potential for inconsistent interpretations. It is useful to separate the discussion of constraints on V's freedom (i) caused by D, from those (ii) not caused by D.

Where D induces apparent consent through threats or deception, he restricts V's freedom of choice. Certain categories of deception will be caught by section 76 and lead to a conclusive presumption of non-consent; certain threats of violence will lead to a rebuttable presumption under section 75. However, there will be many examples of threats or deceptions that, whilst not falling within the presumptions, may nevertheless undermine V's apparent consent under section 74. For example, where D threatens to injure V at some point in the future, but not immediately, unless she submits to a sexual act.

Although a lack of freedom due to threats or deception will often be clear, borderline cases have emerged, and the courts have struggled for consistency. For example, on the one hand we have cases stating that non-disclosure of HIV will not undermine consent, and judges stating that deception as to 'wealth' will 'obviously not be sufficient to vitiate consent'.[63] A striking example of this arose in *R (Monica) v DPP*,[64] where an undercover police officer had, under his assumed identity, conducted a sexual relationship with V (a protestor). The High Court held that that deception of V did not vitiate consent within section 74. However, on the other hand, we have had a flurry of cases where deception (outside the conclusive presumptions) has been enough to undermine consent within section 74, such as *Assange* (deception as to the use of a condom),[65] *F v DPP* (deception as to intentional internal ejaculation),[66] and *McNally* (deception as to gender).[67] Some of this lack of consistency can be explained by the distinction between active deception (more likely to undermine consent) and passive deception (less likely to undermine consent), but this 'rule' is not consistently applied, and presents problems.[68] The latest case to engage with this issue, which presents a new rule for distinguishing categories of deception, is *Lawrance*.[69]

 Lawrance [2020] EWCA Crim 971

D knowingly and falsely assured V that he had had a vasectomy, and therefore no condom was required to prevent the risk of pregnancy. On this basis, and following reassurance from D, V consented to sex. D was charged with rape.

- Crown Court: guilty of rape. V's consent was not free and informed, and was therefore legally invalid.
- Court of Appeal: appeal allowed. V was not deceived as to the 'sexual intercourse itself' but only as to the 'broad circumstances' surrounding it. The latter category of deception does not undermine consent.

---

[63] *McNally* [2013] EWCA Crim 1051, per Leveson LJ.
[64] [2018] EWHC 3508 (Admin). See Clement, 'Deception and Consent to Sex' [2019] 78 CLJ 264.
[65] [2011] EWHC 2849 (Admin).
[66] [2013] EWHC 945 (Admin).
[67] [2013] EWCA Crim 1051.
[68] Sharpe, 'Expanding Liability for Sexual Fraud Through the Concept of "Active Deception": A Flawed Approach' (2015) 80 JCL 28; cf Ryan, '"Active Deception" v Non-Disclosure: HIV Transmission, Non-Fatal Offences and Criminal Responsibility' [2019] Crim LR 4. See generally, Gibson, 'Deceptive Sexual Relations: A Theory of Criminal Liability' (2020) OJLS 82.
[69] See Rogers, '*R v Lawrance*—The Right Outcome' (2020) 8 Arch Rev 4.

Lawrance is important for two principal reasons. First, the court explicitly rejects the express/implied distinction as a mechanism for identifying legally relevant deception, stating that whether D's deception is express or not 'makes no difference'.[70] Secondly, a new test is derived from the case law, distinguishing deception as to the physical sexual activity (will undermine consent—eg promise not to ejaculate; to wear a condom; etc) from deception as to the broader circumstances (will not undermine consent—eg promise as to HIV status; marital status; etc). Considerable time is taken to set out how this test should be applied, and the case warrants careful reading on this basis. However, less time is taken to explain why this test strikes the correct moral distinction in terms of deserved liability; and academic critique is likely to follow. The need for Supreme Court or (less likely) legislative clarification of this area remains clear.[71]

V's freedom of choice may also be restricted by circumstances that are not caused by D. In certain cases D will not be the cause of V's lack of freedom, but he may take advantage of it in order to induce V to submit to a sexual act. This is a difficult area because V is likely to be under many pressures in everyday life, including financial pressure; pressures from wanting to maintain a relationship; wanting to start a family; etc, and these pressures may well cause her to accept a sexual act that she would not otherwise have chosen. This will not, ordinarily, undermine consent. However, there are extreme examples where such pressures will undermine V's freedom of choice and thus her consent. For example, in *Kirk*,[72] a homeless teenager, V, agreed to sex with D in exchange for £3.25 to buy food. The Court of Appeal held that V was not consenting.

The general definition of consent set out in section 74, and the factors of 'freedom' and 'capacity', therefore provide *some* codified guidance for juries. But considerable discretion remains.

 Extra detail . . .

When discussing non-consent across sections 74, 75, and 76, voluntary intoxication has emerged as a particularly problematic area (where it does not come within the presumptions). We discuss this further when considering potential reforms to the current law (**8.9**).

8.2.2 Mens rea of s1

The requirement of mens rea in rape reflects the criminal law's focus on D's wrongdoing, as opposed to the compensation of V which is the focus of the civil law. If the actus reus is completed, V has suffered a serious wrong. But *only* if the mens rea is satisfied will the law attribute that wrong to D, constituting the offence of rape.

8.2.2.1 Mens rea as to penetration

D does not commit rape unless, at the time of penetration, he intends to penetrate V's vagina, anus, or mouth.[73]

---

[70] At [41].
[71] See generally Ormerod, 'Rape and Deception (Again)' [2020] Crim LR 877.
[72] [2008] EWCA Crim 434 (decided under pre-2003 Act offence).
[73] Discussed in *Gabbai* [2019] EWCA Crim 2287: D claimed that any anal penetration of D was accidental.

8.2.2.2 Mens rea as to V's non-consent

To be liable for rape or the other sexual offences requiring non-consent, D must have mens rea as to V's non-consent. It is important to remember that D's appreciation of V's non-consent (mens rea) is a separate requirement from non-consent in fact (actus reus). Here, we are only concerned with D's mens rea.

Prior to the SOA 2003, D would only be liable where he foresaw a risk of non-consent or did not care about the issue.[74] Thus, where D believed that V consented he could avoid liability even if that belief was unreasonable. Criticisms of this approach often focus on the case of *Morgan*.[75]

Morgan [1976] AC 182 (pre-SOA 2003)

D and others had sex with V after being told by her husband that they should do so, and that her apparent resistance would only be done to increase her enjoyment. Each was charged with rape. They claimed that they honestly (though unreasonably) believed V consented.

- Crown Court: guilty of rape. D's belief in consent must be *reasonable*.
- Court of Appeal: appeal dismissed.
- House of Lords: appeal dismissed. There was a misdirection at the Crown Court—belief in consent does not have to be reasonable (as long as it is honest). However, no jury could have found their belief to be honest.

Although liability was found in *Morgan*, the possibility that an unreasonable belief of this kind could have led to an acquittal (if honestly held) was heavily criticised. Commentators contended that some objectivity (reasonableness) was required: recognising the seriousness of sexual offences, as well as the ease through which D could ask V about consent.[76]

The response within the SOA 2003, whilst short of the purely objective test mooted at the time,[77] nevertheless incorporates a considerable objective dimension. As with the actus reus of non-consent, the mens rea is dealt with over multiple sections.

Presumptions of mens rea as to non-consent

Just as sections 76 and 75 create presumptions of non-consent in the context of the actus reus, the same sections also create mens rea presumptions. Thus, where the facts of a case come within section 76 (discussed earlier) this will establish D's mens rea as to V's non-consent; where the facts come within section 75 (discussed earlier) there will be a rebuttable presumption that D satisfies the mens rea.

Assessment matters . . .

If your discussion of non-consent in the context of actus reus finds that one of the presumptions is engaged, the same presumption will always also apply to mens rea.

[74] *Taylor* (1984) 80 Cr App R 327 (pre-SOA 2003).
[75] Farmer, '*DPP v Morgan*' in Handler, Mares, and Williams (eds), *Landmark Cases in Criminal Law* (2017).
[76] Wells, 'Swatting the Subjectivist Bug' [1982] Crim LR 209.
[77] Early versions of the Bill even included a reversed burden of proof. See **Chapter 1.1.7.2**.

General approach to mens rea as to non-consent

Where the presumptions do not apply at all (or, in the context of section 75, are rebutted) we must consider the general approach. This is set out separately within each of the non-consent-based offences, but the same form of words is used in each. Mens rea will be satisfied where:

> [D] does not reasonably believe that [V] consents.[78]

The requirement of a 'reasonable belief' in consent represents a largely objective approach to mens rea. D will satisfy this aspect of the mens rea where he:

- intends V to lack consent;
- knows V lacks consent;
- is reckless as to consent;
- does not consider consent; or even
- honestly but unreasonably believes that V consents.

Where the last of these arises, the jury must consider whether a reasonable person in D's position would have believed (as he did) that V was consenting. Where the answer is 'no', as it would have been if *Morgan* was decided under the current law, mens rea will be satisfied.

The test is not, however, *purely* objective. This is because, for each offence, the reasonable belief requirement is qualified with subjective considerations.

> Whether a belief is reasonable is to be determined having regard to all the circumstances, including any steps [D] has taken to ascertain whether [V] consents.[79]

The question for the jury is not 'would a reasonable person have believed that V consented' but, rather, 'would a reasonable person sharing D's characteristics have believed that V consented'. The difference is not intended to weaken the objective (reasonableness-based) approach, but it will allow the jury to consider characteristics that genuinely affect D's ability to appreciate V's non-consent, such as D's age, sexual experience, learning disabilities,[80] or other factors of this kind. The law is imposing a duty on D to take reasonable steps to ensure that V is consenting, it is not expecting D to take steps that he is not physically or mentally equipped to take.

The rule, however, is not consistently applied across all conditions and characteristics. For example, it has long been accepted that D's voluntary intoxication will not be a relevant characteristic (ie the test is whether a reasonable *sober* person would have believed that V consented),[81] and more recently, mirroring similar developments in self-defence,[82] D will also not be able to rely on a 'delusional belief' in consent caused by a mental disorder.[83] When applying the reasonable belief in consent requirement, taking account of D's circumstances, it is important to remember these exceptions.

[78] SOA 2003, s1(1)(c).
[79] Ibid, s1(2).
[80] *TS* [2008] EWCA Crim 6.
[81] See discussion of the intoxication rules at **Chapter 13.2**.
[82] See **Chapter 14.5**.
[83] *B* [2013] EWCA Crim 3. Child and Sullivan, 'When Does the Insanity Defence Apply? Some Recent Cases' [2014] Crim LR 788.

8.3 SOA 2003, s2: assault by penetration

Section 2 of the SOA 2003 criminalises assault by penetration, carrying a maximum sentence of life imprisonment.[84]

2(1) A person (D) commits an offence if—

    (a) he intentionally penetrates the vagina or anus of another person (V) with a part of his body or anything else,

    (b) the penetration is sexual,

    (c) V does not consent to the penetration, and

    (d) D does not reasonably believe that V consents.

The elements of assault by penetration are set out in **Table 8.2**.

Table 8.2 SOA 2003, s2

	Actus reus	**Mens rea**
Conduct element	Penetration of V's vagina or anus	Intention
Circumstance element	V does not consent	D lacks a reasonable belief in consent
	Penetration is sexual	None
Result element	None	None

8.3.1 Actus reus of s2

The actus reus of section 2 overlaps with the actus reus of rape considerably. As with rape, D must perform an act that penetrates the vagina or anus of V without V's consent. These requirements are defined in the same way as they are for rape, discussed previously. When discussing the element of non-consent, consideration must be given to the following:

• Do the facts come within the conclusive presumptions of non-consent (s76)?

• If not, do the facts come within the rebuttable presumptions of non-consent (s75)?

• If not, or if a section 75 presumption is rebutted, the general definition of consent (s74) should be applied.

There are, however, notable differences between the actus reus of rape and the section 2 offence. Most importantly, for section 2, D's act of penetration does not need to be by his penis. D (male or female) will be liable where they penetrate V (male or female) with *any* body part (eg fingers, tongue, etc) or with 'anything else' (eg bottle, knife, etc).

---

[84] SOA 2003, s2(4).

Not only does this offence recognise the seriousness of non-penile penetration,[85] but it is also useful in cases where V is unsure whether she was penetrated with D's penis or another object, or lacks the capacity to distinguish.[86] The offence covers penetration of V's vagina or anus. Non-penile penetration of V's mouth will not be caught within this section, although it may constitute a sexual assault under section 3.

 Extra detail . . .

The broad definitions of 'penetration' and 'vagina', discussed in relation to rape, will have even more of an impact for section 2. For example, where D performs non-consensual oral sex upon V's vagina, this will be caught within the section 2 offence because D's tongue will have penetrated V's vulva.

8.3.1.1 Penetration must be sexual

The other notable difference between the actus reus of rape and the section 2 offence is that, for section 2, the prosecution must prove that D's act was 'sexual'. Penile penetration, as required for rape, is self-evidently sexual and so this extra element is not required. However, there may be examples of non-penile penetration of the vagina or anus that are not self-evidently sexual, for example medical examinations. Where V is penetrated without her consent and the sexual element is present, it is correct to apply sexual offences. Where it is not present, where D's conduct is non-sexual, the non-fatal offences against the person should be applied.[87] The term 'sexual' is defined by section 78 of the SOA 2003:

> 78. . . . penetration, touching or any other activity is sexual if a reasonable person would consider that—
>
> (a) whatever its circumstances or any person's purpose in relation to it, it is because of its nature sexual, or
>
> (b) because of its nature it may be sexual and because of its circumstances or the purpose of any person in relation to it (or both) it is sexual.

Many cases within section 2, involving non-consensual penetration of V's vagina or anus, will satisfy the sexual element because of the nature of D's conduct (s78(a)). This is where D's acts are self-evidently (objectively) sexual, irrespective of the circumstances or purposes of D, and irrespective of whether D would consider them to be sexual. For example, in *Hill*,[88] D forcefully inserted his fingers into his partner's vagina during a violent argument. Although the Court of Appeal described his acts as violent 'rather than sexual', D pleaded guilty to a sexual offence and it is likely that his acts would have been viewed as sexual under section 78(a) without consideration of his purposes.

Where D's act of penetration is not sexual by its nature (eg because of the medical context in which it occurs), section 78(b) should be considered. As penetration of the vagina or anus always '*may* be sexual', the jury will consider whether the circumstances or D's purposes make it sexual. For example, if D (a doctor) recommends certain penetrative examinations of V in circumstances where such examinations have no medical role, and/or for reasons of personal sexual gratification, his conduct will be sexual under section 78(b).

---

[85] The offence separates acts of this kind from the more general offence of sexual assault (**8.4**).
[86] See *Minshull* [2004] EWCA Crim 2673: V was severely disabled.
[87] See **Chapter 7**.
[88] [2006] EWCA Crim 2575.

Extra detail . . .

Where D's acts may be sexual and the sexual requirement is satisfied by his accompanying purposes (s78(b)), this is an example where an actus reus requirement seems to be satisfied by D's mind as opposed to an external fact.[89]

8.3.2 Mens rea of s2

Mens rea for the section 2 offence is the same as for rape, discussed earlier. When penetrating V, D must:

- intend the act of penetration (see **8.2.2.1**); and
- lack a reasonable belief that V is consenting (see **8.2.2.2**).

There is no corresponding mens rea to the actus reus requirement that D's conduct is 'sexual'. D's liability does not require him to be aware (or even negligent) that his conduct is sexual.[90]

8.4 SOA 2003, s3: sexual assault

Section 3 of the SOA 2003 criminalises a broad range of conduct within the offence of sexual assault, carrying a maximum sentence of 10 years on indictment.[91]

3. A person (D) commits an offence if —

   (a) he intentionally touches another person (V),

   (b) the touching is sexual,

   (c) V does not consent to the touching, and

   (d) D does not reasonably believe that V consents.

The elements of sexual assault are set out in **Table 8.3**.

Table 8.3 SOA 2003, s3

	Actus reus	**Mens rea**
Conduct element	Any conduct that causes the result	Voluntary
Circumstance element	V does not consent	D lacks a reasonable belief in consent
	Touching is sexual	None
Result element	Touching of V	Intention

[89] Sullivan, 'Bad Thoughts and Bad Acts' [1990] Crim LR 559. Cf Child, 'The Structure, Coherence and Limits of Inchoate Liability: The New Ulterior Element' (2014) 34 LS 537.

[90] Although, of course, where D's conduct is only potentially sexual, it may be made sexual by D's purposes (s78(b)).

[91] SOA 2003, s3(4).

8.4.1 Actus reus of s3

As with section 1 and 2 offences, a central element of sexual assault is that V does not consent to the contact from D. Again, this will involve consideration of the conclusive presumptions of non-consent (s76), rebuttable presumptions (s75), and (if necessary) the general definition of consent (s74).

However, beyond non-consensual penetration, sexual assault also includes non-consensual sexual touching of any kind. D and V may be male or female.

8.4.1.1 Touching

The label 'sexual *assault*' implies that D must commit a technical assault or battery,[92] however, this is not the case. Rather, a 'touching' is all that is required. Touching is defined broadly within section 79(8) to include 'touching, (a) with any part of the body, (b) with anything else, (c) through anything'. Touching does not need to be firm or prolonged, and may be satisfied even where V is unaware of it.[93] The leading case is *H*.

_H_ [2005] EWCA Crim 732

D approached V as she walked across some fields and asked her 'Do you fancy a shag?' D then grabbed her tracksuit bottoms by the fabric and attempted to pull her towards him. V escaped. D was charged with sexual assault.

- Crown Court: guilty of sexual assault. Touching V's clothes amounted to touching V.
- Court of Appeal: conviction upheld on appeal.

Although it is clear that touching 'through' clothes will amount to touching V,[94] *H* confirms that it also includes cases where D *only* makes contact with V's clothes. This interpretation is welcomed, and consistent with the interpretation of touching for battery.[95] It is also likely that 'touching' can be performed by omission if D omits to act in breach of a recognised duty (eg where D allows a child to touch his genitals).[96]

Despite this broad interpretation of 'touching', it will not include cases where D makes no contact with V, even where this amounts to an assault. For example, if D threatens V and makes her remove her clothes, this will not be a sexual assault unless he also makes some physical contact.

8.4.1.2 Touching must be sexual

We have already discussed the meaning of 'sexual' in the context of section 2 (**8.3.1.1**), and the same two-stage approach (set out in s78) also applies here. D's conduct will be 'sexual' if (a) the jury consider it to be sexual by its 'nature' independent of other factors, or (b) if they consider it to be potentially sexual and made sexual by the 'circumstances' or D's 'purposes'. This is illustrated in **Table 8.4**.

---

[92] See **Chapter 7.2**.
[93] *Bounekhla* [2006] EWCA Crim 1217.
[94] *Swinscoe* [2006] EWCA Crim 2412: D touched an eight-year-old girl through her underwear.
[95] See **Chapter 7.2.2**.
[96] *Speck* [1977] Crim LR 689 (pre-SOA 2003).

Table 8.4 Defining 'sexual'

Section 78(a) D's conduct is sexual by its nature = sexual
Section 78(b) D's conduct may be sexual + made sexual by circumstances or D's purposes = sexual

Where D's conduct is sexual because of its nature (s78(a)), this requirement will be straight-forward to apply. However, unlike section 2 cases where D's conduct will often be sexual because of its nature, this is considerably less likely for cases discussed within section 3. As sexual assault encompasses any sexual touching, the full definition of 'sexual' becomes much more important, including section 78(b). A classic illustration of this is *Court*.

> **_Court_** [1989] AC 28 (pre-SOA 2003)
>
> D, a shop assistant, pulled a 12-year-old girl across his knee and spanked her clothed bottom. When asked why, he said 'buttock fetish'. D was charged with indecent assault (equivalent to sexual assault).
> • Crown Court: guilty of indecent assault—assault was made indecent (sexual) by D's sexual purpose.
> • Court of Appeal: conviction upheld on appeal.
> • House of Lords: appeal dismissed.

Court is a useful example where D's touching is unlikely to be considered sexual by its nature, but is potentially sexual, and made sexual by the purposes of D. Similarly, in *H* (discussed earlier at **8.4.1.1**), grabbing V's clothing is not sexual by its nature, but is potentially sexual, and made sexual by the circumstances (ie whilst asking V for 'a shag').

The two-part approach within section 78(b), however, creates some uncertainty in relation to niche sexual fetishes. In *George*,[97] for example, D had a foot fetish and attempted to remove a girl's shoe for reasons of sexual gratification. If decided today, as D's conduct is not sexual by its nature (s78(a)), it could only come within the offence if it satisfied the sexual element through section 78(b). It is clear that the second part of section 78(b) would be satisfied as D is acting for sexual gratification. However, would the case get beyond the first part of the test in section 78(b)? Objectively viewed, without considering D's purposes, is the removal of a shoe potentially sexual? If the answer is 'yes', and such conduct may be sexual, then it is difficult to imagine any form of touching that would not satisfy this part of the test. As fetishism knows no bounds, the first part will be redundant and we will always look to the circumstances and D's purposes. If the answer is 'no', and such conduct is not considered potentially sexual, then this first part of the test will maintain an active role, but it will be very difficult to see where the line should be drawn: what is required for conduct to be potentially sexual?[98] It is likely that the former, more expansive, view of 'sexual' will be preferred.

---

[97] [1956] Crim LR 52 (pre-SOA 2003).
[98] Bantekas, 'Can Touching Always be Sexual When There is No Sexual Intent?' (2008) 73 JCL 251.

8.4.2 Mens rea of s3

The mens rea for sexual assault includes two main elements. First, D's conduct (touching) must be intentional. Thus, for example, if D *accidentally* makes contact with V on a busy train he will not commit sexual assault even if the touching is sexual in nature, as where his hand touches her breast. Secondly, D must lack a reasonable belief that V is consenting to the touching. This was discussed previously in relation to rape (8.2.2.2). Although the actus reus of section 3 includes a 'sexual' requirement, D does not require any corresponding mens rea to this element.[99]

8.5 SOA 2003, s4: causing a person to engage in sexual activity without consent

Section 4 of the SOA 2003 creates an offence for D where he or she causes V to engage in sexual activity without consent. The offence carries a maximum life sentence where sexual penetration is involved, or 10 years on indictment for other cases.

4(1) A person (D) commits an offence if —

    (a) he intentionally causes another person (V) to engage in an activity,

    (b) the activity is sexual,

    (c) V does not consent to engaging in the activity, and

    (d) D does not reasonably believe that V consents.

The elements of section 4 are set out in **Table 8.5**.

Table 8.5 SOA 2003, s4

	Actus reus	Mens rea
Conduct element	Any conduct that causes the result	Voluntary
Circumstance element	V does not consent	D lacks a reasonable belief in consent
	The activity is sexual	None
Result element	V engages in an activity	Intention

8.5.1 Actus reus of s4

Unlike offences under sections 1–3, section 4 does not require D to have any physical contact with V or even be present at the time of the sexual activity. Rather, the offence focusses on D who causes V to engage in some form of non-consensual sexual activity.

---

[99] Although where D's conduct is only potentially sexual, it may be made sexual by D's purposes (s78(b)). See *Attorney General's Reference No 1 of (2020)* [2020] EWCA Crim 1665 [45].

The offence will cover D (a woman) who causes V (a man) to penetrate her without consent, as well as cases of sexual activity with a third party,[100] or even self-masturbation.[101] In each case, although D need not make physical contact with V, a causal link must be proven between D's conduct (which could be words alone) and V engaging in the sexual activity.

Beyond D's causal role, other elements of the actus reus must be demonstrated that have already been discussed in relation to sections 1–3. These include:

- V's activity as caused by D must be 'sexual' (s78). As discussed for section 2 (**8.3.1.1**) and section 3 (**8.4.1.2**), conduct may be sexual because of its nature, or be potentially sexual and made sexual by the circumstances or D's purposes;

- the sexual activity must also be without V's consent. As discussed for rape (**8.2.1.4**), this element requires consideration of the conclusive presumptions of non-consent (s76), rebuttable presumptions (s75), and (if necessary) the general definition of consent (s74).

It should be remembered that the actus reus of section 4 will only be satisfied when all these elements are complete. For example, if D threatens V to compel her to perform a sexual activity at some point in the future, the actus reus is not satisfied until that future activity is completed.

8.5.2 Mens rea of s4

The mens rea for section 4 includes two central elements. First, D must intend the conduct which caused V to engage in a non-consensual sexual activity. Secondly, as with offences under sections 1–3, D must have lacked a reasonable belief that V consented to the sexual activity. This is discussed earlier in relation to rape (**8.2.2.2**). Although the actus reus of section 4 includes a sexual element, D does not require any corresponding mens rea to this element.

 Assessment matters . . .

Unlike sections 1–3, the actus reus of section 4 allows for the possibility of a gap in time between D's conduct and the sexual activity carried out by V (eg where D threatens V over the phone or internet to complete sexual acts with another person on a later date, the offence is only complete when that activity on the later date occurs). It should be remembered that although the actus reus of an offence can be spread in this manner, the same is not true of mens rea.[102] We must identify all mens rea requirements at the time that D completes the conduct element of the actus reus. Thus, while performing the acts that cause V's later sexual activity, D must be intending to cause that activity and lack a reasonable belief that V will consent to it.

8.6 Sexual offences against children under 13 years

The four offences in this category (ss5–8) closely mirror the four offences discussed earlier (ss1–4). However, crucially, these offences do *not* require the prosecution to prove that V lacked consent, or that D lacked a belief in V's consent.[103] Offences in

[100] *Basherdost* [2009] EWCA Crim 2883.
[101] *Devonald* [2008] EWCA Crim 527.
[102] See **Chapter 3**.
[103] Spencer, 'The Sexual Offences Act 2003: Child and Family Offences' [2004] Crim LR 347.

this category are not claiming that a child under 13 is incapable of consent. Rather, they are constructed to make the issue of consent irrelevant; it is not an offence element.

8.6.1 SOA 2003, s5: rape of a child under 13

The section 5 offence, commonly referred to as 'statutory rape', criminalises D who penetrates the vagina, anus, or mouth of V *aged 12 or under* with his penis. The offence carries a maximum sentence of life imprisonment.[104]

5(1) A person commits an offence if—

(a) he intentionally penetrates the vagina, anus or mouth of another person with his penis, and

(b) the other person is under 13.

The elements of section 5 are set out in **Table 8.6**.

Table 8.6 SOA 2003, s5

	Actus reus	**Mens rea**
Conduct element	Penile penetration of V's vagina, anus, or mouth	Intention
Circumstance element	V is aged 12 or under	None
Result element	None	None

In common with the section 1 offence of rape (**8.2**), this offence requires penile penetration of V's vagina, anus, or mouth. The actus reus of section 5 differs from section 1 in that V's consent or non-consent is irrelevant; and although D may be of any age,[105] V must be aged 12 or younger. In terms of mens rea, D must intend to penetrate V. However, beyond this, there are no mens rea requirements for the section 5 offence. As V's consent is irrelevant, there is no mens rea requirement in relation to it. There is also no mens rea required as to V's age (ie no need to prove D was aware, or even should have been aware, that V was under 13). This was confirmed in *G*.[106]

 G [2008] UKHL 37

D (15) had sexual intercourse with V (12). V consented to the intercourse, and D argued that he reasonably believed that V was over 13 (he claimed she told him so). D was charged with a section 5 offence.

---

[104] SOA 2003, s5(2).
[105] Provided D is over the age of criminal responsibility (10 years old).
[106] Ashworth, Commentary [2008] Crim LR 818.

- Crown Court: guilty of section 5 offence.
- Court of Appeal: conviction upheld on appeal.
- House of Lords: appeal dismissed. Issues of consent and D's belief in V's age are irrelevant to the offence. Also confirming that section 5 is compatible with Article 6 ECHR (right to a fair trial) and Article 8 (right to respect for family life).

8.6.2 SOA 2003, s6: assault of a child under 13 by penetration

Section 6 criminalises any sexual penetration of V's vagina or anus, where *V is aged 12 or under*. The offence carries a maximum sentence of life imprisonment.[107]

6(1) A person commits an offence if—

(a) he intentionally penetrates the vagina or anus of another person with a part of his body or anything else,

(b) the penetration is sexual, and

(c) the other person is under 13.

The elements of section 6 are set out in **Table 8.7**.

Table 8.7 SOA 2003, s6

	Actus reus	**Mens rea**
Conduct element	Penetration of V's vagina or anus	Intention
Circumstance element	Penetration is sexual	None
	V is aged 12 or under	None
Result element	None	None

In common with the section 2 offence of non-consensual assault by penetration (**8.3**), section 6 targets the intentional sexual penetration of V's vagina or anus with any part of D's body or anything else. In contrast with section 2, however, this offence does not require V to lack consent to penetration or for D to lack a belief in V's consent. As long as D sexually penetrates V in the proscribed manner, and V is under 13 years old, D will be liable for the offence. D will be liable even if he reasonably believes that V is aged 13 or over: mens rea as to the age of V is strict.

---

[107] SOA 2003, s6(2).

8.6.3 SOA 2003, s7: sexual assault of a child under 13

Section 7 criminalises the sexual touching of V, where *V is aged 12 or under*. The offence carries a maximum sentence of 14 years' imprisonment.[108]

7(1) A person commits an offence if—

(a) he intentionally touches another person,

(b) the touching is sexual, and

(c) the other person is under 13.

The elements of section 7 are set out in **Table 8.8**.

Table 8.8 SOA 2003, s7

	Actus reus	Mens rea
Conduct element	Any conduct that causes the result	Voluntary
Circumstance element	Touching is sexual	None
	V is aged 12 or under	None
Result element	Touching of V	Intention

As with the section 3 sexual assault offence (**8.4**), this offence requires D to have intentionally touched V and for that touching to be sexual. However, as with the other child sex offences, this offence will only apply where V is aged 12 or under. V's non-consent and D's belief as to V's consent are irrelevant to liability, as is D's belief as to V's age.

8.6.4 SOA 2003, s8: causing or inciting a child under 13 to engage in sexual activity

Section 8 criminalises D who causes *or incites* sexual activity with V, where *V is aged 12 or under*. The offence carries a maximum sentence of 14 years' imprisonment.[109]

8(1) A person commits an offence if—

(a) he intentionally causes or incites another person (V) to engage in an activity,

(b) the activity is sexual, and

(c) V is under 13.

Section 8 creates two separate offences, set out in **Tables 8.9** and **8.10**.[110]

[108] Ibid, s7(2)(b).
[109] Ibid, s8(3)(b).
[110] *Walker* [2006] EWCA Crim 1907.

Table 8.9 SOA 2003, s8

	Actus reus	Mens rea
Conduct element	Any conduct that causes the result	Voluntary
Circumstance element	V is under 13	None
	The activity engaged in by V is sexual	None
Result element	V engages in an activity	Intention

Table 8.10 SOA 2003, s8

	Actus reus	Mens rea
Conduct element	Communication with V	Voluntary
Circumstance element	V is under 13	None
	D's communication with V incites her to engage in an activity	None
	The activity incited is sexual	None
Result element	None	None

The first of these offences (set out in **Table 8.9**) mirrors the section 4 offence of causing another person to engage in sexual activity without consent (**8.5**): criminalising D who causes V to engage in any sexual activity. As with the other child sexual offences, the offence is only committed where V is 12 or under, and issues of non-consent, belief in consent, and belief in age, are irrelevant.

The second offence within section 8 (set out in **Table 8.10**) does not mirror the section 4 offence. Rather, it criminalises D for inciting (encouraging) V to engage in sexual activity where V is aged under 13. D is liable as soon as he has completed the conduct of encouragement, and there is no requirement that sexual activity ever takes place. Further, although D's communication with V must be voluntary, there is no additional mens rea: D's beliefs in relation to V's willingness to engage in the activity; her age; and even whether he truly intends the sexual activity to ever come about, are all irrelevant to liability. This construction of section 8 was charged in *Walker*.

 Walker [2006] EWCA Crim 1907

D spoke on the phone to a child whilst looking at her. He told her 'show us your fanny'. He was charged with a section 8 offence of inciting sexual activity.

- Court: guilty of section 8 offence.
- Court of Appeal: conviction upheld on appeal. Whether D intended the sexual activity to happen (disputed in this case) is irrelevant to D's liability.[111]

---

[111] The correctness of this decision should be doubted, but it remains a valid precedent.

It is also clear from the case of *Jones*[112] that incitement under section 8 does not require the targeting of a particular child: in this case, a note left in a public toilet asking for sex with any child who read it.

Although the incitement offence provides additional protection against those encouraging children to perform sexual acts,[113] the broad nature of the actus reus and the use of strict liability has the potential to cause problems. For example, what if D writes on an open internet blog about the joys of sex and comments that people should have sex as soon as they are in a relationship. D is not intending to encourage children to have sex and he does not foresee that children will even be reading his post. However, he has voluntarily completed an act that has the potential to encourage those aged 12 or under to engage in a sexual activity. D's conduct satisfies the elements of the offence, and he must rely on prosecutorial discretion to avoid liability.[114]

8.6.5 Sexual offences against children under 13 *by children*

The offences within sections 5–8 can only be committed against children aged 12 or under. However, provided D is over the age of criminal responsibility (10 years old), his age is irrelevant. Therefore, although paradigm examples of these offences will focus on adult offenders, the offences apply equally where D is a similar age (or even younger) than V. As a result, because the consent of V is irrelevant to these offences, they have the potential to criminalise sexual experimentation between young people that we may wish to keep outside the criminal law. For example, at the extreme end, it would be possible to view a kiss between two consenting 12-year-olds as acts *from both parties* of sexual assault against someone aged 12 or under (contrary to section 7).[115]

Foreseeing this possibility when the SOA 2003 first gained Royal Assent, the Home Secretary stated in a press release that there would be no prosecutions of children under 16 years old where sexual activity was genuinely consensual. This restriction seems sensible. However, by not including the restriction within the offences themselves, *which would have been quite straightforward to do*, we rely on the much less consistent process of prosecutorial discretion.[116] The result has been unwelcome and unnecessary inconsistency. In certain cases (eg *R(S) v DPP*[117]) prosecutors have been willing to abandon charges against young people where consent is found. However, in others, such as *G*[118] (discussed at **8.6.1**), prosecutors have pursued cases through to conviction despite the potential that V was consenting.

Assessment matters . . .

If you are presented with problem question facts involving sexual contact between apparently consenting young people, some mention of prosecutorial discretion is advised. Although we do not usually discuss prosecutorial discretion in the context of the substantive law, the statement by the Home Secretary

---

[112] [2007] EWCA Crim 1118.
[113] The problems in this area for the general offence of incitement (now assisting and encouraging) are discussed in **Chapter 11.4**.
[114] See discussion of the CPS in **Chapter 1.1.7.1**.
[115] Bohlander, 'The Sexual Offences Act 2003 and the *Tyrrell* Principle Criminalising Victims' [2005] Crim LR 703.
[116] See discussion of the CPS in **Chapter 1.1.7.1**.
[117] [2006] EWHC 2231 (Admin).
[118] [2008] UKHL 37.

provides a clear guide that should limit the substantive application of this offence. Having said this, it will still be necessary for you to apply the section 5–8 offences as appropriate to the facts: in light of G and other prosecutions in conflict with the guidance, you cannot be sure that a prosecution will not be brought. When applying the offences, as both consent and knowledge of age are irrelevant, liability is likely.

8.7 Sexual offences against children under 16 years

Offences in this category target offending against victims under 16 years old, which is the age of sexual consent. Victims of this age are also covered by the offences in sections 1–4, and the lower end of the age range (under 13 years old) are also covered by the offences in sections 5–8. In this manner, we will often see considerable overlap, where a single event could lead to liability under a number of different offences.

Extra detail . . .

There is a high degree of overlap between offences within the SOA 2003. However, overlap is common in many areas of the criminal law. The advantage of overlap is that it can minimise gaps between offences where D's conduct (although wrongful) does not quite come within the elements of an offence. However, on the other side, overlap can create confusion for prosecutors (and students!) trying to choose which offence to apply, and can lead to a lack of precise labelling between the different mischiefs. We discuss this, and provide a guide to selecting the appropriate offence, when discussing assessments later (**8.10**).

As with the offences against children discussed (at **8.6**), V's possible consent and D's possible belief in that consent are not relevant to these offences. In this manner, the protection of young victims where consent is irrelevant is extended beyond those aged 12 and under (ss5–8) to include those up to 15 years old.

As we will see, however, these offences include two major differences from those within sections 5–8. First, where the victim is aged between 13 and 15, D will only commit the offence if he does not reasonably believe that V is aged 16 or over. Secondly, for the first time in this chapter, offences in this category are classified differently depending upon the age of D. We summarise the offences in the following sections with reference to those age restrictions.

8.7.1 Adults offending against children under 16

The four offences set out in sections 9–12 apply to adults (aged 18 or over) who offend against children (aged under 16).

8.7.1.1 SOA 2003, s9: sexual activity with a child

Section 9 focusses on sexual touching. The maximum sentence varies depending upon the nature of the touching.[119]

9(1) A person aged 18 or over (D) commits an offence if—

    (a) he intentionally touches another person (V),

    (b) the touching is sexual, and

---

[119] SOA 2003, s9(2) and (3).

(c) either—

    (i)   B is under 16 and A does not reasonably believe that B is 16 or over, or

    (ii) B is under 13.

The elements of section 9 are set out in **Table 8.11**.

Table 8.11 SOA 2003, s9

	Actus reus	**Mens rea**
Conduct element	Any conduct that causes the result	Voluntary
Circumstance element	D is aged 18 or over	None
	Touching is sexual	None
	V is aged 12 or under	None
	Or	
	V is aged 13–15	Lack of reasonable belief that V is aged 16 or over
Result element	Touching of V	Intention

Where V is aged 12 or under, the elements of this offence mirror the offence under section 7 precisely other than as to the restriction on D's age. D is liable if he intentionally touches V; the touching is sexual;[120] and V is aged 12 or under. D and V may be male or female.[121] Issues of consent (actus reus or mens rea) are irrelevant, as are D's beliefs as to the sexual nature of his conduct, and the age of V.

Where V is between 13 and 15, D will avoid liability if he held a reasonable belief that V was aged 16 or over. Aside from this additional element of mens rea, the other elements of the offence are the same as where V is aged 12 or under.

8.7.1.2 SOA 2003, s10: causing or inciting a child to engage in sexual activity

Section 10 focusses on D's causing V to engage or inciting V to engage in sexual activity. The maximum sentence will vary in line with the type of activity caused or incited.[122] The offence is commonly used to prosecute the senders of explicit text messages,[123] and in certain cases of sexual grooming.[124]

10(1) A person aged 18 or over (D) commits an offence if—

    (a) he intentionally causes or incites another person (V) to engage in an activity,

[120] *Lister* [2005] EWCA Crim 1903: confirming again that passionate kissing will suffice.
[121] *Angela C* [2006] EWCA Crim 1781: 43-year-old woman having sex with 14-year-old boy.
[122] SOA 2003, s10(2) and (3).
[123] *Howell* [2007] EWCA Crim 1863.
[124] Gillespie, 'Indecent Images, Grooming and the Law' [2006] Crim LR 412.

(b) the activity is sexual, and

(c) either—

(i) V is under 16 and D does not reasonably believe that V is 16 or over, or

(ii) V is under 13.

It is useful to view this section as two separate offences, set out in **Tables 8.12** and **8.13**.

Table 8.12 SOA 2003, s10

	Actus reus	**Mens rea**
Conduct element	Any conduct that causes the result	Voluntary
Circumstance element	D is aged 18 or older	None
	The activity in which V engaged is sexual	None
	V is aged 12 or under	None
	Or	
	V is aged 13–15	Lack of reasonable belief that V is aged 16 or over
Result element	V engages in an activity	Intention

Table 8.13 SOA 2003, s10

	Actus reus	**Mens rea**
Conduct element	D communicates with V	Voluntary
Circumstance element	D is aged 18 or older	None
	D's communication with V incites her to engage in an activity	None
	The activity incited is sexual	None
	V is aged 12 or under	None
	Or	
	V is aged 13–15	Lack of reasonable belief that V is aged 16 or over
Result element	None	None

Where V is aged 12 or under, the elements of this offence mirror section 8 precisely except that D must be over 18. D will be liable either because he has intentionally caused V to engage in a sexual activity that has come about (offence in **Table 8.12**); or because he has incited (encouraged) V to engage in a sexual activity whether or not it later comes about (offence in **Table 8.13**). In each case, the consent of V; D's belief as to consent; D's belief as to the sexual nature of the conduct; and D's belief as to V's age, are all irrelevant.

Where V is between 13 and 15, D will avoid liability if he held a reasonable belief that V was aged 16 or over. Aside from this additional element of mens rea, the other elements of the offence are the same.

8.7.1.3 SOA 2003, s11: engaging in sexual activity in the presence of a child

Section 11 criminalises D who engages in a sexual activity in order to gain sexual gratification from being witnessed by a young person. For example, it will apply to D who masturbates in front of a child,[125] as well as 'doggers' (individuals who have sex in public because they enjoy being observed) where the activity can be viewed by children.[126]

11(1) A person aged 18 or over (D) commits an offence if—

    (a) he intentionally engages in an activity,

    (b) the activity is sexual,

    (c) for the purpose of obtaining sexual gratification, he engages in it—

        (i) when another person (V) is present or is in a place from which D can be observed, and

        (ii) knowing or believing that V is aware, or intending that V should be aware, that he is engaging in it, and

    (d) either—

        (i) V is under 16 and D does not reasonably believe that V is 16 or over, or

        (ii) V is under 13.

The elements of section 11 are set out in **Table 8.14**.

Table 8.14 SOA 2003, s11

	Actus reus	**Mens rea**
Conduct element	Any activity	Voluntary
Circumstance element	D's activity is sexual	None
	D is aged 18 or over	None
	V is present or can observe D	None
	V is aged 12 or under	None
	Or	
	V is aged 13–15	Lack of reasonable belief that V is aged 16 or over
Result element	None	None

[125] *Chevron* [2005] All ER 91: D masturbating in view of a 12-year-old on the beach.

[126] *WT* [2005] EWCA Crim 2448: husband and wife having their nine-year-old daughter photograph them during sex.

| Ulterior mens rea element | * | Intends, knows, or believes that V is aware he is engaging in the activity |
| | | Intends to gain sexual gratification from V's presence and awareness |

The actus reus of section 11 catches D (aged 18 or over) where he performs a sexual activity whether alone or with another, and V is present or can observe D. The construction of 'present' *or* 'can be observed' is important (eg where V is viewing the activity on a webcam, she is not present but can observe). It is unclear whether V must be viewing the activity in real time, and this will have to be clarified by the courts. For example, will it apply where D posts images of his sexual activity on the internet for children to view at a later point? The actus reus also requires that V is aged 15 or under.

The mens rea of section 11 contains three core elements. First, D must be acting intentionally. Secondly, D must at least believe that V is aware he is engaging in the activity (note that recklessness is *not* sufficient). Thirdly, the prosecution must prove that the sexual activity was for the *purpose of obtaining sexual gratification*; it is insufficient for the prosecution to prove that a child just happened to be present when sexual activity was taking place.[127] These second two elements are examples of ulterior mens rea because they do not correspond to elements within the actus reus: D must believe that V is aware and must intend to gain sexual gratification, but it is *irrelevant* whether V actually is aware or whether D is sexually gratified.

Where V is aged 12 or under, no further mens rea is required. However, where V is between 13 and 15, it must be proved that D lacked a reasonable belief that V was aged 16 or over.

8.7.1.4 SOA 2003, s12: causing a child to watch a sexual act

Section 12 creates an offence where D, aged 18 or over, causes V, aged 15 or younger, to view the sexual activity of another or view the image of a sexual act, doing so to gain sexual gratification. The primary target of this offence will be paedophiles who use sexual imagery, whether of themselves or others, as part of a grooming process.[128]

12(1) A person aged 18 or over (D) commits an offence if—

    (a) for the purpose of obtaining sexual gratification, he intentionally causes another person (V) to watch a third person engaging in an activity, or to look at an image of any person engaging in an activity,

    (b) the activity is sexual, and

    (c) either—

        (i) V is under 16 and D does not reasonably believe that V is 16 or over, or

        (ii) V is under 13.

---

[127] *B and L* [2018] EWCA Crim 1439. See Comment by Laird [2020] CrimLR 261.

[128] *L* [2006] EWCA Crim 2225: D sent images of himself masturbating to V's phone.

The elements of section 12 are set out in **Table 8.15**.

Table 8.15 SOA 2003, s12

	Actus reus	**Mens rea**
Conduct element	Any conduct that causes the result	Voluntary
Circumstance element	The activity viewed (directly or through an image) is sexual	None
	D is aged 18 or over	None
	V is aged 12 or under	None
	Or	
	V is aged 13–15	Lack of reasonable belief that V is aged 16 or over
Result element	V watches a third party engage in an activity or looks at an image of an activity	Intention
Ulterior mens rea element	*	Intends to gain sexual gratification from V's presence and awareness

D completes the actus reus where he (aged 18 or over) causes V (aged 15 or under) to watch an activity or view images of an activity; and that activity is sexual. Where D caused V to view an image of a person engaging in a sexual activity, the term 'image' has been defined broadly to include moving or still images, 3D images,[129] and even cartoons, etchings, and computer-generated pseudo-images.

The mens rea requires that, at the time of acting, D must intend that his conduct will cause V to watch another person engage in an activity or to view images of an activity. The statute does not specify any mens rea requirement as to the 'sexual' nature of the conduct/image, implying that as long as it is considered sexual by the court (actus reus) then D's belief/awareness is irrelevant.[130] However, D must intend to gain sexual gratification from V viewing the activity. Interestingly, 'intention to gain sexual gratification' has been interpreted very broadly to include both the intention to gain immediate gratification (eg from viewing the child or knowing that the child is viewing the activity), as well as the intention to gain sexual gratification later (eg where causing V to view the activity is part of a grooming process leading to a possible sexual encounter between D and V).[131]

---

[129] SOA 2003, s97(4).
[130] This could cause problems, particularly in relation to artwork.
[131] *Abdullahi* [2006] EWCA Crim 2060.

8.7.2 Young people offending against children under 16

A common feature of the offences in sections 9–12 is that D must be aged 18 or over. However, by section 13 of the SOA 2003, the same conduct will also be an offence if committed by someone under 18 years old.

8.7.2.1 SOA 2003, s13: child sex offences committed by children or young persons

Section 13 creates an offence for D (aged 17 or under) where he completes any of the conduct proscribed by sections 9–12. The difference between liability under section 13 and liability under sections 9–12 is that the maximum sentence for section 13 is considerably lower.[132]

> 13(1) A person under 18 commits an offence if he does anything which would be an offence under any of sections 9 to 12 if he were aged 18.

The elements of this offence are exactly the same as discussed in relation to sections 9–12, the only difference being the age of D.

Returning to the issue of overlapping offences and prosecutorial discretion, it would be interesting to know the extent to which this offence with its lower maximum sentence is used in favour of more serious offences where D is under 18 years old. It is contended that this offence (s13) should usually be preferred. However, this does not rule out the possibility of other offences being used *which may be a criticism of overlapping offences*. A good illustration of this is the case of *G*[133] (discussed at **8.6.1**), where D (aged 15) had consensual intercourse with V (aged 12), believing that she was over 13 years old. D was convicted with the offence of raping a child (s5), where issues of consent and the age of D are both irrelevant. On appeal, D claimed that if he was to be prosecuted at all, which he claimed would be contrary to the Home Office guidance (**8.6.5**), it should have been for an offence under section 13. This was rejected by the House of Lords: D satisfied the elements of the section 5 offence, and it was not for him to decide which offence to charge.

 Assessment matters . . .

If the facts of a problem question involve an event that could be charged as more than one offence, the general rule is that you discuss the most serious of the potential offences first, and stop your discussion if you find the offence elements to be satisfied (eg if D stabs and kills V, within this single act D may have committed assault; battery; ABH; GBH; manslaughter; etc, but you should begin with a discussion of murder, and if murder is committed you do not need to discuss the others). However, where D is under 18 years old and committing a sexual offence, because of the prosecutorial guidance it is best to begin with a discussion of section 13. You should highlight if D may be alternatively guilty of a section 5 offence, for example, and note the case of *G*, but submit that it is likely that section 13 will be preferred.

---

[132] SOA 2003, s13(2).
[133] [2008] UKHL 37.

8.7.3 Preparatory offences against children under 16

The final two offences in this category (ss14 and 15) criminalise behaviour that is likely to lead to sexual contact with a child. By creating offences that deal with preliminary behaviour, there is an opportunity for investigation and prosecution before sexual contact has occurred.

8.7.3.1 SOA 2003, s14: arranging or facilitating commission of a child sex offence

Section 14 criminalises D (of any age) who arranges or facilitates conduct that would amount to an offence under sections 9–13 by himself or another, intending or believing that that future offence will come about. This offence is targeted at those who facilitate sexual offences against children, either by arranging meetings (eg transporting the child) or in other ways (eg providing a venue).

14(1) A person commits an offence if—

(a) he intentionally arranges or facilitates something that he intends to do, intends another person to do, or believes that another person will do, in any part of the world, and

(b) doing it will involve the commission of an offence under any of sections 9 to 13.

The elements of section 14 are set out in **Table 8.16**.

Table 8.16 SOA 2003, s14

	Actus reus	Mens rea
Conduct element	Any conduct that causes the result	Voluntary
Circumstance element	The activity would amount to an offence under ss9–13	None
Result element	Arranging or facilitating an activity	Intention
Ulterior mens rea element	*	Intention to carry out the activity personally Or Intention or belief that another person will carry out the activity

The actus reus of section 14 requires D to have arranged or facilitated a future activity that will amount to an offence within sections 9–13, whether this future offence is to be committed by D or another. As with all preparatory or inchoate offences, this future offence does not need to come about for D to be liable for the offence under section 14: he is liable for the separate prior mischief of arranging or facilitating it.

The central terms 'arranges' and 'facilitates' are not defined in the statute, but are interpreted widely to include a broad range of behaviour leading to potential future offences. For example, in the case of *R*,[134] D asked an adult sex worker (X) whether she could arrange a 12-year-old girl for him. D was eventually convicted of 'arranging' under section 14 despite reaching no agreement with X, and despite asking her to do the arranging for him. Making contact in this manner was sufficient. On this basis, it seems that the offence is even wide enough to catch D (aged 18) who asks to meet his girlfriend (aged 15) for sex, even where she says no.

D satisfies the mens rea of a section 14 offence where he intends to arrange or facilitate the activity, and where he either intends to carry it out himself or intends or believes that another will do so. The mens rea will not be satisfied if D arranges or facilitates, and merely foresees a risk that the offence will come about: for example, D rents a hotel room to a man and young girl foreseeing that it *may* be used for abuse.

Statutory exception to s14

Following concern that section 14 might criminalise youth or health workers and teen magazine columnists providing advice to teens on safe sexual practices, Parliament inserted a wide-ranging exception into the statute.

14(2) A person does not commit an offence under this section if—

    (a) he arranges or facilitates something that he believes another person will do, but that he does not intend to do or intend another person to do, and

    (b) any offence within subsection (1)(b) would be an offence against a child for whose protection he acts.

  (3) For the purposes of subsection (2), a person acts for the protection of a child if he acts for the purpose of—

    (a) protecting the child from sexually transmitted infection,

    (b) protecting the physical safety of the child,

    (c) preventing the child from becoming pregnant, or

    (d) promoting the child's emotional well-being by the giving of advice,

    and not for the purpose of obtaining sexual gratification or for the purpose of causing or encouraging the activity constituting the offence within subsection (1)(b) or the child's participation in it.

Terms such as 'emotional well-being' are ambiguous and require interpretation by the courts. However, it seems that as long as D is acting with the intention to assist V in an accepted context, and does not actively want V to engage in sexual practices for reasons of personal sexual gratification or otherwise, he will avoid liability under section 14.

8.7.3.2 SOA 2003, s15: meeting a child following sexual grooming, etc

The much publicised grooming offence under section 15 criminalises D (aged 18 or over) who communicates with V (aged 16 or under) and then travels or arranges to meet V with the intention to commit a sexual offence. The offence is primarily targeted at adults who groom children through internet chat forums, etc.

---

[134] [2009] EWCA Crim 1472. See Gillespie, 'Case Comment: Attempting to Find a Child Prostitute' (2009) 73 JCL 378.

15(1) A person aged 18 or over (D) commits an offence if—

(a) D has met or communicated with another person (V) on one or more occasions and subsequently—

(i) D intentionally meets V,

(ii) D travels with the intention of meeting V in any part of the world or arranges to meet V in any part of the world, or

(iii) V travels with the intention of meeting D in any part of the world,

(b) D intends to do anything to or in respect of V, during or after the meeting mentioned in paragraph (a)(i) to (iii) and in any part of the world, which if done will involve the commission by D of a relevant offence,

(c) V is under 16, and

(d) D does not reasonably believe that V is 16 or over.

The elements of section 15 are set out in **Table 8.17**.

Table 8.17 SOA 2003, s15

	Actus reus	**Mens rea**
Conduct element	Meeting or communicating with V	Voluntary
Circumstance element	D is aged 18 or over V is aged 15 or younger	None Lack of reasonable belief that V is aged 16 or over
Result element	Meeting V, travelling to meet V, or V travelling to meet D	Intention
Ulterior mens rea element	*	Intention to commit a sexual offence with V at the meeting or after it

To satisfy the actus reus of section 15, D (aged 18 or over) must first meet or communicate with V (aged 15 or younger).[135] Despite the offence label of 'sexual grooming', the initial communication(s) need not be sexual.[136] Following this initial contact, it must also be proved that D subsequently met V *or* travelled to meet V *or* V travelled to meet D. The drafting is such that the offence can be completed without D ever meeting V.

D must intend the prior meeting/communication with V, as well as the subsequent meeting/travelling to meet. With regard to this second meeting/travel, D must also

[135] As amended by the Criminal Justice and Courts Act 2015, s36. Prior to this, D had to meet or communicate with V on at least two occasions.
[136] *Gaviria* [2010] EWCA Crim 1693.

intend to commit a sexual offence—either on or after this occasion. Additionally, D must lack a reasonable belief that V is aged 16 or over; this mens rea is required (unlike other offences) even where V is aged 12 or under.

Section 15A offence

The section 15 grooming offence has been supplemented with a new offence of sexual communication under section 15A of the SOA 2003.[137] This offence applies where D (aged 18 or over) communicates with V (aged 15 or younger) for the purpose of sexual gratification; the communication is sexual or intended to encourage a sexual communication; and D does not reasonably believe V is aged 16 or over. In this way, the new offence applies to conduct short of the full grooming offence, because it does not require an intention to commit a sexual offence.

8.8 Status-based and relationship-based sexual offences

Just as offences in the previous category (ss5–15) are constructed to protect a V who is vulnerable on the basis of youth, other categories of sexual offences are designed in relation to similar vulnerabilities. These include cases where D is in a position of trust; where D is a family member; as well as where V has a mental disorder impeding choice. In this section, we provide only a brief overview of these offences.

8.8.1 Sexual offences abusing a position of trust

Sections 16–19 create four offences that mirror those of sections 9–12 (discussed at **8.7.1**) almost entirely, applying where D:

- sexually touches V (s16);
- causes or incites V to engage in sexual activity (s17);
- engages in sexual activity in V's presence for the purpose of sexual gratification (s18); or
- causes V to watch a sexual activity or image for the purpose of sexual gratification (s19).

Two differences at once expand and narrow liability in comparison to sections 9–12. First, expanding potential liability, sections 16–19 apply to victims up to the age of 17 (ss9–12 only apply to victims up to the age of 15).[138] Secondly, narrowing potential liability, sections 16–19 will only be committed by D who holds a position of trust over V. 'Position of trust' is defined in great detail within sections 21 and 22: including, for example, teachers, care-home workers, guardians, etc.

 Point to remember . . .

Mirroring sections 9–12, issues of V's consent are irrelevant to D's liability under sections 16–19. Thus, where V is 16 or 17 years old, although she may legally consent to sexual intercourse, her consent to intercourse with D (who holds a position of trust) will not prevent his liability under sections 16–19.

---

[137] Amended by the Serious Crime Act 2015, s67.
[138] *Wilson* [2007] EWCA Crim 2762: teacher engaged in sex with 15- and 16-year-olds.

There are two important exceptions to liability.

A) **Marriage exception (s23):** D will not commit an offence under sections 16–19 if V is aged 16 or over and D proves that (*note the reverse burden of proof*) they are legally married.

B) **Prior sexual relationship exception (s24):** D will not commit an offence under sections 16–19 if he proves that (*note the reverse burden of proof*) they were involved in a sexual relationship immediately prior to the position of trust arising, and that V was aged 16 or over throughout this period. This will cover cases, for example, where D is involved in a legitimate sexual relationship with V (aged 17), becomes V's teacher (position of trust), and continues the relationship.

8.8.2 Sexual offences within a family relationship

There are two sets of offences within the SOA 2003 that focus on sexual activity within a family relationship: sections 25 and 26 deal with child family relationships; and sections 64 and 65 deal with adults. V's potential consent is not relevant to either set of offences.

Section 25 (mirroring s9, discussed at **8.7.1.1**) creates an offence for D who intentionally touches V sexually. In contrast with section 9, this offence applies to D of any age, and will apply even where V is aged 16 or 17, as long as D does not reasonably believe that V is older. It must, however, be demonstrated that D and V have a family relationship (defined in s27), and that D knows or could reasonably be expected to know that they have this relationship. Section 26 is similarly constructed, but focusses on D who incites or causes V, aged 17 or under and with a family relationship, to engage in a sexual activity. As with the 'abuse of a position of trust' offences (**8.8.1**), these offences also include exceptions where D and V are lawfully married (s28) and where they had a lawful sexual relationship prior to the family relationship (s29).

 Extra detail . . .

The definition of 'family relationship' in section 27 goes well beyond blood relations to include stepchildren, foster children, adopted children, and even where D and V simply cohabit in circumstances where D cares for V in the manner of a family member.[139] This demonstrates a move in these offences, away from the criminalisation of heterosexual incest, and towards gender-neutral offences based on sexual exploitation.

The second set of offences, set out in sections 64 and 65, are much more controversial.[140] These offences criminalise D (aged 16 or over) who intentionally and sexually penetrates with his penis the vagina, anus, or mouth of V (a relative aged 18 or over), or penetrates the vagina or anus of such a person with anything else. They also criminalise D (aged 16 or over) who consents to being sexually penetrated by V (aged 18

---

[139] Brackenridge and Williams, 'Incest in the "Family" of Sport' (2004) 154 NLJ 179.

[140] Bowsher, 'Incest—Should Incest Between Consenting Adults be a Crime?' [2015] Crim LR 208; Spencer, 'Sexual Offences Act 2003: Child and Family Offences' [2004] Crim LR 347.

or over) in the same manner. In each case, the definition of 'adult relative' is considerably narrower than the definition of 'family relationship' discussed earlier, and D will avoid liability if he did not know and could not have reasonably been expected to know that he was V's relative. These offences are particularly controversial when you consider that if adult relatives D and V have a consensual sexual relationship, they are both committing an offence: one for penetration (s64) and one for consenting to being penetrated (s65). Where this is the case, it is difficult to identify the *victim* the law is seeking to protect.

8.8.3 Sexual offences against people with a mental disorder impeding choice

There are a number of offences in this category, designed to protect those with a mental disorder from exploitation and abuse. In each case, the consent or non-consent of V, as well as the gender and ages of D and V, are not relevant offence elements.

A) Sections 30–33: These sections criminalise D who intentionally sexually touches V (s30); intentionally incites or causes V to engage in a sexual activity (s31); intentionally engages in a sexual activity in the presence of V for the purposes of sexual gratification (s32); or intentionally causes V to watch a sexual act or view a sexual image for the purposes of sexual gratification (s33). In each case, V must have a mental disorder that makes her *unable to refuse*, and D must know or reasonably be expected to know that V has a disorder that may cause such inability. This was at issue in *C* (discussed at **82.1.4**).

 C [2009] 1 WLR 1786

V had a history of mental disorders manifesting themselves in manic episodes and delusions involving irrational fears for her safety. D befriended V, gave her crack cocaine, and made her perform acts of oral sex on him and another. V claimed that she only consented out of fear for her safety.

- Crown Court: guilty of the section 30 offence. Capacity undermined by fears originating from mental illness.

- Court of Appeal: allowing D's appeal. Capacity not undermined by a condition of this kind.

- House of Lords: conviction reinstated—capacity can be undermined where V understands the nature of the act but a mental condition prevents her making a real choice, even if the inability to refuse is temporary.

B) Sections 34–37: These sections criminalise the same conduct as sections 30–33, but this time, instead of the inability to refuse, V's mental disorder must be accompanied by an agreement from V that is caused by D's *threats or deception or inducement*. D must know or be reasonably expected to know that V has a relevant disorder. Particularly in the context of 'inducements', these offences go considerably further than the conclusive presumptions of non-consent discussed in relation to sections 1–4.

C) Sections 38–41: Again, these offences focus on the same range of conduct as sections 30–33. Here, the additional factor is that V is mentally disordered, and that D is in a *relationship as a carer*.

8.9 Reform

The emotive nature of sexual offences, as well as the continued low reporting[141] and conviction rates,[142] means that discussions of potential reform in this area are always high on the agenda. The SOA 2003 represented a comprehensive reform of the previous law, broadly welcomed for its gender-neutrality, broadening of liability, specific labelling, and use of modern and appropriate language.[143] However, the SOA 2003 was never likely to represent the final word in terms of reform, and such debates continue.[144] Some of these debates focus on new areas for potential criminalisation, targeting forms of sexual assault/abuse that were less prevalent in 2003 or were wrongly assumed to be captured by other offences.

The Serious Crime Act 2015 introduced the section 15A offence discussed at **8.7.3.2** (sexual communication with a child). More recently a new offence was created of 'upskirting' (ie taking non-consensual pictures beneath V's clothing to view their genitals or buttocks) under the Voyeurism (Offences) Act 2019. This Act amends the Sexual Offences Act 2003 by inserting a new section section 67A (which came into force on 12 April 2019). It applies to those who, without consent or reasonable belief in consent, operate equipment or record images from beneath the clothing of another person, for the purpose of observing or recording images of the buttocks or genitals, whether covered with underwear or not. The offender's purpose may be either sexual gratification or causing humiliation, alarm, or distress to the victim. Both offences are triable either way and punishable on indictment by up to two years' imprisonment. Further reform in this area could also usefully embrace wider forms of image-based sexual abuse (eg including so-called revenge porn).[145]

Even setting debates about potential new areas of criminalisation to one side, reform debate has focussed equally upon perceived weaknesses within current offences. We provide some brief discussion of three such areas: the appropriate boundaries of liability for rape; the specific problem of voluntary intoxication and consent; and the issue of undue complexity.

A) Boundaries of rape: The offence of rape (s1) is one of the most well-known and highly stigmatising within the criminal law. Partly because of this, the boundaries of rape (both actus reus and mens rea) are a common focus of academic attention. This has arisen particularly within two interesting debates.

The first debate of note focusses on the role of consent within the offence of rape. Under the current law, as we discussed previously, the non-consent of V is central to the mischief of D's conduct: consensual penile penetration is a social good, whereas non-consensual penile penetration is rape. But the central role of non-consent can be problematic. It is problematic when trying to prove a lack of consent: in the absence of force, there will often be little evidence. And it is problematic in that 'consent' is a difficult concept to define with the degree of objectivity and consistency that is required for such a central role. The current law has attempted to mitigate this with a definition

---

[141] Consistently evidenced within the British Crime Survey (victims survey).

[142] Consistently evidenced within Home Office Crime Statistics. Such statistics can, of course, be misleading, and should be treated with caution.

[143] Home Office, *SOA 2003: Stocktake* (2006).

[144] For a comparative review of rape legislation in a range of jurisdictions, see McGlynn and Munro (eds), *Rethinking Rape Law* (2010).

[145] See McGlynn and Rackley, 'Image-Based Sexual Abuse' (2017) 37 OJLS 534. The Law Commission commenced work on this area in 2019.

across three statutory sections (ss74, 75, and 76), but despite this the definition is rightly criticised for its lack of precision. These problems have given rise to a number of interesting academic alternatives. Some of these have focussed on redefinitions of consent, attempting to provide a more robust concept for the task.[146] More radically, others have sought to reduce the centrality of non-consent by reinterpreting the act of penetration as inherently wrongful, shifting the focus to circumstances that must be observed by D to make his wrongful act acceptable as, for example, the *active* willingness of V.[147] Inevitably, debates about D's mens rea as to V's non-consent play an important role in this debate.[148]

The second debate in this area concerns the label of 'rape' and its role within potential reform. On one side of this debate, the powerful label and its stigmatising effect can be presented as positive aspects of the criminal law: sending a clear message about unacceptable behaviour and condemning those who offend. However, on the other side, a powerful and well-known label can hamper reform. For example, where the definition of rape has been expanded to include anal and oral penetration, there is discussion not only about whether this conduct is wrongful in an equivalent manner to be included within the offence, but also whether it will be acceptable within the common meaning of 'rape'.[149] Part of the concern is that by widening the offence beyond its common understanding, the label will be misunderstood or undermined. In extreme cases, jury members with strong impressions of what rape is may be less inclined to find liability outside their personal understanding, even where the legal elements are satisfied.[150] Entrenched common understandings of offences like rape can also lead to the entrenchment of rape myths (eg that stranger rape is more serious), as well as prejudicial attitudes (eg relating to V's sexual history).[151] This is part of the reasoning behind the decision in Canada, for example, to abandon the label of rape entirely.[152]

B) Voluntarily intoxicated consent: The general policy of the law towards D who acts in a state of voluntary intoxication is that an intoxicated intention is still an intention: D may regret his intoxicated actions when sober, he may even claim that he would not have done them if he had not been intoxicated, but as long as he possessed the required mens rea when intoxicated then his liability is clear.[153] In relation to rape and other sexual offences, the law will *also* often have to deal with V who has become voluntarily intoxicated and then provides some form of consent to sexual activity with D. In such a case, should we follow the same harsh approach applied to defendants and hold that intoxicated consent is still consent, or should we provide additional protection for the intoxicated V who has *albeit voluntarily* become vulnerable to sexual abuse?

---

[146] Conaghan, 'The Essence of Rape' (2019) OJLS 151; Gardner, 'The Wrongness of Rape' in *Offences and Defences* (2007); 'The Opposite of Rape' (2018) 38 OJLS 48; Munro, 'An Unholy Trinity?' (2010) 63 OJLS 45; Huigens, 'Is Strict Liability Rape Defensible?' in Duff and Green (eds), *Defining Crimes* (2005) 196; Tadros, 'Rape Without Consent' (2006) 26 OJLS 515.

[147] Wall, 'Sexual Offences and General Reasons Not to Have Sex' (2015) 35 OJLS 777; Dempsey and Herring, 'Why Sexual Penetration Requires Justification' (2007) 27 OJLS 467. Cf Greasley, 'Sex, Reasons, Pro Tanto Wronging, and the Structure of Rape Liability' (2020) CrimL&P.

[148] See Daly, 'Knowledge or Belief Concerning Consent in Rape Law' [2020] Crim LR 478.

[149] Home Office, *Setting the Boundaries* (2000).

[150] Ashworth and Temkin, 'Rape, Sexual Assault and the Problems of Consent' [2004] Crim LR 328.

[151] Elvin, 'The Concept of Consent under the Sexual Offences Act 2003' (2008) 72 JCL 516.

[152] Gotell, 'Canadian Sexual Assault Law' in McGlynn and Munro (eds), *Rethinking Rape Law* (2010) 209.

[153] The intoxication rules are discussed at **Chapter 13.2.**

The current law does not provide a clear answer to this question. Where V is so intoxicated that she becomes unconscious, or where she is tricked into consuming an intoxicant against her will, the SOA 2003 creates a rebuttable presumption that V is not consenting (s75). However, no presumption will apply where V has become heavily voluntarily intoxicated but not yet unconscious. In such cases, the general definition of consent in section 74 (focussing on freedom and capacity) will be applied, and the jury must decide whether V consented or not whatever level of intoxication is present.[154] Whether V in this scenario should be provided with further protection, and whether the law should send a clearer message to men (in particular) that taking sexual advantage of intoxicated people is not acceptable, is a contentious debate.[155]

C) Undue complexity: Modern criminal statutes have generally become longer and this is not necessarily a bad thing: drafting in a way that sets out the detail of an offence increases the likelihood that the public understand the nature of the offence and are more accurately warned. Clarity of drafting should also reduce the need for appeal courts to clarify ambiguous offence elements. However, certain statutes have become unduly and unhelpfully complex, and this is certainly a criticism that can be levelled at the SOA 2003.[156]

The SOA 2003 does not define offences simply in relation to general harms, but rather provides multiple elements that set out each specific form of conduct that will be caught by the offence. In doing so, individual offences can become difficult to follow, and care must be taken to work methodically through the elements when applying them to factual cases. A useful example of this, from an offence we have not discussed in this chapter, is voyeurism (s67). D, for the purpose of obtaining sexual gratification, observes or records or enables another to observe (with equipment or otherwise) V doing a 'private act' knowing V does not consent to observation for that purpose.[157] By section 68, 'private acts' are those 'in a private structure in which one would expect privacy and V's genitals, buttocks or breasts are exposed or covered only with underwear, or V is using the lavatory, or V is doing a sexual act not of a kind ordinarily done in public'!

Where offences are set out in this level of detail, we may question how effectively they are providing a warning for the general public.[158] They are also likely to cause problems in practice, with prosecutors identifying the wrong offences and/or failing to apply each of the essential elements.[159]

 Extra detail . . .

In view of the criticism of undue complexity, it is perhaps even more glaring and unsatisfactory that central concepts such as 'consent' have been defined so briefly and ambiguously within the statute.

---

[154] *Bree* [2007] EWCA Crim 804.
[155] Usefully discussed in *Kamki* [2013] EWCA Crim 2335. See also Wallerstein, 'A Drunken Consent is Still a Consent—Or Is It?' (2009) 73 JCL 318; Wertheimer, 'Intoxicated Consent to Sexual Relations' (2001) 20 Law & Phil 373.
[156] Spencer, 'The Drafting of Criminal Legislation: Need it Be So Impenetrable?' (2008) 67 CLJ 585.
[157] See recently *Richards* [2020] EWCA Crim 95: offences committed against sex workers covertly recorded by D when having sex with them.
[158] See **Chapter 1.4.1**.
[159] eg *Gillard v The Queen* [2014] HCA 16: Australian case where there was confusion of elements between non-consent offences and abuse of position offences.

8.10 Eye on assessment

The complexity of the offences within the SOA 2003 and the quantity of offences make their application to problem facts challenging. However, as long as you adopt the methodical approach that we have repeated throughout this textbook, they need not cause you too many problems.

STEP 1 Identify the potential criminal event in the facts

This should be simply stated (eg 'The first potential criminal event arises where D touches V'). The role of this stage is to highlight which part of the question you are answering before you begin to apply the law.

STEP 2 Identify the potential offence

Again, state this simply (eg 'When touching V, D may be liable for sexual assault'). The role of this stage is to highlight which offence you are going to apply.

Certain problem questions will specify an offence that should be applied (eg 'Discuss D's potential liability for rape'), and where this is the case, only the specified offence should be considered. Others may specify a certain range of offences (eg 'Discuss D's potential liability under sections 1–4 of the SOA 2003') and, again, the limited range will make it much easier to identify which offence should be applied.

However, there may be problem questions that simply require you to consider 'D's liability for sexual offences' generally. In this case, identifying which offence to apply becomes very important. To help with this task, **Table 8.18** sets out each of the offences that have been discussed in this chapter, with a guide for how the appropriate offences can be identified quickly.

Using **Table 8.18**:

(a) First look to the age of V; this will identify the correct row of potential offences in the table. Many of the sexual offences will only apply to certain ages, or apply different rules depending upon the age of V.

(b) Next you must look (in very general terms at this stage) at the sort of factors that *may* be present in the facts (ie non-consent; D is in a position of trust; D is a family member; or V has a mental disorder impeding choice). This will identify the correct column in the table.

(c) The intersection of V's age (row) and other relevant factor (column) will identify the offences that should be applied. The following should be noted:

　(i)　where two or more relevant factors are present (eg D is a family member and V does not consent), then both sets of offences can be applied;

Table 8.18 Identifying which sexual offence to charge

Age of V	V consents	D is in a position of trust	D is a family member	V has a mental disorder impeding choice	V does not consent
18+	No offence	No offence	ss64–65 (requires D's MR as to familial status)	ss30–33 (requires D's MR as to disorder)	ss1–4 (requires D's MR as to non-consent)
16–17	No offence	ss16–19 (requires D's MR as to position of trust)	ss25–26 (requires D's MR as to familial status)	ss30–33 (requires D's MR as to disorder)	ss1–4 (requires D's MR as to non-consent)
13–15	ss9–15 (requires D's MR as to V's age)	**(ss16–19)** *But easier to apply the non-specific offences:* ss9–15	**(ss25–26)** *But easier to apply the non-specific offences:* ss9–15	ss30–33 (requires D's MR as to disorder) *May be easier to apply* ss9–15	ss1–4 (requires D's MR as to non-consent) *May be easier to apply* ss9–15
0–12	ss5–8 ss10–14 s15 (requires D's MR as to V's age for s15) **(s9)**	**(ss16–19)** *But easier to apply the non-specific offences:* ss5–8, 10–14, 15	**(ss25–26)** *But easier to apply the non-specific offences:* ss5–8, 10–14, 15	**(ss30–33)** *But easier to apply the non-specific offences:* ss5–8, 10–14, 15	**(ss1–4)** *But easier to apply the non-specific offences:* ss5–8, 10–14, 15

(ii) where certain offences are in bold font, this means that they can be applied but it will be easier to apply the non-specific offences (ie those within the first column, labelled 'V consents'). For example, where V is aged 12 or younger and does not consent to sexual contact, the offences within sections 1–4 can be applied, but it will be easier to apply offences such as sections 5–8 where the same conduct is criminalised (with the same maximum sentences) but there is no need to prove the absence of consent.

Assessment matters . . .

Even when using this table, there is likely to be more than one offence that could apply to a particular factual scenario. Where this is the case, you should follow the rule of thumb to apply the most serious offence first. If you find all the elements of that offence satisfied then you need not explore alternatives. Where there is a doubt (where an element of the offence may not be satisfied) it may be useful to go on to explore the next most serious offence that could apply as an alternative.

The only exception to this, in the context of sexual offences, is where D is under 16 years old. In this case, although D may be liable for a more serious offence, prosecutorial guidance suggests that you should first explore the offence designed for younger defendants (s13).

STEP 3 Applying the offence to the facts

Having highlighted a possible offence, STEP 3 requires you to both identify the actus reus and mens rea of that offence, *and* apply them to the facts.

In this section we provide an outline of how you should structure your analysis of the actus reus and mens rea of rape. The same structure is easily transferrable to the other non-consent-based offences (ss1–4), and can be adapted for the other offences as well. As we are dealing with statutory offences, your identification of the law in order to apply it to the problem facts should *always* begin with the statute. Case law should be used to inform and clarify the statute within your discussion, but the statute provides your most authoritative framework.

- **Actus reus**

  o As with all offences, you should begin with the conduct element. For rape, it is enough to ask simply whether, on the facts, D penetrated V's vagina, anus, or mouth with his penis.

  o Next you should consider the circumstance element: did V consent to the penetration?
    – Do the facts of the case come within the conclusive presumptions of non-consent (s76)? If yes, you can conclude that V lacked consent. If not . . .
    – Do the facts of the case come within the rebuttable presumptions of non-consent (s75)? If yes, D must provide evidence that V was consenting. If not, all burdens (legal and evidential) remain on the prosecution. However, either way, you should . . .
    – Consider the general definition of consent (s74), considering issues of freedom and capacity. The definition in section 74 leaves considerable discretion to the jury, so remember to talk in terms of *likely* outcomes.

- **Mens rea**

  o The first part of the mens rea will usually be straightforward: did D penetrate V intentionally? Where the answer is a simple yes, there is no need to discuss in any great detail; where there is some doubt (eg D was being physically manipulated by another), you should discuss in more detail.

  o The second part is to question whether D lacked a reasonable belief in V's consent. Remember to keep this element (mens rea as to non-consent) separate from the issue of whether V did in fact consent (actus reus). You should again consider the presumptions of non-consent (ss76 and 75) as these are also mens rea presumptions. If these do not apply (or a s75 presumption is rebutted), the mens rea question can be usefully analysed as two questions:

– Would a reasonable person in D's position have believed that V was consenting? If no, then D satisfies the mens rea. If yes, . . .
– Did D hold this belief at the time of penetration? If no, D satisfies the mens rea. If yes, D does not satisfy the mens rea and is not liable for rape.

 Point to remember . . .

Particularly when discussing consent, we have referenced several cases that pre-date the SOA 2003. These cases will have informed the SOA 2003 and can provide a useful point of discussion where the statute is unclear. However, remember that they are no longer authoritative precedent as to what the law is now, which can only be found from the SOA 2003 itself and the cases coming after it.

AR and MR are satisfied	AR and/or MR are not satisfied
Continue to STEP 4.	Return to STEP 2, and look for an alternative offence. If none, then skip to STEP 5, concluding that no offence is committed.

STEP 4 Consider defences

The word 'consider' here is important as you should not discuss every defence for every question. Rather, think whether there are any defences (eg duress) that *could* potentially apply. If there are, discuss those only.

STEP 5 Conclude

This is usually a single sentence either saying that it is likely that D has committed the offence, or saying that it is not likely either because an offence element is not satisfied or because a defence is likely to apply. It is not often that you will be able to say categorically whether or not D has committed the offence, particularly when applying concepts such as consent, so it is usually best to conclude in terms of what is more 'likely'.

STEP 6 Loop

Go back up to STEP 1, identifying the next potential criminal event. Continue until you have discussed all the relevant potentially criminal events.

ONLINE RESOURCES

www.oup.com/he/child-ormerod4e

This chapter is accompanied by a selection of online resources to help you with this topic, including:

- **Self-test questions** and **scenario questions**
- **Videos** from the authors
- **Audio introduction** to the topic
- **Chapter summary sheet**
- Two **sample examination questions** with answer guidance
- **Further reading and weblinks**

Also available on the online resources are:

- A selection of **videos** from the authors containing general advice on problem questions and essay questions
- **Legal updates**

9

Theft and other property offences

9.1 Introduction

Having discussed offences against the person, fatal (**Chapters 5** and **6**), non-fatal (**Chapter 7**), and sexual (**Chapter 8**), this chapter and **Chapter 10** move to consider offences against property. Offences within this category are many and varied, criminalising conduct such as the taking of another's property (eg theft, robbery, etc), possessing stolen or criminal property (eg handling stolen goods, money laundering, etc), as well as damaging another's property (eg criminal damage, arson, etc). Beyond such crimes, there are also a number of specific technical offences designed to protect particular property rights, such as those relating to intellectual and/or online property, vehicle misuse, and so on. Through such offences, the criminal law provides protection for the full range of civil law property rights, supporting the system of rules governing civil ownership in its function.[1]

Within the wide range of property crimes, this chapter focusses on a selection of core offences:

- **Theft:** D dishonestly appropriates V's property.
- **Robbery:** D uses force to steal V's property.
- **Burglary:** D trespasses onto V's property, committing (or intending to commit) an offence.
- **Handling stolen goods:** D deals in specified ways with V's property, which has been stolen.
- **Blackmail:** D threatens V in order to gain her property.
- **Criminal damage:** D damages V's property.

Each of these offences is defined by statute, and often in considerable detail.

In **Chapter 10**, still focussing on property crimes, we analyse the fraud offences as defined within the Fraud Act 2006. The fraud offences are distinct from most other property offences because they are conduct crimes, criminalising D for acting with the intention to interfere with V's property rights, rather than for actually doing so.

9.2 Theft

Theft is defined in section 1(1) of the Theft Act 1968 (TA 1968), with further detail provided over sections 2–6. The maximum penalty on indictment is seven years' imprisonment.[2]

> 1(1) A person is guilty of theft if he dishonestly appropriates property belonging to another with the intention of permanently depriving the other of it . . .

The elements of theft are set out in **Table 9.1**.

---

[1] Ormerod and Williams, *Smith's Law of Theft* (9th edn, 2007) and *Smith, Hogan, and Ormerod's Criminal Law* (16th edn, 2021) Chs18–27.
[2] Theft Act 1968, s7.

Table 9.1 Theft

	Actus reus	**Mens rea**
Conduct element	Any conduct causing the result	Voluntary
Circumstance element	What is appropriated is property	Knowledge
	It belongs to another	Knowledge
	D's appropriation is dishonest	In the context of D's knowledge and belief
Result element	D appropriates V's property	Intention
Ulterior mens rea element	*	Intention permanently to deprive V of her property

To simplify the relatively complex structure of the theft offence, courts and commentators typically distil the detail from **Table 9.1** into the discussion of five core elements, as in **Figure 9.1**. This approach also reflects the statutory sections of the TA 1968.

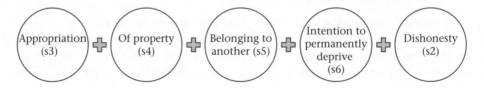

Figure 9.1 Theft

We discuss each of these offence elements in turn. Liability requires the prosecution to prove that D satisfied *every* element, and for these elements to have coincided (ie occurred at the same time).

9.2.1 Appropriation

Appropriation is defined in section 3 of the TA 1968.

> 3(1) Any assumption by a person of the rights of an owner amounts to an appropriation, and this
> includes, where he has come by the property (innocently or not) without stealing it, any later
> assumption of a right to it by keeping or dealing with it as owner.

Despite the relative clarity of section 3(1), the meaning of 'appropriation' has generated considerable dispute in the appellate courts, including four cases in the House of Lords. In resolving these disputes, the courts have generally preferred to interpret the term broadly. Three central points of debate have arisen: whether D must appropriate all the rights of the owner; whether consensual appropriation will satisfy this element; and whether D appropriates where V has given the property as a valid gift in civil law.

9.2.1.1 Assuming the rights of an owner

Section 3(1) is clear that assuming the rights of an owner will amount to an appropriation. The most obvious cases will be where D takes V's property and treats it as her own. However, what if D only assumes certain ownership rights, but not others? For example, what if D sells V's property (assuming rights of legal ownership), but does not physically interfere with it (does not assume rights of possession or control)? Where cases of this kind emerge, it forces us to recognise ownership rights as a bundle of rights and not a singular concept. The case of *Morris* confirms that the assumption of any one property right will be sufficient to find an appropriation.

Morris [1984] AC 320

D switched labels on supermarket goods in order to purchase the more expensive goods at the (false) lower price. He proceeded to the checkout and paid the lower price. D was charged with theft.

- Crown Court: guilty of theft.
- Court of Appeal: conviction upheld on appeal.
- House of Lords: appeal dismissed. When swapping the labels, D assumed 'a' right of the owner (the right to price the goods) and this was sufficient to amount to an appropriation at that point.

It has been cogently argued that *Morris* represents an incorrect interpretation of the TA 1968 and that appropriation should only be found where D assumes all of the rights of an owner.[3] However, the approach in *Morris* has been confirmed subsequently by the House of Lords in *Gomez*,[4] and so, for better or worse, this is the approach that should be applied.

Adopting this approach to appropriation requires an examination of each stage of the defendant's conduct. Although a criminal event may involve a single actor and a single item of property, there may be several separate 'acts' of appropriation. For example, D takes an item from V with the intention of borrowing it and returning it later, *appropriating* at the point she assumes physical possession and control; later, D decides to keep the item, *appropriating* further rights of legal ownership (note here the potential for appropriation by omission/decision to treat V's property as her own).[5] In each case, D only appropriates where she intends/knows what she is doing (eg D does not

---

[3] For discussion of this and support for the decision, see Melissaris, 'The Concept of Appropriation and the Offence of Theft' (2007) 70 MLR 581.

[4] [1993] AC 442.

[5] Indeed, this second appropriation (where D decides to keep the property) is explicitly catered for in the latter part of s3(1): 'this includes, where he has come by the property (innocently or not) without stealing it, any later assumption of a right to it by keeping or dealing with it as owner'.

appropriate where her child takes something from a shop without her knowledge, unless or until she *then* decides to keep it),[6] but the potential for multiple acts of appropriation remains a real one.

 Assessment matters . . .

The potential for multiple acts of appropriation makes it crucial to identify precisely which act of appropriation you are discussing when answering a problem question in this area. This is particularly important where only one of D's appropriations coincides with the other offence elements, making liability possible on that conduct alone. We explore this further when discussing assessments below (**9.9**).

A final point should be clarified regarding the time span of an appropriation.[7] In most cases of theft, the act of appropriation is best analysed as a single and instantaneous event: for example, D steals V's bag when she grabs it from V and runs away; she does not continue to steal it when using it several days or weeks later. However, if we follow the logic of *Morris*, we could say that appropriation starts and finishes the moment that D touches the bag, concluding before D even begins to run away. This issue can be important where there is uncertainty about territorial jurisdiction: for example, where D takes V's car whilst abroad and imports it to England, can we say that theft occurred in England? It will also be important in the context of other offences such as robbery, where violence must be shown to accompany the act of theft. The shorter the duration of the theft, the less likely robbery can be found (**9.3**). In such cases, courts have sensibly interpreted appropriation as existing beyond an instant, to include the time where D is still 'on the job', probably including D's running away but not her use of the property on following occasions.[8]

9.2.1.2 Appropriation with consent

Paradigm cases of theft will involve a non-consensual appropriation: D taking V's property without her knowledge or against her wishes. In line with this, a requirement of 'adverse' appropriation has often been assumed by the courts, such as in *Morris*.[9] However, the wording of the TA 1968 does not expressly limit the offence in this way, stating generally that 'any assumption' of rights will constitute an appropriation. In light of this drafting, other cases such as *Lawrence* have held that the consent or non-consent of V is irrelevant.[10] The question, and the inconsistent approach of previous cases, was eventually addressed by the House of Lords in *Gomez*.

---

[6] *Broom v Crowther* (1984) 148 JP 592.

[7] See Williams, 'Appropriation: A Single or Continuous Act?' [1978] Crim LR 69.

[8] *Atakpu* [1994] QB 69: no appropriation in England where cars were stolen in Frankfurt or Brussels and brought to England days later.

[9] [1984] AC 320. Lord Roskill (*obiter*) 'appropriation involves not an act expressly or impliedly authorised by the owner but an act by way of adverse interference with or usurpation of those rights'.

[10] *Lawrence* [1972] AC 626: D, a taxi driver, took extra money from V for a fare. V did not speak much English and 'allowed' the extra money to be taken from his wallet. The House of Lords held that there was an appropriation: it did not matter that V consented to the taking.

Gomez [1993] AC 442

D was the assistant manager of an electrical goods shop. He convinced his manager to allow a customer to buy items using cheques that D knew were stolen and therefore worthless. The manager consented to the 'sale'. D was charged with theft.

- Crown Court: guilty of theft.
- Court of Appeal: appeal allowed. Following *Morris*, the consent of V undermines the element of appropriation.
- House of Lords: appeal allowed, reaffirming D's liability and following *Lawrence*. With Lord Lowry dissenting, the Lords confirmed that V's consent was irrelevant: D appropriated where he tricked V and assumed ownership rights.

The decision in *Gomez* sparked considerable academic debate,[11] not least because the irrelevance of V's consent created a substantial overlap with other property offences: with offences of obtaining by deception at the time of *Gomez* (since repealed),[12] and now with the fraud offences.[13] Indeed, the prosecution of *Gomez* for an offence of obtaining property by deception (what would today be fraud by false representation) would have been straightforward. However, for reasons unknown, the prosecutors chose to charge theft and so the question of consent in relation to theft had to be resolved.[14] *Gomez* (again, for better or worse) confirms that as long as D assumes a right of ownership over V's property, there will be an appropriation. V's consent or non-consent is irrelevant.

9.2.1.3 Appropriation with full civil title

Gomez confirmed that D could appropriate V's property regardless of V's consent in circumstances of deception (ie D lied about the cheques). However, the question remained open whether D's assumption of rights would still be an appropriation where V consented and there was no deception. The court in *Gomez* indicated that appropriation would be found even in the absence of deception, both through the examples they employed,[15] as well as other cases they overruled, but this did not form part of the ratio of the case.

The decision that appropriation could be found despite a lack of deception was confirmed in the case of *Hinks*. *Hinks* provides that, where D assumes ownership rights from V, this may be an appropriation even where the property is consensually transferred from V with full title (where the transfer is valid and not voidable in civil law[16]). Thus, D may be liable for theft of property in criminal law, but be entitled to keep that same property in civil law.

---

[11] Heaton, 'Deceiving Without Thieving' [2001] Crim LR 712; Davies, 'Consent After the House of Lords: Taking and Leading Astray the Law of Theft' (1993) 13 LS 308; Cooper and Allen, 'Appropriation after *Gomez*' (1993) 57 JCL 186.

[12] TA 1968, s15. Repealed by the Fraud Act 2006.

[13] Fraud Act 2006. See **Chapter 10**.

[14] The same charging error was made more recently in *Gimbert* [2018] EWCA Crim 2190. We discuss the overlap between theft and fraud offences further in **Chapter 10.8.3**.

[15] eg of a person switching labels in a supermarket, where the court said there would be appropriation at the moment D touches the labels. At that point there is no full deception offence.

[16] Transfers become voidable if there is a 'vitiating factor'. These include duress, misrepresentation, undue influence, and so on.

Hinks [2000] UKHL 53

D befriended V who was a man described by the court as naive, trusting, and of limited intelligence. Over a six-month period she took V to his building society almost every day where he withdrew and gave to her £300 (the maximum withdrawal), eventually totalling over £60,000. At the point of arrest, D had taken almost all of V's money as well as his television. D was charged with theft.

- Crown Court: guilty of theft.
- Court of Appeal: conviction upheld on appeal.
- House of Lords: appeal dismissed, with Lord Hutton and Lord Hobhouse dissenting. Although the transfer of money may not have amounted to a civil wrong, this does not preclude it being an appropriation and a theft.

 Extra detail . . .

It may have been arguable that the facts of *Hinks* involved a voidable contract. In other words, it could have been argued that V was mentally incapable of making a valid gift or that there must have been some undue influence from D. If the gift was voidable then D's conviction for theft (following *Gomez*) would have been uncontroversial. However, importantly, the accepted facts for the House of Lords were such that the gift was valid in civil law.

To appreciate the full implications of *Hinks*, it is useful to highlight the two main arguments raised and rejected by the appeal courts:

A) Distinguishing *Hinks* and *Gomez*: The first line of argument was that *Hinks* should be distinguished from *Gomez* because *Hinks* involved a full and valid transfer of property in civil law. Indeed, even following *Gomez*, in *Mazo*,[17] it was accepted by the Court of Appeal to be 'common ground that the receiver of a valid gift *inter vivos* could not be the subject of a conviction for theft'.[18] This argument was supported by the apparent absurdity of D being potentially liable for theft and yet, as a matter of civil law, remaining the owner of the property stolen.[19] However, this argument was rejected in *Hinks*, and *Mazo* was overruled. The court found the law clearly stated in *Gomez*. On the issue of inconsistency between civil and criminal law, Lord Steyn, with the majority, stated that:

> The purposes of the civil law and the criminal law are somewhat different. In theory the two systems should be in perfect harmony. In a practical world there will sometimes be some disharmony between the two systems. In any event, it would be wrong to assume on priori grounds that the criminal law rather than the civil law is defective.

The House of Lords therefore recognised the inconsistency, but rejected it as a reason for finding no appropriation. This is particularly interesting if we consider the rationale

---

[17] [1996] Crim LR 435.
[18] In *Mazo*, this led to the acquittal of D on similar facts to *Hinks*.
[19] Beatson and Simester, 'Stealing One's Own Property' (1999) 115 LQR 372.

of property offences to be for the protection of the civil system of ownership rights. Following the decision in *Hinks*, theft is not being used to protect ownership rights; quite the opposite, it is punishing D for gaining valid ownership.[20] Theft is now targeting dishonesty or exploitation more generally. We discuss the apparent changing rationale of theft when discussing potential reform of theft (**9.8.1**).

B) **Challenging *Gomez*:** The second line of argument in *Hinks* was that the definition of appropriation had become too easy to satisfy following *Gomez*, rendering it of negligible significance within the offence. The idea here is that the consensual touching of another's property does not, of itself, target the mischief of theft, and so other offence elements are having to do the work of narrowing the scope of criminal liability that used to be done (at least in greater part) by appropriation.[21] The main 'other' element to bear the brunt of this narrowing has been 'dishonesty' (discussed later) and, the argument goes, the current definition of dishonesty is not suitable on its own for this task. However, the court reasoned that any fundamental change of this kind (reconsidering *Gomez*) could lead to the offence becoming unacceptably narrow. It is clear that the court wanted to find liability in cases such as *Hinks* and so, taking some comfort from one alternative academic opinion,[22] they dismissed this line of argument as well.

 Point to remember . . .

Gomez and *Hinks* led to considerable debate about the appropriate role and construction of theft, and some of these points will be discussed further in the context of potential law reform (**9.8.1**). However, by avoiding technical distinctions based on the civil law, the requirement of appropriation is usually straightforward to apply: we ask simply, did D assume any right of ownership over V's property? For example, if D goes to a supermarket to steal an item, she will have appropriated (and committed theft) at the first moment she comes into contact with the item. The fact that D is permitted by the shop to touch the item at this point (ie the shop consents) is irrelevant.

9.2.1.4 The bona fide purchaser exception

Section 3(2) of the TA 1968 creates an exception where no appropriation will be found. This arises where D purchases property in good faith (bona fide), believing that she is gaining full civil title, it then transpires that full title has not been transferred (eg because the goods were stolen), but D continues to treat the item as her own. In such a case, D appears to have assumed the rights of the owner and thus come within the definition of appropriation, however, this section prevents that from being the result in law.

---

[20] For an alternative view, that *Hinks* provides indirect protection for property rights, see Shute, 'Appropriation and the Law of Theft' [2002] Crim LR 445.

[21] Smith, 'Theft or Sharp Practice: Who Cares Now?' (2001) 60 CLJ 21.

[22] Gardner, 'Appropriation in Theft: The Last Word' (1993) 109 LQR 194.

It should be remembered that this exception only applies to property acquired by D for value, so it does not apply to gifts. Further, even though D is excused from theft by section 3(2), she remains potentially liable for handling stolen property,[23] and/or fraud if she presents herself as the owner (eg to sell the property to another).[24]

9.2.2 Property

For theft to be committed, D must have appropriated something legally recognised as 'property'. Unlike the definition of appropriation, the definition of property is generally not controversial. However, care must be taken to understand exactly what is included. Section 4 of the TA 1968 provides a general definition of property (founded on civil law concepts), and then lists specific exclusions relating to land, things growing wild, and wild creatures.

> 4(1) 'Property' includes money and all other property, real or personal, including things in action and other intangible property.

Before moving to consider the specific exceptions to this definition, its key terms require some unpacking:

A) **Real property** is a reference to land. Thus, subject to the specific exclusions discussed later, D can be liable for the theft of certain land rights.

B) **Personal property** is a reference to all property that is not land and that includes property that is illegal or prohibited. For example, D commits theft where she appropriates controlled drugs from V, even where they are illegally possessed by V.[25]

C) **Things in action** is a reference to a category of intangible property where D has the right to sue another for a particular sum. This is most commonly associated with bank accounts. Although we commonly refer to having 'money in the bank', this is, of course, not accurate: there is no specific pile of money in a bank belonging to any individual customer.[26] Rather, depositing money to a bank creates a form of intangible property, each customer's right to sue the bank for that specific sum. This property right is a 'thing in action'. Therefore, where D dishonestly causes the bank to transfer funds from V's account, D does not steal any physical money belonging to V, she steals a thing in action (ie she steals part of V's right to sue the bank for a sum of money).[27] The same is true where D has transferred money from V's overdraft.[28] The only exception in such cases is where D has transferred funds from V's account that V had no right to sue for (ie where V had no thing in action). This can arise where D has transferred funds in excess of V's overdraft, or where D takes from her own account in excess of her overdraft.[29]

---

[23] See **Chapter 9.5**.
[24] *Wheeler* (1990) 92 Cr App R 279.
[25] *Smith* [2011] EWCA Crim 66.
[26] Discussed in *Davenport* [1954] 1 All ER 602.
[27] *Chan Man-sin v AG for Hong Kong* [1988] 1 All ER 1.
[28] *Kohn* [1997] 2 Cr App R 445.
[29] *Hilton* (1979) 69 Cr App R 395; Griew, 'Stealing and Obtaining Bank Credits' [1986] Crim LR 356.

D) Other intangible property allows the definition of intangible property to extend beyond the most common things in action. An example can be seen in *AG of Hong Kong v Chan Nai-Keung*,[34] in which D, a director of company A and company B, sold export quotas from one company to the other at a gross undervalue. Although the export quotas did not represent a thing in action, they were held to constitute other intangible property and were therefore capable of being stolen.

An interesting problem of categorisation has emerged in relation to the stealing of cheques.[35] A cheque which is given by V for consideration creates a thing in action as it creates the right to sue V's bank for the specified sum. So if V is tricked, for example, into writing a cheque in D's favour, that creates a right for D to sue V's bank. However, on receipt of the cheque D has not taken V's right to sue, unlike electronic bank transfers discussed earlier. Instead, the thing in action which D has gained is property which has never belonged to V and cannot be the subject of theft.[36] What D gains is her own brand-new item of property—a right to sue V's bank. We could wait for a theft to arise when D presents the cheque and thereby causes a bank transfer so that V's bank account—a thing in action—is diminished. The problem is that D does not commit theft until she presents the cheque and causes the transfer, not allowing earlier intervention. Alternatively, we could focus on the cheque as a piece of paper (tangible property) and say that D stole that from the outset. However, as D does not intend to keep the paper, in fact she intends to present it to the bank, she does not satisfy a different offence element (intention to permanently deprive): so this cannot ground our case for theft either.[37] Our final option to find liability in theft[38] is to say

---

[30] [2018] EWCA Crim 1009.
[31] Discussed in **Chapter 10**.
[32] On innocent agents, see **Chapter 12.2.3**.
[33] Discussed in **Chapter 10.8.3**.
[34] [1987] 1 WLR 1339, exploring identical provisions in the law of Hong Kong.
[35] Smith, 'Obtaining Cheques by Deception or Theft' [1997] Crim LR 396.
[36] *Preddy* [1996] AC 815.
[37] *Graham* [1997] 1 Cr App R 302.
[38] D may commit fraud if she dishonestly induces V to write the cheque for her, see **Chapter 10**.

the cheque is a 'valuable security', a piece of property that creates or guarantees certain financial rights.[39] This approach has been accepted in Australia by the Supreme Court of Victoria[40] and, although not yet accepted in this jurisdiction, may well (and should) be followed in the future.

 Extra detail . . .

The decline in the use of cheques generally has made this problem less acute. However, the same issues can arise in relation to the stealing of paper tickets.

9.2.2.1 Exceptions

Section 4 provides specific exceptions to the definition of property:

Land (s4(2))

Where D takes V's land without severing it, she may have appropriated property within the civil law, but this will not constitute property for the purposes of theft.[41] For example, D moves her garden fence a few inches into V's garden.

Only certain specified land rights will amount to property within the offence of theft. First, section 4(2)(a) allows for theft of land by a trustee of property.

> 4(2)(a) when he is a trustee or personal representative, or is authorised by power of attorney, or as liquidator of a company, or otherwise, to sell or dispose of land belonging to another, and he appropriates the land or anything forming part of it by dealing with it in breach of the confidence reposed in him

Therefore, where D is the trustee of property and disposes of that property dishonestly for her own advantage, she may commit theft.[42]

Secondly, section 4(2)(b) allows for theft of land by D who severs part of that land, as long as D does not possess rights of ownership.[43]

> 4(2)(b) when he is not in possession of the land and appropriates anything forming part of the land by severing it or causing it to be severed, or after it has been severed

The fence moving example was not theft because D did not sever (remove) the part of V's land that she appropriated. Where there is such severance, however, these items will constitute property for the purposes of theft. For example, D takes some of V's topsoil, her plants, her garden shed, etc.

Thirdly, section 4(2)(c) allows for theft of land by a tenant who appropriates a fixture or structure from the land.

> 4(2)(c) when, being in possession of the land under a tenancy, he appropriates the whole or part of any fixture or structure let to be used with the land.

---

[39] *Arnold* [1997] 4 All ER 1.
[40] *Parsons* [1998] 2 VR 478.
[41] It was felt that civil remedies would be more appropriate to deal with cases of this kind.
[42] See *Gimbert* [2018] EWCA Crim 2190: D's appeal against conviction for theft of land was allowed as he was not a trustee of the property.
[43] This includes eg the children of a tenant.

Unlike D with no rights to the land, a tenant will not commit theft where she removes certain items such as topsoil. However, where she appropriates a fixture (eg bath, sink, etc) or a structure (eg garden shed, greenhouse, etc), these items will constitute property for theft. In such cases, simple appropriation is all that is required, there is no additional requirement for severance.

Wild mushrooms and flowers (s4(3))

The second exception, where items treated as property in civil law will not amount to property for the purposes of the TA 1968, relates to wild mushrooms and flowers. This is defined liberally to include all fungi, and any plant or tree.

> 4(3) A person who picks mushrooms growing wild on any land, or who picks flowers, fruit or foliage from a plant growing wild on any land, does not (although not in possession of the land) steal what he picks, unless he does it for reward or for sale or other commercial purpose.

As with land, this exception from the definition of property is also not absolute. Although D may *pick* 'flowers, fruit or foliage', if D takes or digs up the *whole plant*, that will still amount to property and may be theft. The exception also only applies to things growing wild, so cultivated flowers or fungus are not included. Finally, the exception only applies to those picking for non-commercial reasons.[44] Thus, where D picks berries to make jam for sale, she is picking property and may commit theft; where D is picking for her own use only, the berries are not property within the offence. How D makes use of the items picked is a useful indication of her intentions at the time of picking, but remember that it is her intention when picking (regardless of what happens later) that is crucial for coincidence and therefore liability. For example, if D picks berries to make jam for herself then she does not commit theft, even if she *later* decides to sell the jam.

Wild creatures (s4(4))

The final specified exception relates to wild creatures.

> 4(4) Wild creatures, tamed or untamed, shall be regarded as property; but a person cannot steal a wild creature not tamed nor ordinarily kept in captivity, or the carcase of any such creature, unless either it has been reduced into possession by or on behalf of another person and pos-session of it has not since been lost or abandoned, or another person is in course of reducing it into possession.

Note the caveats within this exception: non-wild creatures are to be treated as property, as are wild creatures that are killed or trapped (usually the property of the person who killed or trapped them). Thus, where D kills and removes a wild animal from V's land (eg a pheasant), whilst D may be guilty of a poaching offence,[45] she will not be guilty of theft. To keep a creature in 'captivity', thus making it property, requires more than the regular feeding of a wild creature, even if the eventual aim is to trap and/or kill the creature.[46]

---

[44] Welstead, 'Season of Mists and Mellow Fruitfulness' (1995) 145 NLJ 1499.
[45] Night Poaching Act 1828; Game Act 1831.
[46] *Cresswell v DPP* [2006] EWHC 3379 (Admin): involving the feeding of wild badgers.

Other common law exceptions

Alongside the TA 1968, the common law has developed further exemptions from the definition of property in theft. These include the following:

A) **Electricity:** Electricity is not property for the purposes of theft[47] but there is a separate offence within section 13 of the TA 1968 of wasting or diverting another's electricity.

B) **Confidential information:** Information does not amount to property within section 4.[48] In *Oxford v Moss*,[49] a university student who unlawfully acquired an examination paper, read and returned it, could not be liable for theft. There may be alternative offences under the Computer Misuse Act 1990, where the information is taken from a computer, and the Law Commission once provisionally proposed a new offence of misuse of trade secrets.[50] However, there is no theft in these cases.

C) **Services:** A service (eg a manicure, taxi journey, theatre performance, etc) is not property within section 4, and so failure to pay for a service is not theft. Such conduct is likely to be an offence of obtaining services dishonestly under section 11 of the Fraud Act 2006.

D) **Bodies:** Traditionally, human bodies and/or parts of bodies have not been classed as property within section 4.[51] However, this view is changing in certain areas. For example, it has been held that bodily products which are intended to be held or controlled can amount to property (eg urine samples,[52] sperm deposits,[53] etc). Stealing blood from a blood bank is therefore likely to constitute theft.

9.2.3 Belonging to another

The offence of theft is not designed simply to prevent D dishonestly assuming property rights (ie appropriating property), but to protect the ownership rights of *others*. Therefore, it is always essential to demonstrate that the property appropriated belonged to another at the point of appropriation. The general rule is set out in section 5(1) of the TA 1968.

> 5(1) Property shall be regarded as belonging to any person having possession or control of it, or having in it any proprietary right or interest (not being an equitable interest arising only from an agreement to transfer or grant an interest).

Before we explore the terms used within section 5, it should be highlighted that 'belonging to another' does not necessarily mean that V possessed exclusive ownership of the property appropriated. Having introduced the idea of multiple different ownership rights (**9.2.1.1**), it is important to recognise that D still appropriates V's property where V only possesses one of these rights. For example, V lends a book to X, X gives the book

---

[47] *Low v Blease* [1975] Crim LR 513.
[48] Christie, 'Should the Law of Theft Extend to Information?' (2005) 69 JCL 349; Davies, 'Protection of Intellectual Property—A Myth?' (2004) 68 JCL 398.
[49] (1978) 68 Cr App R 183.
[50] Law Commission, *Misuses of Trade Secrets* (Consultation 150, 1997).
[51] *Sharpe* (1857) D & B 160.
[52] *Welsh* [1974] RTR 550.
[53] *Yearworth v North Bristol NHS Trust* [2009] EWCA Civ 37.

to Z to hold, and D snatches the book from Z and makes off with it. Here, D appropriates property belonging to V (proprietary ownership), X (possession), and Z (control). Even if only one of these could be proved, D's charge for theft of property belonging to another would be satisfied. What matters is that someone has *some* proprietary right or interest which is appropriated by D.

9.2.3.1 'possession or control'

V has possession or control of property where she intends to control or possess it, and maintains some degree of control over it in fact. For example, the owners of a vending machine will possess the coins inside the machine even if they do not know the quantity; and a landowner will possess the contents of their buildings even if they are not aware of every item.[54] The question in each case, turning on civil law concepts, is whether V demonstrates a sufficient claim of possession. This is illustrated in *Rostron*.

Rostron [2003] EWCA Crim 2206

D and others trespassed onto a golf course at night, with diving apparatus, and took lost golf balls from a lake which was part of the course driving range. D was charged with theft of the balls.

• Crown Court: guilty of theft.

• Court of Appeal: conviction upheld on appeal. The jury were entitled to find that the balls belonged to the golf course. Although the course owners did not intend to collect the balls themselves, they still maintained possession and control over them.

An interesting problem emerges where D is the owner of the property and she takes it from another who has possession or control. Does D commit theft of her own property? The requirement of dishonesty (discussed later) makes theft in these circumstances very unlikely. However, it is now clear that where V legitimately maintains possession or control of D's property, a dishonest taking by D may amount to theft. This is illustrated in *Turner (No 2)*.

Turner (No 2) [1971] 2 All ER 441

D had his car repaired by V at a garage. On collecting his car, D used a spare set of keys to take his car without paying the bill. D was charged with theft of the car.

• Crown Court: guilty of theft.

• Court of Appeal: conviction upheld on appeal. The garage was in possession and control of the car and so, although D was the legal owner, he was still taking property that belonged to another (the garage).

The reasoning in *Turner (No 2)* was expressed too widely, indicating that appropriation in *all* such circumstances would amount to the taking of property belonging to another. This cannot be right. For example, if V snatches D's bag in the street and D takes it back, even though V takes brief control of the bag, D's re-taking is not a taking

---

[54] *Woodman* [1974] QB 754.

of property belonging to another: D has every right to take it back. This was recognised in *Meredith*, where D's dishonest appropriation of his car from a police compound was not theft.[55] *Turner (No 2)* does provide a useful illustration, however, of theft in circumstances where D does not have the right to demand his car be returned in civil law (until he pays the bill).

9.2.3.2 'proprietary interest'

Proprietary interests are determined by reference to civil law rules of ownership. In most cases ownership is clear, as with the owner of the book in our opening example. However, the civil law rules are not always straightforward, as illustrated in *Marshall*.[56]

 Marshall [1998] 2 Cr App R 282

D obtained part-used tickets from underground transport users and resold them. London Underground Ltd (V) claimed ownership of the part-used tickets, making D's reselling an appropriation of their property. D was charged with theft.

- Crown Court: guilty of theft.
- Court of Appeal: conviction upheld on appeal. The question was whether a clause on the back of the ticket stating V's continued ownership of the ticket was sufficiently clear to buyers. If yes, then it remained V's property in civil law, but if not, then V had no interest. The court found that the clause was sufficiently clear.

As with *Marshall*, decisions in this area may turn on the subtle rules of civil ownership. For example, property may be found to belong to the Crown if it comes within the rules of 'treasure',[57] property may belong (in equity) to beneficiaries of a trust,[58] property ownership may pass on contract despite V never receiving the goods,[59] and so on. Although identifying the proprietary interest may involve close scrutiny of civil rules, once such an interest is identified, it will always satisfy this element of theft. This will be the case even where D also has a proprietary interest in the property, as where one business partner takes all the value out of a corporate partnership.[60]

9.2.3.3 Specific examples within s5

Alongside the general definition of 'belonging to another' in section 5(1), further subsections go on to clarify certain potentially problematic examples:

A) **Section 5(2):** This subsection clarifies that where D, a trustee, dishonestly appropriates from that trust, she takes property of another. This is true where the trust has individual beneficiaries (overlapping with section 5(1)), as well as purpose trusts (eg charitable trusts) where others can enforce the trust.[61]

[55] [1973] Crim LR 253.
[56] Smith, 'Stealing Tickets' [1998] Crim LR 723.
[57] *Waverley Borough Council v Fletcher* [1995] 4 All ER 756: using a metal detector, D found a gold brooch on the council's land.
[58] *Clowes (No 2)* [1994] 2 All ER 316; Davies, 'After *R v Clowes No 2*' (1997) 61 JCL 99.
[59] *Rose v Matt* [1951] 1 KB 810.
[60] *Bonner* [1970] 1 WLR 838.
[61] *Dyke and Munro* [2002] Crim LR 153. In the context of charitable trusts, the AG has the right of enforcement.

Point to remember . . .

There is an obvious overlap with section 5(1) and (2) where the agreement between D and V creates a trust, or V retains equitable proprietary rights. In such a case, either provision may be used.[62]

B) Section 5(3): This subsection deals with property given to D for a particular purpose as, for example, where V provides D (her cleaner) with money to buy cleaning products. Even though the property is passed to D here, if she deals with it in an improper manner, for example keeping it for herself, this will constitute taking the property of another.

To come within section 5(3), D must be under a legal, as opposed to a merely moral, duty to deal with the property in a particular way. This is a question of law for the judge.[63] In the context of money, the question is often whether D was expected to use specific money for a specific purpose (s5(3) applies), or whether the money was a general payment to D in exchange for future conduct that may be paid for from other funds (s5(3) does not apply). For example, where a travel agent receives deposits for a trip, there is an expectation that the agent will organise and pay for the trip, but no expectation that they will do so with the particular monies provided. Thus, even where the company dishonestly fails to provide the trip or a refund there is no theft, although there is a breach of a civil/contractual obligation.[64] On the other side of this fine line are cases where D receives money in sponsorship, on the understanding that it will be passed to a relevant charity. These cases are now likely to fall within section 5(3): those sponsoring are not paying D, they expect her to pass that money to the charity.[65]

C) Section 5(4): This subsection applies where D receives property by mistake and is under an obligation to return it or its value, for example where D receives an overpayment of wages. Where D appropriates such property and refuses to make restoration, she takes the property of another, illustrated in *Gresham*.[66]

Gresham [2003] EWCA Crim 2070

D's mother died and yet D, who had power of attorney, did not inform her pension provider (V) who continued to make payments for 10 years. D used this money as his own. D was charged with theft.

- Crown Court: guilty of theft.
- Court of Appeal: conviction upheld on appeal.[67] D had a duty under section 5(4) to return the money to V, and so his use of it amounted to taking another's property.

---

[62] *Hallam* [1995] Crim LR 323.
[63] *Clowes (No 2)* [1994] 2 All ER 316.
[64] *Hall* [1972] All ER 1009.
[65] *Wain* [1995] 2 Cr App R 660.
[66] See also *AG's Reference (No 1 of 1983)* [1985] QB 182: theft of overpaid wages.
[67] Two of the 12 counts were overturned for lack of appropriation, but these are not relevant to the current discussion.

Where V mistakenly transfers property to D, this will *also* often result in V retaining some equitable proprietary ownership. In such cases, section 5(4) *and* (1) will apply.[68]

D) **Section 5(5):** This subsection clarifies that a legal person (a corporation) can own property. Therefore, if directors of a company dishonestly appropriate company property, for example, they are taking the property of another (the company).[69]

9.2.3.4 Abandonment by V

Where property owned by V is abandoned, it becomes ownerless, and therefore cannot be the subject of theft. It should be emphasised, however, that such abandonment is very rare: V must leave the property and be indifferent as to *any* future appropriation. For example, where V throws property into the bin, intending it to be collected and disposed of by authorised collectors, it is not abandoned; and D's taking of the property, where D is not an authorised collector, can amount to theft.[70] This is why in *Rostron* (discussed earlier), the golf course had not abandoned lost golf balls even though they had no intention of collecting the balls themselves. Other examples of *non*-abandonment include V who loses jewellery and gives up the search; and V who leaves property for a specific charity to collect.

9.2.3.5 The *Hinks* problem

The case of *Hinks*, discussed earlier (**9.2.1.3**), provides an interesting problem in relation to the requirement that the property must belong to another. It will be remembered that *Hinks* involved money being given to D by V, who was a vulnerable adult. These payments were dishonestly received, but nevertheless, crucially, represented valid gifts in civil law. Thus, at the moment the property was passed to D, D gained exclusive ownership rights. The question arises whether, at the moment of appropriation, the property belonged to D or V? If it belonged to D then there is no appropriation of another's property—no coincidence in time—and, therefore, no theft.

In *Hinks*, this point was given little consideration and the property was assumed to belong to V at the moment of transfer. This is a useful indication that, when appropriation and the passing of property ownership are simultaneous, the courts will take a permissive approach to potential problems of coincidence. However, facts could arise that test such indulgence. For example, what if V in *Hinks* had sent the money to D by post, with D only appropriating it when later picking up her mail inside her house. In such a case, if the money is a valid gift, then when it sits in D's house it is entirely her property: thus, her appropriation of it could not, surely, be theft.

9.2.4 Intention permanently to deprive

The next major element of theft is the requirement that when appropriating the property of another, D did so with an intention permanently to deprive V of it. Section 1(2) of the TA 1968 explicitly clarifies that theft need not be for D's benefit, so this element includes an intention to give V's property to another. However, V must be deprived of her property, and, D must intend that deprivation to be permanent.

---

[68] *Shadrokh-Cigari* [1988] Crim LR 465; McCormack, 'Mistaken Payments and Proprietary Claims' [1996] Conv 86.
[69] *A v Snaresbrook Crown Court* (2001) 165 JPN 495.
[70] *Williams v Phillips* (1957) 121 JP 163.

The requirement of an intention permanently to deprive is an ulterior mens rea element:[71] whether D permanently deprives V in fact is irrelevant, the prosecution only need demonstrate an intention. D's conduct after the appropriation, whether she returns the property and/or how she deals with it, is only relevant insofar as it provides evidence of D's intention at the moment of appropriation. For example, if D dishonestly takes V's watch intending to keep it, but later discovers the sentimental value of the watch to V and returns it, she still commits theft: all the elements of the offence coincided at the moment of appropriation. Conversely, where D takes the watch intending to return it, but later loses it or changes her mind, there was no theft at the moment the watch was taken.[72]

 Assessment matters . . .

In an assessment it is very easy to slip up when applying this element by focussing on whether D has permanently deprived V or not. Remember, *all* discussion of this element should be focussed on D's intentions at the point of appropriation only.

9.2.4.1 TA 1968, s6(1): extensions

Section 6(1) of the TA 1968 sets out a broad, and not entirely clear,[73] definition of what it means to intend to permanently deprive.

> 6(1) A person appropriating property belonging to another without meaning the other permanently to lose the thing itself is nevertheless to be regarded as having the intention of permanently depriving the other of it if his intention is to treat the thing as his own to dispose of regardless of the other's rights; and a borrowing or lending of it may amount to so treating it if, but only if, the borrowing or lending is for a period and in circumstances making it equivalent to an outright taking or disposal.

Several areas of uncertainty have arisen in the application of this section, and it is useful to trace how the courts have responded to them:

A) **Intention to ransom or sell property back to V:** Where D appropriates V's property with the intention of selling it back, or ransoming it to V, it is arguable that D does not intend *permanently* to deprive V of it. However, not surprisingly, the courts have consistently held such conduct to be caught by section 6(1): D intends to treat the property as her own, and this is equivalent to an intention to take outright.[74] The same principle applies, for example, where D steals a ticket from a theatre, intending to return the ticket only when granted entry to the theatre (ie only when the theatre provides consideration).

B) **Intention to replace with identical property:** Where D takes V's property intending to keep it, her intention to deprive V permanently is not undermined by an intention to replace the property with an identical equivalent. This applies to any property.

---

[71] See **Chapter 4.2.1.2**.

[72] Prosecution for theft here would rely on finding a second appropriation when D decides to keep the watch.

[73] Spencer, 'The Metamorphosis of Section 6 of the Theft Act' [1977] Crim LR 653.

[74] *Raphael* [2008] EWCA Crim 1014: D stole V's car and then offered to sell it back.

For example, if D takes a celebrity's sunglasses and replaces them with an identical pair, D has intended to deprive V permanently of the sunglasses. Importantly, and somewhat controversially, the rule also applies to money. For example, D takes money from a till at work, intending to replace it the following day with equivalent money, albeit not exactly the same notes or coins taken. This is discussed in *Velumyl*.

Velumyl [1989] Crim LR 299

D, an employee, took money from the company safe, intending to return it after the weekend. D was charged with theft.

• Crown Court: guilty of theft.
• Court of Appeal: conviction upheld on appeal. D did not intend to return the exact notes or coins taken, so he must have intended to permanently deprive his employers of them.

It should be noted that although liability was found in *Velumyl*, many cases of this kind will fail for lack of dishonesty (discussed later). It is an odd principle for the criminal law to adopt given the fungibility of cash (ie one note or coin can usually be substituted for another in law).

C) **Intention to remove value from the property:** If D's intention is to take property and return it to V with *all* its value removed, then there is, straightforwardly, an intention permanently to deprive. For example, D returns an animal after killing it; a car after setting it on fire; a sports season ticket at the end of the season; etc. Such conduct may be described, within section 6(1), as borrowing equivalent to an outright taking or disposal.[75] However, as illustrated in *Lloyd*, difficult questions of degree emerge where D intends only to take *some* of the value from V's property.

Lloyd [1985] 3 WLR 30

D, who worked as a cinema projectionist, appropriated films with the intention of making illegal copies to sell elsewhere, but to return the originals. D was charged with theft.

• Crown Court: guilty of theft.
• Court of Appeal: appeal allowed. D's intention was merely to remove some of the value from the films, and was not sufficient to be equivalent to an outright taking.

Each case will turn on its facts. Where, for example, D intends to return the sporting season ticket halfway through the season, or the car when damaged but not destroyed, the question for the court will be one of degree: did D's intended conduct amount to an intention to remove sufficient value to be equivalent to an outright taking?

D) **Intention to abandon the property:** There will be clear cases where an intention to abandon V's property will amount to an intention to dispose of it, as where D intends to throw V's pin into a haystack. However, where D's intended abandonment may allow V to regain her property, the question is again one of degree. This is illustrated in *Mitchell*.

[75] *DPP v J* [2002] EWHC 291 (Admin): intention to return headphones after breaking them.

Mitchell [2008] EWCA Crim 850

D and three others forcibly took V's car, having crashed their own, whilst attempting to escape from the police. The car, largely undamaged, was later abandoned on the road with its hazard lights on. D was charged with robbery, which requires D to have committed theft.

- Crown Court: guilty of robbery.
- Court of Appeal: appeal allowed. The circumstances of the intended abandonment made it likely that the car would be returned to V and thus did not indicate an intention to permanently deprive.

The question in each case will focus on how D *intended* to abandon the property at the moment of appropriation.

E) Conditional intentions: This final problem case emerges where D appropriates property with a conditional intention to permanently deprive V of it. Examples include intention to keep V's jewellery only if the stones are genuine; to keep V's season ticket only if the team keeps winning; etc. Despite doubt created by early case law,[76] it is now clear that D's conditional intention will constitute a valid intention, confirmed in *AG's References (Nos 1 and 2 of 1979)*.

 AG's References (Nos 1 and 2 of 1979) [1980] QB 180

Combined cases involving Ds who were arrested whilst trying to break into buildings. Both were charged with burglary, requiring an intention to steal.

- Crown Court: not guilty of burglary, a conditional intention to steal (if there was anything worth taking) is insufficient.
- Court of Appeal: the Crown Court was wrong: both Ds had an intention to steal, even if they had no specific property in mind. The court explicitly extended its judgment to standard theft cases.

The older case of *Easom* provides useful facts to explain how the current law should be applied. In that case, D picked up a woman's handbag and looked through it for valuables, but then replaced it having taken nothing. D's conviction for theft of the handbag and its contents was quashed because D's conditional intention was deemed insufficient for liability. Following *AG's References (Nos 1 and 2 of 1979)*, there remains no theft of the bag: D never intended (even conditionally) permanently to deprive V of the bag. There will, however, be theft of the bag's contents: although D decided not to keep the contents because of their lack of value, he still appropriated them with the conditional intention of keeping them had they been valuable. If the bag had been empty, there would be no property for D to intend conditionally permanently to deprive, and therefore no theft. There would, however, be liability for attempted theft.[77]

9.2.4.2 TA 1968, s6(2): intention to risk the property

Although most borderline issues within section 6 have been left to the common law, one area has been clarified by section 6(2) of the TA 1968.

---

[76] *Easom* [1971] 2 QB 315; *Husseyn* (1977) 67 Cr App R 131.
[77] See **Chapter 11.2**.

6(2) Without prejudice to the generality of subsection (1) above, where a person, having possession or control (lawfully or not) of property belonging to another, parts with the property under a condition as to its return which he may not be able to perform, this (if done for purposes of his own and without the other's authority) amounts to treating the property as his own to dispose of regardless of the other's rights.

This subsection makes clear that where D intends to part with V's property and cannot be sure of its return, her intention amounts to an intention permanently to deprive. For example, where D intends to risk V's money by gambling with it, or pawning it in circumstances where she is not positive of its return, her intention amounts to an intention permanently to deprive even if she hopes to be successful and give the property back.[78]

9.2.5 Dishonesty

The final element of theft is the requirement of dishonesty. D must appropriate property belonging to another, with the intention permanently to deprive V of it, and that appropriation must be dishonest. With many of the other elements of theft being interpreted widely by the courts, and potentially applying to apparently innocent conduct, the role of dishonesty is crucial in narrowing the offence to its target mischief only. Unfortunately, despite its importance, dishonesty is not defined in the TA 1968. Rather, section 2 provides three situational examples where D is *not* dishonest. These will always be the starting point for a discussion of dishonesty: if the case comes within one of the examples then the discussion stops there—there is no dishonesty and therefore there is no theft.

9.2.5.1 Statutory examples of no dishonesty

The first situation applies to cases where D believed she had a legal right to the property she appropriated (s2(1)).

2(1)(a) if he appropriates the property in the belief that he has in law the right to deprive the other of it, on behalf of himself or of a third person;

D's belief need not be reasonable,[79] and it does not have to be based on an accurate understanding of the law.[80] As long as D *honestly* believed she had a legal (and not merely moral) right to the property, she will not be dishonest. Most commonly, this will arise where D takes V's property believing that it is hers as, for example, where D takes the wrong umbrella when leaving a restaurant.

The second example applies where D believed that V would have consented to the appropriation (s2(1)).

2(1)(b) if he appropriates the property in the belief that he would have the other's consent if the other knew of the appropriation and the circumstances of it;

Again, D's belief need not be accurate or reasonable. As long as D honestly believed at the time of appropriation that V would have consented, then her conduct is not dishonest. Circumstances of this type are common, for example with family or friends using each other's property in the belief that the other would consent.

---

[78] *Fernandes* [1996] 1 Cr App R 175.
[79] *Terry* [2001] EWCA Crim 2979.
[80] *Bernhard* [1938] 2 KB 264.

The final example applies where D appropriates property believing that the owner is undiscoverable (s2(1)).

> 2(1)(c) (except where the property came to him as trustee or personal representative) if he appropriates the property in the belief that the person to whom the property belongs cannot be discovered by taking reasonable steps.

This example is intended to deal with those who discover seemingly abandoned property. D is not dishonest if she appropriates that property, as long as she honestly (though not necessarily reasonably) believes that the owner cannot be found using reasonable steps. Note here that believing an owner cannot be found using *reasonable* steps is not the same as believing it is impossible to find them. For example, D may believe she could find the owner of a watch if she spent weeks searching and paid for television adverts, but this is clearly more than would be reasonable to expect of her. The value of the property will thereby affect what constitutes reasonable steps in each case.[81]

As the subsection makes clear, this example does not apply to trustees and trust property. Here D must rely on one of the other examples, or the general common law definition of dishonesty.

 Point to remember ...

Section 2(2) clarifies that D may be dishonest even where she pays for the property. This is necessary to accommodate situations such as D taking her neighbour's barbeque on a hot day, but leaving some money to compensate. The subsection only provides that D 'may' be dishonest in such cases, however, so the common law definition must be applied.

9.2.5.2 Common law definition of dishonesty

In the absence of a statutory definition of what dishonest *is*, much has been left to the common law. In this regard, courts will often leave dishonesty undefined.[82] For example, where D accepts that the conduct would be dishonest but denies the conduct;[83] or D accepts that she performed apparently dishonest conduct but claims to have done so absent-mindedly (ie so the question is whether we believe her).[84] Where dishonesty is at issue, however, a definition has been required.

Following some initial uncertainty, the definition of dishonesty was settled by the Court of Appeal in *Ghosh*,[85] which (despite academic criticism[86]) was applied consistently for 35 years. However, in 2017, the Supreme Court revised the *Ghosh* test in the new leading case of *Ivey*.[87]

---

[81] *Sylvester* (1985) CO/559/84: D unsuccessfully raised s2(1)(c) in relation to a car he was stripping for parts.

[82] *Roberts* (1985) 84 Cr App R 177.

[83] *Cobb* [2005] EWCA Crim 1549: D denied taking money from a till.

[84] *Atkinson* [2004] Crim LR 226.

[85] [1982] QB 1053.

[86] See eg Griew, 'Dishonesty—The Objections to *Feely* and *Ghosh*' [1985] Crim LR 341.

[87] See commentary from Laird [2018] Crim LR 395. See also Griffiths, 'The Honest Cheat' (2020) 40(2) LS 252, discussing *Ivey* in the context of historical interpretations of dishonesty.

Ivey v Genting Casinos Ltd [2017] UKSC 67

D (a professional gambler) made a civil claim against X (a casino) for withheld winnings. D used a technique called 'edge-sorting' to improve his odds of winning a card game: asking the casino dealer to turn 'bad' cards differently from 'lucky' cards, noting the minor printing imperfections on the back of the cards, and thereby distinguishing such cards in subsequent games. D won £7.7 million. D admitted edge-sorting, but denied this was cheating. The casino refused to pay and D brought an action for breach of contract. The casino argued that there was a breach of the implied contractual term not to cheat.

- High Court: rejecting D's claim—edge-sorting for this game is cheating.

- Court of Appeal: dismissing D's appeal.

- Supreme Court: dismissing D's appeal. In a unanimous judgment delivered by Lord Hughes, the court confirmed that D's conduct was cheating; and dishonest in civil law. Crucially, the court also found (*obiter*) that the civil and criminal definitions of dishonesty should be interpreted consistently. Replacing *Ghosh*, juries should be directed to answer the following: (a) What was the actual state of D's knowledge or belief as to the facts? (b) In the context of (a), was D's conduct dishonest by the standards of ordinary decent people?

Although *Ivey* involved a civil law dispute, the test set out for dishonesty was clearly intended to apply to future criminal cases,[88] and has been confirmed by the criminal courts,[89] including a specially constituted five-member Court of Appeal in *Barton*.[90] It is usefully analysed and applied across two steps:[91]

Step 1: What was the actual state of D's knowledge or belief as to the facts? This first step is subjective, and focusses on the mind of D. The issue here is not whether D believes her conduct is honest or dishonest; the court in *Ivey* make clear that assessments of this kind are not determinative to the definition of dishonesty. This is consistent with the pre-*Ivey* case *Hayes*.

Hayes [2015] EWCA Crim 1944

D, a banker, manipulated banking investment rates (LIBOR rates) to benefit his company. D admitted his conduct, but later claimed that it was not dishonest because it was widely condoned and even encouraged within the industry at that time. D was charged with conspiracy to defraud, an offence requiring dishonesty.

- Crown Court: guilty of conspiracy to defraud. Different personal standards, or within specific industries, are not relevant to the objective standard of dishonesty.

- Court of Appeal: conviction upheld on appeal. Confirming the judgment of the lower court, it was clarified (at [30]) that 'honesty is determined by objective standards of honest and reasonable people; persons are not free to set their own standards'.

---

[88] At [74].

[89] See *DPP v Patterson* [2017] EWHC 2820 (Admin), [16]; *Pabon* [2018] EWCA Crim 420.

[90] [2020] EWCA Crim 575.

[91] For the practical implications of the *Barton* decision see Ormerod and Laird [2020] *Archbold Review* (6), available at www.archbolde-update.co.uk/PDF/2020/Archbold%20Review%20Issue%206%20PRESS.pdf.

Despite this, however, D may hold (or lack) certain knowledge or belief that is relevant to an assessment of her conduct. The court in *Ivey* gives the example of a tourist who comes from a country where public transport is free, and reasonably believes that it is free in the UK as well. This reasonably held belief can and should influence a jury's evaluation of D's conduct (eg when boarding public transport without paying) under the second objective step.[92]

Step 2: In the context of step 1 knowledge and beliefs, was D's conduct dishonest by the standards of ordinary decent people? This second step is objective, and now the primary focus of the dishonesty test. Taking account of D's knowledge and beliefs, the jury must assess D's conduct against a societal standard of dishonesty; a standard that is assumed as common knowledge rather than further defined. The appeal and reliance upon a common understanding of dishonesty is not new to *Ivey*, having played a central role within the previous *Ghosh* definition. However, it is an assumption that has been cogently criticised, with academics highlighting the lack of common understanding in practice, and the resulting risk of inconsistent application.[93] Post-*Ivey*, this remains a fundamental problem with the test for dishonesty.

Extra detail . . .

How does the *Ivey/Barton* test differ from the old test in *Ghosh*? The precise nature and extent of change from *Ghosh* to *Ivey* has given rise to debate.[94] Most importantly, whereas *Ivey/Barton* asks us to assess D's conduct in light of her knowledge and beliefs, *Ghosh* was formulated to assess the dishonesty of D's conduct *and then* to ask if D knew her conduct was dishonest by the standards of reasonable people. Asking whether D knew her conduct was dishonest (per *Ghosh*) was intended to deal with examples such as the ill-informed tourist using public transport discussed earlier. However, a concern, highlighted again in *Ivey*, was that *Ghosh* could allow those with a warped sense of dishonesty to avoid liability. Taking a common Robin Hood example, a jury applying *Ghosh* could find dishonesty where Robin (despite belief in his cause) understood that robbing from the rich was dishonest by reasonable standards, but could not find dishonesty where Robin believed that all right-minded people would agree with him.[95] *Ivey* resolves this potential problem by removing the requirement for D to know her conduct is dishonest; simply assessing D's conduct in light of relevant knowledge and beliefs. Although this might be thought a useful change, it is perhaps unfortunate that the court in *Ivey* were so exercised by this theoretical problem with *Ghosh*, and yet the demonstrable problem of basing the test upon an assumed common understanding of dishonesty was left unresolved.[96]

---

[92] At [60].

[93] See Norrie, *Crime, Reason and History* (2014) 42; Griew, 'Dishonesty—The Objections to *Feely and Ghosh*' [1985] Crim LR 341.

[94] See eg Laird [2018] Crim LR 395; Laird and Ormerod, '*Ivey v Genting Casinos*—Much Ado About Nothing?' in Clarry (ed), *Supreme Court Yearbook* (2019); Virgo, 'Cheating and Dishonesty' (2018) 77 CLJ 18; Dyson and Jarvis, 'Poison *Ivey* or Herbal Tea Leaf?' (2018) 134 LQR 198.

[95] Instead of Robin Hood, we might consider environmental protesters taking GM crops; peace protesters taking property from military bases; and so on.

[96] Lord Hughes sets out other criticisms of *Ghosh* (at [53]), including that juries find it puzzling to apply; it was inconsistent with the definition of dishonesty at civil law; it represented a significant departure from the pre-TA 1968 position; and was not compelled by previous authority. However, the weight of such criticisms may be questioned, particularly given the long-standing application of *Ghosh* without common law or legislative amendment.

Definitions of dishonesty have always required an evaluation of D's conduct as well as her subjective beliefs, but the test in *Ivey* has taken this considerably further. The new test for dishonesty may note D's subjective knowledge and beliefs within step 1, but it is the second objective step evaluating her conduct that is now determinative. By subordinating D's subjective beliefs in this way (ie by not requiring D to be aware others would think her conduct dishonest), it is likely that prosecutions will become more straightforward, particularly of corporate defendants.[97] However, subjective mens rea is generally vital for criminal offences to ensure culpability, to ensure that the law punishes a blameworthy choice.[98] The *Ivey/Barton* test runs contrary to this principle of criminalisation: if D's conduct is judged dishonest, the fact that she chose to act believing her conduct was honest is now irrelevant. It should be remembered that this change in the law has come about through *obiter* statements in a civil law case (without thorough review of the criminal context); despite parliamentary endorsement of the old *Ghosh* test, which has been assumed as the standard in subsequent legislation; and despite the unresolved uncertainty of the objective measure.

9.3 Robbery

Robbery is defined in section 8(1) of the TA 1968. The maximum sentence on indictment is life imprisonment.[99]

> 8(1) A person is guilty of robbery if he steals, and immediately before or at the time of doing so, and in order to do so, he uses force on any person or puts or seeks to put any person in fear of being then and there subjected to force.

The elements of robbery are set out in **Table 9.2**.

Table 9.2 Robbery

	Actus reus	**Mens rea**
Conduct element	Any conduct causing the results	Voluntary
Circumstance element	What is appropriated is property	Knowledge
	What is appropriated is property belonging to another	Knowledge
	D's appropriation is dishonest	In context of D's knowledge and belief

---

[97] See Laird and Ormerod, '*Ivey v Genting Casinos*—Much Ado About Nothing?' in Clarry (ed), *Supreme Court Yearbook* (2019).

[98] See **Chapter 3.1.2**.

[99] TA 1968, s8(2).

Result element	D appropriates the property (D uses unlawful force against another, or causes another to apprehend immediate unlawful force)	Intention Intention or recklessness
Ulterior mens rea element	*	Intention permanently to deprive V of her property Intention that force or threat of force will facilitate the theft (Where D does not use or cause another to apprehend unlawful force, she may still be liable if seeking to make another so apprehend)

The elements of robbery are more simply illustrated in **Figure 9.2**.

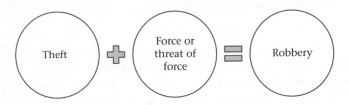

Figure 9.2 Robbery

9.3.1 Theft

D must commit theft as an essential part of the offence of robbery.[100] If D does not commit theft because any of element of theft (**9.2**) is absent then D does not commit robbery. Where there is unlawful force but no theft, D may still be liable for an offence against the person,[101] or for an offence of assault with intent to rob,[102] but not robbery.

9.3.2 Force or the threat of force

The requirement of 'force' can be satisfied in any one of three ways: actual application of force; causing an apprehension that force will be used; and/or seeking to cause the apprehension that force will be used. We discuss each in turn.

---

[100] *Guy* (1990) 93 Cr App R 108.
[101] **Chapter 7.**
[102] TA 1968, s8(2).

Point to remember . . .

The requirement of force or threat of force shares several similarities with the offences of assault and battery.[103] However, as we will see, these similarities are not complete, and so the requirement of force within robbery should not be equated with assault and battery.

9.3.2.1 Force

Most straightforward cases of robbery will involve D using force against V in the course of theft. Such force must be against V's body and not simply against V's property. It must be more than negligible, but need not be serious.[104] For example, minor bodily contact when picking V's pocket will not satisfy this element,[105] but any pushing or shoving of V is likely to do so.[106] This is illustrated in *P v DPP*.

 P v DPP [2012] EWHC 1657 (Admin)

D snatched a lit cigarette from V's hand. No contact was made with V. D was charged with robbery.

- Youth Court: guilty of robbery.
- High Court: appeal allowed, and conviction for theft substituted. D's snatching of the cigarette did not amount to sufficient 'force' to satisfy robbery.

D's appeal was allowed in *P v DPP* because of a lack of sufficient force, not because of the lack of direct bodily contact. It has been recognised for some time that although force against another's body is required, such force may be indirect. For example, where D wrenches a shopping basket or a handbag from V's grip, causing force to be applied despite the lack of direct physical contact, robbery may be found.[107]

9.3.2.2 Fear of force

Section 8 describes putting V in 'fear' of being subjected to force. However, the term 'fear' is problematic to the extent that it suggests something beyond the apprehension of force. It would not be desirable, for example, for D's liability to depend on the robustness or bravery of V. Therefore, courts have interpreted 'fear' as the apprehension that force will be used.[108]

V must be caused to apprehend that force will be used 'then and there'. Thus, there was no robbery in *Khan*[109] where V handed money to D fearing that if he did not do so D would be in trouble with a third party (X), and that D may return and use force against

---

[103] Offences of assault and battery are discussed in **Chapter 7.2**.

[104] It has been argued that different levels of force should lead to different levels of liability: Ashworth, 'Robbery Reassessed' [2002] Crim LR 851.

[105] *Monaghan and Monaghan* [2000] 1 Cr App R 6: pickpocketing and 'jostling' charged as theft.

[106] *Dawson* (1976) 64 Cr App R 170: theft and a 'nudge' charged as robbery.

[107] *Clouden* [1987] Crim LR 56; *Symons* [2009] EWCA Crim 83.

[108] *R v DPP* [2007] EWHC 739 (Admin): robbery despite evidence from V that he was not afraid.

[109] [2001] EWCA Crim 923.

V. The apprehension here was of future not present force. Where D threatens that force will be used in the future to gain V's property, the appropriate charge is blackmail.[110]

9.3.2.3 Seeking fear of force

D can alternatively satisfy this element of robbery if she 'seeks' to put V in fear of force. Even where D does not use force against V, or cause V to apprehend the use of force (both actus reus), D may still be liable if she acts with the intention to cause V to so apprehend (ulterior mens rea).[111] For example, robbery will be committed if D uses a fake gun to threaten V and take property, even if V realises the gun is fake.

Point to remember . . .

Where D causes another to apprehend force, or seeks to do so, the person threatened must be aware of it. For example, where D threatens V directly, or where D threatens V's family member X whilst X is present, robbery may be committed. However, where D threatens V that she will attack one of V's family, and that family member is not present and not aware of the threat, robbery is not committed.[112]

9.3.3 Link between theft and force

Links are required between theft and force (eg an offence against the person) to turn two separate offences into a single robbery. A link in terms of victim/target is *not* required: it is not necessary for force to be used against the owner of the property stolen (eg there will be robbery where D overpowers a security guard of shop A to prevent her seeing and reporting D's thefts from shop B). Links are required, however, in terms of time and intention:

A) **Temporal link:** Section 8 states that the force must be 'immediately before' or 'at the time of' the theft. This means that there is no robbery where there is a large time gap between the two. However, a common-sense application of the law, as in *Hale*, allows some minor gaps in time, even where the force comes after the act of appropriation.

Hale (1978) 68 Cr App R 415

D1 and D2 broke into V's house. Whilst D1 stole V's jewellery, D2 tied V up. D1 and D2 were charged with robbery.

- Crown Court: guilty of robbery.
- Court of Appeal: convictions upheld on appeal. Even if the appropriation by D1 might have occurred fractionally before the force used by D2, the act of theft can be interpreted as a continuing act. The elements of robbery therefore coincided in time.

Just as the courts have interpreted the 'act' of theft broadly to find that the elements coincide in time, the same has been true of the element of 'force', particularly in threat

---

[110] See **Chapter 9.6**.
[111] *Tennant* [1976] Crim LR 133.
[112] *Taylor* [1996] 10 Arch News 2.

of force cases. For example, there will be robbery where D threatens V on day one and then takes property from V on day two, knowing that the threat is still operating on V (ie when approached on day two, V may fear immediate force if she refuses because of the earlier threat).[113]

B) **Intentional link:** D must use the force 'in order to' steal. Therefore, accidental infliction of force during a theft is not robbery. Indeed, where D assaults V with no intention to steal, but then takes the opportunity to remove V's property, there is no robbery. There may be a theft and an assault in such a case, but there is no intentional link between them.[114]

9.4 Burglary

The offence of burglary is set out in section 9 of the TA 1968. The maximum sentence on indictment is 10 years' imprisonment, or 14 years where the burglary takes place in a dwelling.[115]

9(1) A person is guilty of burglary if—

   (a) he enters any building or part of a building as a trespasser and with intent to commit any such offence as is mentioned in subsection (2) below; or

   (b) having entered any building or part of a building as a trespasser he steals or attempts to steal anything in the building or that part of it or inflicts or attempts to inflict on any person therein any grievous bodily harm.

(2) The offences referred to in subsection (1)(a) above are offences of stealing anything in the building or part of a building in question, of inflicting on any person therein any grievous bodily harm therein, and of doing unlawful damage to the building or anything therein.

The offence of burglary is more complex than its common (mis)understanding as simply breaking and entering to commit theft. In fact, the offence is best understood by splitting it into two separate offences, both leading to conviction for burglary. The first offence is set out in section 9(1)(a); the second in section 9(1)(b).

9.4.1 TA 1968, s9(1)(a): burglary by trespassing with intent

Section 9(1)(a) creates an inchoate offence: targeting D who trespasses with *intent* to commit theft, cause GBH, or commit criminal damage. D is liable at the point of entry provided she has the requisite intent. Whether she goes on to commit the intended future offence is irrelevant to her liability under this subsection. As with other inchoate offences,[116] the rationale for this offence is to facilitate early intervention by the police, imposing liability *before* the harms associated with theft, GBH, or criminal damage have come about. The offence is set out in **Table 9.3.**

---

[113] *Donaghy and Marshall* [1981] Crim LR 644.

[114] *James* [1997] Crim LR 598.

[115] TA 1968, s9(3). On the meaning of 'dwelling', see *Hudson v CPS* [2017] EWHC 841 (Admin); [2017] Crim LR 703; Laird, 'Conceptualising the Interpretation of "Dwelling" in Section 9 of the Theft Act 1968' [2013] Crim LR 656.

[116] See **Chapter 11.**

Table 9.3 Burglary: TA 1968, s9(1)(a)

	Actus reus	**Mens rea**
Conduct element	Any conduct causing the results	Voluntary
Circumstance element	D is a trespasser	Intention/knowledge or recklessness
Result element	Entry into a building or part of a building	Intention
Ulterior mens rea element	*	Intent to commit theft; cause GBH; or commit criminal damage

9.4.1.1 Actus reus of s9(1)(a) burglary

The actus reus of section 9(1)(a) burglary is deceptively simple: entry to a building, or part of a building, as a trespasser. However, within this, areas of complication have arisen:

A) **Entry:** D 'enters' a building, or part of a building, if any part of her person crosses the threshold. In the case of *Collins*,[117] discussed in the following section, Edmund Davies LJ said that entry must be 'effective and substantial'. However, such terms are not useful, as they erroneously suggest that D must have fully entered or that her entry must be such that she could commit the intended offence. As illustrated in *Ryan*, such a degree of entry is not required.[118]

> *Ryan* [1996] Crim LR 320
>
> D attempted to break into V's house but became wedged in the kitchen window with his arm and head inside the building. D was charged with section 9(1)(a) burglary.
>
> • Crown Court: guilty of burglary.
> • Court of Appeal: conviction upheld on appeal. Although most of D's body was not inside the building, and although he was not in a position to commit the intended offence, the jury were still entitled to find a valid entry.

Under the (pre-1968) common law, entry could also be found indirectly as where D used an instrument such as a long hook rather than her body to enter the building. It is uncertain whether such conduct could constitute entry under the current law, and there is no authority directly on this point. In such cases, where D uses the instrument to commit

---

[117] [1973] QB 100.
[118] See also *Brown* [1985] Crim LR 212: entry where D stood outside a shop, but was reaching through a window.

the intended offence (eg theft), it is better to charge that intended offence rather than burglary, or an attempt of the intended offence where it is not carried out.[119]

B) Building or part of a building: The word 'building' is given its ordinary meaning by the courts.[120] However, a judge must still advise the jury whether the structure entered by D is capable of being found to be a building. This is not always straightforward. A typical house is clearly a building whether occupied or not, as are work buildings; outhouses; sheds; and so on. The term has been interpreted broadly to include part-built or damaged structures, as well as semi-permanent containers.[121] Section 9(4) also extends the term to include 'inhabited' vehicles or vessels whether occupied or not, which includes caravans, houseboats, and so on. However, where the vehicle or vessel is not inhabited, or the structure is insufficiently permanent (eg a tent), a court may find that there is no building and therefore no burglary.[122]

 Don't be confused . . .

The orthodox interpretation of a 'building' includes the entire structure. Where D breaks into Flat 1 in order to gain access to Flat 2 to commit theft, D commits section 9(1)(a) burglary at the point of entry to the building that houses the two flats (we do not have to wait until she enters Flat 2).[123]

Reference to 'part of a building' is included to deal with cases where D has permission to enter the building (eg the shop) but not into certain areas (eg behind the counter).[124] Where such areas constitute 'part of a building', D may be liable under section 9(1)(a) for entering them as a trespasser with the required mens rea. As with the definition of 'building', there are core examples such as separate rooms within a house or hotel; behind a shop counter; etc, but there will also be uncertainty, as with a roped-off area within a shop.[125]

C) As a trespasser: Where D enters a building without permission from the owner or possessor, or the owner or possessor's family, or some other legal authorisation,[126] she enters as a trespasser. Trespass is a concept from the law of tort, but its definition in the criminal law need not be identical to that in tort.[127] Whether D is a trespasser will usually be clear, but two cases should be highlighted. First, where V mistakenly permits D to enter (eg V thinks D is the plumber), D enters as a trespasser.[128] Secondly, where D enters in excess of her permission, she is also trespassing. This is illustrated in *Jones and Smith*.

---

[119] See **Chapter 11.2.**
[120] *Brutus v Cozens* [1973] AC 854.
[121] *B & S v Leathley* [1979] Crim LR 314: a freezer container disconnected from its chassis could be a building.
[122] *Norfolk Constabulary v Seekings and Gould* [1986] Crim LR 167: a freezer container that was still connected to its chassis was a (non-inhabited) vehicle and not a building.
[123] *Headley v Webb* [1901] 2 Ch 126: two semi-detached houses can constitute a single building.
[124] *Walkington* [1979] 2 All ER 716: D trespassed behind a shop counter.
[125] Discussed in *Walkington*. Where the barrier is clear, it is likely to create a separate part of the building.
[126] eg police entering property with a warrant.
[127] *Collins* [1973] QB 100.
[128] Ibid.

Jones and Smith [1976] 3 All ER 54

D and another entered D's father's house, at night, with the intention to steal. D had a general permission to enter, but not for the purposes of stealing. D was charged with burglary.

• Crown Court: guilty of burglary.

• Court of Appeal: conviction upheld on appeal. D entered the building in excess of the general permission given by his father, thus as a trespasser.

The logical conclusion from this is that D commits burglary whenever she enters a shop with intent to steal: she is a trespasser because her permission to enter does not extend to entry for the purposes of theft.[129] This seems correct on the law. However, prosecutors have been, and are likely to remain, reluctant to prosecute shoplifting as burglary unless D enters a specifically restricted area within a shop.[130]

Extra detail . . .

Interesting problems emerge where D enters with permission which is subsequently withdrawn. Where D fails to leave in a reasonable time, she becomes a trespasser. However, as she has not 'entered' as a trespasser, we would still need some kind of crossing of a boundary (eg into a new area of the building) as a trespasser in order for D to be potentially caught within burglary.

9.4.1.2 Mens rea of s9(1)(a) burglary

There are two major elements to the mens rea of section 9(1)(a) burglary. First, D must be at least reckless as to the facts that make her a trespasser; secondly, D must intend to commit one of the offences listed in section 9(2).

A) Intention/reckless as to trespass: In most cases D will be aware when she enters a building as a trespasser. However, particularly in mistaken consent cases, and cases of entry in excess of permission, mens rea may be harder to demonstrate. Take the case of *Collins*.

Collins [1973] QB 100

D, naked apart from his socks, climbed a ladder up to V's window. D's intention was to have sex with V. Seeing the silhouette of D in her window, V mistook D for her boyfriend, invited him in, and they engaged in sexual intercourse. V turned on the light and discovered her mistake. D was charged with burglary (at this time burglary included entry as a trespasser with 'intent to rape').

• Crown Court: guilty of burglary.

• Court of Appeal: appeal allowed. Although V's mistake meant that D entered without true permission, the jury were not directed to ask the separate mens rea question: was D at least reckless as to V's mistake (ie did he at least foresee a risk of the mistake and continue unreasonably to run that risk)?

---

[129] Smith, 'Shoplifting and the Theft Acts' [1981] Crim LR 586.

[130] *Walkington* [1979] 2 All ER 716.

Although *Collins* avoided liability due to (possible) lack of mens rea, this will not always be the case. For example, in *Jones and Smith* (discussed in the previous section), the fact that the youths waited to enter D's father's house at night provided evidence that they realised that they were entering in excess of their permission.

B) **Intent to steal, cause GBH, or commit criminal damage:** This element is an example of ulterior mens rea: D must intend to commit one of these offences at the time of entry, but whether she goes on to carry it out is irrelevant.[131] This element is pivotal to the mischief targeted by section 9(1)(a). Without this intention, D merely commits the civil wrong of trespass; with the intention, D commits burglary, a serious criminal offence. As a form of ulterior intention, it is clear that a conditional intention is sufficient, as where D intends to steal if she finds anything worth stealing.[132] However, nothing short of intention as to every element of the future offence will suffice.[133]

Assessment matters . . .

What if D intends to take an item from the building and damage it elsewhere (does D intend to commit criminal damage 'therein'?), or to take a person from the building and cause GBH elsewhere (does D intend to cause GBH 'therein'?). These questions have not arisen in the case law, but provide an interesting problem. As with all legal unknowns, if arising in a problem question, you should highlight the lack of authority and say what you think the likely outcome would be, based on the rationale of the offence and the general approach of the courts.[134]

9.4.2 TA 1968, s9(1)(b): burglary by offences committed following trespassory entry

Section 9(1)(b) burglary will often overlap with section 9(1)(a), but is quite different. Section 9(1)(b) applies where D enters a building or a part of a building as a trespasser and then commits theft, attempted theft, causes GBH, or attempts to cause GBH. Where D enters with the intent to commit one of these offences, and then does so, she commits burglary under *both* sections 9(1)(a) and 9(1)(b). However, where she enters with intent to commit one of the listed offences, but does not commit or attempt to commit it, there is a section 9(1)(a) burglary only. Where she enters without the intent to commit one of the listed offences, but then does commit such an offence after having entered, there is a section 9(1)(b) burglary only.

To come within section 9(1)(b), D must complete the offence of theft, attempted theft, a GBH offence, or an attempted GBH offence. The elements of these offences are discussed elsewhere in this book.[135] In addition to this base offence, the other elements of section 9(1)(b) are set out in **Table 9.4.**

---

[131] See **Chapter 4.2.1.2.**
[132] *AG's References (Nos 1 and 2 of 1979)* [1979] 3 All ER 143.
[133] *A v DPP* [2003] All ER 393: recklessness is not sufficient.
[134] White, 'Lurkers, Draggers and Kidnappers' (1986) 150 JP 37.
[135] For theft, see **9.2**; GBH, see **Chapter 7.5–7.6**; and for attempts, see **Chapter 11.2.**

Table 9.4 Burglary: TA 1968, s9(1)(b)

	Actus reus	Mens rea
Conduct element	Any conduct causing the results (and conduct required for the base offence)	Voluntary
Circumstance element	D is a trespasser (and circumstances required for the base offence)	Recklessness (and any mens rea required for the base offence)
Result element	Entry into a building or part of a building (and any results required for the base offence)	Intent (and any mens rea required for the base offence)

Section 9(1)(b) burglary is more simply illustrated in **Figure 9.3**.

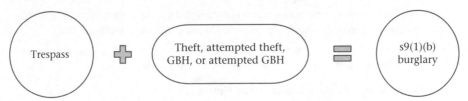

Figure 9.3 Burglary: TA 1968, s9(1)(b)

 Point to remember . . .

The listed offences in sections 9(1)(a) and 9(1)(b) are different. Importantly, criminal damage is a listed offence under section 9(1)(a) but not under section 9(1)(b). So, where D trespasses without the intention to commit criminal damage, but commits criminal damage whilst inside the building, she does not commit burglary. She will, of course, be liable for criminal damage.

9.4.2.1 Actus reus of s9(1)(b) burglary

D must enter a building or a part of a building as a trespasser. These elements were discussed above in the context of the section 9(1)(a) offence (**9.4.1.1**).

When inside the building, D must then complete the actus reus of theft, a GBH offence, or attempt either. We discussed the elements of theft above (**9.2**); and GBH offences and criminal attempts are discussed in other chapters.

9.4.2.2 Mens rea of s9(1)(b) burglary

D must be at least reckless as to the facts that make her entry a trespass. We discussed this previously in relation to the case of *Collins* (**9.4.1.2**).

When committing one of the listed offences within the building, D must act with the mens rea required for that offence. For example, if committing theft, D must intend to permanently deprive V of her property, and do so dishonestly (**9.2**). The mens rea for GBH offences and attempts are discussed in separate chapters.

Extra detail . . .

As section 9(1)(b) does not specify a particular GBH 'offence', it was held in *Jenkins*[136] that as long as D caused GBH there was no need to demonstrate *any* mens rea. However, this interpretation has been heavily criticised and is unlikely to be followed by future courts. For example, D trespasses into V's house, thinking V is away; V hears someone in the house and suffers a shock-induced heart attack. D has committed the trespass, but surely not burglary.

9.4.3 Aggravated burglary

A burglary becomes aggravated burglary under section 10 of the TA 1968 if it is committed with the use of a listed weapon. The maximum sentence for aggravated burglary on indictment is life imprisonment.[137]

10(1) A person is guilty of aggravated burglary if he commits any burglary and at the time has with him any firearm or imitation firearm, any weapon of offence, or any explosive; and for this purpose—

(a) 'firearm' includes an airgun or air pistol, and 'imitation firearm' means anything which has the appearance of being a firearm, whether capable of being discharged or not; and

(b) 'weapon of offence' means any article made or adapted for use for causing injury to or incapacitating a person, or intended by the person having it with him for such use; and

(c) 'explosive' means any article manufactured for the purpose of producing a practical effect by explosion, or intended by the person having it with him for that purpose.

The structure of the offence is illustrated in **Figure 9.4**.

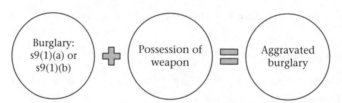

Figure 9.4 Aggravated burglary

We have already discussed the elements of burglary, and much of the possession requirement is self-explanatory from the text of section 10. However, three points should be stressed.

First, it will not always be clear if what D possesses is a 'weapon' within the meaning of section 10. Section 10(1)(b) is particularly ambiguous, but has been interpreted broadly. For example, even an otherwise innocent item such as a screwdriver will become a weapon within this section if D is carrying it to use as a weapon.[138] Note that section 10(1)(b) also extends to 'incapacitation'. Thus, carrying sleeping pills to drug the owner of the building, or socks to tie her up, etc, will all be caught by the offence.

Secondly, the requirement that D must have the weapon 'at the time' of committing the burglary means that it is important to identify whether D is committing burglary under section 9(1)(a) or 9(1)(b). D commits section 9(1)(a) burglary at the point of entry to the building with the requisite intention. Thus, for aggravated section 9(1)(a)

---

[136] [1983] 1 All ER 1000.
[137] TA 1968, s10(2).
[138] *Kelly* [1993] Crim LR 763.

burglary, D must have the weapon at this point.[139] D commits section 9(1)(b) burglary at the point she commits theft, a GBH offence, or attempts either. Thus, for aggravated section 9(1)(b) burglary, D must have the weapon at this point.[140]

Thirdly, the requirement of possession ('has with him') simply means that D must be in control of the weapon and must be aware of it.[141] It is irrelevant whether D intends to use the weapon during the burglary. For example, in *Stones*,[142] D's conviction was upheld where he was carrying a kitchen knife, even though he claimed to have the knife for defensive purposes only.

9.5 Handling stolen goods

The offence of handling stolen goods is set out in section 22 of the TA 1968. The maximum sentence on indictment is 14 years' imprisonment.[143]

22(1) A person handles stolen goods if (otherwise than in the course of the stealing) knowing or believing them to be stolen goods he dishonestly receives the goods, or dishonestly undertakes or assists in their retention, removal, disposal or realisation by or for the benefit of another person, or if he arranges to do so.

The elements of the offence are illustrated in **Table 9.5**.

Table 9.5 Handling stolen goods

	Actus reus	**Mens rea**
Conduct element	Any conduct causing the result	Voluntary
Circumstance element	The goods are stolen	Knowledge or belief
	D's conduct is dishonest	In context of D's knowledge and belief
Result element	D receives the goods,	Intention
	Or	
	Undertakes or assists in their retention, removal, disposal, or realisation by or for the benefit of another person, or arranges to do so	Intention

---

[139] *Wiggins* [2012] EWCA Crim 885.
[140] *Chevannes* [2009] EWCA Crim 2725; confirmed in *Eletu and White* [2018] EWCA Crim 599.
[141] *Russell* (1985) 81 Cr App R 315.
[142] [1989] 1 WLR 156.
[143] The high maximum of 14 years (theft carries a maximum of seven years) is set to discourage trade in stolen goods and thereby discourage future thefts: *Shelton* (1993) 15 Cr App R 415.

9.5.1 Actus reus of s22

Handling stolen goods is an extremely wide-ranging offence, extending well beyond the paradigm where D takes physical possession of V's recently stolen goods from the thief (P). Core questions within the actus reus relate to the meaning of 'goods'; 'stolen'; and 'handling'.

9.5.1.1 Goods

The definition of 'goods' for this offence is set out in section 34(2)(b) of the TA 1968.

> 34(2)(b) 'goods', except in so far as the context otherwise requires, includes money and every other description of property except land, and includes things severed from the land by stealing.

This section explicitly links the definition of 'goods' to that of 'property', defined in section 4 and discussed earlier (**9.2.2**). Therefore, (almost) everything that qualifies as property under section 4 will also be 'goods' for the purposes of section 34, including things in action (eg bank account credit).[144] The only exception to the equivalence between property and goods is in relation to land: certain non-severed fixtures are capable of constituting property, whereas they will not be goods for the purpose of this offence unless severed.

9.5.1.2 Stolen

For the handling offence to apply, it must be demonstrated that the goods were in fact 'stolen'.[145] This is set out in section 24 of the TA 1968.

> 24(4) For purposes of the provisions of this Act relating to goods which have been stolen . . . goods obtained in England or Wales or elsewhere either by blackmail or . . . by fraud . . . shall be regarded as stolen; and 'steal', 'theft' and 'thief' shall be construed accordingly.

The types of property that are classed as stolen goods for the purposes of this offence extend beyond those that are acquired by theft. Goods can be stolen through theft (**9.2**), robbery (**9.3**), burglary (**9.4**), blackmail (**9.6**), or fraud.[146] D need not personally have committed the relevant offence (leading to the 'stolen' status), but it must be demonstrated that someone did. This is discussed in *Defazio v DPP*.

 Defazio v DPP [2007] EWHC 3529 (Admin)

V's missing credit card was found in D's house. D was charged with handling stolen goods.

- Magistrates' court: guilty of handling stolen goods.
- Divisional Court: appeal allowed. The fact that the card was found does not mean that it was stolen; D had claimed that he found the card on the street and merely forgot to hand it in.

Where goods are found and there is some doubt as to their status, the fact that D has been told by another that they are stolen is not sufficient to demonstrate that they are

---

[144] *AG's Reference (No 4 of 1979)* [1981] 1 All ER 1193.

[145] If the goods are not stolen, but D believes they are, she may be liable for an attempted handling offence (*Haughton v Smith* [1975] AC 476), see **Chapter 11**.

[146] See **Chapter 10**.

stolen in fact.[147] However, other material evidence, such as D witnessing the goods being stolen; buying them in extremely suspicious circumstances; and/or for an unrealistically low price, may be sufficient.[148]

The types of goods that can be classed as stolen under this section also extend beyond the property that was originally acquired through theft, robbery, etc. This is set out in section 24(2) of the TA 1968.

> 24(2) For purposes of those provisions references to stolen goods shall include, in addition to the goods originally stolen and parts of them (whether in their original state or not),—
>
> (a) any other goods which directly or indirectly represent or have at any time represented the stolen goods in the hands of the thief as being the proceeds of any disposal or realisation of the whole or part of the goods stolen or of goods so representing the stolen goods; and
>
> (b) any other goods which directly or indirectly represent or have at any time represented the stolen goods in the hands of a handler of the stolen goods or any part of them as being the proceeds of any disposal or realisation of the whole or part of the stolen goods handled by him or of goods so representing them.

This means that, in certain cases, it will be necessary to trace the stolen goods and their proceeds. This is best illustrated by way of example. Let us imagine that P steals an iPhone and sells it to X for £100, and X then sells the phone to D. In line with section 24(2)(a), despite gaining the phone third-hand, D may still be liable for handling stolen goods if she has the requisite mens rea. This will be the case even if X did not commit the offence of handling because her conduct was not accompanied by mens rea. In line with section 24(2)(b), it is also possible to trace the proceeds of stolen goods. Thus, the money P receives from X (the proceeds of the stolen goods) becomes stolen property in its own right; this will also be the case for D if she goes on to sell or exchange the goods bought from X.[149]

Section 24(3) sets out when goods cease to be stolen, and thus cannot form the basis of the offence when handled.

> 24(3) But no goods shall be regarded as having continued to be stolen goods after they have been restored to the person from whom they were stolen or to other lawful possession or custody, or after that person and any other person claiming through him have otherwise ceased as regards those goods to have any right to restitution in respect of the theft.

The result of this section is that where the police (or owner) regain lawful possession, the goods cease to be stolen. In such a case, where D retakes control of the goods, she is guilty of theft rather than handling stolen goods. Interesting questions emerge about what constitutes being 'restored' to an owner or custody, as in *AG's Reference (No 1 of 1974)*.

---

[147] This is evidence of D's belief only: *Marshall* [1977] Crim LR 106.
[148] *Korniak* (1983) 76 Cr App R 145: D buying jewellery from a stranger for a very low price.
[149] However, D's money received by X (who did not commit a handling offence in relation to the original goods) does not constitute stolen goods: the money received by X is not money 'in the hands of a handler of stolen goods'.

AG's Reference (No 1 of 1974) [1974] 2 All ER 899

A police officer immobilised D's car while D was absent from it and kept watch for D's return, correctly suspecting the car contained stolen goods. D returned, and was questioned by the officer. In view of his unsatisfactory responses, D was arrested and the car searched. D was charged with handling stolen goods.

• Crown Court: not guilty of handling stolen goods. When immobilising the car, the police officer effectively took control of (restored) the goods. When D came to the car, the goods were no longer stolen.

• Court of Appeal: whether the officer had restored the goods was a question of fact for the jury, taking account of the officer's intentions. The judge at first instance was therefore wrong not to allow this issue to be decided by the jury.

9.5.1.3 Handling

The section 22 offence specifies a number of ways (as many as 18) by which stolen goods may be handled.

22(1) A person handles stolen goods if . . . he . . . receives the goods, or . . . undertakes or assists in their retention, removal, disposal or realisation by or for the benefit of another person, or if he arranges to do so.

Several of these terms require explanation.

A) **Receives or arranges to receive:** This is the only form of handling that does not have to be 'by or for the benefit of another person'. Therefore, in any case where D is not acting for another, this is the only potential route to liability. D receives goods where she gains possession or control from another.[150] This will typically involve physical possession, but is wide enough to include joint control, as where the goods are held by X, but X is acting as an agent of D.[151] Acts of arranging to receive will also be included, as where D agrees to receive the goods from X.[152] However, the simple fact that the goods are found on D's premises will not be sufficient; it must be shown that they are there by D's invitation or agreement: receiving requires D's active participation.[153]

B) **Retention, removal, disposal, realisation:** Alongside receiving, these terms represent the other form of handling. 'Retention' requires D to act in a manner that will make it more likely that stolen goods are kept (eg storing them for X);[154] simple use of the goods is not sufficient.[155] 'Removal' requires D to assist with moving the goods from one location to another even if D never gains possession or control.[156] 'Disposal' requires D to destroy or sell/exchange the stolen goods.[157] 'Realisation' requires D to exchange the goods for money or other property, and as such, overlaps with disposal.[158]

---

[150] 'From another' is important. Where D simply finds stolen goods, she does not receive them: *Haider* (1985, unreported).

[151] *Miller* (1854) 6 Cox CC 353; *Smith* (1855) Dears CC 494.

[152] *King* [1938] 2 All ER 662.

[153] *Cavendish* [1961] 2 All ER 856.

[154] *Pitchley* (1972) 57 Cr App R 30.

[155] *Sanders* (1982) 75 Cr App R 84: D used a stolen heater and battery charger in his father's garage.

[156] *Gleed* (1916) 12 Cr App R 32.

[157] *Watson* [1916] 2 KB 385.

[158] *Bloxham* [1983] 1 AC 109.

C) **Arranging or assisting:** Just as 'receiving' extends to arranging to receive, the same is true of the other forms of handling defined above. For example, D arranges to dispose when she agrees with another to sell the stolen goods. However, beyond that which is applicable to receiving, D may also handle stolen goods under these other headings through acts of assisting or encouraging the retention, removal, disposal, or realisation of the goods (eg lying to the police to allow the goods to be retained by X).[159] To assist, it must be shown that D actively encouraged or helped X; simply benefiting from another's handling is not sufficient.[160] When combined, these qualifications even allow for handling where D arranges to assist X to retain, remove, dispose, or realise.

D) **For the benefit of another:** Apart from cases of receiving or arranging to receive (as in point A above), it must be shown that D has acted (handled) for the benefit of another. This requirement keeps the offence within limits, avoiding every theft also being an incident of handling, and the requirement has been interpreted narrowly in cases such as *Bloxham*.

 Bloxham [1983] 1 AC 109

D purchased a car from P, unaware that it was stolen. D later came to suspect that the car was stolen and sold it to X. D was charged with handling stolen goods.

- Crown Court: guilty of handling stolen goods.
- Court of Appeal: conviction upheld on appeal.
- House of Lords: appeal allowed. D clearly disposed of the stolen goods, but did not do so for the benefit of another. Although the buyer of the car (X) may have benefited, it was not sold by D for X's benefit.

9.5.2 Mens rea of s22

There are two main mens rea elements: knowledge or belief that the goods are stolen, and dishonesty.

9.5.2.1 Knowledge or belief that the goods are stolen

Knowledge and belief are subjective mens rea terms and, as such, it will not be sufficient to show that a reasonable person would have believed or known.[161] It must be proved that D believed or knew.[162]

---

159 *Kanwar* (1982) 75 Cr App R 87.
160 *Coleman* [1986] Crim LR 56: D's knowledge that his wife was using stolen money to pay their joint solicitor's fees did not, of itself, amount to assisting.
161 See **Chapter 3.4.2–3.4.3**. Griew, 'States of Mind, Presumptions and Inferences' in P Smith (ed), *Criminal Law: Essays in Honour of JC Smith* (1987) 63.
162 *Atwal v Massey* [1971] 3 All ER 881.

It is clear that suspicion or recklessness that the goods are stolen will never be sufficient.[163] Interestingly, it has also been held that wilful blindness will not be sufficient either.[164] Thus, where D is suspicious but in order to remain ignorant she actively avoids looking deeper, although this may amount to a form of knowledge in other contexts,[165] it will not suffice for the purposes of handling stolen goods.

9.5.2.2 Dishonesty

The requirement of dishonesty requires us to apply the *Ivey* test discussed previously (**9.2.5**). We ask (a) what was the actual state of D's knowledge or belief as to the facts? And (b), in the context of (a), was D's conduct dishonest by the standards of ordinary decent people? In most cases where D handles stolen goods knowing or believing that they are stolen, it will not be difficult to demonstrate dishonesty. The exception may be where D handles the goods with an intention to return them to the owner or the police.[166]

 Extra detail . . .

Similar and overlapping offences of money laundering are used in tandem with the offence of handling stolen goods. The main offences of money laundering are found in the Proceeds of Crime Act 2002. We do not discuss these offences further in this book.[167]

9.6 Blackmail

The offence of blackmail is defined in section 21 of the TA 1968. The maximum sentence on indictment is 14 years' imprisonment.[168]

21(1) A person is guilty of blackmail if, with a view to gain for himself or another or with intent to cause loss to another, he makes any unwarranted demand with menaces; and for this purpose a demand with menaces is unwarranted unless the person making it does so in the belief—

(a) that he has reasonable grounds for making the demand; and

(b) that the use of the menaces is a proper means of reinforcing the demand.

The elements of blackmail are set out in **Table 9.6**.

---

[163] *Forsyth* [1997] Crim LR 581.
[164] *Griffiths* (1974) 60 Cr App R 14.
[165] See **Chapter 3.4.2.1**.
[166] *Matthews* [1950] 1 All ER 137.
[167] See *Smith, Hogan, and Ormerod's Criminal Law* (16th edn, 2021) Ch34.
[168] TA 1968, s21(3).

Table 9.6 Blackmail

	Actus reus	**Mens rea**
Conduct element	D makes demands	Voluntary
Circumstance element	D uses menaces	Knowledge
Result element	None	None
Ulterior mens rea element	*	D intends to make a gain or cause a loss to another
		D does not believe that she has reasonable grounds to make the demands,
		Or
		D does not believe that the use of menaces is a proper means of reinforcing the demand

Blackmail has an interesting structure: criminalising harmful conduct (ie the demand with menace), but also a significant ulterior element (ie D must intend to make a gain or cause a loss, but this need never come about, the offence requires no actual results at all). There is no single rationale for the offence of blackmail. It can be seen as necessary to protect V from threats of unpleasant consequences; her privacy from invasive demands;[169] and her property which is the subject of the demand.[170]

9.6.1 Actus reus of s21

The actus reus of blackmail is formed of two principal elements: the making of a demand, and the use of menaces.

 Extra detail . . .

Although the 'unwarranted' nature of D's demand may appear to be an actus reus element, and is often described by courts in these terms, it is better understood as part of D's mens rea. This is because the question of whether D's demands are unwarranted depends solely upon her intentions and beliefs (ie her state of mind).

---

[169] Alldridge, 'Attempted Murder of the Soul: Blackmail, Privacy and Secrets' (1993) 13 OJLS 368.

[170] Lamond, 'Coercion, Threats and the Puzzle of Blackmail' in Simester and Smith (eds), *Harm and Culpability* (1996) Ch10.

9.6.1.1 Demands

It must be proved that D made a demand as to another's property. This can be express or implied, as where D points a gun and asks if V might like to hand over her wallet; and it can be made by any means of communication, including orally, written, gesture, via an intermediary, etc.[171] Also, although the word 'demand' might imply some form of harsh words, it is clear that the manner of the request, however polite, will still constitute a demand. In *Robinson*,[172] for example, 'Sir, I am now only making an appeal to your benevolence' was capable of being a demand. The requirement of a demand is satisfied as soon as it is made, regardless of whether V is aware of it, such as in cases where a letter is lost in the post, or where V is deaf, etc.[173]

The lack of a demand for property will be fatal to the offence. Where D catches V committing a crime (or doing anything she would rather keep secret), and V asks D if she will accept some property in exchange for her silence, there is no demand from D and therefore no blackmail. Equally, even where there is a demand from D, but that demand does not relate to property, such as where D demands sexual acts from V, again there is no blackmail.[174]

9.6.1.2 Menaces

A menace has been defined as 'any action detrimental to or unpleasant to the person addressed'.[175] Therefore, beyond threats of violence to persons or property, any threat of an unpleasant character (eg to reveal compromising information) can amount to a menace. The only restriction, preventing the offence applying in trivial circumstances, is that the menace must be 'of such a nature and extent that the mind of an ordinary person of normal stability and courage might be influenced or made apprehensive so as to accede unwillingly to the demand'.[176] This is a relatively low threshold (note the use of 'might'), but it is an objective one. Three situations should be distinguished:

A) V does not accede, but a reasonable person would: The use of an objective standard means that D's threats constitute a menace even if V is not intimidated in fact because, for example, she is particularly brave.[177]

B) V accedes, but a reasonable person would not: Again, the objective standard means that V's reaction is largely irrelevant and the question is whether a reasonable person *might* have acceded. Thus, in this context, there will be no menace, and therefore no blackmail.[178]

C) V accedes due to known vulnerabilities, but a reasonable person would not: Where D has personal knowledge of V's vulnerability, such as V's infirmity, youth, timidity, etc, and so D realises that her threat will be particularly menacing to V, a menace will be found.[179]

---

[171] *Treacy v DPP* [1971] AC 537.
[172] (1796) 2 East PC 1110.
[173] *Treacy v DPP* [1971] AC 537: the demand was made when the letter was posted.
[174] Although D may be committing a sexual offence: **Chapter 8**.
[175] *Thorne v Motor Trade Association* [1937] AC 797, 817.
[176] *Clear* [1968] 1 All ER 74, 80.
[177] *Moran* [1952] 1 All ER 803.
[178] *Harry* [1974] Crim LR 32: V felt threatened by a note from a student charity event offering shopkeepers immunity from 'inconvenience' for payment: not sufficiently menacing.
[179] *Garwood* [1987] 1 All ER 1032: where D must have been aware of V's extreme timidity.

Provided D's threats meet the objective standard required, it is irrelevant whether the menace is directed at V or another, whether the menace is carried out, or even whether it is possible for D to carry it out. This is illustrated in *Lambert*.

Lambert [2009] EWCA Crim 2860

D phoned his grandmother pretending to have been kidnapped, and asking her to send money to have him freed. D was charged with blackmail.

• Crown Court: guilty of blackmail.

• Court of Appeal: conviction upheld on appeal. D communicated a menace to V. The fact that D was also the victim of that menace, and that the whole scenario was untrue, did not matter.

9.6.2 Mens rea of s21

There are two core mens rea elements: D's demands must be unwarranted, and they must be made with the intention to make a gain or cause a loss. Both requirements are ulterior as they do not correspond to elements within the actus reus.[180]

Point to remember . . .

Unlike the property offences discussed earlier, blackmail does not require an element of dishonesty.

9.6.2.1 Unwarranted demands

Not all demands with menaces will constitute blackmail (eg D demands payment of a debt from V and threatens civil legal action). Demands will only come within blackmail if they are unwarranted. To apply this element, we do not look to the content of the threat or the demands, although these will be useful evidence, but, rather, we look to the state of mind of D. It must be demonstrated by the prosecution that (A) D did not believe that she had reasonable grounds to make the demands *or* (B) that D did not believe that the use of menaces was a proper means of reinforcing the demand.[181] Lack of either belief will suffice for liability.

Extra detail . . .

The unwarranted requirement attempts to mitigate what some describe as the 'blackmail paradox'. The paradox is evident because D is legally entitled to make certain demands of V (eg ask V for money). D is also legally entitled to do certain things that are unpleasant for V (eg expose V's immoral activities). However, where D threatens the latter in exchange for the former, her conduct becomes criminal.[182]

---

[180] See **Chapter 4.2.1.2**.

[181] *Ashiq* [2015] EWCA Crim 1617: discussing unwarranted demands, and the prosecution's legal burden.

[182] Lindgren, 'Unraveling the Paradox of Blackmail' (1984) 84 Col L Rev 670.

A) Lack of belief in reasonable grounds for the demand: Even where D believes that it is proper to use menaces, she must also believe that she has reasonable grounds for her demands. The question is not whether she thinks her demands are correct, but whether she believes that others would agree they are reasonable.

B) Lack of belief in the propriety of menaces: More common is the case where D believes that her demands are reasonable, but lacks belief in the propriety of her menaces. For example, in *Kewell*,[183] although D believed in the reasonableness of demanding the return of a debt, it was easy for the prosecution to show that D did not honestly believe that threatening to reveal embarrassing photos of V was a proper means of enforcing that debt. It has been argued that whenever D realises that her threat will involve committing a criminal offence, such as threats of unlawful violence, this will automatically undermine any claim of belief in propriety.[184] However, although this is undoubtedly very strong evidence that D did not believe that her threats were proper, it is unlikely to be conclusive in every case.

Extra detail . . .

Structuring this element in terms of mens rea can lead to two interesting results. First, even where (objectively) D's demands and use of menaces are entirely reasonable, if D lacks belief of the reasonableness she will still satisfy the offence. Conversely, even where (objectively) D's demands and use of menaces are entirely unreasonable, unless the prosecution prove that D knew that either was improper, she will not satisfy the offence.

9.6.2.2 A view to a gain or a loss

Although D need not make a gain or cause a loss in fact,[185] it is necessary that she made the demands with this intention. Gain and loss are defined in section 34(2)(a) of the TA 1968, confining the offence to focus on property only.[186]

> 34(2)(a) 'gain' and 'loss' are to be construed as extending only to gain or loss in money or other property, but as extending to any such gain or loss whether temporary or permanent; and
>
> > (i) 'gain' includes a gain by keeping what one has, as well as a gain by getting what one has not; and
> >
> > (ii) 'loss' includes a loss by not getting what one might get, as well as a loss by parting with what one has . . .

An intention to make a gain *or* cause a loss is sufficient. For example, this element will be satisfied where D intends to cause a loss to V even though D makes no gain by, for example, demanding that V destroys an item of property. The same is true where D intends to make a gain but not to cause a loss by, for example, demanding to be promoted, but intending to do a good job. It has been argued that where D demands something to which she is legally entitled, such as the payment of a debt, she cannot be intending

---

[183] [2000] 2 Cr App R 38.

[184] *Harvey, Ulyett and Plummer* (1981) 72 Cr App R 139.

[185] *Dooley* [2005] EWCA Crim 3093, see Ormerod, Commentary [2006] Crim LR 544.

[186] As stated earlier, a demand of a sexual nature or other non-property demand will not come within the offence.

to make a gain or cause a loss.[187] However, the court in *Lawrence and Pomroy*,[188] without specific discussion, seem to have assumed that such demands will still satisfy this element.

9.7 Criminal damage

In this section we discuss offences of criminal damage, arson, and aggravated criminal damage.[189] The basic offence of criminal damage is contained in section 1(1) of the Criminal Damage Act 1971.[190] The maximum sentence on indictment is 10 years' imprisonment.[191]

> 1(1) A person who without lawful excuse destroys or damages any property belonging to another intending to destroy or damage any such property or being reckless as to whether any such property would be destroyed or damaged shall be guilty of an offence.

The elements of criminal damage are set out in **Table 9.7**.

Table 9.7 Criminal damage

	Actus reus	**Mens rea**
Conduct element	Any conduct causing the result	Voluntary
Circumstance element	What is damaged is property	Intention/knowledge or recklessness
	The property belongs to another	Intention/knowledge or recklessness
Result element	Damage or destruction	Intention or recklessness

Following the enactment of the TA 1968 just three years earlier, the Criminal Damage Act 1971 attempts to create a coherent scheme of liability where D damages as opposed to appropriates another's property.

---

[187] Hogan, 'Blackmail' [1966] Crim LR 474.

[188] (1971) 57 Cr App R 64.

[189] There are also various offences of threatening criminal damage (Criminal Damage Act 1971, s2), possession of anything with intent to commit criminal damage (Criminal Damage Act 1971, s3), as well as more specific offences relating to dangerous materials such as explosives. These offences will not be discussed in this book. See further *Smith, Hogan, and Ormerod's Criminal Law* (16th edn, 2021) Ch27.

[190] Following Law Commission recommendations: *Offences of Damage to Property* (No 29, 1970).

[191] Criminal Damage Act 1971, s4(2).

9.7.1 Actus reus of s1(1)

D commits the actus reus of criminal damage where she 'damages' 'property' 'belonging to another'. Each of these three elements requires discussion.

9.7.1.1 Damage

Damage is not defined in the statute and is intended to carry its ordinary meaning.[192] Short of destruction, damage requires that property is rendered unusable and/or involves a physical interference that reduces the value of property or costs money to repair.[193] The benefit of this open-textured approach has been necessary flexibility, allowing similar acts to be considered as damage in one context but not another. For example, we may want to say that spitting in food is damage, but spitting on the pavement is not. However, the courts have struggled to maintain coherence.

A) **Undermining usability:** In *Drake v DPP*,[194] it was held that wheel clamping did not amount to damage because, although it prevents use of the vehicle, the physical integrity of the vehicle is not affected. Contrast *Fiak*,[195] where D stuffed blankets from his prison cell in the toilet and flushed repeatedly to cause a small flood. The fact that the blankets and the cell were rendered temporarily unusable led the courts to find that damage was caused.

B) **Reduction in value:** Equating damage with actions that reduce value seems apt in examples such as the scratching of a car: the car remains usable but there is clearly some damage.[196] However, this approach has been criticised and has largely fallen out of favour.[197]

C) **Cost of repair:** Recent cases have tended to focus on the cost of repair as opposed to any reduced value of the property. However, again, courts have struggled for coherence. In *A (A Juvenile)*,[198] there was no damage where D spat on a policeman's raincoat because the spittle could be easily removed with a damp cloth. Contrast *Samuels v Stubbs*,[199] where D jumped on a policeman's hat, and whilst the hat could be restored to its original state with little difficulty, the court still found that damage was caused. A useful case, demonstrating the problems for the court, is *Hardman v Chief Constable of Avon and Somerset Constabulary*.

 Hardman v Chief Constable of Avon and Somerset Constabulary [1986] Crim LR 330

D painted silhouettes on the pavement using water-soluble paints. The paint would have washed away in a few days, but the council paid for a jet wash to remove it. The issue was whether the painting constituted damage.

- Crown Court: taking account of the cost of removal, the painting constituted criminal damage.

---

[192] *Roe v Kingerlee* [1986] Crim LR 735.
[193] See Grevling, 'Damaging Property' [2020] CrimLR 497.
[194] [1994] RTR 411. Note, this may now constitute a separate offence.
[195] [2005] EWCA Crim 2381.
[196] *Foster* (1852) 6 Cox CC 25.
[197] Smith, *Property Offences* (1994) para 27.16.
[198] [1978] Crim LR 689.
[199] [1972] 4 SASR 200.

This case seems correct in that there was a cost to the council in removing the paint. However, it opens several unanswered questions. For example, would it still have been damage if the council had left the paint to be removed by the rain? What about other mess that we leave for the council (or rain) to clear up?[200] What about graffiti that people appreciate, and D anticipates will be appreciated?[201]

 Assessment matters . . .

When applying this element to the facts of problem questions, it is important to acknowledge the inconsistent approach of the courts and areas of uncertainty. Compare your problem facts with those of decided cases, discuss relevant academic debate, and conclude whether you think it is likely that damage will be found or not.

9.7.1.2 Property

Property is defined by section 10(1) of the Criminal Damage Act 1971.

10(1) In this Act 'property' means property of a tangible nature, whether real or personal, including money and—

(a) including wild creatures which have been tamed or are ordinarily kept in captivity, and any other wild creatures or their carcasses if, but only if, they have been reduced into possession which has not been lost or abandoned or are in the course of being reduced into possession; but

(b) not including mushrooms growing wild on any land or flowers, fruit or foliage of a plant growing wild on any land.

For the purposes of this subsection 'mushroom' includes any fungus and 'plant' includes any shrub or tree.

This definition, particularly subsections (a) and (b), is broadly consistent with the definition of property in the TA 1968 (**9.2.2**). However, there are three important differences:

• Land cannot generally be the subject of theft. However, the same logic does not apply to criminal damage. For example, D may not be able to steal her neighbour's garden, but can certainly damage it. Land is property in this context.

• Intangible property, such as bank account credit, copyright, etc, is property for theft, but will not constitute property for criminal damage. Criminal damage is isolated to physical damage to tangible property only.

• Wild plants/fungi can be property for theft if picked with a commercial intention, but this will not be the case for criminal damage. Plants/fungi growing wild will not be property for the purposes of criminal damage.

9.7.1.3 Belonging to another

It is not an offence under section 1(1) for D to damage her own property. Belonging to another is defined in section 10(2)–(4) of the Criminal Damage Act 1971.

---

[200] Alldridge, 'Incontinent Dogs and the Law' (1990) 140 NLJ 1067.
[201] Edwards, 'Banksy's Graffiti: A Not So Simple Case' (2009) 73 JCL 345.

10(2) Property shall be treated for the purposes of this Act as belonging to any person—

    (a) having the custody or control of it;

    (b) having in it any proprietary right or interest (not being an equitable interest arising only from an agreement to transfer or grant an interest); or

    (c) having a charge on it.

    (3) Where property is subject to a trust, the persons to whom it belongs shall be so treated as including any person having a right to enforce the trust.

    (4) Property of a corporation sole shall be so treated as belonging to the corporation notwithstanding a vacancy in the corporation.

As with 'belonging to another' in the context of theft (**9.2.3**), it is not fatal to a conviction if D had some proprietary interest in the property, as long as another person also had some proprietary interest. Thus, this element will be satisfied where D damages property that she co-owns with another, or in which another has even a minor proprietary interest as, for example, where the property is loaned to V.[202]

9.7.2 Mens rea of s1(1)

There are two principal elements to the mens rea. First, it must be shown that D intended, or was at least reckless, as to causing damage to the property. Secondly, D must also have intended/known or been reckless as to the fact that the property belonged to another. This second element of the mens rea should not be forgotten, as illustrated in *Smith*.

 Smith [1974] QB 354

At the end of D's tenancy, he removed a length of wiring that he had installed, causing £130 worth of damage. Under civil law, following its installation, the wiring belonged to D's landlord. However, D was unaware of this, believing that it belonged to him. D was charged with criminal damage.

- Crown Court: guilty of criminal damage.
- Court of Appeal: appeal allowed. D did not know, and did not foresee a risk, that the wiring did not belong to him. D lacked an essential element of the mens rea.

The mens rea terms 'intention' and 'recklessness' were discussed in **Chapter 3**. It will be remembered that much of the debate and flux relating to the definition of recklessness has focussed on criminal damage cases, including the leading case of *G*.[203]

9.7.3 Defences to criminal damage

In addition to the general defences such as duress, necessity, etc,[204] section 5 of the Criminal Damage Act 1971 also provides two specific defences: belief in consent; and protection of property.

---

[202] This does not extend to insurers of goods, as they hold no proprietary interest: *Denton* [1982] 1 All ER 65.

[203] [2004] AC 1034.

[204] See **Chapters 13** and **14**.

5(2) A person charged with an offence to which this section applies, shall, . . . be treated for those purposes as having a lawful excuse—

(a) if at the time of the act or acts alleged to constitute the offence he believed that the person or persons whom he believed to be entitled to consent to the destruction of or damage to the property in question had so consented, or would have so consented to it if he or they had known of the destruction or damage and its circumstances; or

(b) if he destroyed or damaged . . . in order to protect property belonging to himself or another or a right or interest in property which was or which he believed to be vested in himself or another, and at the time of the act or acts alleged to constitute the offence he believed—

(i) that the property, right or interest was in immediate need of protection; and

(ii) that the means of protection adopted . . . were . . . reasonable having regard to all the circumstances.

(3) For the purposes of this section it is immaterial whether a belief is justified or not if it is honestly held.

(4) For the purposes of subsection (2) above a right or interest in property includes any right or privilege in or over land, whether created by grant, licence or otherwise.

9.7.3.1 Belief in consent defence

Section 5(2)(a) provides a belief in consent defence. As confirmed by section 5(3), the test is simply whether D honestly believed that the owner did or would have consented to her causing damage, even if that belief was not reasonable. In *Denton*,[205] for example, there was no criminal damage where D honestly believed that the owner of a mill had encouraged him to burn it down, even though the reason for that belief was based on insurance fraud. However, honest belief that God is the owner, and would have consented, will not be sufficient.[206]

It should be remembered that even where the owner would not have consented and/or the person consenting does not have the authority to do so, and even where this would have been clear to a reasonable person, D may still satisfy the defence if she *honestly* believes that both requirements are satisfied. One of the more controversial mistake cases is *Jaggard v Dickinson*.[207] In this case, D had permission from X to treat X's house as her own. However, when arriving heavily intoxicated at what she mistakenly believed was X's house, and finding herself unable to gain entry, D broke into V's house through V's window. Her defence to criminal damage under section 5(2)(a) was accepted. Although rather shocking, the problem with this case may be the court's treatment of her intoxicated state (concluding that it made no difference) rather than the defence itself. We discuss this further when exploring the intoxication rules.[208]

9.7.3.2 Belief in protection of property defence

Section 5(2)(b) creates a defence for belief in the protection of property, as where D damages a fence in order to protect/enforce her right of way, or shoots a dog to protect cattle, etc.[209] There are three main elements to this defence: belief that D or another has a vested

---

[205] [1982] 1 All ER 65.
[206] *Blake v DPP* [1993] Crim LR 586.
[207] [1980] 3 All ER 716. See criticism in *Magee v CPS* [2014] EWHC 4089 (Admin).
[208] **Chapter 13.2.**
[209] The 'threat' protected from need not be a criminal act: *Jones* [2005] QB 259.

interest in the property protected; belief that that property is in immediate need of protection; and belief that the means of protection (ie the damage caused) is reasonable. D must have belief as to all three.

A) **Belief in vested interest:** D must believe that she or another has a vested interest in property that she is acting to protect by damaging other property.[210] She must also believe that her action is necessary 'in order to' protect that property. This sounds like a subjective requirement (did D honestly believe?), but following *Hunt*, has been given a mixed subjective/objective meaning.

 Hunt (1977) 66 Cr App R 105

D, who was assisting his wife as a warden at a set of retirement flats, set fire to some bedding to draw attention to the defective fire alarms. D claimed a section 5(2)(b) defence, saying that he was acting to protect the properties from future risks. D was charged with arson which requires proof of criminal damage.

- Crown Court: guilty of arson.
- Court of Appeal: conviction upheld on appeal. Whether D's acts were capable of protecting the property (were 'in order to') is an objective question. Here, D's acts provided no protection.

It is counter-intuitive to interpret a requirement of 'belief' in an objective way. However, *Hunt* has been confirmed in further judgments.[211] What is necessary, therefore, is to ask what D believes (subjectively), and then to ask if this belief in protection has any reasonable (objective) basis.

 Extra detail . . .

It is open to future courts to interpret this element purely subjectively, which would be preferable. Defendants in cases like *Hunt* should not be able to claim the defence because they would lack belief in 'immediate' need; there is no need to read in an objective limb here.

B) **Belief in immediate need:** This element has been interpreted to be part subjective and part objective. First, the court must ascertain the subjective beliefs that D held at the time: how soon did she believe, reasonably or not, that the property would be in danger? Secondly, the court must decide (objectively) whether D's belief amounted to a belief of an 'immediate' need. Whether D would classify it as immediate is irrelevant.[212]

C) **Belief in reasonableness of methods:** This is a subjective requirement: we ask whether D believed her methods were reasonable, not whether others would so regard them. Even where D cuts down large parts of her neighbour's trees to protect her right to light, if she honestly believes that this is a reasonable method, and the jury believe she is or may be telling the truth, then the defence will be available.[213]

---

[210] *Cresswell v DPP* [2006] EWHC 3379 (Admin).
[211] *Hill and Hall* (1988) 89 Cr App R 74: D could not use the defence when damaging an air-force base in order to protect surrounding properties from being targeted by enemy forces.
[212] *Jones* [2005] QB 259.
[213] *DPP v Unsworth* [2010] EWHC 3037 (Admin).

9.7.4 Arson

Arson is preserved as a separate offence from simple criminal damage by section 1(3) of the Criminal Damage Act 1971. The maximum penalty on indictment is life imprisonment.[214]

1(3) An offence committed under this section by destroying or damaging property by fire shall be charged as arson.

The structure of arson is illustrated simply in **Figure 9.5**.

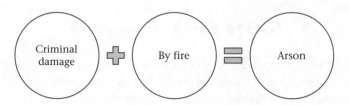

Figure 9.5 Arson

All elements of the criminal damage offence must be satisfied. Additionally, it must be demonstrated that D caused the damage by fire, and that she intended to cause or was reckless as to causing the damage by fire. Thus, where D causes damage other than by fire, such as smoke damage, or intentionally causes damage to property that results unexpectedly in fire, there will be no liability for arson, although D may still be liable for criminal damage.[215]

9.7.4.1 Defences to arson

D may rely on the general defences such as duress, necessity, etc.[216] D may also rely on the specific defences under section 5 discussed earlier (**9.7.3**).

9.7.5 Aggravated criminal damage

Aggravated criminal damage and aggravated arson are also separate offences under section 1(2) of the Criminal Damage Act 1971. The maximum sentence on indictment is life imprisonment.[217]

1(2) A person who without lawful excuse destroys or damages any property, whether belonging to himself or another—

(a) intending to destroy or damage any property or being reckless as to whether any property would be destroyed or damaged; and

(b) intending by the destruction or damage to endanger the life of another or being reckless as to whether the life of another would be thereby endangered;

shall be guilty of an offence.

---

[214] Criminal Damage Act 1971, s4(1).
[215] *Drayton* [2006] Crim LR 243.
[216] **Chapters 13** and **14**.
[217] Criminal Damage Act 1971, s4(1).

The structure of aggravated criminal damage/arson is illustrated simply in **Figure 9.6**.

Figure 9.6 Aggravated criminal damage

Aggravated criminal damage can be constructed upon either criminal damage or arson, even where the damage is to D's own property. The aggravating element is that D must intend or be reckless as to the endangerment of life by the damage caused.

9.7.5.1 Actus reus of aggravated criminal damage

The actus reus of aggravated criminal damage, for the most part, simply mirrors that of criminal damage or arson. However, crucially, the actus reus of this offence may also be satisfied where damage is caused to D's own property (eg D burns down her own house, or takes a hammer to her own car).[218]

Although, as we discuss later, D must intend or be reckless as to the endangerment of life, there is no need for endangerment of life in fact. This is not part of the actus reus. In *Parker*,[219] for example, D was liable for aggravated criminal damage where he started a fire in his semi-detached house and foresaw a risk to the lives of his neighbours. This was the case even though his neighbours were unharmed, and even though they were not in their house at the time such that the fire could not have endangered them in fact.

9.7.5.2 Mens rea of aggravated criminal damage

The mens rea of aggravated criminal damage requires D to satisfy all the mens rea requirements of the base offence of criminal damage or arson discussed previously. *Additionally*, it must be proved that D acted with the intention or was reckless as to the possibility of another person's life being endangered.[220]

D must intend or foresee endangerment arising *from the damage of property* that she intended or was reckless that she might cause (this is the nexus to the property offence), and so foresight of endangerment from D's acts alone is not sufficient: it has to be *by* the damage which D intended or was reckless about causing. This was discussed in *Steer*.

---

[218] *Merrick* [1996] 1 Cr App R 130: D, with the owner's permission, exposed a cable reckless as to endangerment. There are also several cases of attempted suicide reckless as to endangerment, eg where D burns down her own house, eg *Brewis* [2004] EWCA Crim 1919.

[219] [1993] Crim LR 856.

[220] Foresight of self-endangerment is not sufficient. *Thakar* [2010] EWCA Crim 2136: D set fire to his car when depressed following divorce.

Steer [1988] AC 111

D shot a rifle at the windows of V's house, against whom he had a grudge, breaking the windows (criminal damage) and foreseeing the endangerment of V. D was charged with aggravated criminal damage.

- Crown Court: guilty of aggravated criminal damage.
- Court of Appeal: appeal allowed. D was reckless as to the endangerment of V from his acts (ie shooting the rifle), he was not reckless as to the endangerment of V 'by the destruction or damage of property' (ie from the broken glass from the window). Aggravated criminal damage is only satisfied by the latter.
- House of Lords: appeal dismissed, confirming the reasoning of the Court of Appeal.

This interpretation means that D will be liable for aggravated criminal damage where she foresees the endangerment of life *by* the damage she intended (eg demolishing a building that might fall on someone, breaking a gas pipe that might poison someone, etc[221]); but not where the damage is simply incidental (eg throwing a bat that might hit someone, and may also damage property). This may seem a fine and perhaps unnecessary distinction, but the House of Lords recognised that to hold otherwise would lead to undesirable results. Lord Bridge in *Steer* provided the following example:

> If A and B both discharge firearms in a public place, being reckless as to whether life would be endangered, it would be absurd that A, who incidentally causes some trifling damage to property, should be guilty of an offence punishable with life imprisonment, but that B, who causes no damage, should be guilty of no offence.

The point being made here is that our criminal law does not recognise a general offence of endangerment which would apply to reckless acts where no harm is caused,[222] and aggravated criminal damage should not be manipulated/misapplied into filling that role.

9.7.5.3 Defences to aggravated criminal damage

D may rely on general defences such as duress, necessity, etc.[223] However, the specific defences under section 5 do not apply to aggravated criminal damage: belief in the owner's permission and/or protection of property will not excuse causing damage that might endanger a person's life.

9.7.6 Criminal damage and racial or religious aggravation

Separately from aggravated criminal damage and arson offences under section 1(2) CDA 1971, a 'simple' section 1(1) criminal damage offence can also be 'aggravated' if it is accompanied by racial or religious hatred.[224] We discussed the mechanism for this form of aggravation as it applies to non-fatal offences against the person,[225] and the same principles apply for racially or religiously aggravated criminal damage.[226]

---

[221] *Cunningham* [1957] 2 QB 396: breaking a gas pipe.
[222] Duff, 'Criminalising Endangerment' in Duff and Green (eds), *Defining Crimes* (2005) Ch3.
[223] **Chapters 13** and **14**.
[224] Crime and Disorder Act 1998, s30.
[225] See **Chapter 7.9.2**.
[226] *DPP v M* [2005] Crim LR 392.

9.8 Reform

There are numerous areas of confusion and apparent incoherence within the property offences, and many of the academic articles referred to in this chapter are calling for some manner of reform. In this section we focus on just one of these debates: how to define the offence of theft. However, we use this debate to highlight questions that are common among other property offences.

When considering reform of property offences it is useful to note that, despite powerful criticism in certain specific areas and despite a flurry of appeals cases between the 1970s and 1990s in particular, the law has been relatively settled for nearly 20 years—at least until *Ivey*. Relative stability of this kind does not necessarily make reform undesirable, but it should caution against reform that is likely to result in renewed uncertainty.

9.8.1 The mischief in theft

In order to evaluate the offence of theft, and to consider reform, it is necessary to first identify the mischief: what is the offence designed to target? The most obvious answer to this, and the one we began the chapter with, is that theft is designed to protect property rights. The mischief of theft is therefore any violation of those rights. However, this is not sufficient. Where V lends D her car, for example, D gains possession and so interferes with V's property rights, but there is nothing wrongful here, and certainly nothing deserving of criminalisation. Thus, there must be something more, beyond simple interference with property rights, that justifies the use of criminal law.

At one time, this additional wrong or harm may have been identified in D's 'manifestly criminal' appropriation: theft being a *non-consensual* interference with property rights.[227] However, following *Gomez*,[228] an appropriation can be found even where V consents. Without this additional 'wrong' within the actus reus of the offence, much of the work necessary to isolate theft to those deserving of criminalisation is instead done within the mens rea, and particularly the requirement of dishonesty. Some believe that this has led to the offence becoming unacceptably broad in its application, potentially applying to minor acts of appropriation that outwardly suggest little wrongdoing, such as touching an item in the supermarket with the requisite mens rea;[229] arguing that an element of non-consent should therefore be re-introduced to the interpretation of appropriation.[230]

Perhaps the most controversial point of the mischief debate, however, relates to cases where theft has been found even though there has been no breach of civil law and no property rights have been infringed. The clearest example of this is *Hinks*,[231]

---

[227] The term manifest criminality was coined by Fletcher, *Rethinking Criminal Law* (1978) 82. It means that D's external conduct is obviously wrongful.

[228] [1993] AC 442.

[229] For a good summary of the debate, see Shute, 'Appropriation and the Law of Theft' [2002] Crim LR 445.

[230] For a recent example, see Tamblyn, 'Reforming Theft: Taking Without Consent' [2020] Crim LR 597.

[231] [2000] 4 All ER 833.

where D dishonestly took advantage of a vulnerable person although the gifts from V were valid in civil law. Cases like *Hinks* are central to our identification and understanding of the mischief of theft, suggesting that the offence is targeting dishonest appropriation more generally, and not, as had generally been assumed, being structured by civil property rules. There have been various responses to *Hinks*. For some, the inconsistency with civil law is unproblematic, and the criminal law of theft should go beyond the wrongs of civil law to protect against dishonest appropriation more generally.[232] However, a majority of commentators have seen the developing split from civil law as problematic. Within this group, many have criticised *Hinks* as a wrong turn losing sight of the specific mischief (anchored by civil law breaches) that theft should be targeting.[233] There has also developed an interesting line of analysis that sees the split as problematic, but places the fault for that split with unduly narrow interpretations of the civil law.[234]

A final, but vital part of this first debate relates to the overlap between the expanding mischief of theft and fraud offences. We discuss fraud in **Chapter 10** and will return to this debate there. Basically, the argument is that theft and fraud are designed to protect property rights in different ways, targeting and separately labelling different mischiefs: theft should target non-consensual appropriation, whereas fraud should target deceptive consensual appropriation. On this view, the expansion of theft in *Gomez* and *Hinks* has broken down the distinction, potentially leading to inappropriate convictions and labelling.[235] The argument against this, from Gardner in particular, has been that overlapping offences are useful to ensure all criminally deserving cases are covered, particularly in relation to protection of the vulnerable where it may be difficult to demonstrate deception.[236] Although this argument is well put, following the reform of fraud offences by the Fraud Act 2006, where proof of deception is not required, it is debatable whether this justification for overlap still holds.

 Point to remember . . .

Debate about the identification of the rationale of an offence is also central to academic discussion of several other property offences discussed in this chapter. This is particularly true where the offence contains a requirement of harm or endangerment of a person, leading us to consider whether the gravamen of the offence is the protection of property or the person.[237]

---

[232] Bogg and Stanton-Ife, 'Theft as Exploitation' (2003) 23 LS 402.

[233] Simester and Sullivan, 'The Nature and Rationale of Property Offences' in Duff and Green (eds), *Defining Crimes* (2005).

[234] Green, 'Theft and Conversion—Tangibly Different' (2012) 128 LQR 564: discussing the interpretation of 'property' within the two regimes.

[235] Shute and Horder, 'Thieving and Deceiving: What is the Difference?' (1993) 56 MLR 548; Melissaris, 'The Concept of Appropriation and the Offence of Theft' (2007) 70 MLR 597; Green, *Thirteen Ways to Steal a Bicycle* (2012).

[236] Gardner, 'Appropriation in Theft: The Last Word?' (1993) 109 LQR 194.

[237] eg robbery. Ashworth, 'Robbery Reassessed' [2002] Crim LR 851.

9.8.2 Defining theft

The second part of the debate, having discussed what the offence is attempting to achieve, analyses the appropriateness of its elements. If we agree that the offence of theft should be protecting against the dishonest appropriation of all property rights, or dishonest appropriation more generally, then it may be contended that the current rules are too narrowly drawn. Glanville Williams, for example, made the case that even where D's intention is to deprive V temporarily (ie not permanently) of her property, this may still have a similarly detrimental effect on V's rights, and be deserving of criminalisation.[238] Lacey, Wells, and Quick go even further to suggest that the elements of theft could be expanded to protect other rights, such as environmental and welfare rights.[239]

A related discussion, if the wrong of dishonesty lies at the heart of theft and many other property offences, is whether the current definition of dishonesty is sufficient to distinguish between those deserving and not deserving of liability. When discussing the definition of dishonesty and the *Ivey* test (**9.2.5**), we highlighted problems with relying on the jury to identify common standards of honesty without legislative guidance. Analysing the same point of uncertainty within the pre-*Ivey* test, Griew observed a lack of consistency, the lack of objectivity, a tendency towards longer and more complex trials, etc.[240] Interestingly, not only does the recent decision in *Ivey* fail to resolve these problems, but by removing the second limb of the old test (asking whether D knew her conduct was dishonest by the standards of reasonable people) it can be argued that the definition of dishonesty has become more uncertain: D's self-moderation in line with her belief about common standards of honesty will no longer be determinative, and although the court will take account of D's knowledge and beliefs (step 1 of the *Ivey* test) exactly *how* and *when* this will impact the objective assessment of dishonesty in step 2 remains unknown. Indeed, it is possible that such uncertainty will lead to a renewed Article 7 ECHR challenge.[241]

Finally, a further discussion relating to the construction of theft and other property offences focusses on whether there should be some distinction between amounts or types of property appropriated. Whilst offences against the person are typically constructed to take account of the *degree* of harm suffered by V,[242] and only exceptionally in terms of the *method* of that infliction, property offences tend to be the opposite. And this is despite research showing that the public does see a moral difference between different degrees of theft, such as the values of the property taken and/or types of property.[243] Rearranging property offences to reflect degrees of harm would represent a fundamental shift from current practice.

---

[238] Williams, 'Temporary Appropriation Should Be Theft' [1981] Crim LR 129.

[239] Lacey, Wells, and Quick, *Reconstructing Criminal Law* (4th edn, 2010) 399.

[240] Griew, 'Dishonesty: The Objections to *Feely* and *Ghosh*' [1985] Crim LR 341.

[241] Article 7 guarantees that 'legal provisions which interfere with individual rights must be adequately accessible, and formulated with sufficient precision to enable the citizen to regulate his conduct', *G v Federal Republic of Germany* (1989) 60 DR 252, 262.

[242] See **Chapters 5–7**.

[243] Green and Kugler, 'Community Perceptions of Theft Seriousness' (2010) 7 J Em LS 511.

9.9 Eye on assessment

In this section we consider the potential application of property offences within a problem question, using the structure of analysis discussed in previous chapters.

STEP 1　Identify the potential criminal event in the facts

This should be simply stated (eg 'The first potential criminal event arises where D takes the iPhone'). The role of this step is to highlight which part of the question you are answering before you begin to apply the law.

For most criminal offences, this stage is quite straightforward. However, particularly in relation to property offences, you need to take extra care. This is because, as well as obvious potential criminal events (eg D snatches V's wallet, D smashes V's vase, etc), many of the offences discussed can arise from what might appear externally to be quite innocent conduct. For example, as long as mens rea is present, any touching of another's property could be theft, any trespass could be section 9(1)(a) burglary, and so on. Take care not to miss potential crimes; read the question facts carefully.[244]

In addition, when dealing with a potential theft, it should be remembered that a single taking might include more than one act of appropriation. For example, where D takes physical control of the property (appropriation by control) and then later decides to keep it (appropriation of ownership rights). Although there may be only one crime in these cases, you are given a choice of conduct elements: a choice of where to identify the potentially criminal event. You should focus on the one that is most likely to find liability. Thus, in our example, if the first act of taking control was not accompanied with an intention to keep the item, then this appropriation will not be theft because, at this point, there is no coinciding intention permanently to deprive. You should therefore highlight the second act of appropriation (D's decision to keep the item) as the one that is most likely to lead to liability, and therefore focus your discussion of the offence on that moment.

STEP 2　Identify the potential offence

Again, state this simply (eg 'When taking V's iPhone, D may be liable for theft'). The role of this stage is to highlight which offence you are going to apply.

Identifying the relevant offence can be challenging for property offences, partly because of the overlap between offences and partly because of the common use of aggravating elements. Where more than one offence could apply to the same potentially criminal event, our advice in previous chapters has been to apply the most serious potential offence first. This advice also holds true for property offences. However, having identified the most serious potential offence based on D's conduct, make sure to also consider potential aggravating factors that may lead to variations in the charge. This is illustrated in **Table 9.8**.

---

[244] Also, as always, be guided by the question as well as the facts (eg if the question asks you to consider theft only, then these potential criminal events are the only relevant ones to highlight).

Table 9.8 Identifying and applying property offences

Starting offence	Offence following aggravation
Where D appropriates property—first consider liability for **theft**	If D satisfies the elements of theft, go on to consider the following potential aggravations: • Does D use force—robbery • Is D trespassing—s9(1)(b) burglary • Where there is s9(1)(b) burglary, does D use a weapon—aggravated burglary
Where D trespasses into another's building or part of a building—first consider liability for **s9(1)(a) burglary**	If D satisfies the elements of s9(1)(a) burglary, go on to consider the following potential aggravations: • Does D have a weapon—aggravated burglary
Where D has trespassed into another's building or part of building, and then harms someone or attempts to harm someone or attempts to steal—first consider liability for **s9(1)(b) burglary**	If D satisfies the elements of s9(1)(b) burglary, go on to consider the following potential aggravations: • Does D use a weapon—aggravated burglary
Where D comes into possession of stolen property, or the proceeds of stolen property—consider liability for **handling stolen goods**	*
Where D threatens V, making demands in relation to property—consider liability for **blackmail**	*
Where D damages another's property—first consider liability for **s1(1) criminal damage**	If D satisfies the elements of s1(1) criminal damage, go on to consider the following potential aggravations: • Is there any racial or religious hatred—racial or religiously aggravated criminal damage • Is the damage caused by fire—arson • Is D at least reckless as to the endangerment of others' lives—aggravated criminal damage
Where D damages her own property—first consider liability for **s1(2) aggravated criminal damage**	If D satisfies the elements of s1(2) aggravated criminal damage, go on to consider the following potential aggravations: • Is the damage caused by fire—aggravated arson

When applying the law to problem facts, you therefore need to choose between the 'starting offences' in the left-hand column, applying the most serious potential offence. If the elements of that offence are satisfied, you should go on to consider whether that offence can be upgraded by one of the aggravating elements detailed in the right-hand column.

When discussing aggravating elements, it is common for courts and commentators to describe the process as 'constructing' upon the base offence. This is accurate, but you should take care not to confuse it with 'constructive liability', which is a specific label given to offences that include a constructive strict liability element.[245] The offences discussed in this chapter are not constructive crimes in this more specific sense. To avoid confusion and mislabelling, it may be best to avoid language like 'construction' in the context of property offences entirely.

STEP 3 Applying the offence to the facts

Having identified the relevant offence, make sure you discuss each of the required elements.

Actus reus: What does the offence require? Did D do it?

Mens rea: What does the offence require? Did D possess it?

AR and MR are satisfied	AR and/or MR are not satisfied
Continue to STEP 4.	Return to STEP 2, and look for an alternative offence. If none, then skip to STEP 5, concluding that no offence is committed.

STEP 4 Consider defences

The word 'consider' here is important as you should not discuss every defence for every question. Rather, think whether there are any defences (eg duress) that *could* potentially apply. If there are, discuss those only.

When considering and discussing potential defences, remember to consider any specific defences (ie those statutory defences that only apply to certain offences) as well as the general defences (discussed in **Chapters 13** and **14**).

STEP 5 Conclude

This is usually a single sentence either saying that it is likely that D has committed the offence, or saying that it is not likely either because an offence element is not satisfied or because a defence is likely to apply. It is not often that you will be able to say categorically whether or not D has committed the offence, particularly when applying concepts such as dishonesty, so it is usually best to conclude in terms of what is more 'likely'.

---

[245] See **Chapter 4.2.1.1**.

> **STEP 6 Loop**
>
> Go back up to STEP 1, identifying the next potential criminal event. Continue until you have discussed all the relevant potentially criminal events.

 ONLINE RESOURCES

www.oup.com/he/child-ormerod4e

This chapter is accompanied by a selection of online resources to help you with this topic, including:

- **Self-test questions and scenario questions**
- **Videos** from the authors
- **Audio introduction** to the topic
- **Chapter summary sheet**
- Two **sample examination questions** with answer guidance
- **Further reading and weblinks**

Also available on the online resources are:

- A selection of **videos** from the authors containing general advice on problem questions and essay questions
- **Legal updates**

10

Fraud

10.1 Introduction

Fraud offences are designed to criminalise D's dishonest conduct—her lies, her withholding of information, and/or her abuse of position—where she intends V to lose or risk losing property and/or to gain property herself. This has been contrasted with theft where, put simply, D dishonestly appropriates the property of another. However, the extent to which these offences operate to target *distinct* mischief is a matter of contention, particularly since theft has been held to include consensual appropriation.[1]

Fraud is an offence under section 1 of the Fraud Act 2006 (FA 2006). Prior to the FA 2006, conduct that we would now charge as fraud was criminalised through a variety of deception offences within the Theft Acts 1968 (TA 1968), 1978 (TA 1978), and 1996 (TA 1996), which have now been repealed. Those deception offences were heavily and consistently criticised, both for their unnecessary complexity as well as their overly restrictive application.[2] For example, under the pre-FA 2006 law, the prosecution had to demonstrate a 'representation' from D; that that representation *caused* V to form a false belief; that that false belief *caused* V to act in a specified manner, such as transferring property; and that V's behaviour thereby benefited D or another. Demonstrating each causal link within this chain was often very difficult for prosecutors, and, more importantly, it was argued that D's behaviour may have been equally blameworthy even when certain elements were missing (eg where D failed to deceive V, but still gained the advantage[3]).

The FA 2006, based upon Law Commission recommendations,[4] recast this area of the law. Moving away from the previous result-based deception offences, the fraud offence focusses on D's dishonest conduct combined with her intention to make a gain and/or cause a loss or risk of a loss to V. It is therefore a conduct crime, committed regardless of whether V was deceived or any other consequences were caused. In this manner, the fraud offence represents a move away from the property harms discussed in **Chapter 9** (eg theft, criminal damage, etc), and shares many more characteristics with the inchoate offences to be discussed in **Chapter 11**.

The offence of fraud is set out in section 1 of the FA 2006. The maximum sentence on indictment is 10 years' imprisonment (three years more than theft).[5]

1(1) A person is guilty of fraud if he is in breach of any of the sections listed in subsection (2) (which provide for different ways of committing the offence).

(2) The sections are—

(a) section 2 (fraud by false representation),

(b) section 3 (fraud by failing to disclose information), and

(c) section 4 (fraud by abuse of position).

Fraud under section 1(1) of the FA 2006 is a single offence that can be committed in three separate ways, set out across sections 2–4. To examine the offence, it is useful to analyse each of these individually. Following this, the chapter will discuss offences of obtaining services dishonestly (FA 2006, s11) and possession of articles for use in frauds (FA 2006, s6). We will also provide a brief overview of other related fraud and deception offences that remain active within the current law.

---

[1] We discuss this later in the context of potential reform to the law (**10.8.3**).

[2] For an overview of this criticism, see Law Commission, *Fraud and Deception* (Consultation 155, 1999).

[3] *Edwards* [1978] Crim LR 49.

[4] Law Commission, *Fraud* (No 276, 2002). See also Home Office, *Fraud Law Reform* (Consultation, 2004).

[5] FA 2006, s1(3)(b).

10.2 FA 2006, s2: fraud by false representation

The first route to liability for fraud under section 1 of the FA 2006 is fraud by false representation, defined in section 2. The offence elements within section 2 are exceptionally wide, and this route to fraud is prosecuted most often in practice.[6]

2(1) A person is in breach of this section if he—

    (a) dishonestly makes a false representation, and

    (b) intends, by making the representation—

        (i)   to make a gain for himself or another, or

        (ii) to cause loss to another or to expose another to a risk of loss.

The elements of section 2 are illustrated in **Table 10.1**.

There is fraud under section 2 where D makes a false representation dishonestly, with the intention thereby to make a gain or cause a loss, or risk of loss, to another. Whether V is actually deceived by D's representation, and/or whether V loses or D gains, is irrelevant (ie no results need to be demonstrated).

10.2.1 Actus reus of s2

The actus reus of section 2 requires D to have made a representation, and for that representation to be false.

Table 10.1 FA 2006, s2

	Actus reus	**Mens rea**
Conduct element	Making a representation	Voluntary
Circumstance element	D's representation is false	Knowledge or foresight of a possibility
	D's representation is dishonest	In context of D's knowledge and belief
Result element	None	None
Ulterior mens rea element	*	Intention, by the making of the representation, to make a gain or cause a loss to another or expose another to a risk of loss

---

[6] Ormerod, 'The Fraud Act 2006—Criminalising Lying' [2007] Crim LR 193.

10.2.1.1 Making a representation

It must be shown that D made a representation. Three important aspects of a 'representation' require comment: the subject of the representation; the recipient; and the method:

A) The subject of the representation: Paradigm cases will involve false representations as to facts. For example, D assures V that the painting she is selling is genuine; that the car is not stolen; that she has sufficient funds to pay for the meal; and so on. However, section 2 is not limited to representations as to facts.

> 2(1) 'Representation' means any representation as to fact or law, including a representation as to the state of mind of—
>
> (a) the person making the representation, or
>
> (b) any other person.

D makes a representation as to law where she informs someone about a legal detail, such as a contractual matter;[7] and as to a state of mind where she states her intentions or beliefs or those of another (eg her intention to pay for goods on delivery).

Difficulty has arisen in relation to statements of opinion. For example, D exaggerates the quality of sale goods; tells V that her roof would benefit from retiling; etc. Under the pre-FA 2006 law, cases of this kind were decided inconsistently, with certain cases falling short of a representation,[8] whilst others were caught.[9] It is submitted that, under the current law, matters of opinion should *always* be treated as representations of D's belief as to facts. The focus then shifts, in such cases, to whether that opinion was honestly held.

B) The recipient of the representation: Representations will usually be made to a person (V). Where this is the case, there is a question whether V must be aware of the representation for it to be complete. For example, what if V does not hear D's spoken comments, because, unknown to D, she is deaf; or V does not see D's email because it is blocked by V's email filters; etc? There is no case yet directly on this point, but it is likely that the courts will interpret 'representation' broadly to be satisfied even where V remains oblivious. This is supported by a similarly broad interpretation given to 'communication' in other areas of the law,[10] a term which is arguably more likely than 'representation' to require acknowledgement from V.

 Point to remember . . .

Although V does not need to be aware of the representation, this does not mean that D will commit the offence when she makes intentionally private representations (eg notes something

---

[7] Note that it is for the judge, and not the jury, to decide the legal status of matters such as a contractal term: *Whatcott* [2019] EWCA Crim 188.

[8] *Bryan* (1857) Dears & B 265: saying spoons were as good as Elkington's (a famous brand) was a mere exaggeration.

[9] *Smith v Land and House Property Corporation* (1884) 28 Ch D 7: saying a tenant was 'most desirable' where there was a consistent history of non-payment of rent.

[10] *Collins* [2006] UKHL 40: discussing the offence of grossly offensive communications under the Communications Act 2003, s127.

inaccurate in her diary). Other elements of the offence, such as the required intention to make a gain or cause a loss by the representation, mean that the offence will only catch representations that are aimed at influencing others (ie D must intend to make a representation to another or a machine).

Although D's representations will usually be aimed at a person, this need not be the case. Under the pre-FA 2006 law, it was held that 'deception' entailed the deception of a person, and so liability in cases where D deceived a machine, such as a banking system, became highly problematic.[11] Under the current law, this is addressed by section 2(5).

2(5) For the purposes of this section a representation may be regarded as made if it (or anything implying it) is submitted in any form to any system or device designed to receive, convey or respond to communications (with or without human intervention).

Despite rather complex drafting, this subsection clearly allows for fraud by false representation where there is no intended human recipient. If anything, it may be too broadly drafted. Read literally, it may even apply where D drafts an email containing a misrepresentation and saves (submits) it to her computer (any system).

C) **The method of the representation:** Section 2 can apply regardless of how D chooses to communicate with V, whether orally; in writing; by gestures; etc. D may even make a representation indirectly via an agent. This is illustrated in *Idrees v DPP*.

 Idrees v DPP [2011] EWHC 624 (Admin)

Having failed his driving theory test on multiple occasions, D arranged for another person (P) to impersonate him, and pass the test on his behalf. D was charged with fraud by false representation, the false representation being P's impersonation whilst acting as D's agent.

- Magistrates' court: guilty of fraud.
- High Court: appeal dismissed. D was making a false representation (via P), and was doing so with the intention to make a gain (pass the test).

As well as catching different methods of physical communication, section 6(2) also clarifies that both express and implied representations will be caught. Thus, just as D makes a false representation when she tells a shop assistant falsely that she has authority to use a credit card, the same is also true where D simply presents the card for payment, thereby implying that she has authority to do so.[12] The case of *Barnard*, although pre-FA 2006, provides a memorable illustration.

---

[11] *Holmes* [2004] EWHC 2020 (Admin).
[12] For a similar interpretation pre-2006, see *Lambie* [1982] AC 449.

Barnard (1837) 7 C & P 784 (pre-FA 2006)

D entered an Oxford cobblers and requested boots and straps. D was wearing a cap and gown (of the type then worn by Oxford University students), and requested the student discount. D was not a student of the university and was charged with a deception offence.

- Crown Court: guilty. D clearly deceived through an express note which claimed that he was a student. However, Bolland B went on to say that even if D did not present the note, his dress provided an implied deception sufficient for liability.

Despite section 2 being wide enough to encompass different methods of representation, one area of uncertainty has emerged. Given that section 3 of the FA 2006 specifically criminalises fraud by omission, does section 2 also cover implied representations by omission?

It is contended that for section 2, two scenarios involving omissions can, and should, be distinguished. In the first scenario, D makes a true representation to V, the facts then change, but D omits to inform V of this change. In these circumstances, it is possible that D's representation will be interpreted as a continuing act to include her failure to inform V after the facts change, and thus it is possible that section 2 will apply. Pre-FA 2006, such implied representations were found whether D was responsible for the change of facts, or simply became aware of them.[13] This is illustrated in *DPP v Ray*.

 DPP v Ray [1974] AC 370 (pre-FA 2006)

D and others ordered and consumed a meal at a Chinese restaurant. They did so intending to pay. However, at the end of the meal they changed their minds. They continued to sit in the restaurant until the waiter left the room, and then ran out. D was charged with a deception offence relating to his debt to the restaurant.

- Crown Court: guilty of the deception offence.
- Divisional Court: appeal allowed—D's omission was not a deception.
- House of Lords: (3:2) appeal allowed. D's representations to be a paying customer continued from his ordering and eating the food (positive acts) and included his continuing to sit in the restaurant after he had decided not to pay (omission). Thus, there was coincidence of deception and mens rea.

In cases such as *Ray*, recognition of an implied continuing representation is essential to liability and, under the FA 2006, the potential for implied representations of this kind has been confirmed in *Government of the United Arab Emirates v Allen*.[14] However, in this case, the Divisional Court cautioned that implied continuing

---

[13] *Rai* [2000] 1 Cr App R 242: D failed to inform the local authority that his mother had died, and allowed them to install the disability aids to which he was no longer entitled.

[14] [2012] EWHC 1712 (Admin).

representations would only be found where it was 'reasonable' to read such a representation into the conduct of another. Stressing the fact-specific nature of this inquiry, the court rejected that a representation was made where D failed to inform her bank that she was no longer able to honour a security cheque deposited when she received a loan.

In the second omission scenario, D becomes aware that V is mistaken about a certain fact, but fails to correct her mistaken belief. For example, V says 'it will be great to buy a car which has only had one owner', where D, who is selling the car, knows the car has had many more owners. In such cases it could be argued that, despite no express false representation, D's silence could amount to an implied representation that V's beliefs are correct. However, it is contended that this route to liability should be avoided. In line with CPS charging guidelines,[15] the criminal law should take care not to undermine the civil rules of *caveat emptor* (buyer beware), and maintain a difference between active representations and a simple failure to report faults. In the most serious cases of this kind there will generally be a legal duty upon D to disclose the omitted information, and in such cases section 3 of the FA 2006, and not section 2, provides the appropriate route to fraud liability.

10.2.1.2 The representation must be false

Section 2(2) defines what is meant by a 'false' representation.

2(2) A representation is false if—

    (a) it is untrue or misleading, and

    (b) the person making it knows that it is, or might be, untrue or misleading.

The first part of this provision, section 2(2)(a), extends the meaning of 'false' beyond core cases of outright untruth to include representations that are misleading. A representation may be misleading, and thus come within this part of the actus reus, even if it is literally true. For example, if V asks D, a car dealer, if there has been any reported problem with a particular model of car in the last year, and D answers honestly that there has not, this may still be misleading if D omits to mention the several hundred reported problems every other year. Equally, where D displays a fake painting among genuine classics, even if she does not state that the fake is genuine, her choice of display may still be misleading.[16]

Where D believes that her statement is false, but it is in fact true, there will be no fraud. This was the case in *Deller* (pre-FA 2006),[17] where D agreed to sell his car 'free of encumbrances' in the belief that he had mortgaged the car (ie it was encumbered). However, as the proposed mortgage was unsuccessful, his statement turned out to be true. In such cases, the appropriate charge is attempted fraud.[18]

[15] www.cps.gov.uk/legal-guidance/fraud-act-2006.
[16] *Hill v Gray* (1816) 1 Stark 434.
[17] (1952) 36 Cr App R 184.
[18] Discussed at **Chapter 11.2**.

10.2.2 Mens rea of s2

The mens rea of section 2 is made up of three core elements: D must at least foresee a risk that her representation is false; she must act dishonestly; and she must intend to make a gain, cause a loss, or cause a risk of loss to another. Each element must coincide with (ie must be present at the point in time of) D's false representation.

10.2.2.1 Knowledge that the statement is, or might be, false

This element is satisfied where D *either* knows her representation is false or misleading, *or* foresees that it might be (s2(2)(b)). In either case, subjective mens rea is required: simple negligence (ie a reasonable person would have foreseen) will not be sufficient. This has been confirmed in *Augunas*,[19] and will include cases where D *deliberately* closes her eyes to a risk or deliberately avoids confirming facts when she has at least foreseen a risk of falsity.

Including the foresight of a risk makes this element of mens rea extremely wide. For example, it will be satisfied where an art dealer, D, advertises a painting for sale as an original, being aware of the risk, which seems unavoidable in the art world, that it might be a fake. As a result, the requirement of 'dishonesty' is once again crucial for avoiding liability in such cases.

10.2.2.2 Dishonesty

The FA 2006 does not provide a definition of dishonesty, and there is also no equivalent to section 2 of the TA 1968 which provides examples of conduct not to be deemed dishonest.[20] Therefore, in the absence of any statutory guidance, the term is left exclusively to the common law definition and the *Ivey/Barton* test.[21]

We have already discussed the *Ivey/Barton* test for dishonesty in detail in the context of theft, which will not be repeated here.[22] The *Ivey/Barton* test, which replaces the old common law test in *Ghosh*,[23] requires the jury to engage with two questions of fact:

- **Question 1:** What was the actual state of D's knowledge or belief as to the facts?

- **Question 2:** In the context of Question 1, was D's conduct dishonest by the standards of ordinary decent people?

There are several general problems with the *Ivey/Barton* test, not least the unpredictability of asking a jury to identify a common standard of honesty. Added to these criticisms, it should be noted that the FA 2006 was created under the explicit understanding that 'dishonesty' would be defined and applied according to the old *Ghosh* test, making the change at common law particularly troubling.[24]

An important question has emerged within the academic literature on fraud and dishonesty: is lying always dishonest?[25] If the answer were 'yes', then the section 2 offence would be rendered hopelessly wide. When television adverts, for example, imply that the spraying

---

[19] [2013] EWCA Crim 2046.
[20] See **Chapter 9.2.5**. The TA, s2 states that there will be no dishonesty in theft where D thinks she has a legal right; D thinks V would consent; or D thinks V is untraceable by reasonable steps.
[21] [2017] UKSC 67.
[22] See **Chapter 9.2.5.2**.
[23] [1982] EWCA Crim 2.
[24] See Laird and Ormerod, 'Ivey v Genting Casinos—Much Ado About Nothing?' in Clarry (ed), *Supreme Court Yearbook* (2019) 380, including the potential to challenge the *Ivey* judgment on this basis.
[25] Ormerod, 'Criminalising Lying' [2007] Crim LR 193.

of a deodorant will make the wearer sexually irresistible, or that an energy drink can make you play sport like a professional, such representations are clearly false, but it is unlikely that they would be considered dishonest by a reasonable person. Ironically in such cases, the more extreme the lie, and thus the less plausible, the less likely it is to be found dishonest. However, there is a clear grey area, for example occupations such as market trading and used car dealerships where trade patter and exaggeration is common.[26] Such cases will be left to the case-by-case application of the test in *Ivey*, with the likely outcomes far from clear.

10.2.2.3 Intention to make a gain or cause a loss (or risk of loss)

Section 2 does not require D to make a gain, or to cause or risk a loss to another in fact (ie these are not actus reus elements). However, D must act with the ulterior intention to achieve at least one of these ends. For example, where D starts a false rumour about a competitor's business, this element of the offence will be satisfied as long as D at least intends to risk causing a loss to that competitor, even if she does not intend to gain anything.[27]

The definitions of 'gain' and 'loss' are set out in section 5 of the FA 2006.

5(2) 'Gain' and 'loss'—

    (a) extend only to gain or loss in money or other property;

    (b) include any such gain or loss whether temporary or permanent;

    and 'property' means any property whether real or personal (including things in action and other intangible property).

  (3) 'Gain' includes a gain by keeping what one has, as well as a gain by getting what one does not have.

  (4) 'Loss' includes a loss by not getting what one might get, as well as a loss by parting with what one has.

As made clear in section 5(2)(a), D's intentions must relate to property, so an intention to gain something other than property, for example sexual favours, will not be sufficient. However, the definition of property here is very wide, including all tangible and intangible property, and without the exclusions that exist under the TA 1968.[28]

The final point to remember is one that is easily overlooked: D's intention must be causal. D must intend to *cause* the gain or loss by her conduct. This is illustrated in *Gilbert*.

> **Gilbert** [2012] EWCA Crim 2392
>
> D and others set up a bank account in order to facilitate their company's activities—developing and selling real estate. In doing so, they made false representations about their financial position. D was charged with fraud by false representation.
>
> • Crown Court: guilty of fraud.
>
> • Court of Appeal: appeal allowed. Although a false representation was made, the court failed to direct the jury clearly that D must intend to make a gain *from* that representation.

---

[26] It should be remembered that the standard for 'honesty' is universal, and not industry-specific. The fact that a certain lie is common within an industry is no excuse for dishonesty: *Hayes* [2015] EWCA Crim 1944.

[27] Usually the prosecution will allege that D either intended to gain *or* expose V to a risk of loss, but if they allege one specifically they are obliged to prove that intention: *Bush* [2019] EWCA Crim 29.

[28] eg land and wild creatures. These (and other examples) are not property in the context of theft because they are excluded by the TA 1968, s4. However, they are property in the context of fraud.

Importantly, the court in *Gilbert* did not rule out the possibility that D intended her false representation to cause a gain in allowing her to finance the company, thereby allowing her to make a profit. However, D's conviction in the Crown Court was unsafe because the need to demonstrate this intention-based causal link was not clarified for the jury.

 Point to remember . . .

The requirement for D to intend her conduct to 'cause' a gain or a loss provides a further (potential) tool for limiting liability. Consider the problem examples of extreme advertising, market traders, and used car salesmen discussed earlier. In such cases, where the trader makes an extreme puff (eg 'these sunglasses are the same as those worn by David Beckham'), it may be contended that she does not intend this representation to 'cause' V to buy the goods. Rather, perhaps, such comments are intended simply as friendly trade banter or humour.[29]

10.3 FA 2006, s3: fraud by failure to disclose information

The second way D commits fraud under section 1 of the FA 2006 is fraud by failure to disclose information, set out in section 3.

3. A person is in breach of this section if he—
    (a) dishonestly fails to disclose to another person information which he is under a legal duty to disclose, and
    (b) intends, by failing to disclose the information—
        (i) to make a gain for himself or another, or
        (ii) to cause loss to another or to expose another to a risk of loss.

The elements of section 3 are illustrated in **Table 10.2**.

Table 10.2 FA 2006, s3

	Actus reus	**Mens rea**
Conduct element	Failing to disclose information	Voluntary
Circumstance element	D has a legal duty to disclose the information	None
	D's failure to disclose is dishonest	In the context of D's knowledge and belief

---

[29] Ormerod and Gardner discussed this point in [2007] Crim LR 660.

Result element	None	None
Ulterior mens rea element	*	Intention, by failing to disclose, to make a gain or cause a loss to another or expose another to a risk of loss

As with section 2, section 3 is a conduct crime, where no gain or loss needs to be demonstrated within the actus reus. However, D must dishonestly fail to disclose information where there is a legal duty to do so, and D must intend thereby to make a gain or cause a loss or risk of loss to another.

10.3.1 Actus reus of s3

The actus reus of section 3 requires a failure to disclose information where D has a legal duty to do so.

10.3.1.1 Identifying a legal duty to disclose information

The question whether a legal duty exists is one of law for the judge. There is no definition of 'legal duty' in the statute. However, quoting from the original Law Commission report,[30] the FA 2006 explanatory notes make clear that 'legal duty' should be interpreted in line with the civil law.

> 7.28 . . . Such a duty may derive from statute (such as the provisions governing company prospectuses), from the fact that the transaction in question is one of the utmost good faith (such as a contract of insurance), from the express or implied terms of a contract, from the custom of a particular trade or market, or from the existence of a fiduciary relationship between the parties (such as that of agent and principal).

> 7.29 For this purpose there is a legal duty to disclose information not only if the defendant's failure to disclose it gives the victim a cause of action for damages, but also if the law gives the victim a right to set aside any change in his or her legal position to which he or she may consent as a result of the non-disclosure. For example, a person in a fiduciary position has a duty to disclose material information when entering into a contract with his or her beneficiary, in the sense that a failure to make such disclosure will entitle the beneficiary to rescind the contract and to reclaim any property transferred under it.[31]

The second paragraph of this guidance is particularly informative, clarifying that a legal duty to disclose will arise whenever D's failure to disclose information would render a contract, or relevant part of a contract, voidable. Clear examples will include a failure to disclose medical conditions when taking out life insurance; failure to disclose a criminal

---

[30] Law Commission, *Fraud* (No 276, 2002) paras 7.28–7.29.
[31] FA 2006 Explanatory Notes, s3.

record when applying for a job; failure, as in *Mashta*, to reveal a change of financial position when in receipt of State benefits; and so on.[32]

Mashta [2010] EWCA Crim 2595

D continued to receive asylum support on grounds of destitution whilst in gainful employment. Among other charges, D was charged with fraud by failing to disclose his employment.

• Crown Court: guilty of fraud.
• Court of Appeal: appeal on sentence allowed, but conviction upheld.

It is important to note that not all financial relationships entail a legal duty to disclose information, and it is essential for the prosecution to be able to point to a specific legal duty owed by D. Where, for example, D ceased paying her council tax having told the council, falsely, that she had moved and was renting the property to another party, she was not liable under section 3 because the prosecution could find no statutory duty on D to inform the council she remained living in the property.[33] Anything short of a clear legal duty to disclose will be insufficient.[34]

Assessment matters . . .

In most cases D's failure to disclose could also be presented as a false representation (a representation that there is nothing to disclose), and so could be prosecuted under section 2. In clear cases of a failure to disclose, section 3 is likely to be preferred because it provides the most accurate label for D's conduct. However, where the presence of a duty is more difficult to identify, it is likely that section 2 will generally be preferred because there is no requirement within section 2 to demonstrate a duty. We discuss this further below in the context of writing assessments (**10.9**).

10.3.1.2 When does D fail to disclose

D's failure to disclose will often be obvious on the facts. For example, D has a duty in *Mashta* to disclose any gainful employment whilst receiving benefits; D does not disclose; so D has 'failed' to do so. However, it is important to remember that a failure to disclose is satisfied not only where D discloses nothing at all, but also where D fails to disclose *sufficient* information in a manner that renders relevant parts of a contract voidable. Thus, even partial disclosure may still satisfy the actus reus of this offence. Again, this question will involve the judge in a detailed analysis of the relevant civil law obligation.

[32] See Salter, 'It's Criminal Not to Disclose' (2007) 37 Fam L 432: discussing divorce proceedings where D fails to disclose the true extent of her assets. See also *Razoq* [2012] EWCA Crim 674: D (a doctor) failed to disclose disciplinary hearings and suspension from hospital to other locum (ad hoc medical work) agencies.
[33] *D* [2019] EWCA Crim 209.
[34] The Law Commission had originally recommended a wider conception of 'legal duty to disclose', including 'moral duties'. However, this was rejected by the Home Office: *Fraud Law Reform* (Consultation, 2004) paras 18–25.

10.3.2 Mens rea of s3

The mens rea of section 3 requires (i) D to have acted dishonestly, and (ii) to have intended by her failure to disclose to make a gain or to cause a loss or risk of loss to another. These two core elements have been discussed above in relation to section 2 (**10.2.2**), and should be interpreted in exactly the same way for section 3.

It should be noted that whilst the section 2 offence required mens rea of knowledge or awareness of a risk that D's representation was false, section 3 does not contain any equivalent requirement in relation to the duty to disclose. Therefore, D may be liable under section 3 even if she did not know or even foresee a possibility that she was under a legal obligation to disclose information. However, although this seems unacceptably broad, the possibility for unfairness is limited by the requirement of dishonesty and the *Ivey* test. This is because where D is unaware of a legal duty to disclose, her failure to do so is much less likely to be considered dishonest by the standards of reasonable and honest people.

10.4 FA 2006, s4: fraud by abuse of position

The final way D commits fraud under section 1 of the FA 2006 is fraud by abuse of position, set out in section 4.

4(1) A person is in breach of this section if he—

  (a) occupies a position in which he is expected to safeguard, or not to act against, the financial interests of another person,

  (b) dishonestly abuses that position, and

  (c) intends, by means of the abuse of that position—

   (i) to make a gain for himself or another, or

   (ii) to cause loss to another or to expose another to a risk of loss.

The elements of section 4 are illustrated in **Table 10.3**.

Table 10.3 FA 2006, s4

	Actus reus	**Mens rea**
Conduct element	Acts or omissions	Voluntary
Circumstance element	D occupies a position in which she is expected to safeguard the financial interests of another	None
	D abuses that position	None
	D's abuse of position is dishonest	In the context of D's knowledge and belief

(Continued)

Table 10.3 Continued

Result element	None	None
Ulterior mens rea element	*	Intention, by abuse of position, to make a gain or cause a loss to another or expose another to a risk of loss

As with sections 2 and 3, section 4 is a conduct crime. D must dishonestly abuse a position in which she is expected to safeguard the financial interests of another, D must intend thereby to make a gain or cause a loss or risk of loss to another, but no such gain or loss needs to be demonstrated in fact.

10.4.1 Actus reus of s4

The actus reus of section 4 requires D, by act or omission,[35] to abuse a position in which she is expected to safeguard the financial interests of another.

10.4.1.1 Identifying the relevant positions

The first element of the actus reus requires D to occupy a position in which she is expected to safeguard the financial interests of another. Unfortunately, again, this core element is not defined in the statute.

The most obvious interpretation of the required 'position' is where D owes a 'fiduciary duty' to another (ie a civil law duty to act within the interests of another). Indeed, most of the examples provided by the Law Commission and government have involved such duties. For example, employees using insider knowledge to make secret profits; those taking advantage of vulnerable people whose finances they have agreed to administer; and so on. *Marshall* provides a useful illustration.

 Marshall [2009] EWCA Crim 2076

D was a manager of a residential care home for people with extreme learning difficulties, and in that position had control over a particular resident's (V's) finances. Over a period of time, D withdrew over £7,000 from the resident's account and used it for her own benefit. D was charged with fraud by abuse of position.

• Crown Court: guilty of fraud.
• Court of Appeal: appeal on sentence (12 months) dismissed.

Beyond cases of this kind, however, the FA 2006 Explanatory Notes indicate that the offence will not be limited to abuse of a fiduciary duty.

---

[35] FA 2006, s4(2).

The necessary relationship will be present between trustee and beneficiary, director and company, professional person and client, agent and principal, employee and employer, or between partners. It may arise otherwise, for example within a family, or in the context of voluntary work, or in any context where the parties are not at arm's length. In nearly all cases where it arises, it will be recognised by the civil law as importing fiduciary duties, and any relationship that is so recognised will suffice. We see no reason, however, why the existence of such duties should be essential. This does not of course mean that it would be entirely a matter for the fact-finders whether the necessary relationship exists. The question whether the particular facts alleged can properly be described as giving rise to that relationship will be an issue capable of being ruled upon by the judge and, if the case goes to the jury, of being the subject of directions.[36]

The guidance maintains that the question of relevant position is one for the judge, but by breaking away from the civil law concept of fiduciary duty, the task for the judge identifying a relevant position can be very difficult. Potentially, whenever D is in a position of trust, or expresses some form of loyalty to another, they may satisfy this element.[37] This question was explored in *Valujevs*.

Valujevs [2014] EWCA Crim 2888

D and others were gangmasters (they controlled a group of casual agricultural workers, supplying accommodation and travel). In order to secure personal gain, D made unwarranted deductions from workers' pay, grossly inflated rents, and withheld work in order to force workers into debt. D was charged with fraud by abuse of position, along with specific unlicensed gangmaster offences.

- Crown Court: guilty of gangmaster offences; but no case to answer in relation to fraud. Although D treated the victims very poorly, he was not 'expected to safeguard' their 'financial interests', and so did not fall within the terms of section 4.
- Court of Appeal: allowing appeal. D's conduct is capable of falling within the scope of section 4.

The Court of Appeal clarified a number of key points in this judgment. First, it was confirmed that the duty to safeguard the financial interests of another is an objective question for the court. In other words, we are not talking about legitimate expectations from D's or V's perspective, but from the perspective of the reasonable person. This is sensible, not allowing D to avoid a duty unfairly, and not allowing V to impose one artificially. Secondly, the court clarified that although such a duty arose in this case, this was because D had collected the pay of his workers and was therefore responsible for delivering it to them. Crucially, the duty did not arise simply because D was charging inflated rents or paying poor wages, and such conduct alone will not be sufficient.[38]

10.4.1.2 When does D abuse this position

Once established to the satisfaction of the judge that the position D occupies qualifies in law as a relevant one, it is then a question of fact for the jury whether she abused this position. Where D owes a fiduciary duty to V, establishing abuse will involve directing the

---

[36] FA 2006 Explanatory Notes, s4. Quoting from Law Commission, *Fraud* (No 276, 2002) para 7.38.
[37] See Collins, 'Fraud by Abuse of Position: Theorising Section 4 of the Fraud Act 2006' [2011] Crim LR 513.
[38] Collins, 'Fraud by Abuse of Position and Unlicensed Gangmasters' (2016) 79 MLR 354.

jury on potentially complex civil law rules relating to breach of duty. Beyond this, as the offence extends past formal relationships of this kind, the term 'abuse' has had to remain flexible. As a result, the term is undefined. This is justified in the Explanatory Notes as a conscious choice to maintain flexibility.[39] Unfortunately, what is gained in flexibility from not defining such a crucial term is almost certainly lost in lack of certainty and consistency when the offence is applied by the courts. This is illustrated in *Pennock and Pennock*.

 Pennock and Pennock [2014] EWCA Crim 598

A husband and wife (D1 and D2) opened a joint bank account with an uncle (V) aged 90. £100,000 of V's money was subsequently transferred into the account and later used to buy a house to be owned by D1 and D2's daughter (X). V later claimed to have no knowledge of the account, the transfer, or the use of the money. D1 and D2 were charged with fraud under section 4 as to (a) the money transfer, and (b) transferring the title of the property to X.

- Crown Court: guilty of fraud.
- Court of Appeal: appeal allowed. The evidence and detail of abuse was not sufficiently clear on the facts, the trial judge having failed to direct the jury that D1 and D2 were free to make use of funds from a joint account (where this was free of restrictions) and that the transfer of property title did not undermine V's equitable interest because X was not a bona fide purchaser. Although the court made clear that the facts could have resulted in liability under section 4, the lack of clear direction from the trial judge as to the civil law involved rendered the convictions unsafe.

10.4.2 Mens rea of s4

The mens rea of section 4 requires D to have (i) acted dishonestly, and (ii) to have intended *by* her abuse of position to make a gain or to cause a loss or risk of loss to another. These two core elements have been discussed previously in relation to section 2 (**10.2.2**), and should be interpreted in exactly the same way for section 4.

The additional circumstances for the section 4 offence are strict liability elements, as we saw with section 3 as well. Thus, although D must occupy a position in which she is expected to safeguard the financial interests of another, and although D must abuse that position, it is not necessary to prove that D had any specific mens rea as to either of these actus reus elements. D may therefore commit the offence even where she is unaware that she holds such a position.[40] However, as with section 3, although this seems unacceptably broad, the possibility for unfairness is limited by the requirement of dishonesty and the *Ivey* test. This is because where D is unaware that she occupies a relevant position, her potential abuse of it is much less likely to be considered dishonest by the standards of reasonable and honest people.

 Point to remember . . .

We discussed in **Chapter 9** the central role of 'dishonesty' within most of the property offences, and highlighted criticism of its inability to perform this role effectively. Within the core fraud offences the same, and arguably even greater, reliance is apparent.

---

[39] FA 2006 Explanatory Notes, s4.
[40] The term 'abuse' implies some form of conscious or intentional wrongdoing. However, there is nothing in the statute to make such mens rea a requirement.

10.5 FA 2006, s11: obtaining services dishonestly

Beyond the core fraud offence, set out across sections 1–5, the FA 2006 contains several separate complementary offences. Obtaining services dishonestly is set out at section 11 of the FA 2006.[41] The maximum penalty on indictment is five years' imprisonment.[42]

11(1) A person is guilty of an offence under this section if he obtains services for himself or another—

   (a) by a dishonest act, and

   (b) in breach of subsection (2).

 (2) A person obtains services in breach of this subsection if—

   (a) they are made available on the basis that payment has been, is being or will be made for or in respect of them,

   (b) he obtains them without any payment having been made for or in respect of them or without payment having been made in full, and

   (c) when he obtains them, he knows—

     (i)   that they are being made available on the basis described in paragraph (a), or

     (ii) that they might be,

  but intends that payment will not be made, or will not be made in full.

The elements of section 11 are set out in **Table 10.4**.

Table 10.4 FA 2006, s11

	Actus reus	**Mens rea**
Conduct element	Acts causing the result	Voluntary
Circumstance element	D's obtaining of services is dishonest	In the context of D's knowledge and belief
	Payment is required for the services	Knowledge or foresight of that being the case
	No (or insufficient) payment is provided	Intention
Result element	Services are obtained for D or another	Intention

Unlike the offence of fraud discussed earlier, section 11 creates a result crime: D's dishonest acts must *cause* services to be obtained in circumstances where payment is knowingly withheld.

---

[41] Replacing the old offence 'obtaining services by deception' (TA 1978, s1). Withey, 'The Fraud Act 2006—Some Early Observations and Comparisons with the Former Law' (2007) 71 JCL 220.

[42] FA 2006, s11(3).

10.5.1 Actus reus of s11

The actus reus of section 11 requires D to have acquired services for which payment is required, and to have failed to pay for these services in full. Paradigm examples will include cases where D uses an illegal device (decoder) to watch satellite TV without paying; where D takes goods on hire without intending to pay for them; where D gains entry to a sporting or music event by climbing over a fence; and so on. Indeed, where the service requires payment, the offence will even cover D who opens a bank account using false details, or continues to use her account having had her authority to do so removed.[43]

Two points should be emphasised. First, as section 11 is a result crime, causation is crucial. Thus, where D obtains services, for example, gaining entry to a sporting event, with the intention of paying, but decides after the event that she will not do so, she does not commit a section 11 offence. This is because, at the time she acts to *cause* the services to be obtained, she is not yet dishonest; and when she is later dishonest, she has already obtained the services. The correct charge in these circumstances, discussed later, would be making off without payment (**10.7**).[44]

Secondly, it must be shown that D acquired a 'service'. This is not defined in the statute, but is clearly distinct from and considerably wider than 'property'. The only restriction is that the service must be one for which payment is required. Thus, where D acts dishonestly to gain a gratuitous service D does not commit a section 11 offence: as, for example, where D lies about his age to obtain a free car wash for the elderly.

10.5.2 Mens rea of s11

To satisfy the mens rea of section 11, D must know that payment for the service is or might be required; must intend to obtain the service without paying; and must act dishonestly. The first two of these requirements are relatively straightforward, but should be carefully applied. For example, where D lies about her religion or postcode to access a selective fee-charging school, she will not commit a section 11 offence if she intends to pay the fees: she acts dishonestly to obtain a service, but she does not intend to avoid payment.[45] The final element requires us to apply the *Ivey* test for dishonesty. This was discussed earlier in the context of section 2 (**10.2.2.2**), and the same approach applies here.

10.6 Fraud preparation offences

Sections 6 and 7 of the FA 2006 criminalise acts in preparation for fraud. Section 6 proscribes possession of articles for fraud; and section 7 proscribes the making or supplying of articles for use in frauds. In both cases, the law is trying to facilitate early intervention by the police, targeting D before she has caused or attempted to cause harm.

[43] *Sofroniou* [2003] EWCA Crim 3681.
[44] Where D has obtained the services and continues to represent that she is willing to pay, there will be an alternative charge under the FA 2006, s2.
[45] Monaghan, 'Fraudsters? Putting Parents in the Dock' (2010) 174 CL&JW 581 and 'School Application Forms and the Criminal Law' [2015] Crim LR 270.

Extra detail . . .

It should be remembered that, under the current law, the principal fraud offence is also drafted in an inchoate or pre-emptive fashion, criminalising D where she falsely represents, fails to disclose, or abuses her position with the intent to make a gain or cause a loss, but not requiring that gain or loss (the substantive harm) to be caused. The offences under sections 6 and 7 criminalise of even earlier conduct.

10.6.1 FA 2006, s6: possession of articles for use in frauds

The maximum penalty for section 6 on indictment is five years' imprisonment.[46]

6(1) A person is guilty of an offence if he has in his possession or under his control any article for use in the course of or in connection with any fraud.

The elements of section 6 are set out in **Table 10.5.**

Table 10.5 FA 2006, s6

	Actus reus	**Mens rea**
Conduct element	Possessing or controlling an article	Voluntary (ie known) possession
Circumstance element	None	None
Result element	None	None
Ulterior mens rea element	*	Intention to use the article in connection with fraud

As **Table 10.5** illustrates, section 6 creates an extremely broad offence, criminalising the possession or control of any article with intention to use it in connection with fraud. It is irrelevant for this offence whether any fraud is completed or not.

10.6.1.1 Actus reus of s6

The two core elements of the actus reus are that D (A) has possession or control of (B) an article.

A) **Possession or control:** Straightforward cases will involve physical possession of an article on D's person. This will include, for example, where D is found with fake bank notes; with a decoding machine facilitating the illegal viewing of paid satellite television; etc.[47] It will also include, as in *Nimley*, items that might be otherwise innocent, such as an iPhone.

---

[46] FA 2006, s6(2).
[47] *Kazi* [2010] EWCA Crim 2752: possession of paper that was to be used to make fake banknotes; *Ciorba* [2009] EWCA Crim 1800: possession of a memory stick used to download data from ATM machines.

Nimley [2010] EWCA Crim 2752

D was caught recording cinema films on his iPhone. D had already successfully recorded and uploaded three previous films to the internet for free consumption. D was charged with offences including possession of articles (the iPhone) for use in fraud.

- Crown Court: guilty of section 6 offence.
- Court of Appeal: appeal against sentence allowed, removing the custodial element of the sentence and replacing it with community service.

Possession or control are not, however, limited to examples of physical possession. For example, where D has relevant articles stored in her house, in her office, or in other premises, these too will be in her possession or control. In this manner, we are in possession or control of many thousands of articles at any one time.[48]

B) **Articles:** As noted earlier, relevant articles found in D's possession may be otherwise innocent as long as D intends to use them in connection with fraud. Thus, the iPhone in *Nimley* constituted a relevant article just as much as an item, such as a decoding machine, where the sole function is to facilitate fraud. Everyday articles such as pens and paper will therefore constitute relevant articles as long as D possesses them with the required mens rea. Section 8(1) of the FA 2006 also expressly includes 'any program or data held in electronic form' as articles. Thus, where D possesses certain software or a document held in electronic form, and intends to use it in connection with fraud, she commits a section 6 offence. We wait to see how widely these terms will be interpreted by the courts. For example, does D have possession of all the information on the internet simply by her ability to access it? Surely not.

Extra detail . . .

Another aspect of the offence that gives it a wide reach is that the possession only has to be 'for use in connection with any fraud' (ie not necessarily for use to commit fraud). When looking for the coincidence of elements, this means the offence applies even where D creates the 'article' after the fraud has taken place, with the intention of covering her tracks.[49]

10.6.1.2 Mens rea of s6

The two core mens rea elements are D's (A) knowledge of possession or control, and (B) intention to use the article in connection with fraud.

A) **Knowledge of possession:** It is not clear from the statute whether D must have knowledge, or indeed any mens rea, as to the fact of possession. However, in line with other possession offences, particularly drug offences, it is contended that such a requirement should be found by the courts. In most cases, the fact that D must intend to use the article in connection with fraud will require in effect that D has knowledge of possession; but not always. For example, where D plans to use a piece of software without realising that the software is already installed on her computer. In such cases, it is contended that D should avoid liability under section 6.

---

[48] *Montague* [2013] EWCA Crim 1781.
[49] *Smith* [2020] EWCA Crim 38.

B) Intention to use the article in connection with fraud: This is a common law supplement to the wording of the statute, narrowing the offence to more acceptable limits. However, the intention requirement remains broadly constructed. For example, the phrase 'in connection' clearly allows for cases where D does not plan to use the article as a tool for the fraud, but simply in some related role as, for example, to help cover her tracks; or gain access to the necessary tools; etc.[50] It is also unclear how widely 'fraud' should be interpreted: the term clearly covers an intention to commit an offence under section 1, and most likely sections 9 and 11, but beyond this it remains uncertain. One useful clarification in *Sakalauskas*[51] is that although there needs to be an intention, it can be as to any (unspecified) fraud.

10.6.2 FA 2006, s7: making or supplying articles for use in frauds

The maximum penalty for section 7 on indictment is 10 years' imprisonment.[52]

7(1) A person is guilty of an offence if he makes, adapts, supplies or offers to supply any article—

    (a) knowing that it is designed or adapted for use in the course of or in connection with fraud, or

    (b) intending it to be used to commit, or assist in the commission of, fraud.

The elements of section 7 are set out in **Table 10.6**.

Table 10.6 FA 2006, s7

	Actus reus	*Mens rea*
Conduct element	Making, adapting, supplying, or offering to supply an article	Voluntary
Circumstance element	None	None
Result element	None	None
Ulterior mens rea element	*	Knowing the article is designed or adapted for use in connection with fraud Or Intending the article to be used to commit or assist the commission of fraud

Section 7 creates an offence capable of numerous constructions (eg making; adapting; supplying; offering; with knowledge; with intent; etc). As such, it should be applied carefully, ensuring that the correct construction is identified in relation to each particular factual event. However, at its core, the offence is designed to criminalise D who is either preparing articles for the commission of fraud herself, or doing so to assist another.

---

[50] *Smith* [2020] EWCA Crim 38.
[51] [2013] EWCA Crim 2278.
[52] FA 2006, s7(2).

10.7 Related fraud and deception offences

There are a number of fraud-related offences within the criminal law, including false accounting;[53] making false statements as company directors;[54] suppression of documents;[55] and the common law offence of cheating the public revenue.[56] However, in this section we provide a brief account of only two such offences: conspiracy to defraud and making off without payment.

10.7.1 Conspiracy to defraud

Conspiracy to defraud is a common law offence that criminalises D who agrees with another (D2) on a dishonest course of conduct that risks prejudice to another's property rights.[57] This is a spectacularly wide offence, with the potential to criminalise an agreement to complete conduct that may not be a crime or even a civil wrong if simply undertaken by an individual. The exact boundaries of the offence are also far from certain. As a result, unsurprisingly, it has attracted considerable criticism.[58] The Law Commission recommended abolition of conspiracy to defraud within its recommendations for the FA 2006.[59] However, concerned about possible lacunae within the new statute, and bearing in mind the popularity of the offence with prosecutors, the government favoured retention.[60] There are currently no signs that the offence will be abolished.

The elements of conspiracy to defraud are set out in **Table 10.7**. The maximum sentence is 10 years' imprisonment.

Table 10.7 Conspiracy to defraud

	Actus reus	Mens rea
Conduct element	Agreement with another	Voluntary
Circumstance element	Agreement involves a risk to V's property interests or deception in a public duty	Knowledge
	D's agreement is dishonest	In the context of D's knowledge and belief

---

[53] TA 1968, s17.

[54] Ibid, s19.

[55] Ibid, s20.

[56] Ormerod, 'Cheating the Public Revenue' [1998] Crim LR 627.

[57] Defined in *Scott v Metropolitan Police Commissioner* [1975] AC 919.

[58] Jarvis, '*Evans* and Conspiracy to Defraud: A Postscript' [2015] Crim LR 704; ATH Smith, 'Conspiracy to Defraud' [1988] Crim LR 508; JC Smith, 'Conspiracy to Defraud: Some Comments on the Law Commission's Report' [1995] Crim LR 209.

[59] Law Commission, *Fraud* (No 276, 2002) Draft Bill, cl9.

[60] See commentary in Ormerod and Williams, *Smith's Law of Theft* (2007) paras 5.65 et seq.

Result element	None	None
Ulterior mens rea element	*	Intention that the course of conduct is completed

10.7.1.1 Actus reus of conspiracy to defraud

The core elements of the actus reus of conspiracy to defraud are: (A) an agreement between two or more (B) on a course of conduct that risks the property interests of another or deception in a public duty. This is a conduct-based inchoate offence: the agreement must involve a risk to property interests or deception, but it is irrelevant whether the parties go through with their agreement and whether any property interests are imperilled.

A) **Agreement between two or more:** As with other conspiracy offences,[61] conspiracy to defraud requires an agreement (a meeting of minds) between two or more people. However, the agreement need not involve one of the defendants doing the defrauding themselves. For example, in *Hollinshead*[62] the House of Lords found a conspiracy to defraud where D1 and D2 agreed to produce devices designed to corrupt electricity meters, making them fail to record the electricity used, even though the defrauding would be done by unidentified third parties—the customers using the device.

B) **Risks the property interests of another or deception of someone's public duty:** Agreements to carry out a course of conduct that would amount to an offence under the Theft Acts and/or the FA 2006 would clearly satisfy the requirement of risking another's property interests. Conspiracy to defraud has also been used to criminalise agreements that if carried out would not amount to an offence. For example, agreements relating to the 'temporary' deprivation of another's property (short of theft);[63] to shifting land boundary fences; to dishonestly obtaining transfers of real property that cannot be charged as theft;[64] to inducing another to take a financial risk they would not otherwise have taken (eg gambling);[65] and so on. However, the case of *Evans*[66] has clarified that something unlawful is required under this route: either that the object of the agreement was unlawful, or if the object was lawful, that the means of achieving that object were unlawful.[67]

Alongside agreements that risk property interests, it has long been accepted that the deception of V to act against her public duty will also satisfy this element of the offence. Examples include D deceiving a public official to supply export licences,[68] supply

---

[61] Discussed at **Chapter 11.3**.

[62] [1985] AC 975.

[63] *Scott v Metropolitan Police Commissioner* [1975] AC 919: temporary deprivation of cinema tapes.

[64] *Gimbert* [2018] EWCA Crim 2190.

[65] *Allsop* (1976) 64 Cr App R 29.

[66] [2014] 1 WLR 2817. Upheld by Fulford LJ when the SFO sought to reopen the prosecution: [2014] EWHC 3803 (QB).

[67] Jarvis, 'Conspiracy to Defraud: A Siren to Lure Unwary Prosecutors' [2014] Crim LR 738.

[68] *Board of Trade v Owen* [1957] AC 602.

information,[69] employ unqualified staff,[70] and so on. Certain cases suggest that this construction will also apply outside public officials to those deceived into acting against any contractual duties.[71]

10.7.1.2 Mens rea of conspiracy to defraud

The mens rea of conspiracy to defraud requires (A) knowledge of the risks involved in the agreement; (B) intention that the course of conduct will be carried out; and (C) dishonesty. As with all conspiracy offences, at least two of the parties to the agreement must *both* satisfy the mens rea (ie there must be a meeting of minds).

A) Knowledge of the risks: D must recognise the risks posed to the property interests of another, or the possible deception of V acting in a public duty.[72] D's motives, in this regard, are irrelevant. Thus, in *Wai Yu-tsang*[73] the Privy Council found that D had conspired to defraud the bank he worked for by failing to reveal financial information even though he was acting, he claimed, to protect the bank's interests.

B) Intention that the course of conduct will be completed: If the parties agree on a course of conduct, but do not intend that it will be carried out, then no offence is committed. For example, D agrees, but plans to 'whistle-blow' and prevent the course of conduct happening.

C) Dishonesty: The *Ivey* test applies here, as discussed previously (**10.2.2.2**). The potential for other elements of the offence to catch ostensibly innocent conduct makes the role of dishonesty centrally important, and therefore the widening and objectifying of that concept in *Ivey* particularly troubling.[74]

10.7.2 TA 1978, s3: making off without payment

Making off without payment is an offence contrary to section 3 of the TA 1978. The maximum penalty on indictment is two years' imprisonment.[75]

3(1) Subject to subsection (3) below, a person who, knowing that payment on the spot for any goods supplied or service done is required or expected from him, dishonestly makes off without having paid as required or expected and with intent to avoid payment of the amount due shall be guilty of an offence.

(2) For purposes of this section 'payment on the spot' includes payment at the time of collecting goods on which work has been done or in respect of which service has been provided.

(3) Subsection (1) above shall not apply where the supply of the goods or the doing of the service is contrary to law, or where the service done is such that payment is not legally enforceable . . .

The elements of section 3 are set out in **Table 10.8**.

---

[69] *DPP v Withers* [1975] AC 842.
[70] *Bassey* (1931) 21 Cr App R 160.
[71] *Welham* [1961] AC 103.
[72] *Cooke* [1986] AC 909.
[73] [1992] 1 AC 269.
[74] See Laird and Ormerod, '*Ivey v Genting Casinos*—Much Ado About Nothing?' in Clarry (ed), *Supreme Court Yearbook* (2019) 380.
[75] TA 1978, s4.

Table 10.8 TA 1978, s3

	Actus reus	Mens rea
Conduct element	Making off	Voluntary
Circumstance element	On-the-spot payment is required	Knowledge
	Payment is not supplied in full	Intention
	D's making off is dishonest	In the context of D's knowledge and belief
Result element	None	None
Ulterior mens rea element	*	Intention to avoid payment

Making off without payment was intended to provide a simple offence to target cases where D tries to avoid payment for goods or services by taking flight. For example, running out of a restaurant without paying the bill, jumping out of a taxi without paying the fare, etc. Importantly, there is no need to demonstrate any deception, or that D successfully avoided payment. The offence simply requires D to have dishonestly made off without paying for goods or services that she knows require payment, and doing so with the intention to avoid payment.[76]

10.7.2.1 Actus reus of s3

The actus reus of section 3 requires D to (A) make off; (B) without payment; where (C) on-the-spot payment is required.

A) **Making off:** Making off simply requires D to have physically moved from the location in which payment is required. This will be the case whether D leaves surreptitiously, as where D climbs out of a restaurant's bathroom window, or whether she leaves to the 'sound of trumpets'.[77] However, D must have fully left the relevant location. For example, if D is stopped before leaving the restaurant where payment is required she will not have committed the section 3 offence, although there may be liability in attempt.[78]

One point remains unresolved in the literature—does D 'make off' if V gives her permission to leave?[79] It was held in *Hammond*[80] that, however obtained, the existence of permission was incompatible with the notion of 'making off', and it is contended that

[76] *Vincent* [2001] 1 WLR 1172.
[77] *Brooks and Brooks* (1982) 76 Cr App R 66.
[78] *McDavitt* [1981] Crim LR 843.
[79] Spencer, Letter, 'Making Off Without Payment' [1983] Crim LR 573.
[80] [1982] Crim LR 611.

this approach is correct. Where D is dishonest we may feel that liability is deserved, but as V has allowed her to leave, section 3 is not appropriate. Liability can likely be found under fraud by false representation (**10.2**).

B) Without payment: This element simply requires that D has not paid for the goods or services, or has not paid in full.

C) On-the-spot payment is required: There are two parts to this requirement. First, for payment to be 'required or expected', it must be that goods or services have been supplied.[81] This will include D taking goods that are supplied via self-service display in a supermarket, or fuel at a self-service forecourt.[82] However, where goods have not yet been supplied there will be no offence under section 3 as, for example, where D tries unsuccessfully to trick V out of goods and then runs away.[83] Equally, where goods or services are supplied, but they are of a sufficiently low quality or provided in breach of contract, such that D is not legally obliged to pay for them, there will again be no liability under this section.[84] Section 3(3) also makes it clear that there will be no offence under this section where D makes off without paying for illegal goods or services, for example from a brothel, or having been supplied with controlled drugs.

The second part of this element is that the payment for goods or services must be required or expected 'on-the-spot'. This was the focus of the appeal in *Vincent*.

 Vincent [2001] EWCA Crim 295

D did not settle his bill in full when leaving two different hotels. On each occasion, he dishonestly assured the owners (V) that he was about to come into some money and would pay them later, and on each occasion V allowed him to leave on this basis. D was charged with making off without payment.

- Crown Court: guilty of section 3 offence. Even though V consented to D leaving, D's dishonest obtaining of that consent meant that he still 'made off' from the spot for the purposes of section 3.
- Court of Appeal: appeal allowed. Where V consents to D leaving without payment, even where this is procured by dishonesty, D is not 'making off' for the purpose of section 3.

In *Vincent*, V's consent to later payment meant that payment was no longer required or expected on the spot (ie at that time, in that hotel). Therefore, D's leaving that spot could not amount to making off without payment. Where D acts in this manner, dishonestly avoiding immediate payment with the intention to make a gain or cause a loss in property, the appropriate charge would be fraud by false representation (**10.2**).

10.7.2.2 Mens rea of s3

The mens rea of section 3 requires D to have (A) known that on-the-spot payment was required; (B) intended to avoid payment; and (C) acted dishonestly.

---

[81] 'Goods' are defined by the TA 1968, s34 (made applicable to the TA 1978 by s5(2)). 'Services' are not defined in statute. This may involve an analysis of the civil law: *Wilkinson* [2018] EWCA Crim 2154.

[82] For an alternative view, see Smith, 'Shoplifting and the Theft Acts' [1981] Crim LR 586.

[83] The charge here, if any, would be for fraud or attempted theft.

[84] *Troughton v Metropolitan Police* [1987] Crim LR 138: taxi driver in breach of contract so payment was not required.

A) Knowledge that on-the-spot payment is required: It will often be clear to D that payment for goods or services is required of her on-the-spot. However, the element will be lacking where, for example, D leaves thinking that another party is going to pay, or believing that payment is only required at some later stage.[85]

B) Intention to avoid payment: The text of section 3 requires D to intend to avoid payment, but is unclear whether this means an intention to *permanently* avoid payment or whether intention to avoid payment temporarily will suffice. This was clarified in *Allen*.

 Allen [1985] AC 1029

D left a hotel without settling his bill. His intention was to pay the bill later when he could afford to do so. D was charged with making off without payment.

- Crown Court: guilty of section 3 offence. The trial judge directed the jury that D need only intend to default from payment at that time.
- Court of Appeal: appeal allowed. D must intend to make permanent default.
- House of Lords: appeal dismissed, endorsing the Court of Appeal's reasoning.

It is now clear that D will not come within section 3 unless she makes off with the intention to permanently avoid payment.

C) Dishonesty: The *Ivey* test applies here, as discussed earlier (**10.2.2.2**). It is important to remember that we are looking for dishonesty at the point D makes off.

10.8 Reform

The open-textured drafting of the FA 2006 has given rise to an interesting range of reform opinions and debates. For many, the potential breadth of the fraud offences, and the minimal definitional detail provided as to core concepts, are causes for concern (and perhaps further legislative clarification). In this section, we discuss three areas of debate: the drafting of the FA 2006; the move to conduct crimes; and the disappearing distinction between theft and fraud.

10.8.1 The drafting of the FA 2006

There has been a trend in modern statutes to define offences in an unhelpfully complex manner.[86] We were critical of this in relation to the Sexual Offences Act 2003,[87] and later we discuss similar criticisms in relation to inchoate offences of assisting and encouraging and the Serious Crime Act 2007.[88] In comparison to these other statutes, the FA 2006

---

[85] *Brooks and Brooks* (1982) 76 Cr App R 66.
[86] Spencer, 'The Drafting of Criminal Legislation: Need It Be So Impenetrable?' (2008) 67 CLJ 585.
[87] See **Chapter 8.9**.
[88] See **Chapter 11**.

is remarkably straightforward, defining the three core routes to fraud liability over just five brief sections. It should also be recognised that in the still relatively early years of the statute, despite extensive use in the lower courts, there have been very few appeal cases, demonstrating its general success. In this vein, Virgo comments that:

> Legal analysis needs to strike a balance between principle and pragmatism. The Fraud Act on its face might be criticised for infringing fundamental criminal justice principles, by virtue of its breadth and uncertainty, but if the legislation enables appropriate responses to be reached, assisted by judicial interpretation where appropriate, it can be defended. This is the case with the Fraud Act 2006. Initial concerns about the ambit and interpretation of the legislation have largely proved unfounded. It remains a model of criminal legislation which remains fit for purpose.[89]

Even within Virgo's statements, however, we should note his acknowledgement of 'on its face' uncertainties. The question emerges whether apparent simplicity and success has come at a cost. And three points should be highlighted.

First, to remove complex details from the statute, a number of key terms have been left undefined. We saw this earlier, for example, with terms such as 'dishonesty',[90] 'service',[91] 'position',[92] 'abuse',[93] and so on. With terms of this kind, where ordinary meanings are not self-evident, the choice not to provide a statutory definition creates uncertainty in the law.[94] In this manner, complexity is not avoided but is rather hidden within the case law.

Secondly, by removing complex requirements of deception and causation present in the pre-FA 2006 offences, the current law has defined the core fraud offences in an inchoate manner, criminalising D's dishonest conduct which is *intended* to interfere with property rights as opposed to criminalising successful interferences. Attempting to simplify the law by broadening offence definitions has also been a common practice in recent years (eg sexual offences; inchoate liability; terrorism offences; etc). The disadvantage of this is the potential for over—or inappropriate—criminalisation, which we discuss further in the following sections.

Thirdly, we do not know how many people have simply pleaded guilty to secure a discount in sentence rather than face trial and challenge the language of the Act.

10.8.2 Fraud and the irrelevance of results

Although the fraud offences are undoubtedly simpler than their equivalents were prior to the FA 2006, the move from deception-based result crimes to dishonesty-based conduct crimes has considerably widened the range of conduct caught.[95] Unlike the old deception offences, and unlike other property offences discussed in **Chapter 9**, the actus reus of fraud does not require D to gain property or cause a loss of property to another. For example, for section 2 of the FA 2006, D commits fraud as soon as she makes a false representation with the required mens rea.

---

[89] Virgo, 'The Fraud Act 2006—Ten Years On' [2017] 10 Arch Rev 6.
[90] This term is central to most property offences.
[91] Central to the offence of making off without payment (**10.7.2**) and obtaining services dishonestly (**10.5**).
[92] Required for fraud by abuse of position (**10.4**).
[93] Ibid.
[94] Including potential for challenge under Art 7 ECHR.
[95] See **Chapter 2.4.1**.

The irrelevance of results has broadened liability in two important ways. First, the offence is committed earlier, when the false representation is made rather than when property is transferred. Although this change affects all cases, it has a particular impact on cases in which D fails to deceive V and no property is passed. Under the old law, D either committed an attempt offence or no offence at all. Under the FA 2006, D has completed the full offence of fraud.

Secondly, at the other end of the scale, the irrelevance of results also expands the offence to capture later acts. Under the pre-FA 2006 law, it had to be demonstrated that D's deception caused property to be transferred. Thus, D could not be liable for deceptive conduct that came after the transfer of property. This caused problems in cases, for example, where D filled her car with petrol intending to pay, but then changed her mind and deceived the station attendant (V) to avoid payment. The ownership of the petrol passed to D at the moment it mingled with other petrol in her car; and therefore, by the time D deceived V, there were no property rights to be passed.[96] This has traditionally been dealt with through the offence of making off without payment, and this continues to apply. However, D's conduct will now *also* be fraud by false representation: D dishonestly makes a false representation after filling her tank when she deceives V (this might be as simple as continuing to act as a paying customer), and does so to make a gain (which includes keeping what one has[97]).

Recognising the expansion of liability under the FA 2006, two questions should be considered. First, is the expansion of liability justified: do these cases exhibit a criminal mischief that we want to label as fraud? Secondly, are the central terms of the new expanded offence, particularly 'dishonesty', fit for the purpose of identifying and targeting only the conduct deserving of criminalisation?

10.8.3 Distinguishing theft and fraud

Having discussed the definition of the fraud offences, it is useful to briefly return to the debate about overlap between theft and fraud. As highlighted at the end of the last chapter,[98] there is a concern that the offences of fraud and theft overlap to an unacceptable degree.[99] The argument here is that where theft should target D who takes V's property without consent, fraud should target those who deceive V into parting with their property voluntarily. However, as we have seen, the current law does not reflect this neat division. Rather, following *Gomez* and *Hinks*, as long as D acts dishonestly, theft can now extend to cases in which V consents to the appropriation of her property.[100] And, alongside this, fraud now requires no transfer of property at all.

The question emerging from this is whether the current law is well served maintaining these two separate offences? If the mischief of both offences is now simply focussed on dishonest conduct, would a single dishonesty offence provide a more coherent way forward?[101]

---

[96] *Collis-Smith* [1971] Crim LR 716.

[97] FA 2006, s5(3).

[98] See **Chapter 9.8.1**.

[99] Shute and Horder, 'Thieving and Deceiving: What is the Difference?' (1993) 56 MLR 548; Melissaris, 'The Concept of Appropriation and the Offence of Theft' (2007) 70 MLR 581.

[100] See **Chapter 9.1**. Cf *Darroux* [2018] EWCA Crim 1009 discussed at **Chapter 9.2.2**.

[101] This possibility is discussed (and rejected) by the Law Commission, *Fraud* (No 276, 2002) paras 5.20–5.57. See also the proposal to simplify theft to non-consensual taking and borrowing in Tamblyn, 'Reforming Theft: Taking Without Consent' [2020] Crim LR 597.

10.9 Eye on assessment

In this section we consider the potential application of fraud offences within a problem question, using the structure of analysis discussed in previous chapters.

> **STEP 1 Identify the potential criminal event in the facts**
>
> This should be simply stated (eg 'The first potential criminal event arises where D makes a false benefit claim'). The role of this stage is to highlight which part of the question you are answering before you begin to apply the law.

When identifying a potential criminal event, it is important to remember that the main fraud offence is a conduct crime: the relevant point of potential liability is where D makes the representation (s2), fails to disclose (s3), or abuses her position (s4), not at the point if and when property rights are affected. Where D possesses articles for use in fraud (s6), or makes or supplies such articles (s7), the potential event may be even earlier.

> **STEP 2 Identify the potential offence**
>
> Again, state this simply (eg 'When claiming false benefits, D may be liable for fraud by false representation'). The role of this stage is to highlight which offence you are going to apply.

Identifying the appropriate offence in this area is not easy, and you need to take time to consider your options. Chiefly, this is because many of the offences overlap, and so you will usually have more than one available route to liability. One issue arising here is that it can be possible, and tempting, to answer a whole problem with reference to only one route to fraud (eg section 2). Although accurate, you need to consider the fair labelling of D (and the need to demonstrate knowledge within an assessment), and so it is useful to acknowledge and discuss potential liability under different routes. The one caveat here, as always, is that if the problem question specifies a certain route (eg 'Discuss Dave's potential liability for fraud by failure to disclose') then you should *only* do what the question asks of you.

Table 10.9 sets out the offences we have discussed in this chapter (with the addition of theft), ordered in terms of when they might arise within a problem scenario. On the right, we indicate why you might discuss this offence as opposed to other overlapping options.

Table 10.9 Identifying and applying fraud offences

Possession of articles for use in frauds	• This offence is useful to criminalise acts where D is in possession of something with the required intent before he has done any more towards a full fraud offence.
	• These offences are useful to consider where, for whatever reason, D does not go on to commit the fraud or theft.

Making or supplying articles for use in frauds	• This offence is useful where D makes or supplies articles for fraud with the required intent.
	• Again, these offences are useful to consider where, for whatever reason, D does not go on to commit the fraud or theft.
Conspiracy to defraud	• This offence is useful where D agrees with another person to commit fraud, with the required intent.
	• Again, these offences are useful to consider where, for whatever reason, D does not go on to commit the fraud or theft.
Fraud by false representation	• This way of committing fraud applies at the point D makes a false representation.
	• This offence is extremely wide, covering most of the conduct targeted by the two other routes to fraud liability below. If in doubt, this is probably the one to focus on.
Fraud by failure to disclose	• This way of committing fraud applies at the point D fails (omits) to disclose information where she has a legal duty to do so.
	• Where there is an omission and a clear legal duty, such as a failure to disclose a criminal record when applying for a job, you should try to apply this route to fraud in preference to fraud by false representation.
Fraud by abuse of position	• This way of committing fraud applies at the point D abuses her position with a view to making a gain or causing a loss.
	• Again, although these cases will usually involve a false representation, it is useful to apply this route to fraud in preference to section 2 where the facts are clear (eg a carer taking money from her vulnerable patients).
Theft	• Theft applies at a later time (and more narrowly) than the offences discussed above, occurring only when property has been appropriated by D.
	• Remember that theft requires potentially problematic elements that fraud does not: appropriation; intention to permanently deprive.
	• Where you could apply theft or fraud, you should consider which offence provides the most accurate label for what D has done, but also that fraud is the more serious offence and so should usually be applied in preference.

(Continued)

Table 10.9 Continued

Obtaining services dishonestly	• Like theft, this offence only applies where results are caused: the obtaining of a service.
	• Remember that theft does not apply to services. Thus, where services are obtained, you should either apply this offence or one of the routes to fraud.
Making off without payment	• This offence comes last in our timeline, applying where D has received the goods/services and then makes off.
	• This offence is useful where D's dishonesty does not arise until after the goods have been transferred to D. In such a case, theft will not apply due to a lack of coincidence in time of actus reus and mens rea. However, at the time of making off D will be dishonest and so will come within this offence.

Where, as is likely, you identify more than one possible offence, it is good practice to focus your analysis on the most appropriate, but also to (briefly) acknowledge the other possible routes.

STEP 3 Applying the offence to the facts

Having identified the relevant offence, make sure you discuss each of the required elements.

Actus reus: What does the offence require? Did D do it?

Mens rea: What does the offence require? Did D possess it?

AR and MR are satisfied	AR and/or MR are not satisfied
Continue to STEP 4.	Return to STEP 2, and look for an alternative offence. If none, then skip to STEP 5, concluding that no offence is committed.

STEP 4 Consider defences

The word 'consider' here is important, as you should not discuss every defence for every question. Rather, think whether there are any defences (eg duress) that *could* potentially apply. If there are, discuss those only.

STEP 5 Conclude

This is usually a single sentence either saying that it is likely that D has committed the offence, or saying that it is not likely either because an offence element is not satisfied or because a defence is likely to apply. It is not often that you will be able to say categorically whether or not D has committed the offence, particularly when applying concepts such as dishonesty, so it is usually best to conclude in terms of what is more 'likely'.

STEP 6 Loop

Go back up to STEP 1, identifying the next potential criminal event. Continue until you have discussed all the relevant potentially criminal events.

 ONLINE RESOURCES

www.oup.com/he/child-ormerod4e

This chapter is accompanied by a selection of online resources to help you with this topic, including:

- **Self-test questions and scenario questions**
- Videos from the authors
- Audio introduction to the topic
- **Chapter summary sheet**
- Two **sample examination questions** with answer guidance
- **Further reading and weblinks**

Also available on the online resources are:

- A selection of **videos** from the authors containing general advice on problem questions and essay questions
- **Legal updates**

11

General inchoate offences

11.1 Introduction

'Inchoate' is a term used to describe offences that are, in some sense, unfinished.[1] Whilst standard (principal) offences target completed harms, inchoate offences will generally

---

[1] Introduced in **Chapter 4.2.1.2.**

not require D to have caused significant harm to a person or property. Inchoate offences target defendants who have made some progress towards a harmful end, foreseeing/ intending harm to come about: D's conduct may be inchoate ('just begun'; 'undeveloped'), but because of her potentially harmful ambitions, it is also deserving of criminalisation.

Some statutory offences create specific inchoate forms of liability, including possession offences, modern fraud offences, and so on. These are not the primary focus of this chapter, though some discussion is provided at **11.6**. The chapter centres on the three general inchoate offences that are not defined in relation to any single protected interest, but apply across most principal offences in criminal law:

- **Attempt:** D is criminalised for trying to commit a principal offence;
- **Conspiracy:** D is criminalised for agreeing with another to commit a principal offence; and
- **Assisting or encouraging:** D is criminalised for doing acts capable of assisting or encouraging another (P) to commit a principal offence.

 Point to remember ...

The following terminology will be used throughout **Chapters 11** and **12**:

- principal offence—this refers to the offence (eg murder, theft, etc) that D is attempting/conspiring/ assisting or encouraging. This is also commonly referred to as the 'substantive offence', the 'full offence', or the 'future offence';
- principal offender—where D is assisting or encouraging another to commit a principal offence, the party assisted or encouraged is referred to as the principal offender (P).

In order to understand and apply the general inchoate offences, it is crucial to understand their relationship with principal offences. Two rules stand out as particularly important. First, inchoate offences only operate in combination with a principal offence. For example, D cannot be liable for 'attempt' *simpliciter*, she can only be liable for 'attempted murder' or 'attempted theft' or 'attempted rape', etc. Therefore, when identifying potential liability for one of the general inchoate offences, it is essential also to identify the related principal offence. Secondly, although D's inchoate liability must relate to a principal offence, it is irrelevant (in terms of her inchoate liability) whether that principal offence attempted/conspired/assisted or encouraged ever comes about.[2] D's liability arises as soon as she satisfies the elements of the inchoate offence.

It is universally accepted that the criminal law should include some form of inchoate liability.[3] For example, if D shoots at V with an intention to kill, the criminal law would rightly be criticised if it did not consider D's conduct worthy of criminalisation just because, as a matter of luck,[4] D missed her target. The challenge with these offences is setting the

---

[2] Where D completes the principal offence, however, it would usually be more appropriate in terms of fair labelling to charge that offence (or complicity in a principal offence committed by P, discussed in **Chapter 12**).

[3] Cornford, 'Preventative Criminalisation' [2015] New Crim LR 1.

[4] On the role of 'luck', see Ashworth, 'Criminal Attempts and the Role of Resulting Harm' (1988) 19 Rutgers LR 725.

point at which D's conduct justifies criminal intervention. We discuss this later in the context of potential reform (**11.7**), but the challenge should be kept in mind throughout. As we discuss the different inchoate offences, you should note that there is a necessary balancing of legal priorities, and you should consider which of these priorities you believe is most important in order to start thinking about your evaluation of the current law. We can present this balancing as the relationship between fairness to D and the protection of society.

A) **Fairness to D:** At the point D commits one of the inchoate offences, the principal offence attempted/conspired/assisted or encouraged has not yet come about and may never come about. Thus, in order to identify sufficient blameworthiness which renders it fair to criminalise D, we are not looking for the same mischief as the principal offence, but rather some kind of equivalent in terms of moral blameworthiness. In search of such equivalence, we are likely to favour mens rea requirements that ensure that we only criminalise D where she has fully 'committed' to the principal offence, with intention as to its commission. We are also likely to favour restrictive actus reus requirements, which mean that the inchoate crime is only committed at the moment when D has unequivocally demonstrated dangerous conduct, or conduct very close to the point of committing the principal offence. We want to criminalise D who would have gone on to commit the principal offence, not D who might have changed her mind if left alone.

B) **Protection of society:** If we follow the 'fairness to D' approach to its natural extremes, we end up with a narrow set of inchoate offences that only target conduct very close to the commission of a principal offence. The problem with this, in many cases, is that it will be dangerous to draw the offences so narrowly, forcing investigators to wait for D to have progressed a long way on her criminal enterprise towards the commission of a principal offence before she can be arrested for an inchoate offence. Particularly with the rise of intelligence-led policing, where we might have very good evidence of D's future intentions and planning well before the attack, there are obvious benefits to an intervention at the earliest, and therefore safest, opportunity.

The balancing of these (and other[5]) considerations is central to the offences discussed in this chapter. It is a balancing that shifts over time due to political preferences, changes in policing, and public attitudes. You should consider your own views on this issue now, and keep these in mind when considering the individual offences and cases that follow.

11.2 Criminal attempts

The offence of attempt criminalises D for doing more than merely preparatory acts towards the commission of a principal offence she is trying to commit.[6] Attempt is conventionally charged where D has failed to commit the principal offence (although this need not necessarily be the case[7]). D can fail to commit a principal offence for many reasons: she may have changed her mind before completing the offence; she may have been stopped from doing so; she may have done everything she thought necessary but

---

[5] We discuss the principles of criminalisation in **Chapter 1.4**.

[6] See generally Law Commission, *Conspiracy and Attempts* (Consultation 183, 2007) Parts 12–16; *Conspiracy and Attempts* (No 318, 2009) Part 8; Duff, *Criminal Attempts* (1996); Yaffe, *Attempts* (2010).

[7] If D succeeds in committing the principal offence, she remains liable for the earlier attempt, but it would be inappropriate to charge both: *Webley v Buxton* [1977] QB 481.

failed, for example because her shot misses her target (V) or V is saved by medical intervention. As long as D satisfies the elements for attempt, her reason for not completing or succeeding in completing the principal offence she attempted is irrelevant to liability.[8]

Exactly when D's 'trying to commit' a principal offence becomes a criminal attempt is defined in section 1(1) of the Criminal Attempts Act 1981 (CAA 1981). The maximum sentence for attempt mirrors that of the principal offence which is attempted.[9]

> 1(1) If, with intent to commit an offence to which this section applies, a person does an act which is more than merely preparatory to the commission of the offence, he is guilty of attempting to commit the offence.

The elements of criminal attempt are set out in **Tables 11.1a** and **11.1b**.

Table 11.1a Criminal attempts

	Actus reus	**Mens rea**
Conduct element	Any action	Voluntary
Circumstance element	D's action goes beyond mere preparation towards the commission of a principal offence (on the facts as she believes them to be)	None
Result element	None	None
Ulterior mens rea element	*	Set out in **Table 11.1b**

Table 11.1b Ulterior mens rea element for criminal attempts

Principal offence	**D's ulterior mens rea as to the principal offence**
Conduct element	D must intend to complete the conduct required for the principal offence
Circumstance element	*Possible attempts*: D's required mens rea will mirror that required for the circumstances of the principal offence, but only to a minimum of recklessness Or *Impossible attempts*: D must intend/know the circumstances required for the principal offence
Result element	D must intend to cause the results required (if any) for the principal offence

---

[8] Although it may be relevant at sentencing.
[9] CAA 1981, s4(1).

As **Tables 11.1a** and **11.1b** demonstrate, a major part of the offence of attempt is forward-looking: examining D's ulterior mens rea as to the principal offence she is trying to commit.

11.2.1 Actus reus of attempts

The actus reus of attempt requires D's conduct to have gone beyond mere preparation towards completing a principal offence. Although this sounds relatively simple, several questions must be carefully considered.

11.2.1.1 Can D attempt by omission?

The wording of section 1(1) ('a person does an act') suggests that a criminal attempt cannot be committed by omission.[10] There is also an absence of case law to contradict this.[11] However, it is contended that section 1 can and should be interpreted to allow for this possibility where D is under a legal duty to act. For example, where D starves her child (V) with the intention of killing V, and does so, it is clear that she commits murder.[12] Where V is discovered prior to death and given life-saving treatment, it would surely be appropriate to charge D with attempted murder.[13]

 Assessment matters ...

If faced with an attempt by omission in a problem question, it should be highlighted that liability may not be available within the terms of the CAA 1981. However, if there is a duty to act, as there would be in our example above, you should also acknowledge that a court *may* choose to interpret the CAA 1981 to allow for omissions liability.

11.2.1.2 Which principal offences can be attempted?

Our starting point is that all principal offences may be subject to an attempt. However, from this starting point, there are a number of exceptions where attempts liability will *not* apply.

A) **Summary only offences:** Attempts liability will only apply to indictable and either way offences, excluding summary only offences (ie those triable only in the magistrates' court).[14] Notable examples of summary only offences include assault and battery.[15]

---

[10] Palmer, 'Attempt by Act or Omission: Causation and the Problem of the Hypothetical Nurse' (1999) 63 JCL 158.

[11] *Nevard* [2006] EWCA Crim 2896 provides some discussion of the point: D convicted of attempted murder having attacked his ex-wife and then delayed the attendance of the emergency services.

[12] *Gibbins and Proctor* (1918) 13 Cr App R 134.

[13] The Law Commission has recommended amending the CAA 1981 to make it clear that omissions liability should be possible: Law Commission, *Conspiracy and Attempts* (No 318, 2009) paras 8.142–8.151. A charge of wilful neglect or an offence under the OAPA would be possible.

[14] See **Chapter 1.1.7.3**.

[15] The Law Commission has recommended that attempts should not be extended to include summary only offences: Law Commission, *Conspiracy and Attempts* (No 318, 2009) paras 8.154–8.161.

B) Conspiracy and secondary liability: To avoid criminalising events too far removed from the principal offence, there can be no liability for D who attempts to conspire or attempts to aid and abet another.[16] We discuss this further in the double inchoate liability section later (**11.5**).

C) Other exceptional cases: There are a few examples where attempt liability would be impossible, or at least unlikely, to arise. For example, it is impossible to attempt to commit an involuntary manslaughter offence. This is because attempt requires D to intend the result element of the principal offence (ie in this case, death), and if D intends this element she has committed attempted murder.

11.2.1.3 When are D's acts more than merely preparatory?

The crux of the actus reus of attempt is that D's acts must go 'beyond mere preparation' towards the commission of a relevant principal offence. The phrase is not defined in the CAA 1981 and should be given its natural meaning.[17] However, it is useful to understand the intentions of those drafting the law, before considering how it has been applied in the courts.

The intended role of 'more than merely preparatory'

Before the CAA 1981, the actus reus of the old common law offence of attempt was simply that D needed to have 'attempted'. Without further guidance on what conduct constituted an attempt, the law was open to interpretations across a wide spectrum of behaviour. At either end of this spectrum were what have been termed the last act test and the series of acts test.

A) Last act test: The last act test would only allow for attempt liability where D completed all acts that she believed were necessary to commit the principal offence.[18] Thus, where D set out to shoot and kill V, D would only attempt after having pulled the trigger. Allowing D every opportunity to change her mind and desist, this approach would only criminalise D where she passed the point of no return, when she 'crossed the Rubicon and burnt h[er] boats'.[19] The downside of this approach, of course, is that it may not provide adequate protection for society: where the police can intervene prior to D's 'last act' we would surely want them to do so, and yet we could not always rely on an alternative offence to charge D with.

B) Series of acts test: Applying the series of acts test, formulated by Stephen, would result in liability for attempts where D's act forms 'part of a series of acts which would constitute [the] commission [of a principal offence] if it were not interrupted'.[20] In our attempted murder by shooting example, this would allow for liability well before the firing of the gun, and potentially as far back in time as the act of buying of the gun,

---

[16] CAA 1981, s1(4). On the exclusion of attempting to aid and abet, see Bohlander, 'The Conflict Between the Serious Crime Act 2007 and Section 1(4)(b) Criminal Attempts Act 1981—A Missed Repeal?' [2010] Crim LR 483; Child, 'The Differences Between Attempted Complicity and Inchoate Assisting and Encouraging—A Reply to Professor Bohlander' [2010] Crim LR 924.
[17] *Jones* (1990) 91 Cr App R 351.
[18] Applied in the early case of *Eagleton* (1855) 6 Cox CC 559.
[19] *Stonehouse* [1978] AC 55. Reference to the 'Rubicon' is to the river at the edge of the Roman Empire: when the Rubicon was crossed with armed men, war was declared.
[20] *Digest of Criminal Law* (5th edn, 1894) Art 50.

planning the killing, etc. This approach allows for early criminalisation and thus early intervention by the police to protect potential victims. However, as recognised by Lord Lane CJ in *Gullefer*,[21] the disadvantage is that D's actions at these very early stages may not yet be sufficiently proximate to the completion of the principal offence to be deserving of liability. As D's conduct may also be objectively innocent (eg legally buying a gun), there is also a problem with potential over-reliance on confession evidence and the associated risks of incentivising police malpractice.[22]

C) The CAA 1981 test: Within this spectrum of proximity to the principal offence, the CAA 1981 formulation—'more than merely preparatory'—tries to forge a midway path.[23] Although strictly speaking all acts prior to the last act are done in preparation, the idea is that there are certain acts leading to a principal offence that are sufficiently proximate as to go beyond 'mere' preparation, and are deserving of attempts liability.[24] The ideal of this approach is illustrated in *Jones*.[25]

 Jones (1990) 91 Cr App R 351

D got into the back seat of a car with V, and pointed a sawn-off shotgun at him. Following a struggle, V escaped unharmed. D was charged with attempted murder.

- Crown Court: guilty of attempted murder.
- Court of Appeal: conviction upheld on appeal. Even though D was at least three steps away from completing the principal offence (he still had to remove the safety catch, put his finger on the trigger, and pull it), his acts were still capable of being 'more than merely preparatory'.

Applying 'more than merely preparatory' in practice

The *aims* of the CAA 1981 formulation are relatively clear, but the terminology remains somewhat vague in application. This is understandable, but a legitimate target for criticism. It is unrealistic to expect a precise determination from a test that is applied in practice across a multitude of offences and across an infinite variety of factual circumstances, but the danger is that imprecision leads to unwanted and inconsistent application.[26] This danger does not arise for 'complete attempts': where D has finished the last acts she believes necessary to commit the principal offence, such acts clearly go beyond mere preparation.[27] However, for incomplete attempts, where D still has a number of acts to perform, problems can and do arise. Three areas of concern should be highlighted: (A) the test is being applied too narrowly; (B) the test is being applied inconsistently *between* offences; and (C) the test is being applied inconsistently *within* offences.

---

[21] [1990] 3 All ER 882.
[22] Horder, *Ashworth's Principles of Criminal Law* (9th edn, 2019) Chapter 13.
[23] See, leading to this formulation, Law Commission, *Attempt, and Impossibility in Relation to Attempt, Conspiracy and Incitement* (No 102, 1980) paras 2.19–2.52.
[24] *Tosti* [1997] Crim LR 746: the court held that D's acts were 'preparatory, but not merely so'.
[25] Discussed in Smith, 'Proximity in Attempt: Lord Lane's Midway Course' [1991] Crim LR 576.
[26] Law Commission, *Conspiracy and Attempts* (Consultation 183, 2007) Parts 1, 12–14.
[27] The only exception to this can arise where D is a secondary party to a principal offence.

Extra detail ...

What D has done, and whether these acts are more than merely preparatory, are ultimately questions of fact for the jury. However, the judge has an important filtering role, only allowing the question to go to the jury if the prosecution has provided evidence that is capable of fulfilling the test.[28] This legal decision, on the part of the judge, is invariably the subject of the appeal cases discussed here.

A) **Applied too narrowly:** The first area of concern is that the 'more than merely preparatory' test is being interpreted too narrowly, inadequately weighing the need to protect society from harms and failing to maintain the desired midway course. This was the view of the Law Commission in its most recent consultation,[29] although it subsequently chose not to recommend reform of the current formulation. **Table 11.2** provides an overview of cases that can be used to illustrate this criticism.

Table 11.2 Is the actus reus of attempt applied too narrowly?

Case	Facts	Outcome on appeal
Gullefer [1990] 3 All ER 882	D tried to stop a greyhound race, in which the dog he bet on was losing, by jumping onto the track. He hoped the race would be declared a 'no race' and he would be able to reclaim his bet. D was convicted of attempting to steal the money.	Appeal allowed. D's acts did not go beyond mere preparation: he would still have had to go to the bookmakers, demand his money, etc.
Campbell [1991] Crim LR 268	D was arrested a yard away from the door of a Post Office that he intended to rob. He was carrying an imitation firearm, a threatening note, and he confessed to the planned robbery. D was convicted of attempted robbery.	Appeal allowed. D's acts did not go beyond mere preparation: he had not yet entered the Post Office or made any demands of the cashier.
Geddes [1996] Crim LR 894	D was found in the boys' toilet of a school with various kidnapping paraphernalia. D was convicted of attempted false imprisonment.	Appeal allowed. D's acts did not go beyond mere preparation: D was lying in wait but he had not confronted a potential victim.
K [2009] EWCA Crim 1931	D approached a 6-year-old boy playing near his work and asked him if he wanted to watch pornography on the laptop in his office. D was convicted of attempting to cause a child to watch a sexual act (Sexual Offences Act 2003, s12).	Appeal allowed. D's acts did not go beyond mere preparation: D had not yet led the child to the laptop (if indeed it was there).

[28] CAA 1981, s4(3). Discussed in *Wang* [2005] UKHL 9.
[29] Law Commission, *Conspiracy and Attempts* (Consultation 183, 2007).

B) **Inconsistent between offences:** The second area of concern is that the test is being applied inconsistently, and that despite the restrictive approach exemplified in the cases in **Table 11.2**, certain categories of offence have attracted a considerably broader approach.[30] An example of this is the offence of attempted rape. Although the actus reus of rape is only completed when D achieves penile penetration of V's vagina, anus, or mouth, convictions for attempted rape have been secured on the basis of conduct well short of this. In most such cases, D will be found to have attempted rape at the stage of physical confrontation with V. This is illustrated in the case of *Dagnall*.[31]

 Dagnall [2003] EWCA Crim 2441

D grabbed V with the intention of raping her and forced her against a fence. Fortunately, a passing police officer saw D and intervened. There was no evidence that D had begun to remove V's clothes, let alone attempted the act of penetration. D was charged with attempted rape.

• Crown Court: guilty of attempted rape.

• Court of Appeal: conviction upheld on appeal.

C) **Inconsistent within offences:** The third area of concern is that the test is being applied inconsistently within individual offence groups, and even within individual offences. For example, in the case of *K*, summarised in **Table 11.2**, it was held that discussing watching pornography with a child was mere preparation towards the offence of causing a child to watch a sexual act. However, in *R*,[32] a case which was appealed in the same year, it was held that there could be attempt liability where D sent a text message to a sex worker asking her if she knew of any 12-year-olds available for sex.[33] Similarly, although the court held in *Geddes* (also summarised in **Table 11.2**) that D had not gone beyond mere preparation to kidnapping when he was found in a school toilet, a quite different approach was taken in *Tosti* just a year later.

 Tosti [1997] Crim LR 746

D was found examining the lock of a barn. D's car was also found nearby, containing metal-cutting equipment. D was charged with attempted burglary.

• Crown Court: guilty of attempted burglary.

• Court of Appeal: conviction upheld on appeal.

For those who believe that *Geddes* applied the law too narrowly, the decision in *Tosti* is to be welcomed. However, bearing in mind that in *Tosti* the defendant was simply examining the lock, and would have had to have gone back to his car to collect the cutting equipment, etc, the two decisions are difficult to reconcile.

---

[30] For useful discussion of this, see Clarkson, 'Attempt: The Conduct Requirement' (2009) 29 OJLS 25.
[31] See also *AG's Reference (No 1 of 1992)* (1992) 96 Cr App R 298; *Paitnaik* [2000] 3 Arch News 2; *MH* [2004] WLR 137; *Bryan* [2015] EWCA Crim 433.
[32] [2009] 1 WLR 713.
[33] An attempt to arrange a sexual offence with a child (Sexual Offences Act 2003, s14).

Assessment matters ...

When applying the actus reus of attempts to facts in a problem question, it is important to acknowledge that the test is relatively uncertain and that case law thus far has shown signs of inconsistency. From here, draw on the normal meaning of the words from the test itself, combined with a discussion of relevant case law, and tell your reader what you think the most likely outcome would be.

11.2.1.4 What if the crime D is attempting is impossible for her to commit?

This question arises where D tries to commit a principal offence, *but unknown to her*, the commission of that offence would be impossible. An offence may be impossible for a variety of reasons. However, there are two broad categories that should be distinguished: legal impossibility and factual impossibility.

Legal impossibility

D's attempt is *legally* impossible where she tries to commit a principal offence which, contrary to her belief, is not actually an offence known to law. For example, if D wrongly believes that adultery is illegal, and then tries to seduce one of her husband's friends, we could describe her actions as an impossible attempt: she has gone beyond mere preparation towards the commission of what she believes is a principal offence. She has revealed a criminal character; a willingness to break the law. However, as adultery is not a crime known to English law, and because the actus reus of attempt requires D to have attempted to commit 'an offence', there can be no liability in these circumstances. This was confirmed in *Taaffe*.[34]

Factual impossibility

D's attempt is factually impossible where she tries to commit a principal offence which *does* exist in English law, but the circumstances surrounding her attempt mean it could not come about. This includes cases of physical impossibility where, for example, D tries to kill V who is already dead, or tries to steal from an empty safe, etc; as well as cases of inadequate means, such as where D tries to kill V by putting pins in a voodoo doll, or tries to shoot V with an unloaded gun, etc. In these cases, D has not only demonstrated a general willingness to break the law, but has gone beyond mere preparation—on the facts as she believed them to be—towards committing a valid principal offence. In recognition of this culpability, the current law *will* find liability for attempt. This is confirmed in section 1(2) of the CAA 1981.

> 1(2) A person may be guilty of attempting to commit an offence to which this section applies even though the facts are such that the commission of the offence is impossible.

This subsection does not contradict the requirement for D's acts to have been more than merely preparatory towards the commission of an offence. Rather, it provides an alternative route to satisfy this element. Take the example where D tries to shoot V with a gun that is, unknown to her, not loaded. Applying the actus reus of attempted murder, we first ask whether, viewed *objectively*, D's acts in pulling the trigger have gone beyond mere preparation towards killing V? The answer here may be 'no': D cannot cause an unloaded gun to fire, and so, objectively, the intended shooting still requires D to go and buy bullets etc (ie it is not sufficiently proximate). However, where the answer to this

---

[34] [1983] 2 All ER 625: D attempted to import foreign currency, believing (incorrectly) that this was a crime. No liability for attempt.

first question is 'no', section 1(2) allows us to ask a second question: have D's acts gone beyond mere preparation *subjectively* (ie on the facts as she believed them to be)? Where the answer to this second question is 'yes', as it would be in our example, D will have satisfied the actus reus of the attempt. In this way, the 'more than merely preparatory' requirement can be satisfied objectively and/or subjectively.

In many cases, the application of this rule appears uncontroversial. In our unloaded gun case, for example, D has shown herself willing to complete all the acts she believes necessary to kill another person, demonstrating her culpability, and the mere fact of failure on this occasion does not undermine this judgement. Nor does it deny her future dangerousness. However, isolated from D's intentions/beliefs, impossible attempts will often involve seemingly innocent conduct, such as clicking the trigger of an unloaded gun (*believing it is loaded*), putting sugar in tea (*believing it is poison*), handling goods (*believing them to be stolen*), and so on. Because such cases can seem so innocuous, despite the terms of section 1(2) of the CAA 1981, the courts initially wavered when applying the test. We see this in *Anderton v Ryan*.

 Anderton v Ryan [1985] UKHL 5

D admitted to police that she was in possession of a stolen video recorder. However, the police could not trace the origin of the recorder in order to prove that it was stolen. D was charged with attempting to handle stolen goods.[35]

- Magistrates' court: not guilty of attempting to handle stolen goods—ruled out by impossibility.
- Divisional Court: appeal allowed. The case was sent back with an instruction to convict—an impossible attempt is still an attempt.
- House of Lords: appeal against conviction allowed (Lord Edmund-Davies dissenting)—the majority held that section 1(2) only extended attempts liability to certain cases of factual impossibility and this was not one of them.

Anderton v Ryan created an odd precedent, contrary to the wording of section 1(2). And, indeed, just a year later, in *Shivpuri*, it was overruled. *Shivpuri* confirmed, in line with the statute, that factual impossibility would never undermine attempts liability.[36]

 Shivpuri [1987] AC 1

D was arrested by customs officials with a suitcase which he 'confessed' contained controlled drugs. However, analysis of the contents showed that it actually contained simple vegetable matter (ie not controlled drugs). D was charged with attempting to be knowingly concerned in dealing with a controlled drug.[37]

- Crown Court: guilty of attempting the drugs offence.
- Court of Appeal: conviction upheld on appeal.
- House of Lords: appeal dismissed—*Anderton v Ryan* overruled.

[35] The offence of handling stolen goods is discussed in **Chapter 9.5**.
[36] The court was heavily influenced by Williams, 'The Lords and Impossible Attempts' (1986) 45 CLJ 33.
[37] Customs and Excise Management Act 1979, s170(1)(b).

Post-*Shivpuri*, the legal position on impossible attempts is clear. Even where objectively in fact D's acts do not go beyond mere preparation, they may still satisfy the actus reus of attempts if they go beyond mere preparation subjectively on the facts *as D believed them to be*.

11.2.2 Mens rea of attempts

As illustrated in **Tables 11.1a** and **11.1b**, the major part of D's mens rea relates to her target principal offence (eg murder, theft, handling stolen goods, etc) that need never be completed in fact (ie within the actus reus) for her to be liable for the attempt. This ulterior mens rea is vital to D's liability, representing the gravamen of attempts, and all general inchoate liability. Without such mens rea, D has simply completed acts that may appear entirely innocent, particularly in the context of impossible attempts. With proof of her mens rea, however, D's acts are revealed as culpable acts in pursuit of a principal offence and deserving of criminalisation. For example, D puts sugar in V's tea believing that that substance is poison and intending to kill.

It is on this basis that section 1(1) of the CAA 1981 explicitly requires D to act 'with intent to commit an offence'. In the Law Commission's work preceding the CAA 1981, it was considered that D would only be correctly held liable for an attempt where she was fully committed (ie where she *intended*) to go on to commit every element of the principal offence attempted.[38] This approach was adopted within the statute. However, as we will discuss in the following section, maintaining the requirement that D intends the principal offence has not always been straightforward.

11.2.2.1 Intending the principal offence

The requirement that D acts with the intention to commit the principal offence, subject to the discussion later, applies regardless of the mens rea requirements of that principal offence. This is illustrated in *Whybrow*.

 Whybrow (1951) 35 Cr App R 141

D wired-up a soap dish in his bathroom to give his wife an electric shock. D was charged with attempted murder.

- Crown Court: guilty of attempted murder. The trial judge directed the jury that the mens rea for attempted murder is the same as for murder: intention to kill or cause GBH.
- Court of Criminal Appeal: appeal dismissed. The direction was wrong to include 'intention to cause GBH', but the misdirection did not render the verdict unsafe. The mens rea for attempted murder is intention to kill.

As clarified in *Whybrow*, although the mens rea of murder allows for an intention to kill *or to cause GBH*, the mens rea for attempted murder requires D to intend to complete every element of the actus reus of the principal offence. Thus, as the actus reus for murder requires D to kill V (ie GBH is not sufficient), only an intention to kill will satisfy the mens rea of attempted murder.

[38] Law Commission, *Attempt, and Impossibility in Relation to Attempt, Conspiracy and Incitement* (No 102, 1980).

The same rule applies in relation to principal offences that require a mens rea of less than intention. For example, attempted criminal damage requires an intention to cause damage despite the principal offence requiring only recklessness as to damage;[39] attempted ABH requires an intention to cause ABH despite the principal offence requiring no mens rea as to this harm at all;[40] and so on.[41] Regardless of the mens rea of the principal offence, attempts liability requires D to act with the intention to complete the principal offence.

The mens rea term 'intention' here carries the same meaning as it does at common law: including both direct (purposive) and oblique (defined in *Woollin*) intention.[42] As with all ulterior mens rea, an intention to commit the principal offence also includes a conditional intention to do so. A conditional intention, as we have discussed,[43] arises where D decides to do something (ie in this case, to commit a principal offence) *only if* a certain condition arises or, alternatively, *unless* certain conditions arise. This was discussed in *AG's References (Nos 1 and 2 of 1979)*.

 AG's References (Nos 1 and 2 of 1979) [1980] QB 180

Combined cases in which D (in each case) was arrested in the process of trying to steal non-specified items (ie anything worth stealing) from another's premises. In the first case, D had entered the building and was searching for items of value; in the second, D was arrested when trying to enter the building. Both were charged with attempted section 9(1)(a) burglary.[44]

- Crown Court: not guilty in either case—D did not have an intention to steal specific items but merely a conditional intention to steal items if there were any worth taking.

- Court of Appeal: Crown Court was wrong. D could have been convicted in either case. A conditional intention to steal is still an intention to steal.

The clarification of the law in *AG's References (Nos 1 and 2 of 1979)* seems entirely sensible: just as D intends to steal if she has specific items in mind, so she intends to steal if she has a conditional intention to steal unspecified items.

Prior to the decision in *AG's References (Nos 1 and 2 of 1979)*, there had been confusion as to how such cases should be charged. These earlier cases provide a useful reminder that care must be taken to identify exactly what D is intending. For example, in *Easom*,[45] D rummaged through a woman's handbag in a theatre and then, finding nothing worth taking, put it back. The bag was connected to a policewoman's wrist by a thread. The Court of Appeal correctly held that D did not commit theft or attempted theft because he was not intending to steal (ie to permanently deprive D) of the bag or those contents

---

[39] *Millard and Vernon* [1987] Crim LR 393. See **Chapter 9.7**.

[40] See **Chapter 7.4**.

[41] Horder, 'Varieties of Intention, Criminal Attempts and Endangerment' (1994) 14 LS 335.

[42] Confirmed in *Pearman* (1984) 80 Cr App R 259; *Walker* (1989) 90 Cr App R 226. For discussion of 'intention', see **Chapter 3.4.1**.

[43] See **Chapter 3.4.1.3**. Child, 'Understanding Ulterior Mens Rea: Future Conduct Intention is Conditional Intention' (2017) 76 CLJ 311.

[44] See **Chapter 9.4.1**.

[45] [1971] 2 QB 315; followed in *Husseyn* (1977) 67 Cr App R 131.

specified on the indictment. Rather, D was attempting to steal items of value that he did not find; these were the items of which he intended to permanently deprive V. If the indictment had reflected this by stating 'attempting to steal contents of the handbag' then he could and should have been found liable of an impossible attempt.[46]

Extra detail ...

Try to remember, simply, that a conditional intention as to future acts is still an intention. Indeed, all future intention can be described as conditional to some degree, whether D makes this explicit or not. Taking the example of attempted theft, if we asked any would-be thief if she intends to steal if she discovers she is being watched by the police; if she wins the lottery and becomes a millionaire; etc, the answer is likely to be 'no'—her intention to steal is conditional on these facts not arising. In this way, just because D is explicit about certain conditions in a case will not undermine her intention.

11.2.2.2 Expanding what it means to intend the principal offence

So far, so good: D must act with the intention, which includes conditional intention, to commit the actus reus of the future principal offence. However, unfortunately, the application of this approach in practice has revealed an apparent unfairness, and the courts have reacted to this by reinterpreting the CAA 1981.

This apparent unfairness arose in the context of attempted rape, and the case of *Khan*.

Khan [1990] 2 All ER 783

D and others tried to have sex with V (a 16-year-old girl) who was not consenting. Each of the defendants was reckless as to her non-consent. The defendants who achieved penetration were straightforwardly guilty of rape. However, D did not achieve penetration and was charged with attempted rape.

- Crown Court: guilty of rape—the mens rea for attempted rape is the same as for the principal offence of rape.
- Court of Appeal: *the judgment of the Court of Appeal is discussed below.*

Applying section 1(1) of the CAA 1981 literally, the judgment of the Crown Court in *Khan* appears to be wrong. If attempt liability requires D to intend *every* element of the actus reus of the principal offence, then the mens rea for attempted rape is not the same as the mens rea for rape. The principal offence of rape is satisfied by an intention to penetrate V's vagina, anus, or mouth with a penis, but it requires a lesser mens rea as to the circumstance requirement of V's non-consent (ie recklessness when *Khan* was decided; a lack of reasonable belief in consent under the current law[47]). Adopting a literal interpretation of the CAA 1981, therefore, the charge of attempted rape should require a mens rea of intention as to every element of the actus reus, including intention or knowledge as to this circumstance element.[48]

---

[46] Campbell, 'Conditional Intention' (1982) 2 LS 77.

[47] See **Chapter 8.2**.

[48] As discussed at **Chapter 3.4.2**, in the context of circumstance elements, knowledge and intention are applied as equivalent states of mind.

The problem with adopting such an interpretation in a case like *Khan* is that it would have undermined D's liability for attempted rape: D was *reckless* as to V's non-consent; he did not *intend* or *know* that V was not consenting. However, what D did in trying to have non-consensual intercourse with V, being reckless as to her non-consent, was so similar to those defendants who were liable for rape that a lack of liability for attempted rape would appear unacceptable.[49] The Court of Appeal chose to avoid this problem by reinterpreting and expanding what it means to intend to commit the principal offence.

 Khan [1990] 2 All ER 783

- Court of Appeal: conviction upheld on appeal. Attempts liability requires D to *intend* the physical parts of the principal offence (in this case, the act of penetration), but need not include an intention as to attendant circumstances (in this case, V's lack of consent). Thus, in relation to such attendant circumstances, it is sufficient for D to have the same mens rea as required for the principal offence (in this case, recklessness).

By separating the circumstance element of the principal offence for special treatment, the Court of Appeal were able to find attempted rape liability.

Applying *Khan*, the mens rea of attempt is satisfied where D *intends* the conduct and result elements of the principal offence attempted, and fulfils at least the mens rea requirement of the principal offence (*potentially less than intention*) as to the circumstance element. Applied to an offence of attempted criminal damage, for example, this would require D to intend the result element of causing damage, even though the principal offence would be satisfied by recklessness; but, it would be sufficient for the attempt that D was reckless as to the circumstance element (ie that the property damaged belongs to another), mirroring the mens rea of the principal offence as to this element.

Khan remains part of the current law, subject to the more recent case of *Pace* discussed shortly. The decision in *Khan* was and remains controversial, and this debate is taken up in our reform discussion later (**11.7.2**). However, even at this point it is useful to highlight some problems with the application of *Khan* in practice; to understand what has led the Court of Appeal to further intervention. Four criticisms should be noted.

A) **Difficulty in separating offence elements:** The approach in *Khan* had been mooted by the Law Commission when it was making its recommendations which led to the CAA 1981. However, the approach was rejected at that time, chiefly because of the difficulty of separating principal offences into conduct, circumstance, and result elements.[50] To apply the *Khan* approach, such separation is essential: although mens rea as to the circumstance element can mirror that required for the principal offence, mens rea as to the conduct and result elements are fixed at intention.

---

[49] Williams, 'The Problem of Reckless Attempts' [1983] Crim LR 365.

[50] Law Commission, *Attempt, and Impossibility in Relation to Attempt, Conspiracy and Incitement* (No 102, 1980) paras 2.11–2.13. Buxton, 'The Working Paper on Inchoate Offences' [1973] Crim LR 656; Buxton, 'Circumstances, Consequences and Attempted Rape' [1984] Crim LR 25.

Assessment matters ...

When applying the *Khan* approach to facts in a problem question, you will have to separate the circumstance element of the principal offence. The tables that we use in this book (setting out elements in this way) should help you. However, it is important to remember that the choices we have made in these separations are matters of judgement and would not necessarily be shared by others. With this in mind, when you apply the approach in practice, it is perfectly acceptable to identify what is likely to be considered the circumstance element but to remark that such a choice is not an objective one.

B) Lack of clarity regarding mens rea for the circumstance element: Where the principal offence requires subjective mens rea as to the circumstance element (eg intention, recklessness, etc) then it is clear from *Khan* that the mens rea for attempt should mirror this standard. However, it remains unclear whether the courts will allow a similar mirroring if the circumstance element of the principal offence was satisfied by negligence or strict liability. For example, in a case similar to *Khan* today (ie under the Sexual Offences Act 2003) would D have to be reckless as to V's non-consent, or would it be sufficient to mirror the principal offence mens rea (ie a lack of reasonable belief in consent)? The answer to this is uncertain. However, it is likely that courts would follow the Law Commission's interpretation that there should be a minimum mens rea of recklessness.[51]

C) What if the principal offence includes an ulterior mens rea element? *Khan* helps us to identify the mens rea for an attempt in relation to the conduct, circumstance, and result elements of an offence, but does not tell us what mens rea will be required as to an ulterior mens rea element within a principal offence. This issue arose in *AG's Reference (No 3 of 1992)*.

 AG's Reference (No 3 of 1992) (1993) 98 Cr App R 383

D (and others) threw petrol bombs towards a car containing V, being reckless as to the endangerment of V's life. The bombs missed. D was charged with attempted aggravated arson.[52]

• Crown Court: not guilty of attempted aggravated arson. Although the principal offence allowed for liability where D is merely reckless as to the endangerment of life (ulterior mens rea requirement), an attempt requires D to intend to endanger life.

• Court of Appeal: Crown Court was wrong. D should have been found guilty. Following *Khan*, it is sufficient for D's mens rea in attempt to reflect the mens rea required for the principal offence.

This case is highly problematic. Although the Court of Appeal claimed to be following *Khan*, the element of the principal offence they were dealing with (recklessness as to the endangerment of life) is poorly characterised as a circumstance element. However, if we see it as anything other than a circumstance element (eg as a result element) then *AG's Reference (No 3 of 1992)* represents a further extension of the *Khan* precedent,

---

[51] Law Commission, *Conspiracy and Attempts* (No 318, 2009) para 8.133.
[52] See **Chapter 9.7.5**.

allowing conviction based on some mens rea less than intention in relation to elements other than circumstances. The general confusion surrounding what this case represents makes it unlikely to be followed. It is contended that where a principal offence includes an ulterior mens rea element, this should be *intended* for attempts liability.[53]

D) What if the offence D is attempting is impossible? One of the reasons the Law Commission rejected a *Khan*-like approach when preparing the CAA 1981 was because of a concern about the potential for inappropriate criminalisation, where D's attempt was impossible *and* D was reckless as to circumstances.[54] For example, D intentionally breaks a vase that belongs to her, although at the time of causing the damage she was not sure if it was hers or not. Liability for attempted criminal damage in this case seems unjustified: D did not risk another's property (impossible attempt), and she did not intend to do so (reckless as to ownership).[55] Interestingly, it is this final area of concern that has led to the latest twist in the case law.

11.2.2.3 Re-narrowing what it means to intend the principal offence?

In *Pace*, a case arose that combined an impossible attempt with potential recklessness as to circumstances.

  Pace [2014] EWCA Crim 186

Undercover police officers sold scrap metal at a scrap metal yard to D and another, intimating that the metal was stolen. D purchased the metal regardless. As the metal was not in fact stolen, D was charged with attempting to convert criminal property.[56]

- Crown Court: guilty of attempting to convert criminal property. The fact that the attempt was impossible, because the metal was not criminal property, does not bar liability; and following *Khan* it is sufficient that D had a mens rea of suspicion as to the circumstance element of the principal offence (ie suspicion rather than intention that the property was stolen).

- Court of Appeal: appeal allowed. Attempts liability requires D to intend every element of the principal offence, including any circumstance elements.

The Court of Appeal in *Pace* explicitly rejected the reasoning that led to the outcome in *Khan*, drawing on a number of the criticisms of *Khan* listed earlier. However, crucially, *Pace* could not overrule *Khan*, with both decided by the Court of Appeal. Instead, the court in *Pace* sought to distinguish and limit *Khan* on the dual basis that: (a) *Khan* was not intended to create a general rule for attempts; and (b) *Khan* did not involve an impossible attempt.[57] We are left with a rather unfortunate patchwork of both *Khan* and *Pace*.

---

[53] Child, 'The Structure, Coherence and Limits of Inchoate Liability: The New Ulterior Element' (2014) 34 LS 537.

[54] Law Commission, *Attempt, and Impossibility in Relation to Attempt, Conspiracy and Incitement* (No 102, 1980) paras 2.99–2.100.

[55] Williams, 'The Government's Proposals on Criminal Attempts—III' (1981) 131 NLJ 128.

[56] Contrary to the Proceeds of Crime Act 2002, s327(1).

[57] At [52].

11.2.2.4 Intending the principal offence under the current law

The current law, after the decisions in *Khan* and *Pace*, is at something of a crossroads. Despite the efforts to distinguish the two cases in *Pace*, it is difficult to avoid the conclusion that the two approaches are irreconcilable, representing different interpretations of the 'mischief' of attempt liability. We must therefore wait for an appeal to the Supreme Court, or the unlikely eventuality of legislative reform, to decide between them. Academic opinion is divided on which approach should be preferred.[58]

In the meantime, for the lower courts (*and for answers to problem questions*), we may see the mens rea of attempts diverging between impossible and possible attempts: impossible attempt cases applying *Pace* and requiring intention as to every element of the principal offence attempted, and attempts that are possible applying *Khan* and requiring intention as to conduct and results, but allowing mens rea as to circumstances to mirror that required for the principal offence. To illustrate this distinction, we use the example of attempted criminal damage in **Table 11.3**. Remember that the principal offence of criminal damage has a mens rea of recklessness, both as to circumstances (ownership of the property) and results (damage to the property).[59]

Table 11.3 Applying *Khan* and *Pace*

Facts	Which case to apply?
D intentionally tries to damage property, being reckless as to whether it belongs to her. The property belongs to V.	Possible attempt = apply *Khan*. D is liable for attempted criminal damage because she intended the conduct and result, and her mens rea as to the circumstance mirrored that of the principal offence.
D intentionally tries to damage property, being reckless as to whether it belongs to her. The property does belong to her.	Impossible attempt = apply *Pace*. D is not liable for attempted criminal damage because she does not intend or know every element of the principal offence.
D intentionally tries to damage property that she knows belongs to V.	D is liable for attempted criminal damage (whether the attempt is possible or not) because she intends every element of the principal offence.
D is reckless as to causing damage to property that she knows belongs to V.	D is not liable for attempted criminal damage (whether the attempt is possible or not) because she does not intend the result element of the principal offence.

---

[58] In support of the approach in *Pace*, see Child and Hunt, '*Pace and Rogers* and the Mens Rea of Criminal Attempt: *Khan* on the Scrapheap?' (2014) 78 JCL 220; Mirfield, 'Intention and Criminal Attempts' [2015] Crim LR 142; Simester, 'The Mens Rea of Criminal Attempts' (2015) 131 LQR 169. In support of the approach in *Khan*, see Dyson, 'Scrapping *Khan*' [2014] Crim LR 445; Stark, 'The Mens Rea of a Criminal Attempt' [2014] 3 Arch Rev 7.

[59] See **Chapter 9.7**.

Distinguishing the mens rea of possible and impossible attempts in this way is no more than a temporary position until one approach (*Khan* or *Pace*, or perhaps another) is chosen definitively over the other. Not only does the distinction make the law overly complex,[60] but it is also unprincipled, as the reasoning in the two cases clashes, not being isolated to possible or impossible attempts. The distinction is also contrary to the wording of section 1(3) of the CAA 1981. This subsection states that so long as D has gone beyond mere preparation on the facts as she *believes* them to be, D's intention to commit an impossible attempt should be analysed on the same footing as D's intention to commit any other attempt. How we interpret 'intent to commit an offence' should therefore be our sole focus, choosing between rival interpretations in *Khan* and *Pace*.

11.2.3 Defences to criminal attempts

The general defences discussed in **Chapters 13** and **14** apply to criminal attempts in the same way that they apply to other offences. Beyond this, there are no specific defences.

Certain jurisdictions have recognised a defence of withdrawal, where D has gone beyond mere preparation with the required mens rea (ie she has committed an attempt) but then voluntarily desists from carrying it out. However, withdrawal has never been incorporated as a defence into English law.[61]

11.3 Conspiracy

Conspiracy, defined in section 1 of the Criminal Law Act 1977 (CLA 1977),[62] makes it an offence for two or more defendants (D1 and D2) to agree to commit a future principal offence. As with attempts, D's liability for conspiracy is tied to the principal offence: D is not guilty of conspiracy *simpliciter*, but of conspiracy to murder, conspiracy to commit theft, conspiracy to rape, and so on. And, again, D's liability for conspiracy is not affected by the principal offence being later committed or not: D is liable as soon as the agreement is formed with the required mens rea.

 Extra detail …

It is common to see prosecutions for conspiracy even where D has completed the principal offence agreed upon. There is nothing to prohibit this approach, and it can be advantageous for prosecutors in relation to the rules of evidence.[63] However, this is not good practice in terms of fair labelling; has been consistently criticised by the courts;[64] and has led to problems in practice.[65]

---

[60] It will also be difficult to apply in practice, since it will not always be clear whether an attempt is possible or impossible. Child and Hunt, '*Pace* and *Rogers* and the Mens Rea of Criminal Attempt: *Khan* on the Scrapheap?' (2014) 78 JCL 220.

[61] First rejected in *Taylor* (1859) 1 F & F 511. See also Wasik, 'Abandoning Criminal Intent' [1980] Crim LR 785; Stuart, 'The Actus Reus in Attempts' [1970] Crim LR 505, 519–521.

[62] As amended by the CAA 1981, s5.

[63] Klein, 'Conspiracy—The Prosecutor's Darling' (1957) 24 Brook LR 1.

[64] We see such criticism as far back as *Boulton* (1871) 12 Cox CC 87.

[65] Jarvis and Bisgrove, 'The Use and Abuse of Conspiracy' [2014] Crim LR 261.

Alongside statutory conspiracy (CLA 1977), there also remains a small subset of common law conspiracies. A legacy from the old law of conspiracy pre-CLA 1977, these conspiracies can apply even where D1 and D2 have agreed to do something that may not be a principal offence in its own right. The common law conspiracies which are still recognised within the law are conspiracy to defraud,[66] and conspiracy to corrupt public morals or to outrage public decency. These common law conspiracy offences are highly controversial and the Law Commission has repeatedly recommended their abolition.[67] Each will be discussed briefly, after we have explored the central statutory offence.

The rationale for criminalising conspiracy, as with attempts, is based around the dual logic of (a) allowing for early police intervention to prevent future criminal harms, whilst (b) targeting conduct and mens rea that demonstrates a sufficient mischief to be deserving of liability. This mischief in the context of conspiracy, however, is quite unique. Rather than requiring a certain degree of proximity to the principal offence as with attempts, conspiracy focusses on the agreement between defendants to commit the principal offence. Agreement becomes crucial: it provides powerful evidence of a resolute intention to carry out the principal offence; it signifies the increased danger posed by coordinated group offences (eg gang violence, organised property offences, etc); and psychologically an agreed intention, as opposed to an individual intention, makes D more likely to go through with what she has agreed with another.[68]

The maximum sentence for statutory conspiracy mirrors that of the principal offence D1 and D2 have conspired to commit.[69] The offence is defined in section 1 of the CLA 1977.

1(1) ... if a person agrees with any other person or persons that a course of conduct shall be pursued which, if the agreement is carried out in accordance with their intentions, either—

(a) will necessarily amount to or involve the commission of any offence or offences by one or more of the parties to the agreement, or

(b) would do so but for the existence of facts which render the commission of the offence or any of the offences impossible,

he is guilty of conspiracy to commit the offence or offences in question.

The elements of conspiracy are set out in **Tables 11.4a** and **11.4b**.

Table 11.4a Statutory conspiracy

	Actus reus	**Mens rea**
Conduct element	Any action that causes the agreement	Voluntary
Circumstance element	The agreement involves a course of conduct that will necessarily amount to the commission of an offence (on the facts as D1 and D2 believe them to be)	None

(Continued)

---

[66] Already discussed in **Chapter 10.7.1**.
[67] eg Law Commission, *Fraud* (No 276, 2002).
[68] Law Commission, *Conspiracy and Attempts* (Consultation 183, 2008) Part 2.
[69] CLA 1977, s3.

Table 11.4a Continued

Result element	D1 forms an agreement with D2 to pursue a course of conduct	Intention of D1 and D2
Ulterior mens rea element	*	*Set out in* **Table 11.4b**

Table 11.4b Ulterior mens rea element for statutory conspiracy

Principal offence	**D1 and D2's ulterior mens rea as to the principal offence**
Conduct element	D1 and D2 must intend that the conduct required for the principal offence will be completed by at least one of them
Circumstance element	D1 and D2 must intend/know the circumstances required for the principal offence
Result element	D1 and D2 must intend that the results required (if any) for the principal offence will be completed by at least one of them

As with attempts, the mischief involved in conspiracy relates primarily to D's ulterior mens rea, to her commitment to the future principal offence. However, unlike attempts, conspiracy requires us to identify actus reus and mens rea elements in at least two separate defendants. It requires a meeting of minds. This is not to say that both defendants must be found and convicted for liability to arise (eg D2 might have fled or died). But the court must be satisfied that both parties committed the offence before either can be liable.

11.3.1 Actus reus of conspiracy

The actus reus of conspiracy requires an agreement between D1 and D2 to pursue a course of conduct that will necessarily amount to the commission of a principal offence. These requirements are not defined in any detail within the CLA 1977, but have been the subject of several appellate cases.

11.3.1.1 Agreement to a course of conduct

At its core, the actus reus of conspiracy consists of an agreement between D1 and D2. This does not require the formalities of a contractual agreement valid in civil law, but a *decision* to pursue the criminal course of conduct must have been made.[70] This is illustrated in *Walker*.

---

[70] Orchard, 'Agreement in Criminal Conspiracy' [1974] Crim LR 297.

Walker [1962] Crim LR 458

D1 discussed with D2 and D3 the proposition that they should steal a payroll, but D1 later withdrew from the negotiation. D1 was charged with conspiracy to rob.[71]

- Crown Court: guilty of conspiracy to rob.
- Court of Criminal Appeal: appeal allowed. There was no evidence of a decision, of an agreement being reached.

Negotiation, encouragement, assistance, or even actively pursuing a common goal,[72] all fall short of an agreement and cannot amount to conspiracy. However, once an agreement is found, there is no need to go beyond this to show that D has begun any further preparation towards committing the principal offence: the agreement is sufficient.[73] Such agreements may be oral, written, or by any other means. In charging D1 with conspiracy, it is obviously desirable to have identified D2 and to have direct evidence (eg observation) of their agreement. However, neither of these is essential as long as there is sufficient evidence to show that an agreement was reached between D1 and another.[74]

Care should be taken when identifying the relevant agreement, especially where the agreement involves multiple principal offences and/or multiple defendants. In the context of multiple principal offences, such as an agreement to rob *and* to murder V, it is usually appropriate to treat them as two separate conspiracies, even though they are contained within a single agreement.[75] Where there are multiple defendants, the situation may be more complex. It is not essential for every defendant within a conspiracy to have agreed with every other defendant, or even to have made contact with them. We see this, as in **Table 11.5**, in so-called wheel and chain conspiracies.

Table 11.5 Identifying wheel and chain conspiracies

Wheel conspiracies	Wheel conspiracies take place where there is a core individual or group who make agreements with a series of others. Like spokes on a bicycle wheel, these 'others' do not have contact with one another directly, but they are all joined within a single agreement (conspiracy) by the central figure. This may arise, for example, where D plans a bank robbery and contacts several others to play their parts as get-away drivers, lookouts, etc.
Chain conspiracies	Chain conspiracies take place where D1 agrees with D2, who agrees with D3, who agrees with D4, and so on. Again, although there is no direct communication between defendants beyond those either side of them in the chain, they are all signing up to a single common venture. This may arise, for example, where individuals contact others in order to organise a riot.

[71] Robbery is discussed in **Chapter 9.3**.
[72] eg where both D1 and D2 are trying to kill V.
[73] *Hussain, Bhatti and Bhatti* [2002] Crim LR 407.
[74] *Mehta* [2012] EWCA Crim 2824: conspiracy with persons unknown to defraud the NatWest bank, where there was CCTV evidence of others being involved. See also Smith, 'Proving Conspiracy' [1996] Crim LR 386; Smith, 'More on Proving Conspiracy' [1997] Crim LR 333. More recently, see *Cook* [2017] EWCA Crim 353.
[75] *Taylor* [2002] Crim LR 205.

The examples in **Table 11.5** involve single conspiracies between multiple defendants where, although not all of the defendants are in communication with one another, they have all agreed to a course of conduct with *at least* one other, and they are all aware of the common nature of the enterprise and share the common intention to commit that offence. In such cases, the agreement between all the defendants can be charged as a single conspiracy. However, where there are parallel but separate agreements, those separate agreements should be charged as separate conspiracies. This is discussed in *Shillam*.[76]

 Shillam [2013] EWCA Crim 160

There was evidence of a central figure (D2) who supplied illegal drugs and cutting equipment to several others including D1 (the appellant), D3, and D4. Each was charged with a single conspiracy to supply cocaine.

- Crown Court: guilty of conspiracy to supply cocaine.
- Court of Appeal: appeal allowed. D1, D3, and D4 were not parties to a single grand conspiracy to supply cocaine across the network of dealers. Rather, they were each party to separate conspiracies with D2 in relation to their own supply of cocaine and equipment. Conviction for a conspiracy that spanned all defendants was therefore unsafe.

The same point is made within a useful example from *Griffiths*.[77]

I employ an accountant to make out my tax return. He and his clerk are both present when I am asked to sign the return. I notice an item in my expenses of £100 and say: 'I don't remember incurring this expense'. The clerk says: 'Well, actually I put it in. You didn't incur it, but I didn't think you would object to a few pounds being saved.' The accountant indicates his agreement to this attitude. After some hesitation I agree to let it stand. On those bare facts I cannot be charged with 50 others in a conspiracy to defraud the Exchequer of £100,000 on the basis that this accountant and his clerk have persuaded 500 other clients to make false returns, some being false in one way, some in another, or even all in the same way. I have not knowingly attached myself to a general agreement to defraud.

In this hypothetical scenario, as in *Shillam*, there is evidence of several separate conspiracies. Multiple defendants can only be grouped within a single conspiracy where they are all agreeing to a *common* course of action (as in **Table 11.5**).

Excluded agreements: parties to the agreement

Certain classes of agreement cannot give rise to conspiracy liability. For example, although a company can be party to a conspiracy,[78] there can be no conspiracy between a company and the sole controlling director of that company. This is because where the director (D) acts as the sole controlling mind of the company, any conspiracy between the two would involve D effectively conspiring with herself.[79] Section 2(2) of the CLA 1977 also makes three further specific exclusions:

A) **Spouses or civil partners:** Originating from the common law idea of a married couple as a single person, and currently justified to preserve the stability of marriage, there

---

[76] Jarvis and Bisgrove, 'The Use and Abuse of Conspiracy' [2014] Crim LR 261.
[77] [1966] 1 QB 589. For a more recent discussion of the principles see *Johnson* [2020] EWCA Crim 482.
[78] *ICR Haulage Co Ltd* [1944] KB 551.
[79] *McDonnell* [1966] 1 QB 233. A company could be liable where its guilt depended on the guilt of an individual controlling mind and will of the company even though that individual was not charged: *Alstom* [2019] EWCA Crim 1318.

is no conspiracy where spouses or civil partners agree to commit a principal offence. Of course, where there are other co-conspirators in addition to the spouses, any agreement with these others will qualify as a relevant agreement.[80] The exclusion is also limited to marriage or civil partnership, and does not extend to cohabitation akin to marriage.[81] Despite Law Commission recommendations to abolish this exclusion entirely, it remains effective.[82]

B) Persons under the age of criminal responsibility: Where D1 agrees with a child under the age of 10, there can be no meeting of criminal minds because an infant is not legally capable of forming a criminal intent.[83]

C) The intended victim of the principal offence: There is no conspiracy where D1 agrees with D2 to commit an offence where D2 is the intended victim, and the offence involved is designed to protect D2. For example, there is no conspiracy where D1 and D2 agree to kidnap D2, or to cause GBH to D2.[84]

Excluded agreements: principal offences

Agreements may also be excluded if they relate to certain principal offences. Care should be taken here, as the exclusions do not mirror those in relation to attempts discussed earlier. Significantly, it is possible for D to conspire to commit a summary only offence (it is not possible to attempt summary only offences).[85] This was thought necessary, in the context of conspiracy, to guard against the planning of multiple summary only offences on a wide scale.[86] It is also possible to conspire to commit other inchoate offences, as we discuss later (**11.5**).

The only major exclusion, in the context of conspiracy, is that D cannot conspire to commit an offence as a secondary party. We discuss complicity in **Chapter 12**. For example, where D1 and D2 agree to send a letter to P to encourage her to kill V, and P goes on to kill V, D1 and D2 will not be liable for conspiracy to commit murder as secondary parties. D1 and D2 may, however, be liable for conspiring to commit the inchoate offence of assisting or encouraging murder (**11.5**).[87]

11.3.1.2 Necessarily amount to or involve the commission of a crime

Having established that D1 and D2 have agreed on a course of conduct, it must then be demonstrated that that course of conduct would necessarily amount to or involve the commission of the principal offence by one of the parties.

 Point to remember ...

The last part of this is simple, but easily forgotten. Where D1 and D2 agree that someone outside the agreement will commit an offence, there is no conspiracy. There is only a conspiracy where it is agreed that (at least) one of those party to the conspiracy will commit the future principal offence.

---

[80] *Chrastny* [1991] 1 WLR 1381.

[81] *Suski* [2016] EWCA Crim 24. Foreign marriage will only qualify if valid in English law: *Bala* [2016] EWCA Crim 560.

[82] Law Commission, *Conspiracy and Attempts* (No 318, 2009) para 5.16.

[83] Ibid, para 5.45.

[84] Ibid, para 5.35.

[85] Although consent of the DPP is required: CLA 1977, s4(1).

[86] *Blamires Transport Services Ltd* [1964] 1 QB 278: involving a conspiracy over two years to contravene certain (summary only) Road Traffic Act provisions on multiple occasions.

[87] *Kenning* [2008] EWCA Crim 1534.

But what does it mean for an agreement to *necessarily* amount to or involve the commission of an offence? Three issues in particular have arisen: (a) where D1 and D2's agreement is vague and imprecise; (b) where the agreement is conditional; and (c) where the agreement is impossible to carry out. In each of these cases, there are grounds to argue that D1 and D2's agreement will not *necessarily* amount to or involve the commission of a principal offence. However, a blanket exclusion of this kind would not be in the interests of justice, and so the provision has been interpreted to allow for liability.

What if the agreement is imprecise?

The rule here is relatively simple, but must be applied with care. For D1 and D2 to have agreed to commit a principal offence, there must be sufficient detail within that agreement to be sure that they (i) have agreed to do something criminal, so an agreement to 'get revenge on James' would not be sufficient, and (ii) to identify the offence they have agreed to commit, so an agreement to 'break the law' would be equally insufficient. It should be remembered that conspiracy requires a principal offence to attach to (eg conspiracy to murder) and so, unless we can identify that principal offence, there can be no liability for conspiracy. The agreement must, therefore, cover every element of the principal offence, including any results. For example, an agreement to put poison in V's tea is not a conspiracy to murder unless the agreement is to kill V with that poison: causing death is an essential element of murder and so, for conspiracy to murder, it must be part of the agreement.

Providing it is proved that D1 and D2 agreed that all the elements of a particular offence will be completed, there is no requirement for the agreement to have settled the details of that offence. For example, where D1 and D2 agree to kill V, there may be a conspiracy to murder even though they have not decided when, how, or where the killing will be undertaken. Indeed, as long as they have decided that the principal offence will be carried out by one of the parties to the agreement, they need not have decided which one of them will do it. All that is required is agreement to complete the elements of the principal offence.[88]

What if the agreement is conditional?

Alongside the issue of conditional mens rea discussed later (**11.3.2.2**), conspiracies may also involve explicitly conditional agreements.[89] For example, D1 and D2 agree to rob a bank *if the coast is clear*. The agreement here is conditional on an external factor and, therefore, it could be argued that the agreement is not one that will *necessarily* amount to or involve the commission of robbery (ie if the coast is not clear, there will be no robbery). Where there is an agreement between multiple actors to commit a future principal offence, conditions of this kind are likely.

The basic rule here is that, as long as the condition does not fully undermine the potential for the principal offence being completed, then a conditional agreement will still satisfy the actus reus of conspiracy. This is illustrated in *O'Hadhmaill*.

 O'Hadhmaill [1996] Crim LR 509

D, who was a member of the IRA, was found in possession of explosives and planned targets. D was charged with conspiracy to cause explosions. D claimed that there was no conspiracy, because

---

[88] Ormerod, 'Making Sense of Mens Rea in Statutory Conspiracies' (2006) 59 CLP 185.

[89] See Law Commission, *Conspiracy and Attempts* (Consultation 183, 2007) paras 5.18–5.26.

the plan was not to use the explosives unless the ceasefire, which was then in operation, came to an end.

- Crown Court: guilty of conspiracy to cause explosions.
- Court of Appeal: conviction upheld on appeal—a conditional agreement to commit an offence is sufficient for liability.

In *O'Hadhmaill*, although the agreement might not have led to the use of explosives if the ceasefire held, there remained a conditional agreement to use the explosives if the cease-fire ended. This was sufficient. Even if the condition that leads to the principal offence being committed is unlikely, as long as there is a genuine agreement that, if that condition came about, it would be committed, then there is a conspiracy.[90] Note, however, that the agreement must be to commit the offence under some condition. For example, if D1 and D2 agree to smash a vase *only* if they discover that the vase belongs to them, or to have sexual intercourse with V *only* if V consents, then there can be no conspiracy to commit criminal damage or rape: in each case, the agreement is only to act if an essential element of the principal offence is absent.

When applying the law it is vital to distinguish conditional agreements, which can form valid conspiracies, from ongoing negotiations, which can't. Conditional agreement requires D1 and D2 to have made a firm commitment (agreement) that they *will* (not might) commit a future principal offence on certain conditions. For example, where D1 and D2, who work in a bureau de change, agree to 'transfer money if it is not criminal property' then there can be no conspiracy to launder: there is no agreed position on what they will do if the money is criminal property. However, if they agree to 'transfer the money even if they discover it to be criminal property' then there will be a conspiracy to launder: they have decided that if a certain condition comes about (that the property is criminal) they *will* commit the principal offence.[91]

Another area of potential confusion relates to so-called peripheral conditional agreements. The case of *Reed*[92] provides a useful hypothetical example.

D1 and D2 agree to drive from London to Edinburgh in a time which can be achieved without exceeding the speed limits but only if the traffic which they encounter is exceptionally light.

The question here is whether, alongside the central agreement to meet in Edinburgh at the set time, there is a conditional agreement and potential conspiracy to exceed speed limits if necessary. The court in *Reed* commented that this would not be a conspiracy, because the agreement to speed under certain conditions is incidental to the central agreement. However, if accepted, this reasoning will only encourage uncertainty and incoherence. For example, if D1 and D2 agreed to rob a bank and to kill security guards if necessary, it would be inconceivable for a court to hold the conditional agreement to kill as peripheral and therefore irrelevant.[93] So what does it mean for an agreement to be peripheral?

---

[90] *Jackson* [1985] Crim LR 444: conspiracy to pervert the course of justice where D1 and D2 agreed to shoot V in the leg if V was found guilty of a separate crime, the idea being to encourage judicial lenience at sentencing.

[91] Campbell, 'Conditional Intention' (1982) 2 LS 77.

[92] [1982] Crim LR 819.

[93] Indeed, this was a paradigm example of conditional intention used by the Supreme Court in *Jogee* [2016] UKSC 8, [92]–[94].

Assessment matters …

> If you encounter similar facts in a problem question to the hypothetical scenario in *Reed*, or any other conditional agreement where the principal offence is both conditional and incidental, you should discuss the approach suggested (*obiter*) in *Reed*. You should then decide what you think is more likely for the court to do (ie follow the guidance in *Reed* or apply the rule on conditional agreements strictly).

What if the agreement is impossible?

Just as D may attempt the impossible as discussed at **11.2.1.4** (eg D tries to kill V being unaware that V is already dead), so D1 and D2 may conspire to commit an impossible offence (eg agreeing to kill V, being unaware that she is already dead). As with attempts, although D may conspire to commit a *factually* impossible offence of this kind, there can be no liability for *legally* impossible agreements. For example, agreeing to commit adultery, wrongly believing it is a crime, will not give rise to liability.

This approach is codified in section 1(1)(b) of the CLA 1977:[94]

> 1(1)   … if a person agrees with any other person or persons that a course of conduct shall be pursued which, if the agreement is carried out in accordance with their intentions, either—
>
> (a) will necessarily amount to or involve the commission of any offence or offences by one or more of the parties to the agreement, or
>
> (b) would do so but for the existence of facts which render the commission of the offence or any of the offences impossible,
>
> he is guilty of conspiracy to commit the offence or offences in question.

The actus reus requirement that the agreement must necessarily amount to or involve the commission of a principal offence can therefore be satisfied in two ways: either on the objective facts of the case (s1(1)(a): possible conspiracies) or on the facts as D subjectively, and wrongly, believed them to be (s1(1)(b): impossible conspiracies).

11.3.2 Mens rea of conspiracy

In comparison to the other general inchoate offences, the mens rea for conspiracy is relatively straightforward, and does not require us to identify the separate elements of the principal offence in order to apply it.[95] In relation to her own immediate actions, the sole requirement is that D must intend to form the agreement.[96] It is irrelevant whether D realises that what she is agreeing to is a principal offence; ignorance of the law is no excuse.[97] In relation to the future principal offence, D must intend or know that, in accordance with their agreement, *every* element of that offence will be completed, whether by D or one of her co-conspirators. D and at least one other party to the agreement must have acted with this mens rea.

---

[94] As amended by the CAA 1981, s5. The old law (pre-amendment) barred liability for conspiracy where the principal offence was impossible: *DPP v Nock* [1978] AC 979.

[95] Ormerod, 'Making Sense of Mens Rea in Statutory Conspiracies' (2006) 59 CLP 185.

[96] *Prior* [2004] Crim LR 849.

[97] *Broad* [1997] Crim LR 666.

As with attempts, the aspect of mens rea that has caused the courts the most problems has been the ulterior mens rea requirements relating to the future principal offence. Four main issues should be highlighted.

11.3.2.1 At least two defendants must intend the principal offence

It is clear in section 1(1) of the CLA 1977 that D and *at least one other party to the agreement* must have intended for it to be carried out 'in accordance with their intentions'. Care must be taken when applying this in practice, and it should be remembered we are looking at the parties' intentions at the point they form the agreement. A useful case to illustrate this is *Yip Chiu-Cheung*.

Yip Chiu-Cheung [1995] 1 AC 111

D1 arranged with D2 to traffic illegal drugs between Hong Kong and Australia. Unknown to D1, D2 was an undercover police officer: D2 intended to carry out the plan, but only in order to identify both suppliers and recipients of the drugs, so both could be arrested. However, D2 later missed his flight and the plan failed. D1 was charged with conspiracy to traffic dangerous drugs.

- Hong Kong Court: guilty of conspiracy to traffic dangerous drugs.
- Hong Kong Court of Appeal: conviction upheld on appeal.
- Privy Council: appeal dismissed. Although D2's aim was to arrest D1 at a later stage, at the time of agreeing with D1, he was intending that the principal offence (drug trafficking) would happen. D2's motive for his intention is irrelevant.

This case is discussed at length by the Law Commission.[98] D1 is liable for conspiracy to traffic dangerous drugs because he made an agreement to do so with D2, satisfying the actus reus of conspiracy, and *at the time of that agreement* both D1 and D2 intended that the principal offence would be carried out, thereby satisfying the mens rea of conspiracy. D2's motives are irrelevant. Equally, the fact that D2 later changed his mind after missing his flight is also irrelevant, what matters is the state of mind of both parties at the time of the agreement.

If we vary the facts of *Yip Chiu-Cheung*, the reason for caution is clear. Consider a case where the undercover officer, D2, made the original agreement with the intention of intervening *before* the principal offence took place. On these amended facts there would be no conspiracy. The actus reus of the conspiracy may have been completed by the agreement, but the mens rea is absent because they did not *both* intend that the principal offence be completed. If D1 and D2 were the only parties to the potential conspiracy, a lack of mens rea from D2 would mean that neither party commits the offence: even though D1 intended the principal offence, and even though D1 believed that D2 also intended the offence, if D2 did not intend in fact then there is no common intention. Of course, if there was another party to the agreement who did intend the principal offence (D3), then there could still be a conspiracy between D1 and D3, but not D2.[99]

---

[98] *Conspiracy and Attempts* (Consultation 183, 2007) paras 8.11–8.26.
[99] *McPhillips* (1990) 6 BNIL: D not liable for conspiracy (although others were) when he intended to intervene to prevent the principal offence taking place.

11.3.2.2 A conditional intention is still an intention

At **11.3.1.2** we discussed conditional agreements as part of the actus reus of conspiracy. Where an agreement is conditional, D is also likely to have a conditional intention: an intention to commit the principal offence *only* if certain conditions are present/absent. For example, where D1 and D2 agree to rob a bank as long as the coast is clear, we have both a conditional agreement and, if D1 and D2's intentions are in line with that agreement, a conditional intention. Even where the agreement between D1 and D2 is unconditional (eg simply agreeing to rob the bank), it is still possible for either or both to have a conditional intention, as where D1 agrees but only intends to go ahead with the plan if she can get a gun. Indeed, as the House of Lords recognised in *Saik*, 'In the nature of things, every agreement to do something in the future is hedged about with conditions, implicit if not explicit.'[100]

In line with the approach taken to conditional agreements, the core point here is that a conditional intention to commit a principal offence still amounts to a valid intention to commit it, and will satisfy the mens rea of conspiracy. What we are looking for is a decision from D, at the point of agreement, that if a certain condition arises/is absent then she will commit the principal offence. D is pre-empting a future choice (eg whether to rob the bank) by deciding in advance that if the condition is satisfied she will act with the required intention.[101]

11.3.2.3 The parties must intend *every* element of the principal offence

The wording of the statute—'in accordance with their intentions'—carries the clear implication that D1 and D2 must intend every part of the principal offence will be carried out. This was also the stated policy at the time the 1977 Act was created.[102]

However, as we discussed at **11.2.2.2**, the court in *Khan* reinterpreted the CAA 1981 to be satisfied by something less than intention as to every element of the principal offence, and the wording of the CLA 1977 could be interpreted similarly. The facts of *Khan* itself provide a useful example. *Khan*, it will be remembered, involved a number of defendants raping V, and D trying to do so. Each one was reckless as to V's non-consent, the circumstance element of the principal offence of rape. On these facts, as we discussed, the Court of Appeal held that even though D did not intend or know that V was not consenting, he could still be liable for attempted rape on the basis of his intention to complete the physical elements of rape (penile penetration of V's vagina), combined with a mens rea as to the circumstance element (V's non-consent) which satisfied that mens rea as required by the principal offence. Adjusting these facts, what would happen if the parties had agreed their plan in advance? If conspiracy requires intention or knowledge as to *every* element of the principal offence, then there would be no conspiracy to rape: the parties lacked intention or knowledge as to the circumstance of V's non-consent. However, if the *Khan* approach were applied to conspiracy, liability for conspiracy to rape could be found.

---

[100] [2006] UKHL 18, [5].

[101] See Child, 'Understanding Ulterior Mens Rea: Future Conduct Intention is Conditional Intention' (2017) 76 CLJ 311.

[102] Law Commission, *Report on Conspiracy and Criminal Law Reform* (No 76, 1976) paras 1.41–1.43.

The difference between attempts and conspiracy, however, is that beyond the general requirement of intention, section 1(2) of the CLA 1977 addresses mens rea as to circumstances directly:

1(2)　Where liability for any offence may be incurred without knowledge on the part of the person committing it of any particular fact or circumstance necessary for the commission of the offence, a person shall nevertheless not be guilty of conspiracy to commit that offence by virtue of subsection (1) above unless he and at least one other party to the agreement intend or know that that fact or circumstance shall or will exist at the time when the conduct constituting the offence is to take place.

Under this subsection, a *Khan*-like approach to conspiracy is ruled out: where the principal offence requires a mens rea as to circumstances of anything less than intention or knowledge, D1 and D2 must still intend or know that circumstance for conspiracy liability.

Despite the language of section 1(2), however, in a series of conspiracy cases post-*Khan*, the potential for conspiracy liability where D did not intend or know the circumstance element of the principal offence began to find favour.[103] For example, in *Sakavickas*[104] D was convicted of conspiracy to assist another to retain the benefit of criminal conduct following involvement with a tobacco-importing operation.[105] D claimed that he lacked intention or knowledge that the tobacco had been imported without duty being paid (the circumstance element of the principal offence) but this was held not to be necessary by the Court of Appeal, following *Khan*, as long as he had the mens rea required by the principal offence. This line of cases finally came to a head in *Saik*.

 Saik [2006] UKHL 18

D operated a bureau de change with a turnover of around £1,000 a week. However, from 2001 this increased dramatically to over £8 million in a year. Surveillance of D also witnessed him meeting his alleged co-conspirators in parked cars, rather than in the office, to exchange large sums of money. D was charged with conspiracy to launder the proceeds of crime.[106] D intended the physical elements of the principal offence, and had a mens rea of 'suspicion' as to the criminal origins of the money (the circumstance element of the principal offence) that was sufficient for the principal offence.

• Crown Court: guilty of conspiracy to launder the proceeds of crime.

• Court of Appeal: conviction upheld on appeal. Mens rea as to circumstances can mirror those required by the principal offence.

• House of Lords (Baroness Hale dissenting): appeal allowed, quashing D's conviction. The mens rea of conspiracy requires D to intend or know every element of the principal offence and this is confirmed (in relation to circumstances) in section 1(2).

The House of Lords in *Saik* brought much needed clarity to the law of conspiracy. To be liable, D and at least one other conspirator must intend every element of the principal

---

[103]　Ormerod, 'Making Sense of Mens Rea in Statutory Conspiracies' (2006) 59 CLP 185.
[104]　[2004] EWCA Crim 2686.
[105]　Contrary to the Criminal Justice Act 1988, s93A.
[106]　Contrary to the Criminal Justice Act 1998, s93C(2); and now an offence under the Proceeds of Crime Act 2002, s327.

offence. Therefore, unlike with attempts, it is not necessary to separate the principal offence into its elements in order to identify the mens rea required by D: whether act, circumstance, or result, all elements must be intended.[107]

 Extra detail ...

Baroness Hale dissented in *Saik* claiming that liability could be found using conditional intention: as D intended to convert the money regardless of its origin, this could be described as a conditional intention to launder the money if it was criminal. However, the majority rejected this logic. The problem here is that D did not make a decision to act in the future with intention or knowledge as to the criminal origin of the money, he decided to act in the absence of such knowledge. Therefore, D did not intend or know the circumstance, even conditionally. He was reckless.[108]

11.3.2.4 A problem case: *Anderson*

In *Anderson*, the House of Lords created a great deal of uncertainty for the mens rea of conspiracy from which the current law is still recovering. The case has not been overruled. However, its conclusions have been consistently overlooked and/or ignored to the extent that it should no longer be applied.

 Anderson [1986] AC 27

D was part of a group planning to effect the escape of one of them from prison. D was paid to supply diamond wire capable of cutting through metal bars. D was charged with conspiracy to effect the escape of a prisoner. D claimed that he only wanted to be paid and did not intend the principal offence to be completed. In fact, he did not believe that it would be successful.

• Crown Court: guilty of conspiracy to effect the escape of a prisoner.

• Court of Appeal: conviction upheld on appeal.

• House of Lords: appeal dismissed. Lord Bridge, with whom the other Lords concurred, stated that conspiracy requires an agreement to commit a principal offence and an intention for D to play his part. However, it does not require an additional intention that the principal offence will be committed.

Anderson suggests that an intention to commit the principal offence is not required for conspiracy, but that D must intend to play a role towards that principal offence. Both of these conclusions are highly problematic.

A) D need not intend the principal offence: If the parties to an agreement do not need to intend to commit the principal offence then we have the prospect of a conspiracy to commit an offence where no party actually wants it to come about; this is absurd. The approach has not been applied in subsequent cases.[109] For example, in *Ashton*,[110] the Court of Appeal found that there would be no conspiracy to murder where D did not

---

[107] See discussion in *Thomas* [2014] EWCA Crim 1958.
[108] Law Commission, *Conspiracy and Attempts* (Consultation 183, 2007) Part 5.
[109] *McPhillips* (1990) 6 BNIL; *Edwards* [1991] Crim LR 45; *Harvey* [1999] Crim LR 70; etc.
[110] [1992] Crim LR 667.

intend the murder to take place: D had agreed the plan to kill V, but did not intend that it should come about.

B) D must intend to play an active role in the principal offence: The idea that D must intend to play an active role in the principal offence is equally problematic; it would mean having to prove, in every case, the details of D's role beyond simple agreement. This could lead to problems where D orders others (eg those in a gang) to commit an offence but does not plan to play any active role herself. Again, subsequent decisions have reinterpreted the words of Lord Bridge to, effectively, dismiss this requirement. In *Siracusa*,[111] for example, the Court of Appeal attempted to empty the requirement of any real meaning, holding that it would be satisfied where D does not actively intend to take steps to prevent the offence taking place.

The approach in *Anderson* is not likely to be followed and, we suggest, should not be followed in future cases. D1 and at least one other conspirator must intend the principal offence be committed for them to be liable for conspiracy. Beyond their agreement, as long as it is intended that one of them will commit the principal offence, there is no need to show that all parties will play an active role.[112]

Assessment matters ...

If you encounter facts similar to *Anderson* in a problem question, then the case should be discussed—remember that it is a House of Lords judgment and it has not been overruled. However, it is important that your discussion should acknowledge the criticisms of *Anderson* and the approach of subsequent cases, concluding that it is unlikely to be followed.

11.3.3 Defences to conspiracy

The general defences discussed in **Chapters 13** and **14** apply to conspiracies in the same way they apply to other offences. Beyond this, there are no specific defences.[113] As with attempts, a defence of withdrawal has been mooted (ie a defence where D conspires but then acts in order to cancel her agreement) but has not found favour.[114]

As conspiracy is a multi-party offence, it is possible for situations to arise where D1 alone has a defence such as duress, insanity etc. Where this is the case, D1 will not be liable. However, the same is not necessarily true for D2, even where she has only agreed with D1. D2's liability will depend upon whether D1's defence undermines her ability to form an agreement and to share an intention to commit the principal offence. For example, where D1's defence is insanity, and it is accepted that she was not able to appreciate the nature or quality of her conduct, then it is clear that there could not have been any agreement and neither party will have committed conspiracy. However, where D1's

---

[111] (1989) 90 Cr App R 340.
[112] This corresponds to the Law Commission's analysis of the current law: Law Commission, *Conspiracy and Attempts* (Consultation 183, 2007) paras 4.22–4.41.
[113] The Law Commission has recommended a defence of 'acting reasonably': *Conspiracy and Attempts* (No 318, 2009) Part 6.
[114] *Thomson* (1965) 50 Cr App R 1: confirming that there is no such defence; *McPhillips* (1990) 6 BNIL: providing some support for such a defence.

defence is duress, whereby D1 was threatened by a third party to conspire with D2, it is still possible for D1 to have agreed and to have shared the required intention. Thus, although D1 may be acquitted, D2 remains liable for conspiracy.[115]

11.3.4 Common law conspiracies

Alongside the statutory offence of conspiracy, two examples of common law conspiracy remain active. Preserved by section 5 of the CLA 1977, these offences can apply even where the object of the parties' agreement is not in itself an offence.

- **Conspiracy to defraud:** An agreement between two or more to dishonestly deprive or interfere with the property rights of another, or to deceive a public official into acting contrary to their duty.

- **Conspiracy to corrupt public morals or to outrage public decency:** An agreement between two or more to act in a highly offensive way.

Conspiracy to defraud remains a frequently used offence, and was discussed in the previous chapter.[116] Conspiracy to corrupt public morals or to outrage public decency is also retained, but lacks clear definition in statute or case law. Rather, in the rare cases where it is applied, the reasoning tends to focus on extreme moral distaste for the subject of the agreement.[117] Examples include *Shaw v DPP*,[118] where D was liable for conspiracy to corrupt public morals when publishing a 'Ladies' Directory' detailing the names, addresses, and sexual activities available from various sex workers; and *Knuller*,[119] where, despite the legalisation of homosexual acts, D was convicted of conspiracy to corrupt public morals when publishing adverts facilitating homosexual encounters. The continued existence of this offence is further complicated by debate as to whether corrupting public morals and outraging public decency is itself a principal offence capable of being the subject of conspiracy under the CLA 1977.

 Extra detail ...

Although factual impossibility does not undermine liability for statutory conspiracy, it will undermine liability for a common law conspiracy.[120]

11.4 Assisting or encouraging

Offences of assisting or encouraging are contained within Part 2 of the Serious Crime Act 2007 (SCA 2007).[121] As with the other inchoate offences, D is not liable for assisting or encouraging *simpliciter*, but rather for conduct capable of assisting or encouraging

---

[115] *Matusevich* (1977) 51 ALJR 657.

[116] **Chapter 10.7.1**.

[117] This may be unlikely to survive an Art 7 ECHR challenge for lack of certainty.

[118] [1962] AC 220.

[119] [1973] AC 435.

[120] *DPP v Nock* [1978] AC 979.

[121] Fortson, *Blackstone's Guide to the Serious Crime Act 2007* (2008) Ch6; Ormerod and Fortson, 'Serious Crime Act 2007: Part 2 Offences' [2009] Crim LR 389.

a principal offence, for example assisting murder; encouraging theft; etc. In such cases, D is not trying to commit the offence herself (as in attempts) or necessarily agreeing that it should be committed (as in conspiracy) but she is, nevertheless, criminally blameworthy for her conduct in support of the potential principal offender.[122] D is liable as soon as, with the required mens rea, she carries out conduct capable of assisting or encouraging.

The SCA 2007 offences replaced the old common law of incitement, where D encouraged P to commit a principal offence with the intention that it should be completed. The SCA 2007 offences cover this conduct, but also reach considerably further than the old offence, and considerably further than the Law Commission recommendations that led to the reform.[123] In this regard, although Law Commission material can be useful in understanding the offences, care must be taken to identify points of departure between the Commission's report and the final SCA 2007 offences.

Three separate offences were created within Part 2 of the SCA 2007. The maximum penalty for each mirrors that of the principal offence for which D completed acts capable of assisting or encouraging.[124]

- **Section 44:** Intentionally encouraging or assisting an offence.
- **Section 45:** Encouraging or assisting an offence believing it will be committed.
- **Section 46:** Encouraging or assisting offences believing one or more will be committed.

The actus reus of each offence is the same, so we deal with this collectively. We then explore the different mens rea requirements of each offence in turn. The offences have been rightly criticised for being overly complex in their formulation and have yet to be usefully clarified in the courts; it is therefore essential to work methodically through the offence elements as presented in the statute.

11.4.1 Actus reus of assisting or encouraging

Offences under sections 44, 45, and 46 require the following actus reus. Sections 44(1)(a) and 45(a):

... an act capable of encouraging or assisting the commission of an offence.

Section 46(1)(a):

... an act capable of encouraging or assisting the commission of one or more of a number of offences.

As with attempts and conspiracy, as soon as D completes this actus reus with the required mens rea, D is liable for assisting or encouraging the offence: it is irrelevant whether P (the person assisted or encouraged) goes on to commit the principal offence.[125]

---

[122] For a discussion of the rationale of these offences, see Law Commission, *Inchoate Liability for Assisting and Encouraging Crime* (No 300, 2006) Part 4.
[123] Law Commission, *Inchoate Liability for Assisting and Encouraging Crime* (No 300, 2006).
[124] SCA 2007, s58.
[125] Ibid, s49(1).

Extra detail …

Although irrelevant for the inchoate charge, where P goes on to commit the principal offence D may be liable as an accomplice. We discuss this in **Chapter 12**.

Several aspects of the actus reus are clarified at other points in the statute. Section 65(2) (b) clarifies that D may assist or encourage by act *or omission*. For example, D, a disgruntled security guard, assists by omitting to turn on an alarm system to assist a robbery.[126] Section 65(2)(a) clarifies that assisting or encouraging an offence includes taking steps to reduce the chance of criminal proceedings being brought against P. For example, D acts as a lookout or intimidates potential witnesses of P's offence. Section 67 clarifies that the actus reus may be a 'course of conduct' as well as a one-off act. For example, D sends P a series of weapons components over a period of time.

Despite these useful points of clarification, however, the central terms 'encouraging' and 'assisting' are not fully defined in the statute.

A) Encouraging: Encouraging is intended to mean the same as 'inciting' under the pre-SCA 2007 law.[127] This includes positive acts of instigation, persuasion, or emboldening, as well as negative acts such as threats.[128] Conduct capable of encouraging can include that which is express or implied,[129] and can be targeted at a particular person or addressed to the world at large.[130] Examples under the old law, demonstrating the breadth of the term, include D responding to an advert which invited readers to buy indecent pictures of children, thereby encouraging P to distribute such photos;[131] and where D subscribed to a website showing indecent pictures of children, thereby encouraging the owner of the website to continue their publication.[132]

B) Assisting: The SCA 2007 extended the old common law of incitement to include assisting as well as encouraging. This is useful where D provides P with a tool or with advice, etc, to help with, but not necessarily encourage, the principal offence.[133] As with encouragement, there is no need for D's assistance to be substantial: any act capable of providing any assistance will suffice.

Perhaps the most important aspect of the actus reus is that D does not need to assist or encourage P in fact: D must simply perform acts *capable* of assisting or encouraging P. For example, where D encourages P to kill V, it does not matter whether this convinces

---

[126] For omissions liability, D must have a duty to act. See **Chapter 2.6.2.**

[127] Law Commission, *Inchoate Liability for Assisting and Encouraging Crime* (No 300, 2006) paras 5.32–5.45.

[128] SCA 2007, s65(1).

[129] *Jones* [2010] EWCA Crim 925: implied encouragement to grow cannabis where D gave coded advice on 'growing tomatoes'.

[130] *Parr-Moore* [2003] 1 Cr App R 425: advertising the sale of speed trap blockers, inciting speeding offences.

[131] *Goldman* [2001] Crim LR 894.

[132] *O'Shea* [2004] Crim LR 948.

[133] Law Commission, *Inchoate Liability for Assisting and Encouraging Crime* (No 300, 2006) paras 5.46–5.51; Sullivan, 'Inchoate Liability for Assisting and Encouraging' [2005] Crim LR 1047.

[134] Law Commission, *Inchoate Liability for Assisting and Encouraging Crime* (No 300, 2006) paras 5.27–5.31.

P; whether it has no effect on P at all; or even if P is aware of it; as long as D's acts were capable of encouraging P to kill then the actus reus is satisfied.[134] In the latter case, the Law Commission uses the example of D who places a ladder outside V's house to assist P committing burglary. Even if P fails to discover the ladder, and knows nothing of D's efforts, D's acts are still capable of assisting P to burgle, and so the actus reus of the SCA 2007 offences is complete.

Extra detail ...

Despite extending the offence to cover 'assisting', the SCA 2007 has left a gap where D 'procures' an offence (tries to cause it to happen) without assisting or encouraging. For example, D spikes P's drink intending for P to commit an offence of driving over the prescribed alcohol limit. Where P goes on to commit the offence then D will be liable as a secondary party.[135] However, where P does not (eg because P realises what has happened), it will be difficult to show that D has performed conduct capable of assisting or encouraging the offence.[136]

11.4.2 Mens rea of s44: intentionally encouraging or assisting an offence

As with attempts and conspiracy, the gravamen of assisting or encouraging lies in the mens rea.[137] Unfortunately, the unnecessarily complex drafting of the SCA 2007 expresses this requirement across two sections. Section 44:

44(1) A person commits an offence if ...

   (b) he intends to encourage or assist its commission ...

Section 47:

47(1) Sections 44, 45 and 46 are to be read in accordance with this section.

   (2) If it is alleged under section 44(1)(b) that a person (D) intended to encourage or assist the commission of an offence, it is sufficient to prove that he intended to encourage or assist the doing of an act which would amount to the commission of that offence ...

   (5) In proving for the purposes of this section whether an act is one which, if done, would amount to the commission of an offence—

      (a) if the offence is one requiring proof of fault, it must be proved that—

         (i) D believed that, were the act to be done, it would be done with that fault;

         (ii) D was reckless as to whether or not it would be done with that fault; or

         (iii) D's state of mind was such that, were he to do it, it would be done with that fault; and

---

[135] See **Chapter 12.3.1.2.**

[136] Child, 'The Differences Between Attempted Complicity and Inchoate Assisting and Encouraging—A Reply to Professor Bohlander' [2010] Crim LR 924, 929. D would be liable for a poisoning offence.

[137] Child, 'Exploring the Mens Rea Requirements of the Serious Crime Act 2007 Assisting and Encouraging Offences' (2012) 76 JCL 220; Ormerod and Fortson, 'Serious Crime Act 2007: Part 2 Offences' [2009] Crim LR 389.

(b) if the offence is one requiring proof of particular circumstances or consequences (or both), it must be proved that—

  (i) D believed that, were the act to be done, it would be done in those circumstances or with those consequences; or

  (ii) D was reckless as to whether or not it would be done in those circumstances or with those consequences.

The elements of the section 44 offence are illustrated in **Tables 11.6a** and **11.6b**.

Table 11.6a SCA 2007, s44: assisting or encouraging

	Actus reus	**Mens rea**
Conduct element	Any action or omission	Voluntary
Circumstance element	D's conduct is capable of assisting or encouraging P to commit an offence	Intention to assist or encourage the conduct element of P's offence
Result element	None	None
Ulterior mens rea element	*	Set out in *Table 11.6b*

Table 11.6b Ulterior mens rea element for s44 assisting or encouraging

	D's ulterior mens rea as to P's principal offence
Conduct element	D must intend that P will complete the conduct element of the principal offence
Circumstance element	D must intend, believe, or be reckless as to the circumstance element of P's principal offence
Result element	D must intend, believe, or be reckless as to whether P will cause the results (if any) required by the principal offence
P's mens rea	D must intend, believe, or be reckless as to whether P will act with the mens rea required by the principal offence Or D must have the mens rea for the principal offence herself

Don't be confused ...

The SCA 2007 uses the term 'fault' to mean the same as 'mens rea'; and the term 'consequences' to mean the same as 'results'.

When considering the mens rea for these offences, it is useful to separate what is required by D in relation to her own conduct, and what is required by D in relation to the future conduct and mind of P.

11.4.2.1 D's mens rea as to her own conduct

Section 44(1)(b) states that D must intend that her conduct will assist or encourage P's principal offence. This implies that D must intend to assist or encourage every element of P's offence. However, as sections 47(1) and 47(2) clarify, this is not the case. Rather, 'it is sufficient to prove that [she] intended to encourage or assist the *doing of an act* which would amount to the commission of a crime'.[138]

Therefore, D will satisfy this part of the mens rea if she intends to assist or encourage P, even by some minimal amount, to complete the conduct element of the future principal offence. For example, where D is charged with assisting murder, having provided P with a gun, it is sufficient to prove that D intended her conduct to assist P to shoot that gun (the conduct element of P's offence). There is no additional need within this element to show that D intended to assist P to shoot a person (circumstance), or cause death (result).

11.4.2.2 D's mens rea as to P's principal offence

As well as D's intentions as to the impact of her own conduct, D must act with ulterior mens rea as to the future principal offence of P. Unlike conspiracy, and to a lesser extent attempts, D need not intend that every element of the principal offence should be completed.

Section 44 is silent on this part of D's mens rea, and so we look to section 47. To identify the required mens rea, and to apply it to case facts, it is necessary to separate the elements of P's principal offence.

A) D's mens rea as to the conduct element of P's principal offence: There is no mention of D's mens rea as to the conduct element of P's offence within the statute. However, as D must intend to assist or encourage this conduct element (**11.4.2.1**), it is logical that D must also *intend* that P will complete it.[139] Taking our assisting murder example, D must not only intend to assist P to shoot the gun (own conduct), she must also intend that P will shoot the gun in fact (P's conduct).

B) D's mens rea as to the circumstances of P's principal offence: This is provided by section 47(5)(b): requiring a minimum of *recklessness*. In our example, therefore, D must

---

[138] Emphasis added.

[139] For an alternative possibility, see Child, 'Exploring the Mens Rea Requirements of the Serious Crime Act 2007 Assisting and Encouraging Offences' (2012) 76 JCL 220. See the useful rebuttal in Fortson, 'Inchoate Liability and Part 2 Offences under the Serious Crime Act 2007' in Reed and Bohlander (eds), *Participation in Crime* (2013) 173.

intend for P to shoot the gun and be at least reckless as to whether P shoots a person (the circumstance element of murder).

C) **D's mens rea as to the result element of P's principal offence:** This is also provided by section 47(5)(b): requiring a minimum of *recklessness*. In our example, D must intend for P to shoot the gun and be at least reckless as to whether P shoots a person (circumstance) and causes their death (the result element of murder).

D) **D's mens rea as to P's mens rea when completing the principal offence:** This is provided by section 47(5)(a): requiring a minimum of *recklessness*. In our example, D must intend for P to shoot the gun, be at least reckless as to whether P shoots a person (circumstance) and causes their death (result), and be at least reckless as to whether P will do so with the intention of causing death or GBH (the mens rea of murder).

Where, in an exceptional case, D lacks recklessness as to P's mens rea, D may still be liable if she possesses the mens rea for the principal offence herself. This clause (s47(5) (a)(iii)) will rarely arise, but is designed to address a potential loophole. For example, knowing that V is asleep, D provides P with a gun and encourages her to shoot V, telling P that V is already dead. Could D be charged with assisting and encouraging murder? D clearly possesses mens rea as to her own conduct, as she intends to encourage P to shoot the gun. D also satisfies ulterior mens rea requirements as to the conduct, circumstances, and results of P's principal offence, as she intends P to shoot and kill what she knows to be a living person. However, D is not reckless as to P's mens rea: D knows that P thinks V is dead, and therefore acts with the mens rea for murder. In such a case, D will be liable because, although she knows that P lacks the mens rea for murder, D acts with that mens rea herself.[140]

11.4.3 Mens rea of s45: encouraging or assisting an offence believing it will be committed

Moving beyond intentional assisting or encouraging, this offence expands liability to cases of belief.[141] The mens rea requirements for this offence are spread across sections 45 and 47.

45. A person commits an offence if …

   (a) he believes—

      (i) that the offence will be committed; and

      (ii) that his act will encourage or assist its commission.

47(1)   Sections 44, 45 and 46 are to be read in accordance with this section …

---

[140] This will also apply to encouraging rape where, eg, D encourages P to have sex with V knowing that V will not consent. Even if D assures P that V is consenting, and even if (on some unlikely basis) P has reasonable grounds to believe that V is consenting and so P would lack mens rea when completing the principal offence, D remains liable for encouraging rape because D has the mens rea for rape him/herself.

[141] Child, 'Exploring the Mens Rea Requirements of the Serious Crime Act 2007 Assisting and Encouraging Offences' (2012) 76 JCL 220; Ormerod and Fortson, 'Serious Crime Act 2007: Part 2 Offences' [2009] Crim LR 389.

(3) If it is alleged under section 45(b) that a person (D) believed that an offence would be committed and that his act would encourage or assist its commission, it is sufficient to prove that he believed—

   (a) that an act would be done which would amount to the commission of that offence; and

   (b) that his act would encourage or assist the doing of that act …

(5) [Extracted at **11.4.2**]

The elements of the section 45 offence are illustrated in **Tables 11.7a** and **11.7b**.

Table 11.7a SCA 2007, s45: assisting or encouraging

	Actus reus	**Mens rea**
Conduct element	Any action or omission	Voluntary
Circumstance element	D's conduct is capable of assisting or encouraging P to commit an offence	Belief that it will assist or encourage the conduct element of P's offence
Result element	None	None
Ulterior mens rea element	*	*Set out in **Table 11.7b***

Table 11.7b Ulterior mens rea element for s45 assisting or encouraging

	D's ulterior mens rea as to P's principal offence
Conduct element	D must believe that P will complete the conduct element of the principal offence
Circumstance element	D must believe or be reckless as to the circumstance element of P's principal offence
Result element	D must believe or be reckless as to whether P will cause the results (if any) required by the principal offence
P's mens rea	D must believe, or be reckless as to whether P will act with the mens rea required by the principal offence Or D must have the mens rea for the principal offence herself

11.4.3.1 D's mens rea as to her own conduct

Section 45(b)(ii) states that D must believe that her act will assist or encourage P's principal offence. Again, although this appears to apply to the whole of that offence, it must be read in accordance with sections 47(1) and 47(3). Section 47(3)(b) clarifies that, as with the section 44 offence, D's mens rea need only apply to the conduct element of P's offence.[142]

This part of D's mens rea merely requires her to believe that her conduct will assist or encourage the conduct element of P's principal offence. Using our assisting murder example, this might apply where D sells P a gun simply in order to make a profit. In this case, D may not intend to assist P to fire the gun, indeed she may actively not want her to, and so D will not come within the section 44 offence. However, if she believes that she is assisting P to fire the gun, she will satisfy this part of section 45.

11.4.3.2 D's mens rea as to P's principal offence

Section 45(b)(i) states that D must believe that the principal offence will be completed, implying that D must have belief as to each element of that future offence. However, as section 47(3)(a) subsequently clarifies, this only applies to P's conduct element. Thus, again, it is necessary to separate out the elements of P's principal offence in order to identify the mens rea required of D for each.

A) D's mens rea as to the conduct element of P's principal offence: This is provided by a combination of sections 45(b)(i) and 47(3)(a): requiring a minimum of *belief*. Using our gun-selling example, D not only has to believe that her conduct will assist P to shoot the gun (D's mens rea as to her own conduct), but must also believe that P will shoot the gun in fact (D's mens rea as to the conduct of P).

B) D's mens rea as to the circumstances of P's principal offence: This is provided by section 47(5)(b): requiring a minimum of *recklessness*. In our example, D must believe that P will shoot the gun and be at least reckless as to whether P shoots a person (the circumstance element of murder).

C) D's mens rea as to the result element of P's principal offence: This is also provided by section 47(5)(b): requiring a minimum of *recklessness*. In our example, D must believe that P will shoot the gun, and be at least reckless as to whether P shoots a person (circumstance) and causes their death (the result element of murder).

D) D's mens rea as to P's mens rea when completing the principal offence: This is provided by section 47(5)(a): requiring a minimum of *recklessness*. In our example, D must believe that P will shoot the gun, be at least reckless as to whether P shoots a person (circumstance) and causes their death (result), and be at least reckless as to whether P will do so with the intention of causing death or GBH (the mens rea of murder). As with section 44 discussed earlier, D may alternatively satisfy this element if she has the mens rea for the principal offence herself.

 Extra detail ...

The mens rea requirements for section 44 and 45 offences are the same in many respects. The only difference (intention/belief) relates to the conduct element of the principal offence.

---

[142] The misleading use of the term 'offence' in the SCA 2007 is discussed in Fortson, 'Inchoate Liability and Part 2 Offences under the Serious Crime Act 2007' in Reed and Bohlander (eds), *Participation in Crime* (2013) 173.

11.4.4 Mens rea of s46: encouraging or assisting offences believing one or more will be committed

Section 46 applies where D does acts capable of assisting or encouraging P to commit a number of principal offences but is unsure which offence P will choose.[143] The mens rea is set out over sections 46 and 47.

46(1) A person commits an offence if …

(b) he believes—

(i) that one or more of those offences will be committed (but has no belief as to which); and

(ii) that his act will encourage or assist the commission of one or more of them.

47(1) Sections 44, 45 and 46 are to be read in accordance with this section …

(2) If it is alleged under section 46(1)(b) that a person (D) believed that one or more of a number of offences would be committed and that his act would encourage or assist the commission of one or more of them, it is sufficient to prove that he believed—

(a) that one or more of a number of acts would be done which would amount to the commission of one or more of those offences; and

(b) that his act would encourage or assist the doing of one or more of those acts.

(5) [Extracted at **11.4.2**]

The elements of the section 46 offence are illustrated in **Tables 11.8a** and **11.8b**.

Table 11.8a SCA 2007, s46: assisting or encouraging

	Actus reus	**Mens rea**
Conduct element	Any action or omission	Voluntary
Circumstance element	D's conduct is capable of assisting or encouraging P to commit one or more of a number of offences	Belief that it will assist or encourage the conduct element of one or more of P's offences (but with no belief as to which)
Result element	None	None
Ulterior mens rea element	*	Set out in Table 11.8b

[143] Child, 'Exploring the Mens Rea Requirements of the Serious Crime Act 2007 Assisting and Encouraging Offences' (2012) 76 JCL 220; Ormerod and Fortson, 'Serious Crime Act 2007: Part 2 Offences' [2009] Crim LR 389.

Table 11.8b Ulterior mens rea element for s46 assisting or encouraging

	D's ulterior mens rea as to P's principal offence
Conduct element	D must believe that P will complete one or more conduct elements of one or more principal offences
Circumstance element	D must believe or be reckless as to the circumstance elements of P's principal offences
Result element	D must believe or be reckless as to whether P will cause the results (if any) required by the principal offences
P's mens rea	D must believe, or be reckless as to whether P will act with the mens rea required by the principal offences Or D must have the mens rea for the principal offences herself

In order to explain the mens rea of this offence, it is useful to employ an example. As before, let us imagine that D sells V a gun, motivated purely by profit from the sale. D believes that P will use the gun to attack V. However, D is unsure whether P will use the gun to threaten and rob V,[144] or whether P will use the gun to shoot and kill V.[145] D may be charged under section 46 with assisting robbery and murder.

11.4.4.1 D's mens rea as to her own conduct

Section 46(b)(ii) states that D must believe that her act will assist or encourage P to commit one or more principal offences. Read in accordance with sections 47(1) and 47(4)(b), this requires D to believe that her conduct will assist or encourage (at least) the conduct element of those possible offences. In our example, D must believe that she has assisted the conduct elements of both robbery and murder.

11.4.4.2 D's mens rea as to P's principal offence

Section 46(b)(i) states that D must believe that one or more of P's principal offences will be completed, implying that D must have belief as to each element of those offences. However, as section 47(4)(a) subsequently clarifies, this only applies to P's conduct elements. Thus, again, it is necessary to separate the elements of P's principal offences in order to identify the mens rea required of D in relation to each.

A) D's mens rea as to the conduct elements of P's principal offences: This is provided by a combination of sections 46(b)(i) and 47(4)(a): requiring a minimum of *belief*. In our example, D must believe that P will *either* use the gun to threaten with *or* to shoot. D does not intend either (so section 44 would be inappropriate), does not believe that

---

[144] Theft Act 1968, s8. See **Chapter 9.3**.
[145] The offence of murder is discussed in **Chapter 5**.

P will commit one act over the other (so section 45 would be inappropriate), she believes that P *will* commit one of the acts but is unsure which.

B) **D's mens rea as to the circumstances of P's principal offences:** This is provided by section 47(5)(b): requiring a minimum of *recklessness*. In our example, D must believe that P will shoot or threaten with the gun, and be at least reckless as to whether P shoots or threatens a person (the circumstance element of murder and robbery).

C) **D's mens rea as to the result element of P's principal offences:** This is also provided by section 47(5)(b): requiring a minimum of *recklessness*. In our example, D must believe that P will shoot or threaten with the gun, be at least reckless as to whether P shoots or threatens a person (circumstance), and at least reckless as to whether D will cause death or appropriate V's property (the result elements of murder and robbery).

D) **D's mens rea as to P's mens rea when completing the principal offences:** This is provided by section 47(5)(a): requiring a minimum of *recklessness*. In our example, D must believe that P will shoot or threaten with the gun, be at least reckless as to whether P shoots or threatens a person (circumstance), be at least reckless as to whether D will cause death or appropriate V's property (result), and be at least reckless as to whether P will do so with the mens rea required for murder or robbery. Again, D may alternatively satisfy this element if she has the mens rea for the principal offence herself.

11.4.4.3 Applying s46: the Court of Appeal's guidance in *Sadique*

There is, arguably, a need for an offence like section 46 to cater for assisting and encouraging where D believes an offence will be committed but is unsure which offence it will be. However, as the previous section sets out, the structure of this offence is highly complex. The offence was discussed in *Sadique*.

 Sadique [2011] EWCA Crim 2872

D supplied cutting agents including benzocaine and hydrochloric acid to assist the production and supply of controlled drugs. D was charged with a section 46 offence of assisting the supply of Class A or Class B drugs.

- Crown Court: appeal against charges in preparatory hearing, contending that section 46 is incompatible with Article 7 ECHR.
- Court of Appeal: appeal dismissed.

In confirming that the section 46 offence is sufficiently clear to be compatible with Article 7 ECHR, the Court of Appeal set out their interpretation of the provision. However, their analysis was problematic in two main areas:

A) **Confusing ss45 and 46:** The court held that section 46 requires D to believe that each of the possible offences, assisted or encouraged, *will* be committed by P. Thus, in *Sadique*, D must believe that his acts will assist the supply of Class A drugs and Class B drugs, and an indictment should ideally separate these offences into individual counts. The problem with this, as highlighted by several academics,[146] is that although it makes

---

[146] eg Virgo, 'Encouraging or Assisting More Than One Offence' [2012] 2 Arch Rev 6.

the sentencing exercise clearer, it undermines the purpose of section 46. Although section 45 requires D to believe that an individual offence will come about, section 46 is designed to deal with cases where D only believes that one of a number of offences will be committed (but does not know/believe which). This interpretation (consistent with our discussion at **11.4.4.1–11.4.4.2**) was later accepted by the Court of Appeal following a further appeal in 2013.[147]

B) Mens rea as to circumstances, results and mens rea of the principal offence: Seeking to clarify the requirements of the offence, the court set out the mens rea in simple terms.[148] However, they do so inaccurately, suggesting that D must believe that P will complete *all* elements of the principal offence. As we set out earlier, the statute in fact requires a minimum of recklessness as to P's circumstances, results, and mens rea. The court's confusion on this point is a useful illustration of over-reliance on the Law Commission report which had recommended a minimum of belief, a recommendation that was not adopted within the SCA 2007.[149]

Despite these problems with *Sadique*, much of the blame must be placed with the unnecessary complexity of the legislation. Without significant amendment, further confusions of this kind are inevitable.

11.4.5 Defences to assisting or encouraging

As well as the general defences (discussed in **Chapters 13** and **14**), the SCA 2007 creates two specific defences: acting reasonably and protection of the victim.[150]

 Extra detail ...

These defences only apply to offences under sections 44–46 of the SCA 2007. They do not apply to attempts or conspiracy, or any other offences.

Section 50 of the SCA 2007 creates a specific defence of 'acting reasonably'. This applies where circumstances exist, or D reasonably believes they exist, and these circumstances make it reasonable to act as D did.

This defence is essential in order to narrow liability to acceptable limits. The Law Commission provides the following example: D is driving at 70mph in the outside lane of a motorway but moves in when she sees P's car approaching from behind at greater speed. In this case, without the defence of acting reasonably, the Law Commission recognises that because of the astonishing breadth of the offences created, D may be liable for assisting P's speeding offence: D's act is capable of assisting P by clearing the way; D believes that she will assist P to continue speeding; D believes that P will

---

[147] *Sadique* [2013] EWCA Crim 1150. Commentary by Fortson [2014] Crim LR 61.

[148] *Sadique* [2011] EWCA Crim 2872, [87].

[149] For a more generous interpretation of the case, see Fortson, 'Inchoate Liability and Part 2 Offences under the Serious Crime Act 2007' in Reed and Bohlander (eds), *Participation in Crime* (2013) 173.

[150] Law Commission, *Inchoate Liability for Assisting and Encouraging Crime* (No 300, 2006) Part 6.

continue speeding; and D is at least reckless as to whether P will be over the speed limit, etc. The example is fanciful, of course, since it is unlikely that the SCA would be used to charge a driver in the circumstances. However, it does demonstrate the importance of the defence of acting reasonably. It is unclear whether the defence will generate difficulties in practice, as where D claims that her acts capable of assisting terrorism were reasonable given her beliefs, or her supply of a weapon was reasonable given the previous attacks P had suffered.

Although such examples are used to illustrate the role of the defence, they may also be employed to criticise the overbroad scope of the original offences. As we discussed from the start of **Chapter 1**, the purpose of a criminal offence is to define and punish a criminal mischief. The fact that the assisting and encouraging offences apply to conduct such as the driving in the example above, shows that these offences are not satisfying that task and are effectively switching the burden: requiring D, through the specific defence, to demonstrate the reasonableness of her own conduct to avoid liability. The criminal law would be much simpler for the prosecution if all acts were presumed criminal unless D could justify their reasonableness![151]

Less controversially, section 51 provides a specific defence where D assists or encourages an offence for which she is the intended victim. For example, if D (12 years old) encourages her boyfriend (16 years old) to have sex with her, *she* has a defence to a charge of encouraging rape of a child under 13.

11.5 Double inchoate liability

So-called double (or infinite) inchoate liability arises where D's inchoate offence is targeted at a principal offence which is itself inchoate.[152] For example, where D provides P with access to her house so that P can plan a robbery with a third party, D may be liable for assisting a conspiracy to commit robbery. Although, as in our example, liability of this kind may be justified, it must also be recognised that D's conduct is extremely remote from the potential future harm, being at least two steps removed. Concern that such remoteness will lead to inappropriate criminalisation is limited in two ways.

First, not all combinations of inchoate offences are possible. The potential combinations, illustrated in **Table 11.9**, were expanded dramatically by the SCA 2007, but have developed in the absence of clear principle. For example, the Law Commission has rejected the potential for an offence of attempt to conspire as an overextension of the law, yet conceded that such conduct will almost always amount to encouraging a conspiracy, which is an offence.[153] The table should be read by looking to the left-hand column first.

---

[151] Newman, 'Statutory Defences of Reasonableness' in Reed and Bohlander (eds), *General Defences in Criminal Law* (2014) 145.

[152] Law Commission, *Conspiracy and Attempts* (No 318, 2009) Part 3.

[153] Ibid, para 3.22.

Table 11.9 Double inchoate liability

	Attempt	Conspiracy	SCA 2007, s44	SCA 2007, s45	SCA 2007, s46
Attempt	No offence	No offence CAA 1981, s1(4)(a)	D may attempt a s44 offence	D may attempt a s45 offence	D may attempt a s46 offence
Conspiracy	D1 and D2 may conspire to attempt	D1 and D2 may conspire to conspire	D1 and D2 may conspire to commit a s44 offence	D1 and D2 may conspire to commit a s45 offence	D1 and D2 may conspire to commit a s46 offence
SCA 2007, s44	D may assist or encourage an attempt	D may assist or encourage a conspiracy	D may assist or encourage a s44 offence	D may assist or encourage a s45 offence	D may assist or encourage a s46 offence
SCA 2007, s45	No offence SCA 2007, s49(4)–(5)	No offence SCA 2007, s49(4)–(5)	No offence SCA 2007, s49(4)–(5)	No offence SCA 2007, s49(4)–(5)	No offence SCA 2007, s49(4)–(5)
SCA 2007, s46	No offence SCA 2007, s49(4)–(5)	No offence SCA 2007, s49(4)–(5)	No offence SCA 2007, s49(4)–(5)	No offence SCA 2007, s49(4)–(5)	No offence SCA 2007, s49(4)–(5)

The second way in which double inchoate liability could be limited is through requiring D to intend the future offence. For example, where D assists a conspiracy to commit robbery, she must intend that the robbery is completed. To ensure that this second limitation is applied, courts must require that for D to commit an inchoate offence, she must intend any ulterior mens rea requirement within that principal offence. As noted previously (**11.2.2.2**) when discussing *AG's Reference (No 3 of 1992)*,[154] however, this has not always been the case with attempts, and appears contrary to the wording of the SCA 2007 in relation to the assisting and encouraging offences. Therefore, despite some comments to the contrary, it seems that this second limitation is largely absent from the current law.[155]

[154] (1993) 98 Cr App R 383.
[155] Child, 'The Structure, Coherence and Limits of Inchoate Liability: The New Ulterior Element' (2014) 34 LS 537.

11.6 Principal offences in an inchoate form

We have discussed several offences in this book that could be described as inchoate, and there are a considerable number of such offences within the criminal law. These include, for example, the Fraud Act offences where D acts with the dishonest intention of making a gain or causing a loss, but need not do so in fact to be liable;[156] several of the new sexual offences such as specific offences of inciting sexual activity and grooming, where no sexual contact is required;[157] several possession offences such as D's possession of controlled drugs or prohibited weapons; endangerment offences such as driving over the speed limit, with excess alcohol; as well as D acting in criminal violation of health and safety legislation. In each case, it should be remembered that we are criminalising D for causing the *potential* for future harms.

11.6.1 Assisting or encouraging suicide

The general inchoate assisting or encouraging offences in the SCA 2007 do not apply to suicide, because suicide is not a criminal offence. However, section 2 of the Suicide Act 1961 makes special provision for the criminalisation of acts which assist or encourage it (see **Table 11.10**).[158] The most controversial aspect of this offence relates to the likelihood of prosecution being brought where, for example, D assists P's travel to a jurisdiction in which euthanasia is legal.[159]

Table 11.10 Assisting or encouraging suicide

	Actus reus	**Mens rea**
Conduct element	Any action	Voluntary
Circumstance element	D's conduct is capable of assisting or encouraging P to commit suicide (on the facts as D believes them to be)	Intention to assist or encourage suicide

It should be noted that the offence contains no result element, so it is irrelevant whether P is in fact assisted or encouraged, or whether P commits suicide. There is also no ulterior mens rea requiring D to intend that P will, as a result, commit suicide, so a suicide website owner who writes posts intending to assist P, but does not necessarily desire that P will commit suicide, will still be caught by the offence. The offence, and the prosecution guidance accompanying it, remain controversial.[160]

---

[156] **Chapter 9**.

[157] **Chapter 8**.

[158] Amended by the Coroners and Justice Act 2009, s59.

[159] O'Sullivan, 'Mens Rea, Motive and Assisted Suicide: Does the DPP's Policy Go Too Far?' (2014) 34 LS 96.

[160] See Sanders, 'The CPS, Policy-Making and Assisted Dying: Towards a "Freedom" Approach' in Child and Duff (eds), *Criminal Law Reform Now* (2019) 133; and Comment from Duff at 155. Recent challenges include *R (on the application of Conway) v Secretary of State for Justice & Humanists UK; Not Dead Yet; CNK Alliance Ltd (Interveners)* [2018] EWCA Civ 1431: discussing Art 8 ECHR compatibility; and *R (Kenward and others) v DPP* [2015] EWHC 3508 (Admin): in which the court provides a valuable summary of current debates.

11.7 Reform

The general inchoate offences criminalise conduct at the fringes of the criminal law, and so it should be no surprise that there has been, and remains, considerable debate about their appropriate construction and interpretation. Much of this debate relates to the overarching clash between those who would like to facilitate earlier intervention, to minimise the risk of future harms, and those who are concerned about the over-expansion of criminalisation to remote conduct, which may be insufficient to demonstrate appropriate blameworthiness. In this section we summarise some of the main areas of clash, highlighting academic material that should be followed for greater detail.

11.7.1 The actus reus of attempts

Debate surrounding the actus reus of attempts is probably the most straightforward to understand, but may also be the most intractable. Defensible academic arguments can be made for a wide variety of approaches, from very early to very late criminal intervention, to the abandonment of attempt as an offence of general application:

A) **Early intervention with attempts:** If we believe that the 'mischief' targeted by criminal attempts is D's mental commitment to completing the principal offence, rather than any physical signs of that commitment, then we can justify very early intervention by the criminal law as soon as we have sufficient evidence of that commitment.[161] However, for many, the term 'attempt' is problematic here, requiring D to do more than form an intention. It was on this basis that the Law Commission proposed the creation of a new offence of 'criminal preparation' in 2007.[162] This proposal was problematic and was ultimately rejected following consultation.[163] However, for those who favour early intervention through a general offence, the case for a preparation offence may still be appealing.[164]

B) **Refining the current midway course:** Most academics, and most other jurisdictions, favour something of a midway option between first and last act attempts. In this regard, it may be that an alternative form of words (eg 'substantial step' or 'unequivocal act') should be preferred to the current formulation.[165] Alternatively, or in addition, several academics recommend the use of statutory examples, as used in the US Model Penal Code,[166] to supplement the statute. These could, for example, make it clear that lying in wait, as in *Geddes* (discussed at **11.2.1.3**), should satisfy the actus reus.[167] However, this approach has been resisted in this country, partly because of the difficulty in agreeing suitable examples, and partly because statutory examples have not been part of the drafting history in England and Wales.[168]

C) **Narrowing the actus reus to later acts:** It may be argued that attempts liability should be narrowed from the current formulation to apply only to the most

---

[161] Robinson, 'The Modern General Part: Three Illusions' in Shute and Simester (eds), *Criminal Law Theory* (2003) 92–93.

[162] Law Commission, *Conspiracy and Attempts* (Consultation 183, 2007) Part 16.

[163] Law Commission, *Conspiracy and Attempts* (No 318, 2009) Part 8.

[164] Rogers, 'The Codification of Attempts and the Case for "Preparation"' [2008] Crim LR 937.

[165] There is a very useful discussion of this in Law Commission (No 102, 1980) Part 2D.

[166] Model Penal Code, §5.01(2).

[167] Duff, *Criminal Attempts* (1996) 57.

[168] Law Commission, *Conspiracy and Attempts* (No 318, 2009) para 8.74.

blameworthy cases. For example, a subtle narrowing has been recommended by Duff, who conceptualises attempts as 'attacks' on protected interests, and so would only find an attempt where D's conduct could be described as an attack.[169] More radically, Alexander, Kessler Ferzan, and Morse have recommended that attempts should be narrowed to cases in which D has unleashed a risk, an approach that comes close to the 'last act' test discussed earlier.[170]

D) **Abandoning general application:** A yet more radical option is to abandon attempts as a general offence, replacing it with multiple new bespoke inchoate offences (like those discussed at **11.6**) or by extending existing offences as necessary. This option was mooted by Glazebrook in 1969,[171] and has been debated again recently.[172] The advantage of this approach is that it allows for different points of actus reus (and mens rea) intervention depending upon which principal offence is being attempted. However, this approach introduces new problems of complexity (replacing a single offence with potentially many hundreds) and coherence (how do we understand a varying standard of attempt?).[173]

11.7.2 The mens rea of attempts and conspiracy

Although the current mens rea requirements for attempts and conspiracy differ, it is generally accepted that overlap between the offences means that a consistent approach would be preferable. It was partly on this basis that the court in *Pace* rejected *Khan*, and chose to adopt, for the mens rea of impossible attempts, a position in line with conspiracy (**11.2.2.2–11.2.2.3**). However, a preference for consistency does not tell us what that consistent approach should be. Some of the main options for reform include the following:

A) **Intention approach:** This approach requires D to intend every element of the future principal offence. This approach was preferred and adopted within the CAA 1981 and the CLA 1977. Its benefits include its simplicity, as well as its narrowing of inchoate liability to cases where D is fully committed to completing the principal offence. However, as discussed in *Khan*, it may be too narrow: preventing liability for (eg) attempted rape, where D intends the physical parts of the offence but is reckless as to the circumstance of V's non-consent. A similar alternative may be to offer a mens rea requirement of belief as to every element.[174]

B) ***Khan* approach:** This approach allows D's mens rea as to circumstances to mirror that of the principal offence. This approach has been recommended, with clarification, by the Law Commission for both attempts and conspiracy.[175] Problems with this approach have been highlighted earlier (**11.2.2.2**). To these we may also add that this

---

[169] *Criminal Attempts* (1996) Ch13.

[170] *Crime and Culpability: A Theory of Criminal Law* (2009).

[171] 'Should We Have a Law of Attempted Crime?' (1969) 85 LQR 28.

[172] Eldar, 'Reforming the Law of Criminal Attempts: Take Two' in Child and Duff (eds), *Criminal Law Reform Now* (2019) 75.

[173] Ibid. See Comment from Child at 92.

[174] Preferred in Child and Hunt, 'Mens Rea and the General Inchoate Offences: Another New Culpability Framework' (2012) 63 NILQ 247.

[175] Law Commission, *Conspiracy and Attempts* (No 318, 2009) paras 8.87–8.141.

approach seems to be conceptually confused: requiring less than intention as to circumstances, but not telling us why circumstances as elements of an offence warrant special treatment (beyond the desired result in the individual case).[176]

C) **Conditional intention approach:** This approach stretches a traditional understanding of conditional intention to find intention where D intends to act in the knowledge that her action may be criminal.[177] This has the advantage of focussing on intention, but also allowing for liability in *Khan*-like cases. However, it is problematic, labelling what is essentially recklessness as conditional intention, and struggling to explain why recklessness as to results (as opposed to circumstances) should be treated differently.[178]

D) **Missing element approach:** Stannard has recommended an approach in which D need only intend elements of the principal offence that are not completed despite his trying (eg in *Khan*, as V is not consenting, the only missing element is the sexual penetration; so D must intend the latter, but need not intend the former).[179] This approach was preferred in *AG's Reference (No 1 of 1992)*.[180] However, this approach may be too broad. For example, D borrows V's tools to do a job that risks damaging them; however, in his confusion, he uses his own tools and causes damage. D would be liable for attempted criminal damage: intending the missing element (ownership) and reckless as to the non-missing element (damage).[181]

E) **Mirroring approach:** The Irish Law Commission has recommended that (with the exception of murder) mens rea should mirror that required for the principal offence as to every element.[182] This has the advantage of simplicity but is highly problematic. For example, if D asks a drunken P for a lift home, D may be liable for the strict liability offence of encouraging P to drive with excess alcohol, even if D was not aware that P was intoxicated.[183]

11.7.3 The future of assisting and encouraging

Whatever the merits of the Law Commission's recommendations on assisting and encouraging,[184] the final scheme of offences created within the SCA 2007 (ie the current law) is not fit for purpose. Spread over multiple complex sections, the law lacks clarity and has already caused problems for the appellate courts (**11.4.4.3**). Additionally, although its complex drafting has discouraged its extensive use, the breadth of the offences as drafted (both in terms of actus reus and mens rea) provide for the possibility of inappropriate criminalisation—with only the uncertain defence of 'acting reasonably' to restrain it.[185]

---

[176] Child and Hunt, 'Mens Rea and the General Inchoate Offences: Another New Culpability Framework' (2012) 63 NILQ 247.
[177] Williams, 'Intents in the Alternative' (1991) 50 CLJ 120.
[178] Duff, *Criminal Attempts* (1996) 15–16.
[179] Stannard, 'Making Up for the Missing Element—A Sideways Look at Attempts' (1987) 7 LS 194.
[180] (1992) 96 Cr App R 298.
[181] Duff, *Criminal Attempts* (1996) 14–15.
[182] Irish Law Reform Commission, *Report on Inchoate Offences* (No 99, 2010).
[183] Child and Hunt, 'Mens Rea and the General Inchoate Offences: Another New Culpability Framework' (2012) 63 NILQ 247.
[184] Law Commission, *Inchoate Liability for Assisting and Encouraging Crime* (No 300, 2006).
[185] Ormerod and Fortson, 'Serious Crime Act 2007: Part 2 Offences' [2009] Crim LR 389.

The Justice Committee of the House of Commons engaged a review of these offences in 2013 with a view to post-legislative scrutiny, a process that could end in reform or even repeal of the offences.[186] This has already revealed a consistent dissatisfaction with the law amongst those consulted. However, the Committee concluded that a full review should be delayed to see if the current law can be clarified by future court judgments.

It should be noted that changes elsewhere in the law may result in more charges being brought within the SCA 2007 assisting or encouraging provisions. Most obviously, complicity liability (cases where D assists or encourages an offence which is then committed) has been narrowed in recent years to require intentional assistance, and intention as to elements of P's offence.[187] Defendants who may have previously been charged with complicity offences, but who do not meet the new mens rea requirements, are likely to be charged with SCA 2007 offences.

11.7.4 The inconsistency of law reform

To understand the current state of the law, it is useful to observe the inconsistent approach taken to the reform of general inchoate offences. As we highlighted at various points in this chapter, the codification of attempts (CAA 1981) and conspiracy (CLA 1977) resulted from a fundamental review of inchoate offences by the Law Commission at that time. Between 2006 and 2009, we saw a similar review by the Law Commission and recommendations for a consistent change of direction—particularly through the broadening of mens rea.[188] However, these recommendations were not consistently taken forward into legislation. Rather, the only offences to be reformed on the basis of the later review were those of assisting or encouraging, those in least need of reform and for which reform has proved least satisfactory.

As a result, the current general inchoate offences are imbalanced. Despite the overlap between the offences (eg it is hard to think of an agreement to commit an offence that does not also involve one party encouraging the other), the approach codified within the SCA 2007 is fundamentally different from the current law of attempts and conspiracy. And as the courts seek to bridge this gap, both sides risk further confusion and incoherence. In **Chapter 12** we discuss a similar inconsistency caused by the reform of inchoate assisting and encouraging, and the lack of complementary statutory reform of secondary liability, (again) despite Law Commission recommendations. Finally, a similar criticism can be made in relation to the creation of specific inchoate offences, such as those relating to sexual offences and terrorism, which do not seem to have been created with a view to consistent coexistence with the general inchoate offences.[189]

---

[186] House of Commons, *Post-Legislative Scrutiny of Part 2 of the Serious Crime Act 2007* (2013).

[187] We discuss these changes in **Chapter 12**.

[188] No 300, 2006; Consultation 183, 2007; No 318, 2009.

[189] Child and Hunt, 'Risk, Pre-Emption, and the Limits of the Criminal Law' in Doolin, Child, Raine, and Beech (eds), *Whose Criminal Justice? State or Community?* (2011) 51.

11.8 Eye on assessment

This section provides advice for applying the offences discussed in the context of problem questions. Although the elements of the general inchoate offences are very different from the offences discussed in previous chapters, the basic structure to follow remains the same.

> **STEP 1 Identify the potential criminal event in the facts**
>
> This should be simply stated (eg 'The first potential criminal event arises where D tries to shoot V'). The role of this stage is to highlight which part of the question you are answering before you begin to apply the law.

> **STEP 2 Identify the potential offence**
>
> Again, state this simply (eg 'When shooting at V, D may be liable for attempted murder'). A useful way to identify the principal offence attempted/conspired/assisted or encouraged is to think about what offence D (or D2 or P) would have committed if her plan had been successful. The role of this stage is to highlight which offence you are going to apply.

When answering a question on the general inchoate offences, it is easy to become overwhelmed by the detail. Steps 1 and 2 should be useful reminders to start simply. While looking for a potential offence, keep the basic descriptions of the offences in your mind: for example, has D tried to commit an offence (attempt); has D agreed with another to commit an offence (conspiracy); has D assisted or encouraged another to commit an offence (assisting and encouraging)?

Remember that these offences overlap, and so a single action may amount to more than one of the general offences. In this case, highlight the overlap to your reader and then proceed with the offence you think is most appropriate: either because it more accurately describes what D has done, or because you think there is more chance of finding liability for that offence. Again, tell your reader *why* you have made the choice.

> **STEP 3 Applying the offence to the facts**
>
> Having identified the relevant offence, make sure you discuss each of the required elements.
>
> Actus reus: What does the offence require? Did D do it?
>
> Mens rea: What does the offence require? Did D possess it?

This is the most challenging part of problem questions for the general inchoate offences because there are several stages of analysis that you need to lead your reader through. The most important advice here is to be clear; to separate each part of your discussion; and to be methodical. With reference to our detailed discussion of the offences earlier, the checklist approach in **Tables 11.11**, **11.12**, and **11.13** can provide a useful guide to structuring your answer.

Table 11.11 Applying attempts

Attempts

D decides to cut down a tree, unsure whether it belongs to her or her neighbour V. The tree belongs to V, who stops D just before the first chop of her axe. If D had continued, she would have committed the principal offence of criminal damage.

When D tries to cut down the tree, she may have committed attempted criminal damage:

- Actus reus: Has D's act gone beyond mere preparation towards damaging or destroying V's tree (the actus reus of criminal damage), either in fact or as D subjectively believes to be the case?

- Mens rea: D's attempt is not impossible (ie if D continued as planned, she would have committed criminal damage); therefore we need to apply the mens rea for attempts set out in *Khan*. Does D *intend* the conduct she has performed? Does D *intend* the conduct required for the principal offence of criminal damage (ie the chopping)? Does D *intend* to cause the result of criminal damage (ie damage)? Does D have the same mens rea as criminal damage requires (ie *recklessness*) as to the circumstance (ie that the tree belongs to another)?

Table 11.12 Applying statutory conspiracy

Conspiracy

D1 and D2 agree to smash the window of V's car. If their plan was carried out, they would commit the principal offence of criminal damage.

When D1 and D2 make their plan, they may be liable for conspiracy to commit criminal damage:

- Actus reus: Has D (whichever D you are considering) formed an agreement with another that will necessarily amount to or involve the commission of criminal damage by one of them, either in fact or as D subjectively believes to be the case?

- Mens rea: Do D1 and D2 intend to form the agreement? Do D1 and D2 *intend that every element required for criminal damage will be completed by a party to the agreement?*

Table 11.13 Applying assisting or encouraging

Assisting or encouraging

D sells a can of spray paint to P in her shop. D is concerned that P might use it for graffiti. If P did use it she would commit the offence of criminal damage.

(Continued)

Table 11.13 Continued

When D sells the paint to P, she may commit an offence of assisting criminal damage. As she does not intend the principal offence to come about, and has only one principal offence in mind, the most likely charge would be section 45 of the SCA 2007:

- Actus reus: Has D done an act which is capable of assisting P to commit criminal damage?
- Mens rea: Does D *believe* that her act will assist P to complete the conduct required for criminal damage (ie assist spraying the paint)? Does D *believe* that P will complete the conduct required for criminal damage (ie spraying the paint)? Is D at least *reckless as to whether P will complete the other elements of the principal offence: the results (causing damage), circumstances (that the damaged property belongs to another), the mens rea (that P will be at least reckless as to causing damage to another's property)*?

Remember that with the exception of conspiracy and impossible attempts, you will need to split the principal offence into conduct, circumstances, and results in order to identify and apply the mens rea required of D in relation to each. You will find this division relatively straightforward for certain offences, as with the criminal damage examples in **Tables 11.11, 11.12,** and **11.13.** Where you struggle to find a clear separation, try and do the best you can, but highlight to your reader that the separation is not clear, and reflect on this as a criticism of the law in this area that makes such separation essential.

AR and MR are satisfied	AR and/or MR are not satisfied
Continue to STEP 4.	Return to STEP 2, and look for an alternative offence. If none, then skip to STEP 5, concluding that no offence is committed.

STEP 4 Consider defences

The word 'consider' here is important, as you should not discuss every defence for every question. Rather, think whether there are any defences (eg duress) that *could* potentially apply. If there are, discuss those only.

As well as the general defences, remember that there are also a number of specific defences (as discussed earlier). Remember that where a specific defence applies to a certain offence only (eg acting reasonably for assisting or encouraging), it should *never* be applied to a different offence (eg attempts or conspiracy).

STEP 5 Conclude

This is usually a single sentence either saying that it is likely that D has committed the offence, or saying that it is not likely either because an offence element is not satisfied, or because a defence is likely to apply. It is not often that you will be able to say categorically whether or not D has committed the offence, so it is usually best to conclude in terms of what is more 'likely'.

STEP 6 Loop

Go back up to STEP 1, identifying the next potential criminal event. Continue until you have discussed all the relevant potentially criminal events.

This video discusses how to identify the criminal event when applying property offences and how to deal with overlapping offences in this area:

 ONLINE RESOURCES

www.oup.com/he/child-ormerod4e

This chapter is accompanied by a selection of online resources to help you with this topic, including:

- **Self-test questions** and **scenario questions**
- **Videos** from the authors
- **Audio introduction** to the topic
- **Chapter summary sheet**
- Two **sample examination questions** with answer guidance
- **Further reading and weblinks**

Also available on the online resources are:

- A selection of **videos** from the authors containing general advice on problem questions and essay questions
- **Legal updates**

12

Parties to crime

12.1 Introduction

Crimes are rarely committed by a single defendant acting in perfect isolation. Where P robs a bank, for example, she may have enlisted X as a getaway driver, Y as a lookout, Z to assist gathering the loot, and so on. Even before the robbery begins, these parties and others may have encouraged P or helped her to make plans. In **Chapter 11** we discussed the potential for inchoate liability in these circumstances. Where it can be proved that X, Y, Z, or any other, assisted, encouraged, or conspired with P, with the necessary mens rea, they will be liable for an inchoate offence regardless of what follows. Those inchoate offences apply whether or not the future principal offence (the robbery) ever comes about.

Moving beyond inchoate liability, accomplice liability (or complicity as it is also called) arises where P goes on to complete the principal offence. In these circumstances, the other parties are no longer simply liable for their inchoate roles,[1] but may now be additionally liable as accomplices, as parties to the crime. X, Y, and Z do not need to have done anything more than their previous acts of assistance or encouragement; but their liability as accomplices reflects the additional blameworthiness that is derived from the completion and associated harms of the principal offence. Where X, Y, and/or Z are liable as accomplices, they are labelled and punished in the same way as P. In the example given, each will be charged with 'robbery', and if convicted, sentenced as a 'robber'.

 Extra detail . . .

P may also be assisted after the principal offence (eg hiding money or disrupting police investigations). There are a number of offences to deal with such acts,[2] but they will not be discussed in this chapter. Rather, our focus is on the actions of the parties before P's crime is completed or during its continuance.

Complicity, like the general inchoate offences, creates a form of general liability, applying across the criminal law unless excluded expressly[3] or impliedly.[4] Therefore, just as D may commit an offence as a principal offender, D may be liable for that same offence as an accomplice when helping another to commit it. Where P commits murder, for example, her accomplice D will also be labelled as a murderer, and will be subject to the same mandatory life sentence. Where P commits rape, his accomplice, D, will be labelled and punished as a rapist, even if D is a woman and therefore unable to commit rape as a principal because rape requires penile penetration.[5] Indeed, where D acts as an accomplice, her liability will derive directly from whatever offence is committed by P.

Complicity is largely a common law doctrine, but its basic structure is codified within section 8 of the Accessories and Abettors Act 1861.[6]

8. Whosoever shall aid, abet, counsel, or procure the commission of any indictable offence, whether the same be an offence at common law or by virtue of any Act passed or to be passed, shall be liable to be tried, indicted, and punished as a principal offender.

Despite the important role played by complicity, and perhaps partly because of it, the rules governing liability have not developed consistently within the common law. Rather, as the Law Commission has observed, the law has 'developed haphazardly and is permeated with uncertainty'.[7] There are two main reasons for the unsatisfactory state of this development:

[1] Although each will in theory remain liable for the inchoate offences committed, they would be unlikely to be charged.
[2] Examples include impeding the apprehension or prosecution of offenders (Criminal Law Act 1967, s4); compounding an offence (Criminal Law Act 1967, s5); and the common law offence of refusal to aid a constable.
[3] eg the Corporate Manslaughter and Corporate Homicide Act 2007 expressly excludes complicity of individuals.
[4] *Farr* [1982] Crim LR 745, and commentary.
[5] *Ram and Ram* (1893) 17 Cox CC 609. For the exceptional cases where a woman can commit rape as a principal, see **Chapter 8.2**.
[6] The Magistrates' Courts Act 1980, s44 creates an equivalent provision for summary offences.
[7] Law Commission, *Participating in Crime* (No 305, 2007).

- **Inevitable complexity:** Complicity, like the general inchoate offences, is particularly complex and challenging because it requires discussion of D's actus reus; D's mens rea as to her own conduct; and D's mens rea as to a future principal offence being committed by P. However, beyond inchoate liability, complicity also involves the *commission* of that principal offence by P. Therefore, complicity includes an additional requirement: D's mens rea as to P's principal offence must be sufficiently similar (factually) to that principal offence to ground D's liability for the principal offence itself and not merely inchoate liability. Maintaining a consistent and coherent approach to each of these separate requirements, especially within the common law, is exceptionally difficult.

- **Problem of policy:** The doctrinal rationale of complicity remains uncertain and contested, and so provides little structure for how complicity should be interpreted by the courts. We discuss this later as it impacts on reform (**12.7**). There are also conflicting intuitions and practical policies at play. For example, on one hand the law is correctly concerned with the dangers of group criminality and coordinated law breaking, and so we have seen expansive interpretations of complicity to facilitate findings of liability.[8] However, on the other hand, particularly in recent years, valid concerns have been raised about the potential for expansive interpretations of complicity to create a form of 'guilt by association', inappropriately criminalising peripheral actors with serious offences.

Responding to these and other challenges, the law of complicity has continued to generate a series of appellate decisions seeking clarity and fairness. Central among such decisions is the 2016 judgment of the Supreme Court in *Jogee and Ruddock* (hereafter *Jogee*).[9] *Jogee* has fundamentally changed the mental element of complicity, stating that the previous 30 years of jurisprudence had been the result of a 'wrong turn'. After this recent fundamental reappraisal of complicity liability, this chapter aims to provide a clear explanation of the law of complicity and how it applies. The challenge for courts, academics, and students alike, is to find sufficient coherence within the law to be able to discuss and apply it logically.

12.2 Principal or accomplice?

Where a criminal event involves multiple actors, the division between principal offenders (those committing the offence) and accomplices (those assisting, encouraging, or procuring the offence) is not always obvious. However, as the rules governing the liability of principals and accessories are different, identifying the role of D may be crucial.

12.2.1 D as a principal offender

D is a principal offender if she completes the actus reus and mens rea elements of the principal offence. This is the standard form of liability assumed in our discussion of the substantive offences in previous chapters.

---

[8] See eg the House of Lords case of *Powell and English* [1999] AC 1 where Lord Hutton makes repeated reference to 'practical concerns' outweighing 'strict logic'.

[9] [2016] UKSC 8, [2016] UKPC 7.

12.2.2 D as a co-principal

Where there is more than one actor involved in an offence, this does not necessarily mean that there is a single principal offender and that the other parties are accessories. Rather, where D and another (or others) each complete the actus reus and mens rea of an offence, they act as co-principals. For example, D1 and D2 attack V with the intention to kill or cause GBH, and V dies as a result of this combined attack. As both D1 and D2 cause V's death,[10] and do so with the mens rea for murder, both will be liable for murder as principal offenders.[11]

This contrasts with the situation where D does not commit the actus reus of the offence with P, but she does assist or encourage it. For example, where D hires P as a contract killer to murder V. In this scenario, it may be thought by a layperson that D has caused V's death, but this is not the result in law. Rather, because P has taken the free and informed choice to kill V after D's assistance or encouragement, P's free and voluntary act breaks the chain of causation between D and the killing.[12] Legally, D has not caused P's voluntary acts or their results; P is their sole author. As stated in *Kennedy (No 2)*:

> Principals cause, accomplices encourage (or otherwise influence) or help. If the instigator were regarded as causing the result he would be a principal, and the conceptual division between principals . . . and accessories would vanish. Indeed, it was because the instigator was not regarded as causing the crime that the notion of accessories had to be developed . . . The final act is done by the perpetrator, and his guilt pushes the accessories, conceptually speaking, into the background. Accessorial liability is, in the traditional theory, 'derivative' from that of the perpetrator.[13]

Despite the foundational importance of the distinction between principals and accessories, because both parties (if found guilty) will be labelled and punished in the same way, it is one that is often confused.

The case of *Gnango* provides a useful illustration of this confusion, as well as the general difficulty that courts can find in identifying D's precise role.

 Gnango [2011] UKSC 59

D and P (who was unidentified, but referred to in court as 'Bandana Man') got into a gunfight with each other following a chance meeting in a London estate. Each shot at the other with the intention to kill or to cause GBH. One of P's shots missed D and hit and killed V, an innocent pedestrian passing by. D was charged with murder.

- Crown Court: D guilty of murder on the basis that D and P were jointly concerned with an affray, and D foresaw the chance of murder being committed within this venture.
- Court of Appeal: appeal allowed, quashing D's conviction. There was no common purpose between D and P, and thus no way of connecting P's crime with D.
- Supreme Court: appeal allowed, restoring liability (Lord Kerr dissenting). D was liable because he assisted or encouraged P to shoot (Lords Phillips, Judge, and Wilson); or because he was a principal offender (Lord Clark); or because he was a joint principal with P (Lords Brown, Clark, and Dyson).

[10] See **Chapter 2.7.1**.
[11] *Macklin and Murphy's Case* (1838) 2 Lew CC 225.
[12] See **Chapter 2.7.2.3**.
[13] [2007] UKHL 38, [17], quoting Williams, '*Finis* for *Novus Actus*?' (1989) 48 CLJ 391.

In *Gnango*, D does not shoot V himself, and P's shots are not caused by D, they are free and voluntary acts.[14] In short, D does not commit the actus reus of murder. However, in the Supreme Court, Lords Brown,[15] Clarke,[16] and Dyson[17] each express support for the view that D could be liable as a principal offender; and in the latter's case, this was even after recognising a break in the chain of causation.[18] If these dicta were accepted it would represent a significant change to the law, collapsing the distinction between principals and accessories set out in *Kennedy (No 2)*, and rewriting the rules of causation.[19] It cannot be correct. It is an understandable, but regrettable, confusion of distinct concepts.[20]

12.2.3 D as a principal via innocent agency

Although the free and voluntary acts of a third party will break the chain of causation, this is not the case where the actions of that third party are uninformed. Where D uses a party (X) as a tool to commit an offence, and that party is unaware of the circumstances that would make her acts criminal, D may still be liable as a *principal* offender via the doctrine of innocent agency.[21] For example, D gives X a letter bomb to deliver to V, X does so, and V is killed. In this scenario, if D had informed X that the letter contained a bomb then X's act of delivery becomes a free and voluntary act that breaks the chain of causation between D's acts and the death of V (X becomes the principal to the murder; D the accessory). In contrast, if X is unaware of the letter's contents, then her delivery to V is not an informed act and D remains the cause of V's death (D becomes the principal to the murder; X the innocent agent).

The doctrine of innocent agency is illustrated in *Michael*.[22]

Michael (1840) 9 C & P 356

D, intending to kill her baby (V), gave the nurse caring for the child (Y) a bottle of 'medicine' which she asked Y to administer. The bottle actually contained laudanum, a drug that would kill V if administered at the dose instructed by D. In the event, Y did not administer the drug but left it on the mantelpiece. Whilst Y was absent, her five-year-old son (X) took the drug and administered it to V, causing death. X had no understanding of the drug or its danger. D was charged with murder.

• Assizes: guilty of murder. The actions of Y and X were uninformed (ie they were innocent agents) and so D's act remained the cause of V's death.

A third party will qualify as an innocent agent if she acts without essential knowledge (as with X and Y in *Michael*); where she is under the age of criminal responsibility (as X was in *Michael*); or where she is legally insane. In each case the third party becomes, in effect, a tool of D as opposed to an autonomous agent.

---

[14] Unlike in *Pagett* (1983) 76 Cr App R 279, where return fire from police was held not to break the causal chain, P's shots were not involuntary self-defence. See **Chapter 2.7.2.3**.

[15] At [71].

[16] At [81].

[17] At [105].

[18] At [106].

[19] Sullivan, 'Accessories and Principals after *Gnango*' in Reed and Bohlander (eds), *Participating in Crime* (2013).

[20] Buxton, 'Being an Accessory to One's Own Murder' [2012] Crim LR 275.

[21] Williams, 'Innocent Agency and Causation' (1992) 3 Crim L Forum 289.

[22] See also *Stringer and Banks* [1991] Crim LR 639: fraud via an innocent agent.

The doctrine of innocent agency works well for offences where the principal offender does not require a particular attribute to commit the offence, as for example with murder. However, for certain offences it seems inappropriate to characterise D as a principal offender when acting through an innocent agent. For example, D tells X to have sex with his wife (V) who does not consent; D convinces X that V is consenting and threatens V so that she shows no signs of non-consent to X. Where X then has sex with non-consenting V, does D rape V as a principal offender?[23] The doctrine of innocent agency would suggest this is possible, with X's uninformed acts not breaking the chain of causation. However, section 1 of the Sexual Offences Act 2003 defines rape in terms of D penetrating V's vagina with 'his penis', an act D has not performed. Similar problems arise in the context of bigamy: if D knows Y is married, but induces X (unaware of Y's marital status) to marry Y, it is problematic to say that D has 'married during the lifetime of his wife' (the actus reus of bigamy). In each case, the courts have preferred to describe D as 'procuring' the offence as an accomplice. This affords liability, and avoids the linguistic problems described in relation to rape and bigamy above, but it also begs an obvious question: how can D be an accomplice to X when X has not committed an offence? We discuss 'procuring' at **12.2.3.1**.

Extra detail . . .

The Law Commission has recommended that the doctrine of innocent agency should be codified and reformed to include all cases where D acts through an innocent person. Thus, for the Commission, D should be liable for rape and bigamy as a principal offender in the examples given despite the linguistic problems applying the offence definitions. This would resolve the current need to resort to procuring. However, this recommendation does not represent the current law.[24]

12.2.4 D as an accomplice

D is an accomplice to a principal offence where, rather than completing the actus reus of the offence herself, she aids, abets, counsels, or procures P to commit the offence, and P does so. In modern language, this requires D to have assisted or encouraged P, *or* to have caused P's offence to come about.[25] Each will be discussed in detail later.

Don't be confused . . .

Several terms are used interchangeably in the literature.

• Complicity: the doctrine of complicity is also commonly referred to as accomplice liability; accessorial liability; and secondary liability.

• Accomplices: accomplices are also commonly referred to as accessories and secondary parties.

• Principals: principal offenders are sometimes referred to as perpetrators.

---

[23] This example is based on the facts of *Cogan and Leak* [1976] QB 217, where there was some support for an innocent agency approach.

[24] Law Commission, *Participating in Crime* (No 305, 2007) paras 4.8–4.27. See Taylor, 'Procuring, Causation, Innocent Agency and the Law Commission' [2008] Crim LR 32.

[25] *Ferguson v Weaving* [1951] KB 814.

D's liability for the principal offence is derivative of P's conduct. This does not mean that P must be convicted of the principal offence before D can be liable, or even that P must be identified. D's liability derives from proof of the principal offence, not from P's conviction for it. Thus, D's liability depends on proof that her acts were relevant to a principal offence that has been committed by another party: D's liability *does* derive from P's criminal conduct.[26] This is crucial where, for example, P is unidentified (eg *Gnango*, discussed at **12.2.2**) or even deceased.

12.2.5 Uncertainty whether D is a principal or an accomplice

Even when the greatest care is taken to distinguish between principals and accessories, uncertainties nevertheless arise.

A) Legal uncertainties: Legal problems separating principal offenders and accomplices can emerge, as we have highlighted, in the context of innocent agency (**12.2.3**). Although the doctrine of innocent agency operates logically in relation to most offences, its application to certain offences such as rape and bigamy is strained. As a result, despite D acting through an innocent agent (ie acting as a principal), the courts are more likely to characterise D's conduct as procuring (ie acting as an accomplice).

B) Factual uncertainties: Factual problems separating principal offenders and accomplices can emerge in cases where D's role in the principal offence is unclear. For example, it might be common ground that both D1 and D2 were present at the time V was attacked and killed, but disputed whether both attacked V, or whether only one of the parties attacked V, and disputed between them as to which. Where this is the case, there are two possible outcomes.

First, if it can be proved that D *either* killed V as a principal offender *or* was an accomplice to the killing of V by another, then D may be convicted of the principal offence without the prosecution having to prove which role she played. *Giannetto* provides a useful illustration.

 Giannetto [1997] 1 Cr App R 1

D threatened to kill his wife (V) and hired another party (Y) to kill her. V was killed, but it could not be proved who killed her. D was charged with murder on the basis that he *either* killed V himself as a principal *or* she was killed by someone on his behalf (ie he was an accomplice).

- Crown Court: guilty of murder.
- Court of Appeal: conviction upheld on appeal. D may be liable in these circumstances even where the jury are not unanimous on what role he played, as long as they were sure that he was either a principal or an accessory.

Despite D's uncertain role, because conviction as principal or accessory leads to the same result in the shape of liability for the principal offence, it has been held

---

[26] *Thornton v Mitchell* [1940] 1 All ER 339: no principal offence, and therefore no accessory liability.

that this rule does not breach D's right to a fair trial under Article 6 ECHR.[27] This is often referred to as the 'forensic advantage of complicity', and provides a crucial route to liability in a number of cases.[28] For example, in the context of gang violence and other group offences it may be impossible to prove which member committed the actus reus of the principal offence, namely which member struck the fatal blow, but clear that each member was sufficiently involved.[29] It is also useful for domestic situations involving mistreatment of children: a parent's duty to prevent harm to their child may be enough to implicate them as an accomplice to abuse carried out by the other parent, avoiding the need to identify which parent is the principal offender.[30]

The second possibility of factual confusion arises where evidence places D at the scene of the crime, but it *cannot* be proven that D either committed the offence as a principal or acted as an accessory. In other words, although D may have committed the principal offence, or may have acted as an accomplice, she may also be an innocent party; the evidence is inconclusive. In such a case, D must be acquitted. Where this is the case for both/all parties involved, even though we know one of them must have committed the offence, both/all must be acquitted: simply, it is not possible to prove *beyond reasonable doubt* the guilt of any of them as either a principal or accessory.[31]

12.3 Complicity by aiding, abetting, counselling, or procuring

Where D aids, abets, counsels, or procures P to commit a principal offence, and P does so, D is labelled and punished *as if* she committed the principal offence herself. D's liability goes beyond inchoate liability[32] because the principal offence has been committed; but D does not commit the principal offence as a principal offender because P's choice to commit the offence breaks the chain of causation between D's acts and that offence. D is an accomplice, a secondary party.

Although the precise elements for liability (as an accomplice) remain uncertain within the common law, **Tables 12.1a, 12.1b**, and **12.1c** provide an overview of the likely requirements.

---

[27] *Mercer* [2001] All ER 187.

[28] Law Commission, *Participating in Crime* (No 305, 2007) paras 2.5–2.6 and 3.3–3.4.

[29] *Bristow* [2013] EWCA Crim 1540: D convicted of manslaughter where there was uncertainty which of the group (jointly committing burglary) killed V in their escape. Commentary by Ormerod [2014] Crim LR 457.

[30] Glazebrook, 'Insufficient Child Protection' [2003] Crim LR 541.

[31] *Abbott* [1955] 2 QB 497; *Banfield* [2013] EWCA Crim 1394; Williams, 'Which of You Did It?' (1989) 52 MLR 179.

[32] See **Chapter 11**.

Table 12.1a Complicity by aiding, abetting, counselling, or procuring

	Actus reus	Mens rea
Conduct element	Any acts or omissions causing the result	Voluntary
Circumstance element	Aiding, abetting, or counselling: D's conduct is capable of assisting or encouraging P to commit the principal offence Or Procuring: D's conduct is capable of causing P's principal offence	Knowledge Knowledge
Result element	Aiding, abetting, or counselling: D's conduct assists or encourages P to commit the principal offence Or Procuring: D's conduct causes P's principal offence	Intention None
Ulterior mens rea element		*Set out in* **Table 12.1b**

Table 12.1b Ulterior mens rea element for complicity

	D's ulterior mens rea as to P's principal offence
Conduct element	D must intend that P will complete the conduct element of the principal offence
Circumstance element	D must intend or know the circumstance element of P's principal offence
Result element	D must intend that P will cause the results (if any) required by the principal offence, unless the principal offence is one of constructive liability
P's mens rea	D must intend that P will act with the mens rea required by the principal offence

Table 12.1c P's principal offence

P's principal offence	P's principal offence must be completed in the absence of an overwhelming supervening event

Unlike the general inchoate offences, as P's offence is completed, we do not analyse D's actus reus and mens rea in the abstract. Rather, cases begin by identifying the crime that P has committed, and then discuss D's actus reus and mens rea *in relation to* that principal offence.

12.3.1 Actus reus of aiding, abetting, counselling, or procuring

As illustrated in **Tables 12.1a**, **12.1b**, and **12.1c**, D's actus reus requires us to distinguish between aiding, abetting, or counselling on one hand, and procuring on the other. D's conduct only needs to satisfy one of these terms to complete the actus reus.[33]

In *AG's Reference (No 1 of 1975)*,[34] Lord Widgery CJ stated that the terms 'aid', 'abet', 'counsel', and 'procure' should be given their 'ordinary meaning'. However, this is somewhat misleading, particularly in the context of counselling which should not be interpreted in line with common parlance,[35] and abetting and procuring which are not terms in common use. Rather, we need to identify legal definitions.

12.3.1.1 Aiding, abetting, or counselling

Aiding, abetting, and counselling have been interpreted in modern times[36] to mean no more than assisting or encouraging. This will include, for example, D providing P with tools, with information, acting as a lookout, positively emboldening P, threatening P to commit the principal offence, and so on.

A) Aiding: 'Aiding' should be read as 'assisting'. D may assist at the time P commits the principal offence (eg acting as a lookout, driving the getaway car, etc), or in advance of the offence (eg providing tools, weapons, etc).[37] D may satisfy this requirement even where the assistance is unwanted, or even unknown, to P. For example, D, without P's knowledge, restrains a policeman who would have intervened to stop P's offence.[38]

B) Abetting: 'Abetting' should be read as 'encouraging'. As with inchoate assisting or encouraging,[39] D can encourage positively by instigating or emboldening P (even as one of a number supporting P[40]) or negatively by threatening.

An important line of case law has developed in relation to encouraging by 'mere presence' at the scene of P's offence. This is not the same as omissions liability (discussed later) because D must have *actively* gone to the scene; D simply finding herself unwittingly at the scene of a crime is not sufficient.[41] Despite some legitimate doubt as to whether such non-accidental presence should ever be sufficient, the courts have consistently held that it is capable of constituting an act of encouragement, illustrated in *Clarkson*.[42]

---

[33] *Ferguson v Weaving* [1951] KB 814.
[34] [1975] 2 All ER 684, 686.
[35] We are not talking about D providing P with emotional support or therapy.
[36] Historically, these terms have been interpreted in different ways.
[37] *Nedrick-Smith* [2006] EWHC 3015 (Admin): D was an accessory when driving P to the scene of the crime.
[38] Discussed in *Fury* [2006] EWCA Crim 1258.
[39] See **Chapter 11.4.1**.
[40] *N* [2019] EWCA Crim 2280.
[41] eg *Kousar* [2009] EWCA Crim 139: D was not liable for possession of counterfeit goods simply because her husband was found storing them in the loft of their matrimonial home.
[42] Confirmed in *Jogee* [2016] UKSC 8, [11].

Clarkson [1971] 3 All ER 344

D1 and D2 entered a room in their barracks in which a woman was being raped by other soldiers. There was no evidence that they provided any assistance or encouragement beyond their choice to enter and remain present. They were charged with rape as accomplices.

- Court-Martial: guilty of rape.
- Court-Martial Appeal Court: appeal allowed. Voluntary presence is *capable* of satisfying the actus reus of complicity. However, there was insufficient proof as to mens rea: the prosecution did not prove that D1 and D2 intended to assist or encourage rape by their presence.

Clarkson provides useful clarification on the actus reus of complicity, as well as a reminder to be mindful of mens rea requirements (discussed later). Although voluntary presence is capable of constituting an act of encouragement, such encouragement should not be assumed, and must still be demonstrated on the particular facts. For example, in *Coney*,[43] D's presence at an illegal prize-fight was clearly capable of encouraging those taking part because such fights would not happen without an audience, but his conviction was quashed because the jury were incorrectly directed that such presence was *conclusive* of encouragement.[44] In fact, where encouragement is found, D has often done more than being *merely* present. For example, in *Wilcox v Jeffery*,[45] where D was complicit in P's offence of playing an illegal jazz concert,[46] D was present at the concert, but had also arranged the concert and transported P from the airport.

 Point to remember . . .

Issues relating to mere presence are only necessary where there is no evidence of D's conduct at the scene, or there is evidence of inactivity. Where there is evidence of D encouraging P at the scene (eg clapping at the concert in *Wilcox*), then it will be much easier to find liability on that basis.

   C) Counselling: 'Counselling' should also be read as 'encouraging'. At one time counselling and abetting were distinguished on the timing of D's encouragement, with abetting occurring at the time of the offence and counselling in advance, but this distinction no longer operates.[47]

Can D assist or encourage by omission?

As with inchoate assisting and encouraging, D may also become complicit in P's offence by omission. This arises in two circumstances, both of which are usually analysed as providing P with tacit encouragement.

The first, and most straightforward, case applies where P's omission arises as a breach of a recognised duty to act. We highlighted such duties in our general discussion of omissions liability (ie familial duties; contractual duties; assumed duties; duties arising

---

[43] (1882) 8 QBD 534.
[44] *Allen* [1965] 1 QB 130: D's presence at an affray did not constitute encouragement, even though he held a secret intention to help P if needed.
[45] [1951] 1 All ER 464.
[46] Paid employment was not allowed on the terms of P's permission to visit the UK.
[47] Discussed in *NCB v Gamble* [1959] 1 QB 11.

from the creation of a dangerous situation; and so on).[48] This will include, for example, D who does nothing whilst his wife drowns their child,[49] or a disgruntled security guard who omits to turn on an alarm system.

Controversially, complicity also recognises a second category of omission-based encouragement.[50] It applies where D has a *power or right to control* the actions of P, but deliberately refrains from doing so, illustrated in *Du Cros v Lambourne*.

 Du Cros v Lambourne [1907] 1 KB 40

D was charged with driving a motor vehicle at a dangerous speed. However, it could not be proved whether he was driving or was a passenger.

- Petty Sessions: guilty of driving at a dangerous speed. Conviction in the alternative that he was either driving, or was (as owner of the car) assenting to P's speeding by failing to intervene.
- Quarter Sessions: conviction upheld on appeal.
- King's Bench: appeal dismissed.

More recent cases, confirming the rule, include *Tuck v Robson*, where D (a pub licensee) allowed customers to drink after hours;[51] *Webster*, where D allowed an intoxicated P to drive his car;[52] *Gaunt*, where D (a manager) failed to prevent P (his employee) racially harassing another employee;[53] and *Martin*, where D (supervising a learner driver) allowed P to drive dangerously, resulting in the deaths of P and a passenger.[54] It should be remembered that liability under this rule, although potentially extensive, is restrained by the requirements of mens rea (discussed later), as it will not always be straightforward to prove that the defendant who omitted to perform a relevant act intended thereby to assist or encourage P.

 Extra detail . . .

The Law Commission recommended abolishing omissions liability where D is not in breach of a duty to act, contending that the current law demands too much of D to act as a 'good Samaritan'. The Commission used the example of D who fails to prevent an assault happening on his front lawn when woken by it in the middle of the night.[55]

Must D cause P's offence?

Having established that D's conduct is *capable* of assisting or encouraging P's principal offence, the next question is whether it must do so in fact. We have already highlighted that strict causation between D's conduct and P's offence could never be required: where P acts voluntarily she breaks the chain of causation, and therefore

---

[48] See **Chapter 2.6.2**.
[49] *Russell* [1933] VLR 59.
[50] This second category does *not* apply to inchoate assisting or encouraging offences.
[51] [1970] 1 WLR 741.
[52] [2006] EWCA Crim 415: P crashed the car causing death. D was liable as an accomplice for causing death by dangerous driving.
[53] [2003] EWCA Crim 3925.
[54] [2010] EWCA Crim 1450.
[55] Law Commission, *Participating in Crime* (No 305, 2007) paras 3.39–3.41.

there is no causal link from D's conduct; where P does not act voluntarily (ie she is an innocent agent), then D is a principal rather than an accomplice (**12.2**). It will also be remembered that no causal link is necessary for inchoate assisting or encouraging.[56] However, as D's liability in complicity derives from P's completion of a crime, it might be thought that some causal role is essential to justify that derivation.[57] As stated in *Stringer*:

> It is well established that D's conduct need not cause P to commit the offence in the sense that 'but for' D's conduct P would not have committed the offence. . . . But it is also established by the [common law] that D's conduct must have some relevance to the commission of the principal offence; there must, as it has been said, be some connecting link. The moral justification for holding D responsible for the crime is that he has involved himself in the commission of the crime by assistance or encouragement, and that presupposes some form of connection between his conduct and the crime.[58]

It is on this rather vague basis that the current law of complicity requires *some* causal effect from D's conduct, but does not require full causation of the kind discussed in **Chapter 2**. To understand what this means in practice, it is useful to distinguish assistance from encouragement.

    A) D assists P (eg provides tools, acts as a lookout, etc): It must be demonstrated that D's assistance contributed to P's offence in some way. For example, where D provides P with a gun to kill V, but P ignores the gun and kills V with a knife, there is no assistance: D's acts were capable of assisting P, but provided no assistance in fact. Thus, although D satisfies the actus reus for inchoate liability by her acts capable of assisting or encouraging,[59] D does not assist P for the purposes of complicity.

 Assessment matters . . .

Where P rejects D's assistance (as in our example), the offer of help may nevertheless encourage P to commit the principal offence. With this in mind, even where D's acts look like potential assistance, remember to consider whether they also (or alternatively) encourage P (ie abet or counsel).

Once it is established that D has provided some assistance, the actus reus of complicity will be satisfied. There is no need to show that D's assistance was substantial. For example, D acts as a lookout but no one appears to disturb the crime being committed by P; D supplies weapons that P could have acquired elsewhere; D drives P to the scene but gets lost and is late: in each case D's assistance is minimal, but will still satisfy the actus reus for complicity in P's offence. This element is usefully discussed in *Bryce*.

---

[56] See **Chapter 11.4.1**.
[57] Some have argued that this causal connection is/should be the basis for complicity liability. We discuss this when considering reform of the current law (**12.6**).
[58] [2011] EWCA Crim 1396, per Toulson LJ at [48].
[59] See **Chapter 11.4.1**.

Bryce [2004] EWCA Crim 1231

D drove P to a place to enable P to kill V. D foresaw that P would kill V. P did kill V, but a full 12 hours after D's involvement, and only following discussion with another party. D was charged with murder as P's accomplice.

- Crown Court: guilty of murder.
- Court of Appeal: conviction upheld on appeal. Despite the time delay between D's acts and the killing, and despite other contributory facts, D's acts continued to provide some assistance to the murder.

B) D encourages P (eg emboldens, threatens, etc): To establish a connection between D's encouragement and P's offence, it must be proved that D's encouragement was communicated to P.[60] In other words, P must know that D is encouraging her. For example, D, present as a spectator in a football stadium, shouts for one player (P) to punch another player (V), and P does so. D will only be complicit in P's offence if P hears the shout. If P does not hear, D remains liable for inchoate encouragement (ie her act is *capable* of encouraging P), but will not satisfy the actus reus of complicity.[61]

Once it is demonstrated that P was aware of D's encouragement, even where that encouragement had little effect on P, D will satisfy the actus reus of complicity. The trial judge in *Giannetto*, discussed earlier (**12.2.5**), provided a useful and often repeated example.

If . . . [D] knew that somebody else intended to kill his wife and he just did nothing at all, then he is not guilty because he has not participated . . . Supposing somebody came up to [D] and said, 'I am going to kill your wife', if he played any part, either in encouragement, as little as patting him on the back, nodding, saying, 'Oh goody', that would be sufficient to involve him in the murder, to make him guilty, because he is encouraging the murder.

As this example illustrates, D's encouragement will be sufficient to found her liability as an accessory even where P has already decided to commit the principal offence. It is assumed that D's encouragement, although not changing D's settled plan, still emboldens or fortifies her intention. This assumption is only rebutted if there is evidence that P gained no encouragement from D. For example, where D encourages P to punch V, but before doing so P tells D 'mind your own business'.[62]

12.3.1.2 Procuring

In the alternative to aiding, abetting, or counselling, the actus reus of complicity can be satisfied where D 'procures' P's offence. To procure is to 'produce by endeavour'.

---

[60] *Calhaem* [1985] 1 QB 808.
[61] Example taken from the Law Commission, and discussed in *Stringer* [2011] EWCA Crim 1396, [49].
[62] Law Commission, *Participating in Crime* (No 305, 2007) para B.62.

Procuring will apply even where D has not assisted or encouraged P, as long as D has played a causal role in the principal offence coming about. The leading case is *AG's Reference (No 1 of 1975)*.

AG's Reference (No 1 of 1975) [1975] 2 All ER 684

D surreptitiously laced P's drink with alcohol knowing that P would be driving home. P was unaware of this. P later committed an offence of driving with excess alcohol[63] as the principal offender, and D was charged as an accomplice.

- Crown Court: not guilty of driving offence, because P was unaware of D's role.
- Court of Appeal: on a reference from the AG, D should have been liable. D procured P's offence.

Adopting the reasoning in this case, it is clear that D can procure an offence where P is unaware of D's actions, and even though D is not encouraging or assisting P's acts (ie in this case, P's driving). It is enough that D caused the necessary circumstances of the offence to be present (ie in this case, for P to be over the proscribed alcohol limit), and thus caused P to commit the offence.

Subject to the problem cases discussed in the following section, procuring requires D to have caused P's offence. Thus, liability for procuring will be undermined by any break in the causal chain. In *AG's Reference (No 1 of 1975)*, P's acts in drinking do not break the chain of causation between D's acts and the offence because they are not informed (ie P is unaware of the alcohol lacing his drink). If P was aware of the alcohol and chose to continue, his acts would break the chain, and D would only be liable as an accomplice if it could be shown that his acts also assisted or encouraged P. In *Beatty v Gillbanks*,[64] for example, the Salvation Army knew that a proposed meeting would provoke a violent reaction from a hostile organisation known as the 'Skeleton Army'. Although this proved to be correct, the Salvation Army could not be said to have procured the violence. This is because the free, voluntary, and informed choice of Skeleton Army members broke any potential causal chain. Provocation is not causation.

Extra detail . . .

Although D may assist or encourage by omission, it is very unlikely that D could procure an offence (produce by endeavour) without positive movement.

Problem cases and procuring

Ideally, procuring cases can be logically distinguished from principal offending and other types of complicity as we see in **Table 12.2a**.

---

[63] Contrary to the Road Traffic Act 1972, s6(1), now replaced by the Road Traffic Act 1988, s5.
[64] (1882) 9 QBD 308.

Table 12.2a Identifying procuring

D assists or encourages P who commits a principal offence with mens rea	This is *not* a procuring case because D has not caused P to commit the principal offence. This is a standard case of complicity by D assisting or encouraging P
D causes P to commit the actus reus of a principal offence, P lacks mens rea, as D knows	This is *not* a procuring case because P commits no crime. D will be liable as the principal offender via the doctrine of innocent agency
D causes P to commit a strict liability offence when P lacks any fault in doing so	**This *is* a procuring case. P does commit the principal offence, and D has caused her to do so**

Unfortunately, within the innocent agency category in the second bullet row, certain cases have been decided under the heading of procuring. Thus, as well as standard cases of procuring in **Table 12.2a**, a further category must be added (illustrated in **Table 12.2b**).

Table 12.2b Identifying problem cases of procuring

D causes P to commit the actus reus of a principal offence, P lacks mens rea, as D knows. However, the offence is one that cannot be committed by an innocent agent

As highlighted earlier (**12.2.3–12.2.4**), there are a number of offences that cannot be committed via an innocent agent (eg rape and bigamy). Therefore, for these cases, even though innocent agency might appear the correct approach (D causes P's actus reus but P does not commit an offence because she lacks mens rea), the courts are more likely to describe D's liability as complicity by procuring. This is an unfortunate description. P has not committed an offence and so it cannot be said that D's liability derives from another's crime. This is not to say that D should be acquitted—D has caused P to commit the actus reus of that crime, and D has mens rea—it is simply that the approach used to find liability (ie procuring) seems inappropriate.

The case of *Cogan and Leak* provides a useful illustration.

 Cogan and Leak [1976] QB 217

D told his wife (V) to have sexual intercourse with his friend (P). V was scared of D and so, although she did not consent, she did not resist P. P was unaware that V was not consenting. P was charged with rape, with D as his accomplice.

- Crown Court: guilty of rape (both D and P).
- Court of Appeal: P's appeal allowed—there was a misdirection relating to the mens rea required of P for rape.[65] D's conviction upheld—although P was innocent, D nevertheless procured the offence of rape.

---

[65] See **Chapter 8.2**.

Cogan and Leak is a useful case because the Court of Appeal discusses the possibility of finding liability on the basis of innocent agency, but eventually prefers the procuring approach. Similar reasoning was adopted in *Millward*.[66] In this case D instructed an employee (P) to drive a tractor and trailer knowing that the hitch mechanism connecting them was defective. The hitch broke in transit and the detached trailer killed the driver of an oncoming car (V). P did *not* commit an offence of causing death by reckless driving[67] because he lacked mens rea. However, D *was* convicted of procuring that offence.

 Point to remember . . .

Although these cases allow for complicity by procuring even though P does not commit a principal offence, it is essential that P completes the actus reus of the offence and that D has caused P to do so. We see this in *Cogan and Leak*, and in *Millward*, where D commands or permits conduct from P knowing (but not telling P) that such conduct will satisfy the actus reus of an offence. Where the actus reus of the offence is not completed by P, whatever D's role, there can be no complicity.[68]

12.3.2 Mens rea of aiding, abetting, counselling, or procuring

The mens rea for complicity has not been consistently identified or applied by the courts for many years. The current law is governed by the case of *Jogee*, in which the Supreme Court fundamentally changed the previous law, and (to some extent) clarified the current law moving forward.

 Jogee and Ruddock [2016] UKSC 8, [2016] UKPC 7

Combined cases on appeal. In *Jogee*, D and P went to V's house and began a violent confrontation. P took a knife from the kitchen and killed V. D intended P to confront V with violence, and foresaw the possibility of serious harm being caused, but did not intend serious harm to be caused. In *Ruddock*, D and P were jointly involved in the robbery of V's car. V was tied up, and P killed V. D foresaw that P might act with intention to cause serious harm, but did not intend him to. Jogee and Ruddock were both charged with murder, as accessories.

- Crown Court (and court of first instance in Jamaica): guilty of murder as accessories.
- Court of Appeal (and Court of Appeal of Jamaica): convictions upheld on appeal.
- Supreme Court (and Privy Council): unanimous in allowing the appeal, and ordering retrials of both defendants. Complicity liability requires D to intend to assist or encourage P to commit the principal offence with the required mens rea, foresight is no longer sufficient for liability; it is merely evidence of intent.

---

[66] [1994] Crim LR 527.
[67] Since replaced by the offence of causing death by dangerous driving, discussed at **Chapter 6.4.2.1**.
[68] *Loukes* [1996] 1 Cr App R 444: D was not an accomplice to causing death by careless driving because P (the driver) was not careless and therefore did not satisfy the actus reus of the offence.

The full implications of *Jogee* have attracted considerable academic attention,[69] and are likely to require further clarification in the courts. However, as we discuss below, despite areas of continued uncertainty, the judgment is generally to be welcomed. As a unanimous judgment it avoids the inconsistencies highlighted earlier in the context of *Gnango*, and in its substance it has made positive steps towards narrowing the law to a more acceptable level—particularly for murder.

When discussing D's mens rea, and interpreting the judgment in *Jogee*, it is useful to separate: (a) D's mens rea as to her own conduct, illustrated previously in **Table 12.1a**; and (b) D's mens rea as to the future conduct and state of mind of P, illustrated previously in **Table 12.1b**. We discuss each in turn.

Point to remember . . .

Separating the discussion of D's mens rea in this way was also recommended in relation to inchoate assisting and encouraging.[70] However, the important difference for complicity is to assess D's mens rea with regard to a principal offence which has been completed by P. We do not ask generally whether D had mens rea as to P committing an offence but, rather, whether D had mens rea as to P committing the offence completed. As discussed later, this difference can be important where the offence P commits varies from what D expects.

12.3.2.1 D's mens rea as to her own conduct

This part of D's mens rea contains two requirements. First, as with all criminal liability, D's conduct (ie D's assisting, encouraging, or procuring) must be performed voluntarily. For example, there will be no liability where D inadvertently drops a tool which P then uses to commit a crime, and/or where D omits because she is tied up and unable to move.[71]

Secondly, D must intend that her conduct will assist or encourage P to commit the principal offence; or in the context of procuring, that her conduct will cause the principal offence.[72] Significantly, this is different from a requirement that D must intend that P will commit the principal offence (we discuss D's mens rea as to P's offence later). Where D intends to assist, encourage, or cause an offence she will usually also intend that that offence should be committed, but this is not necessarily the case. For example, if D sells P a gun knowing that P could use it to kill V, D may be motivated purely by payment for the gun and may hope that P does not commit the offence, but she is still 'intentionally assisting' P to commit murder. This was discussed in *National Coal Board v Gamble*, and explicitly endorsed throughout *Jogee*.

---

[69] See eg Krebs (ed), *Accessorial Liability after Jogee* (2020); Ormerod and Laird, '*Jogee*—Not the End of a Legal Saga but the Start of a New One?' [2016] Crim LR 543; Buxton, '*Jogee*: Upheaval in Secondary Liability for Murder' [2016] Crim LR 324; Dyson, 'Shorn-Off Complicity' (2016) 75 CLJ 196 (comment); Stark, 'The Demise of "Parasitic Accessorial Liability": Substantive Judicial Law Reform, not Common Law Housekeeping' (2016) 75 CLJ 550; Simester, 'Accessory Liability and Common Unlawful Purposes' (2017) 133 LQR 73.

[70] See **Chapter 11.4.2–11.4.4**.

[71] *Bryce* [2004] EWCA Crim 1231, [41]–[42].

[72] Duff, 'Can I Help You? Accessorial Liability and the Intention to Assist' (1990) 10 LS 165.

National Coal Board v Gamble [1959] 1 QB 11

D supplied coal to P. At the weigh-station, before P was able to leave with the coal, D found that P's lorry was overladen to the extent that taking the lorry on the road became an offence.[73] Nevertheless D allowed P to leave with the overladen lorry. D was charged as an accomplice to P's offence.

• Court: guilty of overladen offence.

• Divisional Court: conviction upheld on appeal by case stated. Although D may have been indifferent as to P's offence, he must have obliquely intended to assist (knowing that his action, supplying the coal and allowing P to leave, was virtually certain to assist). Slade J dissented, stating that D should only be found to have intended to aid where this was his direct intention (ie oblique intent would be insufficient).

Following *Gamble*, another useful example of obliquely intending to assist or encourage is supplied by *Gnango* where the gunfight between D and P resulted in V being shot (outlined at **12.2.2**). It was clearly not D's direct intention in *Gnango* to encourage P to shoot at him, D would have actively not wanted this, but such encouragement was a fore-seen virtual certainty from D's conduct (ie D obliquely intended it).[74] In summary, then, this element will be satisfied both where D directly intends to assist, encourage, or pro-cure P's offence because it is D's desire or purpose, *and* where it is D's oblique intention because although she may not desire it, D recognises that assistance or encouragement is the virtually certain consequence of her conduct.

Jogee provides further clarification that an 'intention' to assist or encourage can be sat-isfied by both direct and oblique intention, but also emphasises a potential role for con-ditional intention.[75] For example, for the court, D conditionally intends to encourage P to commit murder where D intentionally encourages P to commit a bank robbery and to murder guards if necessary. It is clearly correct that D intends to encourage murder in this example, but it is questionable whether the concept of conditional intention is required to reach that conclusion.[76] In cases of this kind, standard definitions of direct and oblique intention will suffice. Where D's conduct is motivated by a desire to encourage robbery and murder should certain circumstances arise, D directly intends to encourage both offences.

The requirement that D must intend to assist, encourage, or procure P's offence is a settled element of D's liability, but problem cases have emerged. For example, it has been argued that where D supplies P with an article for use within a principal offence, D may be excused accessorial liability if the supply was required under civil law, for example where P demands the return of a gun which was lent to D.[77] However, although liability in these circumstances can appear harsh,[78] it is unlikely that such an exclusion exists.[79] Provided D intends directly or obliquely to assist, encourage, or procure P's crime, she will satisfy this element.

[73] Motor Vehicles (Construction and Use) Regulations 1955, regs 68 and 104.

[74] See also *Lynch v DPP for Northern Ireland* [1975] AC 653, 678: knowingly driving P to murder V is sufficient even where D would prefer the murder not to happen.

[75] At [92]–[95]. Cowley, '*Jogee*, Parasitic Accessory Liability and Conditional Intention' in Krebs (ed), *Accessorial Liability after Jogee* (2020) Ch3.

[76] D is not conditioning her act of encouragement, it is completed. See **Chapter 3.4.1.3**.

[77] Discussed in *National Coal Board v Gamble* [1959] 1 QB 11, 20.

[78] Williams, 'Obedience to Law as a Crime' (1990) 53 MLR 445.

[79] Not least because withholding property in these circumstances would not be a breach of civil law: *K v National Westminster Bank* [2006] EWCA Civ 1039. Discussed in *Bryce* [2004] EWCA Crim 1231, [63].

Extra detail . . .

In most cases, D's intention to assist, encourage, or procure P's offence can be discussed and applied in general terms. However, this is not always required. The following represents the minimum mens rea to satisfy this element.

• Assisting or encouraging: following *Jogee*, it now seems apparent that D must intend to assist or encourage the whole principal offence (with the exception of constructive crimes, discussed later).[80] This contrasts with the law pre-*Jogee*, and that applicable to inchoate assisting or encouraging, where D need only intend to assist or encourage the conduct part of the principal offence.[81]

• Procuring: D must intend to cause the principal offence, but she need not intend to cause every element. For example, in *AG's Reference (No 1 of 1975)* discussed earlier (**12.3.1.2**), where D laced P's drink with alcohol, it was enough that D intended to cause the circumstance element (alcohol level) to come about, there was no additional requirement to intend to cause D's conduct (driving).

12.3.2.2 D's mens rea as to P's principal offence

This element of D's mens rea is the most complex. Unlike inchoate assisting or encouraging where we assess D's mens rea as to a *potential* principal offence in the abstract, complicity requires us to examine D's mens rea in relation to a principal offence that has come about. Therefore, as well as exploring D's state of mind at the time of the assistance or encouragement, we must also assess whether that mens rea will be sufficient where P's actual offence is less serious than D anticipated; more serious; or simply very different. We discuss each of these separately. However, we begin with the case in which P completes the principal offence in line with D's expectations.

A) P commits the principal offence as D expected: The general rule, taken from *Johnson v Youden*,[82] is that at the time of assisting, encouraging, or procuring D must 'know the essential matters' that constitute P's principal offence. This implies that D must have knowledge of what P will go on to do. However, despite consistent endorsement of the quotation from *Johnson*, it has been interpreted to mean something quite different. Rather than a requirement of knowledge, or even belief, courts began to interpret 'knowledge' in this context as being satisfied by mere 'foresight' of a risk (see **Table 12.3**).

Table 12.3 Foresight and complicity

Case reference	Case facts	Outcome
Chan Wing-Siu **[1985] AC 168**	D (and two others) went to V's house with knives to rob him. V was stabbed and killed, and his wife wounded. D foresaw, but did not intend, that one of his co-accused might act with intention to kill.	The Privy Council decided that in cases of this kind (described as Joint Criminal Ventures), D may be liable as an accomplice on the basis of foresight.

(Continued)

---

[80] At [88]–[99].

[81] For pre-*Jogee* complicity, see discussion in *Bryce* [2004] EWCA Crim 1231; for inchoate, see Chapter **11.4.2**.

[82] [1950] 1 KB 544, 546.

Table 12.3 Continued

Powell and English [1999] AC 1	In *Powell*, D, X, and P went to the house of a drug dealer (V) to buy drugs. At the door, one of them shot V dead. In *English*, D and P attacked a police sergeant, V, with wooden posts. P produced a knife which D had not foreseen that P might carry and fatally stabbed V.	Following a line of authority from *Chan Wing-Siu*, including *Slack* [1989] QB 775, *Wakely* [1990] Crim LR 119, and *Hyde* [1991] 1 QB 134, the House of Lords endorsed the view that foresight sufficed for mens rea.
ABCD [2010] EWCA Crim 1622	C organised an attack on V in his home, carried out by A, B, and D. Unable to prove which of the defendants inflicted the fatal blows, they were each charged with murder as a principal or an accomplice.	Court of Appeal clarified that D must foresee every element of the principal offence, including the principal's required mens rea.

This line of authority has been explicitly overruled in *Jogee*, and is no longer good law.[83] Characterising *Chan Wing-Siu* as a 'wrong turn',[84] *Jogee* returned the law on this point to its position 30 years earlier, requiring D intentionally to assist, encourage, or procure, and to know that P will complete the elements of the principal offence.

Unfortunately, in contrast to the clarity of the Supreme Court's rejection of the previous case law, detail of the court's preferred construction was lacking. The court was clear that D must *intend* P to act with whatever mens rea is required for the principal offence,[85] but largely silent on D's required mens rea as to the other elements of P's offence (ie potential circumstance and/or result elements). The court restated the proposition from *Johnson* that D must have 'knowledge' as to the essential elements of P's offence,[86] but did not clarify what was meant by knowledge in this context. Faced with this vacuum, several competing theories remained plausible following *Jogee*, from strict liability as to P's offence elements,[87] belief,[88] and knowledge,[89] to a universal requirement of intention.[90]

---

[83] At [61]–[99].

[84] At [82].

[85] At [90].

[86] At [9] and [16].

[87] A literal reading of *Jogee* would suggest that D does not require any specific mens rea beyond a requirement to intend to assist or encourage the principal offence, and an intention that P should act with the required mens rea.

[88] See Dyson, 'Shorn-Off Complicity' (2016) 75 CLJ 196; 'Principals without Distinction' [2018] Crim LR 296, 310–312.

[89] See Simester, 'Accessory Liability and Common Unlawful Purposes' (2017) 133 LQR 73.

[90] See Ormerod and Laird, '*Jogee*—Not the End of a Legal Saga but the Start of a New One?' [2016] Crim LR 543; Buxton, '*Jogee*: Upheaval in Secondary Liability for Murder' [2016] Crim LR 324; Horder, *Ashworth's Principles of Criminal Law* (2016) 446–453.

The lack of clarity on this point within *Jogee* remains highly regrettable, but subsequent case law has consistently indicated that the last of these interpretations (ie general intention requirement) should be preferred.[91] This seems correct, as it aligns most closely with the stated aim of *Jogee*: to narrow the law from the previous *Chan Wing-Siu* standard. We reflect this interpretation in **Tables 12.1a, 12.1b,** and **12.1c**.

We may now state with some confidence that D must act with intent that P will commit the principal offence. However, in doing so, it is necessary to reflect on the application and the meaning of 'intention' in this context, as further qualifications require discussion. We highlight three issues here, the last of which represents a point of major uncertainty within the current law.

(1) What if D intends P to commit an offence, but is not sure which of a number of offences P will commit, or is unsure of the details of the offence? The answer to this question, confirmed in *Jogee*,[92] is that D may be complicit if P commits any offence among those D intends. In *Bainbridge*,[93] for example, D was liable as an accessory to bank robbery even though, when supplying cutting equipment to P, he was unaware which premises would be targeted and when. The Court of Criminal Appeal clarified that although D did not know the details of the specific offence committed by P, his conviction remained safe because he knew when supplying the equipment that P might use it for breaking and entering. Similar reasoning is also evident in *DPP for NI v Maxwell*.

> **DPP for NI v Maxwell** [1978] 1 WLR 1350
>
> D was a member of the proscribed organisation UVF in Northern Ireland and he assisted P by driving him to a pub. D knew that P intended to attack the pub, but was unsure whether this would involve planting explosives, murder, or robbery. In the event, P damaged the pub using pipe bombs. D was charged as an accessory to the explosives offence.[94]
>
> • NI Crown Court: guilty of explosives offence.
>
> • NI Court of Appeal: conviction upheld on appeal.
>
> • House of Lords: appeal dismissed. D does not need to know the details of P's offence, as long as he knows the essential matters.

Maxwell is a particularly useful case. It provides House of Lords endorsement for the principle in *Bainbridge* that D need not know the details of P's offence. Additionally, although narrowed by *Jogee* to require intention, it confirms that D may be liable even where she is unsure as to which of a number of offences P will commit. Of course, where P commits an offence that was not intended, for example in this scenario rape,[95] then D would not be an accomplice to that offence.

---

[91] *Crilly* [2018] EWCA Crim 168; *Brown* [2017] EWCA Crim 1870; *Johnson* [2016] EWCA Crim 1613. This interpretation of *Jogee* was also assumed in the Australian High Court (*Miller* [2016] HCA 30) and Hong Kong Court of Final Appeal (*Chan Kam Shing* [2016] HKCFA 87).

[92] At [14]–[16].

[93] 1960] 1 QB 129.

[94] Explosive Substances Act 1883, s3(1)(a).

[95] The offence of rape is discussed in **Chapter 8.2**.

(2) What if D intends P to commit a strict liability offence, must D still intend every element of that offence? This question did not arise in *Jogee*, but is likely to follow the previous case law. Although P in this case requires no mens rea, complicity liability nevertheless requires D to intend each element of the principal offence.[96] In *Callow v Tillstone*,[97] a butcher (P) committed a strict liability offence by selling tainted meat. P was liable despite genuinely believing that the meat was fit for sale, a belief based on D's negligent veterinary examination. D was not liable as an accomplice because he was not reckless as to the tainted status of the meat (the law would now require intention). The important point here is that although not every element of P's offence requires P to have mens rea, D must intend all the essential elements to be liable as an accomplice.

(3) Can an intention that P complete the principal offence be found otherwise than by standard definitions of direct and oblique intention? D will intend P to complete the principal offence when she assists, encourages, or procures P with a purpose that the offence be committed, or virtually certain that it will be committed. This accords with established definitions of intention.[98] However, at various points within the judgment in *Jogee*, the Supreme Court implied that an intention standard might be found even outside these core definitions.

Perhaps the clearest example of definitional uncertainty within *Jogee* arises in one of the court's hypotheticals, used to illustrate where liability *should* be found:

> [D] supplies a weapon to [P], who has no lawful purpose in having it, intending to help [P] by giving him the means to commit a crime . . . , but having *no further interest in what he does, or indeed whether he uses it at all.*[99]

This example, confirmed elsewhere in the judgment,[100] is entirely incompatible with a full-offence intention interpretation of *Jogee*: D neither acts in order that P will commit the principal offence, nor foresees that offence as a virtual certainty. The example is either a mistake, or (more drastically) the court were implying a new definition of intention.[101]

The judgment in *Jogee* is also remarkable for its appeal to 'conditional intention' as an alternative route to finding that D intended P to commit the principal offence.[102] The court's use of conditional intention is far from clear, but in order to understand its potential application two scenarios should be distinguished. In the first, *Jogee* tells us that conditional intention should be found where D and P agreed to Crime A (eg a fight) and Crime B (eg murder) *if necessary*.[103] In finding an intention, both as to the fight and

---

[96] The only exception relates to constructive offences, discussed later.

[97] (1900) 83 LT 411.

[98] See **Chapter 3.4.1**.

[99] At [90]. Emphasis added.

[100] At [10].

[101] Discussed in Ormerod and Laird, '*Jogee*—Not the End of a Legal Saga but the Start of a New One?' [2016] Crim LR 543. See also Krebs, 'Oblique Intent, Foresight and Authorisation' (2018) 7 UCL J Law & Juris 1.

[102] At [92], eg 'it will . . . often be necessary to draw the jury's attention to the fact that the intention to assist, and indeed the intention that the crime should be committed, may be conditional'.

[103] Based on an example from *Jogee* at [92].

murder, this example is unproblematic. However, it is questionable whether it is necessary to employ the concept of conditional intention; as before, a simple direct intention appears to be present.[104]

More worryingly, at other points within the judgment in *Jogee*, the court appears to endorse the possibility that conditional intention may alternatively be found where D simply foresees that P *might* commit an *unwanted* Crime B.[105] The potential for conditional intention to apply to Crime B in this kind of example has been echoed in case law post-*Jogee*, including *Johnson*,[106] *Anwar*,[107] and many others, as well as some academic commentary.[108] It is contended that intention (conditional or otherwise) should never be found in such cases: D's conduct is not motivated by a purpose that P's offence should be committed under any circumstances, and it is not foreseen as a virtually certain consequence either. Simply put, labelling D's mental state as a form of intention is to collapse the concept of intention into recklessness. Concern that *Jogee* allows for a finding of intention in such cases has been central to the refusal of high courts in Australia and Hong Kong to follow the Supreme Court's approach,[109] and authoritative clarification in England and Wales is desperately needed.[110]

 Extra detail . . .

One of the obvious concerns of the Supreme Court in *Jogee* was that, having found that the courts had applied the wrong test for 30 years since the legal 'wrong turn', there would be a flood of appeals from those convicted of complicity offences under the old law.[111] It may be that their concern to avoid such appeals contributed to some of the confusions we have discussed, leading the Court of Appeal to qualify its narrowing of liability with a definition of intention that might still apply to many of the older cases (ie preventing appeals). The Court of Appeal continues to resist all but the most exceptional of these cases, and the impact of this resistance is likely to continue to affect the substantive interpretation of the law for some time.[112]

---

[104] See Child and Sullivan, 'The Current State of Murder in English Law: A Critique, Wrong Turns and All' in Reed et al (eds), *Homicide in Criminal Law* (2018) 62, 75–77.

[105] Although not explicitly endorsed in *Jogee*, it is implied from the court's examples involving escalating violence, and certainly left open from the use of vague language such as 'scope of the venture' and 'tacit agreement' ([90]–[95]).

[106] *Johnson and Others* [2016] EWCA Crim 1613: combined cases involving appeals against pre-*Jogee* convictions. See Stark, 'The Taming of *Jogee*' (2017) 76 CLJ 4 (comment).

[107] *Anwar* [2016] EWCA Crim 551. The court stating at para 22 that '. . . the same facts which would have been used to support the inference of mens rea before the decision in *Jogee* will equally be used now'.

[108] See eg Baker, 'Lesser Included Offences, Alternative Offences and Accessorial Liability' (2016) 80 JCL 446, 448; '*Jogee*: Jury Directions and the Manslaughter Alternative' [2017] Crim LR 51 (letter).

[109] See *Miller* [2016] HCA 30 and commentary by Krebs (2017) 76 CLJ 7; *Chan Kam Shing* [2016] HKCFA 87 and commentary by Krebs (2017) 81 JCL 271.

[110] To this end, it is regrettable that the Supreme Court refused leave to appeal in *Johnson*. Subsequently the Court of Appeal has confirmed that it will not grant leave and that an applicant cannot petition the Supreme Court: *Towers* [2019] EWCA Crim 198.

[111] Discussed at [100].

[112] See eg Buxton, 'Joint Enterprise: *Jogee*, Substantial Injustice and the Court of Appeal' [2017] Crim LR 123; Stark, 'The Taming of *Jogee*?' (2017) 76 CLJ 4. Only one murder conviction has been overturned: *Crilly* [2018] EWCA Crim 168.

B) P commits a less serious principal offence than D intended: This situation arises where D assists, encourages, or procures P to commit an offence such as intentional GBH, but P commits a less serious offence such as battery. Regardless of P's conduct, D is likely to be liable for the inchoate offence of assisting or encouraging the more serious offence.[113] D is also likely to be complicit in the offence committed by P. For the latter, it would have to be shown that D either intended P to commit the less serious offence or, as with our example, that the less serious offence is a lesser included offence within the one intended.[114] However, there are certain cases in which D may be liable as an accomplice to the more serious offence intended, even though this offence is not completed by P. We separate our analysis into the three reasons why P may not have committed the more serious offence D intended.

P lacks actus reus: This was the case in our example, where P commits battery rather than GBH. Here, D's liability is limited by P's actus reus and will not go beyond it. D may therefore be an accessory to battery, but not to intentional GBH. This is a logical outcome, and one that remains faithful to the idea of complicity as derivative from P's offence. However, it can appear rather generous to D, particularly where P causes harm as a result of D's assistance or encouragement, but does not complete the actus reus of an offence. This was the issue in *Thornton v Mitchell*.[115]

Thornton v Mitchell [1940] 1 All ER 339

A bus conductor (D) negligently signalled for a bus driver (P) to reverse. Two pedestrians were knocked down by the bus, one of whom (V) was killed. P was charged with careless driving, D as an accomplice.[116]

- Court: P not guilty, as his driving was not careless. D was found guilty, and appealed.
- Divisional Court: appeal by case stated allowed. Where P does not commit the actus reus of an offence, there can be no accomplice liability.

P's commission of the actus reus may therefore limit D's accomplice liability, and where no actus reus is performed by P, it may undermine it altogether. In such cases, however, remember that inchoate liability may still be available.

P lacks mens rea: Mirroring cases of incomplete actus reus, a lack of mens rea from P is also likely to minimise or even extinguish her liability; with D's derivative liability following suit. However, there is an important exception. This applies where, although P lacks mens rea for the principal offence and although D may know that P will lack mens

---

[113] See Chapter **11.4**.

[114] A 'lesser included' offence is one where all of its elements are included within the more serious offence; with the more serious offence also requiring further elements. Thus eg where D intends P to commit intentional GBH by hitting V with a bat, then D must have also intended P to make unlawful physical contact with V (ie battery) as part of that greater offence.

[115] See also *Loukes* [1996] Crim LR 341: lack of actus reus element undermining D's accomplice liability for dangerous driving.

[116] The relevant offence under the current law is causing death by careless driving (see **Chapter 6.4.2.2**).

rea, D will nevertheless be guilty as an accomplice to that offence if she herself acted with the mens rea required for it. Lord Mackay approved the following example in the House of Lords:[117]

> [D] hands a gun to [P] informing him that it is loaded with blank ammunition only and telling him to go and scare [V] by discharging it. The ammunition is in fact live, as [D] knows, and [V] is killed. [P] is convicted only of manslaughter, as he might be on those facts. It would seem absurd that [D] should thereby escape conviction for murder.

In this example, P has not committed murder, and D did not intend that P would do so because D knew that P lacked mens rea. However, although P's lack of mens rea negates his murder liability, it would seem unfair if it also undermined D's liability for murder as an accomplice: P did not intend to kill or cause GBH (the mens rea of murder), but D certainly did. This is the crux of the exception.[118] Indeed, it is an exception that is closely mirrored in the context of inchoate assisting and encouraging as well.[119]

Where P lacks mens rea for *any* crime, it is possible for D to be liable as an accomplice even though P has not committed an offence. Such cases will usually more appropriately be treated within innocent agency: where P lacks any mens rea, she becomes a tool of D's offence, and her conduct does not break the causal chain (**12.2.3**). However, as we have discussed, there are linguistic problems with innocent agency in the context of offences such as rape and bigamy, and so the doctrine of complicity has been preferred. *Cogan and Leak*, discussed at **12.3.1.2**, provides a useful example: D made his wife V submit to sex with P, where P was unaware that V was not consenting. In this case, P was not liable for rape or any other offence because he lacked mens rea. However, D qualified within the exception and was liable as an accomplice to rape because D acted with the mens rea for rape: D knew that V was not consenting.[120]

Alternatively, as in Lord Mackay's example, P may have mens rea for a lesser offence, with D complicit in a more serious one. These examples are more difficult to reconcile with standard complicity rules than those in which P has *no* mens rea, because P's knowledge of the lesser crime is enough to undermine her potential status as an innocent agent. Commentators have characterised P's conduct as a form of semi-innocent agency,[121] but this terminology raises more questions than it answers. Rather, the better approach is to apply the exception, and to ask if D had mens rea for the more serious principal offence. Where she does, as with the murder in Lord Mackay's example, D should be liable as an accomplice to that more serious offence, even though P is only

---

[117] *Burke* [1987] AC 417, 457.
[118] Taylor, 'Complicity, Legal Scholarship and the Law of Unintended Consequences' (2009) 29 LS 1. See critique of the exception in Kadish, 'Complicity, Cause and Blame' in *Essays in Criminal Law* (1987) 180.
[119] See **Chapter 11.4.2.2**.
[120] The minimum mens rea for rape at this time was recklessness as to non-consent. The current law has a minimum of a lack of reasonable belief in consent. See **Chapter 8.2**. See also *Millward* [1994] Crim LR 527: D instructed P to drive a vehicle he knew was unfit for the road. P did so, and an accident led to the death of V. D was complicit in causing death by reckless driving, but P committed no offence.
[121] Williams, *Textbook of Criminal Law* (1978) 373.

guilty of the lesser one. This approach was rejected in *Richards*[122] but, following judicial criticism of that case in *Burke*,[123] it is contended that the exception should (and would) be applied in these circumstances today.

P has a defence: The last possibility, where D is complicit in a more serious offence than P has committed, arises where P has a defence. In this case, as P has committed the intended principal offence assisted, encouraged, or procured by D, our starting point is that they are both liable for that offence. If P has a successful defence, P's liability will be reduced or removed. If D does not satisfy the defence, she will remain complicit in the principal offence, even if P is acquitted.

This rule applies both to partial and complete defences. For the partial defences to murder, the potential for D to be liable for murder despite P's satisfaction of a partial defence has been codified.[124] For the other defences, the rule exists at common law. *Bourne* provides an example in the context of duress.[125]

 Bourne (1952) 36 Cr App R 125

D compelled his wife (P) to have sex with a dog. D was charged as an accomplice to P's offence of buggery. P was not charged because she would have had a defence of duress.

- Court of Assizes: guilty of buggery.
- Court of Criminal Appeal: conviction upheld on appeal. The fact that P had a defence, and so was not liable for the principal offence, does not undermine D's liability as an accomplice.

This rule has the same effect as the last one discussed (where P lacks mens rea) but it applies very differently. In the present case, the standard complicity rules are applied without an exception, with the only difference being that P's liability (but not D's) is reduced by a defence.

C) P commits a more serious offence than D intended: At the other extreme from the cases just discussed, P may act in a way which goes beyond that intended by D. For example, D assists P to commit a simple battery, but P intentionally causes GBH.

Most cases of this kind can be resolved relatively simply. Since D must intend the essential elements of P's offence, D's liability cannot exceed that which was intended. In our example, as P causing GBH is likely to have included a battery in the form of some unlawful contact between P and V, D will be complicit in that battery (which D intended), but only P will be liable for the more serious GBH offence since that was not intended by D.

There is an exception, however, and this applies where P commits a constructive liability offence—an offence, such as unlawful act manslaughter, where an unforeseen result increases P's liability from the base offence intended to a more serious offence.[126] Where P commits an offence of this kind, because P is not required to foresee the result

---

[122] [1974] QB 776.
[123] [1987] AC 417, 457. Cf Kadish, 'Complicity, Cause and Blame' (1985) 73 Cal L Rev 323, 329.
[124] Diminished responsibility, Homicide Act 1957, s2(4); loss of control, Coroners and Justice Act 2009, s54(8).
[125] **Chapter 14.3**.
[126] See **Chapter 4.2.1.1**.

element for liability (in manslaughter that is the death of V), it has been consistently held that D can also be liable as an accomplice where she does not intend or foresee the result either. For example, D encourages P to punch V, with both expecting the punch to result in no more than minor bruising amounting to only a battery. However, when P punches V and commits the base offence of battery, V unexpectedly falls backwards and hits her head on the hard floor, dying as a result. P is now liable for unlawful act manslaughter despite not foreseeing the death.[127] D is liable for unlawful act manslaughter as an accomplice; as with P, despite her lack of intention or foresight that P might cause death.

Extra detail . . .

You may have noticed an inconsistency—where P commits a strict liability offence that does not require her to have mens rea, it has been held that D must nevertheless intend P to complete the actus reus of that offence to be liable as an accomplice; however, where P does not require mens rea as to the result element of a constructive liability offence, the law requires that D may be liable as an accomplice even where she too lacks mens rea as to that result. The best explanation for this inconsistency, as explained by the Law Commission,[128] is that (unlike complicity in strict liability offences) complicity in a constructive crime still requires D to intend P to commit the base offence. Thus, D's intention as to the base offence means that she is not an innocent party, and she (like P) should accept even the unforeseen consequences of her actions.

The application of this rule in manslaughter cases is exemplified in *Bristow*.[129]

Bristow [2013] EWCA Crim 1540

D and others undertook a planned robbery of an off-road vehicle repair yard. The owner of the yard (V) attempted to prevent the robbery and was killed, run over by one or more of the vehicles used for the robbery. It was unclear who was driving the vehicle that hit V. D and the others were charged with unlawful act manslaughter (as principal or accessory).

- Crown Court: guilty of unlawful act manslaughter.
- Court of Appeal: conviction upheld on appeal. D either (a) completed the dangerous and unlawful act (burglary) and caused death (ie acted as a principal), or (b) he assisted others to commit burglary and they caused V's death. D was liable under (a) or (b) even if he did not foresee the chance of death being caused.

Extending the mens rea of constructive liability crimes into complicity liability has been criticised for being too harsh on D. This has been particularly true for accomplices to murder, another example of a constructive liability offence.[130] However, the rule remains valid. In *Jogee*,[131] for example, the Supreme Court makes clear that if D intended to assist or encourage P to cause serious harm to V and P kills V, even though D does not intend

---

[127] See **Chapter 6.3.1**.

[128] Law Commission, *Participating in Crime* (No 305, 2007) para B.97.

[129] [2014] Crim LR 457 and Ormerod Commentary.

[130] Mitchell and Roberts have researched public attitudes to liability in these circumstances, finding an unease at the harshness of liability, *Public Survey of the Mandatory Life Sentence for Murder* (2010).

[131] [2016] UKSC 8.

P to kill, D is still rightly convicted of murder. And if D intends to assist or encourage less serious harm and P kills V, even though D does not intend P to kill, D is still rightly convicted of manslaughter.[132] In this manner, although complicity liability has been narrowed in *Jogee* to require intention, application to constructive crimes still casts the net (perhaps inappropriately) wide.[133]

D) P commits an offence which is different from that D intended: As we have discussed, D's foresight or lack of foresight about the details of P's offence will not affect her liability as long as she intends the essential elements. For example, if D provides P with a gun to murder V on Tuesday, but P kills V on Wednesday, D remains liable for murder as P's accomplice. However, there are occasions where P's crime is so different from that assisted, encouraged, or procured by D that complicity liability would be inappropriate: D should only derive liability from P's crime where that crime is sufficiently similar to the one D intended. Where P's crime operates as an overwhelming supervening event, D remains inchoately liable for her acts of assistance or encouragement, but is not complicit in P's offence. The leading case, establishing this rule, was *English*.[134]

Extra detail . . .

The rule as applied in *English* and other pre-*Jogee* cases was referred to as the 'fundamental difference' principle (ie P's conduct was fundamentally different from that intended by D, so D cannot be convicted as an accomplice to that offence). Post-*Jogee*, the rule is now referred to in terms of an 'overwhelming supervening event' (ie where P's unintended conduct supervenes any assistance or encouragement provided by D, severing the links required for complicity liability). The change in terminology does not alter the basic function of the rule, but as we discuss below, has led to a narrowing of its application.

English [1999] AC 1

D and P attacked a police sergeant, V, with wooden posts. P produced a knife which D had not foreseen that P might carry and fatally stabbed V. D was charged with murder as an accomplice.

- Crown Court: guilty of murder.
- Court of Appeal: conviction upheld on appeal.
- House of Lords: appeal allowed. Even though D was reckless as to P causing GBH with intent (ie sufficient mens rea for complicity in murder at this time), P's conduct (stabbing with a knife) was fundamentally different from that anticipated by D (hitting with posts). Thus, D is not an accomplice to P's offence.

The fundamental difference rule, recast in terms of an 'overwhelming supervening event' (OSE), should now be interpreted and applied in line with *Jogee*.[135] The Supreme Court

[132] At [96] and [101]–[107]. On this basis, the defendant in *Jogee* was convicted of manslaughter following retrial.
[133] See Krebs, 'Joint Enterprise Murder is Dead—Long Live Joint Enterprise Manslaughter?' in Krebs (ed), *Accessorial Liability after Jogee* (2020) Ch6.
[134] The appeal of *English* was combined with *Powell and Daniels*.
[135] [2016] UKSC 8. Sjölin, 'A Step Away from Liability—Withdrawal and Fundamental Difference Post-Jogee' in Krebs (ed), *Accessorial Liability after Jogee* (2020) Ch4.

touched only briefly on this rule as it was not relevant to the case before them, but they clearly suggest that having narrowed complicity liability to intentional assistors and encouragers, there should be less need for the rule to be applied in future cases.

> . . . there will normally be no occasion to consider the concept of 'fundamental departure' as derived from *English*. What matters is whether [D] encouraged or assisted the crime . . . The tendency which has developed . . . to focus on what [D] knew of what weapon [P] was carrying can and should give way to an examination of whether [D] intended to assist in the crime charged. If that crime is murder, then the question is whether he intended to assist the intentional infliction of grievous bodily harm at least . . . Very often he may intend to assist in violence using whatever weapon may come to hand. In other cases he may think that [P] has an iron bar whereas he turns out to have a knife, but the difference may not at all affect his intention to assist, if necessary, in the causing of grievous bodily harm at least. Knowledge or ignorance that weapons generally, or a particular weapon, is carried by [P] will be evidence going to what the intention of [D] was, and may be irresistible evidence one way or the other, but it is evidence and no more.[136]

The OSE rule was recently applied in *Tas*,[137] a case involving a violent group attack in which V was stabbed and killed by one of his attackers. D was part of the attacking group but maintained that he did not stab V and that he was unaware that any member of his group carried a knife. Following the quoted dicta in *Jogee*, the trial judge held that a potentially unknown weapon of this kind could no longer provide the basis for an OSE, and thereby did not put the question to the jury. D was convicted of manslaughter and appealed, partly on the basis that the potential OSE should have been put before the jury to consider; the appeal was rejected. For the Court of Appeal, it was clear that *Jogee* had narrowed the availability of the OSE rule, which will only be available where P's conduct is such that 'nobody in the defendant's shoes could have contemplated might happen and is of such a character as to relegate his acts to history'.[138]

 Extra detail . . .

Whether P's conduct constituted an OSE is ultimately a question of fact for the jury.[139] However, evident in *Tas*, the judge will only put the question to the jury where the judge is satisfied that a reasonable jury might find that there is evidence of that fact.

The narrowing of the OSE rule post-*Jogee* may lead us to question when such a supervening event could ever be found. The answer to this is not entirely clear, and even post-*Tas* further case law is required to provide necessary clarity.[140] However, we may highlight two scenarios where we believe this rule may retain some significance (the assumption being that outside this the rule has no role).

The first and clearest example of a potential OSE, arises where D intentionally assists or encourages an attack on a certain specified target, and P *intentionally* attacks

---

136 At [98].
137 [2018] EWCA Crim 2603.
138 Ibid at [40], quoting from *Morris* [1966] 2 QB 110.
139 *Greatrex* [1999] 1 Cr App R 126.
140 Some discussion is also provided in *Ibrar* [2017] EWCA Crim 1841 and *Brown* [2017] EWCA Crim 1870.

a different target. For example, D encourages P to kill X, but P intentionally kills V; D assists P to damage X's car, but P intentionally damages V's car; and so on. In these circumstances, P's intentional change of target will probably constitute an OSE, and D will not be liable as an accomplice to P's offence.[141] This is illustrated in *Saunders and Archer*.

> **Saunders and Archer** (1573) 2 Plowd 473
>
> P planned to kill his wife, X. D advised P, and on this advice P gave X a poisoned apple. X ate some of the apple, but gave the rest to their child, V, who ate it and died. P saw what happened and did not intervene.
>
> - Court: P is guilty of murder, his intention to kill X being moved to V via the doctrine of transferred malice.[142] X is an innocent agent. D is also not guilty of murder as an accomplice.

Although dicta in *Saunders and Archer* suggest that D will never be liable as an accomplice where P kills the wrong victim, this does not represent the current law. Rather, in line with the *outcome* of this case, D is likely to escape liability because P was aware of the change of victim, had the power to intervene, and did not do so. In such a case the change of target was known to P, was controllable, and therefore not fully unintentional.

Three qualifications should be noted. First, there will be no OSE where P's change of target is unintentional.[143] Where P attempts to kill X, but accidentally kills V, P commits murder because her mens rea—her intention to kill X—is transferred to V. Just as the doctrine of transferred malice operates to secure P's liability, the same is true for D: her mens rea (ie intention of P killing X) is also transferred to V. Secondly, there will also be no OSE if the change is insubstantial. For example, in *Dunning and Graham*,[144] following a grievance between D and V, P offered to set fire to V's house. D accepted, and supplied V's address. In the event, P changed his mind and set fire to V's car instead. Although this was a clear change of target, the court found that it was not a substantial change from the plan envisaged by D, and so he remained complicit. Thirdly, there is unlikely to be an OSE where P carries out the principal offence as planned *and* goes on to commit an additional offence of the same type. For example, D provides P with a jemmy to assist burglary, and P burgles multiple properties; or D supplies a knife for P to kill someone, and P kills two people with it; and so on.[145] In these cases, D is likely to be complicit in the intended offence and the additional offence(s).

The second *potential* basis for establishing an OSE arises where P acts in a considerably more dangerous way than that intended by D. Despite the court in *Jogee* emphasising that we should move away from focussing on knowledge of a weapon, it is still contended that P's conduct, whether related to the use of a weapon or not, must remain broadly in line with D's intentions for D to be fairly held as an accomplice.[146] For example, if

---

141 Recognised in *Powell* [1999] AC 1, and *Reardon* [1999] Crim LR 392.

142 We discuss transferred malice at **Chapter 4.3.1**.

143 Lanham, 'Accomplices and Transferred Malice' (1980) 96 LQR 110.

144 Unreported, December 1985.

145 *Reardon* [1999] Crim LR 392: D was complicit in two murders committed with his knife, despite only foreseeing one of them.

146 *Mendez* [2010] EWCA Crim 516, [42]–[47]. The Court of Appeal in *Johnson* [2016] EWCA Crim 1613 relied on the fact that applicants were aware of the weapons possessed by principal offenders as a basis for rejecting the applicants' arguments for appeals out of time under *Jogee*.

D intends P to use a knife to cut off one of V's fingers, but P uses it to cut V's throat, we may question whether D's potential liability for manslaughter can be fairly derived from P's conduct. *AG's Reference (No 3 of 2004)* provides a useful illustration.

 AG's Reference (No 3 of 2004) [2005] EWCA Crim 1882

D recruited P and another to intimidate V by discharging a firearm near (but not at) him. P intentionally shot and killed V. D was charged with murder as P's accomplice.

- Crown Court: not guilty of murder.
- Court of Appeal: judge was correct to rule as he had to find no liability, as P's act (shooting at V) was fundamentally different from the act intended by D (shooting near V).

The Court of Appeal in *Tas* also highlight *Rafferty*,[147] a case in which D participated in the beating of V, but whilst D was absent from the scene (attempting to obtain money from V's debit card) P intentionally caused V's death by drowning. Again, this is arguably a clear case in which even post-*Jogee* an OSE would be found.

Along with clear examples of this kind, however, are cases that have presented more challenging facts. In *Gamble*,[148] for example, D intended that an attack on V would result in GBH by kneecapping (ie shooting V in the knee joints), though with the specific intention that V would not be killed. In the event, P killed V by cutting his throat and shooting him in the chest. As a result of this, despite D intending that P should cause GBH, the fundamental difference in P's acts meant that D was not liable for murder. In *Gamble* the court held:

> Although the rule remains well entrenched that an intention to inflict grievous bodily harm qualifies as the mens rea of murder, it is not in my opinion necessary to apply it in such a way as to fix an accessory with liability for a consequence which he did not intend and which stems from an act which he did not have within his contemplation. I do not think that the state of the law compels me to reach such a conclusion, and it would not in my judgment accord with the public sense of what is just and fitting.[149]

If this analysis remains correct, it would have significant implications post-*Jogee* for D who intentionally assists or encourages P to commit a non-fatal attack and P intentionally commits murder, challenging the assumption in *Jogee* that D will usually be liable for manslaughter.[150]

In addition to cases of this kind, it is also likely that the rule will arise in the future as a useful (flexible) tool for dealing with unexpected facts. The South African case of *Robinson* provides a useful example.[151] D, P, and V agreed that P would kill V, allowing

---

[147] [2007] EWCA Crim 1846.
[148] [1989] NI 268.
[149] Per Carswell J at 284.
[150] See Simester, 'Accessory Liability and Common Unlawful Purposes' (2017) 133 LQR 73; Child and Sullivan, 'The Current State of Murder in English Law: A Critique, Wrong Turns and All' in Reed et al (eds), *Homicide in Criminal Law* (2018) 62, 77–79.
[151] 1968 (1) SA 666.

D to claim V's life insurance and to avoid V's upcoming fraud prosecution. At the last moment V withdrew consent to being killed, but P killed V regardless. Applying an equivalent to the OSE rule, the South African court found that D was not complicit in the murder because the withdrawal of consent made P's act of killing very different from that agreed to and intended by D. Whether the same approach would be adopted in this jurisdiction is not certain.

Point to remember . . .

The key to the OSE rule is not simply looking for extreme factual differences. Rather, we are looking for factual differences that break the nexus of responsibility between D and the principal offence. For example, a long time delay might appear a significant difference, but is unlikely to undermine D's liability.[152] It should also be remembered that the more specific D's intention as to P's offence (eg specific victim, etc), the more likely a finding of OSE. For example, if D encourages P to kill others in general, and P goes on to kill, there is very little basis upon which D can claim that P's offence supervened her intention.

12.4 Complicity by joint enterprise?

Alongside standard cases of complicity by assisting, encouraging, or procuring,[153] a parallel concept of complicity by joint enterprise (also known as parasitic accessory liability) was developed in the common law.[154] Crucially, as we discuss below, the concept of joint enterprise liability (as a separate route to complicity) was explicitly removed by the Supreme Court in *Jogee*.[155] Cases will now be prosecuted within the standard terms of complicity liability discussed in the previous section or not at all, and the continued use of the language of 'joint enterprise' should be avoided.

Don't be confused . . .

Joint enterprise is also commonly and interchangeably referred to as joint criminal enterprise, joint venture, and/or joint criminal venture.

Joint enterprise has been used to describe a coordination of behaviour between D and P towards a common criminal end. It was classically described as follows: where D and P engaged together with a common purpose to commit Crime A and in the course of that P committed Crime B, then D would also be liable for Crime B if D had foreseen as a possibility that P might commit it with mens rea, and the manner in which P did so

---

[152] *Bryce* [2004] EWCA Crim 1231.
[153] Codified within the Accessories and Abettors Act 1861.
[154] Krebs, 'Joint Criminal Enterprise' (2010) 73 MLR 578.
[155] [2016] UKSC 8, [76]–[78]. See Sullivan, 'Law Reform in the Supreme Court: The Abolition of Joint Enterprise Liability' in Krebs (ed), *Accessorial Liability after Jogee* (2020) Ch1; van Sliedregt, 'Joint Criminal Confusion: Exploring the Merits and Demerits of Joint Enterprise Liability' and Weinberg, 'Extended Joint Criminal Enterprise—"Top-down" or "Bottom-up" Legal Reasoning?' in Krebs (ed), *Accessorial Liability after Jogee* (2020) Chs9 and 10.

was not fundamentally different from what D had foreseen might happen. For example, D and P take part in a fight with a rival gang, and P kills one of its members (V). D is not a co-principal with P in the murder of V because D does not commit the actus reus of the principal offence of murder. It may well also be that D did not provide any obvious assistance or encouragement to the acts of P in killing, and so the standard route to accomplice liability becomes difficult to establish: D has not assisted or encouraged murder directly. However, through her coordinated conduct, the doctrine of joint enterprise provided the basis for accomplice liability. This route has been supported by several commentators.[156]

The problem with joint enterprise was that as soon as one began to explore the actus reus and mens rea in any detail, it began to merge back into standard complicity by assisting, encouraging, or procuring. Take our gang murder example: it is difficult to see how D can coordinate behaviour with P in any meaningful way without either committing the offence with her as a co-principal, or by assisting, encouraging, or procuring her. Where D does none of these, where her conduct is simply being proximate to P, complicity liability should not be possible.[157]

The decision in *Jogee* means that so-called joint enterprise cases should be analysed within the standard rules of complicity. This followed from a previous line of critical Court of Appeal cases,[158] and legal commentary.[159] As Toulson LJ stated in *Stringer*:[160]

> Joint enterprise is not a legal term of art. In *R v Mendez* [2011] QB 876, the court favoured the view that joint enterprise as a basis of secondary liability involves the application of ordinary principles; it is not an independent source of liability. Participation in a joint criminal adventure involves mutual encouragement and assistance.

In line with this view, our earlier discussion of complicity by assisting, encouraging, and procuring has included several cases where courts have used the language of joint enterprise. The term 'joint enterprise' in these cases does not distinguish them as a separate form of complicity liability.

12.4.1 Challenges following the abolition of joint enterprise

For many, the doctrine of joint enterprise will not be missed. It created further layers of complexity within an already overly-complex area of law, and it has become (as the Supreme Court acknowledged), 'understood (erroneously) by some to be a form of guilt by association or of guilt by simple presence without more'.[161]

---

[156] eg Law Commission, *Participating in Crime* (No 305, 2007); Simester, Spencer, Sullivan, and Virgo, *Simester and Sullivan's Criminal Law: Theory and Doctrine* (5th edn, 2013) 244–249.

[157] We would not want to criminalise as accomplices all those within a certain distance of a criminal offence!

[158] *ABCD* [2010] EWCA Crim 1622; *Mendez* [2011] QB 876; *Stringer* [2011] EWCA Crim 1396; *Gnango* [2011] UKSC 59.

[159] Wilson and Ormerod, 'Simply Harsh to Fairly Simple: Joint Enterprise Reform' [2015] Crim LR 3.

[160] [2011] EWCA Crim 1396, [57].

[161] *Jogee* [2016] UKSC 8.

However, advocates of the doctrine remain,[162] and it is useful briefly to survey some of their reasons in order to understand the potential challenges for complicity in the coming years.

A) **Expanding liability in coordinated encounters:** The first argument in favour of joint enterprise is policy-based, claiming that although standard complicity may be narrowed (or even abolished[163]) a wide view of joint enterprise should be maintained to allow the law to tackle coordinated (often gang-related) criminality. In *English*, Lord Hutton describes this as 'not based solely on logic' but justified by 'public policy' and 'practical concerns' in relation to group criminality.[164] This was the basis of the Law Commission's 2007 report, in which joint enterprise would have been retained with a recklessness mens rea standard.[165]

B) **Cases where D coordinates conduct with P but does not obviously assist or encourage her:** Where D intentionally coordinates her conduct with P towards a common criminal end, it is difficult to imagine a scenario in which D does not thereby provide some manner of intentional assistance or encouragement. However, such cases are possible.[166] It is arguable that *Gnango* represents just such a case, where D and P coordinated their conduct, but D does not intentionally assist or encourage P to commit murder. The facts of *Gnango*, it will be remembered (**12.2.2**), involved a shoot-out between D and P, where P shot and killed a passerby (V). In Lord Kerr's powerful dissenting judgment, the point is made that D's intentional conduct within the gunfight did not include an intention to assist or encourage P to return fire so D was not intending to assist or encourage P to commit murder. It is a convincing point: D's plan was to shoot P and thereby *stop* him shooting back, not to encourage it. If this is correct, then D lacked an essential element of mens rea, and liability should not have been found applying the normal rules of complicity discussed above (**12.3.2.1**). However, this approach was not accepted, and a majority within the Supreme Court found that D *did* intend (at least obliquely) to encourage P to shoot back, thereby finding D liable as an accessory to his own attempted murder by P. The approach of the court on this point is not the most intuitive, but it is likely to be adopted by future courts where similar problem facts emerge.

C) **Cases where D assists or encourages an offence, and anticipates P committing a second collateral offence in the course of the first:** Cases of this kind emerge, for example, where D and P rob a bank and, whilst doing so, P kills a security guard. When analysing D's potential accomplice liability as to the second, collateral, offence, the language of joint enterprise became common.[167] *Powell* provides a useful example.[168]

---

[162] It is notable that the courts in Australia and Hong Kong have chosen not to follow *Jogee*, and to retain joint enterprise as a separate route to complicity liability: *Miller* [2016] HCA 30; *Chan Kam Shing* [2016] HKCFA 87.

[163] Sullivan, 'Doing Without Complicity' [2012] JCCL 199.

[164] *English* [1999] AC 1.

[165] Law Commission, *Participating in Crime* (No 305, 2007).

[166] eg P testifies that, although D's acts were capable of assisting or encouraging, she was not assisted or encouraged in fact. Law Commission, *Participating in Crime* (No 305, 2007) paras 3.42–3.45.

[167] Simester, 'The Mental Element in Complicity' (2006) 122 LQR 578, 598–600.

[168] *Powell* was combined with *English* on appeal.

Powell and Daniels [1999] AC 1

D, X, and P went to the house of a drug dealer (V) to buy drugs (the primary offence). At the door, one of them shot V dead (the collateral offence). D was charged with murder either as a principal offender or as an accessory.

- Crown Court: guilty of murder.
- Court of Appeal: conviction upheld on appeal.
- House of Lords: appeal dismissed.

Powell was liable as an accomplice to the collateral offence (murder) in this case despite providing no obvious assistance or encouragement for that crime, ostensibly on the basis that her coordinated conduct with P (ie joint venture) as to the primary offence was sufficient. Post-*Jogee*, the most likely course will be to ask whether D's assistance or encouragement of the primary offence provided some tacit assistance or encouragement for the collateral. This approach was adopted in *Stringer*,[169] for example, and supported in *Jogee*: although D may not want P to commit the collateral offence come what may, she may have expressly or tacitly agreed with P that the collateral offence should be committed if certain circumstances arise.[170]

12.5 The relationship between complicity and inchoate liability

Just as D may be complicit in substantive offences such as rape or murder, for example, D may also be complicit in an inchoate offence such as conspiracy to rape, or assisting murder. This arises where D assists, encourages, or procures the inchoate offence, and P goes on to commit that inchoate offence.[171]

However, it is *no* offence to conspire, or to assist or encourage P to act as an accomplice.[172] There is also *no* offence of attempted complicity.[173]

12.6 Defences

The general defences and denials of offending apply to complicity as they do across other criminal offences, discussed in **Chapters 13** and **14**. Here we focus on two established specific defences, and one that has not yet been recognised by the courts. These are defences to complicity offences only, and will not necessarily relieve D of inchoate liability.[174]

---

[169] [2011] EWCA Crim 1396.
[170] [2016] UKSC 8, [92]–[99].
[171] Smith, 'Secondary Participation and Inchoate Offences' in Tapper (ed), *Crime, Proof and Punishment* (1981) 21.
[172] *Kenning* [2008] EWCA Crim 1534.
[173] Criminal Attempts Act 1981, s1(4)(b). For discussion, see Bohlander, 'The Conflict Between the Serious Crime Act and s4(1)(b) of the Criminal Attempts Act 1981' [2010] Crim LR 483 and Child, 'The Differences Between Attempted Complicity and Inchoate Assisting and Encouraging: A Reply to Professor Bohlander' [2010] Crim LR 924.
[174] See **Chapter 11.4.5**.

12.6.1 Withdrawal

Where D assists or encourages P to commit a principal offence (with mens rea) she is immediately liable for an inchoate offence regardless of P's future conduct.[175] D cannot negate such inchoate liability even if she later 'withdraws' by removing or renouncing her assistance or encouragement.[176] However, if D successfully withdraws in the time between her conduct and P committing the principal offence, D will be able to limit her liability to the inchoate charge and avoid complicity liability. The ability to withdraw and prevent complicity liability in this way provides a useful incentive for D to negate or at least mitigate the effects of her criminal conduct.

What is required of D to withdraw effectively is not entirely clear within the law, and will vary between case facts, but rules have developed to help us to apply the defence. A useful starting point is that mere repentance, without any action, is not sufficient.

 Rook [1993] 2 All ER 955

D and another were recruited by X to kill his wife (V). D further recruited P. On the day of the murder, D was unexpectedly absent but P went ahead with the plan and murdered V. D was charged with murder as P's accomplice.

- Crown Court: guilty of murder.
- Court of Appeal: conviction upheld on appeal. D's absence was not sufficient to withdraw from P's offence.

The court in *Rook* does not specify what D should have done to withdraw successfully, but does state a minimum that he must have served 'unequivocal notice' of his withdrawal to P.[177] The focus of the defence is not on the withdrawal of D as an individual, but the withdrawal of D's assistance or encouragement, and this will always require action.

The most important detail to remember, discussed in *O'Flaherty*,[178] is that the courts will balance the weight of D's assistance or encouragement against the action taken to withdraw. Thus, the more substantial D's involvement in P's offence,[179] and the closer to P's commission of the offence that D attempts to withdraw,[180] the more the courts will require. Where D's assistance or encouragement is relatively minimal, for example where D has simply expressed the view that P's plan is a good one, it may be sufficient for D to withdraw by retracting those comments to P or removing the assistance. Where D's conduct is more substantial, she will have to do more. This does not necessarily mean that she must try and prevent P's crime taking place by going to the police for example,[181] although this will obviously be useful evidence of withdrawal.

---

[175] See **Chapter 11.4**.

[176] Reed, 'Repentance and Forgiveness: Withdrawal From Participation Liability and the Proportionality Test' in Reed and Bohlander (eds), *Participation in Crime* (2013); Smith, 'Withdrawal and Complicity' [2001] Crim LR 769.

[177] Following *Becerra* (1975) 62 Cr App R 212.

[178] [2004] EWCA Crim 526.

[179] *Gallant* [2008] EWCA Crim 111: comparing withdrawal of instigators within gang violence compared to peripheral members.

[180] *Becerra* (1975) 62 Cr App R 212: failure to withdraw at a very late stage.

[181] *Otway* [2011] EWCA Crim 3.

In certain cases D may accept liability as an accomplice for a primary offence, but claim to have withdrawn before a collateral offence was committed. This can occur where D joins an attack on V intending P to kill V, the attack ends with V still alive, D leaves, and then P returns to kill V.[182] D's argument, on these facts, would be that the second attack was not collateral to the first, but was a separate event which D did not intend (ie D lacked mens rea). This is a different claim to standard cases of withdrawal, but can result in the same outcome, extracting D from continued potential liability.

12.6.2 The victim rule

Where an offence is designed for the protection of a specific class of victim,[183] someone within that class is not complicit where they assist, encourage, or procure the offence to be committed *against themselves*. This mirrors similar defences discussed in the context of inchoate assisting or encouraging and conspiracy.[184] Often referred to as the '*Tyrrell* defence', it originated in this case.

Tyrrell [1894] 1 QB 710

D (a girl at some point when aged between 13–16 years) encouraged P to have sexual intercourse with her. D was charged under section 5 of the Criminal Amendment Act 1885 (now the Sexual Offences Act 2003, s9) as P's accessory.

- Central Criminal Court: guilty of the sexual offence.
- Court for Crown Cases Reserved: appeal allowed. The statute was passed for the protection of young girls, not to criminalise them.

How far the victim rule extends, and exactly which offences it applies to, has not been settled. Indeed, modern statutes such as the Sexual Offences Act 2003 can be criticised for not taking full account of the rule.[185] However, it remains an important defence, and one that the Law Commission has recommended be codified in statute.

Two exceptions to the rule should be noted. First, the defence will only apply to offences designed to protect a specific sub-group of the population, not the population as a whole. For example, the defence will not apply to D who encourages P to kill her, as the offence of murder is designed to protect all people.[186] Secondly, the defence will not apply to D within the protected class if she assists or encourages P to commit the offence against *another* person within that class (eg D would have been liable in *Tyrell* had she encouraged P to have sexual intercourse with another girl aged 13).

---

[182] *Mitchell* [1999] Crim LR 496; *Robinson* [2000] 5 Arch News 2 (restricting the approach in *Mitchell*); *O'Flaherty* [2004] EWCA Crim 526.
[183] Williams, 'Victims and Other Exempt Parties in Crime' (1990) 10 LS 245.
[184] See **Chapter 11.3.1.1** and **11.4.5**.
[185] Bohlander, 'The Sexual Offences Act 2003—The *Tyrrell* Principle—Criminalising the Victim' [2005] Crim LR 701.
[186] *Gnango* [2011] UKSC 59.

12.6.3 Acting reasonably?

The courts have not recognised a defence of acting reasonably within the current law, although the Law Commission has recommended a defence of acting to prevent crime or limit harm.[187] Such a defence has, however, been created in the context of inchoate assisting or encouraging.[188] It would be open to the courts to recognise a defence of this kind where, for example, D encourages P to damage V's car in order to convince P not to attack V herself. In the absence of this as a specific defence, D would have to rely on the uncertain general defence of necessity.[189]

12.7 Reform

Any student studying the law of complicity will be struck by its complexity and, in several areas, its incoherence. The number of appellate court cases in recent years provides further demonstration of the uncertainties within the current law; and the judgments themselves seem to have done little to stem the flow. Even following *Jogee*,[190] parliamentary reform and clarification is long overdue.[191]

When seeking legal coherence, however, it is important to understand the basic principles underlying liability (ie what is the 'mischief' complicity seeks to criminalise?).[192] And it is here that we locate the source of the current law's confusion. There are at least two competing rationales for complicity, neither of which is entirely satisfactory. These are the causal theory and the derivative theory.

A) The causal theory: The causal theory holds that D is complicit in P's offence because she has materially contributed to its commission. There is support for this theory within the current law. For example, unlike inchoate assisting and encouraging where D is merely required to perform acts 'capable' of assisting or encouraging, complicity will *not* be found where there is evidence that (despite conduct capable of encouraging or assisting P) D has not assisted or encouraged in fact (**12.3.1.1**). Indeed, in *Mendez*, Toulson LJ stated that 'at its most basic level secondary liability is founded on the principle of causation'.[193] There is also support for a version of this theory from Gardner, who highlights the benefits of a causal theory in terms of respect for D's autonomy: D is liable for what she has done, not simply for her association with the actions of another.[194]

The obvious (and potentially fatal) problem with this theory, however, is that most complicity cases do not require D to have caused P's offence. Where D has caused P's offence, D has either procured P's offence or committed it as a principal

[187] Law Commission, *Participating in Crime* (No 305, 2007) paras 5.10–5.23.
[188] Serious Crime Act 2007, s50.
[189] Discussed at **Chapter 14.6**.
[190] [2016] UKSC 8.
[191] Cf Wilson and Ormerod [2015] Crim LR 3.
[192] Williams, 'What is the Theoretical Basis for Accomplice Liability?' in Krebs (ed), *Accessorial Liability after Jogee* (2020) Ch2.
[193] [2010] EWCA Crim 516, [18].
[194] Gardner, 'Complicity and Causality' (2007) 1 Crim L & Phil 127, 136.

via the doctrine of innocent agency (12.2). For most complicity cases involving assistance or encouragement, P's free, voluntary, and informed choice to commit the principal offence will break any chain of causation between D's conduct and that offence.[195] In view of this, causal theories are forced into the murky realms of 'substantial contribution' rather than full causation.[196] This is problematic: it does not provide clarity on what the offence should require of D, and if less than causation, as must be the case, it is arguable that it undermines the benefits of the theory highlighted earlier.

B) The derivative theory: The derivative theory holds that D's liability is a product of P's liability; D assuming co-responsibility with P because of her association with P's conduct. Again, advocates of the derivative theory can find support within the current law's treatment of D (ie labelling and punishing her in the same way as P), as well as the fact that D's liability hangs on P's completion of the principal offence.

However, the derivative theory is also problematic. In contrast to the causal theory, the derivative theory can be criticised for being too harsh to D and not respecting the principle of autonomy: D seems to be punished for P's choices rather than her own. And, in other areas, it may also be too generous to D. Where P commits a less serious offence than that intended by D, the current law (in certain cases) still allows D to be held liable for the more serious offence intended (12.3.2.2). But surely, if we fully respect a derivative theory, it should not be possible to criminalise D for anything in excess of P's offence.

The current doctrinal uncertainty makes useful reform almost impossible. As Wilson comments, 'the range of problems left uncatered for by this fudging of the theoretical basis to accessorial liability spreads across the whole field of doctrine'.[197]

12.7.1 Abolishing complicity

In view of the doctrinal uncertainty discussed in the previous section, for some commentators the abolition of complicity liability becomes an attractive proposition. This would not result in a complete lack of liability for D, as the inchoate offences of assisting or encouraging and conspiracy would cover almost all cases.[198] Indeed, it is an approach that once found favour with the Law Commission.[199]

However, the most recent Law Commission recommendations rejected this approach for two main reasons.[200] First, it was argued that cases where P goes on to commit the principal offence assisted or encouraged are different (ie more serious) than cases where P does not, such that inchoate liability alone in both cases would fail to mark the distinction in culpability. Secondly, it was highlighted that abolition of complicity would undermine the forensic advantage of, in appropriate cases, being able to charge D as a

---

[195] *Kennedy (No 2)* [2007] UKHL 38.

[196] See brief discussion in *Jogee* [2016] UKSC 8, [12].

[197] Wilson, *Central Issues in Criminal Theory* (2002) 221.

[198] The only exception might be cases of procuring. Child, 'The Differences Between Attempted Complicity and Inchoate Assisting and Encouraging: A Reply to Professor Bohlander' [2010] Crim LR 924.

[199] Law Commission, *Assisting and Encouraging Crime* (Consultation 131, 1993).

[200] Law Commission, *Participating in Crime* (No 305, 2007) paras 1.38–1.40.

principal *or* an accessory where D's exact role is uncertain. On both of these grounds, we agree that the Commission was right to rethink its original proposal.[201]

12.7.2 Law Commission 2007 recommendations

We have made reference to the latest Law Commission recommendations at several points during this chapter.[202] Despite codification of inchoate assisting or encouraging within the Serious Crime Act 2007 (intended to work in tandem with the Commission's complicity recommendations), the Commission's complicity report remains unimplemented, and, particularly post-*Jogee*, is unlikely to be taken forward by government. However, the Commission's report remains a useful and comprehensive source, recommending a route to reform quite different from the current direction of the law. The Commission's 2007 report focusses on three core offences:

- **Clause 1:** Complicity liability where D assists or encourages P to commit an offence that P goes on to commit, intending to assist or encourage, and intending that P should complete at least the conduct element of that offence.

- **Clause 2:** Complicity liability where D forms a joint enterprise with P to commit an offence that P goes on to commit, intending to assist or encourage, and at least reckless as to P completing that offence. *Note the lower 'recklessness' standard required for this offence.*

- **Clause 3:** A new offence of 'causing a no-fault offence' where D causes (ie not just assists or encourages) P to commit a strict liability offence. *This new offence would provide a coherent response to cases where D causes P's offence, but P is not an innocent agent because the conduct she is caused to complete is an offence despite her lack of mens rea.*

Academic responses to the Commission's recommendations have been mixed.[203] In 2015, the Justice Committee of the House of Commons recommended that the Law Commission start a further project on joint enterprise, not adopting its 2007 report. However, at time of writing, post-*Jogee*, this seems most unlikely.

12.8 Eye on assessment

Answering problem questions on complicity is challenging, but the structure is no different to any other essay of this kind. The focus should be on clarity, leading your reader through your analysis, and keeping your discussion as simple as possible—there

---

[201] Interestingly, a variation on the abolition proposal has been mooted by Sullivan in a manner which seeks to address some of these concerns. Sullivan, 'Doing Without Complicity' [2012] JCCL 199.

[202] Law Commission, *Participating in Crime* (No 305, 2007).

[203] Wilson welcomed the proposals in 'A Rational Scheme of Liability for Participating in Crime' [2008] Crim LR 3, but they were criticised in Sullivan, 'Participating in Crime' [2008] Crim LR 19 and Taylor, 'Procuring, Causation, Innocent Agency and the Law Commission' [2008] Crim LR 32. Horder (Criminal Law Commissioner at the time of the Complicity Report) responds to Sullivan's criticism in Ch 6 of *Homicide and the Politics of Law Reform* (2012).

is no need to add to the complexity! The starting point is to identify a criminal offence from P, and then to work backwards to D's potential liability for complicity in that offence.

STEP 1 Identify the potential criminal event in the facts

This should be simply stated (eg 'The first potential criminal event arises where P murders V, having been encouraged to do so by D'). The role of this stage is to highlight which part of the question you are answering before you begin to apply the law.

STEP 2 Identify the potential principal offence

Again, state this simply (eg 'When P kills V, following D's encouragement, D may be liable for murder as P's accomplice'). The role of this stage is to highlight which offence you are going to apply.

STEP 3 Applying the offence to the facts

Having identified the relevant principal offence, make sure you discuss each of the required elements. Begin with the principal offence committed by P: are we sure we have a complete offence that D may be an accomplice to? Having established P's offence, we can now explore D's potential accomplice liability.

Actus reus: What does the offence require? Did D do it?

Mens rea: What does the offence require? Did D possess it?

In order to apply Steps 2 and 3, you need to do two things. First, you need to lead your reader through the most likely route to liability (ie principal offender; co-principal; complicity by assisting or encouraging; by procuring; etc) and, secondly, you need to apply the elements of that offence.

In Figure 12.1 we set out a flowchart to help you to make sense of the different routes to complicity liability. Within each stage represented in the figure, you will need to take account of the detailed commentary set out in the chapter (ie this is a rough guide, not a substitution for engagement with the case law).

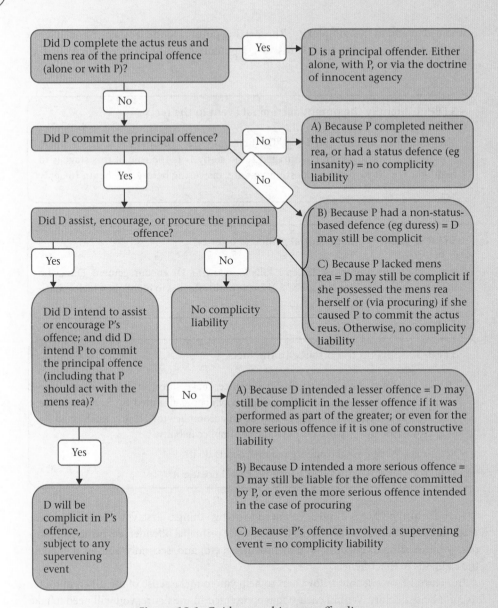

Figure 12.1 Guide to multi-party offending

AR and MR are satisfied	AR and/or MR are not satisfied
Continue to STEP 4.	Return to STEP 2, and look for an alternative offence. If none, then skip to STEP 5, concluding that no offence is committed.

STEP 4 Consider defences

The word 'consider' here is important, as you should not discuss every defence for every question. Rather, think whether there are any defences (eg duress) that *could* potentially apply. This includes the specific defences of withdrawal and the victim rule. If there are any potential defences, discuss those only.

STEP 5 Conclude

This is usually a single sentence either saying that it is likely that D has committed the offence as an accomplice, or saying that it is not likely either because an offence element is not satisfied or because a defence is likely to apply. It is not often that you will be able to say categorically whether or not D has committed the offence, so it is usually best to conclude in terms of what is more 'likely'.

STEP 6 Loop

Go back up to STEP 1, identifying the next potential criminal event. Continue until you have discussed all the relevant potentially criminal events.

 ONLINE RESOURCES

www.oup.com/he/child-ormerod4e

This chapter is accompanied by a selection of online resources to help you with this topic, including:

- **Self-test questions** and **scenario questions**
- **Videos** from the authors
- **Audio introduction** to the topic
- **Chapter summary sheet**
- Two **sample examination questions** with answer guidance
- **Further reading and weblinks**

Also available on the online resources are:

- A selection of **videos** from the authors containing general advice on problem questions and essay questions
- **Legal updates**

13

Denials of an offence

13.1 Introduction

In **Chapters 13** and **14** we shift focus from the discussion of substantive offences and issues of *inculpation*, to denials of liability and issues of *exculpation*. We have already discussed several specific defences in relation to particular crimes (eg withdrawal for complicity, belief in an owner's consent for criminal damage, etc); and some specific partial defences available only to murder (eg loss of self-control and diminished responsibility). The rules discussed in these two chapters are different because, if they apply, they provide a complete defence and acquittal for (almost[1]) any criminal offence.

---

[1] A notable exception is the defence of duress (**Chapter 14.3–14.4**) which does not apply to murder and a small number of related offences.

The classification of criminal law defences is controversial, not least because the term 'defence' is often employed generally to describe all manner of arguments raised by a defendant.[2] In this textbook, between **Chapters 13** and **14**, we distinguish two sets of rules which continue to be commonly referred to as defences. This chapter focusses on the rules regulating D's denial of an offence, a denial of one or more actus reus or mens rea elements. **Chapter 14**, in contrast, focusses on defences properly so called. These rules apply where even if D *has* committed the actus reus and mens rea of the offence charged, she can rely on an independent set of rules (ie a defence) to avoid liability.

Denials of an offence, the focus of this chapter, can come in many forms. Where D relies on an alibi that she was 'out of the country' when alleged to have committed an offence in England, she is denying actus reus; where she admits presence at the scene of the offence, but says she caused harm 'by accident', she is likely to be denying mens rea; and so on. We might talk loosely of these statements as D's 'defence', but D is not relying on a set of exculpatory rules, she is simply denying that she committed the crime; she is denying the prosecution's case. The prosecution bears the burden of proving D's offence beyond reasonable doubt, and so 'denials' by a defendant are not about proving innocence, they are about establishing such doubt in any relevant form. Most of the ways D can deny offending require no special comment, but there are three types of denial that warrant special attention and for which special rules have developed at common law:

- **Intoxication:** D explains her lack of mens rea (including, in extreme cases, her lack of voluntary movement) on the basis of intoxication. For example, D stabs her sleeping friend, drunkenly mistaking her friend for a theatrical dummy.[3] D, in this example, lacks subjective mens rea for any offence against the person.

- **Sane automatism:** D explains her lack of voluntary movement (and associated lack of mens rea) on the basis that she was rendered totally incapacitated by some *external* circumstances affecting her. For example, D drives dangerously when attacked by a swarm of bees, or punches V whilst suffering concussion following a blow to the head.[4] D, in these examples, lacks an essential element of voluntariness that is necessary for all offences.

- **Insanity (as a denial of offending):** D explains her lack of mens rea (including, in extreme cases, her lack of voluntary movement) on the basis of what the law labels insanity.[5] This includes all medical conditions which cause some bodily malfunctioning,[6] which prevent D understanding the nature or quality of her acts. For example, D kills V under the insane delusion that she is breaking a jar.[7] D, in this example, lacks subjective mens rea for any offence against the person.

These three sets of rules require separate discussion from other denials of offending for three main reasons. First, unlike most denials (eg simple alibis, etc), D cannot raise issues of intoxication, automatism, and/or insanity without bringing some evidence that the relevant condition or circumstances applied to her at the time of the alleged offence.[8] This is

[2] Williams, 'Offences and Defences' (1982) 2 LS 233.
[3] Example from Lord Denning in *AG for Northern Ireland v Gallagher* [1963] AC 349, 381.
[4] Examples from Lord Goddard CJ in *Hill v Baxter* [1958] 2 WLR 76, 82–83.
[5] The insanity rules can apply *both* as a denial of offending, and as a defence where D has committed the offence. This chapter discusses the former only, **Chapter 14** discusses the latter.
[6] In the language of the M'Naghten Rules—a defect of reason arising from a disease of the mind.
[7] Example from Stephen, *A Digest of the Criminal Law* (8th edn, 1947) 6.
[8] The nature of this burden differs between the rules, discussed later.

because, although there is a general burden on the prosecution to prove D's liability, there are legal presumptions that our movements are voluntary, that we are sane, etc.[9] Secondly, where D successfully pleads insanity this will not result in an unqualified acquittal, but rather in the special verdict of 'not guilty by reason of insanity'. Thirdly, and most importantly, these rules are special because in circumstances of prior-fault, they *may* provide alternative routes to liability even though D lacks mens rea for the offence charged.

13.1.1 The role of prior-fault

Raising evidence of intoxication, automatism, or insanity may be extremely useful where D seeks to deny an offence. D's honest claim that she did not realise V was a person when she stabbed her, for example, may only seem plausible to a jury with knowledge that D was hallucinating at the time. However, where D's intoxication, automatism, or insanity has resulted from her own prior-fault (eg dangerous drug taking), legal rules have developed *in some cases at least* to find liability regardless of D's denial. In this manner, evidence denying essential elements of an offence (eg denying mens rea) may be used by the prosecution to create a new route to liability; may be used as a method of *inculpation* to construct liability.

 Extra detail . . .

When discussing the potential for prior-fault, it is necessary to distinguish between two points in time: (**T1**) when D performed a blameworthy act—for example, when D became dangerously intoxicated; and (**T2**) when D completed the actus reus of a relevant offence, but lacked an element of mens rea due to intoxication/automatism/insanity. At T1 we ask whether D made a blameworthy choice: whether we have a simple denial of offending, or conduct that also demonstrates prior-fault. Where prior-fault *is* found, our focus shifts to T2, asking whether D's prior-fault is sufficient to substitute for the missing offence elements in order to create liability.

Where intoxication, automatism, and insanity rules are discussed in the context of prior-fault, as potential alternative mechanisms for *finding* liability, their presentation as a 'defence' is even more inappropriate and potentially misleading. For those persevering with this label, and the older case law, analysis can be constructed as follows: D commits the offence because her defence (eg intoxication) is blocked or prevented by evidence of prior-fault. This analysis leads to the correct outcome (ie liability), but is acceptable only if we discount the presumption of innocence: denying a defence surely cannot/ should not lead to an assumption of mens rea; and as we know D lacked mens rea at T2, it should not be possible for the prosecution to prove it was present. Rather, it is submitted, the correct analysis of prior-fault rules is that they apply to construct liability. For example, although D may rely on her intoxicated state to deny mens rea at T2, the prosecution may rely on the same evidence to substitute for that missing mens rea and find liability.[10] As we discuss intoxication, automatism, and insanity in detail, we also consider the implications of prior-fault for each.

---

[9] The use of reverse burdens in these areas is another reason why the terminology of 'defences' has been common.

[10] Simester, 'Intoxication is Never a Defence' [2009] Crim LR 3; Child, 'Prior Fault: Blocking Defences or Constructing Crimes' in Reed and Bohlander (eds), *General Defences* (2014).

13.2 Intoxication

There is an obvious and well-documented link between intoxication, particularly alcoholic intoxication, and crime.[11] Intoxicants can lower inhibitions, warp moral and practical judgements, encourage unpredictable behaviour, and so on. In short, D's conduct when intoxicated may not be a reflection of her character when sober.[12] Being intoxicated is not, however, and never has been, a defence to criminal offences. D's claim that 'it was the drink' may provide some moral mitigation, and may become relevant at sentencing, but it is not an answer to a criminal charge. If it were, there would be a lot more space in prisons!

13.2.1 Intoxication as a denial of offending

The intoxication rules *only* become relevant where, as a result of intoxication at T1, D lacks the prescribed mens rea for the crime charged at T2. This is illustrated in *Kingston* and **Figure 13.1**.

Kingston [1994] 3 All ER 353

P was hired to take compromising photos of D to use for blackmail. P invited V (a 15-year-old boy) to his flat, gave him alcohol and drugs, and left him asleep. He then drugged D's coffee, and encouraged D to indecently assault V as he slept. D did so. D was charged with indecent assault.[13]

- Crown Court: guilty of indecent assault.
- Court of Appeal: appeal allowed. No liability: D only committed the offence as a result of P surreptitiously drugging him and thus lowering his inhibitions.
- House of Lords: appeal allowed, and D's conviction reinstated. A drunken intention is still an intention.

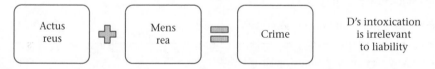

Figure 13.1 An intoxicated mens rea is still a mens rea

In *Kingston*, D's mens rea at T2 was proved irrespective of his intoxication, so his intoxicated state could not provide a denial of offending; and there was no need (or scope) to rely on any special rules of intoxication.[14] Despite the disinhibiting effect of the drugs in this case, D was still able, and did in fact, form an intention to assault V. D acted with the mens

---

[11] Dingwall, *Alcohol and Crime* (2005).

[12] This chapter only discusses the intoxication of D. The intoxication of a victim may affect D's liability (eg where it affects V's consent in sexual offences) but this is a separate issue, discussed in **Chapter 8**.

[13] D's conduct would now be charged under the Sexual Offences Act 2003.

[14] Horder has recommended an alternative approach for cases like *Kingston* based on temporary insanity: Horder, 'Sobering Up? The Law Commission on Criminal Intoxication' (1995) 58 MLR 534.

rea required for the offence. There is no 'defence' of intoxication where D has committed an offence; a drunken intent is still an intent; an intoxicated mens rea is still a mens rea.[15]

D's intoxication only becomes relevant to liability if, as a result of that intoxication, an element of the offence charged is absent. For example, D denies intending to cause harm when she claims that she was so drunk she did not mean to make contact with V, or damage V's property. In more extreme cases, D may even deny voluntary movement. For example, D becomes so intoxicated that she loses consciousness.[16] In all cases of this kind, D's intoxication is relevant as a denial of offending.

 Extra detail . . .

Before the intoxication rules apply, D must lack mens rea as a result of intoxication. However, there is no need to demonstrate further that D was rendered 'incapable' of forming mens rea.[17] For example, if due to her intoxication D kills V mistakenly thinking that V is a theatrical dummy, D may be 'capable' of forming an intention to kill, but her intoxication still provides an explanation for her lack of mens rea in relation to V, and the prior-fault intoxication rules will still apply.

The first question when considering cases where D was intoxicated, is whether D's intoxication led to a lack of mens rea (ie establishes a denial of offending).

13.2.2 Prior-fault intoxication as a method of inculpation

Where, because of her intoxication, the Crown fails to establish that D had mens rea at T2, our starting point is that no liability should be found: D lacks an essential element of the offence. However, where D is responsible for bringing about that state of intoxication, there are strong policy reasons in favour of finding liability (most importantly in the protection of others[18]). The common law response has been the development of prior-fault intoxication rules (**Table 13.1**) capable of substituting for missing mens rea and establishing liability.

Table 13.1 Prior-fault intoxication rules

A) D must be voluntarily intoxicated;
B) D's offence at T2 must have been one of 'basic intent', as opposed to one of 'specific intent';
C) D's intoxicant at T1 must have been 'dangerous' in the sense that it is commonly known to lead to unpredictability or aggression; and
D) D must lack mens rea at T2 *because* of that intoxication.

---

[15] Discussed in *White* [2017] NICA 49, where mens rea for murder was clear despite intoxication.

[16] *Lipman* [1970] 1 QB 152: D took LSD (a hallucinogenic drug). Believing that he was fighting snakes at the centre of the earth, D killed V.

[17] There has been some inconsistency on this point. See *Beard* [1920] AC 479, 501–502; *Kingston* [1994] 3 All ER 353; cf *Sheehan and Moore* [1975] 2 All ER 960.

[18] See **Chapter 1.4.4.**

Where these elements are satisfied, D will be liable *as if* the missing elements were satisfied. This is illustrated in **Figure 13.2**.

Figure 13.2 Intoxication replacing a lack of mens rea

13.2.2.1 Element 1: D must be voluntarily intoxicated

The first stage of the prior-fault intoxication rules requires D to have acted voluntarily in bringing about a state of intoxication at T1, resulting in a lack of mens rea when completing the actus reus of an offence at T2. The focus here is typically upon the requirement of 'voluntariness': it is essential to demonstrate D's T1 *choice* to become intoxicated (and to run the associated risks) in order to demonstrate the culpability necessary for finding liability at T2.[19] D's status as 'intoxicated' is rarely contested, but should also be considered carefully.

Is D intoxicated?

Historically, courts have avoided defining 'intoxication'. The intoxication rules do not require the intoxication to be of any specific type or degree, as long as it is sufficient to establish a reasonable doubt as to whether D had mens rea. The meaning of intoxication has, therefore, not given rise to dispute. However, recent cases have begun to test the boundaries of intoxication, and the courts have been forced to articulate limits. Unfortunately, as we see elsewhere,[20] the courts have struggled to maintain a consistent and coherent interpretation. Four points should be distinguished, with only the first two counting as 'intoxication' in the law:

- Intoxicants directly affecting D's capacity: Typical intoxication cases involve a defendant causing potentially criminal harms under the direct influence of drugs. Such defendants are clearly intoxicated for legal purposes.

- Impact of drug-induced psychosis on D's mental capacity: In *Taj*,[21] a five-member Court of Appeal recently held that D's psychosis at T2, that was attributable to a *previous* state of intoxication, may be caught within the intoxication rules as they apply to self-defence, so that D may be legally 'intoxicated' even after the direct effect of a drug has ended. As *Taj* (discussed at **14.5.4.3**) was concerned with intoxicated mistakes in self-defence, we may question whether the same definition applies where intoxication is used to construct liability (our focus in this chapter). However, it would be exceptional if different interpretations of 'intoxication' were applied, and *obiter*

---

[19] Note the important role of 'choice'. See our discussion of the principle of autonomy in **Chapter 1.4.3**.

[20] eg when regulating 'psychoactive' substances. See Fortson, 'The Psychoactive Substances Act 2016, the "Medicinal Product" Exemption and Proving Psychoactivity' [2018] Crim LR 229.

[21] [2018] EWCA Crim 1743. For critical comment see Laird [2019] Crim LR 167; Dsouza, 'Intoxication, Psychoses, and Self-defence: Evaluating Taj' [2018] Arch Rev 6; Child, Crombag, and Sullivan, 'Defending the Delusional, the Irrational, and the Dangerous' [2020] Crim LR 306.

statements in *Taj* suggest a consistent approach.[22] Broadening the definition of intoxication beyond a case where D is directly affected by the *presence* of intoxicants in her system widens the application of the intoxication rules with as-yet unknown effects on increased criminalisation; it also renders more complex and uncertain the borderline for when intoxication will be relevant to criminal liability.[23]

- **Impact of drug withdrawal on D's mental capacity:** In *Harris*,[24] D developed a pattern of heavy drinking during periods of leave from work followed by sudden abstinence when returning to work. Previously, suddenly stopping drinking had led to episodes of alcohol psychosis, and on one occasion D set fire to his house. D lacked mens rea for the arson offence charged due to his delusional state, but was initially convicted using the prior-fault intoxication rules. However, crucially, D's appeal against conviction was allowed on the basis that psychosis induced by withdrawal from alcohol was not intoxication, and that extending the intoxication rules to apply to his case would represent a 'significant extension' of the law.[25] The *obiter* statements in *Taj* extending the definition of intoxication do not sit well with *Harris*, reaching opposite conclusions despite clear similarities between the defendants' states and the role of alcohol. *Taj* attempts to distinguish *Harris* on the basis that D's psychosis was induced by withdrawal as opposed to consumption, but this is a linguistic rather than a medical distinction, and it is contended that it is not a sustainable one.[26]

- **Impact of drug addiction on D's mental capacity:** Where D is addicted to a drug but does not currently have intoxicants in her system, D will not be caught within the intoxication rules. This is reiterated in *Harris*[27] and *Taj*.[28] This rule seems correct, with analysis of addiction better served within the insanity rules. However, following the judgment in *Taj*, equating intoxication with the ongoing effects of alcohol that has left the system (in the context of self-defence at least), the separate treatment of addicted harm-causers may be identified as an inconsistency.

Was D's intoxication voluntary?

If we are to blame D for her *choice* to become intoxicated, and to run the associated risks of intoxication, we can only do so fairly if D's T1 choice was voluntary.[29] Where D is not responsible for her intoxicated state (ie involuntary intoxication at T1), and where that

---

[22] eg at [56]: '[other intoxication cases] focussed on crime committed while specifically under the influence of drugs or alcohol. Having said that, however, it is difficult to see why the language (and the policy identified) is not equally apposite to the immediate and proximate consequences of such misuse'.

[23] See Crombag, Child, and Sullivan, 'Drunk, Dangerous and Delusional: How Legal Concept-creep Risks Overcriminalization' (2020) 115(12) *Addiction* 2200, and debate responses within the same volume.

[24] [2013] EWCA Crim 223.

[25] At [59].

[26] See Crombag, Child, and Sullivan, 'Drunk, Dangerous and Delusional: How Legal Concept-creep Risks Overcriminalization' (2020) 115(12) *Addiction* 2200, and debate responses within the same volume.

[27] Ibid.

[28] At [60].

[29] Law Commission, *Intoxication and Criminal Liability* (No 314, 2009) Part 4.

involuntary intoxication caused her to lack relevant mens rea at the time of the offence (T2), there is no prior-fault. The legal consequences of involuntary intoxication are illustrated in **Figure 13.3**.

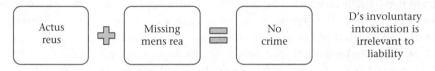

Figure 13.3 Involuntary intoxication

When analysing voluntariness, however, two points should be carefully considered. First, as discussed at **13.2.1**, remember that the intoxication rules do not apply unless elements of the offence cannot be established by the prosecution. The leading case is *Kingston* (discussed earlier), where D was drugged by a third party, and then sexually assaulted a child. Understandably, the House of Lords in *Kingston* had some sympathy for D: he was aware of and claimed to be in control of his paedophilic tendencies when sober, only losing control as a result of the drugs involuntarily administered by P. Where such involuntary intoxication undermines mens rea at T2, D's lack of prior-fault means that no liability will be found. D was liable in *Kingston* because his conduct at T2 *was* accompanied by mens rea.

Secondly, involuntariness has been narrowly defined. D's intoxication is clearly involuntary in cases like *Kingston* where D's drinks are surreptitiously laced with alcohol or other intoxicating drugs,[30] and the same may be true where D is forced to take drugs under duress (ie when threatened if D did not do so). However, as illustrated in *Allen*, where D knows that she is consuming an intoxicant known to create unpredictable behaviour (eg alcohol), this does not qualify as involuntary simply because she is unaware of its quantity or possible effects.

Allen (1988) The Times, 10 June

D committed the actus reus of buggery and indecent assault.[31] He lacked mens rea (he claimed he was not acting voluntarily) because he had consumed a large amount of wine supplied by a friend. D claimed this was involuntary intoxication because he did not realise the strength of the wine. D was charged with the sexual offences.[32]

• Crown Court: guilty of the sexual offences.

• Court of Appeal: convictions upheld on appeal. D's intoxication was voluntary.

A more difficult case arises where D voluntarily consumes an intoxicant, but a further intoxicant is added without her knowledge (eg X gives D a double shot of alcohol rather than the single requested, or X laces D's alcoholic drink with another intoxicating drug). In cases of this kind, the question for the court is likely to be whether the *in*voluntary proportion of D's intoxication overrides the voluntary, such to make it trivial.[33]

---

[30] *Ross v HM Advocate* 1991 SLT 564: D's drink was involuntarily laced with various drugs including LSD, under the influence of which D injured several people. His conviction for offences against the person was quashed on appeal.

[33] Law Commission, *Intoxication and Criminal Liability* (No 314, 2009) paras 3.126–3.127.

[31] Commentary at [1988] Crim LR 698.

[32] For such acts performed today D would be charged under the Sexual Offences Act 2003 (**Chapter 8**).

13.2.2.2 Element 2: D's offence must be one of basic intent

Having established that D was voluntarily intoxicated at T1, focus shifts to the potential offence of which D committed the actus reus (but lacked mens rea) at T2. If D is charged with a crime that is legally classified as a 'specific intent' offence and the prosecution cannot prove mens rea at T2, then D is not guilty of that crime regardless of her intoxication.[34] However, if D is charged with a crime that is classified as a 'basic intent' offence, then D may be liable for that offence on the basis of her prior-fault in voluntarily intoxicating herself at T1.

The crucial two-part classification between basic and specific intent offences has been developed at common law.

 Don't be confused . . .

The terms 'basic intent' and 'specific intent' are misleading, as they do not describe types of intention. Rather, they are simply labels that have been used to distinguish two classifications of offences. We discuss the basis of this distinction later, but suffice to say, it has nothing to do with different types of intention.[35]

A) **Basic intent offences:** Where D is charged with a basic intent offence, the prior-fault in D's voluntary intoxication at T1 *may be* sufficient to replace her lack of mens rea at T2, subject to the other elements within the prior-fault intoxication rules. Section 20 malicious wounding or inflicting GBH[36] is an example of a basic intent offence. Thus, where D wounds V or causes GBH, but lacks mens rea (and even, potentially, lacks voluntariness in her movement) because of her voluntary intoxication, she will still be liable for the offence.[37] This is illustrated in **Figure 13.4**.

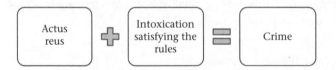

Figure 13.4 Basic intent offences

 Extra detail . . .

Where intoxication is discussed using the language of defences, **Figure 13.4** would be described as the defence of intoxication not being permitted to apply.

B) **Specific intent offences:** Where D is charged with a specific intent offence, D's prior-fault intoxication at T1 will *not* be sufficient to replace her lack of mens rea at T2. Section 18 wounding or causing GBH with intent[38] is an example of a specific intent

---

[34] Unless D had voluntarily intoxicated herself in order to commit the offence—'Dutch courage', discussed later in this section.

[35] For discussion of the origin of these terms, as well as a more general critique, see Gough, 'Intoxication and Criminal Liability: The Law Commission's Proposed Reforms' (1996) 112 LQR 335, 342.

[36] Offences Against the Person Act 1861, s20.

[37] *Aitken* [1992] 1 WLR 1006.

[38] Offences Against the Person Act 1861, s18.

offence. Thus, where D wounds V or causes GBH, but lacks mens rea because of her voluntary intoxication, she will not be liable for this offence.[39] This is illustrated in **Figure 13.5**.

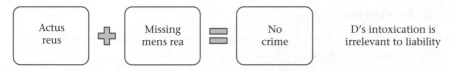

Figure 13.5 Specific intent offences

 Extra detail . . .

Where intoxication is discussed using the language of defences, **Figure 13.5** would be described as the defence of intoxication being permitted to apply.

The logic of separating basic and specific intent offences is that D's voluntary intoxication at T1 is only sufficiently wrongful to replace a lack of mens rea for certain offences and not others. However, there are two major problems with this.

The first problem is that, although D has voluntarily become intoxicated at T1, her conduct is not obviously equivalent to *any* potential subjective mens rea missing at T2; and the prior-fault intoxication rules are not limited to substituting for objective mens rea only.[40] Equivalence with subjective mens rea is assumed within the current law in the context of basic intent offences,[41] but it is difficult to justify logically.[42] Even if we accept that voluntarily taking a dangerous drug means that D *chose* to risk committing a harmful act, that choice is necessarily non-specific. In contrast, subjective mens rea requires D to intend or be reckless as to specific elements of an offence before she is liable for it. In the context of malicious wounding or inflicting GBH, for example, D's foresight that she may become violent in the future is not normally sufficient for the offence; D must perform the act of wounding or causing GBH with malice (akin to recklessness) as to whether that specific act might cause some harm.[43] The criticism, therefore, is that when the prior-fault intoxication rules are used to replace a lack of subjective mens rea (including voluntariness in movement at T2), we are finding liability on the basis of an objective (negligence-based) standard at T1.[44]

The second problem is that the common law has struggled to create a clear set of rules to distinguish basic intent and specific intent offences. It should be acknowledged that in the absence of a justified equivalence between intoxication and a certain level of mens rea, a principled test of this kind is almost impossible, but the law requires one in order to function.

[39] *Davies* [1991] Crim LR 469.
[40] On the subjective/objective mens rea distinction, see **Chapter 3.1**.
[41] *Majewski* [1977] AC 443.
[42] Horder, 'Sobering Up? The Law Commission on Criminal Intoxication' (1995) 58 MLR 534.
[43] See **Chapter 7.5.2**.
[44] Robinson, 'Causing the Conditions of One's Own Defence: A Study in the Limits of Theory in Criminal Law Doctrine' (1985) 71 Vir LR 1, 14–17; Husak, 'Intoxication and Culpability' (2012) 6 Crim L & Phil 363, 366–368; Williams, 'Voluntary Intoxication—A Lost Cause?' (2013) 129 LQR 264, 266–271.

Distinguishing between basic and specific intent offences

The leading case discussing the separation of basic and specific intent offences is *Majewski*.[45]

DPP v Majewski [1977] AC 443

Intoxicated by a combination of dangerous drugs, including alcohol, D was involved in a bar brawl where he assaulted several people. D also assaulted police officers during the course of his arrest. D was charged with assault occasioning ABH, and assaulting a police officer.[46] D claimed that he lacked mens rea due to intoxication.

- Crown Court: guilty of assault offences.
- Court of Appeal: appeal dismissed.
- House of Lords: appeal dismissed. These were basic intent offences, so D's voluntary intoxication can be used as a substitute for the mens rea he lacked at the time of his conduct.

Although *Majewski* is clear in its categorisation of assault as a basic intent offence, the Lords did not provide a unified test to apply to other offences. To the extent that a test is discernible,[47] the Lords seem to treat offences that can be satisfied by recklessness as ones of basic intent, and those requiring intention as specific intent. It is noted by Lord Edmund-Davies that this distinction 'illogical though . . . it may be' has an advantage of 'compromise' where offences are laddered on the basis of mens rea.[48] For example, where D, in her voluntarily intoxicated state lacks mens rea but causes GBH, she is not liable for a section 18 offence (specific intent), but is liable for a section 20 offence (basic intent);[49] where she lacks mens rea but causes death she is not liable for murder (specific intent), but is liable for manslaughter (basic intent); and so on.

This test provides a useful rule of thumb, but where the Lords attempted to be more specific they ran into problems. For example, Lord Simon in *Majewski* discussed a test based on intention as to consequences: where an offence requires intention for the result element, it is a specific intent offence.[50] But this cannot be right. Murder, for example, the paradigm specific intent offence, can be committed without an intention to kill (ie where D intends to cause GBH).

An alternative method of distinction, but equally flawed, was considered in *Heard*.

Heard [2007] EWCA Crim 125

Whilst drunk, D exposed his penis and rubbed it on a police officer's leg. D claimed to lack mens rea due to intoxication (ie a lack of *intentional* touching). D was charged with sexual assault.[51]

- Crown Court: guilty of sexual assault, holding that sexual assault is a basic intent offence.
- Court of Appeal: conviction upheld on appeal.

---

[45] Law Commission, *Intoxication and Criminal Liability* (No 314, 2009) paras 2.2–2.74; Horder, 'The Classification of Crimes and the General Part' in Duff and Green (eds), *Defining Crimes* (2005).

[46] Offences Against the Person Act 1861, s47; Police Act 1996, s89.

[47] In line with *Beard* [1920] AC 479.

[48] [1977] AC 443, 495.

[49] Offences Against the Person Act 1861. Discussed in **Chapter 7**.

[50] [1977] AC 443, 478–479.

[51] Sexual Offences Act 2003, s3. Discussed in **Chapter 8.4**.

Extra detail . . .

Heard should not have been a difficult case. The fact that D did not remember his actions the following day is not a basis for claiming that he did not intend to touch V when intoxicated. There was no need to discuss the classification of sexual assault as a basic or specific intent offence because his appeal to the intoxication rules should have fallen at the first hurdle: an intoxicated mens rea is still a mens rea.

The court in *Heard* took the opportunity to provide an alternative test for identifying basic and specific intent offences.

[C]rimes of specific intent are those where the offence requires proof of purpose or consequence, which are not confined to, but amongst which are included, those where the purpose goes beyond the actus reus (sometimes referred to as cases of 'ulterior intent').

In this passage, Hughes LJ accepts Lord Simon's test in *Majewski* focussing on intention as to results (despite the problems outlined earlier), and builds upon it with reference to ulterior mens rea.[52] For Hughes LJ, any offence which requires ulterior mens rea, even an ulterior mens rea of recklessness (eg criminal damage being reckless as to the endangerment of life[53]), will be one of specific intent.

The test provided in *Heard*, however, is even more problematic than Lord Simon's in *Majewski*. Again, the test is under-inclusive, unable to explain why murder is a specific intent offence despite lacking a requirement of intention as to results and/or ulterior mens rea. But beyond this, and of more importance, the Hughes LJ test also seems to abandon any potential for theoretical underpinning. Although problematic, *Majewski* at least makes a broad implicit claim of moral equivalence, between (a) voluntary intoxication at T1 which causes D to fail to see risks, etc and (b) recklessness at T2, which can be used to explain large parts of the case law. However, in classifying sexual assault as a basic intent offence, despite a mens rea of *intentional* touching, and by classifying recklessness-based offences like aggravated criminal damage as specific intent offences, *Heard* runs counter to the intention/recklessness distinction.

Without guidance beyond these two equally unattractive alternatives, the current law remains in a state of uncertainty. The reaction of several other common law jurisdictions has been to reject the *Majewski* distinction between specific and basic intent.[54] However, we have not yet taken that step in England and Wales.[55] Rather, in the absence of a clear test, the law has developed by categorising offences as they emerge in case law. There is a pattern, with most intention-based offences being classified as specific intent, but this is not systematic:

---

[52] Mens rea going beyond the actus reus of the offence: see **Chapter 4.2.1.2**.
[53] Criminal Damage Act 1971, s1(2). See **Chapter 9.7.5**.
[54] eg Canada in *Daviault* (1994) 118 DLR (4th) 469; Australia in *O'Connor* (1980) 146 CLR 64; New Zealand in *Kamipeli* [1975] 2 NZLR 610; South Africa in *Chretien* 1981 (1) SA 1097.
[55] See the discussion of reform at **13.6.1**.

- **Basic intent:** Manslaughter,[56] malicious wounding or causing GBH (s20),[57] assault occasioning ABH (s47),[58] assault and battery,[59] rape,[60] sexual assault,[61] criminal damage (where only recklessness is alleged),[62] etc.

- **Specific intent:** Murder,[63] wounding or causing GBH with intent (s18),[64] theft,[65] robbery,[66] section 9(1)(a) burglary,[67] attempt to commit a specific intent offence,[68] complicity,[69] etc.

Specific intent offences and Dutch courage

Where an intoxicated D lacks mens rea for a specific intent offence, this is usually the end of the matter: D's intoxication cannot replace her lack of mens rea, so there is no liability for that offence.[70] However, there is one possible exception to this rule. This relates to (so-called) 'Dutch courage' cases, where D becomes intoxicated at T1 *in order to* commit the specific intent offence at T2. In such cases, D's blameworthy conduct is not merely her choice to become voluntarily intoxicated, but her choice to do so in order (ie with intention) to commit the offence. This was discussed in *AG for Northern Ireland v Gallagher*.

AG for Northern Ireland v Gallagher [1963] AC 349

D decided to kill his wife. D drank most of a bottle of whisky and then did so. D claimed that, due to his intoxication, he lacked mens rea for murder as a specific intent offence. D was charged with murder.

- Crown Court: guilty of murder.

- Northern Ireland Court of Appeal: appeal allowed. The court found that D had been wrongly convicted on the basis of his mens rea at T1, rather than focussing on T2.

- House of Lords: appeal allowed, restoring D's conviction. Contrary to the Court of Appeal, the House of Lords held that the trial court had correctly focussed on D's mens rea at T2. Thus, this was simply a case where intoxicated mens rea is still mens rea.

D's conviction in this case did not require an examination of 'Dutch courage' because, despite D's intoxication, it was found that D intended to kill at the time (T2) of killing his wife. However, Lord Denning went on to say that *even if* the Court of Appeal's interpretation was correct (ie that D only had mens rea when becoming intoxicated at T1), it would still be correct in law to find liability, even for a specific intent offence.

> I think the law on this point should take a clear stand. If a man, whilst sane and sober, forms an intention to kill and makes preparation for it . . . and then gets himself drunk so as to give himself

---

[56] *Beard* [1920] AC 479.
[57] *Aitken* [1992] 1 WLR 1006.
[58] *Bolton v Crawley* [1972] Crim LR 222.
[59] *Majewski* [1977] AC 443.
[60] *Grout* [2011] EWCA Crim 299.
[61] *Heard* [2007] EWCA Crim 125.
[62] *Caldwell* [1981] 1 All ER 961.
[63] *Beard* [1920] AC 479.
[64] *Davies* [1991] Crim LR 469.
[65] *Majewski* [1977] AC 443.
[66] Ibid.
[67] *Hutchins* [1988] Crim LR 379.
[68] *Clarkson* [1971] 3 All ER 344.
[69] Ibid, although note some doubt in *Lynch* [1975] AC 653.
[70] See **Figure 13.5**. D may be liable for an alternative basic intent offence.

Dutch courage to do the killing, and whilst drunk carries out his intention, he cannot rely on this self-induced drunkenness as a defence to a charge of murder, nor even as reducing it to manslaughter . . . The wickedness of his mind before he got drunk is enough to condemn him, coupled with the act which he intended to do and did do. A psychopath who goes out intending to kill, knowing it is wrong, and does kill, cannot escape the consequences by making himself drunk before doing it.

The logic of this statement is compelling. Where D becomes intoxicated *in order to* kill whilst in that state, it seems correct that D should be liable for murder even if she lacked mens rea at the moment she caused V's death (due to her intoxication). In line with the views of Lord Denning, this can therefore be presented as an exception to the rule that intoxication cannot replace a lack of mens rea for specific intent offences.

An alternative way of analysing these (rather unlikely) facts, is that D's conduct in becoming intoxicated is the conduct element of her offence. Under this analysis, D's conduct in becoming intoxicated is akin to the shooting of a bullet or the release of a stampeding herd of cattle towards V. In each case, D is in control of the release (ie becoming intoxicated; pulling the trigger; releasing the cattle) and then loses control of the weapon before it makes contact with V (ie her involuntary body; the bullet; the cattle). Analysed in these terms, there is no issue of coincidence, as D has the mens rea for murder whilst completing the conduct element (becoming intoxicated). And there is nothing to break the chain of causation. Thus, whether we recognise an exception to the prior-fault intoxication rules or we rely on standard rules of liability, D is guilty of murder.[71]

13.2.2.3 Element 3: D must have taken a 'dangerous' drug

Having satisfied the first two elements of the prior-fault intoxication rules, we can say that D has made a choice at T1 (through *voluntary* intoxication) that has led to the potential commission of a relevant offence at T2 (a *basic* intent offence). However, to say that V has voluntarily taken an intoxicating substance at T1 is not yet to say that V has acted in a blameworthy manner. Rather, before we can claim any potential equivalence between D's fault at T1 and her missing mens rea at T2, we need to look at the detail of her choice. Was D's choice at T1 a blameworthy choice; did D voluntarily take a *dangerous* drug?[72]

A drug is legally classified as 'dangerous', in this context, where it is commonly known in society, or personally known to D, to cause unpredictability and/or aggression. Alcohol is a clear example where such effects are commonly known, and as established in *Lipman*,[73] other drugs such as LSD will come within the same category. Voluntary intoxication with a dangerous drug provides the blameworthy choice necessary at T1 to construct liability at T2.

Where the intoxicant consumed by D at T1 is *not* commonly known to have effects of this kind, and it is not known to D personally (eg from previous use), then D's choice at T1 will not display sufficient prior-fault to create liability at T2. This is illustrated in **Figure 13.6.**

[71] Child, 'Prior Fault: Blocking Defences or Constructing Crimes' in Reed and Bohlander (eds), *General Defences* (2014).

[72] See discussion in Loughnan and Wake, 'Of Blurred Boundaries and Prior Fault: Insanity, Automatism and Intoxication' in Reed and Bohlander (eds), *General Defences in Criminal Law* (2014) 113, Part 4.

[73] [1970] 1 QB 152.

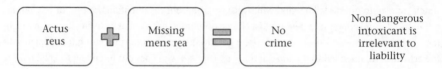

Figure 13.6 Intoxication with a non-dangerous intoxicant

This rule was central in *Bailey*,[74] where D (a diabetic) failed to consume sufficient food after an injection of insulin, and committed a series of serious attacks whilst in an intoxicated state.

> It is common knowledge that those who take alcohol to excess or certain sorts of drugs may become aggressive or do dangerous or unpredictable things, they may be able to foresee the risks of causing harm to others but nevertheless persist in their conduct. But the same cannot be said without more of a man who fails to take food after an insulin injection.[75]

The same reasoning was later applied in *Hardie*.

 Hardie [1985] 1 WLR 64

D took five valium tablets (a sedative drug) to calm himself after being told to leave the house by his partner. D returned, intoxicated by the tablets, and set fire to a wardrobe in the house. D was charged with arson with intention or recklessness as to the endangerment of life.

- Crown Court: guilty of arson. D's lack of mens rea (due to intoxication) was replaced by his voluntary intoxication.
- Court of Appeal: appeal allowed. Valium was not a dangerous drug, and D had no reason to believe it would lead to the actions it caused.

It is only where D has *voluntarily* taken a *dangerous* intoxicant that we have a sufficiently blameworthy choice at T1.

13.2.2.4 Element 4: D must have lacked mens rea *because* of intoxication

Having established that D was voluntarily intoxicated by a dangerous drug at T1, and that she lacked mens rea for the basic intent offence at T2, the final stage of the prior-fault intoxication rules looks for a nexus to connect the two. D's prior-fault voluntary intoxication at T1 will only be sufficient to substitute for her lack of mens rea at T2, creating liability, if her intoxication was the reason she lacked that mens rea. For example, D becomes voluntarily intoxicated with a dangerous drug at T1, and later trips on a hidden tripwire and smashes V's vase in the fall at T2 (basic intent offence of criminal damage). D satisfies the first three elements of the prior-fault intoxication rules in this example, but she fails the fourth element: liability should not be found because D's prior-fault at T1 was not the reason for her lack of mens rea at T2; D would have accidentally damaged the vase even if she was sober.

---

[74] [1983] 1 WLR 760.
[75] Griffiths LJ at 764–765.

This point was at issue in *Richardson and Irwin*.

Richardson and Irwin [1999] 1 Cr App R 392

D and others (university students) picked up V whilst heavily intoxicated and dropped him over a balcony. V fell 10–12 feet, and was injured. D claimed that he did not foresee the potential for injury. D was charged with maliciously inflicting GBH (basic intent offence).[76]

- Crown Court: guilty of section 20 offence, using the intoxication rules to find liability.
- Court of Appeal: appeal allowed. D was convicted because a *reasonable* sober person would have foreseen the risk of injury. However, the correct question for the intoxication rules was whether D would have foreseen the risk of injury if sober.

In some cases, as with *Richardson and Irwin*, it may be difficult to predict what D (as opposed to a reasonable person) would have foreseen if sober. But this is the correct question for the jury.

13.2.3 Intoxication and defences

Just as D's voluntary intoxication can create liability where she lacks mens rea, it can also affect her use of various defences. This does not mean that defences are necessarily unavailable: an intoxicated person may still have good reason to act in self-defence, for example. Problems arise, however, where D makes a mistake due to intoxication. For instance, where D assaults V with the intoxicated belief that she is acting in self-defence, where in fact no defensive force was necessary.

We explore the general defences in **Chapter 14**, and this includes the role of intoxication in their application. However, it is useful here to set out the general rule underpinning these various applications, as well as the exception to the rule. The general rule is that, when relying on a criminal defence, D may not rely on an intoxicated mistaken belief. This is the case even where a defence, as with self-defence,[77] would otherwise allow D to rely on mistaken and even potentially unreasonable beliefs. For example, D may rely on self-defence if she honestly but incorrectly believes force is necessary to repel an attack from V, but she may not rely on an equivalent intoxicated belief.[78]

The only exception to this rule has arisen in the context of criminal damage, where D raises the specific statutory defence that she believed the owner was consenting or would have consented to the damage.[79] As shown in *Jaggard v Dickinson*, here at least D *is* able to rely on her intoxicated mistake.[80]

Jaggard v Dickinson [1981] QB 527

D was told by X, a friend, to use his house as her own. Returning home drunk, D mistakenly tried to enter an identical house on the same street, and when her way was blocked by the owner she gained

---

[76] Offences Against the Person Act 1861, s20.
[77] See **Chapter 14.5**.
[78] Discussed in *Hatton* [2005] EWCA Crim 2951.
[79] Criminal Damage Act 1971, s5(2).
[80] Williams, 'Two Nocturnal Blunders' (1990) 140 NLJ 1564.

access by breaking windows. D was charged with criminal damage, and raised the defence that she believed (at the time) that the house belonged to X, and he would have consented to the damage if he had known the circumstances.

- Magistrates' court: guilty of criminal damage. D may not rely on an intoxicated mistake.
- Divisional Court: appeal allowed. D may use the defence, even if her belief is based on an intoxicated mistake.

This decision is anomalous, and cannot be reconciled with the general rule discussed previously. As a result, although not yet fully reversed, the precedent in *Jaggard* has been limited by subsequent cases. In *Maghee*,[81] for example, D attempted to rely on the rule from *Jaggard* to appeal a conviction for failing to stop after an accident:[82] D claimed his intoxicated state meant he did not realise there had been a collision. The Divisional Court dismissed Maghee's appeal, questioning the continued validity of *Jaggard*, and ruling that D could not rely on his intoxicated mistake.

 Assessment matters . . .

If something similar to *Jaggard v Dickinson* were to arise in problem facts, it is important to remember that this case remains authoritative. However, it would be correct to stress the criticism of this case as anomalous and, following *Magee*, that it is unlikely to be applied outside criminal damage.

In these examples, we are considering defences that apply to D's (intoxicated) conduct at T2. However, where fault is spread across T1–T2, it is useful to recognise that D may also seek to rely on a defence in relation to her T1 conduct when becoming intoxicated. Perhaps the most obvious example would be D who is threatened into taking dangerous drugs at T1 in circumstances of duress.[83] A defence of this kind would undermine D's liability.[84]

13.3 Sane automatism

The 'defence' of sane automatism,[85] as it is commonly referred to, is structured in broadly the same way as the intoxication rules.[86] Where D raises sane automatism, she is making the claim that some external factor affected her body at T1 and caused her to lack voluntariness at T2. For example, 'I drove dangerously, but only because I had just been struck by a flying object'; 'I omitted to feed my child because I was knocked unconscious';

---

[81] [2014] EWHC 4089 (Admin).

[82] Road Traffic Act 1988, s170(4).

[83] We discuss duress in **Chapter 14.3–14.4**.

[84] As we discussed at **13.2.2.1**, cases of this kind may be alternatively analysed as 'involuntary' intoxication. However, the use of 'involuntary' to describe choices made under duress can be misleading (ie D's choice may be extremely unpleasant, but it is still a choice). Rather, we should simply highlight that D has a valid defence as to her conduct at T1.

[85] Law Commission, *Insanity and Automatism* (Discussion Paper, 2013).

[86] Child and Reed, 'Automatism is Never a Defence' (2014) 65 NILQ 167.

'I struck out at the paramedic causing injury because I was suffering the effects of having taken insulin and not having eaten'. As we discussed in the context of mens rea,[87] all criminal offences require voluntary conduct (actions or omission). Thus, D's claim of involuntariness at T2 is a claim that she did not commit an offence, resulting in an unqualified acquittal.

The automatism rules, however, are not simply a shorthand for expressing a lack of voluntary conduct. This is because, even where D successfully denies offending in this way, it is possible for D to be held liable on the basis of her prior-fault in becoming an automaton. As with intoxication, we are again dealing with a two-part set of rules: (i) providing a shorthand for D's denial of offending, and (ii) providing a possible tool of inculpation for the prosecution.

Despite similarities with the intoxication rules, there are three major differences that should be highlighted from the outset. First, the automatism rules will not apply where D's state of automatism is caused by a dangerous drug (as defined within the intoxication rules). Here, only the prior-fault intoxication rules will apply.[88] Secondly, automatism will *only* apply where D loses voluntary control of her conduct. If something external causes D to lack mens rea, but not to lack voluntariness, then the automatism rules will not apply. Thus, automatism arises in far fewer cases than prior-fault intoxication, which applies whenever D's intoxication causes *any* lack of mens rea. Thirdly, as automatism lacks the commonly understood link to violence associated with intoxication, the potential of prior-fault and inculpation is considerably more limited.

13.3.1 Automatism as a denial of offending

Automatism, as a denial of offending, is a shorthand for the claim that D *totally* lacked voluntary control of her conduct at the time of her potential offence, and should therefore be acquitted. Where D acts voluntarily, even if her conduct has been influenced by external factors, automatism will not be found.[89] Just as 'an intoxicated mens rea is still mens rea', so irrational or erratic voluntariness is still voluntariness.[90]

 Extra detail . . .

Although there is a general burden on the prosecution to prove that D completed the elements of the offence charged, there is a legal presumption that a person's movements are voluntary. This creates an evidential burden for D, if she wants to raise automatism, to provide some evidence of involuntariness. After she satisfies this evidential burden, it is then for the prosecution to prove to the criminal standard that her acts were voluntary.[91]

The clearest cases of sane automatism involve D being rendered fully unconscious at T1, as with our dangerous driving example earlier. Where D is fully unconscious, it is clear that she lacks any voluntary control of her body, and so any harm her body causes at T2

---

[87] **Chapter 3.3**.

[88] Mackay, 'Intoxication as a Factor in Automatism' [1982] Crim LR 146.

[89] *AG's Reference (No 4 of 2000)* [2001] Crim LR 578: accidental, but not automatic, conduct.

[90] *Coley* [2013] EWCA Crim 223, [22].

[91] Jones, 'Insanity, Automatism and the Burden of Proof on the Accused' (1995) 111 LQR 475.

cannot be the product of voluntary movement. However, sane automatism is not limited to states of unconsciousness. Indeed, there are several clear examples of conscious automatic behaviour. For example, where X overpowers D and physically manipulates her body to complete certain movements (eg to plunge a knife into V); where D's body spasms uncontrollably (eg causing her to strike V); where D reacts to a sudden noise (eg causing her to drop another's property); where D thrashes her arms about in response to an attack by a swarm of bees (eg causing her to drive dangerously);[92] and so on. In each of these cases, even though D is conscious, she is not in control of her actions. As Lord Denning describes in *Bratty*:

> No act is punishable if it is done involuntarily: and an involuntary act in this context—some people nowadays prefer to speak of it as 'automatism'—means an act which is done by the muscles without any control by the mind, such as a spasm, a reflex action or a convulsion.[93]

Where D's conduct is found to be automatic no liability can result, as illustrated in **Figure 13.7**.

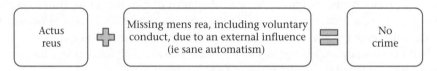

Figure 13.7 Automatism as a denial of offending

Having accepted that conscious behaviour can satisfy automatism, however, the challenge is to identify the line between automatism on the one hand, and non-automatic conduct brought about by external factors on the other.

Automatism, particularly where it arises in driving offences, has been defined very narrowly. This is illustrated in *Broome v Perkins*.

 Broome v Perkins [1987] Crim LR 271

A diabetic (D) failed to take sufficient food after an injection of insulin, and slipped into a hypoglycaemic episode.[94] Whilst in this trance-like state, he drove erratically and collided with another car. D was charged with driving without due care and attention.[95]

• Magistrates' court: not guilty of driving offence due to automatism.

• Divisional Court: appeal allowed. The fact that D was able to coordinate his movements to drive, even though severely impeded, meant that he could not have been in a fully automatic state.

---

[92] Example from *Hill and Baxter* [1958] 1 QB 277, 286.

[93] [1963] AC 386, 409.

[94] Diabetes can lead to involuntariness in two main ways: (a) *hypo*glycaemia—this results from taking insulin (an external cause) and then failing to eat sufficiently; (b) *hyper*glycaemia—this results from failing to take insulin (and so the diabetes acts as an internal cause). As we discuss later, the distinction between these two is vital. This is because although hypoglycaemia causing involuntariness will be treated as a standard form of sane automatism (now under discussion), hyperglycaemia causing involuntariness (because of its internal cause) will be dealt with under the insanity rules.

[95] Road Traffic Act 1988, s3.

This extremely narrow definition of automatism was later confirmed in *AG's Reference (No 2 of 1992)*,[96] where a lorry driver was charged with causing death by reckless driving having suffered a condition known as 'driving without awareness' as a result of long hours on the road.[97] Following D's acquittal on grounds of automatism, the Court of Appeal held that automatism should not have been left to the jury, and that only a 'total destruction of voluntary control' would suffice.

It was once believed that these decisions reflected policy considerations unique to driving offences (ie a reaction to the commonality of people driving when tired or otherwise impaired). This view was supported, to some extent, by non-driving cases such as *Charlson*,[98] where a broader view of automatism seems to have been employed: D's cerebral tumour caused him to act as an 'automaton without any *real knowledge* of what he was doing'.[99] However, a number of more recent cases have reasserted the narrow view of automatism for both driving[100] and non-driving cases.[101] In *Coley*,[102] a non-driving case in which doctors agreed that D would not have been conscious of his movements, the Court of Appeal asserted a particularly restrictive approach:

> [D] was plainly not unconscious, in the sense of comatose. But automatism does not require that, and if it did it would be even more exceptional than it undoubtedly is. On the other hand, his mind may well, if the doctors were right, have been affected by delusions or hallucinations and in that sense his detachment from reality might be described by some as an absence of conscious action. Such condition, however, clearly falls short of involuntary, as distinct from irrational, action. . . . [T]he defendant would, despite their hypothesis of psychotic episode, have been capable of complex organised behaviour. It is plain that a person acting under a delusion may act in such a way, and clearly this defendant did. . . . The doctor said 'He is conscious in a way but it is conscious in the belief that he is a character [in a computer game]. He does not have an awareness of what he is doing.' That is a description of irrational behaviour, with a deluded or disordered mind, but it is not a description of wholly involuntary action.[103]

If automatism is interpreted in line with this statement, it will rarely (if ever) apply outside the context of unconsciousness or physical manipulation.

Coley makes the law easier to apply (ie it creates a clear line between sane automatism and voluntariness), but raises serious questions of fairness. When discussing the voluntariness requirement,[104] we explained the importance of a conscious link between D and the harmful or wrongful events attributed to her; an essential ingredient in the law's respect for individual autonomy. In the circumstances discussed in *Coley*, where D's brain is guiding movement, but that guide is not conscious or rational, it is questionable whether there is a sufficient nexus through which to blame D in criminal law for any

[96] [1994] Crim LR 692.
[97] This would now be causing death by dangerous driving. See **Chapter 6.4.2.**
[98] [1955] 1 All ER 859.
[99] Emphasis added.
[100] *C* [2007] EWCA Crim 1862.
[101] Law Commission, *Insanity and Automatism* (Discussion Paper, 2013) paras 5.24–5.31.
[102] [2013] EWCA Crim 223.
[103] At [23].
[104] **Chapter 3.3.**

harm caused. The current narrow view of sane automatism has therefore attracted considerable academic criticism.[105]

In view of this narrow approach, it will be little surprise that claims of *moral* involuntariness have been consistently rejected as a basis for automatism. We may feel some moral sympathy for D who commits an offence because of an 'irresistible impulse', 'hysterical amnesia', 'hysterical fugue', or where she is unaware of a legal restriction. But D is not treated as acting in an automatic manner in a legal sense.[106] Where D steals alcohol because of an irresistible craving for drink, she still commits theft;[107] where D is provoked to attack V, this is still an assault. These circumstances will be considered as relevant mitigation at sentencing, but they do not affect the liability stage.[108]

It is important to remember, therefore, that not all external impacts effecting D's capacity will give rise to an automatism-based denial of offending. As with many of the cases discussed in this section, where D's conduct is affected by external stimuli but her movements remain voluntary, there is no automatism. This is illustrated in **Figure 13.8**.

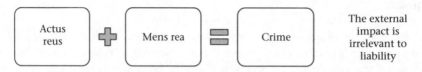

Figure 13.8 External impact not causing automatism

 Extra detail . . .

It is worth noting again that many commentators prefer to describe 'voluntary conduct' as an actus reus element, such that automatism amounts to a denial of actus reus and mens rea. In this book, we prefer to separate conduct (actus reus) from the issue of voluntariness (mens rea), and so automatism does not involve a denial of actus reus. All offences include a voluntariness requirement (including so-called strict or absolute liability offences), and so a denial of voluntariness is a denial of any liability. The different models of analysis do not affect how the law is applied, but should be noted to avoid confusion when reading other sources.

13.3.2 Prior-fault automatism as a method of inculpation

In many cases involving automatism there is no issue of prior-fault. Therefore, automatism, if demonstrated, acts only as a denial of the offence, leading to acquittal. However, where D's automatism at T2 has arisen from blameworthy conduct at T1 (prior-fault), missing offence elements at T2 can be substituted for by this fault, in a similar way to the prior-fault intoxication rules. **Table 13.2** sets out the elements of the prior-fault automatism rules.

---

[105] Horder, 'Pleading Involuntary Lack of Capacity' (1993) 52 CLJ 298; Sullivan, 'Making Excuses' in Simester and Smith (eds), *Harm and Culpability* (1996) 131.

[106] *Isitt* [1978] Crim LR 159.

[107] *Dodd* (1974) 7 SASR 151; Tolmie, 'Alcoholism and Criminal Liability' (2001) 64 MLR 688.

[108] The only exceptions to this are extreme cases which engage defences such as duress (discussed in **Chapter 14**) or loss of control as a partial defence to murder (discussed in **Chapter 6**).

Table 13.2 Prior-fault automatism rules

A) D must have completed the actus reus elements at T2 in a state of automatism;
B) D's automatism must have resulted from D's prior-fault at T1; and
C) D's offence at T2 must have been one of 'basic intent', as opposed to one of 'specific intent'.

 Don't be confused . . .

As with the prior-fault intoxication rules, the inculpatory work of the automatism rules is most commonly described by courts and commentators as a defence (**13.1.1**). For example, in *Coley*,[109] Hughes LJ states that 'the defence of automatism is not available to a defendant who has induced an acute state of involuntary behaviour by his own fault'. We avoid this terminology because it is misleading: saying that D cannot raise the issue of automatism does not make her conduct voluntary or mean that she had mens rea. Rather, the prior-fault automatism rules are replacing a lack of voluntariness and other mens rea with (what the law considers) equivalent prior-fault. The rules are not denying a defence, they are constructing a crime.[110]

13.3.2.1 Element 1: D was in a state of automatism at T2

We discussed this requirement at **13.3.1**. It is important to remember that for the prior-fault automatism rules to apply, D must be in a state of automatism when completing the actus reus of the offence at T2. The narrow conception of automatism within the current law also therefore narrows the potential for prior-fault to inculpate and render D liable for the crime.

13.3.2.2 Element 2: D acted with prior-fault at T1

For the prior-fault intoxication rules, the issue of prior-fault at T1 (ie when becoming intoxicated) was relatively straightforward to establish because of the commonly understood link between intoxication and certain crimes. Thus, where D voluntarily becomes intoxicated with a dangerous drug (one commonly known to create states of unpredictability), we may attribute prior-fault. For automatism, in contrast, there is no equivalent common understanding (and no link in fact) between a lack of voluntariness and the causing of criminal harms.[111] Therefore, more must be required at T1 to establish sufficient prior-fault that might later substitute for missing offence elements.[112]

The law in this area, however, is unfortunately vague and inconsistent. On one hand, cases such as *Bailey*[113] suggest that D will only have sufficient prior-fault where she has

---

[109] [2013] EWCA Crim 223, [24].
[110] Child and Reed, 'Automatism is Never a Defence' (2014) 65 NILQ 167.
[111] *Bailey* [1983] 2 All ER 503, 764–765. For academic discussion of this, see Horder, 'Sobering Up? The Law Commission on Criminal Intoxication' (1995) 58 MLR 534, 544–555.
[112] Law Commission, *Insanity and Automatism* (Discussion Paper, 2013) Ch6.
[113] [1983] 2 All ER 503.

subjectively foreseen at T1 the potential for involuntariness at T2. This would be the case, for example, where D decides to drive foreseeing the chance of an (insulin-induced) hypoglycaemic episode, and foreseeing the chance that this might lead to unconsciousness whilst at the wheel. This approach is endorsed by the Law Commission,[114] and seems to be the most appropriate if D's fault is going to be used to construct liability at T2.[115] On the other hand, however, cases such as *Quick*[116] state that D will have sufficient fault if she *objectively* should have foreseen such risks. Thus, where D is negligent in the management of her diabetes before driving (eg fails to eat sufficiently after a dose of insulin), then this negligence will constitute sufficient prior-fault even where she does not subjectively foresee the risk of hypoglycaemia herself. The Australian case of *Ryan*[117] provides a further example of the objective approach. In this case, D pointed a loaded shotgun at V (whom he had robbed) with one hand, whilst attempting to tie him up with the other. V moved, startled D, and D (according to his account) involuntarily pulled the trigger as a reflex. On Windeyer J's view, D remained liable because of the obvious danger created by his actions at T1, even if D did not subjectively foresee the risk of the involuntary reflex which followed.

 Assessment matters . . .

Where there is inconsistent case law of this kind, you need to take particular care when applying it to problem facts. Do not just choose certain cases and ignore others. Rather, where D subjectively foresees a risk of involuntariness in dangerous circumstances then you can be sure that this is sufficient prior-fault. Where D does not foresee the risk, but was potentially negligent in not doing so, you should highlight cases such as *Quick* and *Ryan* that suggest that this too might be sufficient; but also, ideally, note the academic criticism.

13.3.2.3 Element 3: D is charged with a basic intent offence

Having established prior-fault from D at T1 (when losing voluntary control), our next question is to consider whether the law is prepared to treat that prior-fault as sufficient to replace or substitute for the missing elements of the offence at T2 (when D commits the potential offence). Clearly, D's prior-fault at T1 must be capable of replacing a lack of voluntary conduct at T2: as all cases of automatism include a lack of voluntariness, the ability to substitute for this missing element is essential for automatism to perform any inculpatory role at all. This has been consistently confirmed in all the case law involving prior-fault and automatism.[118]

But what about other mens rea elements beyond voluntary conduct? Where D is effectively or in fact unconscious, she is unlikely to possess any mens rea as to any aspect of

---

[114] Law Commission, *Insanity and Automatism* (Discussion Paper, 2013) paras 6.12–6.28.
[115] Rumbold and Wasik, 'Diabetic Drivers, Hypoglycaemic Unawareness and Automatism' [2011] Crim LR 863.
[116] [1973] QB 910.
[117] (1967) 40 ALJR 488; Elliott, 'Responsibility for Involuntary Acts: *Ryan v The Queen*' (1968) 41 ALJ 497.
[118] Although, as we noted at **13.3.2** ('Don't be confused . . .'), the phenomenon will generally be described as the denial of a defence.

the harm she causes at T2. If the automatism rules are *only* able to substitute prior-fault at T1 for a lack of voluntary conduct at T2, and not these other mens rea elements, then they could only produce liability in the context of strict/absolute liability offences (ie offences that require no mens rea beyond voluntariness). But we know from the case law that prior-fault is used as a substitute for liability for offences beyond this, most commonly for driving offences that often require mens rea as to the dangerous circumstances of D's driving.

Perhaps the most obvious question, in view of the prior-fault intoxication rules (**13.2.3**), is whether prior-fault automatism also makes a distinction between basic and specific intent offences (ie that D's prior-fault can replace a lack of mens rea for a basic intent offence but not for a specific intent offence). The early case law on prior-fault and automatism did not recognise a basic/specific intent distinction; implying a very broad potential for the substitution of missing mens rea elements.[119] However, this position was later clarified, to some extent, in *Bailey*:[120] a case involving the specific intent offence of wounding or causing GBH with intent.[121] The court highlighted that *Quick* should not be interpreted to allow prior-fault automatism to substitute for missing mens rea elements in crimes of specific intent. Unfortunately, following this useful clarification, the court then went further to cast doubt on its ability to substitute for similar elements in crimes of basic intent as well.

> In our judgment, self-induced automatism, other than that due to intoxication from alcohol or drugs, may provide a defence to crimes of basic intent. The question in each case will be whether the prosecution have proved the necessary element of recklessness. In cases of assault, if the accused knows that his actions or inaction are likely to make him aggressive, unpredictable or uncontrolled with the result that he may cause some injury to others and he persists in the action or takes no remedial action when he knows it is required, it will be open to the jury to find that he was reckless.[122]

In view of this confused position, it is likely (and hoped) that the courts will take a lead from the Law Commission Discussion Paper on automatism and insanity.[123] For the Commission, despite reservations as to the specific/basic intent distinction, there is useful recognition that prior-fault for automatism should be consistent with prior-fault for intoxication. Thus, contrary to *Bailey*, prior-fault at T1 leading to automatism when causing harms at T2 *should* result in liability for basic intent offences, but should *not* result in liability for specific intent offences.[124] This is illustrated in **Figure 13.9**.

---

[119] *Quick* [1972] QB 910: 'A self-induced incapacity will not excuse . . . nor will one which could have been reasonably foreseen as a result of either doing, or omitting to do something, as, for example, taking alcohol against medical advice after using certain prescribed drugs, or failing to have regular meals while taking insulin' (at 922). Criticised in Mackay, 'Intoxication as a Factor in Automatism' [1982] Crim LR 146.

[120] [1983] 2 All ER 503.

[121] Offences Against the Person Act 1861, s18. See **Chapter 7.6**.

[122] *Bailey* [1983] 1 WLR 760, 765 (Griffiths LJ).

[123] Law Commission, *Insanity and Automatism* (Discussion Paper, 2013).

[124] Ibid. This is the necessary implication from the flowchart at p 95, and para 6.77.

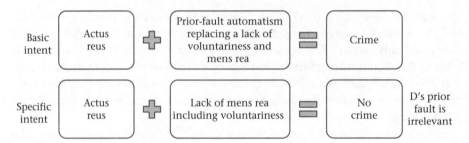

Figure 13.9 Prior-fault automatism

13.3.3 Automatism and defences

In cases where D successfully raises automatism in the absence of prior-fault, she has not committed an offence, and so there is no need to consider potential defences. However, where she does so in circumstances of prior-fault, and the offence is one of basic intent, the prior-fault automatism rules will create liability. Thus, in this latter case, it will become necessary to consider potential defences.

As with our analysis of prior-fault intoxication, it is useful to distinguish defences as they potentially apply at T1 and T2:

A) **Defences applying at T2:** D's involuntariness at T2 is incompatible with the elements of criminal defences discussed in **Chapter 14**.

B) **Defences applying at T1:** Although cases of this kind will be rare, it is possible for defences to apply to D's conduct at T1. For example, where D was subjected to threats to force her to drive in circumstances of duress even though she foresaw the chance of losing consciousness. In such circumstances, D's defence will undermine any finding of prior-fault, and thereby undermine liability at T2.

13.4 Insanity

The final category of denial of offences discussed in this chapter relates to the rules of insanity.[125] This will arise where D claims not to have fulfilled all the elements of the offence because of some malfunctioning of her body—an *internal* factor (eg where D's insane delusions prevent her from appreciating that the thing she is stabbing is a person). Insanity as a denial of offending should be distinguished from two related areas, discussed elsewhere in this book:

• **Unfitness to plead:** This arises where D is mentally and/or physically unfit to stand trial because she is unable to participate effectively in it, discussed in **Chapter 1.5.3**.

Unfitness to plead and insanity focus on two distinct points in the criminal process. Unfitness is focussed on D's mental or physical capacity at trial, whereas insanity is focussed on D's mental capacity when completing the actus reus of the offence charged.

[125] Law Commission, *Insanity and Automatism* (Discussion Paper, 2013).

- **Insanity as a defence:** This arises where D *has* completed the actus reus and mens rea of an offence, and claims she was insane at the time, thereby avoiding liability, discussed in **Chapter 14.2**.

Uniquely, the insanity rules can apply *both* as a denial of offending (the focus here) and alternatively as a defence properly so called. Where D's insanity when completing the actus reus of the crime explains her lack of mens rea (potentially, but not necessarily, including a lack of voluntariness) then insanity is raised as a denial of offending. However, even where D's insanity does not undermine her mens rea, so she completes all elements of the offence charged, insanity may still be raised as an independent defence. The separate roles for insanity have caused confusion in previous case law,[126] but remain essential for the proper application of the law.[127]

> ### Extra detail . . .
>
> Insanity as a defence, and insanity as a denial of offending, are often discussed together because the same rules apply to the application of insanity in either context. We separate them here (between **Chapters 13** and **14**), not to suggest that different rules apply, but to reflect the different role played by the insanity rules in the two different contexts.

Whether insanity is raised as a denial of offending or as a defence, care must be taken to identify the correct burden and standard of proof required. Just as the law presumes that D is sober and in control of her conduct, so the law also presumes that D is sane. Indeed, the presumption of sanity is much stronger. Presumptions of sobriety and voluntariness only create evidential burdens on D, whereas the presumption of sanity creates a legal burden such that D must prove (on the balance of probabilities) that she was insane at the time of the offence.[128] This is extremely controversial, and the Law Commission has considered a reverse evidential burden for insanity instead.[129] Where D raises insanity to deny offending, it is one thing to require evidence to rebut a presumption of common behaviour, but quite another to ask D to prove her innocence![130] But this is what the current law requires.

13.4.1 The special verdict of 'not guilty by reason of insanity'

Uniquely, where D satisfies the insanity rules, either as a defence or denial of offending, she will not receive an unqualified acquittal. Rather, a special verdict applies of 'not guilty by reason of insanity'.[131] The special verdict is a technical acquittal which still allows the court to impose a range of disposal orders.

---

[126] It was held in *DPP v Harper* [1998] RTR 200 that the insanity rules do not apply to strict liability offences, the court reasoning that insanity amounted to a denial of mens rea and strict liability offences do not require mens rea. However, commentators agree that this decision must be wrong. First, insanity can also involve a denial of voluntary movement, which is required for strict liability offences and, secondly, because (as we discuss in **Chapter 14**) insanity can act as a defence as well as a simple denial of offending.

[127] Discussed in *Loake v CPS* [2017] EWHC 2855 (Admin).

[128] *M'Naghten* (1843) 10 Cl & Fin 200, 210, confirmed in *Bratty* [1963] AC 386.

[129] Law Commission, *Insanity and Automatism* (Discussion Paper, 2013) para 4.163.

[130] Jones, 'Insanity, Automatism, and the Burden of Proof on the Accused' (1995) 111 LQR 475.

[131] Trial of Lunatics Act 1883, s2.

Point to remember ...

Although disposal orders can be compulsory, this is not a matter of sentencing. D has been acquitted, and so the terminology of 'disposal' is important.

Before 1991, those found not guilty by reason of insanity (as well as those unfit to plead) had to be ordered to be detained indefinitely in a hospital. Fortunately, with the exception of cases involving murder,[132] this is no longer the case. Disposal is now governed by section 5 of the Criminal Procedure (Insanity and Unfitness to Plead) Act 1991.[133] Under this Act, the judge is provided with three disposal options:

(a) a hospital order (with or without a restriction order);

(b) a supervision order; and

(c) an order for an absolute discharge.

Although these disposal orders are not criminal punishments, the potential for a compulsory order still marks out insanity from other denials of offending and defences that result in unqualified acquittal. Indeed, the inculpatory status of the special verdict is acknowledged by the fact that D (uniquely) can appeal if found not guilty on this basis.[134]

The rationale of the insanity rules, including the special verdict, is that where D lacks responsibility as a result of insanity as opposed to an external influence (eg concussion caused by a blow to the head), D's condition is more likely to reoccur and so the special verdict is required to ensure that the public are protected.[135] How effectively the current insanity rules achieve this rationale is criticised, and considered further in our reform discussion at **13.6.3.**

Extra detail ...

Faced with the uncertain outcome of the special verdict, as well as the stigma of the insanity label,[136] defendants will generally attempt to deny liability without engaging the insanity rules. Rather, it is the judge's role to identify whether the 'defence' D proposes to advance at trial will be left to the jury as one of insanity.[137] Where this is the case, the judge will then inform D, who will choose whether to proceed with a claim of insanity or to change her plea to guilty. As a result, despite some progress being made through the rationalisation of disposal orders, the insanity plea remains underused in the courts.[138]

---

[132] In this case, a fixed hospital order is mandated: Criminal Procedure Act 1991, s5(3).

[133] As amended by the Domestic Violence, Crime and Victims Act 2004.

[134] Criminal Appeals Act 1968, s12.

[135] *Sullivan* [1984] AC 156, 172.

[136] Insanity can be a stigmatising term for those with severe mental conditions but, as will be clear from *Sullivan* (and expanded later), the insanity rules apply well beyond those within this group. When so much progress has been made regarding public attitudes to mental illness more generally, it is staggering that the criminal law retains a label of this kind. The Law Commission has considered whether the special verdict should be amended, holding D 'not criminally responsible by reason of a recognised medical condition' (*Insanity and Automatism* (Discussion Paper, 2013) para 10.15.). The sooner the law is amended in these terms, the better.

[137] *Roach* [2001] EWCA Crim 2698.

[138] Mackay and Kearns, 'The Continued Under Use of Unfitness to Plead and the Insanity Defence' [1994] Crim LR 546; Mackay, Mitchell, and Howe, 'Yet More Facts About the Insanity Defence' [2006] Crim LR 399.

13.4.2 Insanity as a denial of offending

The rationale of the insanity rules, as a denial of mens rea, is essentially forward-looking: D has not committed an offence, and this must be acknowledged with an acquittal, but D has revealed herself as someone who could pose a danger to the public in the future and so may warrant compulsory treatment and/or supervision. Despite some unease about the compulsory treatment of those who have not committed an offence, most commentators accept the public need for a set of rules of this kind.[139] For example, in *Bratty*,[140] D removed a girl's stockings and strangled her with them, in circumstances where (according to medical evidence) his psychomotor epilepsy could have prevented him understanding his actions. Were this to have been the case, D might have been acquitted, but it is surely right that the courts are empowered to put compulsory measures in place to protect others in the future.

The devil, of course, is in the detail; whilst compulsory treatment may be acceptable under certain conditions, those conditions involve the complex weighing of legal and medical priorities, and will inevitably shift alongside medical advancement. Unfortunately, the criminal law has not created a dynamic set of rules capable of balancing these priorities and shifting in line with medical progress. Rather, the insanity rules remain products of the common law, and remain principally based on a set of Law Lords' opinions from 1843.

The current law of insanity was set out in relation to *M'Naghten*. This case involved insanity as a defence (ie D had committed an offence), but the same rules apply where D uses insanity to deny offending.

M'Naghten (1843) 10 Cl & Fin 200

D attempted to murder Sir Robert Peel, who was then Home Secretary, and killed Edward Drummond (Peel's secretary) by mistake. D was charged with murder.

• Crown Court: not guilty of murder by reason of insanity. D was suffering from morbid delusions about the Conservative Party.

M'Naghten's acquittal provoked controversy. It was debated in the legislative chamber of the House of Lords, where the Law Lords were asked questions on the insanity rules.[141] It was the answers given to those questions, and not the case itself, which provide the basis for the modern law on insanity. The '*M'Naghten* Rules', as they have come to be known, were given binding authority by their endorsement in *Sullivan*, a case involving insanity as a denial of offending.

Sullivan [1984] 1 AC 156

Whilst visiting an 80-year-old friend (V), D had an epileptic seizure during which he kicked V in the head and caused GBH. D was charged with GBH offences.[142]

---

[139] For a contrary view, see Slobogin, 'An End to Insanity: Recasting the Role of Mental Illness in Criminal Cases' (2000) 86 Vir LR 1199.

[140] [1963] AC 386.

[141] (1843) 4 St Tr NS 847. See on the history of this Mackay, 'The M'Naghten Rules—A Brief Historical Note' [2019] Crim LR 966.

[142] Offences Against the Person Act 1861, s18 and s20. See **Chapter 7.5** and **7.6**.

- Crown Court: guilty of ABH offence.[143] D attempted to rely on automatism, but the court ruled that his condition amounted to insanity. On this basis, to avoid the insanity rules, D pleaded guilty to ABH.
- Court of Appeal: conviction upheld on appeal.
- House of Lords: appeal dismissed.[144]

The *M'Naghten* Rules, crucially, are not based on a medical definition of insanity. Rather, they provide a set of legal rules to determine if D will be caught within a legal definition of insanity, and directed towards the special verdict. These rules are set out in **Table 13.3.**

Table 13.3 The *M'Naghten* Rules

A) D must suffer from a disease of the mind;
B) This must have caused a defect of reason; and
C) This must have caused a lack of responsibility, *either* because D did not know the nature or quality of her act, *or* she did not know it was wrong

13.4.2.1 Element 1: disease of the mind

The first requirement, that D must have been suffering from a disease of the mind, sounds very much like a medical question. However, although medical experts will be required to provide evidence,[145] the definition they are asked to apply ('a disease of the mind') is a legal one. This is illustrated in *Kemp*.

 Kemp [1957] 1 QB 399

D made a motiveless and irrational attack upon his wife with a hammer, causing GBH. D was suffering from arteriosclerosis, a condition which caused a congestion of blood in his brain and caused him to lapse into unconsciousness at the time of the attack. D was charged with a GBH offence.

- Court of Assizes: not guilty by reason of insanity. The fact that D's condition was physical rather than mental does not prevent the insanity rules applying.

---

[143] Offences Against the Person Act 1861, s47. See **Chapter 7.4.**

[144] *Sullivan* is unfortunately a typical application of a set of rules which, as we will see, are not fit for purpose. A seemingly blameless man would rather plead guilty than be treated under a set of rules designed to acknowledge and protect those not deserving of blame.

[145] Criminal Procedure (Insanity and Unfitness to Plead) Act 1991, s1. This section prevents a jury returning a verdict of not guilty by reason of insanity except on the evidence of two or more registered medical practitioners, of whom at least one must be approved as having special expertise in the field of mental disorder.

Later confirmed in *Sullivan*, *Kemp* provides important clarification that D may be suffering from a disease of the mind (in legal terms) even where there is no degeneration of brain cells. As Devlin J stated:

> In my judgment the condition of the brain is irrelevant and so is the question of whether the condition of the mind is curable or incurable, transitory or permanent. There is no warranty for introducing those considerations into the definition in the *M'Naghten* Rules. Temporary insanity is sufficient to satisfy them. It does not matter whether it is incurable and permanent or not.[146]

Moving away from a medical understanding of mental illness, the legal definition of 'disease of the mind' is rather more concerned with marking the distinction between insanity (leading to the special verdict) and sane automatism or simple lack of mens rea (leading to an acquittal in the absence of prior-fault). In doing so, the law focusses on a single criterion: does D's involuntariness (and/or lack of other mens rea) stem from an internal bodily condition or from an external factor. Where D's condition is internally caused, whatever its medical classification, it will be deemed a disease of the mind for the purposes of the insanity rules.

Although most insanity cases will involve medically recognised mental illnesses (eg schizophrenia being the most common[147]), the central role of the internal/external test has led to a number of unfortunate, and largely indefensible, classifications. Perhaps the most striking of these has arisen in relation to diabetes, where a diabetic coma, and associated involuntariness, can be brought on *internally* by a lack of treatment with insulin (hyperglycaemia), or *externally* by treatment with insulin followed by an insufficient intake of food (hypoglycaemia). The origins of these conditions and their impact upon D are almost identical, but they sit either side of the internal/external divide.[148] This was discussed in *Quick*.

    Quick [1973] QB 910

D, a nurse in a mental hospital, attacked a paraplegic patient causing ABH. D called evidence that he was diabetic and, at the time of the attack, was suffering from hypoglycaemia caused by a lack of food after insulin. D was told that this would amount to a claim of insanity, and so he changed his plea to guilty.

- Crown Court: guilty of assault occasioning ABH.[149]
- Court of Appeal: appeal allowed. D's hypoglycaemia was externally caused, and so he should have been allowed to raise automatism rather than insanity.

Quick can be contrasted with *Hennessy*,[150] where D also raised automatism on the basis of a diabetic coma. However, in *Hennessy* D's coma was induced by a lack of insulin. The ruling, therefore, was that automatism was unavailable because D's condition was internally caused: D could rely on the insanity rules, or (as he did) change his plea to guilty.

---

146 At 407.
147 Mackay, Mitchell, and Howe, 'Yet More Facts About the Insanity Defence' [2006] Crim LR 399.
148 Rumbold, 'Diabetes and Criminal Responsibility' (2010) 174 CL&JW 21.
149 Offences Against the Person Act 1861, s47.
150 (1989) 89 Cr App R 10.

Beyond diabetes, several other conditions have also been (perhaps inappropriately) caught within the insanity rules. Individuals treated in criminal law as insane include epileptics,[151] pre-menstrual syndrome sufferers,[152] sleepwalkers,[153] and so on. These examples are problematic for the simple reason that the term 'insanity' is so obviously inappropriate both medically as well as to the ordinary citizen. But they can also be problematic for a test which seeks a neat, or at least consistent, divide between internal and external causes. In the context of sleepwalking, for example, which has attracted particular attention,[154] it is not always obvious that the cause is purely internal. D's sleep-walking may arise from the external influence of hypnosis or, more trivially, it may be triggered from disturbed sleep or from eating certain foods before sleeping.[155]

Another example of uncertain classification arises in so-called psychological blow cases, where D tries to explain an internal loss of faculties on the basis of a psychologically traumatic event. D's aim here is to characterise the psychological trauma as an external cause, leading to an unqualified acquittal under the automatism rules, and avoiding insanity. One of the first cases where this line of argument was attempted was the Canadian case of *Rabey*.[156] D, a student who became infatuated with a girl (V), discovered that she was not interested in him, and reacted by hitting her on the head with a rock that he had taken from the geology laboratory. D was initially acquitted on the basis of automatism, the court accepting that the psychological blow of rejection had caused him to experience a dissociative state. However, not surprisingly, the prosecution's appeal was later accepted, with the Canadian Supreme Court clarifying that 'the common stresses and disappointments of life which are the common lot of all mankind do not constitute an external cause'.[157] The dissociative state it seems, if accepted, should have constituted evidence of insanity. A more difficult case is *T*.

 T [1990] Crim LR 256

A young woman (D) took part in a violent robbery with two others. She was charged with robbery. It emerged that D had been raped at some point prior to the robbery taking place, and the issue of automatism was raised by the defence: that D was acting in a dissociative state (akin to sleepwalking) as a result of the rape.

• Crown Court: guilty of robbery. Crucially, the court found that the case gave rise to the potential for automatism rather than insanity, and thus accepted the psychological blow as an external cause. However, the jury did not accept that D's conduct was fully involuntary.

This case is useful for two main reasons. First, it demonstrates that psychological blows stemming from extreme circumstances can ground a claim of automatism rather than insanity. But, secondly, it also provides a reminder of how narrowly the law has

---

[151] *Sullivan* [1984] AC 156; Mackay and Reuber, 'Epilepsy and the Defence of Insanity—Time for a Change' [2007] Crim LR 782.

[152] *Smith* [1982] Crim LR 531; Edwards, 'Mad, Bad or Pre-Menstrual' (1988) 138 NLJ 456.

[153] *Burgess* [1991] 2 All ER 769; Mackay, 'The Sleepwalker is Not Insane' (1992) 55 MLR 714.

[154] Wilson et al, 'Violence, Sleepwalking and the Criminal Law' [2005] Crim LR 601 and 614; Mackay and Mitchell, 'Sleepwalking, Automatism and Insanity' [2006] Crim LR 901.

[155] Law Commission, *Insanity and Automatism* (Discussion Paper, 2013) para 1.44.

[156] (1977) 37 CCC 461.

[157] (1980) 54 CCC at 7.

interpreted involuntariness in the context of automatism, making this route very difficult in practice.[158]

Finally, not only can the current internal/external test be criticised for leading to inappropriate labelling and uncertainty, but its practical application is also out of line with its rationale of public protection. The fact that D's condition arises from an internal malfunctioning does not necessarily make her more likely to be dangerous in the future. This is clear, for example, if we compare D1 who suffers an *internal* congestion of blood to the brain that can be treated to prevent reoccurrence, with D2 who suffers an *external* blow to the head that causes permanent brain injury. It is also clear when we compare states of hyper- and hypoglycaemia, conditions sharply distinguished in law, yet conditions which affect D in largely identical ways.

These criticisms of the law are well acknowledged. Indeed, research has shown the Crown Courts will often ignore the detail of the rules where they lead to clear unfairness, and have been willing to apply a more common-sense approach (eg allowing automatism to run in sleepwalking cases).[159]

Assessment matters . . .

Where problem facts involve D causing harm whilst sleepwalking, for example, it is important to follow the established authorities: D's state is internally caused, and thus gives rise to the insanity rules. Acknowledging that the law 'in practice' will often see courts allowing automatism to be run will be an impressive addition to your answer, but should be a secondary point.

13.4.2.2 Element 2: causing a defect of reason

Having established that D's denial of offending is based on an internal cause (a disease of the mind), ruling out the potential application of intoxication and/or sane automatism, our next question is whether D was thereby caused to have a defect of reason. This stage is important. If D's defect of mind caused her to behave absent-mindedly, so she had the ability to reason but did not do so, or simply contributed to an attitude where she chose not think about the dangerous nature of her conduct, then the insanity rules will not apply. The leading case here is *Clarke*.

Clarke [1972] 1 All ER 219

D took articles from a supermarket without paying for them. Evidence was raised that she did so absent-mindedly, partly as a result of mild depression. D was charged with theft. When told that her denial amounted to a plea of insanity, D changed her plea to guilty.

• Crown Court: guilty of theft.

• Court of Appeal: appeal allowed. D's condition did not prevent her being able to reason, and so the insanity rules were not satisfied. D was simply denying mens rea.

---

[158] Horder, 'Pleading Involuntary Lack of Capacity' (1993) 53 CLJ 298, 313–315.

[159] *Lowe* (2005, unreported) and *Pooley* (2007, unreported); Mackay and Mitchell, 'Sleepwalking, Automatism and Insanity' [2006] Crim LR 901.

Clarke was attempting to claim a simple lack of mens rea, which would have resulted in an unqualified acquittal. However, in relying on her depression to explain this lack of mens rea, the insanity rules were engaged.

 Extra detail . . .

Where (as in *Clarke*) D is denying mens rea, her legal representatives will want to avoid the insanity rules. This is because insanity would direct D to the uncertain outcome of the special verdict and, if insanity does not apply, D will be acquitted on the simple basis of lack of mens rea. In contrast, where D accepts that she completed the offence elements and raises insanity as a defence,[160] her default position if the insanity rules do not apply will be that she is liable. Therefore, D is much more likely to want the insanity rules to apply. Remember the insanity rules can operate as both a denial of mens rea or as a defence; context is everything.

13.4.2.3 Element 3: causing a lack of responsibility

The final step in applying the insanity rules requires D's defect of mind to have caused D to lack responsibility for the harms caused, *either* because she did not understand the nature or quality of what she was doing (a denial of mens rea) *or* because she did not know it was wrong (a defence). Our focus in this chapter is the former, but both will be discussed.

The insanity rules will not apply in situations other than these two alternatives. Thus, for example, where D commits an offence as a result of an 'irresistible impulse', if she understands what she is doing and that it is wrong, she will not satisfy the insanity rules. This was considered in *Kopsch*,[161] where D admitted killing his uncle's wife, but evidence was raised that he was acting under the uncontrollable direction of his subconscious mind. The court held that such evidence provided no basis for a denial of criminal responsibility. An irresistible impulse will only be relevant to the insanity rules where it causes D to lack understanding of her actions, or not to know they are wrong.[162]

D does not know the nature or quality of her act

In modern language, this is a claim that D 'did not know what he was doing'.[163] It is a reference to the physical nature of D's conduct, and will not include lesser states of inadvertence (eg to the moral or legal quality of the conduct).[164] It will clearly apply where D is unconscious, but will also include cases where D is acting under a delusion. Oft-repeated examples include where D kills V under the insane delusion that she is breaking a jar,[165] or cuts V's throat believing it is a loaf of bread.[166] However, cases outside clear

---

[160] Discussed in **Chapter 14.2**.

[161] (1925) 19 Cr App R 50.

[162] *AG for South Australia v Brown* [1960] AC 432.

[163] *Sullivan* [1983] 2 All ER 673, 678. See Mackay, '"Nature", "Quality" and Mens Rea—Some Observations on "Defect of Reason" and the First Limb of the M'Naghten Rules' [2020] Crim LR 588.

[164] *Codere* (1916) 12 Cr App R 219; Mackay, 'Some Observations on the Second Limb of the M'Naghten Rules' [2009] Crim LR 80.

[165] Stephen, *A Digest of the Criminal Law* (8th edn, 1947) 6.

[166] Kenny, *Outlines of Criminal Law* (2007) 76.

examples of this kind will be more testing. For example, in the case of B,[167] a paranoid schizophrenic defendant had sex with his wife, without her consent, believing that he had sexual-healing powers. D was rightly convicted of rape on the facts, but interestingly for present purposes, the Court of Appeal also considered what would have happened if D's condition had led him to believe that V was consenting. The court said that nothing would change. But surely this would be an example of D not knowing the nature or quality of his act, consensual intercourse being categorically different from non-consensual intercourse.

In cases where D does not know the nature or quality of her act, the rejection of the insanity rules will generally lead to D's unqualified acquittal: not understanding the nature or quality of one's act is to deny mens rea. With the public's protection in mind, it will be interesting to see if a case with the amended facts of B postulated by the court would end, as the Court of Appeal suggest, outside these rules.[168]

D does not know that her act is wrong

Even where D *does* understand the nature and quality of her conduct, conduct outside rules will still apply if her defect of reason caused her not to know that what she was doing was wrong. This limb of the insanity rules will usually arise where D has committed an offence (both actus reus and mens rea), and raises insanity as a defence. Insanity as a defence, as opposed to a denial of offending, is discussed in **Chapter 14.2**. However, it is useful to provide an overview here.

Crucially, and controversially, D will only satisfy this limb of the insanity rules where she is caused not to know the *legal* wrongfulness of her acts. Where her condition causes her to believe her actions are morally right, but she still understands that they are criminal, she will not come within the insanity rules. This was established in *Windle*.

Windle [1952] 2 QB 826

D's wife was mentally ill, and often spoke to him of suicide. D, described as 'weak willed', became obsessed with this idea. Having discussed it repeatedly with his workmates, one suggested that D should give her a dozen aspirin. D gave his wife 100 aspirin tablets, which she took, and died. Reporting her death, D told the police 'I suppose they will hang me for this'. D was charged with murder.

- Crown Court: guilty of murder. The defence of insanity was withdrawn from the jury because, although there was medical evidence of a defect of mind, it was agreed that D knew that what he did was legally wrong.
- Court of Criminal Appeal: conviction upheld on appeal.

The position in *Windle* has been confirmed in *Johnson*,[169] and so its narrow interpretation continues to apply.[170]

---

[167] [2013] EWCA Crim 3.
[168] Child and Sullivan, 'When Does the Insanity Defence Apply? Some Recent Cases' [2014] Crim LR 787.
[169] [2007] EWCA Crim 1978.
[170] See Manwaring, '*Windle* Revisited' [2018] Crim LR 984.

Criticism of *Windle*, however, has been telling. Bearing in mind that the special verdict still allows for compulsory treatment and therefore restraint, it is difficult to see why a defendant such as Windle should be denied a defence which would recognise his lack of meaningful choice in offending. Other common law jurisdictions, notably Australia,[171] have refused to follow *Windle* in their application of the insanity rules. Indeed, even within this jurisdiction, it seems that the lower courts will often apply the wrongfulness limb without distinction between D's legal and moral awareness.[172]

 Assessment matters . . .

As with other areas, the potential inconsistency here between appellate court authority and the 'law in practice' in lower courts needs to be handled with care. When applying the law to problem facts, always begin by applying the binding authority, which in this context is *Windle*. However, where D is unable to appreciate the moral wrongfulness of her acts, but knows that they are against the law, it is good practice to mention that although *Windle* suggests that the insanity rules will not apply, Mackay et al have found that they are often applied in practice.

13.4.3 Prior-fault insanity as a method of inculpation?

Unlike prior-fault intoxication and prior-fault automatism, the courts have chosen not to explore the reasons for D's insanity as they arose at T1 as a route to liability via doctrines of prior-fault.[173] Such analysis would be possible, and (in some cases at least) the case for liability can be compelling. For example, D intentionally fails to take anti-psychotic medication knowing that this will result in uncontrolled behaviour, and as a consequence D causes serious harm to V. In this case, in line with prior-fault intoxication and prior-fault automatism, although D may lack essential mens rea for an offence against the person at T2, we may want to use her prior-fault in choosing not to take her medication to substitute for her lack of mens rea, constructing liability.[174]

The case for prior-fault insanity rules is perhaps weaker than for intoxication and automatism because the special verdict already allows for compulsory treatment without needing to establish fault. Additionally, there is a risk that prior-fault insanity could lead courts into problematic areas of analysis, such as identifying and weighing the causes of a mental condition that may have affected D for many years. However, in more straightforward cases such as the hypothetical where D chooses not to take medication, a prior-fault approach remains *at least potentially* open for the court.

---

[171] *Stapleton* (1952) 86 CLR 358.

[172] Mackay and Kearns, 'More Fact(s) About the Insanity Defence' [1999] Crim LR 714, 722; Mackay, Mitchell, and Howe, 'Yet More Facts About the Insanity Defence' [2006] Crim LR 399.

[173] See discussion in *Beard* (1920) 14 Cr App R 159 distinguishing intoxication from addiction, endorsed in *Taj* [2018] EWCA Crim 1743.

[174] Discussed in Law Commission, *Insanity and Automatism* (Discussion Paper, 2013) Ch6; Child, 'Prior Fault: Blocking Defences or Constructing Crimes' in Reed and Bohlander (eds), *General Defences* (2014).

13.4.4 Insanity and defences

Where insanity is raised as a denial of offending (ie to explain D's lack of mens rea), D will not require a defence. D has not committed an offence. The question, simply, is whether D should be given an unqualified acquittal as she has not committed a full offence, or if she satisfies the insanity rules, whether she should be given the qualified acquittal of 'not guilty by reason of insanity'.

The only exception to this, potentially, could arise were the courts to recognise a rule of prior-fault for insanity in line with intoxication and automatism. Thus, if D's prior-fault resulted in a state of insanity and criminal conduct, D would be liable for the full offence rather than not guilty by reason of insanity. In such a case, with D now facing liability, defences would come back into play. D could claim a defence to undermine her prior-fault at T1 and thus undermine liability (eg duress, where D is threatened to not take her medication), and/or potentially a defence in relation to her T2 conduct.

We discuss insanity as a defence (as opposed to a denial of offending) in **Chapter 14.2**, and this includes a discussion of how insanity as a defence interacts with other defences. That discussion, however, is not relevant for present purposes.

13.5 Combining intoxication, automatism, and insanity

The three denials of offending discussed in this chapter are mutually exclusive in their application, and will in most cases lead to different outcomes. Identifying which set of rules, if any, should apply is therefore crucial. If D's lack of mens rea stems from an internal factor then *only* the insanity rules should be applied; where it stems from voluntary consumption of a dangerous drug then *only* the prior-fault intoxication rules should be applied; where D's conduct is involuntary as a result of an external factor other than a dangerous drug then *only* the automatism rules should be applied.

Certain cases, however, will test these neat divisions.[175] Causes can be consecutive: for example, D's voluntary intoxication may cause her to fall and hit her head, causing her to commit a criminal act whilst in a state of automatism;[176] repeat intoxication can lead to addiction and a disease of the mind;[177] and so on. Causes can also be concurrent: for example, where an external blow causes automatism by aggravating an internal condition;[178] where D is suffering from a disease of the mind and is intoxicated;[179] and so on. Cases of this kind expose the problems of relying on the internal/external distinction. Courts have tended to take a pragmatic approach, looking for the dominant cause.[180]

---

[175] See Child, Crombag, and Sullivan, 'Defending the Delusional, the Irrational, and the Dangerous' [2020] Crim LR 306.

[176] *Stripp* (1979) 69 Cr App R 318.

[177] *Beard* [1920] AC 479.

[178] *Roach* [2001] EWCA Crim 2698.

[179] *Burns* (1973) 58 Cr App R 364.

[180] For a useful discussion, criticising the 'dominant cause' approach, see Loughnan and Wake, 'Of Blurred Boundaries and Prior Fault: Insanity, Automatism and Intoxication' in Reed and Bohlander (eds), *General Defences in Criminal Law* (2014) 113.

13.6 Reform

The rules on insanity, automatism, and intoxication have attracted sustained academic criticism, and have each been discussed by the Law Commission in terms of potential reform.[181] In this section we provide a brief overview of those reform proposals.

Before dividing our analysis between the three sets of rules, it is useful to highlight an underlying debate that is common between them. The major function of the rules discussed in this chapter is inculpatory in nature.[182] Where D has not completed all the elements of an offence, our starting point must be an unqualified acquittal: D's behaviour is not proscribed by the criminal law, or at least not by the offence charged. The rules governing prior-fault automatism, prior-fault intoxication, the potential for what we might call 'prior-fault insanity', and to a more limited extent the rules covering insanity in general,[183] each operate to construct liability (or the grounds for compulsory treatment) that would not otherwise be available. The underlying debate, then, particularly when we are discussing the construction of liability, is the question of when and how such liability should be constructed.

The dominant language of the current law, discussing automatism, insanity, and intoxication as *defences*, only serves to disguise and confuse this underlying question.[184] If we think of these rules in terms of defences, then it is natural to think about what is required of D to excuse or justify her avoidance of liability (ie liability becomes the default). In contrast, when we accept that these rules are designed to construct liability, or in the context of insanity, at least to provide a route to orders for public protection, the question changes to consider what D has done wrong to deserve liability. The difference between these two may be subtle, but it has a real impact on our interpretation, and potential reform, of the law. For example, whilst the use of objective mental states is common among defences,[185] serious offences will generally require subjective mens rea, holding D liable only where she has *chosen* to commit or risk committing an offence.[186] When we come to consider D's prior-fault for intoxication (objectively based where the drug is a dangerous one) or automatism (case law is uncertain), our perception of the rules as defences or offence constructors is crucial.

---

[181] Law Commission, *Intoxication and Criminal Liability* (No 314, 2009); Law Commission, *Insanity and Automatism* (Discussion Paper, 2013).

[182] Outside this, the rules simply provide a shorthand terminology for saying that D lacks essential elements for the offence charged.

[183] The special verdict of not guilty by reason of insanity provides an acquittal, but its qualified nature (including the potential for compulsory treatment) means that it is still inculpatory in effect.

[184] Simester, 'Intoxication is Never a Defence' [2009] Crim LR 3; Child and Reed, 'Automatism is Never a Defence' (2014) 65 NILQ 167; Child and Sullivan, 'When Does the Insanity Defence Apply? Some Recent Cases' [2014] Crim LR 787; Child, 'Prior Fault: Blocking Defences or Constructing Crimes' in Reed and Bohlander (eds), *General Defences* (2014).

[185] Discussed in **Chapter 14**.

[186] *G* [2003] UKHL 50.

13.6.1 Intoxication

The prior-fault intoxication rules in general, and the *Majewski* principle in particular, have been consistently criticised for their lack of a theoretical basis and their confused application in practice.[187] Where other jurisdictions have abandoned the principle, the English courts have become isolated in clinging to it. It is clear that if reform is to come, it will need to be through Parliament.

When the Law Commission first considered the prior-fault intoxication rules in 1992, it proposed that the *Majewski* principle should be abolished and replaced with an intoxication offence.[188] This would have meant that rather than D's intoxication (at T1) being used to construct liability for an offence where D lacks mens rea (at T2), D's intoxication plus harm would itself constitute a separate offence. However, following criticism on consultation,[189] the Commission changed its stance and recommended codification, with only slight amendment, of the current law.[190] This recommendation was never taken forward into legislation, being widely viewed as unnecessarily complex.

The most recent Law Commission project on intoxication was completed in 2009.[191] In its report, the Commission recommended the abandonment of the *Majewski* distinction between offences of basic and specific intent. However, the Commission did not reject the basic logic underlying the current law that voluntary intoxication with a dangerous drug is equivalent, in culpability terms, to a missing mens rea of recklessness. For the Commission, the main problem with the law was that this principle was not consistently or specifically applied. Thus, rather than a rule distinguishing between offences that might include various mens rea requirements as in *Majewski*, the Commission recommended that each element of each offence should be analysed separately: where the missing element of mens rea is recklessness or less, then D's intoxication can substitute for it (the Commission labelled these 'non-integral' elements), but if the element requires a higher mens rea than recklessness (eg intention, knowledge, etc) then the absence of this cannot be replaced by D's intoxication (the Commission labelled these 'integral' elements). There are a number of merits to this policy as a rationalisation of the current law. However, the Commission's recommendations have also attracted criticism,[192] and have been rejected by government.

As more commentators have accepted that the prior-fault intoxication rules are essentially inculpatory, and that the debate should be about what is required to construct liability, the prospect of an intoxication offence to replace the current prior-fault intoxication rules has regained popularity.[193] Rather than the fiction of the current law, pretending that D possessed mens rea where she did not, the advantage of an intoxication offence

---

[187] Williams, 'Voluntary Intoxication—A Lost Cause?' (2013) 129 LQR 264.
[188] Law Commission, *Intoxication and Criminal Liability* (Consultation 127, 1992).
[189] Gardner, 'The Importance of *Majewski*' (1994) 14 OJLS 279.
[190] Law Commission, *Intoxication and Criminal Liability* (No 229, 1995).
[191] Law Commission, *Intoxication and Criminal Liability* (No 314, 2009).
[192] Child, 'Drink, Drugs and Law Reform' [2009] Crim LR 488.
[193] Simester, 'Intoxication is Never a Defence' [2009] Crim LR 3.

is that it could accurately label and punish D for what she has done: become intoxicated and caused a criminal harm. The detail of such an offence remains contested,[194] but it is contended that this approach offers the best way forward.

13.6.2 Sane automatism

The automatism rules have attracted less academic attention than intoxication, but many of the same debates and criticisms can be applied. The approach of the Law Commission, in its Discussion Paper in 2013,[195] has been an attempt to rationalise the current law in the context of other denials of offending, most notably intoxication and insanity. For example, the Commission explores the wider concept of prior-fault, and looks to identify consistent approaches across the three sets of rules. Focussing on automatism specifically, the Commission also looks to resolve some of the main areas of uncertainty within the current law, discussed earlier, relating to the type of foresight required by D in the context of prior-fault, as well as the degree of involuntariness required to give rise to automatism at all.[196]

As with intoxication, however, if we see the automatism rules as designed to construct liability, an alternative approach could be the creation of a prior-fault automatism offence.[197] This option is not discussed by the Commission. It will be interesting to see what approach is eventually recommended by the Commission.

13.6.3 Insanity

The most widely criticised rules discussed in this chapter relate to insanity.[198] That the law remains governed by the outlined opinions of Law Lords over 175 years ago is nothing short of remarkable; that this should be the case despite dramatic strides in medical and public understanding of mental illness is nothing short of disgraceful.

We have already discussed a number of specific problems with the insanity rules, and there is also a useful summary of these in the Law Commission's Discussion Paper.[199] One of those we have not yet discussed, but a major pressure for reform, derives from the potential incompatibility of the current law with the ECHR.[200] There are three main areas of potential challenge:

- **Articles 2 and 3:** Articles 2 and 3 provide for the right to life and the prohibition of inhuman or degrading treatment. In this regard, the insanity rules have a crucial role

---

[194] Williams, 'Voluntary Intoxication—A Lost Cause?' (2013) 129 LQR 264; Child, 'Prior Fault: Blocking Defences or Constructing Crimes' in Reed and Bohlander (eds), *General Defences* (2014).

[195] Law Commission, *Insanity and Automatism* (Discussion Paper, 2013).

[196] Ibid, Ch5.

[197] Child and Reed, 'Automatism is Never a Defence' (2014) 65 NILQ 167.

[198] Dell, 'Wanted: An Insanity Defence That Can Be Used' [1983] Crim LR 431; Loughnan, 'Manifest Madness: Towards a New Understanding of the Insanity Defence' (2007) 70 MLR 379; Hogg, 'The Insanity Defence: An Argument for Abolition' (2015) 79 JCL 250.

[199] Law Commission, *Insanity and Automatism* (Discussion Paper, 2013) paras 1.30–1.79.

[200] Mackay and Gearty, 'On Being Insane in Jersey—The Case of *AG v Jason Prior*' [2001] Crim LR 560; Mackay, 'On Being Insane in Jersey—Part Two' [2002] Crim LR 728; Mackay, 'On Being Insane in Jersey—Part Three' [2004] Crim LR 219.

to protect mentally disordered individuals from inappropriate prosecution, and also to protect society from potentially dangerous individuals. Where the current law fails in these roles, it is open to challenge in relation to both groups.[201]

- **Article 5:** Article 5 provides the right to liberty and security unless certain circumstances apply, such as where D has committed an offence or requires detention in relation to an 'unsound mind'. Where D lacks mens rea she has not committed an offence, and where the cause of this lack of mens rea is a condition such as diabetes, sleepwalking, etc, it is highly questionable whether this satisfies the Article 5 exception of an unsound mind.[202] Thus, where D, in these circumstances, is caught within the insanity rules and potentially detained against her will, this may be a breach of her Article 5 rights.[203] This ground centres on the current disconnect between legal definitions of insanity and medical definitions of mental illness.

- **Article 6:** Article 6 provides the right to a fair trial, including the presumption of innocence. The presumption of innocence entails placing the burden upon the prosecution to prove the elements of liability. However, where D's denial of offending is based upon a disease of the mind (ie caught within the insanity rules) the current law reverses the legal burden of proof; requiring D to prove that elements of the offence were missing.[204]

In light of the various criticisms levelled at the current law, it is little surprise that it has attracted several reform proposals (almost from its inception[205]). The most recent of these is again contained in the Law Commission's 2013 Discussion Paper.[206] Some of the Commission's main proposals include the following:

- **Proposal 1:** Abolition of the common law rules on insanity.
- **Proposal 2:** Creation of a new statutory test, labelled as 'not criminally responsible by reason of recognised medical condition'.
- **Proposal 3:** Creation of a three-limbed test, where D's recognised medical condition must have caused D to lack capacity: (a) rationally to form a judgement about her conduct or their circumstances; (b) to understand the wrongfulness of what she is charged with, not isolated to legal wrongfulness; or (c) to control her conduct in the relevant circumstances.
- **Proposal 6:** Placing an *evidential* burden on D when raising the reformed rules, but placing the legal burden on the prosecution.

As with the Commission's proposals for automatism, it is important to remember that these are only the provisional proposals within a discussion paper.

---

[201] Law Commission, *Insanity and Automatism* (Discussion Paper, 2013) paras 1.65–1.72.
[202] For discussion of this definition, see *Winterwerp v Netherlands* (1979) 2 EHRR 387.
[203] Although, of course, detention of this kind will require the advice of two medical experts, and would not be ordered for conditions such as diabetes.
[204] *Bratty* [1963] AC 386.
[205] As early as 1923 a committee chaired by Lord Atkin recommended a test based on 'mental disease [which] in substance deprived [D] of any power to resist': Cmd 2005.
[206] Law Commission, *Insanity and Automatism* (Discussion Paper, 2013) paras 4.158–4.168.

13.7 Eye on assessment

In this section we consider how denials of offending based on intoxication, automatism, and insanity should be applied to problem facts. The same basic structure is employed as discussed in previous chapters.

STEP 1 Identify the potential criminal event in the facts

This is unlikely to take more than a sentence, but it is essential to tell your reader where in the facts you are focussing (eg 'The first potential criminal event appears where Mary drunkenly shoots and kills Amir').

It is important to take care at this stage. Where you note from the facts that D may be intoxicated (as in our example) or may be acting involuntarily or may have a mental disorder, it is correct that this should alert you to the potential application of the rules discussed in this chapter. However, Step 1 is not the time to discuss those rules! Many students make the mistake of launching into a discussion of intoxication, automatism, or insanity at this stage but, without having told the reader why these rules need to be discussed, their analysis is likely to be confused.

Rather than discussing rules of denial at this stage, you first need to identify a potential offence (Step 2) and discuss if the elements of that offence are satisfied (Step 3).

STEP 2 Identify the potential offence

Having identified the facts (eg D potentially killing V), you must now identify the offence you are going to apply. Usually, this means identifying the most serious offence that D might have committed, which in this case would be murder.

STEP 3 Applying the offence to the facts

Actus reus: What does the offence require? Did D do it?

Mens rea: What does the offence require? Did D possess it?

If you conclude that D satisfies all the actus reus and mens rea elements of the offence, then the intoxication and automatism rules have no role. This can be highlighted to your reader, for example: 'Although Mary was drunk when she killed Amir, she remains liable for murder because, despite her intoxication, she still possessed the required mens rea.' As the House of Lords confirmed in *Kingston*, 'a drunken intent is still an intent'. The insanity rules as a denial of mens rea will also have no application, although insanity as a defence (discussed in **Chapter 14**) may be relevant.

You should *only* consider the rules discussed in this chapter where D satisfies the actus reus elements of the offence charged, but does not satisfy the mens rea elements including potentially a lack of voluntary action. There are many reasons why D may lack mens rea, but you should now consider the rules of intoxication, automatism, and insanity to see if the reasons relevant to your problem question are caught within one of these sets of rules. Your first task, before applying the rules in detail, is to identify which set of rules should be discussed. **Figure 13.10** provides some guidance on this choice.

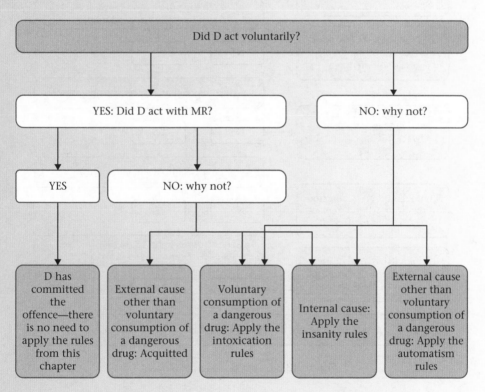

Figure 13.10 How is D denying the offence?

Having identified the correct set of rules to apply, your task is now to discuss the relevant set of rules in detail. Remember that this discussion can lead to a variety of outcomes, with intoxication, automatism, and insanity rules applying *both* to explain D's lack of offending as well as, where prior-fault requirements are satisfied, potentially providing a route to liability. Alongside the detailed discussion of these rules earlier in this chapter, illustrations across **Figures 13.11, 13.12,** and **13.13** can be used to help guide the structure of your analysis.

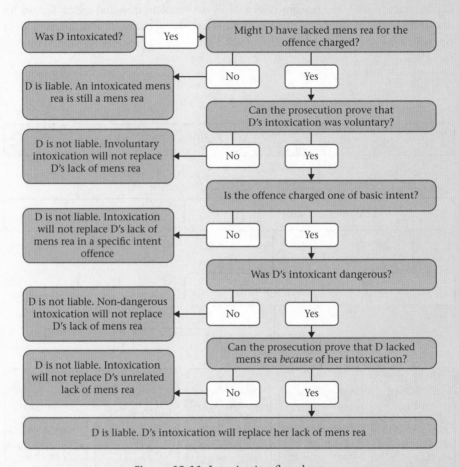

Figure 13.11 Intoxication flowchart

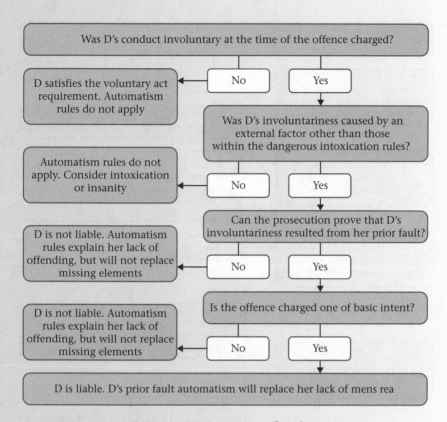

Figure 13.12 Automatism flowchart

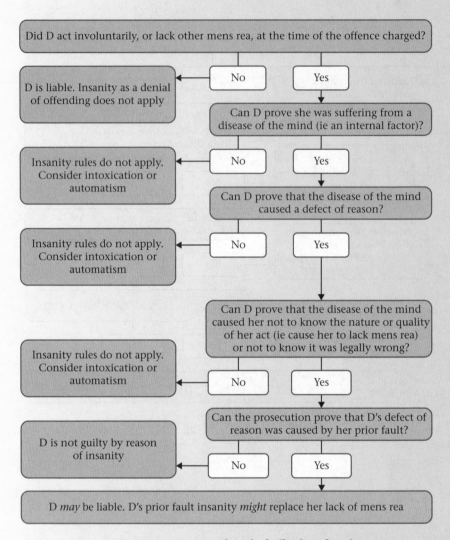

Figure 13.13 Insanity as a denial of offending flowchart

AR and MR are satisfied	AR and/or MR are not satisfied
Continue to STEP 4.	Return to STEP 2, and look for an alternative offence. If none, then skip to STEP 5, concluding that no offence is committed.

STEP 4 Consider defences

The word 'consider' here is important, as you should not discuss every defence for every question. Rather, think whether there are any defences that *could* potentially apply. If you conclude there are, then discuss those only.

Where liability has been constructed on the basis of D's prior-fault at T1, D may rely on a defence to undermine that fault. For example, D may rely on the defence of duress (discussed in **Chapter 14**) to deny responsibility for a failure to take medication (leading to insanity), or for taking something that causes a lack of voluntariness (leading to automatism, or intoxication).

In many cases, as we have discussed, D will have been intoxicated or mentally ill at T2, but still committed all elements of the offence. In these cases, we are not dealing with intoxication and/or insanity as a denial of mens rea because D does satisfy the mens rea. However, although D's condition does not undermine liability, it may have an impact on any defences raised. For example, D will generally not be able to rely on an intoxicated mistake (**13.2.3**) when raising a defence.

STEP 5 Conclude

This is usually a single sentence either saying that it is likely that D has committed the offence, or saying that it is not likely either because an offence element is not satisfied or because a defence is likely to apply. It is not often that you will be able to say categorically whether or not D has committed the offence, so it is usually best to conclude in terms of what is more 'likely'.

STEP 6 Loop

Go back up to STEP 1, identifying the next potential criminal event. Continue until you have discussed all the relevant potentially criminal events.

 ONLINE RESOURCES

www.oup.com/he/child-ormerod4e

This chapter is accompanied by a selection of online resources to help you with this topic, including:

- **Self-test questions** and **scenario questions**
- **Videos** from the authors
- **Audio introduction** to the topic
- **Chapter summary sheet**
- Two **sample examination questions** with answer guidance
- **Further reading and weblinks**

Also available on the online resources are:

- A selection of **videos** from the authors containing general advice on problem questions and essay questions
- **Legal updates**

14

General defences

14.1 Introduction

In this chapter we discuss the general defences. Unlike denials of offending discussed in **Chapter 13**, defences, properly so called, accept that D has committed the elements of an offence, but provide an additional set of rules that D can rely on so as to avoid liability. For example, D accepts that she intentionally pushed V to the ground thereby committing assault occasioning ABH,[1] but denies liability on the basis that she did

---

[1] Offences Against the Person Act 1861, s47. See **Chapter 7.4**.

so only to stop V attacking her child (relying on the public and private defence, discussed at **14.5**).

We have discussed a number of 'specific' defences in previous chapters—defences that only apply to a single offence or a cluster of offences, such as 'belief in owner's consent' for criminal damage.[2] In contrast, the defences discussed in this chapter, as 'general' defences, can apply, with one exception,[3] to offences throughout the criminal law. We have also previously discussed the 'partial' defences to murder—defences which have the potential to reduce liability for murder to manslaughter as, for example, where D was suffering from diminished responsibility.[4] The defences discussed in this chapter, in contrast, are 'complete' defences and, if pleaded successfully, therefore result in D's acquittal.

 Point to remember . . .

When discussing defences, the language of actus reus (guilty act) and mens rea (guilty mind) is not appropriate. These terms are used to describe offences only. Instead, you should refer simply to the elements of defences.

Defences, and the general defences in particular, play a vital role within the criminal law as a concession to the bluntness of the criminal offence. Offence definitions attempt to isolate and identify criminal mischiefs, but, within the infinite variety of circumstances in the real world, it is almost impossible for these definitions to account for every eventuality. Criminal defences provide the next layers of detail; allowing the law to account for exceptional circumstances where (despite D satisfying the elements of the offence charged) liability would be inappropriate. The same analysis can be presented in more positive terms. If criminal offences have a role in guiding the behaviour of society, then relative bluntness in offence definitions is a good thing: offences can provide clear messages about conduct to be avoided, leaving defences to act as a safety net in exceptional circumstances.[5]

Defences can be problematic, however. There is a considerable literature critiquing how defences are defined and applied: whether they are drawn too narrowly, failing to exculpate apparently non-blameworthy defendants; or too widely, allowing blameworthy conduct, inappropriately, to escape liability. Such criticisms are also common of criminal offences, but they may be felt particularly keenly in the context of defences as the 'safety net' or the last set of legal rules that stand between D and a criminal conviction. Indeed, it may be partly because of this that many defences lack clarity in their definitions; opening the potential for inconsistent application and criticism, but also providing flexibility to account for different factual circumstances.

---

[2] Criminal Damage Act 1971, s5(2)(a). See **Chapter 9.7.3**.

[3] The exception is duress, which does not provide a defence to murder and certain related offences. See **14.3** and **14.4**.

[4] Homicide Act 1957, s2. See **Chapter 6.2.2**.

[5] Duff, *Answering for Crime* (2007) Ch11; Wilson, 'The Structure of Criminal Defences' [2005] Crim LR 108; Wilson, 'How Criminal Defences Work' in Reed and Bohlander (eds), *General Defences in Criminal Law* (2014) 7.

In this chapter, we discuss the following defences:

- **Insanity (as a defence):** This arises where a medical condition caused a defect in reason, which prevented D understanding her conduct or understanding that it was wrong. For example, D killed V under the insane delusion that she was required by law to do so.

- **Duress by threats:** This arises where D was threatened by someone that unless she committed the offence she is now charged with she would suffer serious injury or death, D reasonably believed that the threat would be carried out imminently, and a reasonable person in those circumstances would have reacted as D did. For example, D committed robbery because X threatened to kill her if she did not.

- **Duress by circumstances:** This arises where D reasonably believed she faced a threat of death or serious injury, but with the threat arising from D's circumstances rather than explicitly from a person. For example, D broke into another's car and drove away as her only means to escape an approaching tidal wave.

- **The public and private defence (commonly known as self-defence):** This arises where D used force against another in the genuine belief that she needed to do so to protect herself or others, or to prevent crime, and the amount of force used was reasonable in the circumstances as D believed them to be. For example, D assaulted V in the belief she needed to do so to stop V harming her child.

- **Necessity:** This arises where D acted for the greater good, or the lesser evil. This defence, as we will see, is poorly defined and rarely applied. An example of its rare use has been to justify the separation of conjoined twins, killing one to give the other a chance of life.

These defences are not denials of actus reus or mens rea. In an effort to explain why the law does not blame D for her behaviour, courts and commentators have occasionally referred to D's conduct as 'involuntary', or 'morally involuntary'.[6] This terminology is unhelpful. If D's conduct is involuntary then she does not commit an offence, and we apply the rules discussed in **Chapter 13**. Where D relies on a defence, she may have been subject to an impossible choice, such that her voluntary commission of an offence was not blameworthy, but her appeal to defences marks an acceptance that she has committed an offence.[7]

14.1.1 Excuses and justifications

Much of the theoretical writing in this area has focussed on categorising types of defences in order to understand the basis upon which D is exculpated; particularly the division between excusatory and justificatory defences. The language of excuses and justifications originates from a historical question of forfeiture on acquittal: historically a justified killer would not have her goods forfeited, but a merely excused killer would. Forfeiture was abolished in 1828, but academic interest in the division between justifications and excuses continued, and was re-sparked by the seminal work of George Fletcher.[8]

---

[6] *Perka* (1984) 13 DLR (4th) 1: Canadian court discussing duress by threats.
[7] *Hasan* [2005] UKHL 22, [18].
[8] Fletcher, *Rethinking Criminal Law* (1978) Ch10.

The division between excuses and justifications can be stated quite simply, but the detail of its application and relevance to today's law is highly contested. An excusatory defence accepts that D's actions were wrongful all things considered but, because of D's circumstances, challenges the idea that D should be blamed for them; a justificatory defence, in contrast, challenges the wrongfulness of D's actions.[9] As Fletcher put it:

> A justification speaks to the rightness of the act; an excuse, to whether the actor is accountable for a concededly wrongful act.[10]

An excuse, then, *tends* to focus on D herself rather than her actions. For example, if D explains that she committed the offence because voices in her head compelled her to do so, we do not question whether her acts were wrongful (they clearly were), but we may question whether it is right to blame D for those acts, as through the excusatory defence of insanity. As Hart notably stated, 'unless a man has the capacity and fair opportunity or chance to adjust his behaviour to the law, its penalties ought not to be applied to him.'[11] This is the essence of an excusatory defence: whether due to a physical or mental restraint, or whether due to extreme circumstances, D did not have a *fair* opportunity to obey the law.[12] Justifications, on the other hand, *tend* to focus on D's acts. For example, where D assaults V in order to stop V harming her child, D may have completed the elements of an offence, but her acts were permissible. She did the right thing.[13]

There is an appealing logic to the separation of excuses and justification, but beyond some core examples, it can also be problematic.[14] Take the simple example of D who assaults V in order to stop V harming D's child. Although this is a clear example of the justified defence of another, known as 'the public and private defence', D could also rely on this defence if she made a mistake, if she thought V was trying to harm her child but was wrong and V was actually no threat at all. In this case, D's actions are *justified on her beliefs*, but few would call them justified in light of the objective facts. Rather, if we accept the use of the public and private defence on these amended facts, it appears to be *excusing* D's blameworthy conduct on the basis of her mistake. Countless examples of this kind have been difficult to categorise within the excuse/justification framework, and 'bred needless confusion' in the law.[15]

Problems of categorisation have prompted two main responses. Where some commentators question why we should talk of these distinctions at all;[16] others attempt to

---

[9] For criticism, see Gardner, 'Wrongs and Faults' in Simester (ed), *Appraising Strict Liability* (2005) 6–67.

[10] Fletcher, *Rethinking Criminal Law* (1978) 759.

[11] Hart, *Punishment and Responsibility* (1968) 181.

[12] See generally Horder, *Excusing Crime* (2004).

[13] It is problematic to say we 'approve' of D's acts because they still involved the commission of a criminal mischief. However, D's acts should not be condemned; they were permissible. Duff, *Answering for Crime* (2007) Ch11; Westen, 'Offences and Defences Again' (2008) 28 OJLS 563; Dsouza, *Rationale-Based Defences in Criminal Law* (2017).

[14] Even within them there is a question of hierarchy, Husak, 'On the Supposed Priority of Justification to Excuse' (2005) 24 Law & Phil 557.

[15] Duff, *Answering for Crime* (2007) 263.

[16] Williams, 'The Theory of Excuses' [1982] Crim LR 732. Robinson, 'Four Distinctions that Glanville Williams Did Not Make' in Baker and Horder (eds), *The Sanctity of Life and the Criminal Law* (2013).

resolve the issue by becoming ever more fine-grained in their theorising, separating sub-categories of excuses and justifications.[17] This latter approach can be useful to resolve problematic scenarios, but does so at the expense of the simplicity that was one of the initially appealing elements of the separation.

The current law does not rely on the explicit separation of excuses and justifications; the practical result of D's acquittal is the same for both. However, an outright rejection of these classifications, despite their critics, would be premature. First, this is because the debate about these classifications is useful; it forces us to question the basis upon which a defence operates. This aids our evaluation of current defences, questioning their coherence, and leads us towards potential reform options.[18] Secondly, where a separation can be made, it does appear to have certain practical consequences. For example, it seems that it is legitimate for D to use force to defend herself against an excused attacker (eg where V is attacking D under an insane delusion), but it is not legitimate for D to use force to protect herself where the attacker's conduct is justified (eg where V uses force on D to prevent D from harming her child).[19] Further, whilst D1 may be an accomplice to an offence committed by P who is excused from liability, D2 is absolved of liability as an accessory where P was justified in committing the offence.[20] Thirdly, and finally, the distinction seems to make a difference in what the law is trying to communicate to society. Robinson, for example, has discussed the role of defences as rule 'articulators'; that is, telling the public what they should and should not do.[21] For Robinson, whilst excuses are essential concessions to human frailty, they are not rules that the public need to know, they are not designed to guide behaviour. Justifications, in contrast, should be communicated clearly because they tell people when it is permitted to commit certain offences for the greater good.

 Assessment matters . . .

As we have said, the current law does not require an explicit identification of defences as excusatory or justificatory. Therefore, when applying a defence to problem facts, you do not need to use this terminology. However, when evaluating the law, either within a problem question or a more general essay, the terminology will be very useful.

14.2 Insanity as a defence

We have already discussed the insanity rules as a denial of offending,[22] where D raises insanity to explain her lack of mens rea including in extreme cases her lack of voluntary conduct. However, uniquely, the insanity rules can *also* apply as a defence, exculpating

---

[17] For a particularly useful model, see Simester, 'On Justifications and Excuses' in Zedner and Roberts (eds), *Principles and Values in Criminal Law and Criminal Justice* (2012) 95.

[18] This is a common structure within academic writing. See eg Stark, 'Necessity and *Nicklinson*' [2013] Crim LR 949.

[19] Fletcher, *Rethinking Criminal Law* (1978) para 10.1.1.

[20] *Bourne* (1952) 36 Cr App R 125.

[21] Robinson, *Structure and Function in Criminal Law* (1997) Ch5.

[22] **Chapter 13.4.**

D from liability even when she has completed the actus reus and mens rea of the offence charged.[23] The elements of insanity as a defence are the same as those for insanity as a denial of offending. Therefore, our discussion in this section should be read in the context of our more detailed analysis of the insanity rules in the previous chapter. Rather than repeating details from **Chapter 13.4**, this section provides a brief overview of insanity as a defence, before highlighting a few areas where the difference between denial of offending and defence affects the application of the law.

The insanity rules were set out in *M'Naghten*,[24] and confirmed in the House of Lords in its judicial capacity in *Sullivan*.[25] They are illustrated in **Table 14.1**.

Table 14.1 Insanity defence

A) D must suffer from a disease of the mind;
B) This must have caused a defect of reason; and
C) This must have caused a lack of responsibility, *either* because D did not know the nature or quality of her act, *or* she did not know it was legally wrong.

Where D is charged with an offence but her conduct satisfies these elements, she is entitled to a qualified acquittal of 'not guilty by reason of insanity'. We discussed the 'special verdict' in the previous chapter,[26] including the range of disposal orders available to the court. The special verdict ensures that D is protected from inappropriate liability through acquittal, but also that the public can be protected from future danger through disposal options which include compulsory treatment and/or supervision.

Where insanity is raised as a defence as opposed to a denial of mens rea, two main theoretical differences should be noted. The first relates to the application of the elements of the insanity rules, and the second to their interaction with other defences.

14.2.1 The elements of insanity as a defence

The three elements of the insanity defence, set out in **Table 14.1**, are discussed in detail in **Chapter 13.4.2**. It should be noted here, in relation to the third element, that the either/or between 'not knowing the nature or quality of her act' and 'not knowing it was wrong' will often mark the difference between insanity as a denial of offending and insanity as a defence. Where D caused harms without an understanding of her acts as, for example, where D killed V thinking she was breaking a jar, she will not have possessed mens rea. Thus, if mens rea is required for the offence (remember that all offences require at least voluntary conduct), D's plea to the insanity rules will be a denial of offending.[27]

---

[23] Usefully discussed in *Loake v CPS* [2017] EWHC 2855 (Admin).
[24] (1843) 4 St Tr NS 847.
[25] [1984] 1 AC 156.
[26] **Chapter 13.4.1**.
[27] See recently Mackay, '"Nature", "Quality" and Mens Rea—Some Observations on "Defect of Reason" and the First Limb of the M'Naghten Rules' [2020] Crim LR 588.

In contrast, where D has capacity to understand her acts, but her disease of the mind causes her not to know they were legally wrong, she may well possess mens rea. Indeed, understanding the legal wrongfulness of one's conduct is rarely relevant to the mens rea of an offence: ignorance of the law is no excuse.[28] Thus, an appeal to the insanity rules on this basis is likely to be an appeal to insanity as a defence.[29]

A second point that should be noted relates to the first element of the insanity rules, which requires D to suffer from a disease of the mind and the internal/external cause distinction. Importantly, the need to show an internal cause is common to insanity as a denial of offending and insanity as a defence. However, there is likely to be an interesting switch in the priorities of the defendant. Where the plea is one amounting to a denial of offending, D will be particularly keen for the insanity rules not to be applied to her because, if the cause of her lack of capacity is external (ie sane automatism), she will receive an *unqualified* acquittal. This is why, for example, there is so much litigation around the borderline between automatism resulting in an unqualified acquittal and insanity resulting in the special verdict of not guilty by reason of insanity. The same is true in circumstances where D claims a simple lack of mens rea: again, D will gain an unqualified acquittal if her lack of mens rea does not amount to a plea of insanity. In contrast, where the plea arises as a defence, the default position if the insanity rules do not apply is likely to be full criminal liability. Thus, although issues of stigma may still discourage D from raising insanity, a successful plea leading to a qualified acquittal (in modern times at least[30]) is likely to represent a more favourable outcome than the alternative.

14.2.2 Insanity and other defences

Where insanity arises as a denial of offending, it will rarely conflict with other defences.[31] However, where insanity arises as a defence, other alternative defences may also be applicable. For example, imagine a situation where D is visiting V and has a psychotic delusion that V is possessed by the devil and is about to launch a deadly attack upon her. She makes a pre-emptive strike and is charged with assault. D will seek to raise mistaken self-defence (the public and private defence) in this case because, if successful, it would result in an unqualified acquittal. Alongside this, however, it is also clear that D's delusion will qualify for the insanity defence within the *M'Naghten* Rules. This is because D's delusion of self-defence is likely to mean that she did not know that what she was doing was wrong, and the *M'Naghten* Rules also make explicit reference to catching delusions of this kind.[32] For example, in *M'Naghten*, Chief Justice Tindal remarked that D:

> must be considered in the same situation as to responsibility as if the facts with respect to which the delusion exists were real. For example, if under the influence of his delusion he supposes another man to be in the act of attempting to take away his life, and he kills that man, as he supposes, in self-defence, he would be exempt from punishment.[33]

---

[28] *Grant v Borg* [1982] 2 All ER 257; Ashworth, 'Ignorance of the Criminal Law, and Duties to Avoid It' (2011) 74 MLR 1.

[29] Manwaring, '*Windle* Revisited' [2018] Crim LR 987.

[30] See discussion in **Chapter 13.4.1**.

[31] See **Chapter 13.4.4**.

[32] This is sometimes referred to as a third limb of *M'Naghten*: the delusion limb: Williams, *Criminal Law: The General Part* (2nd edn, 1961) 497–507.

[33] *M'Naghten* [1843] UKHL J16, 211.

The reference to being 'exempt from punishment' in this extract is intended to mean that the insanity defence will apply.[34] But this outcome is far from ideal for D. The insanity defence will not result in conviction but in the special verdict and the various disposal options that apply.

The question for the insanity rules is whether D should be allowed to rely on an alternative defence in priority over insanity, or whether the insanity rules should exclude and take preference over alternative defences in order to ensure that the disposal options—compulsory treatment and/or supervision where it is required—are available to the court. If D claims that her belief in the need to use force to protect herself is a belief based on her psychotic state, should D be treated as pleading self-defence, or should the fact that her claim raises insanity mean that self-defence is no longer available to her? Following the approach taken to insanity as a denial of offending, it seems right in principle and in policy that the latter option should be preferred. Whether D would favour an alternative basis for denying offending, or an alternative defence, if her satisfaction of these alternatives relies upon a defect of reason arising from a disease of the mind then the insanity rules should be applied in preference. Just as D is prevented from relying on a simple denial of mens rea where that denial is based on what the law calls insanity, the same forward-looking rationale must apply equally to a choice between alternative defences: there remains a strong interest in protecting the public from future potential harm, as discussed in *Oye*.

 Oye [2013] EWCA Crim 1725

D became gripped by delusions that police officers were agents of evil spirits out to kill him, and launched a series of attacks on officers causing serious harm. D was charged with affray and maliciously inflicting GBH.[35] D raised self-defence (the public and private defence), and the judge instructed that insanity should *also* be left to the jury.

- Crown Court: guilty of affray and GBH offence. The jury rejected both defences.
- Court of Appeal: appeal allowed, substituting a special verdict of not guilty by reason of insanity.

The correct decision was reached in *Oye*, but it remains a problematic case. This is because the trial judge was in error in allowing the defences of mistaken self-defence and insanity to run in parallel. Although any practical problems were avoided because the jury rejected both defences, allowing both to run together is surely wrong in principle: if D was found not guilty on the basis of self-defence, thereby leading to an unqualified acquittal, this should be the end of the matter, and if a judge then wished to impose compulsory treatment under the separate heading of insanity this would give rise to some interesting issues under Article 5 ECHR. The Court of Appeal could have held, in line with our earlier discussion, that raising self-defence on the basis of an insane delusion amounted to raising the defence of insanity alone. However, the court achieved this same

---

[34] The insanity defence should apply on these facts but, worryingly, has not always been applied in practice. See Child, Crombag, and Sullivan, 'Defending the Delusional, the Irrational, and the Dangerous' [2020] Crim LR 306.

[35] Offences Against the Person Act 1861, s20.

result by an alternative route. Focussing on the rules governing self-defence, the Court of Appeal held that insane delusions should be added to the list of grounds which the jury should ignore when considering whether D's use of force was reasonable (an element of the public and private defence, discussed at **14.5.4**).[36]

Don't be confused . . .

The *Oye* case is problematic, but the result (at least) is clear. Where D raises multiple defences including insanity, the insanity defence should be applied ahead of the other options. Following the approach in *Sullivan*[37] (discussing insanity as a denial of offending), it is hoped that future courts will provide clarity as to the priority of defences.

14.3 Duress by threats

Duress, like insanity, is commonly understood as an excusatory defence.[38] D has committed an offence, but she has done so because she was threatened by X with death or serious injury if she refused. We do not agree with her conduct, the commission of the crime was not a justified act, but we can accept that she was placed in an impossible position, and so we can excuse her.

Some commentators go further and describe D's impossible position as a species of involuntariness, and it may be that D herself would protest that she 'had no choice' but to offend.[39] However, as we highlighted earlier, this kind of terminology is unhelpful in the context of defences. Where D seeks to rely on the defence of duress, she is not claiming that she was not in control of her conduct, that would be automatism; nor is she claiming any other lack of mens rea as has been consistently recognised by the courts.[40] Rather, the defence of duress represents a concession to human frailty,[41] an acceptance that although D *did* have a choice between offending or suffering serious harm from X, her decision to offend does not reveal a dangerous character deserving of criminal punishment. We accept, essentially, that D did no more than most of us would have done in her position, and we acquit on the basis that, as the adage goes, 'there, but for the grace of God, go I'.

The defence of duress has developed at common law, and remains uncodified. As illustrated in **Table 14.2**, it consists of three main parts.[42]

---

[36] Child and Sullivan, 'When Does the Insanity Defence Apply? Some Recent Cases' [2014] Crim LR 787.

[37] [1984] AC 156.

[38] Westen and Mangiafico, 'The Criminal Defense of Duress: A Justification, Not an Excuse' (2003) 6 Buff Crim L Rev 833; Huigens, 'Duress is Not a Justification' (2004) 2 Ohio St JCL 303.

[39] The Canadian court in *Perka* (1984) 13 DLR (4th) 1 describe it as 'moral involuntariness'. See Wasik, 'Duress and Criminal Responsibility' [1977] Crim LR 453.

[40] *Fisher* [2004] EWCA Crim 1190; *Hasan* [2005] UKHL 22, [18].

[41] *Howe* [1987] 1 All ER 771, 779–780; *Hasan* [2005] UKHL 22, [18].

[42] Duress by threats is inconsistently presented as containing anything between two and eight elements. This inconsistency does not represent disagreement on the substance of the defence, but simply the presentation.

Table 14.2 Duress by threats

A) Exclusions: duress is not a defence to murder, attempted murder, and certain treason offences, and will not apply in circumstances of prior fault;
B) X's threat and demand: D must have reasonably believed that she or another (for whom she was responsible) was threatened with death or serious injury by X unless D committed the offence; and
C) D's response: committing a crime as D did must be something that a reasonable person in her circumstances would have done. D must show reasonable steadfastness in response to the threat, only committing the offence because her will was overborne.

It is commonly accepted that a defence of duress is a necessary part of the criminal law. For example, where X holds a gun to a bank manger's (D's) head and forces her to open the vault, few would want to hold D liable as X's accomplice.[43] However, it should be highlighted from the start that there is also great concern about the limits of the defence, and scepticism about those raising it. Particularly in the context of criminal organisations and gangs, where threats and intimidation between members are common, duress can be claimed quite easily and be very difficult for the prosecution to disprove.[44] The reaction to this has been twofold. First, as with other defences, D bears an evidential burden when raising duress: only when this burden is satisfied will the court consider the defence, and the prosecution is then under a legal burden to disprove it.[45] In this context, D's evidential burden is only satisfied by evidence that is, in principle, sufficient to justify a jury concluding that duress is or may be established.[46] Secondly, and more controversially, scepticism about the overuse of the defence has led courts to interpret its elements increasingly narrowly. This has led to criticism in the other direction, claiming that the defence has now become overly restrictive and thus unable to apply in certain deserving circumstances.[47]

 Extra detail . . .

The narrowing of duress can be witnessed across multiple cases. However, it is best illustrated by the speech of Lord Bingham in *Hasan*.[48] This speech should be carefully read in full. The minority speech of Baroness Hale, in the same case, provides useful illustration of arguments in favour of a wider interpretation.

---

[43] On accomplice liability, see **Chapter 12**.
[44] Law Commission, *Murder, Manslaughter and Infanticide* (No 304, 2006) paras 6.101–6.111.
[45] *Hasan* [2005] UKHL 22, [37]. The Law Commission has recommended reversing the legal burden of proof where duress is raised as a defence to murder (see discussion at **14.7.1.2**).
[46] *Batchelor* [2013] EWCA Crim 2638. Reaffirmed in *Brandford* [2016] EWCA Crim 1794.
[47] For a useful discussion of this in the context of defendants suffering from domestic abuse, see Loveless, 'Domestic Violence, Coercion and Duress' [2010] Crim LR 93.
[48] [2005] UKHL 22.

14.3.1 Exclusions

There are two areas where duress will be excluded: in relation to certain offences; and in circumstances of prior-fault.

14.3.1.1 Offences to which D cannot raise duress

As a 'general' defence, duress has the potential to apply to offences across the criminal law. However, crucially, the common law has specified exceptions where the defence will not apply. These are:

A) **Treason:** The term 'treason' refers to a collection of offences against the state. Duress *can* be a defence to certain of these offences. In *Purdy*,[49] for example, a British prisoner of war (D) was forced to assist with German propaganda during the Second World War. In doing so, D committed a treason offence, but it was held that he could rely on duress as a defence. However, other more serious treason offences will not allow duress as a defence.[50]

B) **Murder:** Controversially, duress is not a defence to murder.[51] As Blackstone put it, under duress a person 'ought rather to die himself than escape by the murder of an innocent.'[52] This was recognised by a bare majority of the Privy Council in *Abbott*,[53] and later by the House of Lords in *Howe*,[54] where it was also established that duress was no defence to murder as a secondary party.[55] The harsh results of this exclusion are clearly illustrated in *Wilson*.[56]

 Wilson [2007] EWCA Crim 1251

D, a 13-year-old boy, assisted his father to murder his neighbour, fetching an axe and starting a fire on his father's instruction. D claimed that he only did so because of fear of his father's violence. D was charged with murder as his father's accomplice.[57]

- Crown Court: guilty of murder. The defendant, being unable to rely on duress, claimed unsuccessfully that he was so swept up in fear of his father that he was not able to form mens rea.
- Court of Appeal: conviction upheld on appeal.

The Court of Appeal in *Wilson* accepted that the law could be criticised for not providing a defence of duress where a 13-year-old is forced to commit murder by a dominant and violent parent,[58] but were obliged to follow the clear precedent from *Howe*.

---

[49] (1946) 10 JCL 182.
[50] *Steane* [1947] KB 997, 1005.
[51] Law Commission, *Murder, Manslaughter and Infanticide* (No 304, 2006) Ch6.
[52] Blackstone, *Commentaries on the Laws of England* (1765–69) Book 4, 30.
[53] [1977] AC 755.
[54] *Howe* [1987] 1 All ER 771.
[55] Walters, 'Murder Under Duress and Judicial Decision Making in the House of Lords' (1988) 18 LS 61.
[56] Ashworth, Commentary [2008] Crim LR 138.
[57] Accomplice liability is discussed in **Chapter 12.**
[58] At [18].

C) **Attempted murder:** It was recognised in *Gotts*[59] that if duress was no defence to murder then it would be illogical to recognise it as a defence to attempted murder.[60] If the court had found otherwise, the results would have been bizarre: allowing D's acts to be excused, but not the results. This would have been particularly odd if V died sometime after D's attack, as D would be allowed her freedom until the moment of V's death.

Unfortunately, the law remains illogical in allowing duress to apply where D commits an offence of intentionally causing GBH.[61] This is because, as the mens rea of murder includes both an intention to kill or an intention to cause GBH,[62] the same potential for problems arises here as it did in the context of attempted murder. For example, D attacks V under duress, causing V serious injury. D is not prosecuted because she has clearly acted under duress. Months later, or even longer, V dies from the injuries caused by D's original attack. D is now liable for murder, is prosecuted, and has no defence of duress.

It was confirmed by the Crown Court in *Ness* that duress remains a valid defence for conspiracy to murder, and presumably assisting or encouraging murder.[63] Unlike attempted murder, these offences do not involve the direct application of force to V as part of their actus reus. Thus, the defence can be safely recognised in this context without encountering the potential problems just discussed.

 Extra detail . . .

The exclusion of duress as a defence to murder and attempted murder is one of the most controversial aspects of the defence. Echoing academic criticisms, the Law Commission has recommended that duress should be extended to cover these offences.[64] This is discussed further in the reform section at **14.7.1.2**.

14.3.1.2 Exclusion on the basis of prior-fault

The general defences are designed to protect D from liability where she has been placed in a position where her offending is either excused or justified. The reference here to 'has been placed in a position' is important. Where D, either consciously or through negligence, places herself in a position where she requires a defence, the law will be much less willing to recognise that defence.[65] The defence of duress, more than any other general defence, has applied this principle progressively strictly.

Early case law allowed D some leeway where she demonstrated prior-fault by voluntarily associating with X, but on reasonable grounds did not foresee the threat and

---

[59] [1992] 2 AC 412.

[60] Gardner, 'Duress in Attempted Murder' (1991) 107 LQR 389.

[61] Offences Against the Person Act 1861, s18. Discussed in **Chapter 7.6**.

[62] See **Chapter 5.4**.

[63] [2011] Crim LR 645 and Ormerod commentary.

[64] Law Commission, *Murder, Manslaughter and Infanticide* (No 304, 2006) Ch6.

[65] Child, 'Prior Fault: Blocking Defences or Constructing Crimes' in Reed and Bohlander (eds), *General Defences* (2014) 37.

demand which followed.[66] However, subsequent case law has been considerably more restrictive, as illustrated in *Hasan*.

Hasan [2005] UKHL 22

D committed burglary. He did so as a result of threats from X, who was known to be violent. D acted as a minder for X's girlfriend, who was a prostitute. X also acted as a minder for his girlfriend, as well as being involved in drug dealing. D was charged with aggravated burglary.[67]

- Crown Court: guilty of aggravated burglary.
- Court of Appeal: appeal allowed, finding a defence of duress.
- House of Lords: appeal allowed, reinstating conviction. D's voluntary association with X undermined any appeal to duress.

Hasan confirms that duress will be excluded where D voluntarily associated with X in circumstances where a reasonable person would have foreseen (note the objective standard) a risk of future coercion. 'Coercion' is also interpreted widely, not requiring foresight of specifics or even foresight of demands to commit a crime. As Lord Bingham states:

> The policy of the law must be to discourage association with known criminals, and it should be slow to excuse the criminal conduct of those who do so. If a person voluntarily becomes or remains associated with others engaged in criminal activity in a situation where he knows or ought reasonably to know that he may be the subject of compulsion by them or their associates, he cannot rely on the defence of duress to excuse any act which he is thereafter compelled to do by them.[68]

The breadth of this principle was criticised in a powerful minority speech from Baroness Hale, who would prefer a test based on subjective foresight,[69] and it has also attracted cogent academic criticism.[70] However, the majority approach in *Hasan* has been confirmed in *Ali*,[71] and represents the current law.

Extra detail . . .

The quotation above from Lord Bingham includes reference to 'remains associated' as well as becoming associated. The courts have yet to deal explicitly with the potential for prior-fault in these circumstances, but the concept is designed to cover cases where D joins what appears to be a non-criminal

---

[66] *Shepherd* (1987) 86 Cr App R 47: joining a group of burglars does not mean that D should have foreseen being threatened with a gun when trying to leave; *Lewis* (1992) 96 Cr App R 412: joining a group of armed robbers does not mean that D should have foreseen being threatened not to testify against other members when in prison.

[67] Theft Act 1968, s10. See **Chapter 9.4.3**.

[68] At [38].

[69] Hale's approach would only deny duress where D subjectively foresaw that she might be threatened to commit crimes.

[70] JC Smith, 'Comment on *Heath*' [2000] Crim LR 109. Criticising objective foresight of *any* coercion: 'It is one thing . . . to be aware that you are likely to be beaten up if you do not pay your debts, it is another to be aware that you may be required under threat of violence to commit other, though unspecified, crimes, if you do not.'

[71] [2008] EWCA Crim 716.

organisation, discovers that it is criminal and/or violent, but does not take an opportunity to leave. Care must be taken, however, to distinguish between cases where D has a genuine opportunity to leave (such that her choice to stay represents prior-fault), and those for whom leaving the group is not a realistic or safe option (eg children brought up within a terrorist organisation) where D's decision to remain in the group might not represent prior-fault.[72]

14.3.2 Element 1: X's threat and demand

When considering the threat and demand from X, three main issues should be considered: (a) the content of the threat; (b) who made the threat and demand, and who are they directed at; and (c) the content of the demand.

14.3.2.1 The content of the threat

X's threat must be of death or serious personal injury,[73] confirmed by the House of Lords in *Hasan*.[74] In this manner, the gravity of X's threat works as an important threshold for the applicability of the defence. Any threat other than that of death or serious injury, even if it is vastly more serious than the offence X is demanding of D, will not qualify. For example, X threatens D that unless she commits a minor theft of V's property, she will face the much greater theft or damage of her own property. Where D succumbs to the threat and takes V's property, even if a reasonable person in D's position would have done likewise, D will have no defence of duress.[75] Duress is not a 'balance of evils' defence. In circumstances of this kind, where D claims to have committed an offence as a lesser evil, she must seek to rely on the defence of necessity discussed at **14.6**.

When applying the threshold in duress, threats of death are straightforward, but there remains some doubt about what constitutes a threat of serious harm. For example, although a threat to cause non-psychiatric GBH will always be sufficient, there is uncertainty about threats to cause serious psychiatric injury (eg a threat to leave D a nervous wreck).[76] As such harm is now recognised as being capable of constituting GBH for offences against the person,[77] however, the same approach may well be followed for duress. It has also been held (*obiter*) that a threat to rape D will be sufficient to meet the gravity threshold.[78] A threat to cause ABH, however, will not be sufficient (eg where X threatens to punch D unless D commits a crime[79]).

[72] This issue has arisen in the context of trafficked women: *Ajayi* [2010] EWCA Crim 471. However, a specific defence exists in this context: Modern Slavery Act 2015, s45: Laird, 'Evaluating the Relationship between Section 45 of the Modern Slavery Act 2015 and the Defence of Duress: An Opportunity Missed?' [2016] Crim LR 395. See on its application *GB* [2020] EWCA Crim 2.
[73] *Radford* [2004] EWCA Crim 2878.
[74] [2005] UKHL 22.
[75] *Vinh van Dao* [2012] EWCA Crim 1717 (a threat of false imprisonment); *Singh* [1973] 1 WLR 1600 (a threat of blackmail); *M'Growther* (1746) Fost 13 (a threat to property).
[76] *Baker v Wilkins* [1997] Crim LR 497.
[77] *Ireland and Burstow* [1998] AC 147. See **Chapter 7.4.1.3**.
[78] *Ashley* [2012] EWCA Crim 434.
[79] *Aikens* [2003] EWCA Crim 1573.

Extra detail . . .

Although duress is not a balance of evils defence, there is some authority to suggest that where X demands that D commit a particularly serious offence, the gravity of the threat must be even higher (ie of life-threatening harm, or even of death only).[80] The Law Commission has taken a similar approach with its recommendations for duress as a defence to murder, saying that it should only apply where D is threatened with death or 'life-threatening injury'.[81]

A problem can arise where D *believes* that she is being threatened with death or serious injury, but in fact she is not. For example, where X says she will 'do D over' unless D commits a certain crime, D may take this as a threat to her life, and therefore sufficient for duress, when in fact it is a threat to destroy D's property only, which is insufficient for duress. It is clear that duress should be capable of applying, where appropriate, beyond paradigm cases of an objective threat of death or serious injury, as otherwise there could be no duress where X threatens D with an unloaded gun. The *extent* to which D may rely on her mistaken beliefs was usefully clarified in *Safi and others*.

Safi [2003] EWCA Crim 1809

D and others hijacked a plane in Afghanistan, eventually landing in England at Stansted. They claimed duress on the basis that they were fleeing death or serious injury from the Taliban in Afghanistan. D was charged with various offences including hijacking.[82]

• Crown Court: guilty of hijacking offences. The jury were directed that duress was only available where there was objective evidence of a threat, which on the facts there was not, and that D's beliefs in an imminent threat were insufficient.

• Court of Appeal: appeal allowed. There is no need for objective evidence of a threat, as long as D reasonably believed it existed.

Safi clarifies that duress can be founded upon a mistaken belief. Note, however, that an honest belief will not be sufficient unless D's belief is also *reasonable*: a reasonable person in D's position would also have believed that there was a real threat of death or serious injury.[83] More recent case law has endorsed, expressly[84] or implicitly,[85] the objective approach in *Safi*, and so it is very likely that this represents the current law.

In requiring a reasonable belief (objective) in the threat from X, the defence of duress is inconsistent with the public and private defence (discussed at 14.5) where an honest belief (subjective) will suffice. This may be explained on grounds that the defences apply in different circumstances, one as an excuse and the other as a justification.[86] However,

---

[80] *M'Growther* (1746) Fost 13; *Purdy* (1946) 10 JCL 182; *Abbott* [1976] 3 All ER 152.
[81] Law Commission, *Murder, Manslaughter and Infanticide* (No 304, 2006) para 6.76.
[82] Aviation Security Act 1982, s1(1).
[83] At [25].
[84] *Blake* [2004] EWCA Crim 1238, [18]; *Bronson* [2004] EWCA Crim 903, [23].
[85] *Hasan* [2005] UKHL 22.
[86] Lord Bingham expressly rejected the comparison between defences in *Hasan* [2005] UKHL 22.

the origins of the objective approach in duress were guided by the then objective approach employed for the public and private defence.[87] It is therefore at least arguable that a consistent approach favouring one alternative or the other should be preferred.[88]

Extra detail . . .

Does the threat from X have to be criminal for duress to be established? A threat to cause death or serious injury will usually amount to a criminal threat, but the question has arisen whether it *must* be. In *Jones and others*,[89] D raised the defence of duress of circumstance against charges of criminal damage for cutting the fence at an RAF base, claiming that his actions were to prevent the UK government waging an illegal war and killing people in Iraq. The Court of Appeal avoided discussions about the legal status of the war by holding that the defence of duress could only apply to threats of death or serious injury that amounted to crimes in English and Welsh law, which the war was not. This was a convenient approach for the court, but has been cogently criticised and should be isolated to its facts.[90] As we will discuss later, in the context of duress of circumstance in particular, many threats will not be criminal in nature, such as an approaching tidal wave, and the courts are unlikely to follow *Jones* in requiring them to be.

14.3.2.2 Who made the threat and demand, and who are they directed at?

The paradigm case of duress involves X threatening D with death or serious injury unless she commits a particular offence. Cases have emerged, however, to test this paradigm.

Focussing on the source of the threats/demands, it is now clear that these may be directed at D via a third party, so need not come directly from X.[91] However, the threats/demands must still come from another party; they cannot originate from D herself. This was discussed in *Rodger and Rose*.

Rodger and Rose [1998] 1 Cr App R 143

D broke out of prison following news that the tariff period (jail time) of his life sentence had been substantially increased. It was accepted that D did this because he was depressed and suicidal, and believed that he would have committed suicide if he did not escape. D was charged with the offence of 'breaking prison'.

• Crown Court: guilty of breaking prison. Duress was not open to D because the threat was not external from himself.

• Court of Appeal: conviction upheld on appeal.

The Court of Appeal stated that to allow a defence of duress in these circumstances 'could amount to a licence to commit crime dependent on the personal characteristics

[87] *Graham* [1982] 1 All ER 801.
[88] Alldridge, 'Developing the Defence of Duress' [1986] Crim LR 433; Wilson, 'The Structure of Defences' [2005] Crim LR 108, 115–116.
[89] [2004] EWCA Crim 1981. Affirmed in the House of Lords on other grounds [2006] UKHL 16.
[90] Ormerod, Commentary [2005] Crim LR 122.
[91] *Brandford* [2016] EWCA Crim 1794. Although the court confirms the potential for indirect threats and demands, it notes that indirect threats will rarely be sufficiently imminent. See **14.3.3.2**.

and vulnerability of the offender'. The case is useful, therefore, both as a clarification that the threat/demand must come from another person, and to help to understand duress as a concession to *human* frailty as opposed to *individual* frailty.

Moving to the question of who must be the target of X's threat/demand, although both will invariably focus on D herself, there will be occasions where X threatens to kill or seriously harm others to force D to offend. For example, X threatens to kill D's child unless D commits an offence. The common law has taken some time to recognise duress in these circumstances, being concerned that the defence should apply narrowly, but has gradually expanded the defence to accommodate such cases. In *Hurley and Murray*, an Australian court allowed duress to apply where X's threats related to D's de facto wife;[92] in *Wright*, threats against D's boyfriend sufficed;[93] in *Conway*, threats against D's car passenger were enough;[94] and so on. There is some suggestion in *Hasan* that this class of people, other than the defendant, may be limited to 'immediate family or someone close to [D] or for whom [D] is responsible'.[95] But if this is right, it must surely be interpreted liberally. If X, a bank robber, puts a gun to a customer's (Z's) head and instructs the bank manager (D) to open the safe, D may not have any personal connection with Z, but the circumstances of the threat will surely be enough to make D feel 'responsible' for Z; and it would be very harsh to deny D the defence on the basis that she was not sufficiently attached to Z. If this is correct, as *dicta* from other cases suggest,[96] and as the Law Commission has recommended,[97] then the class of people who the threat might be aimed at has no limits at all.

 Extra detail . . .

It is even possible for the person threatening D and the target of that threat to be the same person. This was so in *Martin*,[98] where D's wife threatened to take her own life unless D drove whilst disqualified in order to take their son to work.[99]

14.3.2.3 The content of the demand

Duress by threats arises in its purest form where X makes an explicit demand that D should commit an offence (eg 'rob the bank or else'). However, a demand of criminal activity may also be vague and/or implicit (eg 'have the money by tomorrow or else'). Where, as in our example, X does not specify a crime, it is unlikely that D will be able to rely on duress by threats, although she may be able to rely on duress by circumstances (**14.4**). This was discussed in *Cole*.

---

[92] [1967] VR 526.
[93] [2000] Crim LR 510.
[94] [1989] QB 290.
[95] [2005] UKHL 22, [21].
[96] *Shayler* [2001] 1 WLR 2206, where the Lord Chief Justice approves a statement to this effect from *Abdul-Hussain* [1999] Crim LR 570, [49].
[97] Law Commission, *Defences of General Application* (No 83, 1977) para 2.46.
[98] [1989] 1 All ER 652.
[99] The court discussed this as a duress by circumstances case, but given that there were explicit threats involved it is better analysed as one of duress by threats.

Cole [1994] Crim LR 582

D robbed two building societies in order to repay a debt. The money lenders had hit D with a baseball bat and threatened him and his family unless he repaid the money, although they did not specify what he should do to get it. D was charged with robbery.[100]

- Crown Court: guilty of robbery.
- Court of Appeal: conviction upheld on appeal. Duress did not apply because: (a) D's offence was not specified by the lenders; and (b) there was a lack of imminence between the threat and D's offence.[101]

The line taken in *Cole* is very restrictive, suggesting that duress by threats will only apply where a single crime is clearly demanded. This line has been softened in *Ali*.

 Ali [1995] Crim LR 303

D, a heroin addict, robbed a building society. D claimed that his dealer (X) had threatened him about unpaid debts, provided him with a gun, and told him to get the money from a bank or building society. D was charged with robbery.[102]

- Crown Court: guilty of robbery.
- Court of Appeal: conviction upheld on appeal. Duress did not apply because of D's prior-fault in forming a relationship with X.[103] Obiter: the level of specificity as to the crime to be committed was sufficient for duress.

Following *Cole* and *Ali* it is clear that duress by threats requires X to have provided some indication of the type of crime that D must commit, but precise details of that crime (eg time, place, etc) are not required. Where D's defence fails on this element, the defence of duress by circumstances should be considered (see **14.4**).

14.3.3 Element 2: D's response to the threat

When analysing D's response to the threat and demand, three main issues should be considered: (a) the necessary causal link between X's threat/demand and D's offence; (b) the imminence of threat, and whether D could have avoided committing the offence; and (c) whether a reasonable person would have acted as D did.

14.3.3.1 Causal link between X's threat/demand and D's offence

Duress only provides a defence where D's offence was compelled by X's threats and demands. The language of causation is commonly used here, though we are not applying

---

[100] Theft Act 1968, s8(1). See **Chapter 9.3**.
[101] We discuss the requirement of imminence at **14.3.3.2**.
[102] Theft Act 1968, s8(1). See **Chapter 9.3**.
[103] Prior-fault in the context of duress was discussed at **14.3.1.2**.

strict rules of legal causation.[104] Rather, what we mean is that D must have offended because of X's threat; that she would not have offended in its absence.[105]

Problems can emerge where D has several reasons for committing the offence, and only one of these constitutes a threat qualifying within the duress threshold. This was the case in *Valderrama-Vega*.

 Valderrama-Vega [1985] Crim LR 220

D was involved in trafficking drugs. He claimed that he did so because of threats of serious harm from a mafia-type organisation; because of financial difficulties; and because of threats to expose his homosexuality. D was charged with drug trafficking offences.

- Crown Court: guilty of drug trafficking. The jury were directed that duress could only apply where D acted 'solely' due to the threats of serious injury.
- Court of Appeal: conviction upheld on appeal. However, the court clarified that the 'sole' motive test was wrong. The threats of serious injury had to be a sufficient cause, such that D would not have offended without them, but they need not be the sole cause.[106]

The approach of the court is sensible, and straightforward. Duress will only apply where the qualifying threat caused D to offend. There may have been other causes in addition, but these are irrelevant and should be discounted.

14.3.3.2 The imminence of the threat and opportunities for escape

Related to the requirement of causation, D must have committed the offence because she had no other reasonable option to escape before the threat would be carried out. This is often referred to as a requirement of 'imminence', because the longer the time between X's threat and D's offence, the more opportunity D is likely to have had to escape the threat without offending (eg by going to the police).

Historically, courts were willing to interpret this requirement quite generously for D. For example, in *Abdul-Hussain*[107] the Court of Appeal allowed the appeal of D who had hijacked a plane and come to England to escape deportation and likely execution in Iraq. Although the execution was not going to happen in the 'immediate' future,[108] the threat of execution was the 'imminent' cause of D's offence, and this was sufficient. The court illustrated their approach with a useful and convincing hypothetical:

> If Anne Frank had stolen a car to escape from Amsterdam and been charged with theft, the tenets of English law would not, in our judgment, have denied her a defence of duress . . . , on the ground that she should have waited for the Gestapo's knock on the door.[109]

---

[104] See **Chapter 2.7** on causation. Strictly speaking, X does not cause D to offend because D makes an informed choice to do so.

[105] *DPP v Bell* [1992] Crim LR 176: in terror, D drove while over the alcohol limit. D was planning to drink drive before the threat, but as he may have been talked out of it by his passengers, it was accepted that the threat was the cause.

[106] See *Brandford* [2016] EWCA Crim 1794: pressure from the exploitation of a relationship is not a qualifying threat for duress, but may be relevant to understanding why a qualifying threat caused D to offend.

[107] [1999] Crim LR 570.

[108] This is why duress was rejected at trial.

[109] Here, again, the court is focussing on the imminence of the threat rather than the immediacy of the threatened harm.

A similar approach was adopted in *Hudson and Taylor*.

 Hudson and Taylor [1971] 2 All ER 244

D and another, aged 17 and 19, admitted committing perjury by failing to testify as to the identity of the suspect of a wounding at trial, leading to his acquittal. D claimed that she lied because she was threatened with being 'cut up' if she identified the suspect, and one of those threatening her was in the public gallery when she gave evidence. D was charged with perjury.

- Crown Court: guilty of perjury. Duress did not apply because the threat was not immediate, D was safe in the court and so the threat could not have been carried out there and then.
- Court of Appeal: appeal allowed. Although the harm threatened could not have been carried out immediately, the threat was still imminent and was the operative cause of D's offence. Duress was also not undermined by D's failure to go to the police before the trial because she believed the police could not provide adequate protection.

The test as applied in these cases simply required D to have no effective means of escape. The threatened harm did not need to be immediate, if it was imminent and operative at the time D offended the defence would be allowed. There is much to be said for this approach, but it is unlikely that the courts will continue to be as generous under the current law.

Hudson and Taylor has not yet been overruled, but it has been criticised in a series of more recent cases that have applied a significantly narrower standard. In *Hasan*,[110] Lord Bingham referred (*obiter*) to *Hudson* as having the 'unfortunate effect of weakening' the imminence requirement, referred to as a 'cardinal feature' of duress.[111] Echoing this, Elias LJ went further in *Batchelor*,[112] criticising the court in *Hudson* for distorting legal principles to allow the defence.[113] These cases do not undermine the potential for a threat to be imminent and operative without being immediate, but they do demonstrate a narrowing of the circumstances where this might be found: where it was possible for D to escape X's threat and avoid offending, it is extremely unlikely that duress will be available.

14.3.3.3 The reasonable steadfastness test

The final element of duress applies a further objective standard; requiring that D should display a reasonable fortitude in resisting the threat and demand from X. For example, if an adult, D, is threatened with serious harm from an infant unless she commits an offence, this threat may satisfy the elements discussed previously, but it is likely that D will be expected to resist the threat. Where D commits the offence in these circumstances, duress will not apply: the threat may be real, but a reasonable person would not have had their will overborne by it.[114]

---

[110] [2005] UKHL 22.

[111] At [25]–[27].

[112] *Batchelor* [2013] EWCA Crim 2638, [15].

[113] See *Brandford* [2016] EWCA Crim 1794 and *Khan* [2018] EWCA Crim 78 for more recent examples.

[114] Smith, 'Duress and Steadfastness: In Pursuit of the Unintelligible' [1999] Crim LR 363.

The objective reasonable fortitude test has been consistently highlighted in the case law,[115] and is usefully illustrated in *Graham*.

Graham [1982] 1 All ER 801

D lived in 'a bizarre ménage a trois' with his wife (V) and homosexual partner (X). D suffered from anxiety and took Valium, making him more susceptible to bullying. X had been violent to both D and V in the past. Following a previous attack, X and D tricked V into returning home, X put a flex around V's neck and instructed D to pull. D did so in fear of X, and V died. D was charged with murder.[116] *(Note: at this time duress could be a defence to murder.)*

- Crown Court: guilty of murder.
- Court of Appeal: conviction upheld on appeal. The test for duress asks if a reasonable and sober person would have acted as D did; the fact that D's steadfastness was weakened by alcohol and Valium is therefore irrelevant.

The objective nature of the test is another reflection of duress as a concession to human frailty as opposed to individual frailty. The question whether D's will was overborne is half the story; the defence is only available if a reasonable person in D's position would also have had their will overborne.

A strictly objective test of steadfastness, however, can result in unfairness. Although duress is not a concession to *individual* frailty, there are certain general characteristics, such as age, that will affect D's ability to resist threats and demands. Interestingly, in contrast to the narrowing of other elements of duress, the courts have responded to this concern by gradually expanding the range of D's characteristics that can be taken into account when applying the reasonable steadfastness test. This is discussed in *Bowen*.

Bowen [1996] 2 Cr App R 157

D obtained various electrical goods on credit by deception, with no way of making repayment. D claimed to be acting under duress, having been threatened to obtain the goods by two other men. Expert evidence showed that D had an IQ of 68, putting him in the bottom 2 per cent of the population, and likely to be extremely suggestible. D was charged with obtaining services by deception.[117]

- Crown Court: guilty of obtaining services by deception. The duress steadfastness test was based on a reasonable person of D's age and sex.
- Court of Appeal: conviction upheld on appeal. Characteristics that affect D's ability to resist a threat and demand beyond age and sex may be relevant, but this does not include D's IQ.

The characteristics recognised in *Bowen* as potentially relevant included D's age and sex, pregnancy, serious physical disability, and recognised mental illness or psychiatric condition.[118] Where D possesses these, the test will be whether a reasonable and sober person *sharing these characteristics* might have also had their will overborne. In this way,

---

[115] *Howe* [1987] 1 All ER 771.
[116] **Chapter 5**.
[117] Now obtaining services dishonestly, Fraud Act 2006, s11. See **Chapter 10.5**.
[118] Buchanan and Virgo, 'Duress and Mental Abnormality' [1999] Crim LR 517.

although *Bowen* can be criticised for excluding the relevance of D's low IQ,[119] it has had a highly liberalising impact on this element of duress.

Point to remember . . .

Despite the expanding of this element, the restrictive objectivity of other elements means that duress remains a very narrow defence. The case of *GAC* provides a useful example.[120] In this case D pleaded duress to a charge of importing drugs, having been threatened by her abusive partner (X). It was accepted that D's characteristics could be taken into account, including the fact that she was suffering from battered women syndrome. However, her defence failed on several other grounds, including the fact that the abuse she was suffering did not amount to a threat of death or serious injury.[121]

14.4 Duress by circumstances

Duress by circumstances is essentially an extension of duress by threats. It has been recognised at common law to provide a defence where there is no direct threat and/or demand from another party, but the surrounding circumstances create an equivalent overbearing of D's will. For example, if D sees a tidal wave crashing towards her on the shore, the wave does not tell her to break into a car and escape or she will be killed, but it may be obvious that this is a reasonable choice for her to take.

Don't be confused . . .

Duress by circumstances has caused considerable confusion for the courts, mainly in terms of its place alongside other defences such as duress by threats and necessity. As a result, it has been inconsistently labelled as 'necessity' or 'necessity of circumstances', etc. As we will discuss, duress by circumstances resembles necessity in certain respects and may even be presented as a subset within necessity,[122] but it is important to analyse and apply it as a separate defence. Whereas necessity continues to operate without clear criteria (discussed at **14.6**), duress by circumstances is possible to apply with some precision.

Duress by circumstances was first recognised in *Willer*.

Willer (1986) 83 Cr App R 225

D drove his car slowly onto a pavement in order to escape from a gang of youths who were intent on doing serious injury to him and his passenger. D was charged with reckless driving, and tried to raise the defence of necessity.

• Crown Court: guilty of reckless driving. Necessity does not apply.

• Court of Appeal: appeal allowed. Necessity is irrelevant, but D does have a defence of duress.

---

[119] Although D's low IQ would not make him less resistant to threats, it will make him less able to identify ways of escaping them. Thus, the threat may appear more serious.

[120] [2013] EWCA Crim 1472.

[121] Loveless, 'Domestic Violence, Coercion and Duress' [2010] Crim LR 93.

[122] Gardner, 'Necessity's Newest Invention' (1991) 11 OJLS 125.

In recognising a defence of duress, the Court of Appeal did not distinguish it as a new form of duress by circumstances. However, this was the necessary implication: the youths were not shouting 'drive on the pavement or else', the threats and demands were not specific, they were circumstantial. This was later confirmed, and to some extent clarified, in *Conway*,[123] where D drove dangerously to escape what he believed were two assailants intent on killing his passenger.[124] It was within this case that the language of duress by circumstances (or 'duress of circumstances') began to be used.

The elements of duress by circumstances are set out in **Table 14.3**.

Table 14.3 Duress by circumstances

A) Exclusions: duress is not a defence to murder, attempted murder, and certain treason offences, and will not apply in circumstances of prior fault;
B) Circumstantial threat and demand: D must have reasonably believed that the circumstances posed a threat of death or serious injury which compelled her to commit the offence; and
C) D's response: D must have shown reasonable steadfastness in response to the threat, only committing the offence because her will was overborne.

14.4.1 Relationship between duress by threats and duress by circumstances

When compared to other general defences, duress by circumstances is still very new to the law. However, because of its close relationship with duress by threats, it has been able to establish itself by mirroring most of the elements of that defence. This has led to some confusion in cases such as *Martin*,[125] where D's wife's threats to commit suicide unless he committed an offence were treated as duress by circumstances rather than the more appropriate defence of duress by threats. However, because of the similarities between the defences, both in substance and rationale, such confusions are not overly problematic.

14.4.2 The elements of duress by circumstances

Most of the elements of duress by circumstances mirror those for duress by threats, and so there is no need to repeat that discussion here. However, it is useful to highlight a few key points to illustrate how those elements apply in the context of duress by circumstances.

14.4.2.1 Exclusions

The same exclusions apply for duress by circumstances as apply to duress by threats (discussed at **14.3.1**). Therefore, duress by circumstances is no defence to murder, attempted murder, and certain treason offences. Also, although there is no case on point, it is likely

---

[123] [1989] QB 290.
[124] They were in fact plain-clothes police officers, wishing to interview his passenger.
[125] [1989] 1 All ER 652.

that duress by circumstances will be excluded where those circumstances were brought about by prior-fault. Taking the example of D who breaks into a car to escape a tidal wave, she may therefore lose the defence if she is a storm chaser who has travelled to the coast to witness the devastation. This would be akin to a form of voluntary association in duress by threats.

14.4.2.2 Element 1: circumstantial threat and demand

This element represents the major difference between duress by threats and duress by circumstances. However, it also retains some important similarities. It was discussed for duress by threats at **14.3.2**.

A) **Differences from duress by threats:** Unlike duress by threats, there is no requirement to show that the threat and demand came from a person (**14.3.2.2**). There is also no need to show that a specific crime was demanded (**14.3.2.3**). Both of these requirements have been applied restrictively within the context of duress by threats, so duress by circumstances provides a useful alternative.

B) **Similarities with duress by threats:** Despite the differences, this element still retains two important and restrictive similarities. First, the threat must still be one of death or serious injury (**14.3.2.1**): duress by circumstances retains the high threshold from duress by threats and is not a simple balance of evils defence. Where the circumstances threatening D do not meet this high threshold, this defence will not apply and D will have to appeal to the defence of necessity. Secondly, although the threat does not need to come from another person, it still cannot come from D (**14.3.2.2**). Thus, the principle from *Rodger and Rose* applies.[126] The restrictive application of these requirements in the context of duress by circumstances is illustrated in *Quayle*.[127]

 Quayle [2005] EWCA Crim 1415

Combined cases involving possession, importation, and/or supply of cannabis for the purposes of relieving the pain of those suffering a variety of conditions. The defences of necessity and/or duress of circumstances were raised.

- Crown Court: guilty of drug offences in all but one of the cases, rejecting D's defence. One case allowed the defence to go to the jury and D was acquitted.
- Court of Appeal: convictions upheld on appeal, and the AG's Reference (concerning the acquitted D) was answered to the effect that the defence should not have been allowed to run.

Duress by circumstances was rejected in the *Quayle* appeals for two main reasons. First, the threat, in that case the additional pain resulting from not using cannabis, was not sufficient to constitute a threat of death or serious injury. Secondly, where the drug offences related to personal use, the threat did not emanate from an external source; it was purely internal to D and was therefore disqualified by the principle in *Rodger and Rose*.

---

[126] [1998] 1 Cr App R 143.
[127] Watson, 'Cannabis and the Defence of Necessity' (1998) 149 NLJ 1260.

14.4.2.3 Element 2: D's response to the perceived threats

The requirements are the same here as those for duress by threats, discussed at **14.3.3**. D's offending must have been caused by the threats and demands of X; D must have made reasonable efforts to avoid offending; and D must have demonstrated reasonable steadfastness in resisting X's threats.

One point within this, which is particularly tricky for duress by circumstances, is identifying the beginning and end of D's compelled conduct. Unlike duress by threats, where there is another party directing what D should do and when, duress by circumstances can be rather more fluid and uncertain. For example, where an intoxicated D is compelled to drive in order to escape a tidal wave or gang of youths, how far can D drive with an operative defence of duress by circumstances? A number of cases have encountered this issue, and the general approach has been to allow the defence to operate until D is clear of the danger, such that if D continues to drive she is now committing an offence (driving over the proscribed alcohol limit) without a defence.[128]

14.5 Public and private defence

The public and private defence, commonly referred to as self-defence,[129] provides a complete defence to any charge where D uses otherwise unlawful force to protect her public or private interests.[130] The public and private defence is now often treated as a single defence, but it is useful to recognise that it comes from the amalgamation of two overlapping defences:

- **Private defence:** The private defence developed at common law, providing a defence where D used force to protect herself or another from physical harm,[131] or in the protection of property.[132]

- **Public defence:** The public defence is set out in section 3 of the Criminal Law Act 1967, providing a defence where D used force to prevent a crime,[133] or in effecting or assisting a lawful arrest.

There will be cases where only one of the two applies. For example, D uses force to protect herself from V, a nine-year-old child under the age of criminal responsibility. D may be able to rely on the private defence in this example, but the public defence will not apply because V cannot commit a crime. Equally, where D uses force to assist

---

[128] *DPP v Bell* [1992] Crim LR 176; *DPP v Jones* [1990] RTR 34; *DPP v Mullally* [2006] EWHC 3448 (Admin).

[129] The term 'self-defence' is common, but misleading. The public and private defence is not limited to the use of force to protect oneself.

[130] See generally Leverick, *Killing in Self-Defence* (2006); Sangero, *Self Defence in Criminal Law* (2006).

[131] *Duffy* [1967] 1 QB 63.

[132] Where D damages property to protect other property, this is governed by the Criminal Damage Act 1971, s5(2)(b) (see **Chapter 9.7.3.2**). However, the public and private defence is still necessary where D uses other force to protect property (eg against the person).

[133] This only applies to the prevention of crimes in English law, as opposed to crimes in other jurisdictions or international crimes: *Jones* [2005] Crim LR 122.

police making an arrest, D qualifies under the public defence, but it is quite possible that D does so despite facing no personal threat and would therefore not qualify for the private defence. However, in the majority of cases, both defences will apply simultaneously. For example, D uses force to protect Z from attack by V, where V would commit an offence in attacking Z. Here D acts both to protect Z and to prevent V's crime.[134]

As a result of their common denominator—that each applies only where D uses force—and as a result of the substantial overlap between public and private interests, these defences are now best analysed as a single public and private defence. The integration of the two has been ongoing for many years within the common law, and has been codified within section 76 of the Criminal Justice and Immigration Act 2008 (CJIA) as amended.

> 76(1) This section applies where in proceedings for an offence—
>
> > (a) an issue arises as to whether a person charged with the offence ('D') is entitled to rely on a defence within subsection (2), and
> >
> > (b) the question arises whether the degree of force used by D against a person ('V') was reasonable in the circumstances.
>
> (2) The defences are—
>
> > (a) the common law defence of self-defence; and
> >
> > (b) the defences provided by section 3(1) of the Criminal Law Act 1967 . . .

Where no exclusion applies, the public and private defence requires the satisfaction of two core elements, usefully characterised as trigger and response. We discuss the standard application of these core trigger and response elements, as well as their adapted application to certain exceptional categories of defendant. The structure of the defence, and our analysis that follows, is set out in **Table 14.4**.

Table 14.4 Public and private defence

A) Exclusions: the defence will not apply to an offence committed by D without force, and will not apply in certain circumstances of prior-fault;
B) Trigger: D must have believed (subjective) that force was immediately required in order to protect her public or private interests; and
C) Response: the amount of force used by D must have been reasonable (objective) on the facts as believed them to be.
D) Exceptions: the core elements of the defence may be applied differently where D is a householder, is intoxicated, is insane, and/or is delusional.

After D has raised the defence, the legal burden is on the prosecution to prove beyond reasonable doubt that the elements of the defence are not satisfied.[135]

---

[134] *Clegg* [1995] 1 All ER 334, 343.
[135] *O'Brian* [2004] EWCA Crim 2900.

14.5.1 Exclusions

There are two areas where the public and private defence will be excluded: in relation to certain offences; and in circumstances of prior-fault.

14.5.1.1 Offences where D cannot raise the public and private defence

Unlike duress, the public and private defence is *not* excluded from certain categories of offence.[136] However, although the defence may apply (at least potentially) across all offence categories, it is excluded where an offence is committed without 'force' being used. The requirement of force means that the defence is most commonly applied to murder, robbery, false imprisonment, and the offences against the person more generally. For example, D relies on the public and private defence where she hits V, causing ABH, in order to prevent V stabbing her with a knife.[137]

The requirement of 'force' obliges courts to examine the facts of each case where the defence is raised to identify whether D used force to commit the offence, and so findings in either direction can sometimes turn on fine distinctions. For example, there has been debate in recent years about the potential for the public and private defence to apply to crimes of dangerous or careless driving, crimes that do not typically entail the use of force against the person or property, but may do so in exceptional cases.[138] The requirement of force can also be problematic from a policy perspective, seeming to incentivise more direct and/or damaging methods of defence. For example, in *Blake v DPP*,[139] D was charged with criminal damage having written in felt pen on a concrete pillar outside the Houses of Parliament in protest against the Iraq war. Denying the public and private defence, the court held that D's act was 'insufficient to amount to the use of force', suggesting that D would have had more chance of using the defence if he had caused greater damage.[140] Faced with complexities of this kind, courts have sometimes questioned whether force should remain an essential requirement for the defence.[141] However, the use of force remains essential under the current law; and where force is not used, other defences such as duress of circumstances should be considered.

 Extra detail . . .

Does the public and private defence apply to preparatory acts in anticipation of defensive force? For example, if D knows that V is going to try and kill her in a week's time, can D, in self-defence, purchase a gun without a licence? Or more proximately, if D is caught in a shoot-out and picks up a discarded

---

[136] Usefully reiterated in *Oraki v DPP* [2018] EWHC 115 (Admin): confirming that self-defence can apply to an obstruction of a police officer in the execution of his duty (Police Act 1996, s89(2)). See Laird, Commentary [2018] Crim LR 388.

[137] See **Chapter 7** on offences against the person.

[138] See *Riddell* [2017] EWCA Crim 41. Freer, 'Driving Force: Self-Defence and Dangerous Driving' (2018) 77 CLJ 9. Cf the dangerous driving case of *Bailey* [2013] EWCA Crim 378 where there was no force used, and the defence could not apply.

[139] [1993] Crim LR 586.

[140] The absurdity of this was noted by Brooke LJ in *Bayer v DPP* [2003] EWHC 2567 (Admin). See also *DPP v Stratford Magistrates' Court* [2017] EWHC 1794 (Admin): discussing the actions of those protesting arms sales.

[141] Discussed in *Oraki v DPP* [2018] EWHC 115 (Admin).

gun for protection, can she claim self-defence for this brief moment of unlawful possession? The law would speak with a strange moral voice if it said that D was justified in these cases to use the gun to kill or injure V in defence, but has no defence to her possession of the gun. With this in mind, courts have been willing to extend the public and private defence to cover certain preparatory acts, particularly if they are proximate to or simultaneous with the use of force.[142] To avoid confusing the limits of the public and private defence further, it is contended that such preparatory acts are more appropriately analysed using duress of circumstance.

14.5.1.2 Exclusion on the basis of prior-fault

For duress, as we explained, D's voluntary association where coercion was *objectively* foreseeable undermines D's defence (**14.3.1.2**). However, this very strict rule is not applied to the public and private defence, and it is clear that D may appeal to the defence even where she instigated the violence with V (ie it does not matter 'who started it').[143] The only exception to this is where D has *consciously* manipulated V into attacking her in order to retaliate in 'apparent' defence. In these circumstances, confirmed in *Rashford*,[144] D may not rely on the public and private defence.

14.5.2 Element 1: trigger—the necessity for force

The trigger element within the public and private defence is essentially a threshold question: was it necessary to use *any* force against V on the facts as D believed them to exist? Questions concerning the *degree* of force used should be avoided until the second element. For example, V begins pushing D, and D reacts by shooting V. In this example, D is likely to satisfy the first element since she may well have believed it was necessary to use *some* defensive force; but D will fail on the second element, as shooting V is clearly an unreasonably excessive response.

The trigger element is almost entirely subjective: unlike duress (**14.3.1.2**), we do not ask whether a reasonable person in D's position would have believed that force was necessary; we ask simply whether it was necessary on the facts as D believed them to be. Thus, this element can be satisfied even where D was wrong, and even where her mistake was unreasonable. This approach has raised concerns in relation to ECHR compatibility, particularly where D has killed V, and we return to this when discussing potential reforms to the law (**14.7.1.3**). However, since being established in *Gladstone Williams*, it has been consistently applied in subsequent cases,[145] and is now codified in section 76(4)(b) of the CJIA.

 Gladstone Williams (1984) 87 Cr App R 276

V witnessed X rob a woman in the street. V caught X and held him down, knocking X to the ground on a second occasion when X attempted to get away. D witnessed the second altercation, and thought

---

[142] *AG's Reference (No 2 of 1983)* [1984] QB 456 (making and storing petrol bombs to protect shop); *McAuley* [2009] EWCA Crim 2130 (carrying a knife for self-protection).

[143] *Keane* [2010] EWCA Crim 2514.

[144] [2005] EWCA Crim 3377.

[145] *Beckford v R* [1988] AC 130 (Privy Council).

V was assaulting X. D punched V in the face in an attempt to defend X. D was charged with assault occasioning actual bodily harm.[146]

- Crown Court: guilty of assault occasioning actual bodily harm. The judge directed that, for self-defence, D must have honestly, and on *reasonable grounds*, believed that force was necessary.
- Court of Appeal: appeal allowed. The necessity element must be based on an honest belief, but there is no requirement of reasonable grounds.

The essential question, then, is not whether D's belief in the necessity of force was reasonable, but whether it was honest. The reasonableness of D's belief will provide useful evidence in this regard, but it is not determinative.[147] This is the case whether D was defending against force to the person as in *Gladstone Williams*, property,[148] or in the context of crime prevention or criminal apprehension.[149]

Highlighting the subjective construction of the trigger element, however, does not tell us how to *assess* D's subjective belief. In this regard, we do not simply ask D whether she thought force was necessary. Rather, we take the facts as she subjectively believed them, and our question is whether the jury accepts that *any* force was necessary on those facts. In answering this question, several sub-questions have emerged within the case law.

14.5.2.1 Is it ever necessary to use force pre-emptively?

The answer here is 'yes'. Although the public and private defence will usually apply where D is responding to another's attack, this need not always be the case. In *Devlin v Armstrong*,[150] for example, the Court of Appeal in Northern Ireland held that the defence could apply where D uses force to 'ward off or prevent attack' as long as she honestly believed attack was 'imminent'.[151] The imminence requirement has been interpreted narrowly, and is seen as crucial to ensure that the defence does not extend to cover aggressive, as opposed to defensive, force; as well as excluding certain protest cases where non-forceful democratic processes were available.[152] However, this also has the effect of limiting the defence in the context of abused women who kill their abusers in circumstances where they pre-empt violent attacks which are not imminent.[153]

14.5.2.2 Is it ever necessary to use force where D could have retreated?

There is no duty to retreat, even where D knows that staying at a certain location is likely to result in attack from V and the need for defensive force. Over recent years, courts

---

[146] Offences Against the Person Act 1861, s47. See **Chapter 7.4.**

[147] *Dewar v DPP* [2010] EWHC 1050 (Admin): D's recognition that his use of force was not necessary *after* the event does not undermine his defence (based on his beliefs at the time of the event).

[148] *Faraj* [2007] EWCA Crim 1033: D forcefully detained a gas repair man (V), believing he was a burglar.

[149] *Morris* [2013] EWCA Crim 436: D injured V with his taxi, wrongly believing that V was trying to make off without payment.

[150] [1971] NI 13.

[151] At 33.

[152] See *DPP v Stratford Magistrates' Court* [2017] EWHC 1794 (Admin): the defence should not have been available to arms sales protestors who blocked highways accessing a sales convention.

[153] McColgan, 'In Defence of Battered Women Who Kill' (1993) 13 OJLS 508.

have treated a willingness to retreat as evidence in D's favour, suggesting that the force D then used was necessary; but force may still be necessary even where D has chosen to remain.[154] This is now confirmed, and codified, in section 76(6A) of the CJIA.

14.5.2.3 Is it ever necessary to use force against innocent/lawful force?

It is generally not permissible to use force against lawful actions. In other words, it is not necessary for D to use force against another party who is acting in lawful self-defence, or against a police officer making a lawful arrest. However, this rule is not absolute. Where D is attacked by a child under 10 or someone who is insane, the attacker may not be committing an offence, but it still may be necessary to use some defensive force.[155] Equally, the defence may apply where D has made a mistake, and we have to assess the events on the basis of D's honest beliefs. For example, where D believes that she is defending against an unlawful attack or preventing crime, but in fact V is acting lawfully, the necessity element may still be satisfied.[156]

 Extra detail . . .

There was interesting use of this principle in *Re A*,[157] where Ward LJ held that the public and private defence could be employed to justify the separation of conjoined twins. The weaker twin (V) relied on her sibling's organs for survival, but this resulted in increasing strain being put upon those organs that would inevitably lead to the death of both twins. In this manner, although V was clearly an innocent party, the idea was that separation (resulting in V's immediate death) could be justified *in defence* of her sibling. This approach offered one way of resolving a complex and tragic case, but it is contended that the public and private defence is not suitable in these circumstances; any implication that V's life amounted to a forceful attack upon her sibling is inappropriate.

14.5.2.4 Is it ever necessary to use force where the justifying reasons are unknown to D?

With the trigger element based on D's subjective appreciation of the facts, an interesting problem emerges where D's force is in fact objectively justified but she is unaware of this. For example, D forcefully attacks V, unaware that V was about to attack D. D's force was, as a matter of fact, necessary, but she did not know this was the case. Where D uses force in these circumstances, it has been held in *Dadson* that she will *not* be able to rely on the public and private defence.[158] If D had been aware of the justifying circumstances (eg that she was about to come under attack, that V was about to commit a crime, etc) then her use of force would be necessary; but the focus on D's subjective knowledge (the facts as she believes them to be) means that the defence cannot apply where such circumstances are unknown.

---

[154] *Bird* [1985] 2 All ER 513, 516; *Duffy v DPP* [2007] EWHC 3169 (Admin).
[155] *Bayer v DPP* [2003] EWHC 2567 (Admin).
[156] *Gladstone Williams* (1984) 87 Cr App R 276.
[157] [2000] 4 All ER 961.
[158] (1850) 2 Den 35. Funk, 'Justifying Justifications' (1990) 19 OJLS 630; Christopher, 'Unknowing Justification and the Logical Necessity of the *Dadson* Principle in Self-Defence' (1995) 15 OJLS 229.

14.5.3 Element 2: response—a reasonable degree of force

Having established the trigger that *some* force was necessary on the facts as D believed them to be, the second element of the public and private defence focusses on the degree of force used by D. This is a jury question.[159] Where the degree of force used was *reasonable*, or *proportionate*,[160] even if it equated to more force than was threatened by V,[161] the defence will be satisfied and D will be acquitted. Where D's degree of force was unreasonable, the defence will fail in all cases.

To identify 'reasonable force', the courts have adopted a middle ground between subjective and objective approaches.

- **Subjective:** A purely subjective approach, asking whether D believed the amount of force she used was reasonable, would be inappropriate. For example, D may honestly believe that it is reasonable to shoot V in response to being pushed, but this is not justified force.

- **Objective:** A purely objective approach, asking what degree of force would have been used by a reasonable person in D's circumstances, would be equally inappropriate. This is particularly true where D has made an honest mistake (eg incorrectly believing that V is about to attack her). An approach to reasonable force that only takes account of the objective facts would always deny the defence in such cases: where V is not in fact threatening or involved in an offence, then no degree of force is reasonable.

The current law combines these approaches by asking whether the degree of force D used was *objectively* reasonable based on the *subjective* facts as D believed them to be.[162] Thus, for example, where D mistakenly believes V is about to shoot her, and so responds by stabbing V, the question for the jury is whether D's force (stabbing) was objectively reasonable based on D's belief that she was about to be shot. As confirmed and codified within section 76(3)–(4) of the CJIA, this will be the case regardless of whether D's mistaken belief was reasonably or unreasonably held, as long as it was honestly held.

When applying this element, it is important to remember that the focus is on the degree of *force* employed by D and not the degree of *harm* caused. For example, suppose V attempts to steal D's handbag in the street, and D reacts by pushing V away. It is likely, here, that D's force (the push) is both necessary and reasonable. However, what if V trips as a result of the push, hits her head on the pavement, and dies? The answer is, from the perspective of the public and private defence, that nothing has changed: the focus is on the reasonableness of the force (the push) and not the resulting harm (death). Thus, where D's force involves an obvious risk of causing death or serious harm as, for example, where D pushes V off a cliff, shoots V, etc, then this is likely to make D's force unreasonable.[163] However, just because D's reasonable use of force results in an unforeseen unreasonable degree of harm, this will not undermine D's defence.[164]

---

[159] *AG's Reference (No 1 of 1975)* [1976] 2 All ER 937, 947.
[160] The terms 'reasonable' and 'proportionate' can be used interchangeably in this context.
[161] The public and private defence is not a balance of evils defence.
[162] *Owino* [1996] 2 Cr App R 128; *Harvey* [2009] EWCA Crim 469.
[163] It will rarely, if ever, be reasonable to use deadly force to protect property.
[164] *Keane* [2010] EWCA Crim 2514; *Noye* [2011] EWCA Crim 650, [9] and [55].

When assessing the objective reasonableness of D's degree of force, on the facts as she subjectively believed them to be, the jury must also take account of the circumstances surrounding the use of that force. Essentially, this involves a margin of appreciation for D; acknowledging that where she was in a pressured and stressful situation, she may not have been able to think entirely rationally about the level of force to be used. This rule has been expressed by the courts in various ways, including: 'it will be recognised that a person defending himself cannot weigh to a nicety the exact measure of his necessary defensive action';[165] 'one did not use jewellers' scales to measure reasonable force';[166] and so on. It is also confirmed, and codified, within section 76(7) of the CJIA.

Even acknowledging D's margin of appreciation, however, it should always be remembered that where the degree of force used by D is unreasonable the defence will fail. This was famously illustrated in the case of *Martin*.

 Martin [2001] EWCA Crim 2245

D lived in a remote farmhouse in Norfolk. He was woken by two people trying to burgle his premises, disturbed them, and then shot them as they tried to escape. One was killed and the other seriously injured. D was charged with murder and a serious offence against the person.[167]

- Crown Court: guilty of murder and wounding offence. The public and private defence was rejected by the jury.
- Court of Appeal: appeal allowed, substituting murder for manslaughter. Public and private defence was not satisfied because of the excessive force used by D. However, new evidence provided the basis for a partial defence of diminished responsibility.

Martin is an important case for a number of reasons. First, it provides a useful example of the limits of the public and private defence: use of force by D was clearly necessary both to protect himself and his property, and to prevent crime, but the force he used was excessive and so the defence failed. Secondly, it demonstrates the role that the partial defences can play where D's defensive force is excessive: in this case diminished responsibility.[168] And, thirdly, the case was also a catalyst for public, and ultimately political, concern about the operation of the defence in the context of householders who use force against unlawful intruders.

14.5.4 Exceptions: special categories of defendant

The public and private defence has attracted considerable scrutiny in its application to certain categories of defendant, and this has led to adaptations both in the common law and through statute. In particular, the application of the defence may be different where D is a householder, where D is voluntarily intoxicated, and/or where D is insane or delusional.

---

[165] *Palmer* [1971] AC 814.
[166] *Reed v Wastie* [1972] Crim LR 221.
[167] For murder, see **Chapter 5**; for offences against the person, see **Chapter 7**.
[168] Wake, 'Battered Women, Startled Householders and Psychological Self-Defence' (2013) 77 JCL 433.

14.5.4.1 Householder defendants

Following *Martin*, the public, fuelled by inaccurate media commentary, became concerned that householders were not adequately protected by the public and private defence where force is used against a trespasser. This issue became politicised, and despite the enactment of the CJIA clarifying the current law, there continued to be calls for a wider defence in these circumstances.[169] The result, contained within section 43 of the Crime and Courts Act 2013, was the amendment of section 76 of the CJIA in the context of householders (non-trespassers[170]) who use defensive force against those they believe to be trespassers[171] within the relevant domestic property.[172]

> 76(5A) In a householder case, the degree of force used by D is not to be regarded as having been reasonable in the circumstances as D believed them to be if it was grossly disproportionate in those circumstances.

The amendment made clear that 'grossly disproportionate' force will never be 'reasonable', and so will always fail the second element of the defence.

In line with the political aims of the amendment, it might be assumed that householders (unlike non-householders) who use 'disproportionate' force, but not 'grossly disproportionate' force, would be treated as having acted reasonably. However, this straightforward interpretation has not been accepted by the courts. In *Collins*,[173] the Divisional Court found that where D's defensive force was 'disproportionate' in a householder case, this merely provides discretion for the jury to find that the force was reasonable, it does not mandate that outcome. The reasonableness assessment will take account of the householder's unique position (eg the court will be more understanding of a failure to retreat, and perhaps her greater feelings of panic and vulnerability), but a finding of unreasonable force remains possible. This interpretation has been confirmed in *Ray*.[174]

Ray [2017] EWCA Crim 1391

D was at home with X, the former partner of V. V and X had had a volatile and violent relationship, and V was unhappy about X's new relationship with D. V arrived at X's house at night, angry and threatening violence. D tried to make V leave, and following a violent struggle fatally stabbed V. D was charged with murder and raised the public and private defence (as a householder), claiming that he thought V had a weapon and intended to harm him and X.

---

[169] Skinner, 'Populist Politics and Shooting Burglars' [2005] Crim LR 275.

[170] Including guests: *Day* [2015] EWCA Crim 1646.

[171] It is not necessary that V is in fact a trespasser, it is sufficient for D to rely on the defence that he is not a trespasser and he believes V to be so: *Cheeseman* [2019] EWCA Crim 149.

[172] The householder defence does not apply where D has pursued V out of the property before inflicting violence: *Williams* [2020] EWCA Crim 193.

[173] *R (Collins) v Secretary of State for Justice* [2016] EWHC 33 (Admin): D held a burglar in a headlock, causing serious injury, before police arrived. Dsouza, 'Understanding the "Householder Defence": Proportionality and Reasonableness in Defensive Force' (2016) 75 CLJ 192; Laird, Commentary [2016] Crim LR 438.

[174] Laird, Commentary [2018] Crim LR 432.

- Crown Court: guilty of murder. The trial judge directed the jury, in line with *Collins*, that they should first consider whether the degree of force was grossly disproportionate, and then, if it was not, separately consider whether it was reasonable.
- Court of Appeal: appeal dismissed, and conviction for murder upheld.

It was argued in *Ray* that *Collins* had effectively undermined the householder amendment; that the decision (contrary to the intentions of the legislature) treated the householder in the same way as the non-householder. This argument was rejected by the Court of Appeal, confirming the interpretation in *Collins*, but also clarifying the different position of householders. The court highlighted that whereas disproportionate force from a *non*-householder will always be unreasonable, the same force from a householder will not be determinative of reasonableness, which may be assessed by the jury with reference to all surrounding facts. *Ray* thereby provides some useful clarification, but the application of the defence to householders remains complex and problematic. Most importantly, where the question of proportionate force is separated from our evaluation of reasonable force, it is difficult to identify the content of the latter. Further clarification is still required to explain where force may be disproportionate and yet reasonable.

14.5.4.2 Intoxicated defendants

Although D may well seek to rely on honest but unreasonable mistakes when raising the public and private defence (**14.5.2**), this will *not* be permissible where such beliefs result from voluntary intoxication. Where D is voluntarily intoxicated, the defence will only apply where a reasonable sober person would have made the same mistake as D. For example, if D takes a hallucinogenic drug which causes her to mistakenly believe she is being attacked, the reasonableness of her defensive force will be judged in relation to the threat that would be perceived by a reasonable and sober person in her place. This was held in the case of *Hatton*,[175] and has been confirmed, and codified, within section 76(5) of the CJIA.

 ***Hatton* [2005] EWCA Crim 2951**

Heavily intoxicated, having drunk more than 20 pints of beer, D killed V with several blows of a sledgehammer. D raised self-defence on the grounds that he thought V (who had told D that he was an SAS officer) had attacked him with a stick that D, in his intoxicated state, thought was a samurai sword. D was charged with murder.

- Crown Court: guilty of murder. The court did not allow D to rely on his intoxicated mistake as a basis for self-defence.
- Court of Appeal: conviction upheld on appeal. The lower court was correct not to allow D to rely on his intoxicated mistake.

The decision in *Hatton*, and the policy it follows, have been subject to criticism.[176] It seems strange, for example, that although other unreasonable beliefs can ground

---

[175] [2005] EWCA Crim 2951.
[176] Dingwall, 'Intoxicated Mistakes About the Need for Self-Defence' (2007) 70 MLR 127; Spencer, 'Drunken Defence' (2006) 65 CLJ 267.

self-defence, an intoxicated mistake is singled out for special treatment. However, it is a public policy decision (reflecting a general concern about intoxicated offenders) that has been consistently endorsed.[177]

14.5.4.3 Insane or delusional defendants

In addition to cases of intoxicated defendants, the law has developed rules to deal with defendants who seek to rely on mistakes induced by mental disorders. The courts have concluded that D may *not* rely on mistakes, however honest, that have been caused by such disorders. In these cases, the reasonableness of D's defensive force will be assessed on the basis of a reasonable (non-delusional) person's assessment of the threat. When considering this exception, two alternative cases should be distinguished, with the latter being more controversial:

A) **Insane delusions:** Although D will not be able to rely on an insane delusion to establish the public and private defence, the insanity defence offers a route to qualified acquittal. Indeed, when considering D's welfare (and the protection of others) the disposal orders within the special verdict will often be more appropriate for D than an unqualified acquittal. This is explored in *Oye* (discussed earlier at **14.2.2**).[178]

B) **Non-insane delusions:** Where D forms a delusional belief due to mental illness, but does not satisfy the insanity defence, preventing D relying on that belief may be to exclude all defence options. This was apparent in *Martin* (discussed earlier at **14.5.3**),[179] where D was not able to rely on psychiatric evidence that he perceived threats to be greater than a normal person would, mitigated in that case only by the availability of the partial defence of diminished responsibility. It also arose in the recent case of *Taj*.

 Taj [2018] EWCA Crim 1743

D came across V's broken-down vehicle, and stopped to help. In a paranoid state (resulting from a drug-induced psychosis) D became convinced that V, who was entirely innocent, was a terrorist intending to detonate a bomb. D called the police, who arrived and reassured D, and he was asked to move on. However, D had 'ruminating thoughts' that V was a terrorist and returned after the police had gone, attacking V and causing serious injuries. D raised self-defence as an answer to charges of attempted murder.

- Crown Court: guilty of attempted murder. D could not rely on his mistaken belief because it was induced by voluntary intoxication.
- Court of Appeal: conviction upheld on appeal.

Liability is confirmed in *Taj* on the application of the intoxication rule codified in section 76(5) of the CJIA, discussed earlier at **14.5.4.2**. The application of intoxication rules is controversial in *Taj* because D was not under the direct influence of drugs, but was suffering from psychosis induced by previous drug-taking.[180] Significantly for present

---

[177] See eg Law Commission, *Intoxication and Criminal Liability* (No 314, 2009) para 3.53.
[178] [2013] EWCA Crim 1725. Child and Sullivan, 'When Does the Insanity Defence Apply? Some Recent Cases' [2014] Crim LR 787.
[179] [2002] Crim LR 136.
[180] See discussion at **Chapter 13.2.2.1**.

purposes, the lack of present drug-taking also opened the possibility that D's psychosis (and mistaken belief) was caused by an underlying condition distinct from intoxication. For the court, even if this were the case, the 'equally apposite' precedent from *Oye* may still be applied to deny self-defence.[181] The problem with these decisions, and why they are not apposite to *Oye*, is that D has no alternative route to acquittal.[182]

14.6 Necessity

The definition of the defence of necessity in English law remains an enigma, but it is clear that the criminal law needs to provide such a defence. It is best understood as an imperfect safety net, a complete and general defence of last resort where no other defence is available but liability would be inappropriate. In this way, the necessity defence represents an acceptance that within the infinite variety and complexity of human events, those crafting the criminal law will never be able to predict and account for every variation. Where unexpected facts lead to an inappropriate acquittal, this is to be regretted but tolerated. In such a case there is no broad overarching category of offences that should be applied to catch those who might otherwise avoid liability. That would be intolerable. In contrast, where unexpected facts could lead to inappropriate liability, the law rightly sacrifices principles of coherence to find an acquittal. The principal vehicle for this has become the defence of necessity.[183]

 Extra detail . . .

Alongside necessity, other approaches have been developed to achieve the same outcome. Most notably, this has included the use of prosecutorial discretion simply to avoid bringing those who commit necessary crimes within the criminal system,[184] as well as the use of necessity in the guise of other defences or legal rules.[185] However, both approaches can be criticised,[186] and, arguably, the defence of necessity provides a preferable route.

The defence of necessity has had an interesting history: its existence has often been denied by courts and commentators, but then gratefully deployed in times of legal

---

[181] At [61]–[64].

[182] For critical analysis of the case, see Dsouza, 'Intoxication, Psychoses, and Self-Defence: Evaluating Taj' [2018] Arch Rev 6; Child, Crombag, and Sullivan, 'Defending the Delusional, the Irrational, and the Dangerous' [2020] Crim LR 306.

[183] Williams, 'Necessity' [1978] Crim LR 128.

[184] Following the Zeebrugge disaster eg no charges were brought against the corporal who ordered a man to be forcefully detached from an escape ladder (the man was frozen with fear and cold, and was blocking the escape of others): Leverick, *Killing in Self-Defence* (2006) 6–11.

[185] *Gillick* [1986] AC 112 provides a notable example, where the court applied flawed reasoning about medical judgement not being compatible with a guilty mind, in order to avoid liability where a doctor (D) prescribed the contraceptive pill to an underage girl. See **Chapter 3.4.1.2**.

[186] On prosecutorial discretion, see Rogers, 'Restructuring the Exercise of Prosecutorial Discretion in England and Wales' (2006) 26 OJLS 775.

need.[187] Where it has been recognised and applied, it seems to operate on a simple balance of evils: if D's evil (ie the offence she commits) is less serious than the evil avoided by committing it, then she is entitled to the defence; we might even say she has done the right thing.[188]

The problem lies in setting limits on the defence. If we define necessity in greater detail, then we risk sacrificing its utility as a safety net that can apply to unexpected facts. However, if the only rule defining the offence is a balance of evils test, then the defence becomes potentially impossibly wide, allowing D to raise the defence whenever she believes she has acted for good reason. The reaction of the courts has been pragmatic, to resist further definition and restriction, but to apply the defence reluctantly, and always with its potential indeterminate dangers in mind. The words of Lord Denning and Edmund Davies LJ in *Southwark London Borough v Williams* provide a useful illustration of this, discussing the potential application of necessity where a homeless person steals food or enters another's premises for shelter:

> [I]f hunger were once allowed to be an excuse for stealing, it would open a door through which all kinds of lawlessness and disorder would pass . . . If homelessness were once admitted as a defence to trespass, no one's house would be safe. Necessity would open a door which no man could shut ... The reason for such circumspection is clear—necessity can very easily become simply a mask for anarchy.[189]

The problem with this approach to necessity, however, is that it sends a mixed and complicated message to the public; some might even say a contradictory message. And, in this way, it can provide false hope. We have seen, for example, the defence of necessity employed on numerous occasions in an effort to justify drug offences committed to relieve severe pain,[190] and in even more extreme cases to justify assisted suicide or euthanasia.[191] Such cases, of course, were never likely to succeed. Although a case can be made for both on a balance of evils test, the courts are extremely circumspect about fundamental shifts that bring into question legislative codes and policy decisions. Despite its potential breadth, the necessity defence is only likely to succeed if a case arises where its precedent can be contained; only where there is a genuine belief that its unique facts have been missed or not catered for within the current law; only where it is exceptional.

Despite these problems, and despite judicial reluctance, the defence of necessity has been applied within a number of exceptional cases. It has been applied, for example, to justify detention of a person suffering from a mental disorder;[192] to justify the jettisoning of cargo from a ship to save the lives of those on board;[193] to justify the force-feeding of

---

[187] Stephen went as far as to say that rules of necessity could never be laid down in advance: *A History of the Criminal Law* (1883) vol 2, 108.

[188] Where necessity is recognised, it is generally understood to operate as a justification as opposed to an excuse.

[189] [1971] 2 All ER 175, 179–181.

[190] *Quayle* [2005] EWCA Crim 1415.

[191] *R (Nicklinson) v Ministry of Justice* [2014] UKSC 38; Stark, 'Necessity and *Nicklinson*' [2013] Crim LR 949; Ost, 'Euthanasia and the Defence of Necessity' [2005] Crim LR 255.

[192] *Bournewood Trust* [1998] 3 All ER 289.

[193] *Mouse's Case* (1608) 12 Co Rep 63.

prisoners;[194] to justify procuring an abortion to save the mother;[195] to justify a police officer instructing cars to travel the wrong way on a one-way-street to allow ambulances access;[196] and so on.[197] The circumstances of necessity are usefully illustrated, and discussed, in *F v West Berkshire Authority*.[198]

 F v West Berkshire Authority [1989] 2 All ER 545

V, a 36-year-old patient in a psychiatric hospital, formed a sexual relationship with another patient. Medical evidence found it would be 'disastrous' from a psychiatric perspective if she became pregnant, but there were problems ensuring the use of ordinary contraception. In order to allow V to continue her relationship, V's mother, acting as her next friend, applied for a court declaration that the performance of a sterilisation operation without V's consent (she was unable to consent) would be lawful.

- Court: declaration granted.
- Court of Appeal: appeal dismissed.
- House of Lords: appeal dismissed. The doctors' actions would be protected by the defence of necessity. Duress by circumstances is not available here because the 'threat' (ie pregnancy) does not meet the threshold of death or serious injury.

Interestingly, following many of these cases, where it has been accepted that the courts were correct to apply a defence, legislation has followed to create a specifically tailored defence to apply in the future. In many ways, this is the ideal situation for necessity: catching the exceptional case within the imperfect safety net, alerting to the need for a defence, and then for a precise defence to be created. On a slightly grander scale, this is one way to characterise the creation of duress by circumstances at common law.

However, there remain cases where necessity has been recognised and the creation of a specific defence has not followed. For these cases, and other exceptional cases in the future, the necessity defence remains their only imperfect option. Chief among these is necessity as a defence to murder, largely because of the inapplicability of duress by threats or circumstances in this context.

14.6.1 Necessity as a defence to murder

When considering necessity as a defence to murder, it is useful to begin with the case of *Dudley and Stephens*.

194 *Leigh v Gladstone* (1909) 26 TLR 139.
195 *Bourne* [1939] 1 KB 687.
196 *Johnson v Phillips* [1975] 3 All ER 682.
197 The case for expanding necessity further is made in Edwards, 'Good and Harm, Excuses and Justifications, and the Moral Narratives of Necessity' in Reed and Bohlander (eds), *General Defences in Criminal Law* (2014) 75.
198 This case should now be read with the Mental Capacity Act 2005 in mind.

Dudley and Stephens (1884) 14 QBD 273

D1, D2, and V were shipwrecked, and spent 18 days drifting in an open boat. After several days without food or water, D1 and D2 decided to murder V (the cabin boy) and eat him in order to survive. They did so, and four days later they were rescued. D1 and D2 were charged with murder.

- Assizes: on instruction from the judge, the jury returned a special verdict, making findings of fact that D1 and D2 would probably have died if they had not eaten V, and that V (being very weak already) would certainly have died. The case was then adjourned to the Royal Courts of Justice.
- High Court: guilty of murder, with a sentence of death. [The prisoners were afterwards respited and their sentences commuted to six months' imprisonment without hard labour.]

The rationale for rejecting the necessity defence in *Dudley and Stephens* is disputed, but two main reasons are often highlighted from the court's judgment.[199] The first is that, at this time, necessity was not thought to provide a defence to murder. Following more recent case law, although the point is not settled, it is likely that necessity can be a defence to murder. The second reason, however, has continued to influence the application of the defence. This was the fact that D1 and D2 *chose* to kill V. This is unlike the hypothetical case of the mountain climber, D, whose partner, V, has fallen from the cliff face and is pulling D with her: D must cut the rope (causing her partner to fall) in order to prevent them both being dragged from the cliff. In contrast, the defendants in *Dudley and Stephens* picked the cabin boy to be killed when it could have been any of their number who was selected to die. There has been some discussion of whether the drawing of lots would have led to a different legal result (as it was held it would have done, *obiter*, in a US case[200]) but even this was found to be unacceptable.[201]

Following this, it is notable that on the few occasions where the necessity defence has been successfully applied there has been no problem of victim selection analogous to *Dudley and Stephens*. The most famous of these is the case of *Re A*.

 Re A (Children) [2000] 4 All ER 961

J and M were conjoined twins. Although they had separate vital organs, medical evidence established that the stronger twin (J) was sustaining the life of M through their common artery. If left conjoined, J's heart would fail within months and they would both die; if separated, J had the potential for a healthy life but M would die within minutes. J and M's parents refused on religious grounds to consent to an operation to separate the twins. Doctors applied for a declaration that separating the twins (killing M) would not be unlawful.

- Court: declaration granted.
- Court of Appeal: appeal dismissed.

---

[199] See generally Simpson, *Cannibalism and the Common Law* (1984).
[200] *US v Holmes*, 26 Fed Cas 360 (1841).
[201] *Dudley and Stephens* (1884) 14 QBD 273, 285.

The reasoning of the court in *Re A* is varied, but it is clear that Brooke LJ based his decision on necessity. He set out three requirements for the defence:

(a) the act is needed to avoid inevitable and irreparable evil;

(b) no more should be done than is reasonably necessary for the purpose to be achieved;

(c) the evil inflicted must not be disproportionate to the evil avoided.

These requirements provide useful points of reference for the application of necessity. However, importantly, they remain vastly over-inclusive and should not be misunderstood as criteria for the defence: they are required, but they are not sufficient. This was confirmed in the case itself, where each of the judges was obviously keen to limit the case to its particular facts. A useful illustration of the over-inclusivity of the requirements set out by Brooke LJ is also provided by Dennis:

Suppose P, a hospital patient, urgently needs a blood transfusion to survive, but she has a very rare blood group. As it happens, Q, the patient in the next bed, has the same rare blood group, but refuses to make a donation of blood even though she could do so without risk to herself. May, D, the doctor treating P, take the blood from Q without her consent?[202]

As Dennis goes on to explain, it is arguable that if D forcefully takes blood from Q, she will satisfy the requirements set out in *Re A*. The 'rare' blood type also makes this a case, unlike *Dudley and Stephens*, where there is no problem of selection. However, if we respect the autonomy of Q, if we believe that people 'have rights to be treated as ends in themselves and not as means to the achievement of other social goals', we would surely not want such action to go unpunished by the criminal law. In short, *Re A* confirms the presence of the necessity safety net, but the problematic nature of even the barest attempt at criteria also confirms that that safety net is imperfect.[203]

 Extra detail . . .

Although it has not been considered by a court, it is clear that the UK government (along with many others) believes that necessity can be a defence to murder where a hijacked passenger jet is shot down. Such action involves the intentional killing of innocent passengers, but is performed in order to limit the potential damage if the plane were to be crashed into a populated area or other target.[204]

14.7 Reform

The general defences have attracted considerable academic attention and criticism, as we have discussed, but parliamentary reform has often been piecemeal, as with the partial codification of the public and private defence, or non-existent. In this section, we first

202 Dennis, 'On Necessity as a Defence to Crime' (2009) 3 Crim L & Phil 29, 44–45.
203 Huxtable, 'Separation of Conjoined Twins: What Next for English Law?' [2002] Crim LR 459; Rogers, 'Necessity, Private-Defence and the Killing of Mary' [2001] Crim LR 515.
204 Hörnle, 'Hijacked Planes: May They Be Shot Down?' [2007] New Crim LR 582; Bohlander, 'In Extremis? Hijacked Airplanes, Collateral Damage and the Limits of Criminal Law' [2006] Crim LR 579. Also recognised in *R (Nicklinson) v Ministry of Justice* [2014] UKSC 38.

consider the potential reform of each of the defences covered in this chapter. We then widen out to discuss the current inconsistencies between defences and the importance of achieving coherence.

14.7.1 Reforming the individual defences

Each of the general defences has attracted individual comment and criticism. We consider each in turn.

14.7.1.1 Insanity as a defence

We have already considered the potential reform of the insanity rules at **Chapter 13.6.3**, and we do not repeat that discussion here. However, when evaluating the insanity rules it is useful to bear in mind the distinction between insanity as a denial of offending and insanity as a defence. Indeed, in the context of our discussion of potential human rights compatibility, the difference can be crucial. For example:

- **Article 6:** Article 6 ECHR provides a right to a fair trial including the presumption of innocence. The reverse burden of proof for insanity must be justified in this context. This is particularly important in the context of insanity as a denial of offending: because the Crown has not established the elements of the actus reus and mens rea, then by definition the case for reversing the burden is much weaker because there is no criminal mischief. In contrast, where D has committed an offence and raises insanity as a defence, there is stronger ground for a reverse burden: D has been found to have performed the actus reus and mens rea of an offence, and therefore no longer needs to be presumed innocent. However, the lesser burden—an evidential burden—may still be preferred.[205]

- **Articles 2, 3, and 5:** Criticisms under Articles 2, 3, and 5 will apply in largely the same way to insanity as a denial of offending and insanity as a defence. The defence of insanity, as with insanity as a denial of offending, is designed to protect the right to life, to liberty, and to protect against inhuman and degrading treatment. To the extent that the current law fails to do this, by drawing the defence too narrowly or too widely, or through its disconnect with medical knowledge about mental illness, it is rightly subject to criticism.[206]

14.7.1.2 Duress

The rules on duress by threats, and now duress by circumstances, are reasonably well established within the common law. However, as we have discussed previously, the current law has been criticised for being drawn too narrowly, excluding those deserving of an excuse.[207] Academic opposition to this narrowing has questioned the merits of criminalising people for failing to resist pressures that they are subjectively unequipped to resist, especially where those pressures may objectively have affected others in a similar way.[208] Following recent case law, it is clear that these concerns are only likely to be

[205] Law Commission, *Insanity and Automatism* (Discussion Paper, 2013).
[206] Ibid, paras 1.30–1.79.
[207] This stems from cases such as *Hasan* [2005] UKHL 22.
[208] Lippke, 'Chronic Temptation, Reasonable Firmness and the Criminal Law' (2014) 34 OJLS 75; Reed, 'Duress and Normative Moral Excuse' in Reed and Bohlander (eds), *General Defences in Criminal Law* (2014) 93.

addressed, if at all, through legislation. However, such reform does not appear on the current agenda. If and when this changes, the Law Commission has already provided a useful set of reform proposals.[209]

In contrast with this general lack of legislative attention, one area within the defence has attracted considerable debate: whether duress should be a defence to murder. The arguments in favour of such an extension reflect the general arguments in favour of a defence of duress to *any* crime. In simple terms, if D is threatened with death or serious harm to a degree that a reasonable person in her position would have done likewise to avoid it, D's actions are still wrong, but we can excuse the actor and sympathise with the impossible position in which she was placed. Against this, a number of arguments have been formulated to reject any extension of duress. These are most clearly stated in the reasoning of the court in *Howe*.[210] However, none of these arguments seems to hold up under analysis.

- The ordinary person of reasonable fortitude should sacrifice herself rather than take the life of an innocent.[211] *If the defence of duress were extended to cover murder, it would only apply where a jury found that a reasonable person would have yielded to the threat. If the criminal law is defining a 'reasonable' person as a hero, it is surely expecting too much.*

- One who takes the life of an innocent person cannot claim to be choosing the lesser of two evils.[212] *This is not necessarily the case. For example, if D takes a single life to avoid X's threat to kill multiple people, this looks like the lesser evil. Also, the defence of duress is generally conceived as a concession to reasonable human frailty (an excuse) rather than a balance of evils defence (a justification).*

- The Law Commission had previously recommended that duress should be a defence to murder,[213] but this was not acted upon by Parliament.[214] *This proves little, as the Commission's previous recommendations were not put before Parliament to consider. We could equally claim that the failure of Parliament to overrule the House of Lords' decision in* Lynch, *which suggested duress could be a defence to murder, demonstrated their approval of that approach.*

- Hard cases can be avoided though prosecutorial discretion (ie by not prosecuting).[215] *The morally innocent should not be left to the uncertain mercy of administrative discretion.*

The Law Commission has considered these arguments and others, and has recommended that the duress defence should be extended to apply to murder.[216] However, in doing so the Commission has taken the controversial step of recommending a reversed

---

[209] Law Commission, *A Criminal Code for England and Wales*, 2 vols (No 177, 1989) cll42 and 43, and most recently *Offences against the Person and General Principles* (No 218, 1993) Part 4.

[210] [1987] 1 All ER 771.

[211] At 779–780.

[212] At 780.

[213] Law Commission, *Defences of General Application* (No 83, 1977).

[214] At 784 and 788.

[215] At 780–781 and 790–791.

[216] Law Commission, *Murder, Manslaughter and Infanticide* (No 304, 2006) Ch6.

burden of proof in cases of this kind,[217] and an increased threshold so that the defence will only apply where D is threatened with death or 'life-threatening' harm; in other words serious, non-life-threatening harm will be insufficient.[218] Whether or not the Law Commission's scheme is ever adopted, it is contended that the arguments in favour of extending the defence of duress to murder are overwhelming.[219]

14.7.1.3 The public and private defence

Unlike the other general defences, the public and private defence has attracted the relatively recent attention of Parliament. However, as discussed earlier, the reasons for this attention have been unfortunate, being based chiefly upon public and media misunderstanding about the limits of the defence. The reaction of Parliament in partially codifying the common law within section 76 of the CJIA can be welcomed as a useful clarification, although a complete codification would have been preferable. However, the more recent amendments to this section in relation to householder cases, allowing for disproportionate force to be used in this context, demonstrate the worst features of populist unprincipled law reform.[220] This process has also distracted from two areas of potential reform that should be highlighted regarding (a) the human rights compatibility of the current law, and (b) the potential for a new defence of excessive self-defence.

Concerns have been raised about the compatibility of the current public and private defence with rights enshrined within the ECHR. In particular, this debate has focussed on the potential for the defence to apply where D has killed V, and done so on the basis of an unreasonable mistaken belief that force was necessary (discussed at **14.5.2**). As long as D's response in killing V was reasonable *on the facts as she believed them to be*, the defence will apply and D will be acquitted. However, what of V's Article 2 right to life?[221] As various commentators have set out,[222] although Article 2 is not an absolute right, it only permits life to be taken when it is 'absolutely necessary',[223] with the ECtHR clarifying that this requires 'good grounds' in circumstances of self-defence.[224] Arguably, D's unreasonably mistaken belief, albeit an honest one, does not constitute good grounds. It should be highlighted that neither the ECtHR[225] nor any domestic court[226] has yet found the public and private defence to be in breach of Article 2, and there are also

---

[217] At paras 6.87–6.141.

[218] At paras 6.73–6.76.

[219] Reed, 'The Need for a New Anglo-American Approach to Duress' (1996) 61 JCL 209. See also Arenson, 'The Paradox of Disallowing Duress as a Defence to Murder' (2014) 78 JCL 65.

[220] Editor, 'Defending Self-Defence' [2010] Crim LR 167.

[221] Although debate has focussed on killing and Art 2, it could equally apply where D causes lesser harm in similarly unreasonable circumstances (potentially infringing Arts 3 and/or 5).

[222] De Than and Elvin, 'Mistaken Private Defence: The Case for Reform' in Reed and Bohlander (eds), *General Defences in Criminal Law* (2014) 133; Leverick, 'Is English Self-Defence Law Incompatible with Article 2 of the ECHR?' [2002] Crim LR 347.

[223] Art 2(2) ECHR.

[224] *McCann v UK* (1996) 21 EHRR 95.

[225] *Da Silva v UK* (2016) 63 EHRR 12; *Bubbins v UK* (2005) 41 EHRR 458.

[226] *R (Bennett) v HM Coroner for Inner London* [2007] EWCA Civ 617; *Duggan* [2014] EWHC 3343 (Admin).

good reasons for favouring the current subjective test over an objective alternative.[227] However, it should also be acknowledged that a case of killing under an unreasonable mistaken belief has not yet made its way to the European Court, and so the potential for a breach to be found is still very much alive.

A second area of topical debate is the potential for a new partial defence for murder where D acts with excessive force in self-defence. The public and private defence will not apply to D in these circumstances: although D's use of force may be necessary in the circumstances as she believes them to be, if they are excessive because the degree of force used is unreasonable, then the complete defence will fail. The potential for a new partial defence that would reduce D's liability from murder to manslaughter was considered by the House of Lords in *Clegg*.[228] However, the court concluded that a change of this kind, if it were required, would have to come from Parliament. Such reform has not been forthcoming. However, the potential for a partial defence of this kind has found consistent favour with the Law Commission and there are sound reasons for its recommendation.[229] Under the current law, someone who kills in excessive self-defence may be able to rely on one of the existing partial defences (as in *Martin*, discussed at **14.5.2**), and this potential has been increased by the expansion of the loss of control defence to include a trigger based on fear of serious violence.[230] However, there will still be defendants who kill without having lost control, and who do not qualify for the partial defence of diminished responsibility, and there remains a case to be made that these defendants also warrant partial mitigation on the basis of their (semi-)defensive motivations.[231]

14.7.1.4 Necessity

At one time, the Law Commission went as far as to recommend the abolition of necessity as a defence.[232] However, as we discussed earlier, such a policy is surely ill-conceived, severely limiting the ability of the courts to deal with exceptional cases where liability is inappropriate but other defences do not apply. The recommendation was severely criticised,[233] and has been dropped. Subsequently, the Commission has recommended that necessity should remain a defence but, unlike the other defences, it should not be codified.[234] This seems to be the correct approach, allowing the necessity defence to perform

---

[227] Although mistaken, D's belief in the need for extreme force was honest and so does not reveal a blameworthy character. See the ECtHR discussion in *Da Silva v UK* (2016) 63 EHRR 12, on the death of Jean Charles de Menezes.

[228] [1995] 1 All ER 334. Kaye, 'Excessive Force in Self-Defence: After *Clegg*' (1996) 61 JCL 448.

[229] Law Commission, *A Criminal Code for England and Wales*, 2 vols (No 177, 1989) cl59; Law Commission, *Murder, Manslaughter and Infanticide* (No 304, 2006) para 1.53.

[230] See **Chapter 6.2.1**.

[231] Stannard, 'In the Spirit of Compromise: The Irish Doctrine of Excessive Defence' in Reed and Bohlander (eds), *General Defences in Criminal Law* (2014) 171; Smith, 'Excessive Defence—A Rejection of Australian Initiative' [1972] Crim LR 524. Australian law now recognises a partial defence of this kind, adopting the English position in *Zecevic* (1987) 61 ALJR 375. See also, in the context of abused women who kill in excessive self-defence, Wake, 'Battered Women, Startled Householders and Psychological Self-Defence' (2013) 77 JCL 433.

[232] Law Commission, *Defences of General Application* (No 83, 1977).

[233] Williams, 'Necessity' [1978] Crim LR 128; Huxley, 'Proposals and Counter Proposals on the Defence of Necessity' [1978] Crim LR 141.

[234] Law Commission, *Offences against the Person and General Principles* (No 218, 1992) cl36(2).

its role as an imperfect safety net without the restraint of codification. Indeed, we see a similar approach in most other common law jurisdictions.[235]

14.7.2 Coherence between defences

It is not an objection to the current general defences that they apply in variously different circumstances. However, there may be a problem where the defences are inconsistent in their approach to common issues to an extent that the overall approach of the law becomes incoherent. This is undoubtedly a problem within the current law, and one in which, within denials of offences at least, the Law Commission has begun to take an interest.[236]

It is useful to provide a brief overview of some of the main areas of inconsistency within the current general defences. These inconsistencies can be explained on the basis of common law development that lacks a unifying theory of defences, and the conflict between excusatory and justificatory rationales.[237] However, although they can be explained on this basis, the law must still aim for coherence. After all, unifying theories are elusive in any area of the law.[238]

- **Subjective and objective approaches:** Probably the most striking area of inconsistency between the defences discussed in this chapter relates to their use of subjective and objective elements. For example, whereas duress requires D to have an *objectively* reasonable belief in the presence of a serious threat requiring D to offend, the public and private defence requires the equivalent belief in the necessity of force to be *subjectively* honest. If this difference was based on stated principles then it would be acceptable, but it actually originates from the defences unsuccessfully attempting to run in tandem.[239]

- **Characteristics of the defendant:** Where an objective standard is applied, there are no obvious principles underpinning the approach to which of D's characteristics can be taken into account when applying that standard. For example, for duress, it now seems that almost all of D's physical and psychiatric characteristics can be taken into account when deciding whether a reasonable person with those characteristics would have been compelled to offend (**14.3.3.3**).[240] In contrast, for the public and private defence, the objective degree of force test does not allow characteristics beyond age and sex to be taken into account, and explicitly excludes psychiatric characteristics (**14.5.3**).[241]

---

[235] eg Canada (*Perka* (1984) 13 DLR (4th) 1); Australia (*Loughnan* [1981] VR 443); across the Oceanic countries (Forsyth, 'The Divorce and Marriage of Morality and Law' (2010) 21 Crim L Forum 121); and so on. One exception, where codification has been attempted, is the United States of America (Model Penal Code, §3.02), on which, see Alexander, 'Lesser Evils: A Closer Look at the Paradigmatic Justification' (2005) 24 Law & Phil 611; Berman, 'Lesser Evils: A Less Close Look' (2005) 24 Law & Phil 681.

[236] Law Commission, *Insanity and Automatism* (Discussion Paper, 2013).

[237] Lacey, 'Space, Time and Function: Intersecting Principles of Responsibility Across the Terrain of Criminal Justice' (2007) 1 Crim L & Phil 233.

[238] Tadros, 'The Character of Excuse' (2001) 21 OJLS 495.

[239] The court in *Graham* [1982] 1 All ER 801 equated duress with self-defence and so adopted an objective approach in line with (what was then) the accepted approach for self-defence. However, less than two years later the court in *Gladstone Williams* [1987] 3 All ER 411 opted for a subjective approach to self-defence. See also Alldridge, 'Developing the Defence of Duress' [1986] Crim LR 433.

[240] *Bowen* [1996] 2 Cr App R 157.

[241] *Martin* [2001] EWCA Crim 2245.

- **Approaches to prior-fault:** The approach to prior-fault, and its potential to undermine D's appeal to a defence is also inconsistent. For example, duress will be excluded where D voluntarily associates with others in circumstances where she *objectively* should have foreseen a risk of coercion (**14.3.1.2**).[242] In contrast, the public and private defence will only be similarly excluded where D has *consciously* manipulated the circumstances in order to attack V under the guise of defensive force (**14.5.1.2**).[243] Again, reasons for the inconsistency are not clearly articulated by the courts.[244]

An extreme response to the issue of inconsistency would be to collapse each of the general defences into a single defence, with a single set of rules and principles. A model for this approach has been set out by Clarkson.[245] However, the problem here is that a single defence becomes nothing more than a vague statement of necessity, unifying only in its inevitable preference for the lowest common denominator. Although we acknowledge that a defence of this kind (necessity) is essential as an imperfect safety net below other defences, it is surely right that other defences should exist which are capable of greater clarity and precision.

A better approach, it is contended, following the lead of the Law Commission in relation to automatism, intoxication, and insanity, is to identify common elements between the defences and make sure that the reform of any one takes account of the others, whether this means principled consistency or principled inconsistency. Wilson's work on the structure of defences provides a good example of this approach.[246]

14.8 Eye on assessment

In this section we consider the application of the general defences to problem facts. We employ the same structure as we have discussed throughout the book. However, here perhaps more than ever, it is vital to read carefully what the question is asking you to do. In most cases, questions involving defences will be no different from any other question: they will ask you to discuss potential liability and so you will have to go through every step of the structure (which we set out later) and remember to only discuss the potential for a defence when it becomes necessary to do so, that is *only after* you have established that D is likely to have committed the actus reus with the mens rea for the offence. However, exceptionally, a question may tell you that D has committed an offence and ask you to consider potential defences only. In this case, you should skip from Step 1 (you still need to identify the criminal event) straight to Step 4 (discussion of defences).

---

[242] *Hasan* [2005] UKHL 22.
[243] *Rashford* [2005] EWCA Crim 3377.
[244] Child, 'Prior Fault: Blocking Defences or Constructing Crimes' in Reed and Bohlander (eds), *General Defences* (2014).
[245] Clarkson, 'Necessary Action: A New Defence' [2004] Crim LR 81.
[246] Wilson, 'The Structure of Defences' [2005] Crim LR 108.

Assuming that we are dealing with a standard question, the following structure should be applied.

STEP 1 Identify the potential criminal event in the facts

This should be simply stated (eg 'The first potential criminal event arises where D punches V'). The role of this stage is to highlight which part of the question you are answering before you begin to apply the law.

STEP 2 Identify the potential offence

Again, state this simply (eg 'When punching V, D may be liable for assault occasioning ABH'). The role of this stage is to highlight which offence you are going to apply.

STEP 3 Applying the offence to the facts

Having identified the relevant offence, make sure you discuss each of the required elements.

Actus reus: What does the offence require? Did D do it?

Mens rea: What does the offence require? Did D possess it?

AR and MR are satisfied	AR and/or MR are not satisfied
Continue to STEP 4.	Return to STEP 2, and look for an alternative offence. If none, then skip to STEP 5, concluding that no offence is committed.

STEP 4 Consider defences

The word 'consider' here is important, as you should not discuss every defence for every question. Rather, think whether there are any defences (eg duress) that *could* potentially apply. If there are, discuss those only.

Figure 14.1 is designed to help you to identify which defence you should apply.

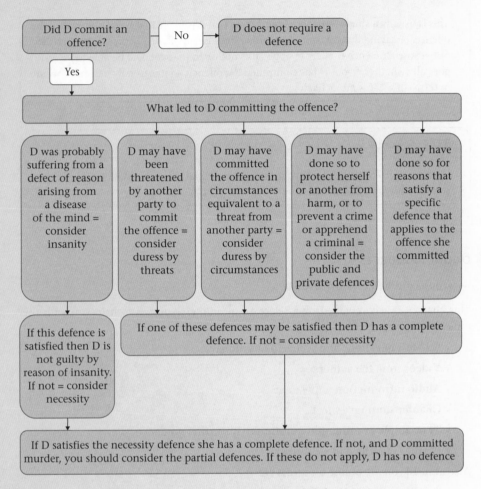

Figure 14.1 Applying the general defences

Note that, if insanity applies, D will usually be directed to the special verdict. If insanity does not apply, you should consider duress, the public and private defence, and/or any specific defences. Remember that there is often an overlap between defences including duress and self-defence, so it may be necessary to apply more than one to the facts. Finally, if these defences do not apply, you should consider necessity as the imperfect safety net beneath. If D is liable for murder and none of the complete defences applies, you should also go on to consider the partial defences.[247]

Remember, analysis of the defences is mainly a mental process. Particularly in an exam, you will not have time to lead your reader through the elements of each defence to say why each does not apply. Rather, keep **Figure 14.1** in mind to help you identify any defences that might apply (ie there are facts in the problem that suggest it might apply) and lead your reader through those defences only.

---

[247] See **Chapter 6.2.**

STEP 5 Conclude

This is usually a single sentence either saying that it is likely that D has committed the offence, or saying that it is not likely, either because an offence element is not satisfied or because a defence is likely to apply. It is not often that you will be able to say categorically whether or not D has committed the offence, so it is usually best to conclude in terms of what is more 'likely'.

STEP 6 Loop

Go back up to STEP 1, identifying the next potential criminal event. Continue until you have discussed all the relevant potentially criminal events.

 ONLINE RESOURCES

www.oup.com/he/child-ormerod4e

This chapter is accompanied by a selection of online resources to help you with this topic, including:

- **Self-test questions and scenario questions**
- **Videos** from the authors
- **Audio introduction** to the topic
- **Chapter summary sheet**
- Two **sample examination questions** with answer guidance
- **Further reading and weblinks**

Also available on the online resources are:

- A selection of **videos** from the authors containing general advice on problem questions and essay questions
- **Legal updates**

Index